Criminal Procedure

Criminal Procedure

An Introduction for Criminal Justice Professionals ▪ Second Edition

NEAL R. BEVANS, J.D.

Wolters Kluwer

Published by Wolters Kluwer in New York.

Wolters Kluwer Legal & Regulatory U.S. serves customers worldwide with CCH, Aspen Publishers, and Kluwer Law International products. (www.WKLegaledu.com)

Cover Image Credits: Upper left: Shutterstock/Inked Pixels; Upper center: iStock.com/DNY59; Upper right: iStock.com/aijohn784; Background: iStock.com/artisteer

To contact Customer Service, e-mail customer.service@wolterskluwer.com, call 1-800-234-1660, fax 1-800-901-9075, or mail correspondence to:

Wolters Kluwer
Attn: Order Department
PO Box 990
Frederick, MD 21705

Printed in the United States of America.

1 2 3 4 5 6 7 8 9 0

ISBN 978-1-5438-2477-3

Library of Congress Cataloging-in-Publication Data

Names: Bevans, Neal R., 1961- author.
Title: Criminal procedure : an introduction for criminal justice
    professionals / Neal R. Bevans, J.D.
Other titles: Criminal law and procedure
Description: Second edition. | New York : Wolters Kluwer, [2021] | Includes
    bibliographical references and index. | Summary: "Introduction to
    Criminal Procedure"— Provided by publisher.
Identifiers: LCCN 2020032210 (print) | LCCN 2020032211 (ebook) | ISBN
    9781543824773 (paperback) | ISBN 9781543824780 (ebook)
Subjects: LCSH: Criminal law—United States. | Criminal procedure—United
    States. | Criminal justice personnel—United States—Handbooks, manuals, etc.
Classification: LCC KF9219.85 .B49 2021 (print) | LCC KF9219.85 (ebook) |
    DDC 345.73—dc23
LC record available at https://lccn.loc.gov/2020032210
LC ebook record available at https://lccn.loc.gov/2020032211

SUSTAINABLE FORESTRY INITIATIVE Certified Sourcing www.sfiprogram.org SFI-00756

About Wolters Kluwer Legal & Regulatory U.S.

Wolters Kluwer Legal & Regulatory U.S. delivers expert content and solutions in the areas of law, corporate compliance, health compliance, reimbursement, and legal education. Its practical solutions help customers successfully navigate the demands of a changing environment to drive their daily activities, enhance decision quality, and inspire confident outcomes.

Serving customers worldwide, its legal and regulatory portfolio includes products under the Aspen Publishers, CCH Incorporated, Kluwer Law International, ftwilliam.com and MediRegs names. They are regarded as exceptional and trusted resources for general legal and practice-specific knowledge, compliance and risk management, dynamic workflow solutions, and expert commentary.

For my wife Nilsa Bevans, and my stepchildren Tamara Tigani and Camilo Lopez Escobar, *con todo mi amor*

Summary
of Contents

Contents		xi
Preface		xxix
Acknowledgments		xxxi

Chapter 1	Criminal Law and the U.S. Constitution	1
Chapter 2	Introduction to the Criminal Justice System	19
Chapter 3	Fourth Amendment: Stop and Frisk and Other Detentions	41
Chapter 4	Fourth Amendment: Probable Cause and Arrest	55
Chapter 5	Fourth Amendment: Search and Seizure	81
Chapter 6	Constitutional Issues in the Use of Evidence	99
Chapter 7	The Exclusionary Rule	123
Chapter 8	Fifth Amendment: Grand Jury and Indictment	143
Chapter 9	Fifth Amendment: Interrogation and Confessions	167
Chapter 10	Sixth Amendment: Right to Trial and Associated Rights	187
Chapter 11	Eighth Amendment: Initial Appearance, Bail, and Preliminary Hearings	215
Chapter 12	Arraignment and Discovery	233
Chapter 13	The Trial	261
Chapter 14	Defenses to Criminal Prosecutions	289
Chapter 15	Eighth Amendment: Sentencing	317
Chapter 16	Appeals	341

Appendix A. Answers to Review Questions and Practice Questions for Test Review	357
Appendix B. The Constitution of the United States	401
Glossary	419
Index	427

Contents

Preface   xxix
Acknowledgments   xxxi

1 CRIMINAL LAW AND THE U.S. CONSTITUTION   1

Chapter Objectives ■ *Chapter Outline*   1

I. SOURCES OF LAW FOR THE CRIMINAL JUSTICE SYSTEM   2

   A. The U.S. Constitution   2
     State Constitutions   2
   B. Statutory Law   3
     Ordinances   4
   C. Judicial Decisions (Case Law)   4
     Case Law and the United States Supreme Court   4
   D. Stare Decisis   5
   E. Court Rules   5
   F. Agency Rules and Regulations   5
   G. Common Law   6
     What is the Common Law?   6
       "Possession is 9/10ths of the Law"   7
     The Importance of Common Law   7
     The Uses of Common Law   8

II. FEDERAL VS. STATE COURT SYSTEMS   9

   A. The Levels of the Federal Court System   9
     Federal District Courts   9
     Appellate Courts: Courts of Appeal   10
     U.S. Supreme Court   11
   B. The Levels of the State Court System   12
     Trial Courts   12
     Appellate Courts   12
     State Supreme Court   13

III. FEDERAL PROSECUTIONS VS. STATE
      PROSECUTIONS   13

      A. Federal Jurisdiction   13
      B. State Jurisdiction   14
         State-Level Prosecutions   14
      C. Differences Among States   15

   Chapter Summary   15
   Key Terms and Concepts   15
   End of Chapter Exercises   16
   Practice Questions for Test Review   17
   Endnotes   18

2 INTRODUCTION TO THE CRIMINAL JUSTICE SYSTEM 19

Chapter Objectives ■ *Chapter Outline*   19

   I. INTRODUCTION TO THE CRIMINAL JUSTICE
       SYSTEM   20

  II. THE CRIMINAL SYSTEM   20

       A. Verdicts in Criminal Cases   20
       B. Verdicts in Civil Cases   21
       C. The Burden of Proof   22
       D. The Pleadings   23
       E. Classes of Crimes: Felonies vs. Misdemeanors   24

 III. OVERVIEW OF PROCEDURAL STEPS IN
       A CRIMINAL PROSECUTION   26

       A. Arrest   26
          Arrest and Probable Cause   26
       B. Interrogation   27
          Miranda Warnings   28
       C. Evidence   29
       D. Initial Appearance   30
       E. Preliminary Hearing   30
       F. Grand Jury   31
          True Bill vs. No Bill   31
       G. Arraignment   31
       H. Trial   32
          Basic Overview of a Criminal Trial   32
       I. Sentencing   33
          Prison vs. Probation   33

Case Excerpt: *State v. Summers*   34

Chapter Summary   36
Key Terms and Concepts   36
End of Chapter Exercises   37
Practice Questions for Test Review   38
Endnotes   39

3 FOURTH AMENDMENT: STOP AND FRISK AND OTHER DETENTIONS   41

Chapter Objectives ▪ *Chapter Outline*   41

I. INTERACTIONS BETWEEN POLICE AND INDIVIDUALS   42

   A. Continuum of Contacts and Their Constitutional Requirements   42
   B. Voluntary Interactions Between Police and Individuals   43
   C. Police Interactions with Constitutional Implications   44

II. *TERRY* STOPS   44

   A. Detention Under *Terry*   44
   B. What is "Reasonable Suspicion?"   45

III. STOP AND FRISK   45

   A. What are the Police Permitted to Do in a Stop and Frisk?   46
   B. The Scope of Stop and Frisk   47
   C. Abuse of the Stop and Frisk Provision   48

IV. ARREST   48

Case Excerpt: *State v. Krannawitter*   48

Chapter Summary   51
Key Terms and Concepts   52
End of Chapter Exercises   52
Practice Questions for Test Review   53
Endnotes   54

4 FOURTH AMENDMENT: PROBABLE CAUSE AND ARREST

55

Chapter Objectives ■ *Chapter Outline*   55

I. THE FOURTH AMENDMENT'S REQUIREMENT OF PROBABLE CAUSE

56

A. Probable Cause   56
   What is Probable Cause?   57
   Degree of Proof Needed to Establish Probable Cause   58
B. Specific Acts That Establish Probable Cause   58
   Description Over the Radio   59
   Suspicious or Unusual Behavior   59
   Information Provided by Confidential Informants   59
   Anonymous Phone Calls   60
   Stops at Sobriety or Roadside Check Points   60
   Pretextual Stops   60
   Flight   61
   Presence at a Crime Scene   61
   "Gut Feelings" or Hunches   62

II. ARREST

62

A. Arrest and Probable Cause   63
B. Who Can Arrest?   64
   Arrests by Police Officers and Others   64
   Arrests Outside of the Officer's Jurisdiction   65
   Citizen's Arrest   65
C. Making an Arrest   66
D. Determining When the Suspect is Under Arrest   66
   Court Tests to Determine the Moment of Arrest   66

III. ARREST WARRANTS

67

A. Courts Have a Preference for Warrants   67
B. The Fourth Amendment Only Applies to Government Conduct   68
C. Applying for an Arrest Warrant   69
   The Magistrate   70
   Drafting the Warrant   70
   Legally Sufficient Arrest Warrant   70
   The "Four Corners" Test   71
   Identifying the Person to Be Arrested   71
D. What Happens After the Warrant is Issued?   72

Case Excerpt: *People v. Howlett*   72

Chapter Summary   76
Key Terms and Concepts   76

End of Chapter Exercises 76
Practice Questions for Test Review 78
Endnotes 79

5 FOURTH AMENDMENT: SEARCH AND SEIZURE 81

Chapter Objectives ■ *Chapter Outline* 81

I SEARCH WARRANTS 82

A. Standards for Issuing Search and Seizure Warrants 82
B. The Good Faith Exception 83
C. Exceptions to the Search Warrant Requirement 84

II. SEARCHES WITHOUT A WARRANT 84

A. Plain View 84
B. Open Fields 85
C. Dropped Evidence 86
D. Abandoned Property 86
E. Contraband 87
F. Stop and Frisk 87
G. U.S. Border Searches 87
H. Canine Officers 87
I. Consent 88
J. Exigent Circumstances 88

III. SEARCH WARRANT LIMITATIONS 88

A. General Searches Not Allowed 89
B. Stale Warrants 89
C. Vagueness 90
D. Overbreadth 90
E. Challenging a Warrant 90
F. The Exclusionary Rule 90

Case Excerpt: *U.S. v. Young* 91

Chapter Summary 94
Key Terms and Concepts 95
End of Chapter Exercises 95
Practice Questions for Test Review 96
Endnotes 97

6 CONSTITUTIONAL ISSUES IN THE USE OF EVIDENCE

99

Chapter Objectives ■ *Chapter Outline* 99

I. EVIDENCE LAW 100

II. THE FIRST AMENDMENT AND EVIDENCE 100

A. Establishment and Free Exercise Clauses 100
B. Freedom of Speech 101
  Freedom of Speech and Incitement to Riot 101
  Freedom of Speech vs. Freedom of Expression 102
  Prosecutions for Pornography 103
    Pornography and Obscenity 103
    The Miller Test 104
    Possession of Obscene Material 104
    Child Pornography 104
C. The Right of the Press 104

III. FOURTH AMENDMENT EVIDENTIARY ISSUES 105

IV. FIFTH AMENDMENT AND EVIDENTIARY ISSUES 105

A. The Grand Jury 105
  Use of Hearsay Evidence at Grand Jury 106
B. Self-Incrimination and Pleading the "Fifth" 107
C. Self-Incrimination and Identification 107

V. SIXTH AMENDMENT AND EVIDENTIARY ISSUES 107

A. The Right to Confront Witnesses 108
B. The Right to an Attorney 108
  Right to an Attorney at a Lineup 109
    The Importance of an Eyewitness Identification 109
    Just How Accurate is Eyewitness Testimony? 109
  Constitutional Limits on Lineups 110
  Right to Counsel at Lineup 110
  Participants in a Lineup 110
    Single-Suspect Lineups 110
    One-Person Show-ups 110
  Photographic Lineups 111
  Constitutional Sanctions for Improper Lineups 111
C. The Right to a Public Trial 111
  Closing a Trial to the Public 112

**VI. OTHER EVIDENTIARY ISSUES WITH
CONSTITUTIONAL IMPLICATIONS**   112

   A. DNA   112
      Using DNA as Evidence   113
      Gathering DNA Samples into a Database   113
   B. Fingerprinting   113
   C. Polygraph Tests   114

Case Excerpt: *State v. Homan*   114

Chapter Summary   118
Key Terms and Concepts   118
End of Chapter Exercises   118
Practice Questions for Test Review   120
Endnotes   121

---

7   THE EXCLUSIONARY RULE   123

Chapter Objectives ■ Chapter Outline   123

  I. THE EXCLUSIONARY RULE   124

   A. Practical Aspects of the Exclusionary Rule   125
      Motions to Suppress   125
      Standing   127
   B. Historical Development of the Exclusionary Rule 128
   C. The Purpose of the Exclusionary Rule   129
   D. Does the Exclusionary Rule Work?   129
   E. Fruit of the Poisonous Tree   130

  II. EXCEPTIONS TO THE EXCLUSIONARY RULE   130

   A. Independent Source Doctrine   131
   B. Attenuation   131
   C. Inevitable Discovery   132
   D. Good Faith   132

Case Excerpt: *Collins v. Commonwealth*   133

Chapter Summary   138
Key Terms and Concepts   139
End of Chapter Exercises   139
Practice Questions for Test Review   140
Endnotes   141

8   FIFTH AMENDMENT: GRAND JURY AND INDICTMENT   143

Chapter Objectives ■ *Chapter Outline*   143

I. CHARGING DECISION   144

  A. Ask for Additional Investigation   144
  B. Bring Additional Charges Against the Defendant   144
  C. Dismiss the Case   146

II. GRAND JURY   146

  A. True Bill vs. No Bill   151
  B. History of the Grand Jury   151
  C. The Purpose of the Grand Jury   152
  D. How is the Grand Jury Composed?   154
      Challenging the Composition of the Grand Jury   155
  E. Function of the Grand Jury   155
  F. Presenting a Case to the Grand Jury   156
      Only the State's Witnesses Appear Before the Grand Jury   157
  G. Subpoena Powers of the Grand Jury   157
      Objecting to a Grand Jury Subpoena: Witness Privilege   158
      Pleading the "Fifth Amendment" Before the Grand Jury   158
      Motion to Quash   158
  H. Immunity Powers of Grand Juries   159

III. AFTER THE GRAND JURY PROCEEDINGS   159

Case Excerpt: *State v. Kent*   159

Chapter Summary   163
Key Terms and Concepts   164
End of Chapter Exercises   164
Practice Questions for Test Review   165
Endnotes   166

9   FIFTH AMENDMENT: INTERROGATION AND CONFESSIONS   167

Chapter Objectives ■ *Chapter Outline*   167

I. ACTIONS FOLLOWING ARREST   168

  A. Interrogation   168
      Oral and Written Statements   169
      Miranda   169
        Background on the *Miranda* Decision   170

When *Miranda* Does Not Apply 170
Background or Routine Police Questioning 171
Exigent Circumstances 171
Voluntary Statements 171
When it is Lawful to Use Trickery 171
Traffic Stops 172
B. Invoking the Right to Remain Silent 172
C. Requesting an Attorney 172
D. Reinitiating Questioning 173
E. Procedure After Arrest 174

II. **SPECIAL RULES REGARDING INTERROGATION** 174

A. Instances Where Defendant Will Not Be Interrogated 174
B. *Jackson v. Denno* Hearing 175

Case Excerpt: *State v. Perry* 176

Chapter Summary 182
Key Terms and Concepts 182
End of Chapter Exercises 182
Practice Questions for Test Review 184
Endnotes 185

10 SIXTH AMENDMENT: RIGHT TO TRIAL AND ASSOCIATED RIGHTS

187

Chapter Objectives ▪ *Chapter Outline* 187

I. **THE DEFENDANT'S RIGHTS PRIOR TO TRIAL** 188

A. The Right to an Attorney 188
Hiring an Attorney 189
Gideon v. Wainwright 189
Court-Appointed Attorney vs. Public Defender Systems 190
When the Defendant Cannot Afford an Attorney 191
The Right of a Defendant to Represent Himself 191
B. The Right to Be Presumed Innocent 192
Presumptions vs. Inferences 193

II. **THE DEFENDANT'S RIGHTS DURING A TRIAL** 193

A. The Right to a Fair Trial 193
B. The Right to a Jury Trial 194
Number of Jurors Used in the Trial 195
Times When Nonunanimous Verdicts are Permitted 195

            Six-Person Juries   196
          Exceptions to the Right to a Jury   196
            Criminal Infractions Where the Sentence is Six Months or Less 196
        C. The Right to a Public Trial   196
          When Can a Judge Close a Trial to the Public?   197
            Jury Selection   197
            Preliminary Hearings   198
            Sensitive or Underage Witnesses   198
        D. The Right to Confront Witnesses   198
        E. The Right to Be Present   200
          Trials in Absentia   200
          Continuing a Trial After the Defendant Flees   200
          When the Defendant Waives His or Her Right to Be Present   201
          When the Judge May Remove the Defendant From the
            Courtroom   201
        F. The Right to Wear Civilian Clothing During the Trial   201
          Prison Attire Not Permitted   201
        G. The Right to Present Evidence   202
        H. The Right to Present a Defense   203

   III. PROVING THE DEFENDANT GUILTY   204

        A. Proof Beyond a Reasonable Doubt   204
        B. Explaining the State's Burden of Proof   204

   IV. CRIMINAL TRIALS AND THE PRESS   204

   Case Excerpt: *Shorter v. U.S.*   205

   Chapter Summary   211
   Key Terms and Concepts   211
   End of Chapter Exercises   211
   Practice Questions for Test Review   213
   Endnotes   214

11 EIGHTH AMENDMENT: INITIAL APPEARANCE, BAIL, AND PRELIMINARY HEARINGS

                                                                                       215

   Chapter Objectives ∎ *Chapter Outline*   215

   I. INITIAL APPEARANCE   216

        A. Purpose of the Initial Appearance   216
        B. Right to an Attorney at Initial Appearance   217

II. BAIL AND BOND   217

   A. Bonding Companies   219
       Bounty Hunters   220
   B. Recognizance Bond   221
   C. Factors to Consider in Setting Bond   221
       Defendant's Ties to the Community   221
       Seriousness of the Offense   222
       Defendant's Likelihood of Flight to Avoid Prosecution   222
       Danger of the Defendant to Victim or Community   223
       Defendant's Burden in a Bail Hearing   223
   D. Bond Forfeiture   223
   E. The Push to Eliminate Bond   223

III. PRELIMINARY HEARING   224

   A. The Purpose of the Preliminary Hearing   224
   B. The Procedure Followed at the Preliminary Hearing   224
   C. Evidentiary Issues and Rules During Preliminary Hearings   225
   D. Decision at the Preliminary Hearing   225
   E. The Defendant's Role at the Preliminary Hearing   226
   F. Negotiations Between Prosecutors and Defense Attorneys at
      Preliminary Hearings   226

Case Excerpt: *Atkins v. State*   227

Chapter Summary   229
Key Terms and Concepts   229
End of Chapter Exercises   230
Practice Questions for Test Review   231
Endnotes   232

12   ARRAIGNMENT AND DISCOVERY   233

Chapter Objectives ▪ Chapter Outline   233

I. ARRAIGNMENT   234

   A. Importance of the Arraignment   234
   B. Purpose of the Arraignment   235
   C. Filing Motions at Arraignment   235
   D. Waiving Arraignment   236
   E. Bench Warrants   236

II. DISCOVERY   237

   A. Purpose of Discovery   238

          Changes to Discovery Rules   239
    B. Material Provided in Discovery   239
          Witness List   240
          Statement of Defendant   240
          Statement of Codefendant   241
          Defendant's Criminal Record   241
          Documents and Tangible Objects   241
          Scientific Reports   241
          Statements of Witnesses   242
    C. Open File Policy   242
    D. Variations Among States in Discovery Rules   242
    E. Information That is Normally Not Discoverable by the
          Defendant   243
          Work Product   244
          Criminal Records of State Witnesses   244
    F. *Brady* Material   245
          In Camera Inspections   246

III. DEFENSE MOTIONS BASED ON DISCOVERY   246

    A. Motions to Suppress   246
    B. Motion to Sever   247
    C. Motion *in Limine*   247
    D. Motion to Reveal the Deal (*Giglio*)   248
    E. Motion to Reveal Identity of Confidential Informants   248

IV. OTHER DEFENSE MOTIONS   248

    A. Motion to Change Venue   249
    B. Motion for Continuance   249
    C. Plea of Former Jeopardy   249
    D. Bill of Particulars   250
    E. Speedy Trial Demand   250
          Dismissing a Case for Failure to Receive a Speedy Trial   250
          How Speedy Must a "Speedy Trial" Be?   251
          When the Defendant May Not Want a Speedy Trial After all   251
          When is the Right to a Speedy Trial Triggered?   251

V. PROSECUTION MOTIONS   252

    A. Similar Transactions   252
    B. Aggravation of Sentence   253
    C. Motion to Join   253

    Case Excerpt: *Ohio v. Magwood*   254

    Chapter Summary   257
    Key Terms and Concepts   257
    End of Chapter Exercises   258

Practice Questions for Test Review   259
Endnotes   260

---

13 THE TRIAL   261

Chapter Objectives ▪ Chapter Outline   261

I. THE COURTROOM   262

    A. The Jury Box   262
           Jury's Deliberation Room   263
    B. Witness Stand   263
    C. Judge's Bench   263
    D. Location of Defense and Prosecution Tables   264
    E. Clerk of Court   264
    F. Court Reporter   264

II. JURY SELECTION   265

    A. Peremptory Challenges   267
    B. Challenges for Cause   267
    C. *Batson* Challenges   268
    D. Striking the Jury   268
           Silent Strikes   269
    E. Alternate Jurors   269
    F. Final Steps for the Jury Before the Trial   269

III. OPENING STATEMENTS   270

IV. DIRECT EXAMINATION   271

    A. Questioning Witnesses During Direct Examination   272
    B. Introducing Evidence During Direct Examination   272

V. CROSS-EXAMINATION   273

    A. How is Cross-Examination Different from Direct Examination?   273
    B. Impeachment   274

VI.   REDIRECT EXAMINATION   274

VII. DIRECTED VERDICT   274

VIII. DEFENSE CASE-IN-CHIEF   275

IX.   REBUTTAL   276

X.   MISTRIAL   276

XI.   CHARGE CONFERENCE   276

XII. CLOSING ARGUMENTS   277

XIII. JURY INSTRUCTIONS   279

XIV. DELIBERATIONS   279

XV.   VERDICT   280

       A. Various Types of Verdicts in Criminal Cases   280
           Guilty   281
           Guilty but Mentally Ill   281
           Not Guilty   281
           Not Guilty by Reason of Insanity   281
       B. Polling the Jury   281
       C. Excusing the Jury   282

Case Excerpt: *People v. Murphy*   282

Chapter Summary   284
Key Terms and Concepts   284
End of Chapter Exercises   285
Practice Questions for Test Review   286
Endnotes   287

14   DEFENSES TO CRIMINAL PROSECUTIONS   289

Chapter Objectives ■ *Chapter Outline*   289

I.   SIMPLE DEFENSES   290

       A. Constitutional Defenses   290
           Double Jeopardy   290
           Privilege Against Self-Incrimination   292
           Due Process   292
           Equal Protection   292
           First Amendment   292
       B. Technical Defenses   292
           Vagueness and Overbreadth   293
           Ex Post Facto   294

Statute of Limitations   294
Errors in Charging Documents   295
   Allegata vs. Probata   295
   Technical Deficiencies in Charging Documents   296

II. AFFIRMATIVE DEFENSES   296

  A. Asserting Affirmative Defenses   296
  B. Specific Affirmative Defenses   298
     Age   298
     Alibi   299
     Battered Woman's Syndrome   299
     Coercion   299
     Consent   300
     Defending Property   300
     Duress   300
     Entrapment   301
     Insanity   301
       Historical Development: M'Naghten Rule   302
       Modern Definitions of Insanity After M'Naghten   303
       Determining the Moment of Insanity   303
       Raising the Insanity Defense   304
       Burden of Proof for the Defendant When Raising the Insanity
       Defense   304
       Diminished Capacity   304
     Intoxication   305
     Mutual Combat   305
     Necessity   306
     Self-Defense   306
       Defendant as Aggressor   307
       Defense of Others   307
       "Stand Your Ground" Laws   307
       Rebutting a Claim of Self-Defense   308
     Other Defenses   308

Case Excerpt: *McElrath v. State*   308

Chapter Summary   312
Key Terms and Concepts   312
End of Chapter Exercises   312
Practice Questions for Test Review   314
Endnotes   315

15 EIGHTH AMENDMENT: SENTENCING

15   **EIGHTH AMENDMENT: SENTENCING**   317

Chapter Objectives ■ *Chapter Outline*   317

I. GUILTY PLEAS   318

    A. Procedure   318
       Voluntariness of the Plea   320
    B. *Alford* Plea   320
    C. Nolo Contendere   320
    D. Conditional Plea   321
    E. First Offender Treatment   321

II. PLEA BARGAINING   322

    A. Federal Sentencing Negotiations   323
       Federal Sentencing Guidelines   323
    B. State Plea Negotiations   324
       State Sentencing Guidelines   324
    C. The Controversy Surrounding Plea Bargaining   324

III. SENTENCING   325

    A. Judicial Discretion   325
       Judicial Procedure in Imposing Sentences   325
         Statutory Minimum and Maximum Sentences   325
         Concurrent Sentencing   326
         Consecutive Sentencing   326
    B. Presentence Investigation   326
    C. Sentencing Hearing   326
       Victim Impact Statements   326
       Aggravation of Sentence   327
       Mitigation of Sentence   327
    D. Possible Punishments   327
       Death   328
         Procedures in Death Penalty Cases   328
         Sentencing in Death Penalty Cases   328
         Aggravating Factors   329
       Life in Prison Without the Possibility of Parole   329
       Life in Prison   329
       Sentence for Years   330
         Alternative Prisons   330
       Probation and Parole   331
       Fines   332
       Community Service   332
       Restitution   332

IV. CONSTITUTIONAL ISSUES IN SENTENCING   332

    A. Cruel and Unusual Punishment   333
    B. "Three Strikes and You're Out"   333

Case Excerpt: *McCloon v. State*   334

Chapter Summary   336
Key Terms and Concepts   337
End of Chapter Exercises   338
Practice Questions for Test Review   339
Endnotes   340

16   APPEALS

APPEALS   341

Chapter Objectives ▪ Chapter Outline   341

I. THE APPELLATE SYSTEM   342

    A. Motion for New Trial   342
    B. Notice of Appeal   342
        The Record   343
        The Docket Number   343
    C. Appellate Procedure   343
        The Brief   344
        Contents of the Appellant's Brief   344
          Title Page   344
          Statement of Facts   344
          Enumerations of Error   345
          Argument   345
          Conclusion   346
        The Appellee's Brief   346
        Moving Through the Appellate System   346
        Certiorari   347
          Standards Used to Determine Granting Cert.   347
          Granting Cert.   348
          Denial of Cert.   348
    D. The Powers of the Appellate Courts   348
    E. *Habeas Corpus*   349

II. ORGANIZATION OF THE APPELLATE SYSTEM   350

    A. The U.S. Supreme Court   350
    B. The U.S. Supreme Court is the Final Authority for Both Federal
       and State Courts   351

Case Excerpt: *Commonwealth v. O'Brien*   351

Chapter Summary   353
Key Terms and Concepts   353
End of Chapter Exercises   354
Practice Questions for Test Review   355
Endnote   356

**Appendix A. Answers to Review Questions and Practice
Questions for Test Review**   357
Appendix B. The Constitution of the United States   401
Glossary   419
Index   427

Preface

Criminal procedure is the core of all criminal justice programs. Unlike other texts on this topic, this book is written with the student, the instructor, and the criminal justice professional in mind. The author has extensive experience not only in teaching the topic, but also in living it. As an Assistant District Attorney in a major city, the author handled all types of cases from misdemeanors to murder trials. He brings his extensive knowledge of the topic to bear on each issue in this text. In *Criminal Procedure: An Introduction for Criminal Justice Professionals*, the author offers in-depth and current research on criminal topics, as well as a personal view of the criminal justice system gleaned from years as both a prosecutor and a criminal defense attorney. The book provides a balance between theoretical discussions and practical, down-to-earth examples of law in action at every phase of a criminal proceeding. The text emphasizes the practical aspects of criminal law and procedure and provides real-world examples, while still discussing the theoretical and academic bases of every aspect of a criminal case from the elements of offenses to procedural steps to the trial and subsequent appeal of a criminal case.

Features of the textbook include the following:

- Chapter objectives that are stated clearly and succinctly
- Terms and legal vocabulary set out in bold in the body of the text and defined immediately in the margin for the ease of student comprehension
- Scenarios to help students develop their understanding of the material
- Excerpts from seminal or otherwise noteworthy appellate cases
- End-of-chapter questions, hypothetical questions, web assignments, and sample quizzes to hone the students' understanding of the materials
- Web surfing to allow students to expand beyond the scope of the material presented in the text and further their research into specific topics

TEXTBOOK RESOURCES

The companion website for this text at wklegaledu.com includes additional resources for students and instructors.

Acknowledgments

I would like to acknowledge the tremendous help, effort, and support that the following individuals provided in bringing this book to its final form: my wife, Nilsa Bevans; my stepdaughter, Tamara Tigani; and Jordan Jepsen and the excellent Betsy Kenny.

Criminal Law and the U.S. Constitution

- Explain the structure of the U.S. court system
- Describe the significance of *stare decisis*
- Define the basic steps in a criminal prosecution
- List and explain the differences between the federal and state systems
- Describe various sources of law for the U.S. system

I. Sources of Law for the Criminal Justice System
   A. The U.S. Constitution
      State Constitutions
   B. Statutory Law
      Ordinances
   C. Judicial Decisions (Case Law)
      Case Law and the United States Supreme Court
   D. *Stare Decisis*
   E. Court Rules
   F. Agency Rules and Regulations
   G. Common Law
      What Is the Common Law?
      The Importance of Common Law
      The Uses of Common Law

II. Federal vs. State Court Systems
   A. The Levels of the Federal Court System
      Federal District Courts
      Appellate Courts: Courts of Appeal
      U.S. Supreme Court
   B. The Levels of the State Court System
      Trial Courts
      Appellate Courts
      State Supreme Court

III. Federal Prosecutions vs. State Prosecutions
   A. Federal Jurisdiction
   B. State Jurisdiction
      State-Level Prosecutions
   C. Differences Among States

SOURCES OF LAW FOR THE CRIMINAL JUSTICE SYSTEM

Whenever we discuss criminal law and criminal procedure, we must first address where law enforcement gets its authority to arrest individuals who have committed crimes, where prosecutors get the power to bring charges against defendants, where courts get the power to seat juries and hear cases, and finally, why the courts have the authority to sentence defendants who have been found guilty. What is the source of this authority? What are its limits? In criminal law, we have several different places we can look to answer this question:

- The U.S. Constitution
- Statutory law
- Judicial decisions
- Court Rules
- Agency rules and regulations
- Common law

A. THE U.S. CONSTITUTION

The Constitution of the United States provides that the government has the power to protect the welfare of its citizens and to pass laws that regulate behavior and punish those who break criminal statutes. This is the so-called police power of the Constitution, and it is the source of both federal and state criminal laws. However, as is often the case with the U.S. Constitution, there is no specific language empowering Congress to enact criminal statutes and to authorize federal courts to impose sentences on criminal defendants. Similarly, the Constitution makes no reference to the states' power to do the same thing. This power has been inferred as a necessary and indisputable right of the government to set boundaries on the behavior of its citizens. Without such power, there would be little need for any kind of government. (You will find the complete text of the U.S. Constitution in Appendix B.) What the U.S. Constitution does spell out is that it is the source of the federal government's power to take action to protect the health, safety, and welfare of the citizens, and creating criminal statutes is a necessary offshoot of that power.

STATE CONSTITUTIONS

A state constitution functions for the state in virtually the same manner as the U.S. Constitution does for the federal government. However, unlike the U.S. Constitution that governs the entire nation, a state constitution governs only those actions occurring within the state's boundaries. The dual nature of the United States often causes some confusion for those not familiar with the process. There is a federal government and there are individual state governments. Most provisions of the U.S. Constitution apply to state residents, and the state constitution certainly applies to the state residents. Interestingly enough, state constitutions are permitted to give greater freedoms to their citizens than those

FIGURE 1-1

Section 2: This Constitution, and the Laws of the United States which shall . . . be the supreme Law of the Land; and the Judges in every State shall be bound thereby, any Thing in the Constitution or Laws of any State to the Contrary notwithstanding.

FIGURE 1-1

Article VI, U.S. Constitution

that are given under the federal Constitution. A state constitution cannot, however, take away any of the rights granted to citizens under the U.S. Constitution. What happens, though, when there is a conflict between the U.S. Constitution and the provisions of a particular state's constitution? In most situations, the U.S. Constitution will prevail. The framers of the Constitution anticipated such problems and included the Supremacy Clause to address this issue. The Supremacy Clause is found in Article VI of the Constitution.

There are times when a crime comes under both state and federal jurisdiction. This means that either the federal or state governments could prosecute. In such a situation, a conflict often arises as to which government takes priority. Fortunately, the **Supremacy Clause** also helps to clear up any problems of who gets priority in prosecuting the defendant. This constitutional provision dictates that when there is a conflict between federal and state law, federal law takes priority. When a person has committed an offense that could be seen as both a federal and a state law violation, the federal authorities have priority and may prosecute the defendant first (see Figure 1-1).

Sidebar

The Supremacy Clause of the U.S. Constitution gives the federal authorities priority over state authorities in criminal actions.

Supremacy Clause
The provision in Article VI of the U.S. Constitution that the U.S. Constitution, laws, and treaties take precedence over conflicting state constitutions or laws.

B. STATUTORY LAW

Statutes consist of bills that are voted on by the legislative branch of government and enacted by the executive branch. Once a bill has been enacted, it is referred to as a **statute**. On the federal level, the U.S. Congress is the legislative branch, and it votes on bills before sending them to the president for signature. If the president signs the legislation, it becomes a binding law and thus a statute. On the state level, the legislature votes on bills and submits them to the governor for signature. In both instances, the laws that are created are referred to as statutes. It is tempting to think that statutes are the one and only source of laws that govern criminal activity, but that is not the case. Statutory law is only one part of the entire scheme of rules that govern criminal behavior.

Not all statutes involve criminal activity. There are many statutes created every year on both the federal and state levels that have nothing to do with criminal law. The statutes that deal with crime are usually grouped together in the federal and state codes for ease of reference. A **code** is a collection of laws, enacted by the legislative and executive process, that has been published in bound volumes and is usually also available on the Internet. Most crimes are violations of state, not federal statutes. There are comparatively few federal crimes, but there are 50 states, and each state has its own set of criminal statutes. As a result, most of the crime in the United States is prosecuted on the state, not the federal level.

Statute
A law that is voted on by the legislative branch of government and enacted by the executive branch.

Code
A collection of laws.

Ordinance
A law passed by a local government, such as a town council or city government.

Case law
The written decisions by appellate courts explaining the outcome of a case on appeal.

ORDINANCES

As we have seen, statutes are laws passed by a state or federal government. However, there is an entire class of laws passed by local governments, such as municipalities and towns, that regulate behavior at a local level. These are not referred to as statutes. Instead, they are called ordinances. An **ordinance** has limited application. It has a strict geographic limit, such as the town limits or the county boundary. Ordinances cannot conflict with statutes. If they do, the ordinance is ruled unconstitutional and the statute takes precedence. Examples of ordinances include regulations regarding excessively loud automobiles, illegal parking, failure to leash a dog, and so on.

People who are charged with ordinance violations are usually given citations and told to report to a local court, where they may face a small fine. Generally, there is no right to a jury trial for an ordinance violation.

C. JUDICIAL DECISIONS (CASE LAW)

In addition to statutory law, there is another, and equally important, source of law: case law. **Case law** is the huge body of published judicial decisions by appellate courts. People who are not familiar with the legal process often do not realize the significance of case law. When an appellate court reaches a decision in a case on appeal, the reasons for the decision are encapsulated in a written opinion. This opinion discusses not only the facts of the case on appeal, but also how the statutes and facts interact with one another. In some ways, case law is like binding commentary on the statutes; it can amplify, refine, or restrict the application of a statute, based on its interpretation by the appellate courts. For attorneys and police officers, case law is just as important as statutory law, and sometimes even more important. Case law generated by the U.S. Supreme Court has had a huge impact on criminal law and procedure and will continue to do so for the foreseeable future. In later chapters, we will examine many of the important U.S. Supreme Court cases that have had a major impact on criminal law.

CASE LAW AND THE UNITED STATES SUPREME COURT

What makes case law so important is not simply that it interprets statutory law, but also that a case decision can invalidate an entire statute. If the U.S. Congress decided to create a statute that no longer required police officers to read suspects their *Miranda* rights, this statute could (and probably would) be interpreted to be a violation of the U.S. Constitution. In such a scenario, the U.S. Supreme Court can, and often has, invalidated a statute that has been voted on by the legislative branch and enacted by the executive branch. This is part of the checks and balances system found in the U.S. Constitution and is often lauded for maintaining the balance of power among the three branches of government.

This is not to say that the only case law of importance is that created by the U.S. Supreme Court. Although the decisions of this court are binding on all U.S. courts, there are appellate courts on both the federal and state levels that also interpret statutes every day and also make rulings on specific cases. Unless and until a higher court overrules a court's interpretation of a statute, it remains binding.

D. *STARE DECISIS*

All courts are bound by the principle of **stare decisis**, the principle that previously decided cases that have similar facts and issues will have similar results.[1] Often referred to as the rule of precedent, it underlies almost all appellate law as a bedrock principle. In deciding their cases, judges must show how their decision comports with the rule of precedent. *Stare decisis* is the Latin term for stand by decided cases. It is an old but still very useful concept. When a court states that it will stand by decided cases, it is saying that if there is a prior decision by a court that dealt with the same issue, this court will rule the same way as that prior court, even if this court doesn't like the ruling. *Stare decisis* is really an issue of continuity. Judges abide by *stare decisis* to give everyone who appears before them some sense of predictability about what the court will do. If judges decide that they will not follow the decision in the prior case, they must show how this case is different from the prior case. With a different case, you can have a different ruling.

When courts review a case on appeal, as we will discuss in much greater depth in Chapter 16, they are guided by some straightforward rules: Has the issue in the current case ever been considered by a previous court? If so, what was the result? Is there any reason to deviate from the previous court's ruling?

Stare decisis
The principle that courts will reach results similar to those reached by courts in prior cases involving similar facts and legal issues.

E. COURT RULES

In addition to statutes and case law, courts also create their own internal rules that are extremely important to litigants in either civil or criminal cases. Court rules often focus on procedural steps, such as when and where a particular action can be filed and the types of motions that the parties to a case may file in a pending case. We will examine motions practice in much greater detail in Chapter 12.

F. AGENCY RULES AND REGULATIONS

Once a statute has been created, a governmental agency may create an administrative rule or regulation to put that statute into effect. For example, the Sixteenth Amendment gave the federal government the power to levy and collect income taxes but provided no details on how the process should actually be carried out. The U.S. Department of the Treasury, an agency authorized under

---

FIGURE 1-2

Sixteenth Amendment,
U.S. Constitution

The Congress shall have power to lay and collect taxes on incomes, from whatever source derived, without apportionment among the several states, and without regard to any census or enumeration.

the federal government, has the power to create its own rules and regulations to enforce the Sixteenth Amendment. These rules and regulations carry the same force as a statute (see Figure 1-2).

Those who violate the U.S. Treasury's rules and regulations in regard to nonpayment of taxes can face serious prison time and fines. They may also have their property confiscated by the government.

G. COMMON LAW

Common law
All case law or the case law that is made by judges in the absence of relevant statutes, or the legal system that originated in England and is composed of case law and statutes.

In addition to constitutional law, statutory law, ordinances, court rules, and agency regulations, there is a final source of law that we must examine in detail: **common law**. The development of the common law in the United States has a very interesting history.

In 1776, when the newly formed colonies of the Americas rebelled against the monarchy in Great Britain and decided to form their own country, they were immediately faced with some very pragmatic problems. Besides the issue of how a democracy would be organized, there was the more general question of what law would govern in the new United States of America. The Founding Fathers made up many of the rules for this new type of government as it was evolving, but they were not operating in a vacuum. They based many of their decisions on examples from Ancient Greece and even former colonies in the Americas, but when it came to the law, they opted to take the easy route. Rather than reinvent the wheel, they chose to adopt the law with which they were most familiar: English common law.

WHAT IS THE COMMON LAW?

England has existed for centuries, and for most of that time many of its citizens were illiterate. Passing statutes and codifying them in books, although it was done, was not of much use to a citizenry that could not read or interpret these laws. Instead, the citizens relied on judges to tell them what the law was and to dispense justice. In centuries past, English (and later American) judges, rode on horseback from town to town, dealing with both civil and criminal issues. Although they may have been accompanied by a few learned treatises, most of the rules of justice were in their heads. Many times, judges were faced with unique situations that no written law had been created to address. In the absence of a written law, a judge would decide the case for himself. These decisions carried as much weight as a written law created by Parliament. Judges from various jurisdictions would come together in meetings and would discuss their decisions in their cases. Over time, as identical legal issues were presented, judges began to create a uniform system of rules that would help them and future judges to reach fair decisions. As there was no written law to interpret, the judges would come up with guidelines of their own. To show the legal system was fair, judges agreed that each judge would be bound by decisions of other judges on specific issues. Many of these rules became known to the common people and thus were referred to as common law.

There is nothing particularly unusual or unique about common law. All of us have unwritten rules that we tend to follow. Many of these rules are understood to apply, even though they are not written down. When strangers meet for the first time, they often shake hands. There is no written rule requiring this behavior, but we all tend to do it and may take offense if someone refuses to offer his or her hand. English common law took this basic philosophy and elevated it to binding legal precedent. When the English colonies of the Americas became the United States of America, many of the states adopted this large body of rules, sayings, guidelines, and interpretations as American common law. We will examine only one of hundreds of common law "rules" to illustrate how common law works.

"Possession is 9/10ths of the Law." Possession is 9/10ths of the law is a maxim we have probably all heard, although probably not entirely understood. This is actually a common law rule. The origin of this law arises from a very common problem in both rural England and rural America: wayward domestic animals.

Suppose that a judge is presented with a case in which a cow has wandered away from one farm and has been found by another farmer. In the Old West, for example, calves that had not yet been branded were referred to as mavericks and could be claimed by anyone who found them. If the cow had no identifying marks on it, how was the judge to decide who actually owned the animal? Farmer A might be correct in claiming that the cow is Betsy that he's owned for years, but Farmer B might just as easily claim that the cow is Belle and that he has also owned her for years. Rather than try to delve into the internal workings of the farms and who may or may not have seen the cow in one farmer's presence, judges fashioned a rule that stated that when ownership of an item of a property—in this case a cow—cannot be confirmed to one person over another, then whoever has possession of it now is allowed to keep it.

This is but one example of the vast body of common law that arose over centuries of judicial decisions. It was this system that our country adopted shortly after its creation. One might be tempted to think that common law makes an interesting, if outdated, historical footnote, but that assumption would be incorrect. Common law is alive and well in the United States today.

THE IMPORTANCE OF COMMON LAW

Common law was adopted to create a body of law that the early colonial court systems could use as a ready-made legal framework. The common law found a valued place in situations where no other law was applicable. Common law was originally adopted by the 13 colonies that later became the first 13 states.

Many of those states took some or all common law principles, enacted them as legislation, and then revoked the original English common law to avoid the confusing situation of having statutory law existing side by side with common law. However, several states never got around to the second part of that equation and never abolished common law. As a result, in those states, common law is as relevant as it ever was and does exist side by side with statutes, causing confusion for people not schooled in the meaning and importance of common law.

Some states, like Virginia and North Carolina, abolished only part of the common law and kept other parts. This means that for people in common law states, it is possible to have two different kinds of criminal violations. For instance, in a common law state, a defendant can be charged with two separate crimes for a single offense. A defendant could be charged with common law burglary and statutory burglary, for example. However, when the case is resolved, the defendant can only be sentenced on one of the counts.

Proving someone guilty of a common law offense involves different evidence than would be required to prove someone guilty of a statutory offense. Under common law burglary,[2] the state must prove the following elements beyond a reasonable doubt:

- Breaking and entering
- Of a house
- At night and with the intent to commit a felony or theft

However, the elements of statutory burglary are different. Under statutory burglary, the state must prove that there was:

- Breaking and entering
- Of a dwelling
- With the intent to commit a theft or felony

As you can see, the elements of common law burglary and statutory burglary are different. The most conspicuous difference is that common law burglary can only be committed "at night." There is no such element in statutory burglary. Given the differences between the two crimes, one might ask why anyone would bother charging common law offenses when the statutory offenses appear to be broader in scope. The simple answer is that for some common law offenses, the sentence can be longer than the statutory offense. Common law offenses may also track the actual details of the crime better than the statutory offense. Finally, prosecutors may use both charges as a bargaining tool during plea negotiations, by offering to reduce the crime to the one with the lower possible punishment, whether it happens to be the common law crime or the statutory crime.

THE USES OF COMMON LAW

Although most states have abolished common law in favor of statutory law, a surprising number have either abolished only some aspects of common law while keeping others (e.g., abolishing all common law crimes but keeping common law marriage), and others have not abolished common law at all. In those states, there are powerful arguments for keeping common law, including sentencing and new legal issues.

When it comes to sentencing, a judge must follow the statutory guidelines for imposing the sentence. However, what happens when a legislature enacts a law but fails to provide a sentence? In that situation, a state that has abolished common law may find itself in a legal quandary that will require additional legislation. In common law states, however, a judge is permitted to use common law sentencing guidelines.

We have all heard that there is nothing new under the sun. Whether or not you believe that statement, there is no question that common law dates back for centuries. Since that time nearly every type of legal question that has arisen has been addressed by a judge at one time or another. A judge who is presented with a seemingly new question could peruse the old common law to see if a similar argument has ever been raised. In such a situation, the judge could benefit from hundreds of years of cases and the accumulated wisdom of thousands of judges to help him or her decide the best course in a current case.

FEDERAL VS. STATE COURT SYSTEMS

When we discuss the organization of the state and federal court systems, the material might, at first, appear daunting in its complexity. However, this is not the case. All court systems, whether on the state or federal level, are built on a simple premise: The actions of a lower court can be reviewed by a higher court. Seen this way, all court systems in the United States could be visualized as pyramids, with the lower courts forming the base and the higher courts forming the upper portions of the pyramid. The **U.S. Supreme Court** is the highest court in the federal system and so sits at the top of that pyramid.

U.S. Supreme Court
The name for the highest court of the United States federal and state court systems.

A. THE LEVELS OF THE FEDERAL COURT SYSTEM

We will now examine the pyramidal structure of the court system on the federal level by looking at the base and then moving slowly up toward the top of the pyramid, the U.S. Supreme Court.

FEDERAL DISTRICT COURTS

The Federal Court system has courts that cover the entire United States and its territories. There are 94 United States District Courts with at least one for each state and some that share jurisdiction over U.S. territories. Federal District Courts are the workhorses of the federal system. These are the courts where trials are held, where motions are heard, where defendants are sentenced, and where probationers may have their probation revoked, among many other procedures.

FIGURE 1-3

Map of Federal Circuits

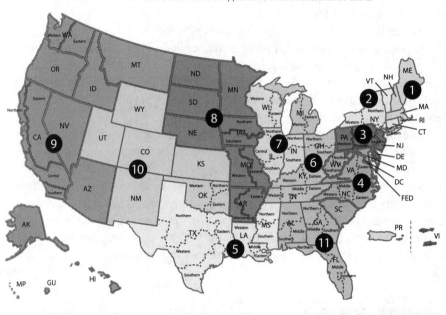

Geographic Boundaries
of United States Courts of Appeals and United States District Courts

Federal District Courts are placed all over the United States, but the system is based on population, not geography. In places where there are few people, there tends to be less crime. In more densely populated areas, crime rates tend to be correspondingly higher. As a result, the East Coast and the Northeast in particular have higher numbers of Federal District Courts as opposed to portions of the western part of the United States, which have comparatively few. See Figure 1-3 for a map showing the location of the Federal Circuits. The courts are organized in 12 different circuits that encompass the entire United States and its territories. Any Federal District Court is identified by its affiliation with a particular circuit and a district within that circuit. A person who is charged with a federal offense in Raleigh, North Carolina, for example, would be tried in the North Carolina Eastern District Court for the 4th Circuit, whereas a man who is charged with a federal crime in Jacksonville, Florida would be charged in the Florida Middle District for the 11th Circuit.

APPELLATE COURTS: COURTS OF APPEAL

Each Federal District Court is established inside a particular circuit. The circuits of the federal judiciary encompass the entire United States and its territories. In criminal cases, when the defendant is found guilty, he or she will appeal the verdict to an appellate court. In the federal system, there are 12 separate circuits that are responsible for hearing appeals from the district courts located within their territory. (There is a 13th circuit, but it is reserved for special cases arising out of the DC Circuit.) When a case is heard on appeal from any district court, the case goes to the corresponding court of appeals for that circuit. The U.S.

Courts of Appeal are the midlevel or intermediate courts between the trial courts (Federal District Court) and the U.S. Supreme Court. A judge who sits on any of the U.S. Circuit Courts of Appeals is nominated by the president and must be confirmed by the Senate before he or she can take the seat.

U.S. SUPREME COURT

The U.S. Supreme Court is the highest court in the federal system. It hears all appeals from the various Federal Circuit Courts of Appeal located around the country. As we will see later in this text, the U.S. Supreme Court is not required to hear all appeals presented to it. The Court may pick and choose, in most situations, which cases it will hear and which cases it will not hear. See Figure 1-4 for a current list of the U.S. Supreme Court Justices.

Justices of the U.S. Supreme Court, once selected for the position, are allowed to serve as a Justice for the rest of their lives. They cannot be fired by the president or anyone else and may only be removed if they commit some crime and are impeached. When a position becomes vacant on the court, either through death or retirement, the president has the authority to nominate a replacement who must then be approved by the Senate. The U.S. Supreme Court building is located in Washington, DC, directly across from the Capitol. The Court begins its session on the first Monday in October and continues through the first Monday of the following May. The Court is in recess from June through October (see Figure 1-5).

The U.S. Supreme Court is unlike any other court in the United States. For one thing, it is both the highest federal court and the highest state court, making it the final authority on all issues dealing with both state and the federal Constitution.

Sidebar

The average salary of a Federal Circuit Court of Appeals judge is $180,000 per year.

- John G. Roberts, Jr., Chief Justice
- Clarence Thomas, Associate Justice
- Ruth Bader Ginsburg, Associate Justice
- Stephen G. Breyer, Associate Justice
- Samuel A. Alito, Jr., Associate Justice
- Sonia Sotomayor, Associate Justice
- Elena Kagan, Associate Justice
- Neil M. Gorsuch, Associate Justice
- Brett M. Kavanaugh, Associate Justice

FIGURE 1-4

The Current Members of the Supreme Court

The judicial Power of the United States, shall be vested in one supreme Court, and in such inferior Courts as the Congress may from time to time ordain and establish.

FIGURE 1-5

Article III, §1, U.S. Constitution

B. THE LEVELS OF THE STATE COURT SYSTEM

The state court systems are often—but not always—similar to the federal system. There are trial courts where juries are empaneled and reach verdicts in criminal cases, and there are intermediate courts of appeal where a defendant may bring an appeal from that conviction. There is also a top state court that determines all issues of state law and is responsible for interpreting the state and the U.S. Constitution. One of the problems inherent in any examination of state court systems is the variation seen among the states. All states have trial courts, but they do not go by the same name or have the same powers as courts in other states.

TRIAL COURTS

In some states, there are State Courts that are empowered to hear misdemeanor cases, before juries of six people, while Superior Courts hear felony cases before juries of 12 individuals. In other states, there are no juries for misdemeanor cases and the defendant may appeal to the Superior Court for a new trial (and a jury) if he or she is convicted in State Court.

Because there is such variation among the states, we will simplify the process of examining state trial courts by using terms that are used by a majority of states and, for the moment, avoid the usage in the minority of states. For our purposes, we will assume that there is only one type of trial court on the state level, even though many states have two or more, each with different names. We will call our hypothetical trial court Superior Court.

Superior Court is the court where criminal trials occur. Juries are brought into this courtroom, and defendants are brought to trial. These are the cases that you can see almost any night on television. In the fictionalized versions of Superior Court, witnesses often admit to committing the crime and attorneys give brilliant, and remarkably short, closing arguments. The real world is considerably different, though, and we will be focusing on the real world of criminal law and procedure throughout this text.

If a defendant is found not guilty in Superior Court, he or she is released and there is no appeal. (The state is not allowed to appeal a not guilty verdict.) If a defendant is found guilty, then he or she will likely bring an appeal to the State Court of Appeals.

APPELLATE COURTS

Each state has its own version of an appellate court. Most states follow the federal model of a trial court, an intermediate court of appeals, and a state supreme court, but not all states use these names to refer to these courts. In most states, the intermediate appellate court is referred to as the State Court of Appeals. It may resemble the federal system closely. Defendants who are found guilty in Superior Court bring their appeal to this court. However, whereas there are 12 different Federal Circuit Courts of Appeal around the United States, there is only one State Appellate Court. If either the defendant or the prosecution loses the appeal at this level, either can bring an appeal to the State Supreme Court.

STATE SUPREME COURT

At the top of the state hierarchy is a court that hears all appeals from the State Court of Appeals. This court has the final say on all state law matters and is also empowered to interpret the U.S. Constitution. Although this court is not always called the State Supreme Court, we use this term to refer to the states' highest court. In most cases, a criminal appeal will end at this level, but as we have already seen, there are provisions that allow the U.S. Supreme Court to reach final and binding decisions on state law as well.

FEDERAL PROSECUTIONS VS. STATE PROSECUTIONS

A prosecution can occur at either the state or federal level. There are state crimes and federal crimes. A person may be prosecuted by the federal government or the state government or, in limited circumstances, by both. This dual arrangement sometimes causes confusion for individuals new to the criminal justice field.

There are provisions that allow the federal government to charge a defendant with one crime and a state to charge a different crime for the same transaction. Examples abound, including the sniper attacks in the Washington, DC area several years ago, where two men shot victims at random. In that case, the men were in violation of both state and federal laws. They were prosecuted by Maryland first, then prosecuted by the federal authorities, all based on the same actions. Why is this not a violation of the rule against **double jeopardy**?

Double jeopardy
A Constitutional provision that prohibits a person from being tried twice for the same crime.

The Fifth Amendment provides that a person cannot be tried twice for the same offense. If a defendant is found not guilty of a crime, the government that tried him is not permitted to try the defendant again. However, this rule applies to the specific jurisdiction that tried the defendant. The federal government and state governments are two different jurisdictions. Because of this, the federal authorities can prosecute a person who has committed a federal offense, and then the state may also prosecute based on a state statute.

In the previous paragraph, we saw the first instance of the use of the word **jurisdiction**. This is an excellent point to explain just what jurisdiction is and how it affects criminal prosecutions.

Jurisdiction
The persons about whom and the subject matters about which a court has the right and power to make decisions that are legally binding.

A. FEDERAL JURISDICTION

When we use the term jurisdiction, we are referring to power or authority. If a court has jurisdiction, it can control the actions of the parties and make decisions that bind all parties in the prosecution. If a judge has jurisdiction and rules that certain evidence produced by the prosecutor will not be admissible, then the evidence will not be allowed. Federal courts are courts of limited jurisdiction, a term that we will examine later. Essentially this means that there are only a limited number of actions in which a federal court may become involved. Barring any statute expressly granting federal courts jurisdiction over a matter, the criminal action defaults to the states.

B. STATE JURISDICTION

State jurisdiction is based on the state's constitution and its own police power. However, simply because the U.S. Constitution imposes certain minimum standards on the states to allow for specific procedural steps, that does not mean that the states are uniform in how they prosecute cases. In fact, states vary considerably in their procedural steps, hearings, and even the names that they apply to charging documents, law enforcement officials, and prosecutors. Because states have their own authority, they are free to develop any procedures that do not violate the U.S. Constitution or their own state constitution, even if this procedure is different from that used by another state.

States have the power to enact their own laws, not only to criminalize behavior, but also to include different procedural steps. Because most criminal prosecutions occur on the state level, we will spend a great deal of time discussing state-based procedural steps, but you should keep in mind that there is a great deal of variation among the states. Simply because an activity is illegal in one state does not mean that it is illegal in another state. Many states have legalized growing, production, and sale of marijuana within their state boundaries. However, at the time of this writing, marijuana continues to be listed as a scheduled narcotic. The practical effect of this situation is that a person may legally possess marijuana in one state but guilty of a crime when crossing state boundaries. This is one example of many disparities between federal and state law.

Throughout this text, we address specific states and how they proceed with certain steps following the arrest of a suspect and continuing through to sentence and appeal. However, there is no way to address the differences among all the states, so we limit our discussion to the most commonly found procedural steps and constitutional safeguards, occasionally addressing the differences in particular states.

STATE-LEVEL PROSECUTIONS

Most prosecutions occur on the state level. There are, after all, 50 states but only one federal government. This explains why there are more state-level prosecutions than federal-level prosecutions. The number of states is not the only reason there are more state-based prosecutions, though. As we have already seen, federal courts have limited jurisdiction, but the states do not have that same limitation. States are free to criminalize any behavior they see fit, again, so long as it does not violate any of the rights guaranteed in the state or U.S. Constitution.

Most attorneys are members of one or maybe two bar associations at most. The reason is that procedures, rules, and hearings vary so much from state to state that it would be difficult to stay current on many different states' laws and variations.

C. DIFFERENCES AMONG STATES

Individuals who are trained based on national standards are often surprised to learn just how regional some legal procedures are. States not only follow different sequences in prosecuting defendants; they even refer to their charging documents by different names and use different procedures. There is very little uniformity among the states and, as a result, an attorney who has been admitted to practice in one state might have difficulty adjusting to the differences in another state. In fact, many states limit the options that an attorney has to transfer his or her license from one state to another. Referred to as reciprocity, some states allow an attorney who is a member in good standing to simply transfer his or her legal license to a new state, but a fair number require the attorney from one state to retake the bar exam for the new state. This fact tends to keep attorneys practicing in one or two states at most.

CHAPTER SUMMARY

There are various sources of authority for criminal law proceedings, including the U.S. Constitution, statutory law, case law, agency rules, and common law. Although common law is not found in all states, it remains an important part of legal history and is actively followed in a handful of states.

The court system is organized as a hierarchy, with trial courts at the bottom, appellate courts in the middle, and a supreme court at the top. On the state level, there is a court that examines appeals and makes final determinations of state law. The federal system is organized along the same lines, with Federal District Courts at the trial level, U.S. Courts of Appeals as the intermediate appellate courts, and the U.S. Supreme Court as the nation's highest court. The U.S. Supreme Court enjoys a unique position in that it is the court of last resort for both federal and state systems.

KEY TERMS AND CONCEPTS

Supremacy Clause	Case law	Double jeopardy
Statute	*Stare decisis*	Jurisdiction
Code	Common law	
Ordinance	U.S. Supreme Court	

END OF CHAPTER EXERCISES

Review Questions

See Appendix A for answers

1　What is the Supremacy Clause?
2　Explain statutory law.
3　What are ordinances?
4　Explain case law and its significance.
5　Are federal and state agencies able to create their own rules and regulations? Explain.
6　What is the common law?
7　Provide an example of a common law rule.
8　What is the function of the judge?
9　What is the role of a defense attorney?
10　How do federal prosecutions differ from state prosecutions?
11　Explain "jurisdiction."
12　Provide a brief description of the organization of the federal court system.
13　What is the name of the highest court in United States?

Web Surfing

1　Locate the website for your state's court system. How is your court system organized? Is it similar or different from the description given in the text?

2　Go to the Federal Judiciary homepage and answer the following questions:
- How many justices serve on the U.S. Supreme Court? How long has each Justice served? Who appointed each Justice?
- How many Federal District Courts exist in United States?

Questions for Analysis

1　Should the court systems in the United States be simplified and streamlined? Do we have too many courts? Explain your answer.

2　In the states that still have common law, should it be abolished? Justify your answer.

Hypothetical

The fictional State of Placid has enacted a recent law that allows the medicinal use of marijuana for those suffering from cancer and chronic pain. Federal law prohibits the sale of marijuana for any reason and does make an exception for medicinal uses. Given the existence of the Supremacy Clause, what is the likely outcome of a dispute between federal and state authorities over whether medical marijuana is legal in Placid?

PRACTICE QUESTIONS FOR TEST REVIEW

See Appendix A for answers

Essay Question

Explain the concept of *stare decisis*.

True-False

1 **T   F**   The U.S. Supreme Court has nine justices.

2 **T   F**   Case law carries as much weight as statutory or common law.

3 **T   F**   Common law is not followed in any states in the United States.

Fill in the Blank

1   A law that is voted on by the legislative branch of and enacted by the executive branch is _____.

2   The written decisions by appellate courts explaining the outcome of a case on appeal are called _____.

3   The principle that courts will reach results similar to those reached by courts in prior cases involving similar facts and legal issues is _____.

Multiple Choice

1   The principle that courts will reach results similar to those reached by courts in prior cases involving similar facts and legal issues.
   A   *Stare decisis.*
   B   *Caveat emptor.*
   C   *Res ipsa loquitor.*
   D   *Pro hac vice.*

2   A Constitutional provision that prohibits a person from being tried twice for the same crime.
   A   Possession is 9/10ths of the law.
   B   Separation of powers.
   C   Dead man's rule.
   D   Double jeopardy.

3   The trial court on the federal level is called:
   A   Superior Court.
   B   Magistrate Court.
   C   Demands Court.
   D   District Court.

ENDNOTES

1. *State v. Peeler,* 321 Conn. 375, 140 A.3d 811 (Conn. 2016).
2. *Clark v. Com.,* 472 S.E.2d 663, 22 Va.App. 673 (Va. App. 1996).

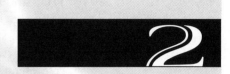

Introduction to the Criminal Justice System

- Explain the differences between civil and criminal cases
- Define the initial procedures following an arrest
- Describe the importance of the *Miranda* decision
- Compare and contrast preliminary hearings and grand jury sessions
- List and explain the basic steps in a criminal trial

I. Introduction to the Criminal Justice System

II. The Criminal System
   A. Verdicts in Criminal Cases
   B. Verdicts in Civil Cases
   C. The Burden of Proof
   D. The Pleadings
   E. Classes of Crimes: Felonies v. Misdemeanors

III. Overview of Procedural Steps in a Criminal Prosecution
   A. Arrest
      Arrest and Probable Cause
   B. Interrogation
      Miranda *Warnings*
   C. Evidence
   D. Initial Appearance
   E. Preliminary Hearing
   F. Grand Jury
      True Bill vs. No Bill
   G. Arraignment
   H. Trial
      Basic Overview of a Criminal Trial
   I. Sentencing
      Prison vs. Probation

INTRODUCTION TO THE CRIMINAL JUSTICE SYSTEM

The world of criminal law is highly specialized and extremely interesting. Although there is a tendency to think about law as only involving an interpretation of statutes and appellate cases, criminal law is all about people. People commit crimes; other people investigate these crimes; and still others prosecute, represent, incarcerate, and monitor those accused of a crime. Criminal law is really about the interactions among and between human beings. In this text, we will cover all of the procedural steps that occur in a criminal prosecution from an initial stop by a police officer through arrest, followed by a thorough discussion of appeals. At every step of the process, during the collection of evidence, arresting the defendant, obtaining a statement from the defendant, arraigning, trying, and eventually sentencing guilty defendants, there are critical steps that must be followed and situations where the defendant is protected by rights guaranteed by the U.S. Constitution and individual state law.

THE CRIMINAL SYSTEM

Guilty
The verdict in a criminal case when the jurors have determined that the defendant has committed a crime.

Criminal law is different than other branches of law. In fact, we could make a broad distinction and say that there are really two overall categories of law: criminal law and civil law. In a criminal case, the government brings charges against a defendant. If a jury believes, beyond a reasonable doubt, that the defendant has committed the crime, then they may vote to find him or her guilty.

When a person is found **guilty** in a criminal case, that person faces imprisonment, fines, restitution, probation, or parole. That is not the situation in a civil case. At the conclusion of a civil case, a person may be found **liable**. A party who is found liable may be required to pay monetary damages to the opposing parties. However, no one who has lost a civil case will go to prison or face a term on probation or parole. See Figure 2-1 for examples of various types of civil and criminal cases.

Liable
A finding in a civil case that a party has a duty or obligation to the other party to pay damages or to carry out some other action.

Verdict
A jury's factual determination; a jury's finding.

A. VERDICTS IN CRIMINAL CASES

The findings in a criminal case are guilty and not guilty; in a civil case they are liable or not liable.

A **verdict** is the jurors' determination of what they believe the facts of the case to be. The verdict is, in fact, the jury's final determination about who is telling the truth in the case and who is not. Looked at another way, the verdict refers to who wins and who loses. As we have already mentioned, the verdicts in civil and criminal cases are very different. At the conclusion of a civil trial, the losing party is found liable to the other party. The verdicts in a criminal case are of a completely different order. At the conclusion of a criminal trial, a defendant

Examples of Civil Cases	Examples of Criminal Cases	**FIGURE 2-1**
■ Slander ■ Property boundary disputes ■ Personal injury cases: when a person injured in a car wreck sues the other driver ■ Medical malpractice	■ Murder ■ Rape ■ Arson ■ Armed robbery ■ Forgery ■ Battery ■ Aggravated assault ■ Theft ■ Criminal damage to property	Examples of Civil and Criminal Cases

may be found guilty, **not guilty**, **guilty but mentally ill,** or **not guilty by reason of insanity**. When a jury reaches a verdict of guilty in a criminal case, it means that the jurors believe that the defendant, to a level of proof beyond a reasonable doubt, committed the crime. This finding of guilt subjects the defendant to a possible prison sentence, probation, parole, fines, or some combination thereof. The defendant may also be required to pay restitution to the victim during the course of his or her probation. A verdict of not guilty means that the jurors do not believe that the defendant committed the crime, or that the state failed to prove that the defendant was guilty beyond a reasonable doubt. The final two verdicts, guilty but mentally ill and not guilty by reason of insanity, are not available in all jurisdictions. When the jury finds the defendant is guilty but mentally ill, the court must sentence the defendant to a facility that includes some psychiatric counseling or monitoring. A finding of not guilty by reason of insanity is a verdict we will explore in much greater depth when we discuss defenses later in this text. At its simplest, the verdict simply means that the defendant lacks the mental capacity to know and understand the difference between right and wrong and therefore cannot be found guilty. Such defendants are often diverted to facilities that care for individuals suffering from severe mental disturbances.

When a defendant has been found not guilty, he or she will be set free (assuming that there are no other cases pending against the defendant). A not guilty verdict has specific legal and constitutional implications. For example, a defendant who has been found not guilty cannot be retried for the same offense. The Fifth Amendment to the U.S. Constitution specifically prohibits this practice under its double jeopardy clause. See Figure 2-2 for the entire text of the Fifth Amendment.

Not guilty
The jury's determination that the state has failed to prove that the defendant committed the crime beyond a reasonable doubt.

Guilty but mentally ill
A finding that the defendant is guilty of the crime charged but has some mental problems or mental disease that mitigate his or her guilt to a small degree.

Not guilty by reason of insanity
A finding that the defendant did not understand the difference between right and wrong when he or she committed the offense and therefore lacks the mental capability to commit a crime.

B. VERDICTS IN CIVIL CASES

In a civil trial, the jury can award monetary payments from one party to another. For instance, a jury can award compensatory **damages**—monetary payments from the defendant designed to compensate the plaintiffs for their

Damages
Money that a court orders paid to a person who has suffered damages by the person who caused the injury.

FIGURE 2-2

Fifth Amendment, U.S.
Constitution

No person shall be held to answer for a capital, or otherwise infamous crime, unless on a presentment or indictment of a Grand Jury, except in cases arising in the land or naval forces, or in the Militia, when in actual service in time of War or public danger; nor shall any person be subject for the same offence to be twice put in jeopardy of life or limb; nor shall be compelled in any criminal case to be a witness against himself, nor be deprived of life, liberty, or property, without due process of law; nor shall private property be taken for public use, without just compensation.

Restitution
Money that a court orders a criminal defendant to pay to the victim of a crime for damage or destruction of the victim's property.

losses. A civil jury can also award punitive damages and other types of damages against a defendant. Punitive damages are monetary assessments designed to punish the defendant and send a message to the community that behavior similar to that of the defendant will not be tolerated. Damages are not available in criminal cases. Instead, the state may seek **restitution** for the victim's out-of-pocket expenses in repairing property destroyed by the defendant, but there are no provisions for punitive damages in criminal law. Instead, the punitive provisions come in the form of fines and prison time.

Unlike criminal cases, in civil cases while the plaintiff who brings suit against a defendant will attempt to prove that the defendant is liable to the plaintiff, a defendant may also bring proof that the plaintiff is actually liable to him or her. In the end, a jury can as easily find the plaintiff liable to the defendant as it could the defendant liable to the plaintiff.

Sidebar

In civil cases, either party may seek monetary damages from the other; in criminal cases, the defendant may be found guilty or not guilty, but is not required to pay civil damages to the state.

C. THE BURDEN OF PROOF

Burden of proof
The amount of proof that a party must bring to sustain an action against another party. It is different in civil and criminal cases.

Preponderance of the evidence
The standard of proof most closely associated with a civil case where a party proves that his or her version of the facts is more than likely to be true.

When we discuss the **burden of proof** in a legal action, we are referring to the minimum level of evidence and facts that one party must establish as true against the other party. Standards of proof have been developed over centuries of legal hearings so that participants will understand what must be established as fact before another party can be liable in a civil case or guilty in a criminal case. Prosecutors in criminal cases have a much higher standard to meet in criminal cases than plaintiffs in civil cases.

The burden of proof is a phrase that refers to one side's obligation to prove the allegations against the other side. In most civil cases, that burden is **preponderance of the evidence**. This means that when a plaintiff brings a civil suit against a defendant, the plaintiff must prove his or her allegations are more likely true than not. Many commentators have compared this burden of proof to an old-fashioned scale, where putting more weight on one side makes the scale dip in one direction. When the plaintiff makes the scales tip in his or her direction, the plaintiff has met the civil standard of proof.

The standard that a prosecutor has to meet to convict someone is much higher than in civil cases. It is **proof beyond a reasonable doubt**. Although difficult to quantify, a reasonable doubt refers to the type of doubt that a person would have that might prevent him or her from making a major life decision. Proof beyond a reasonable doubt has been defined in various ways for centuries, but as most jurors learn at the conclusion of a criminal trial, this burden simply means that the state must prove each and every element of the offense against the defendant. If, at the end of the trial, a juror still believes that the state has failed to do that, and the juror has a specific, reasonable point of contention with the state's case, the juror is not only encouraged but required to find the defendant not guilty. This doubt has to be based on common sense and not mere fancy. Proving that someone has committed a crime beyond a reasonable doubt is quite a high standard. The individuals who founded our society based their legal model on the English system, which also required proof beyond a reasonable doubt to convict a person. The reason that the standard is so high is that it should not be an easy thing to deprive a person of his or her liberty or even the person's life. Conviction of a crime carries it with many legal and social consequences and creating a low standard of proof would make it easy for prosecutors to prove that almost anyone is guilty of some offense. Judges often instruct jurors that even if they believe that the defendant committed the crime, but the state has failed to prove it, then they must vote a not guilty verdict.

There is an unfortunate use of legal terminology when it comes to discussing the parties to civil and criminal cases. The term used to refer to the person who is being sued in a civil case (in most jurisdictions) is the defendant. This is also the term that the state uses when it refers to a person charged with a crime. Because the terms are identical, it can sometimes lead to confusion when discussing a case. Often, it is necessary to ask if the defendant is being sued or is a person charged with a crime. However, even though both of these parties are referred to as defendants, it is not proper to refer to the state as a plaintiff in a criminal action. States rarely sue individuals. It is far more likely that when the state brings an action against a person that the state is pursuing a criminal charge against the defendant.

A criminal prosecution is brought by federal or state governments in the name of their citizens. A private individual brings a civil lawsuit. A crime is a violation of law, usually set out as a statute, and is viewed as an infraction against society as a whole. Although there may be a specific victim, the prosecutor represents the government and brings charges in the name of the government. In the final analysis, a crime is a wrong committed against all of society. A civil action, on the other hand, is generally personal to the parties involved in the lawsuit. It is a private wrong and therefore a private lawsuit. These differences carry over into the pleadings or court documents filed in the different types of cases.

Proof beyond a reasonable doubt The burden of proof in a criminal case; when one has a reasonable doubt, it is not mere conjecture but a doubt that would cause a prudent, rational person to hesitate before finding a defendant guilty of a crime.

Sidebar

In criminal cases, the burden of proof is always on the state to prove that the defendant is guilty beyond a reasonable doubt. The defendant is never required to prove his or her innocence.

D. THE PLEADINGS

A civil action is usually based on a private wrong suffered by an individual. The individual brings suit when he or she has suffered a financial, emotional, or physical loss. The right to bring a civil suit is not limited to natural persons only.

Style
The caption, title, or heading listing the parties to the case.

Corporations and businesses may also sue in their own right. When cases from appellate courts are published, the first detail that is reported is the style, or caption, of the case. This is always given with the names of the parties involved. Civil cases are captioned Plaintiff A v. Defendant B. Because the government always brings criminal cases, the government is listed by name, not as a plaintiff. Criminal cases are captioned Government (or State) v. Defendant. The **style** of a case can tell you, usually within seconds, if the case is civil or criminal. There are times, however, when individuals also bring civil suits against the government, so it is important to examine additional details of the case, not just the style. See Figure 2-3 for an example of the style in a criminal case and how it compares to the style found in a civil case.

Pleadings
1) In a civil case, the pleadings set out the wrong suffered by the parties against one another; 2) in a criminal case, the pleadings are often referred to as indictments (in felony cases) and accusations/ information(s) (in misdemeanor cases), where the state sets out an infraction by the defendant that violates the law.

Pleadings refer to the legal documents that describe the nature of the claim against the parties. In a civil lawsuit, most states refer to the plaintiff's pleading as a **complaint** (also known as a petition). This document sets out the plaintiff's factual allegations against the defendant and requests the jury to award monetary damages to the plaintiff as a result of the defendant's actions. The defendant, on the other hand, responds with an **answer**, also known as a reply. In the answer, the defendant denies the plaintiff's factual allegations and also denies any responsibility for the plaintiff's injuries. In civil pleadings, the defendant may also request damages against the plaintiff.

Complaint
The document filed by the plaintiff and served on the defendant that sets out the plaintiff's factual allegations that show the defendant is responsible for the plaintiff's injuries.

In criminal cases, the state files charges against a defendant through various means. Although the defendant may have initially been arrested on a warrant or given a citation by a police officer, the prosecutor is allowed to alter the charges against the defendant, as long as they are supported by the evidence. In most states, prosecutors charge defendants with felonies through **indictments**. An indictment lists the known facts of the offense, including date, time, and location, as well as the name of the crime and the statute that the defendant is alleged to have violated. Should a prosecutor decide to charge the defendant with a lesser count, the prosecutor might use a different charging document. We will discuss charging decisions and charging documents in a later chapter.

Answer
The defendant's written response to the complaint, usually containing denials of the defendant's responsibility for the plaintiff's injuries.

Indictment
An official charge against a defendant accusing him or her of a felony.

E. CLASSES OF CRIMES: FELONIES VS. MISDEMEANORS

Felony
A crime that can be punished with a sentence of one year or more.

Crimes are broken down into two general classifications: felonies and misdemeanors. A **felony** is a crime punishable by more than one year in custody and often a substantial fine. These crimes include all of the major crimes against people, such as murder, manslaughter, sex crimes such as rape, and theft crimes involving automobiles or items of a certain value. The definition also encompasses crimes as disparate as arson and habitual offending (recidivism). The maximum sentence under a felony is the death sentence, life in prison without the possibility of parole, or a term of years and parole, to name just a few options. By contrast, a **misdemeanor** is a less serious crime, punishable by less than a year in custody. In many states, misdemeanors also have a maximum limit of a $1,000 to $5,000 fine that may be imposed. Examples of misdemeanor offenses include driving while under the influence of alcohol, speeding, minor theft, and some forms of battery and assault, among many others.

Misdemeanor
A criminal offense that is punished by a maximum possible sentence of one year or less in custody.

FIGURE 2-3

Style of Criminal and Civil Cases

Style of a Criminal Case

STATE OF XANADU
COUNTY OF BURKE
SUPERIOR COURT OF BURKE COUNTY

INDICTMENT NO: 20CR-12345

STATE OF XANADU   )
)
)
            v.   )
)
)
CHARLES FOSTER KANE,   )
)
Defendant.   )
)
_____)

Style of a Civil Case

IN THE STATE OF PLACID
COUNTY OF BEVANS

IN THE GENERAL COURT OF JUSTICE
SUPERIOR COURT

Theo Baldwin,   *
                                   *
Plaintiff,   *
                                   *
            v.   *   COMPLAINT FOR DAMAGES
                                   *
                                   *   Civil Action File No.: 12CV-213
                                   *
Randall Nosepuncher,   *
                                   *
Defendant.   *
                                   *
_____ *

OVERVIEW OF PROCEDURAL STEPS IN A CRIMINAL PROSECUTION

In this text, we will cover all of the procedural steps that occur in a criminal prosecution, from an initial stop by a police officer through arrest, and then a thorough discussion of appeals. Here we provide an overview of these steps, which are discussed in detail in the following chapters.

A. ARREST

Arrest
Detention and restraint of a suspect by a law enforcement official; a person who is under arrest is not free to leave.

In almost all situations, a criminal case begins with an **arrest**. To arrest someone is to detain a person suspected of committing a crime. Only law enforcement officers are empowered to make arrests. But what actually is the legal definition of arrest? To arrest a person is to place him or her in custody and prevent him or her from leaving the area. When a person is under arrest, he or she is often physically restrained and the person's liberty is taken away. The suspect is also handcuffed or restrained in some other way. Consider Scenario 2-1. In later chapters, we will examine all of the aspects of when and under what circumstances a person is under arrest, but determining the precise point when a person is considered to be under arrest has important constitutional law consequences. A person who is under arrest has the right to an attorney, the right to petition for bond, the right to be told about the charges against him or her, and the right to remain silent, among many others. When a suspect is under arrest, any statement that he or she makes can be used against him or her.

SCENARIO 2-1

ARREST?

Mike calls the local police after he finds that his roommate, who is currently away, has a substantial amount of cash and what appears to be marijuana hidden under the kitchen sink. The officer who takes the call tells Mike that based on what he has told him, his roommate should be placed under arrest and should surrender himself at the police station. The officer tells Mike to relay this information to his friend. Is the roommate under arrest?

Answer: No. A police officer must personally interact with a suspect to arrest him or her. There is no such thing as a telephonically relayed arrest.

ARREST AND PROBABLE CAUSE

Probable cause
The constitutional requirement that law enforcement officers have reasonable belief that a person has committed a crime.

For an arrest to be legally valid, it must be supported by **probable cause**. The Fourth Amendment requires that when a suspect is placed under arrest, the officer making that arrest must have probable cause to believe that the person committed a crime (see Figure 2-4).

FIGURE 2-4

Fourth Amendment,
U.S. Constitution

The right of the people to be secure in their persons, houses, papers, and effects, against unreasonable searches and seizures, shall not be violated, and no Warrants shall issue, but upon probable cause, supported by Oath or affirmation, and particularly describing the place to be searched, and the persons or things to be seized

If we were called upon to come up with the simplest definition of probable cause, we might rely on how courts have defined it. According to numerous court decisions, probable cause refers to the reasonable belief that the suspect has committed a crime. An officer must have probable cause before arresting a suspect and cannot wait to develop facts later that justify the initial arrest. The existence of probable cause to arrest is based on objective standards and is determined from the viewpoint of what a prudent person would believe when presented with the same facts and circumstances as the officer. If a hypothetical, reasonable person would believe, based on the facts presented, that the suspect had committed a crime, then a police officer would also have probable cause and can make an arrest. The Fourth Amendment was written in such a way as to make sure that officers could not arrest anyone on a whim or based on a "gut feeling." See Scenario 2-2.

Sidebar

Probable cause, in its simplest form, refers to the objective evidence that a crime has been or is about to be committed.[1]

HUNCHES

SCENARIO 2-2

Officer John Doe is on patrol one evening and sees a car being driven by an African American male. Officer Doe is familiar with this area of town and knows that very few African Americans live in this area. He pulls the man over and arrests him. Does he have probable cause?

Answer: No. It is not a crime to be an African American in a car driving through a predominately white neighborhood. Without additional evidence, there is no probable cause for the arrest.

B. INTERROGATION

We tend to think that everyone who is arrested is immediately interrogated by the police. However, this is not the case. There are numerous instances where a defendant will not be interrogated. Before an **interrogation** can be carried out, police must determine that the defendant is not under the influence of drugs or alcohol, which would affect the accuracy, quality, and veracity of his or her statements. Consider Scenario 2-3.

Interrogation
The questioning by law enforcement of a suspect concerning the commission of a crime.

SCENARIO 2-3

UNDER THE INFLUENCE

Sally has been arrested for driving under the influence of alcohol. She is very intoxicated as a breath test has confirmed. Can or should the police interrogate Sally?

Answer: No. First of all, police will not need to question Sally. Why should they? She has been arrested for operating a motor vehicle under the influence. What additional questions do they need to ask? Even if they did, Sally is demonstrably under the influence of alcohol. If the police wished to question her, then they would have to wait until she sobered up.

However, when police do wish to interrogate someone who has been arrested, there are strict rules that they must follow. The most obvious—and most famous—is administering the *Miranda* warnings.

MIRANDA WARNINGS

Miranda warnings
Rights that are required to be read to persons who have been placed under arrest and who the police intend to interrogate; required by the U.S. Supreme Court.

As we have already seen, once defendants have been placed under arrest they have several constitutional rights that immediately protect them. Among them are the right to remain silent and the right to have an attorney present when they are being interrogated. Anyone who watches TV shows or movies about police work should be familiar with **Miranda warnings**. The U.S. Supreme Court decision in *Miranda v. Arizona*[2] requires police officers to read a suspect a summary of his or her rights before law enforcement can interrogate that suspect. One version of the *Miranda* rights is provided in Figure 2-5.

One of the biggest myths about arrest and *Miranda* warnings is that an arrest is somehow invalid if the police do not read the *Miranda* warnings to the suspect. This is not true. As we have already seen, there are many times when the police have no intention of questioning a suspect after arrest. Police officers are only required to read a suspect the *Miranda* warnings when they intend to question a suspect. If there is no need to question the suspect, then there is no need to provide the *Miranda* warnings. Don't the police question suspects in all cases? Not necessarily. If the suspect has been arrested for driving under the influence or violation of probation, there may be no need to ask any further questions and thus no need for *Miranda* warnings.

FIGURE 2-5

The *Miranda* Rights Warning

> You have the right to remain silent. If you give up this right to remain silent, anything you say can and will be used against you at trial. You have the right to an attorney during any questioning. If you cannot afford an attorney, one will be appointed to represent you. Do you understand these rights?

C. EVIDENCE

In deciding what charges to bring against a suspect, police and prosecutors must review the available **evidence**. Although we explore the issues of evidence in Chapter 6, in this introductory chapter, we will examine the basic concepts of the use of evidence in criminal trials. Evidence refers to anything that tends to prove or disprove any fact in a case. Both prosecutors and defense attorneys rely on evidence to establish facts in a case, or to question the veracity of the other side's evidence.

> **Evidence**
> Any type of information, including testimony, documents, and physical objects, that is presented during a trial to prove or disprove a point in contention.

The first way to approach to evidence is to categorize it into two categories: direct and circumstantial. **Direct evidence** refers to any object or testimony that has an immediate connection with the facts in the case. The defendant's fingerprints found on the murder weapon constitute an example of direct evidence. The fingerprints directly link the defendant to the murder weapon and form part of the proof that the defendant committed the crime, beyond a reasonable doubt. **Circumstantial evidence**, on the other hand, suggests conclusions and inferences but has no direct connection with the facts of the case. An example of circumstantial evidence that has been used in law schools for years is the famous "trout in milk" scenario. Suppose that you wake up one morning and find a trout sticking out of a glass of milk in your kitchen. What conclusions can you reach? Obviously, your first conclusion is that someone must have put the fish in your glass of milk. You may not be able to immediately discern who put the trout there, but there is no doubt that someone did. Consider Scenario 2-4.

> **Direct evidence**
> Evidence that proves a fact without the need to resort to any other fact. Direct evidence that the defendant held the murder weapon would be his or her fingerprints on the object.
>
> **Circumstantial evidence**
> Facts that suggest a conclusion or indirectly prove a main fact in question.

BLOODY HANDS

SCENARIO 2-4

Maria walks into an all-night grocery store and finds the clerk slumped behind the cash register. He has been severely beaten and the cash register drawer is open and empty. Maria takes out her cellphone and calls the police. Just as she does, she sees a man outside the store. He has blood on his hands and on the front of his shirt. He looks very guilty. At this point, without any additional testing, would you classify the man's appearance as direct or circumstantial evidence?

Answer: Circumstantial evidence. Without more evidence, such as a test showing that the blood on the man matches the clerk's blood, this evidence is merely suggestive of guilt.

Although circumstantial evidence is often considered to be weaker than direct evidence, any trial will have a combination of both types of evidence. The problem with circumstantial evidence is that under criminal law, circumstantial evidence must not only suggest a conclusion, but also exclude every other reasonable possibility. It is possible to convict a person on circumstantial evidence alone, but the evidence must prove that the defendant committed the crime beyond a reasonable doubt and meet the other requirement: The evidence excludes every reasonable possibility other than the defendant's guilt.

FIGURE 2-6

Types of Evidence

Physical evidence	Refers to objects and things that are relevant to the issues in a case
Documentary evidence	Writings that contain facts or data that tend to prove or disprove that a defendant committed a crime
Testimonial evidence	Evidence given by a person under oath
Demonstrative evidence	Pictorial displays, charts, scale models, and other displays designed to persuade the jury

Direct evidence can be broken down into subcategories, as shown in Figure 2-6.

D. INITIAL APPEARANCE

Initial appearance
A hearing that takes place within days of the suspect's arrest, where the suspect is advised of his or her constitutional rights and given the opportunity to request a court-appointed attorney, and where the court can confirm the defendant's identity.

In some jurisdictions, the **initial appearance** is also called the preliminary examination. No matter what the term, the purpose of the hearing is the same. Shortly after the defendant is arrested, the defendant is brought before a judge—often a magistrate judge—and again reminded of his or her rights and also asked if it will be necessary to appoint an attorney to represent the defendant.

During the initial appearance, the magistrate will often advise the defendant of the charges currently pending against him or her. These are often preliminary charges, and the defendant may have additional charges added once the prosecution team has had an opportunity to review the defendant's case.

The final purpose of the initial appearance is to ensure that the defendant has been correctly identified. The judge will confirm that the person the state believes that it has in custody is in fact the person being held. To that end, the judge may order fingerprint comparisons or some other procedure to properly identify the defendant.

Sidebar

The primary purpose of the initial appearance is to ensure that the defendant is aware of his or her constitutional rights.

E. PRELIMINARY HEARING

Preliminary hearing
A court hearing that determines if there is probable cause to believe that the defendant committed the crime with which he or she is charged.

Within a few days of the initial appearance (the actual time period varies by state), the defendant will be brought before another magistrate or other court officer. However, this hearing is not an initial hearing. Instead, the court will hold a hearing to determine if there is sufficient probable cause to believe that the defendant committed the crime. The **preliminary hearing** (also known as a probable cause hearing) is held within days of the defendant's arrest. It is a hearing where the defendant will appear, represented by an attorney, and the case will be presented by a prosecutor. Preliminary hearings are usually reserved only for felony cases. Misdemeanor cases, in most states, do not have preliminary hearings.

During this hearing, the prosecutor will call witnesses to the stand, swear them in, and then ask them some basic questions about the case. The purpose of the preliminary hearing is not to determine the defendant's guilt. Instead, it is to establish that the police had probable cause to arrest the defendant. This is a relatively low threshold to meet, and winning a preliminary hearing is not difficult for the prosecution.

F. GRAND JURY

If a defendant is charged with a felony, the next step in the criminal process is to convene a **grand jury** to consider the charges against him or her. Grand juries are required under the U.S. Constitution, and most states, but not all, follow this example.

The grand jury is not the same as the jury that hears a criminal charge. Instead, the grand jury is composed of 16 to 23 persons, and they consider the basic facts of the prosecution's case. The purpose of the grand jury is to act as a buffer between the state and the defendant. The grand jury considers witness testimony and then makes a ruling as to whether or not the case should continue. If the grand jurors determine that there is a **prima facie** case of guilt, then they will authorize continued prosecution.

Grand jury
A group of citizens who consider felony charges against defendants and make a determination of whether there is sufficient evidence to warrant further prosecution.

Prima facie
Facts that are considered true as presented until they are disproven by some contrary evidence.

TRUE BILL VS. NO BILL

When the grand jurors reach a decision that the prosecution against a particular defendant should continue, they record their vote as a **true bill**. A true bill authorizes the prosecution to bring formal charges against the defendant and to summon him or her to trial. On the other hand, if the grand jurors do not believe that a case should continue, then they vote **no bill**. A vote of no bill effectively stops the prosecution in its tracks. At this point, the prosecution can either wait until a new grand jury is empaneled, which could be as long as a year or more, or seek to charge the defendant with a misdemeanor.

If the grand jury returns a true bill against a defendant, the next step in the prosecution is the arraignment.

True bill
A grand jury's determination that there is sufficient probable cause to continue the prosecution against the accused.

No bill
A grand jury's determination that there is insufficient probable cause to continue the prosecution against the accused.

G. ARRAIGNMENT

Once a grand jury has returned a true bill, the defendant will be summoned to court for an **arraignment**. The arraignment is normally scheduled several weeks or even months after the grand jury meets. In some jurisdictions, a defendant can be arraigned on the day of the trial, but most follow a pattern that sets the arraignment several weeks before the next scheduled trial date. At the arraignment, the defendant is told exactly what the charges are against him or her and

Arraignment
A court hearing where the defendant is informed of the charges against him or her and given the opportunity to enter a plea of guilty or not guilty.

is given an opportunity to enter an official plea. The defendant may plead guilty or not guilty. If the defendant pleads guilty, he or she may be sentenced immediately. However, if the defendant enters a not guilty plea, the case will be scheduled for trial.

H. TRIAL

If a defendant pleads not guilty, his or her case will be scheduled for trial. We will examine the trial of a criminal case in depth in Chapter 13, but a few words here about a criminal trial are also important.

A defendant enters a trial with several presumptions in his or her favor. For instance, a defendant is presumed innocent unless and until the prosecution can prove, beyond a reasonable doubt, that the defendant committed the crime. If the state fails to meet this burden, the jurors are instructed that they must vote a not guilty verdict.

BASIC OVERVIEW OF A CRIMINAL TRIAL

Trials proceed in a similar pattern all across the United States. When the defendant's case is called for trial, the judge will summon local citizens who will act as jurors in the case. Jury selection will occur prior to trial.

Once a jury is empaneled, the parties will give their opening statements. The usual pattern is for the prosecutor to go first, outlining the evidence that it has against the defendant and the witnesses who will testify in the case. Once the prosecutor has finished his or her opening statement, the defense will have its opportunity. A defense attorney will often use the opening statement as a way to introduce the defense in the case or to simply challenge the state's version of events.

Following the opening statements, the case actually begins. The prosecutor calls witnesses to the stand, questions them about the case, and establishes the basic facts against the defendant. After each witness has answered questions posed by the prosecutor, the defense attorney is allowed to question the witnesses to dispute their version, question their veracity, or show that they have some bias against the defendant. The case proceeds in this fashion, with the state calling a witness, the witness testifying, and the prosecutor using the witness as a means to present direct or circumstantial evidence. Each witness can be questioned by the defense. When the state has presented all of its witnesses and evidence, it rests its case.

At this point, the defense has two options. The defense attorney can present witnesses and evidence to support the defendant's version of the case or to establish a legally recognized defense, or the defense can simply rest without presenting anything. Jurors are instructed that simply because the defense presented no evidence, they are not permitted to infer that the defendant admits guilt. In fact, the jurors are told just the opposite. The burden of proving that the defendant is guilty is always on the state, and it never shifts to the defendant to prove that he or she is not guilty.

When the case concludes, the prosecutor and defense attorney will address the jury in one last presentation, referred to as a closing argument. During the closing argument, the prosecutor will argue how the evidence proves the defendant guilty beyond a reasonable doubt. When it is the defense attorney's turn, he or she will undoubtedly argue that the state's version is incorrect and that the prosecution has failed to meet the burden of proving the defendant guilty beyond a reasonable doubt.

Following closing arguments, the judge instructs the jurors about what law applies to the crime with which the defendant is charged, and then the judge sends the jurors out to deliberate. The jurors will then go into the jury room. No one else is allowed to be present while they discuss the case. In most states, the jury's verdict must be unanimous. If even one juror does not vote for the defendant's guilt, and the other jurors cannot change that juror's mind, the judge will have no choice but to suspend the proceedings. The prosecution can then decide whether or not to schedule a new trial against the defendant.

If the jurors reach a unanimous verdict of guilty, then the court moves on to the next stage in the criminal process: sentencing.

I. SENTENCING

At the conclusion of a criminal trial, if a defendant is found guilty, the judge usually sentences him or her. Although there are provisions that allow juries to recommend sentences in some states, the most common method is for the judge to impose a **sentence** based on the applicable statutes. In most jurisdictions, the judge has specific restrictions on the ultimate sentence that he or she can impose on the defendant. The legislature imposes maximum sentences on all types of crimes, and a judge may not exceed the statutory limit. As part of the sentence, a judge may impose a prison term, parole, or probation, as well as fines that the defendant must pay over the course of his or her probationary sentence.

Sentence
The punishment, which can consist of some combination of prison time and probation, that is imposed on a defendant who has been found guilty at trial or who has pled guilty.

PRISON VS. PROBATION

When a judge sentences a defendant to a term in prison, he or she may order that the sentence be served consecutively to other prison terms or concurrently with other terms. When a defendant is released from prison, he or she will often continue to serve the balance of his or her sentence on **probation** or parole. For the purposes of this chapter, we will consider probation and parole to be the same thing. However, we will learn in a later chapter that although these terms are similar, they are different in the way that they are handled. Probation officers ensure that the defendant follows the conditions of his or her sentence. For instance, if the defendant has been ordered to pay fines or restitution, the probation officer is the person who monitors these payments. In addition, the probation officer also makes sure that the probationer obtains employment and refrains from drug use, among other conditions.

A judge may sentence a defendant to a strictly probationary sentence, without any prison time. If a defendant violates the terms or conditions of his or her

Probation
Allowing a person convicted of a criminal offense to avoid serving a jail sentence imposed on the person, so long as he or she abides by certain conditions (usually including being supervised by a probation officer).

probation, the judge may revoke the defendant's probation and have him or her serve the balance of the sentence in prison.

CASE EXCERPT

STATE v. SUMMERS

62 N.E.3d 451 (2016)

After being ordered to register as a sex offender in Illinois for ten years, Charles Summers moved to Indiana.

Summers later registered as a sex offender in Indiana. When Indiana applied its tolling statute to Summers (in order to extend Summers' registration period by the amount of time he was incarcerated in Indiana for new crimes committed), Summers claimed that applying the statute to him violated Indiana's prohibition against ex post facto laws. He argued that when he committed his underlying offense in Illinois, Indiana had not yet enacted its tolling statute. Because Summers was under a tolling requirement in Illinois, we find no punitive burden to maintaining that requirement across state lines. Because there is no ex post facto violation, we reverse the trial court and remand this case.

FACTS AND PROCEDURAL HISTORY

On April 27, 2005, Summers, age 13, was adjudicated a juvenile delinquent in Illinois for "Criminal Sex Abuse." Appellant's App. p. 29. He was placed on probation and ordered to register as a sex offender in Illinois for ten years. As a sex offender, if Summers became incarcerated for an unrelated conviction or adjudication, his registration period was tolled for that time period according to Illinois statute.

Summers moved to Indiana "several years" after his April 27, 2005 delinquency adjudication.

Effective July 1, 2006, the Indiana General Assembly amended the Sex Offender Registration Act's (SORA) definition of sex offender to include "a person who is required to register as a sex offender in any jurisdiction." P.L. 140–2006, §13; P.L. 173–2006, §13; see Ind.Code §§ 11–8–8–4.5(b)(1), –5(b)(1). Then, effective July 1, 2008, the General Assembly amended SORA to provide that the registration period is tolled during any period that a sex offender is incarcerated. P.L. 119–2008, §8; see Ind.Code §11–8–8–19(a).

On August 26, 2010, Summers was convicted of two counts of robbery in Miami County, Indiana, and sentenced to the Indiana Department of Correction. After Summers was released from the DOC in 2015, he registered as a sex offender in Cass County, Indiana, and was told by the DOC that SORA's tolling statute, Indiana Code section 11–8–8–19(a), extended his duty to register from April 27, 2015, to January 28, 2019, which was the amount of time that he had been incarcerated in the DOC.

On August 2, 2015, police went to Manor Motel in Logansport to verify the address that Summers had provided when he registered as a sex offender in Cass County, and management told police that Summers had moved out a few days earlier. Thereafter, the State charged Summers with Level 6 felony failure to register as a sex offender and Class A misdemeanor failure of a sex offender to possess identification under Cause No. 09D01–1508–F6–233.

Summers filed a motion to dismiss the criminal charges, arguing that SORA's tolling provision, as applied to him, violated Indiana's prohibition against ex post facto laws because Indiana's tolling provision was enacted three years after his delinquency adjudication in Illinois. Following a hearing, the trial court dismissed the criminal charges against Summers.

The same day that the criminal charges were dismissed, Summers, pursuant to Indiana Code section 11–8–8–22, filed a petition to remove his name from Indiana's sex-offender registry under Cause No. 09D01–1510–MI–70. The State later filed a motion to correct error in the criminal case, and the trial court held a joint hearing on the State's motion to correct error and Summers' petition to remove his name from the registry. Following the joint hearing, the court denied the State's motion to correct error and found that Summers' name should be removed from the registry.

The State filed a notice of appeal in both cause numbers, and this Court granted the State's motion to consolidate the appeals.

DISCUSSION AND DECISION

The State contends that SORA's tolling provision, as applied to Summers, does not violate Indiana's constitutional prohibition against ex post facto laws. Accordingly, the State asks us to "reverse the trial court's judgment" and "remand with instructions to proceed with Summers' criminal case and restore his sex offender registration requirement.

The fundamental principle to the prohibition against ex post facto laws is that people have a right to fair warning of the criminal penalties that may result from their conduct. *Tyson v. State*, 51 N.E.3d 88, 92 (Ind.2016). Specifically, our Constitution provides, "No ex post facto law . . . shall ever be passed." Ind. Const. art. 1, §24. We review questions of law and constitutionality de novo. *Tyson*, 51 N.E.3d at 90. As the party challenging the constitutionality of a statute, Summers bears the burden of proof and all doubts are resolved against him. *Id.* at 91.

In *Tyson*, our Supreme Court addressed whether a thirteen year old, who was adjudicated a delinquent in Texas in 2002 and required to register as a sex offender there until 2014, was required to register as a sex offender when he later moved to Indiana in 2009. The Court concluded that because Tyson was required to register as a sex offender in Texas, he was a sex offender in Indiana and required to register here for the duration of his Texas requirement.

Our Supreme Court also addressed Tyson's argument that his obligation to register as a sex offender in Indiana violated Indiana's prohibition against ex post facto laws because when he committed the underlying offense in Texas, Indiana's statutory definition had not yet been amended to include him. Applying the intent-effects test—which analyzes whether the statute imposes a punishment or whether the statute is merely part of a non-punitive, regulatory scheme—the Court found no ex post facto violation. We simply cannot say that transferring the obligation upon moving is any more punitive than lengthening it to potentially last a lifetime.

We reach the same conclusion here. First, as in *Tyson*, Summers was a sex offender in Illinois; by moving across state lines, Summers merely maintained his sex-offender status. Second, although Indiana adopted its tolling provision several years after Summers was adjudicated a juvenile delinquent in Illinois, Summers was already under a tolling requirement in Illinois. There is no punitive burden to maintaining both of these requirements across state lines. Because Summers has not established an ex post facto violation, we reverse the trial court's dismissal of the criminal charges against Summers in Cause No. F6–233 and reverse the trial court's grant of Summers' petition to remove his name from the sex-offender registry in Cause No. MI–70.

Reversed and remanded.

---

1 How did Summers first become a registered sex offender?
2 The state alleges that Summers failed to register as a sex offender in Indiana after moving there. What was the requirement of the statute?
3 Summers, in his appeal, claimed that the imposition of Indiana's sex-offender registry was a violation of the ex post facto rule. How did the trial court rule on his motion to dismiss the case?
4 What is the fundamental principle espoused in the ex post facto prohibition?
5 Why did the appellate court rule that the legislation in question was not a violation of the ex post facto prohibition?

CHAPTER SUMMARY

Criminal cases follow a specific pattern. Once a suspect is placed under arrest, he or she is processed by the system in a series of hearings. The initial appearance is the suspect's first contact with a judge. The preliminary hearing is where the state presents enough evidence, in the judgment of a magistrate, to establish probable cause to believe that the defendant committed the crime. Following the preliminary hearing, the defendant will be arraigned. During the arraignment, the defendant will be told the official charges pending against him or her and given a chance to enter a plea. If the defendant pleads not guilty, then he or she will be scheduled for a trial.

A criminal trial also follows a specific procedure. Once the parties give opening statements, the prosecution presents evidence to convince the jury that the defendant is guilty beyond a reasonable doubt. If the jury convicts, then the judge is responsible for sentencing the defendant.

KEY TERMS AND CONCEPTS

Guilty	Guilty but mentally ill	Restitution
Liable	Not guilty by reason of	Burden of proof
Verdict	insanity	Preponderance of the
Not guilty	Damages	evidence

Proof beyond a reasonable doubt	Arrest	Grand jury
Style	Probable cause	*Prima facie*
Pleadings	Interrogation	True bill
Complaint	*Miranda* warnings	No bill
Answer	Evidence	Arraignment
Indictment	Direct evidence	Sentence
Felony	Circumstantial evidence	Probation
Misdemeanor	Initial appearance	
	Preliminary hearing	

END OF CHAPTER EXERCISES

Review Questions

See Appendix A for answers

1 What is the difference between a verdict of guilty and a verdict of liability?
2 What is a verdict?
3 What four verdicts are available in criminal trials?
4 What is the burden of proof?
5 Explain preponderance of the evidence.
6 Explain proof beyond a reasonable doubt.
7 What is the style of a case?
8 How does the style of a criminal case compare to that of a civil case?
9 What is an indictment?
10 Explain the difference between felonies and misdemeanors.
11 What is the definition of arrest?
12 Explain probable cause.
13 Explain *Miranda* warnings.
14 What is the difference between an initial appearance hearing and a preliminary hearing?
15 What is the purpose of the grand jury?
16 What is an arraignment?
17 Explain the difference between prison and probation.

Web Surfing

Visit your state's criminal court websites. Does your state use a grand jury? What procedures are followed in your state following a suspect's arrest? How much time do statutes allow for the prosecution to conduct a preliminary hearing (also known as a probable cause hearing)?

Question for Analysis

Should criminal and civil cases be more similar or continue to be very different from one another? Is justice served by the current model followed in criminal cases? Explain your answer.

Hypotheticals

1 Tia is approached by a police officer and questioned. The officer doesn't like her answers, handcuffs her, and puts her in the back of a police car. Later, he takes her to a cell. Based on your reading of the definition of arrest in this chapter, is Tia under arrest?

2 Does your answer change if the officer who detained Tia testifies that he never once considered Tia to be under arrest and that, as far as he was concerned, she was free to leave at any point?

PRACTICE QUESTIONS FOR TEST REVIEW

See Appendix A for answers

Essay Question

What are three important differences between civil and criminal law?

True-False

1 T F Criminal juries can return a verdict of guilty or not guilty.

2 T F The primary focus of a preliminary hearing is to determine guilt or innocence.

3 T F The proof required in a criminal case to convict a defendant is proof beyond a shadow of a doubt.

Fill in the Blank

1 A(n) ——— is what prosecutors use to charge a person with a felony.

2 A jury's factual determination; a jury's finding: ———.

3 Money that a court orders paid to a person who has suffered legally recognized losses by the person who caused the injury in a civil trial: ———.

Multiple Choice

1 The jury's determination that the state has failed to prove that the defendant committed the crime beyond a reasonable doubt.

   A Guilty.
   B Liable.
   C Not liable.
   D Not guilty.

2   The standard of proof most closely associated with a civil case where a party proves that his or her version of the facts is more than likely to be true.

   A   Preponderance of the evidence.
   B   Clear and total evidence.
   C   Proof beyond a reasonable doubt.
   D   Proof beyond all doubt.

3   The amount of proof that a party must bring to sustain an action against another party. This is different in civil and criminal cases.

   A   Burden of proof.
   B   Burden of the case.
   C   Case in chief.
   D   Theory of the case.

ENDNOTES

1. *Terry v. Ohio,* 392 U.S. 1 (1968).
2. 384 U.S. 436, 86 S.Ct. 1602, 16 L.Ed.2d 694 (1966).

3

Fourth Amendment: Stop and Frisk and Other Detentions

Chapter Objectives

- Describe the circumstances where a police officer can engage in a brief detention of a suspect
- Explain a *Terry* stop
- Define stop and frisk
- Describe how evidence acquired during a detention or stop and frisk can be used in a prosecution
- Explain the various types of interactions between police and suspects and the constitutional standard required in each

Chapter Outline

I. Interactions Between Police and Individuals
   A. Continuum of Contacts and Their Constitutional Requirements
   B. Voluntary Interactions Between Police and Individuals
   C. Police Interactions with Constitutional Implications

II. *Terry* Stops
   A. Detention Under *Terry*
   B. What Is Reasonable Suspicion?

III. Stop and Frisk
   A. What Are the Police Permitted to Do in a Stop and Frisk?
   B. The Scope of Stop and Frisk
   C. Abuse of the Stop and Frisk Provision

IV. Arrest

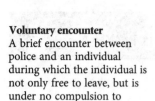

INTERACTIONS BETWEEN POLICE AND INDIVIDUALS

Voluntary encounter
A brief encounter between police and an individual during which the individual is not only free to leave, but is under no compulsion to answer any of the police officer's questions.

Police and individuals interact every day in the United States. Classifying these interactions is important because they require different levels of justification by the police. At its simplest, police can have a **voluntary encounter** with a person. Such a situation might develop when a police officer observes someone and asks what he or she is doing. At this point, the person is free to leave. The person can respond to the question or refuse, although most people would feel a certain compulsion to answer the question. Police officers have the right to ask routine questions and make general inquiries. That is, after all, part of their duties. The important point is that a police officer is not required to offer a legal justification for asking this question. On the other end of the spectrum is an arrest. When a police officer makes an arrest, the Fourth Amendment to the U.S. Constitution requires that law enforcement have probable cause to do so.

However, there are other interactions between police and individuals that do not neatly fall into either category: the brief detention. This is something beyond a voluntary encounter, although not as drastic as an arrest. Brief, investigative stops or detentions by the police were first authorized in *Terry v. Ohio*[1] and have since become known as *Terry* stops. During a *Terry* stop, police are allowed to ask more invasive questions and to prevent a person from leaving, but this detention does not amount to an arrest. Because of that, a *Terry* stop does not qualify as an arrest and therefore the police are not required to show probable cause for the detention. During this brief detention, police are not only allowed to ask questions, but also to take other actions, including patting down the person to see if the person is carrying weapons. This is called stop and frisk and has come under great scrutiny in recent years.

This chapter examines these three categories of police–individual interactions, explains what constitutes a *Terry* stop, and then expands on what police are allowed to do in the context of a stop and frisk.

A. CONTINUUM OF CONTACTS AND THEIR CONSTITUTIONAL REQUIREMENTS

There is a continuum of contacts between individuals and police officers. Each of these interactions carries its own dangers and its own constitutional standards. We will break these interactions down into four disparate settings:

- Voluntary interactions between police and individuals
- *Terry* stops
- Stop and frisk
- Arrests

B. VOLUNTARY INTERACTIONS BETWEEN POLICE AND INDIVIDUALS

There are times when a person might choose to interact with a police officer on a purely voluntary basis. A person might simply ask a police officer a question. The officer might also ask an individual a question. In either of these scenarios, there is no legal requirement that the police must meet before they can engage in voluntary interactions.[2] The Fourth Amendment does not prohibit voluntary interaction between citizens and the police.[3]

The Fourth Amendment was designed to protect people, not locations. To that extent, a person walking down the street has just as much protection from unlawful search and seizure as someone sitting in his or her home.[4] This question often arises in an interaction between a police officer and an individual: When does the situation change from a voluntary encounter to a *Terry* stop to an arrest? Even more important, what are the legal standards that police must meet at each of these stages?

The simplest point to answer is the one concerning voluntary encounters. Police do not need any special reason or meet any constitutional standard to initiate a voluntary encounter.[5] However, things can get complicated quickly and during that give-and-take of an encounter, does the interaction take on a different legal complexity? Is there a bright line test to determine when the police have crossed over from a voluntary encounter to a *Terry* stop? Courts have consistently refused to provide a strict, by-the-numbers test for such scenarios. There is no "litmus-paper test for distinguishing a consensual encounter from a seizure." Why? Because "there will be endless variations in the facts and circumstances, so much variation that it is unlikely that the courts can reduce to a sentence or a paragraph a rule that will provide unarguable answers to the question whether there has been an unreasonable seizure in violation of the Fourth Amendment."[6] Consider Scenario 3-1.

VOLUNTARY INTERACTION

SCENARIO 3-1

Officer Mike is walking down the street, and he meets a man going in the opposite direction. Officer Mike asks the man, "Where you headed?"

The man answers, "I'm heading home."

Later, the man seeks to challenge Officer Mike's actions as unconstitutional. Are they?

Answer: No. A police officer is free to ask questions such as this without having to show any legal basis. Similarly, the person being asked is under no compulsion to answer the question.

There would be nothing gained, and a great deal lost, if the police were required to have a legal basis for asking a simple question such as "What's your name?" However, if the officer wishes to detain the person briefly, there is a legal requirement: reasonable suspicion. These brief detentions are referred to as *Terry* stops.

C. POLICE INTERACTIONS WITH CONSTITUTIONAL IMPLICATIONS

Terry **stop**
A brief detention of a suspect to follow up on specific investigative issues.

A police officer may briefly detain a person to ask questions and conduct a short investigation. This detention is not an arrest, and therefore probable cause is not required. This type of stop is a middle ground between a voluntary encounter and a full-blown arrest. They are called *Terry* **stops** because of the case in which the concept was developed: *Terry v. Ohio*.[7] Under the *Terry* ruling, an officer who does not have probable cause may briefly detain a suspicious individual to determine his or her identity or to gather more information. The U.S. Supreme Court, in creating this new category of interaction between police and individuals, did not include specific time periods for how long such a "brief" detention should last.

Stop and frisk
The right of a law enforcement officer to pat down a person's outer clothing for weapons, whether the person is under arrest or not.

In some situations, a police officer is authorized to actually pat down the outer clothing of an individual he or she has briefly detained. Patting down, or a **stop and frisk**, is permitted under various U.S. Supreme Court decisions, especially *Terry v. Ohio*. However, *Terry* only authorizes such a frisk when it is supported by a reasonable belief that the suspect is armed and dangerous.[8] During a *Terry* stop, an officer can engage in behavior that would normally be considered a seizure of the suspect's person, specifically by patting the suspect down and removing potentially dangerous items from his or her person.[9]

The final type of interaction between individuals and police is an arrest, which must be supported by probable cause. A person who is under arrest is not free to leave and, at the moment that he or she is arrested, a host of constitutional protections are triggered. These protections will be discussed in future chapters.

 ## *TERRY* STOPS

Because voluntary interactions with police carry no constitutional issues, we will move directly into the second category of police–individual interactions: the brief detention or *Terry* stop. What is a *Terry* stop? The U.S. Supreme Court's own wording explains it best: "Not all personal interactions between policemen and citizens involve seizures of persons. Only when the officer, by means of physical force or show of authority, has in some way restrained the liberty of a citizen have the Courts concluded that a seizure has occurred."[10] Under this ruling, police do not have to establish probable cause to briefly detain a suspect.

A. DETENTION UNDER *TERRY*

In *Terry v. Ohio*, 392 U.S. 1 (1968), the Supreme Court held that there was a middle ground between voluntary interactions and full-blown arrests. This category became known as the brief detention and was nicknamed the *Terry* stop for the case in which it was first implemented. Under *Terry*, police may detain a person when they have reasonable suspicion that a crime has occurred. Appellate courts have specifically held that, "If, from the totality of the circumstances, a law enforcement officer reasonably suspects that criminal activity may be afoot, the officer may temporarily detain a person."[11]

B. WHAT IS REASONABLE SUSPICION?

Reasonable suspicion consists of specific, articulable facts that a police officer can point to that gave rise to the conclusion that a crime was committed or was about to be committed.[12] "Reasonable suspicion is a less demanding standard than probable cause not only in the sense that reasonable suspicion can be established with information that is different in quantity or content than that required to establish probable cause, but also in the sense that reasonable suspicion can arise from information that is less reliable than that required to show probable cause."[13]

How do courts evaluate an officer's actions and determine if reasonable suspicion existed? They look to the facts of the case. "The determination of reasonable suspicion must be based on commonsense judgments and inferences about human behavior, and due weight must be given to the reasonable inferences the officer is entitled to draw from the facts in light of his experience."[14] As we will see in the discussions in Chapter 4 about probable cause and arrest, a brief detention cannot be based on arbitrary factors, gut hunches, or "feelings." A court will review the officer's actions in the totality of the circumstances surrounding the stop and the "specific and articulable facts . . . taken together with rational inferences from those facts."[15]

Reasonable suspicion can arise from an officer's personal observation. It can also arise from other sources. A police officer can base a brief detention based on tips from "members of the public, including a known or unknown informant, a victim, an eyewitness, or a concerned citizen."[16]

Another way to define reasonable suspicion is to show what is not required. As we will see in discussing probable cause, the Fourth Amendment requires reasonable belief that a crime has occurred. That is not required for reasonable suspicion. Reasonable suspicion, as a standard, is less demanding than probable cause, and the evidentiary showing required to demonstrate reasonable suspicion is "considerably less than a preponderance of the evidence."[18]

STOP AND FRISK

During a *Terry* stop, an officer is permitted to pat down and then "intrude beneath the surface only if he confirms his reasonable belief or suspicion by coming upon something which feels like a weapon."[19] The idea behind pat down and frisk is that when a police officer briefly detains a suspect, there is a greater chance that violence might ensue. The only way to minimize the potential for violence is to allow police officers to pat down the suspect and remove any weapons that they find. "A *Terry* investigation . . . involves a police investigation at close range, when the officer remains particularly vulnerable in part because a full custodial arrest has not been effected, and the officer must make a quick decision as to how to protect himself and others from possible danger."[20] Consider Scenario 3-2.

SCENARIO 3-2

THE GUN

During a stop and frisk, a police officer discovers that a suspect has a concealed weapon for which he has no permit. Does this give the officer probable cause to arrest?

Answer: Yes. Because the defendant did not indicate that he had the weapon, an officer in a *Terry* stop can establish probable cause to arrest when the officer recovers a concealed weapon.[21]

When the suspect and the officer are dealing with one another face-to-face, it only makes sense that the officer can take some precautions for his or her safety. Pat downs and frisks are not considered to be searches, and police may not use the pretext of a pat down under *Terry* as carte blanche to search anyone that they please.[22]

A. WHAT ARE THE POLICE PERMITTED TO DO IN A STOP AND FRISK?

During a stop and frisk, police are permitted to check for weapons. At the same time, they are also permitted to continue asking questions. They may even engage in asking incriminating questions and not have a Fourth Amendment issue arise.[23] However, the primary purpose of the stop and frisk is the officer's safety. The stop and frisk was never designed as a means to circumvent the Fourth Amendment or allow police officers to wholesale stop individuals to see if they are committing crimes. Stop and frisk has a specific purpose: the officer's safety.[24] During the frisk, an officer is allowed to pat down the person's outer clothing. If the officer feels something that might be a weapon, he or she is authorized to take it out of the person's clothing.

Contraband
An object that is illegal to possess, including child pornography, certain types of weapons, and illegal narcotics, among others.

Suppose that the officer conducts a pat down, feels a lump or a bulge, and although realizes that it is not a weapon, recognizes that is it **contraband**, such as narcotics? Is the officer obligated to ignore the information relayed from his or her touch? Courts have consistently said no, but with a great many reservations. If the officer can testify that he or she knew what the item was, based on prior training and experience as a police officer, then the seizure during a pat down and frisk will be admissible.[25] Consider Scenario 3-3.

CONTRABAND

Officer Pat is on patrol. She sees Rick walk out of an abandoned house that is known throughout the neighborhood as a place used by methamphetamine sellers and buyers. She stops him and asks him a couple of questions. His answers are vague and contradictory. At this point, Officer Pat decides to conduct a frisk. While she is patting down Rick's outer clothes, she feels a small lump. It is obviously not a weapon, and after she readjusts her fingers several times, she is pretty certain it is small tabs of meth. She removes the items from Rick's pocket and confirms that they are contraband. Officer Pat puts Rick under arrest for possession of narcotics. Later, Rick's attorney challenges the frisk based on the fact that as soon as the officer concluded that Rick was not carrying a weapon, she exceeded the scope of a stop and frisk by removing an article that she knew wasn't a weapon and couldn't, in her experience, testify was anything other than an unidentifiable lump. How is the court likely to rule?

Answer: The court will almost certainly rule that the frisk exceeded its purpose. *Terry* created the stop and frisk exception for the officer's safety, not as a method for checking an individual's pockets to see if they might have incriminating evidence in their possession. The trial court suppresses the evidence of the methamphetamine.[26]

B. THE SCOPE OF STOP AND FRISK

Because the doctrine of stop and frisk was developed under *Terry* as a means to protect police officers and not as another means for police to gather evidence, appellate courts have imposed some strict rules governing the scope of a stop and frisk. According to the court, for an item other than a weapon to be seized and used against the defendant at trial:

"1. The officer must have a valid reason for the search, i.e., the patdown search must be permissible under *Terry*.
"2. The officer must detect the contraband while the *Terry* search for weapons legitimately and reasonably is in progress.
"3. The incriminating nature of the object detected by the officer's touch must be immediately apparent to the officer so that before seizing it the officer has probable cause to believe the object is contraband."[27]

In situations where the police go beyond the confines of simply checking a person for weapons, they run the risk of having the evidence obtained ruled inadmissible. "If the protective search goes beyond what is necessary to determine if the suspect is armed, it is no longer valid under *Terry* and its fruits will be suppressed."[28]

However, the opposite is also true. If, during a pat down and frisk, the officer identifies something that in his or her training and experience is contraband, then *Terry* and its line of cases authorizes seizing the material.[29] When an officer feels something that is clearly identifiable to him or her in a pat down and frisk, courts have been consistent in allowing the evidence to be presented at trial. In such a scenario, the evidence would be admitted under the "plain feel" doctrine, discussed at length in Chapter 5.[30]

C. ABUSE OF THE STOP AND FRISK PROVISION

In recent years, stop and frisk policies implemented in large cities, especially New York City, have come under sharp criticism. What began as an attempt to curb a perception of increased crime and violence in densely packed cities quickly turned into a program that was disproportionately targeted against persons of color, especially young men. Michael Bloomberg, the former mayor of New York City, later apologized for this program during his tenure as mayor.

IV   ARREST

As we will see in Chapter 4, all arrests must be supported by probable cause. They are specifically mentioned in the Fourth Amendment. We will discuss the role of probable cause, arrests without a warrant, and arrests with a warrant in the next chapter.

CASE EXCERPT

STATE v. KRANNAWITTER
305 Neb. 66 (2020)

I. INTRODUCTION

Amy J. Krannawitter was charged with third-offense driving under the influence. Her motion to suppress was denied, and she was convicted. Krannawitter then filed a motion for new trial on the basis of newly discovered evidence. That motion was denied, and she was sentenced. Krannawitter appeals. We affirm.

II. FACTUAL BACKGROUND

At approximately 6 a.m. on July 4, 2017, Deputy Dennis Guthard of the Lancaster County Sheriff's Department was leaving his home to report for work. Guthard was driving a marked cruiser. He noticed a black Nissan Altima driving slowly down the street of his neighborhood, of which he had been a resident for 16 years. Guthard's house was located on the corner of a street and a neighborhood circle. He drove from the circle onto the nearby through street and emerged behind the Altima. The Altima pulled into the driveway of Guthard's neighbors' house.

Guthard did not recognize the Altima or its driver, who he testified was a "younger woman" later identified as Krannawitter. Guthard testified that the occupants of the neighbors' house were a 70-year-old woman and her 96-year-old mother and that it was his experience that these two women did not wake until around 8:30 a.m. Guthard also testified that he considered keeping an eye on his neighborhood to be part of his job and that he was therefore aware of many of the vehicles belonging to persons who visited the neighborhood.

As Guthard drove down the street, he noticed, using his side and rear view mirrors, that the Altima was "just parked there" in the driveway. Guthard thought that was suspicious, but he also allowed for the possibility that the Altima's driver was lost, because it was a "confusing neighborhood."

Guthard pulled into the driveway about 5 feet behind the Altima, but did not activate his cruiser's siren or lights. Guthard made contact with the driver, Krannawitter. Immediately before Krannawitter opened the door of the Altima, Guthard observed Krannawitter was "very disheveled" and had droopy eyelids. When she opened the door, Guthard smelled a strong odor of alcohol and further noted Krannawitter's bloodshot eyes and slurred speech.

Krannawitter's breath test, administered approximately 90 minutes later, showed a concentration of .235 grams of alcohol per 210 liters of breath. Krannawitter was charged with aggravated driving under the influence, third offense. Krannawitter's motion to suppress was denied. The district court concluded that the initial stop of Krannawitter was a tier-one police-citizen encounter and that even if it was a seizure, there was reasonable suspicion to support a brief investigative stop.

Following a jury trial, Krannawitter was found guilty of driving under the influence.

III. ASSIGNMENTS OF ERROR

Krannawitter assigns, restated and consolidated, that the district court erred in (1) denying her motion to suppress and (2) denying her motion for new trial.

IV. STANDARD OF REVIEW

In reviewing a trial court's ruling on a motion to suppress based on a claimed violation of the Fourth Amendment, an appellate court applies a two-part standard of review. Regarding historical facts, an appellate court reviews the trial court's findings for clear error, but whether those facts trigger or violate Fourth Amendment protection is a question of law that an appellate court reviews independently of the trial court's determination.

V. ANALYSIS

1. MOTION TO SUPPRESS

In her first assignment of error, Krannawitter assigns that the district court erred in denying her motion to suppress. In so denying, the district court noted that in its view, the interaction between Guthard and Krannawitter was a tier-one police-citizen encounter, but that in any case, the encounter was supported by reasonable suspicion. Krannawitter takes issue with both findings.

There are three tiers of police encounters under Nebraska law. The first tier of police-citizen encounters involves no restraint of the liberty of the citizen involved, but, rather, the voluntary cooperation of the citizen is elicited through noncoercive questioning. This type of contact does not rise to the level of a seizure and therefore is outside the realm of Fourth Amendment protection. The second category, the investigatory stop, as defined by the U.S. Supreme Court in *Terry v. Ohio*, is limited to brief, nonintrusive detention during a frisk for weapons or preliminary questioning. This type of encounter is considered a "seizure" sufficient to invoke Fourth Amendment safeguards, but because of its less intrusive character requires only that the stopping officer have specific and articulable facts sufficient to give rise to reasonable suspicion that a person has committed or is committing a crime. The third type of police-citizen encounters, arrests, is characterized by highly intrusive or lengthy search or detention. The Fourth Amendment requires that an arrest be justified by probable cause to believe that a person has committed or is committing a crime. Only the second and third tiers of police-citizen encounters are seizures sufficient to invoke the protections of the Fourth Amendment to the U.S. Constitution.

A seizure in the Fourth Amendment context occurs only if, in view of all the circumstances surrounding the incident, a reasonable person would have believed that he or she was not free to leave. In addition to situations where an officer directly tells a suspect that he or she is not free to go, circumstances indicative of a seizure may include the threatening presence of several officers, the display of a weapon by an officer, some physical touching of the citizen's person, or the use of language or tone of voice indicating the compliance with the officer's request might be compelled.

We need not decide whether this encounter might have been a tier-one police-citizen encounter, because we conclude that in any case, it was a seizure supported by reasonable suspicion.

In this case, Guthard was familiar with the neighborhood where the seizure took place because he lived in it. Specifically, Guthard testified that he was aware of those individuals who frequented the house of the neighbors in question, but did not recognize Krannawitter or her Altima. Because of this personalized knowledge regarding his own neighborhood, Guthard testified that the fact that Krannawitter was parked in the driveway in question at 6 a.m. was suspicious. Guthard thought it was possible that the driver might be lost, but his suspicion about the Altima and its occupants was reinforced when he circled back to check on the Altima and witnessed it begin to back out of the driveway, only to pause for an unknown reason and abruptly drive back into the driveway just as he approached in his marked cruiser. In his interaction with Krannawitter, Guthard indicated that he thought he should check on the property and on her, to be sure that she and her passengers were not attempting to break into the property.

Guthard witnessed what appeared to him to be evasive behavior when Krannawitter pulled out of and then immediately back into the neighbors' driveway. Based on his knowledge of the neighbors and the neighborhood in question, Guthard did not believe Krannawitter was visiting or acquainted with those neighbors such that there was a reason for her Altima to be parked in that driveway in the early morning hours. Guthard testified he considered it to be part of his job to keep an eye on his neighborhood. We conclude that when the totality of the circumstances is considered, Guthard's seizure of Krannawitter was supported by a particularized and objective basis for suspecting the particular person stopped of criminal activity.

VI. CONCLUSION

The judgment and sentence of the district court are affirmed.

AFFIRMED.

---

1 Why was the defendant detained by the police officer in this case?
2 How did the court characterize this level of interaction between the police officer and the defendant? Does this level of interaction amount to a seizure under the Constitution?
3 What is the second tier of police–citizen interaction? What is required under the Constitution by the police to justify this interaction?
4 What is the third tier of interaction and what is required by the police to justify it?

CASE QUESTIONS

CHAPTER SUMMARY

This chapter examined the various interactions between police and individuals. There are three different types of interactions that police can have with suspects: voluntary actions, *Terry* stops, and arrests. Two out of the three interactions must be justified by the police. A voluntary action carries no constitutional implications. Police officers do not have to justify a voluntary action between themselves and individuals. Prior to 1968, the only other type of interaction that was permissible was a full-blown arrest. However, in *Terry v. Ohio*, the U.S. Supreme Court carved out the third category of interaction, the *Terry* stop. A *Terry* stop is a brief detention of an individual that gives police time to investigate and follow up on their reasonable suspicion that a crime has occurred. Courts have been reluctant to provide a specific time limit for this interaction and will, instead, rely on the totality of circumstances of the case itself. During the *Terry* stop, officers are authorized to conduct a pat down and frisk for their own safety. Although it was originally created within the context of a *Terry* stop, the stop and frisk policy has become so prevalent that it has become a category unto itself. During a stop and frisk, police are authorized to pat down the outer clothing of the individual to check for weapons. During that pat down they can remove any item that they believed to be a weapon. However, stop and frisk was never designed as an alternative means for the police to conduct a separate inquiry and to find incriminating evidence. In recent decades, stop and frisk policies have come under a great deal of criticism because of police attitudes and policies that encourage stop and frisk in a variety of situations that it was never designed to address. The remaining category of interaction with the police is arrest. As we will see in Chapter 4, arrest carries with it a complex web of issues. At its simplest, however, all arrests must be supported by probable cause.

KEY TERMS AND CONCEPTS

Voluntary encounter   Stop and frisk
Terry stop   Contraband

END OF CHAPTER EXERCISES

Review Questions

See Appendix A for answers

1 Is a person who has been asked a question by a police officer during a voluntary encounter obliged to remain in position and answer the question? Why?
2 What is a *Terry* stop?
3 How would you define reasonable suspicion?
4 Prior to the decision in *Terry v. Ohio*, what were the two types of interactions permitted between police and individuals?
5 In a *Terry* stop, police may detain an individual for a brief period of time. How brief is brief?
6 The *Terry* case authorized a pat down and frisk. Why?
7 What is a stop and frisk?
8 During a stop and frisk, what rules are the police obliged to follow?
9 What is the scope of a stop and frisk?
10 How have stop and frisk policies been abused in some areas of the country?

Web Surfing

Do an Internet search about the abuse of stop and frisk policies. How has the stop and frisk rule been abused by some cities?

Visit the Bureau of Justice statistics website (www.bjs.gov) and search for arrests. What can you learn about the arrest rate in major cities beginning in the 1980s? Can you show a relationship between stop and frisk policies and arrest rates?

Question for Analysis

There was, unquestionably, an excessive use of the stop and frisk policy in some major cities. What was the impact of that policy on the relationship between the police and the citizenry in those cities?

Hypothetical

Based on your reading in this chapter, if you are approached by a police officer and asked a general question, could you refuse to answer and not put yourself in legal jeopardy?

PRACTICE QUESTIONS FOR TEST REVIEW

See Appendix A for answers

Essay Question

Explain Terry stops.

True-False

1   **T   F**   To justify a voluntary encounter, a police officer must show probable cause.

2   **T   F**   It is illegal to possess contraband, but not to sell it.

3   **T   F**   Stop and frisk was originally authorized under *Terry v. Ohio*.

Fill in the Blank

1   A brief detention of a suspect to follow up on specific investigative issues is called ——.

2   The right of a law enforcement officer to pat down a person's outer clothing for weapons, whether the person is under arrest or not is known as ——.

3   An object that is illegal to possess, including child pornography, certain types of weapons, and illegal narcotics, among others is ——.

Multiple Choice

1   The constitutional basis for a *Terry* stop is:

   A   There is no constitutional basis.
   B   Probable cause.
   C   Reasonable belief.
   D   Reasonable suspicion.

2   A police officer engages an individual in a voluntary encounter. Which of the following statements is true?

   A   The person is free to leave at any point.
   B   The person is under arrest.
   C   The person must remain still and answer all questions.
   D   The person can resist the unlawful arrest.

3   Which of the following statements is true about stop and frisk?

   A   Police may pat down a person's outer clothing to check for weapons.
   B   The police may take a person to police headquarters for additional questioning.
   C   The police may search all of the person's belongings.
   D   The police can use stop and frisk as an excuse to search a person's home.

ENDNOTES

1. 392 U.S. 1 (1968).
2. *Florida v. Bostick*, 501 U.S. 429, 434 (1991).
3. *Coolidge v. New Hampshire*, 403 U.S. 443, 91 S.Ct.2022, 29 L.Ed.2d 564 (1971).
4. *Katz v. United States*, 389 U.S. 347, 351 (1967).
5. *United States v. Ringold*, 335 F.3d 1168 (10th Cir. 2003).
6. *Florida v. Royer*, 460 U.S. 491 (1983).
7. 392 U.S. 1, 88 S.Ct.1868, 20 L.Ed.2d 889 (1968).
8. *Adams v. Williams*, 407 U.S. 143 (1972); *Terry v. Ohio*, 392 U.S. 1, 88 S.Ct.1868, 20 L.Ed.2d 889 (1968).
9. *Adams v. Williams*, 407 U.S. 143, 92 S.Ct.1921, 32 L.Ed.2d 612 (1972).
10. *Terry v. Ohio*, 392 U.S. 1, 88 S.Ct.1868, 20 L.Ed.2d 889 (1968).
11. *State v. Johnson*, 246 N.C. App. 677, 686, 783 S.E.2d 753, 760 (2016).
12. *People v. Magallanes*, 409 Ill. App. 3d 720, 725 (2011).
13. *Alabama v. White*, 496 U.S. 325, 330 (1990).
14. *Prado Navarette v. California*, 572 U.S. 393, 134 S. Ct. 1683 (2014).
15. *Terry*, 392 U.S. at 21.
16. *People v. Nitz*, 371 Ill. App. 3d 747 (2007).
17. *People v. Linley*, 388 Ill. App. 3d 747 (2009).
18. *State v. Thomas*, 291 Kan. 676 (2011).
19. *Hayes v. State*, 202 Ga. App 204, 414 SE2d 321 (1991).
20. *Michigan v. Long*, 463 U.S. 1032, 103 S.Ct.3469, 77 L.Ed.2d 1201 (1983).
21. *U.S. v. Pontoo*, 666 F.3d 20 (1st Cir. 2011).
22. *U.S. v. Berry*, 670 F2d 583 (5th Cir. 1982).
23. *Florida v. Bostick,* 501 U.S. 429 (1991).
24. *State v. Blassingame*, 338 S.C. 240, 525 S.E.2d 535 (Ct. App. 1999).
25. *Minnesota v. Dickerson*, 508 U.S. 366, 113 S.Ct. 2130, 124 L.Ed.2d 334 (2019).
26. *Id.*
27. *Gardner v. State* (Ala. Crim. App. 2019)
28. *Sibron v. New York*, 392 U.S. 40, 65-66, 88 S.Ct. 1889, 20 L.Ed.2d 917 (1968).
29. *Minnesota v. Dickerson*, 508 U.S. 366, 113 S.Ct. 2130, 124 L.Ed.2d 334 (2019).
30. *Id.*

Fourth Amendment: Probable Cause and Arrest

Chapter Objective

- Define probable cause
- List and explain circumstances that give rise to probable cause
- Provide a definition of when a suspect is under arrest
- Describe who has the power to arrest
- Explain how an arrest warrant is obtained

Chapter Outline

I. The Fourth Amendment's Requirement of Probable Cause
   A. Probable Cause
      What Is Probable Cause?
      Degree of Proof Needed to Establish Probable Cause
   B. Specific Acts That Establish Probable Cause
      Description over the Radio
      Suspicious or Unusual Behavior
      Information Provided by Confidential Informants
      Anonymous Phone Calls
      Stops at Sobriety or Roadside Check Points
      Pretextual Stops
      Flight
      Presence at a Crime Scene
      "Gut Feelings" or Hunches

II. Arrest
   A. Arrest and Probable Cause
   B. Who Can Arrest?
      Arrests by Police Officers and Others
      Arrests Outside of the Officer's Jurisdiction
      Citizen's Arrest
   C. Making an Arrest
   D. Determining When the Suspect Is Under Arrest
      Court Tests to Determine the Moment of Arrest

III. Arrest Warrants
   A. Courts Have a Preference for Warrants
   B. The Fourth Amendment Only Applies to Government Conduct
   C. Applying for an Arrest Warrant
      The Magistrate
      Drafting the Warrant

Legally Sufficient Arrest Warrant
The "Four Corners" Test
Identifying the Person to Be Arrested
D. What Happens After the Warrant Is Issued?

THE FOURTH AMENDMENT'S REQUIREMENT OF PROBABLE CAUSE

The right of the people to be secure in their persons, houses, papers, and effects, against unreasonable searches and seizures, shall not be violated, and no Warrants shall issue, but upon probable cause, supported by Oath or affirmation, and particularly describing the place to be searched, and the persons or things to be seized.

The 54 words in the Fourth Amendment created an enormous body of law and guaranteed that suspects who were detained or were searched had rights that they could assert against law enforcement. The men who wrote the U.S. Constitution had recently survived under a different form of government and many of their concerns with the overreach of the British criminal justice system are reflected in how they wanted to proceed under the new United States of America. The Fourth Amendment makes clear that no one can be subjected to unreasonable searches and seizures (arrests) unless probable cause exists. When law enforcement officials request a warrant to search or arrest, the warrant must also be supported by probable cause.

A. PROBABLE CAUSE

As we will saw in the previous chapter, there are circumstances in which the police are authorized to detain people, briefly, to investigate a possible crime. Those short detentions are authorized as an exception to the general rule that to detain someone the police must always show probable cause.

Because the Fourth Amendment requires probable cause for searches, arrests, and the issuance of warrants, the definition of this phrase takes on great importance. As is true in many other places in the U.S. Constitution, the framers do not define many of the terms that they used. This is also true with probable cause. Although the Constitution is a model of brevity, there have often been times when judges, legislators, and attorneys have wished that its authors spent more time explaining what they meant by phrases like "probable cause." Because the Constitution does not define the phrase, it falls to the court system in general and the U.S. Supreme Court in particular to define the phrase. Because society continues to evolve and technology achieves things that the framers of the Constitution could never have anticipated, the court system is often called on to update and expand on a phrase that originated in a document more than 200 years ago.

WHAT IS PROBABLE CAUSE?

At its simplest, **probable cause** refers to the reasonable belief that a crime has occurred or is about to occur,[1] given that a particular set of facts is true. In this particular case, the set of facts is that a police officer believes that a suspect has committed a crime. Although an officer does not need to prove that the defendant committed an offense beyond a reasonable doubt, the officer cannot base probable cause on mere suspicion, gut feelings, or hunches.[2] Instead an officer must have reasonable suspicion that a crime has occurred.[3] The existence of probable cause to arrest is based on objective standards and is determined from the viewpoint of what a prudent person would believe when presented with the same facts and circumstances as the officer.

Probable cause exists if, at the time of the arrest, the officers had knowledge and reasonably trustworthy information about facts and circumstances sufficient to warrant a prudent man in believing that the defendant had committed the offense. If the officer can demonstrate that he or she had such objective facts at the time that he or she made the arrest, then the courts are likely to rule that probable cause existed and the arrest was constitutionally valid.

Determining probable cause is often not a simple matter. "In dealing with probable cause . . . as the very name implies, we deal with probabilities. These probabilities are technical; they are the essentially factual and practical considerations of everyday life on which reasonable and prudent men, not legal technicians, act."[4] Probable cause at the time of arrest means that at the moment the arrest was made, the officers had reasonable belief that a crime had been (or was about to be) committed.

What is the process for making the determination of probable cause? First, it must exist at the moment of arrest. An officer may be called on to testify about specific, articulable facts that led him or her to believe that a crime had occurred (or was occurring). The standard to prove probable cause is that the facts and circumstances, at the moment of the arrest, "warrant a man of reasonable caution in the belief that an offense had been committed."[5] Probable cause must be based on something more substantial than mere rumor or speculation.[6] This means that police officers must often independently verify facts related to them before they will have sufficient probable cause to make an arrest. Probable cause is a middle ground between proof beyond a reasonable doubt and mere suspicion that a criminal act occurred. Police officers must be able to articulate the precise elements that made them believe that a crime was occurring.

Courts have consistently described probable cause as a factor of the "totality of the circumstance," including the location, time of day, and suspect's demeanor, all viewed through the eyes of a reasonable, prudent police officer.[8] However, this chapter will go beyond these generalities and explore the law of arrest in much greater depth.

If we were called on to come up with the simplest definition of probable cause, we might rely on how courts have defined it. According to numerous court decisions, probable cause refers to the reasonable belief that the suspect has committed a crime. An officer must have probable cause before arresting a

Probable cause
The constitutional requirement that law enforcement officers have reasonable belief that a person has committed a crime.

Sidebar

"*A finding of probable cause to arrest does not require proof beyond a reasonable doubt. However, there must be reasonable cause to believe that a crime was or is being committed, and the defendant committed the crime. Conduct which is, at most, equivocal and suspicious, is not sufficient to establish probable cause to arrest.*"[7]

suspect and cannot wait to develop facts later that justify the initial arrest. The existence of probable cause to arrest is based on objective standards and is determined from the viewpoint of what a prudent person would believe when presented with the same facts and circumstances as the officer. If a hypothetical, reasonable person would believe, based on the facts presented, that the suspect had committed a crime, then a police officer would also have probable cause and can make an arrest. The Fourth Amendment was written in such a way as to make sure that officers could not arrest anyone on a whim or on a "gut feeling." See Scenario 4-1.

SCENARIO 4-1

HUNCHES

Officer John Doe is on patrol one evening and sees a car being driven by an African American male. Officer Doe is familiar with this area of town and knows that very few African Americans live in this area. He pulls the man over and arrests him. Does he have probable cause?

Answer: No. It is not a crime to be an African American in a car driving through a predominately white neighborhood, and without additional evidence, there is no probable cause for the arrest.

DEGREE OF PROOF NEEDED TO ESTABLISH PROBABLE CAUSE

Police officers are not required to establish that a suspect is guilty of a crime beyond a reasonable doubt. That standard must be met by the prosecutor during the trial, not by the police officer at the scene of the arrest. The officer must have probable cause that is based on something more substantial than mere rumor or speculation.[9] This means that police officers must often independently verify facts related to them before they will have sufficient probable cause to make an arrest. Probable cause is a middle ground between proof beyond a reasonable doubt and mere suspicion that an action may be a criminal act.

B. SPECIFIC ACTS THAT ESTABLISH PROBABLE CAUSE

This section will examine specific factual scenarios to determine whether they do or do not establish probable cause, including the following:

- Description over the radio
- Suspicious or unusual behavior
- Information provided by confidential informants
- Anonymous phone calls
- Stops at sobriety or roadside checkpoints

- Pretextual stops
- Flight
- Presence at a crime scene
- "Gut feelings" or hunches

DESCRIPTION OVER THE RADIO

The Court has stated that an arresting officer does not need personal or direct knowledge of the facts that support probable cause. For instance, an officer may arrest a person simply because he or she matches a description relayed over the police radio.[10] Consider Scenario 4-2.

PROBABLE CAUSE?

Officers Smith and Jones are on patrol when they receive a description of an alleged armed robber's clothing and the car he was driving when he committed the robbery. Smith and Jones stop a car that matches the description and a person who matches the description of the armed robber. They conduct a *Terry* stop and find a bag in the car that has the same name on it as the gas station where the robbery occurred. They arrest the man. Do they have probable cause?

Answer: Yes. A prudent officer would have believed that the defendant had committed the crime of armed robbery and had reasonable suspicion that a crime had occurred.[11]

SUSPICIOUS OR UNUSUAL BEHAVIOR

Officers who observe individuals acting in strange or bizarre ways may conduct a *Terry* stop. Suspicious behavior, coupled with additional information about a crime having occurred, will provide probable cause.[12]

INFORMATION PROVIDED BY CONFIDENTIAL INFORMANTS

In *Illinois v. Gates*,[13] the U.S. Supreme Court determined that probable cause may be based on an informant's tip. However, probable cause will only exist if "under the totality of the circumstances, including the veracity and basis of knowledge of the informant, there is a fair probability that contraband or evidence of a crime will be found in a particular place."[14] Corroboration of the informant's tip can come from the officer's previous knowledge of the defendant's criminal activities and other investigations.[15] The rules change, though, when the informant is another police officer. In that situation, the reliability of the information is presumed as a matter of law.[16]

ANONYMOUS PHONE CALLS

When police receive an anonymous phone call stating that a specific individual has committed a crime, that fact coupled with the officers' independent investigation or corroboration can provide sufficient probable cause. However, anonymous phone calls by themselves cannot establish probable cause.[17] Courts give them a much higher degree of scrutiny. The U.S. Supreme Court ruled that an arrest was unconstitutional when police officers responded to a location after receiving an anonymous phone call and immediately arrested the suspect. Because they did not corroborate the details of the anonymous call independently, they lacked probable cause.[18]

Even when the anonymous phone caller gives detailed descriptions, probable cause may not be established. Additional investigation is still required. Courts will look to questions such as, "Can the anonymous caller state with specificity what the defendant's actions would be?" What the courts are looking for with confidential informants is some indication the caller had inside information on the defendant.[19]

STOPS AT SOBRIETY OR ROADSIDE CHECKPOINTS

It is very common for police to set up roadblocks to check drivers to see if they have their drivers' licenses and to incidentally determine if anyone is operating under the influence of alcohol or some other drug. Such roadblocks have been ruled constitutional, as long as the officers follow specific procedures. For instance, police must determine how they will stop cars before they set up the roadblock and then follow that procedure during the roadblock. If they have determined that they will stop every car, then they must follow that procedure. Law enforcement is not permitted to single out specific cars for special treatment or to set up a roadblock as subterfuge to catch a particular defendant. Consider Scenario 4-3.

| SCENARIO 4-3 | FAKE ROADBLOCK |

Several police officers have strong suspicions that Calvin is transporting narcotics. They decide that they will set up a roadblock checkpoint near Calvin's home and then not bother to stop any drivers until Calvin comes along. The roadblock will just be a ruse to find an excuse to talk with Calvin and perhaps see what he has in his car. Is this roadblock constitutional?

Answer: No. Officers cannot use a roadblock as a way to secretly check on one motorist. Once the checkpoint is established, they must stop every car or follow the procedure that they instituted at the beginning.[20]

PRETEXTUAL STOPS

A police officer's decision to stop a suspect for the commission of a traffic violation is not unlawful merely because the officer had reason to believe that the suspect was implicated in committing other crimes. The officer must have a valid reason to pull over a suspect, independent of the officer's suspicion regarding the other crimes. Police officers are authorized to stop motor vehicles, even if the reason that they are doing so is something other than a traffic violation. These are referred to as **pretextual stops** and are constitutional, as long as the stop is based on a real violation.[21]

Pretextual stops
The detention or arrest of a person for a minor offense when the officer really suspects that the defendant has committed a more serious crime.

FLIGHT

One question that often comes up is what happens when the police encounter a person on the street, and after they begin to question him or her, the person flees? Courts have ruled that flight gives the officers probable cause to arrest.[22] See Scenarios 4-4 and 4-5.

FLIGHT

SCENARIO 4-4

Officer Jo has been alerted that a white male, approximately 50 years of age with black hair, has been reported to have committed a murder in a specific neighborhood. Officer Jo spots a man who roughly matches the description. The man is walking into a store. Officer Jo gets out of her car and confronts the man, asking him to show his hands. Instead, the man runs into the store. Officer Jo tackles the man and arrests him. However, he is not the murder suspect. Does she have probable cause anyway?

Answer: Yes.[23] Because the man ran away from Officer Jo, he displayed flight, which satisfies probable cause.

FLIGHT?

SCENARIO 4-5

Officer Dan is on patrol when he receives a call that a man has been seen in a neighborhood, threatening residents with a gun. The officer cruises the neighborhood and sees a man who roughly resembles the 911 description. He stops the man and arrests him, recovering a weapon. It turns out that the man is not the suspect who had threatened others. Does Officer Dan have probable cause to arrest?

Answer: No. Unlike the previous example, the man did not flee when confronted by the officer, so there was no independent action by the suspect that would give the officer probable cause. Officer Dan could have done a *Terry* stop, but he did not have sufficient facts to establish probable cause.[24]

PRESENCE AT A CRIME SCENE

Simply the presence of a person at the scene of a crime does not give police the probable cause to arrest. Consider Scenario 4-6.

SCENARIO 4-6

WRONG PLACE, WRONG TIME

Jimmy is at a party and someone has called the police. When the police arrive, they pat down the man standing next to Jimmy and recover drugs from him. The police then arrest everyone in the immediate area, including Jimmy. Do police have probable cause under these facts?

Answer: No. Mere presence when drugs are recovered from another individual does not give the police probable cause to arrest other people.[25]

"GUT FEELINGS" OR HUNCHES

Although we often see portrayals of fictional police officers following "hunches" or "gut feelings," the real world is more complex. An officer may well have a feeling that a particular person has committed an offense, but until he or she can present some proof to substantiate it, that feeling cannot form the basis for probable cause, and any arrest based on a hunch will be ruled unconstitutional.

 ## ARREST

Arrest
Detention and restraint of a suspect by a law enforcement official; a person is detained and is not free to leave.

In almost all situations, a criminal case begins with an **arrest**. To arrest someone is to detain a person suspected of committing a crime. Only law enforcement officers are empowered to make arrests. But what actually is the legal definition of arrest?

To arrest a person is to place that person in custody and prevent him or her from leaving the area. When a person is under arrest, he or she is often physically restrained and the person's liberty is taken away. The suspect is also handcuffed or restrained in some other way. Consider Scenario 4-7. Determining the precise point when a person is considered to be under arrest has important constitutional law consequences. A person who is under arrest has the right to an attorney, the right to petition for bond, the right to be told about the charges against him or her, and the right to remain silent, among many others. When a suspect is under arrest, any statement that he or she makes can be used against him or her.

SCENARIO 4-7

ARREST?

Mike calls the local police after he finds that his roommate, who is currently away, has a substantial amount of cash and what appears to be marijuana hidden under the kitchen sink. The officer who takes the call tells Mike that based on what he has told him, his roommate should be placed under arrest and should surrender himself at the police station. The officer tells Mike to relay this information to his friend. Is the roommate under arrest?

Answer: No. A police officer must personally interact with a suspect to arrest him or her. There is no such thing as a telephonically relayed arrest.

A. ARREST AND PROBABLE CAUSE

An arrest occurs when the police detain a suspect for a crime and the suspect is not free to leave. All arrests must be supported by probable cause, either based on the police officer's observations, some other information, or an arrest warrant.

The U.S. Constitution places strict limits on the arrest powers of police officers. The Fourth Amendment requires that when police arrest someone either with or without a warrant, they must have probable cause. Probable cause is a reasonable belief that the suspect has committed a crime. In some cases, probable cause is described differently.

An arrest can occur under a wide variety of situations. There is no requirement that the police must use the word "arrest" before a detention is considered to be an arrest. The problem with defining arrest is that there are so many interactions between police and suspects in so many varied locations—and under such a wide variety of circumstances—that simply defining arrest as taking someone into custody is not sufficient. The real issue with defining arrest has to do with constitutional rights. There are vital constitutional issues that figure into the arrest of a suspect. Before a person is legally considered under arrest, he or she does not have the right to a trial by jury, the right to have an attorney present during questioning, or many other rights.

There is a natural tension between suspects and police when it comes to defining the precise moment when an arrest occurred. Suspects would, quite naturally, want that moment to occur as early in the interaction with police as possible. Police, on the other hand, would like to delay the official moment of arrest as long as possible, to sidestep some of the limitations that are placed on them when that moment occurs. Because of this, courts do not look to the subjective belief or intent of either the suspect or the police officer in determining when the exact moment of arrest occurred. Instead, courts will look to the surrounding circumstances. A person is under arrest when a third party, viewing the facts and circumstances, would believe that the suspect was not free to leave.[26] This classification of not being free to leave is the linchpin of the definition of arrest, and it this definition that defines precisely when a suspect's numerous postarrest rights are triggered (see Figure 4-1).

The right of the people to be secure in their persons, houses, papers, and effects, against unreasonable searches and seizures, shall not be violated, and no Warrants shall issue, but upon probable cause, supported by Oath or affirmation, and particularly describing the place to be searched, and the persons or things to be seized.

FIGURE 4-1

Fourth Amendment, U.S. Constitution: Search and Seizure

B. WHO CAN ARREST?

In the United States, hundreds of individuals are arrested on a daily basis. Law enforcement officers make arrests in all types of situations. Some are inherently dangerous, such as serving an arrest warrant on a person who is armed and dangerous. Arrests may occur without warrants, such as when officers have reason to believe that a person has committed a crime.

In the typical situation, an arrest is made under the authority of an arrest warrant, which is discussed later in this chapter. Police officers are also allowed to make arrests without warrants, however, and they do so every day in this country.

ARRESTS BY POLICE OFFICERS AND OTHERS

In most situations, a certified law enforcement officer is the only person who can make an arrest. These officers are specifically empowered by the local, state, or federal government to conduct arrests and have been through extensive training before being given that power. When a person becomes a police officer, he or she is authorized to make arrests either on duty or off duty, either in uniform or in civilian clothes. No matter the circumstance, though, the arrest must be supported by probable cause.

When people desire to become police officers, they usually attend a police academy that is governed and supervised by state agencies. Their trainers are older, more experienced police officers and attorneys. Police officers train the recruits in the methods of carrying out the physical actions involved in arrests, hostage situations, and gun battles, whereas attorneys train officers in the complexities of constitutional law and how to make sure that they abide by the law in their professional lives.

After graduating from a police academy or other training program, new officers are usually subject to a probationary period. They ride with other, more seasoned officers who go out on patrol. They watch and observe other officers in the normal course of their day-to-day activities. While the new officer learns, he or she is also being closely monitored and observed for reactions in stress situations and other police activities. Not everyone is cut out to be a police officer. Some cannot handle the stress. Some cannot handle the power of their positions.

Once officers are fully authorized to carry out arrests, they are normally limited to a specific geographic region where they are allowed to make arrests. This term is frequently—and somewhat incorrectly—referred to as an officer's jurisdiction. The term jurisdiction is a legal term that refers to a person's or a court's power to take some action. In most cases, the geographic limitations of that power are referred to as **venue**, a term that designates the limits of where a court or a police officer can carry out his or her duties. However, because jurisdiction is the most commonly used term, this text will use it from this point forward. Just as a judge cannot make a ruling that binds a judge in some other county, a police officer is usually barred from making arrests in another

Venue
The particular geographic area where a court or an official can exercise power; an example of venue would be the county's borders.

county (assuming that the venue is limited to county, not state, boundaries, which is the most common limitation).

ARRESTS OUTSIDE OF THE OFFICER'S JURISDICTION

Although the general rule is that police officers cannot arrest a person outside their territorial jurisdiction, there are exceptions. One such exception is the **fresh pursuit doctrine**. Under this ruling, if a police officer is pursuing a suspect who has committed a felony, then the officer can chase that person across county or state lines and arrest that suspect, even though the officer has no lawful authority to arrest in that jurisdiction. Of course, the fresh pursuit doctrine has its own limitations, including rulings on just how "fresh" the pursuit must be. It is obviously not fresh pursuit if the officer arrests the suspect hours or even days after the pursuit has ended. In court rulings, fresh pursuit means just what it suggests: an ongoing, immediate pursuit that happens to cross some boundary. Without that showing of immediacy, officers would have no greater authority to arrest someone outside their jurisdiction than would a citizen.

Fresh pursuit doctrine
A court-created doctrine that allows police officers to arrest suspects without warrants and to cross territorial boundaries while they are still pursuing a suspect.

CITIZEN'S ARREST

In some situations, individuals who are not police officers can detain a suspect. This is often referred to as **citizen's arrest**, but the term is misleading. Citizens, or anyone else, can detain a person who has committed a crime and then hand that person over to the police, but citizens do not make arrests. An arrest has a very specific meaning and involves constitutional rights, none of which apply when one or more citizens detain a criminal for the police. However, this term has been in popular use for decades, so this text will continue to use it. Many states allow citizens to make arrests when a crime has been committed in the citizen's presence or within his or her immediate knowledge. Some states even go so far as to say that private citizens have as much power to arrest a felon—in an emergency situation—as does a police officer. Private citizens can make a citizen's arrest—in most states—for a felony occurring in their presence. They might also have the right to arrest someone to prevent a felony from occurring. Generally, there is no right of citizen's arrest to prevent a misdemeanor. Usually the citizen can only arrest a person if the citizen actually saw the person commit the crime. Many states have dramatically curtailed the right of citizen's arrest, preferring to leave it in the hands of the people who have been specifically trained to carry it out, namely, police officers.

Citizen's arrest
A legal doctrine that holds harmless a citizen who detains a person observed to have committed a crime.

Under the citizen's arrest doctrine, persons have the right to physically restrain a person who has committed a crime in their presence and hold this person for the police. A citizen's arrest is used most commonly in cases of shoplifting—a store manager or employee detains a person suspected of shoplifting until the police arrive. This doctrine has more importance in the area of civil law, where it protects the citizen from being sued for battery in restraining the individual and holding him or her until the police arrive to make a real arrest.[27]

Sidebar

Citizen's arrest is not actually an arrest at all. Citizens are not empowered to arrest anyone. The phrase should, more correctly, be called citizen's detention.

C. MAKING AN ARREST

Although in some countries a police officer must actually touch a person before he or she is considered to be under arrest, that is not true in the United States. Here police officers can make a legal arrest simply by giving a verbal command to a suspect. In most cases, of course, the officer does touch the person, usually by restraining him or her. Often, the officer will place the suspect in handcuffs and transport the suspect to police headquarters, so there is no question that the person has been restrained and is not free to leave, the two most important factors in determining when an arrest has been made.

There is no requirement that police use force to make an arrest. Conversely, if a police officer must use force, that force must be reasonable and only that force necessary to effect an arrest and nothing more. A person can always voluntarily submit to an arrest. When this happens, the person is considered legally arrested.

D. DETERMINING WHEN THE SUSPECT IS UNDER ARREST

If a person is arrested without probable cause, then the arrest is unconstitutional. There is often no direct penalty against the officer for making an unconstitutional arrest, so why is the issue of arrest so important? If an arrest is not supported by probable cause, or if some other irregularity occurs during the arrest, then the primary punishment faced by law enforcement is not a civil suit, but the exclusionary rule. This rule, developed by the U.S. Supreme Court in *Weeks v. U.S.*,[28] holds that any evidence obtained after an unlawful arrest (or in violation of the suspect's rights) is not admissible. We will explore the application of the exclusionary rule in Chapter 7.

COURT TESTS TO DETERMINE THE MOMENT OF ARREST

> **Sidebar**
>
> *The test to determine when a person is under arrest is when a reasonable person, reviewing the facts, would believe that the suspect is not free to leave.*

The question of when a person is under arrest is critically important for the entire criminal process. Because the result of an unlawful arrest is so drastic—the suppression of any evidence obtained from that point onward—police and prosecutors are very keen to pinpoint the precise moment when an arrest occurred and to make sure that police officers know how that law applies to factual scenarios. To determine the precise moment when an arrest has occurred, the U.S. Supreme Court has created a test that does not rely on the subjective impressions of either the suspect or the officer to make the determination. As discussed earlier, both of these individuals have vested interests in stating that the moment of arrest occurred at different times. The defendant will attempt to say that an arrest occurred as early as possible in the interaction between the suspect and the officer so that any evidence obtained after this point may be challenged. An officer, on the other hand, has a vested interest in delaying the moment of arrest as long as possible, because officers have more latitude in what they are permitted to do before the suspect is considered to be under arrest.

Courts have created an objective test to determine when an arrest has occurred. The elements of the test are whether under the circumstances at the time, a reasonable person would believe that he or she was under arrest and not free to leave. The subjective beliefs of the police officer and the suspect are irrelevant under this test. As an example, a police officer testifying during a pretrial motion might state unequivocally that the suspect was not under arrest and that he or she was free to leave, but the objective facts might give a completely different interpretation. Consider Scenario 4-8.

FREE TO LEAVE?

Andrew has been asked to come to the police department to answer some questions about burglaries in his neighborhood. He voluntarily comes to the police department, and during questioning a detective accuses him of being the person who has committed the burglaries. As he is being questioned, a uniformed officer stands in front of the door to the interrogation room with a gun drawn and pointed at the floor. Andrew asks if he is under arrest and the detective says, "Absolutely not. You can walk out any time you want." Is Andrew under arrest as that term is defined by the courts?

Answer: Yes. Despite what the detective says, the physical actions of the police speak louder than their words. The fact that there is a uniformed officer standing in front of the door with a gun drawn would suggest to a reasonable person that Andrew is under arrest.

 ARREST WARRANTS

So far, our discussions have centered around situations where police view an incident and then make an arrest. The arrest must be supported by probable cause and that will often mean that, at some point, they will testify about specific, articulable facts that they observed that established a reasonable belief that a crime had occurred. However, there is another broad category of arrests where individual police officers are not required to go through this analysis. That is because someone else has already made a determination about probable cause. That person is a judge.

A. COURTS HAVE A PREFERENCE FOR WARRANTS

Courts have always preferred that an arrest or a search be conducted with a **warrant**.[29] The reasoning behind this approach is painfully simple: When a warrant is issued, some third party—specifically a magistrate or other judge—has reviewed the facts and made a determination that probable cause exists.

Warrant
An order issued by a judge that authorizes a police officer to arrest a suspect or conduct a search.

This takes the factual evaluation of probable cause out of the hands of the police and places it in the judiciary. Having a neutral, third party review the facts is far more likely to result in a ruling that will follow the law. Having a warrant does not eliminate the need for probable cause. Instead, it changes the point where probable cause is determined. Instead of a split-second decision by a police officer on patrol, a magistrate will review the facts, affidavit, and any other evidence to make a determination that probable cause exists before issuing an arrest warrant. This determination takes an officer's discretion out of the equation and places it squarely in the hands of a magistrate.

A magistrate's determination that probable cause exists does not always mean that probable cause exists, but a judicial determination raises a presumption that this is the case. Arrests without warrants are always given greater scrutiny than those made pursuant to a warrant.

The simple fact is that a police officer who carries out an arrest has greater freedom to operate without a warrant than the same officer would have when it comes to a search.[30] Human beings are mobile, dangerous, and can flee a scene. As such, it doesn't make sense to require an officer to spend an hour or more obtaining an arrest warrant before any arrests could be made. However, the same philosophy applies in exactly the opposite manner when it comes to searches. Structures, places, and secured automobiles have none of the characteristics of a live person. These places can be secured and police will be required to wait until a search warrant has been issued—unless the search falls within some narrowly defined exceptions to the search warrant requirement. We discuss those exceptions in Chapter 5.

Although probable cause to arrest and probable cause to search have generally been considered to be more or less the same thing, the day-to-day experience of police officers reveals a wide gap between theory and practice. Probable cause to arrest goes to the ultimate issue of the guilt of the defendant. Probable cause to search boils down to the likelihood of finding evidence in a particular place. For arrests, the rule that has been followed for centuries is that police officers can arrest without a warrant for serious offenses or offenses that have been committed in their presence, but must seek arrest warrants in other situations.[32] Some commentators have even suggested that probable cause to arrest is actually a higher standard than the probable cause necessary to justify a search warrant. Certainly, the consequences to the defendant are different. In one, he or she loses his liberty, in another, his or her property.

Sidebar

"Whether or not a warrant has been issued, all arrests and search warrants must be based on probable cause."[31]

B. THE FOURTH AMENDMENT ONLY APPLIES TO GOVERNMENT CONDUCT

It is important to note at the outset that the arrest warrant requirement only applies to the government, or more specifically, law enforcement. Private individuals are not required to seek arrest warrants. They may go before a magistrate or other judicial official to request that the court issue an arrest warrant, but the court is under no obligation to do so.

C. APPLYING FOR AN ARREST WARRANT

When police officers wish to obtain an arrest warrant, they usually appear before a local judge or magistrate. Because the terminology varies considerably from state to state, we will use the term **magistrate** to refer to the judicial position that is authorized to issue warrants. The normal practice is for the officer to fill out a warrant application and include an affidavit to support the facts contained in the application. An **affidavit** is a written statement that contains an oath by the person who made the document that it is correct and contains no perjury. For an arrest, the officer must create a sworn statement that lists the actions carried out by the suspect and why these activities establish probable cause and justify the court in issuing a warrant for the suspect's arrest. (Note that this procedure can vary from jurisdiction to jurisdiction.) Affidavits for arrest warrants are often required by state constitutions.[33] When courts review affidavits, they interpret the language contained in a liberal manner. Hearsay and other evidentiary objections are not considered when evaluating the evidence provided in the affidavit.[34] There is no requirement that a police officer put the precise legal wording in the affidavit. The ultimate charge to be brought against the suspect is the province of the district attorney. An affidavit violates the Fourth Amendment when the officer knowingly includes false statements.[35]

Once the application and affidavit have been provided to the magistrate, he or she must evaluate the facts and make a determination that probable cause exists to arrest the defendant. The arrest warrant must be based on the warrant application and the sworn statement that accompanies it, and not on information known only to the magistrate or not communicated through the documents. The facts presented must be sufficient to justify a neutral and detached magistrate to reach the conclusion that the suspect has committed a crime. When a judge makes a probable cause determination, it must be based on the facts presented by the officer, not a gut feeling or a personal bias on the part of the magistrate. If the warrant is later challenged by a defendant, appellate courts will only require that the judge had a "substantial basis" for reaching the conclusion that probable cause existed. Courts will only make this ruling when the judge is "clearly wrong." The chances of overturning a warrant on appeal are very low. Consider Scenario 4-9.

Magistrate
A judge who has limited power and authority.

Affidavit
A written statement where a person swears an oath that the facts contained are true.

> Sidebar
>
> *An arrest warrant is issued by a magistrate after a law enforcement has made a sufficient showing that there is probable cause to believe that the suspect has committed a crime.*

SUSPECT IS GUILTY

SCENARIO 4-9

Danny Detective has applied for a warrant and in his affidavit, he declares, "Suspect John Doe is guilty of selling Schedule II narcotics." Is this language sufficient for a magistrate to determine probable cause?

Answer: No. When an affidavit simply states that the suspect committed a crime, it is not enough.[36] The affidavit must provide facts that a magistrate can review and then use to reach a decision about the existence of probable cause.

Unlike other procedural steps that we will discuss in this text, a defendant is not entitled to know that a warrant has been issued for his or her arrest. The obvious reason for this rule is that if a person knew that a warrant had been issued, he or she might flee the area.[37]

THE MAGISTRATE

In addition to the requirements placed on law enforcement officers to provide sworn testimony to support a warrant, there are also requirements placed on the magistrate. Magistrates must be neutral and detached from the proceedings. Magistrates cannot have a vested interest in having a person arrested.[38] They cannot, for example, receive a bonus for every warrant that they issue. Although the people who issue warrants are often referred to as magistrates, there is considerable variation among the states in the name of this position. By whatever name, this individual must be legally empowered to issue warrants and must be neutral and detached. Individuals who are authorized to issue warrants include magistrates, judges, or judicial officers. The magistrate cannot be a prosecutor or a police officer. The individual must operate independently from both. In many states, magistrates are not lawyers or judges. These states allow citizens to serve in the capacity of magistrates, once they have received training from the state about the duties and responsibilities of the office.

DRAFTING THE WARRANT

The warrant must state the crime that law enforcement maintains the suspect has violated, but there is some flexibility here. As we will see later in our discussions about indictments, the wording of indictments (discussed in Chapter 8) must be precise, but warrants are held to a more liberal standard. This means that if the officer incorrectly lists the name of the offense or commits some other typographical error in describing the offense, the warrant will not be considered invalid.[39] So long as the warrant closely follows the wording of the statute, it will be considered legally sufficient.[40]

LEGALLY SUFFICIENT ARREST WARRANT

What makes a warrant legally valid? Here are the features of a valid warrant. It must:

- Be prepared in the correct form
- Be issued by a magistrate or other court that has authority to issue warrants
- Be issued by a court that has jurisdiction over the suspect
- Bear the name of the person to be arrested or provide a description that identifies a specific person

A warrant remains legally sufficient even if it contains typographical errors, including incorrect dates and times.[41] Arrest and search warrants are given a certain amount of latitude. If the warrant is sufficient on its face or has an obvious and explainable error, then it will still be considered valid. However, there are some features that must appear in a warrant. For example, applying the preceding list, if a warrant is issued by a court that has no jurisdiction to do so, it will be invalid. Similarly, a warrant must be signed by the magistrate to be effective. Consider Scenario 4-10.

FRIENDLY JUDGE

Danielle Detective knows a " 'friendly' " judge who will issue warrants without inquiring too seriously into the details presented in sworn testimony. Danielle appears before the judge, but before the warrant is officially issued and signed, the judge is called away. Danielle is in a hurry, and takes the unsigned warrant, and uses it to arrest Sally Suspect. Is this a legally sufficient warrant?

    Answer: No. An arrest based on unsigned warrant is not legally valid.[42]

THE "FOUR CORNERS" TEST

A magistrate must limit his or her review of the warrant application to the materials presented. This is the so-called **"Four Corners" test**, which essentially means that the magistrate's decision must be based on the material presented within the four corners of the application and affidavit. The affidavit and accompanying sworn testimony must be sufficient on its face to authorize the magistrate to issue the warrant. (There are jurisdictions that allow a magistrate to base the warrant not only on the evidence presented, but also the magistrate's personal knowledge, but these are in the minority.[43])

"Four Corners" test
A judicial requirement that a warrant affidavit contain all necessary information in the materials before the warrant was issued.

IDENTIFYING THE PERSON TO BE ARRESTED

A person whose first and last names appear on the warrant can be validly arrested, even if he or she is known by some other name or alias. Courts have even held that warrants that drastically misspell the suspect's name, but are close to his or her name phonetically, will still be considered constitutional.[44] Consider Scenario 4-11.

DIFFERENT NAMES

Officer Tate has applied for a warrant. To the best of his knowledge, the suspect in a series of armed robberies is known as Jorge Luis Escobar Henao. However, when the warrant is issued, the judge writes the name was George Louis Escobar Henao. Is this warrant legally valid?

    Answer: Yes. As long as the warrant sufficiently describes the person to be arrested and, even if the warrant spells the person's name incorrectly, the names—at least as they would be pronounced in English—sound the same. The officer may proceed.

Suppose that law enforcement does not know the suspect's name. In such a case, they can draft a warrant that uses the suspect's nickname, as long as the description includes enough detail that the defendant can be identified with reasonable certainty.[45]

D. WHAT HAPPENS AFTER THE WARRANT IS ISSUED?

Once the warrant has been issued, it must be served on the suspect as soon as possible or within a reasonable period of time. A warrant to arrest a person may remain active for a much greater period of time than a warrant to search a location. However, this does not mean that an arrest warrant remains valid forever. New evidence might arise in the case that could cause law enforcement and prosecutors to reevaluate the need to arrest a specific person.

CASE EXCERPT

PEOPLE v. HOWLETT

2019 NY SLIP OP 50780(U) (N.Y. CITY CT. 2019)

NICHELLE A. JOHNSON, J.

Defendant is charged by superseding misdemeanor information with Criminal Possession of Marihuana in the Fourth Degree and Criminal Possession of Marihuana Fifth Degree.

FINDINGS OF FACT

The People called one witness at the hearing namely Mount Vernon Police Officer Avion Lee. At the hearing, Mount Vernon Police Officer Avion Lee testified that she has been a member of the police force for six years and has been assigned to the Narcotics Unit for one and a half years. She has received HIDTA (High Intensity Drug Traffic Area) training. HIDTA is training for the detection of drugs, including marijuana. Officer Lee testified that over the course of her career she has made over one hundred marijuana arrests. On May 17, 2018, she was working with her partner Officer Joseph Valente and patrolling South Fifth Avenue in Mount Vernon in an undercover police car, a yellow cab. At approximately 5:37 pm she was driving southbound in the vicinity of 657 South Fifth Avenue, Mount Vernon, New York when she observed the defendant's vehicle parked on South Fifth Avenue facing northbound. She testified that "maybe" one week prior, the Mount Vernon Police Department received an anonymous complaint that a black male was selling narcotics from his car in front of the Garden Bar on South Fifth Avenue in Mount Vernon. She testified that her supervisor assigned her to investigate the tip "maybe" one week before she arrested the defendant. Officer Lee stated she, personally, was not the officer or person who received the anonymous tip, and that she received information about it from her Supervisor. Officer Lee testified that the printout of information for the anonymous tip provided the vehicle information, that being a black vehicle bearing license plate # HHJ8881, a description of the seller, and his street name. According to the tip, the seller would hang out in front of the Garden Bar and go to his car to retrieve the drugs. Officer Lee testified that after receiving the information, she did purposely drive by the location a few times while on duty, as well as the rest of the city. On those prior occasions she never saw defendant or his vehicle in the area.

Officer Lee testified that on May 17, 2018 at 5:37 pm she observed the defendant's vehicle bearing license plate # HHJ8881 as she and her partner were traveling south-bound on Fifth Avenue. Officer Lee testified that they made a U-turn and pulled up next to defendant's vehicle. The defendant appeared to meet the description of the person from the anonymous tip and was in the driver's seat of a car bearing the license plate New York # HHJ8881 in close proximity to the Garden Bar. Officer Lee testified that defendant was parked two or three houses down from the Garden Bar. After observing the defendant's vehicle, the officers pulled over next to defendant's vehicle and exited their vehicle. Officer Lee testified that the officers then approached the defendant's vehicle. She stated that the windows were down and as they approached she smelled what appeared to be marijuana emanating from the vehicle but did not observe anyone smoking. She further testified that she smelled marijuana emanating from the defendant's person. Officer Lee testified that marijuana has a distinct odor and that in her opinion the smell of burning marijuana is the same as unburnt marijuana. She also testified that she can smell marijuana through a ziplock bag. Officer Lee testified that she asked the defendant for his identification. She testified that when defendant reached into his right pants pocket for his identification, she observed a ziplock bag of marijuana in his pocket. Defendant then was asked to exit the vehicle and placed under arrest. After defendant was placed under arrest, Officer Lee recovered seven more bags of marijuana from his left pants pocket. They asked the defendant if he had any more marijuana in the vehicle, to which he said yes there is more marijuana in the car. They recovered a backpack that contained seven large ziplock bags and nineteen smaller ziplock bags of mari-juana. Officer Lee testified that they also recovered twenty additional ziplock bags inside of a satchel and a jar of loose marijuana and a digital scale from the center console of the vehicle. Defendant was transported to headquarters.

During Officer Lee's cross examination, the defense introduced a video of the approach to defendant's vehicle by the officers. As the People stated during the trial, the camera appears to be at the end of the street and was too far to capture if the defendant's tinted windows were up or down. However, a close view of the video does demonstrate that the officers pulled up alongside defendant's vehicle, essentially blocking him from moving the vehicle front or back, and activated police "like" lights on the undercover yellow cab. The video also demonstrates that when the officers exited their vehicle, which now also had lights activated, defendant opened the front driver's side door but did not immediately exit. It was clear that Officer Lee was standing very close to the defendant—as his car door was open—which restricted his ability to get out of the car.

CONCLUSIONS OF LAW

In evaluating the constitutionality of police-initiated encounters with motorists the court must decide whether the approach of the vehicle was justified from its inception and at every subsequent stage of the encounter. *People v. De Bour*, 40 N.Y.2d 210, 222 (1976). Under the graduated four-level test announced by the Court of Appeals in *De Bour*, "level one permits a police officer to request information from an individual and merely requires that the request be supported by an objective, credible reason, not necessarily indicative of criminality; level two, the common-law right of inquiry, permits a somewhat greater intrusion and requires a founded suspicion that criminal activity is afoot; level three authorizes an officer to forcibly stop and detain an individual, and requires a reasonable suspicion that the particular individual was involved in a felony or misdemeanor; level four, arrest, requires probable cause to believe that the person to be arrested has committed a crime." *People v. Moore*, 6 N.Y.3d 496, 498-499 (2006).

The Court of Appeals has made clear that "the right to stop a moving vehicle is distinct from the right to approach the occupants of a parked vehicle." *People v. Spencer*, 84 N.Y.2d 749, 753, (1995). The approach of occupants of a stopped, parked vehicle to request information is analyzed under the first tier of the *DeBour* inquiry. When law enforcement approaches an occupied parked motor vehicle to speak with its occupants, they need an objective credible reason for doing so, not necessarily indicative of criminality. A level one request for information may include basic, non-threatening questions regarding, for instance, identity, address, or destination. All that is required is that the intrusion be predicated on more than a hunch, whim, or idle curiosity. The police may restrain the occupants of a parked vehicle based on "some articulable facts, which initially or during the course of the encounter, established reasonable suspicion that the person is involved in criminal acts or poses some danger to the officers." *People v. Harrison*, 57 N.Y.2d at 476.

Here the arresting officer testified that when she initially encountered the defendant on May 17, 2018 she did not observe him engaging in any illegal activity or committing a traffic infraction. Officer Lee acknowledged that the defendant was legally parked on the street at the time she first observed his vehicle. She testified, however, that the defendant's vehicle and license plate matched the information provided by an anonymous complaint "maybe" a week prior. The officer testified that she did not receive the tip herself, but that her supervisor had assigned her to investigate it "maybe" one week prior to defendant's arrest. As stated above, the video of the approach to defendant's vehicle demonstrates that the officers pulled alongside of defendant's vehicle and activated the lights on the undercover police car as they were exiting the vehicle. Defendant could not move his vehicle and was stopped from exiting the car. Under these circumstances, the Court finds that the police escalated the encounter with defendant. Defendant was constructively stopped and seized before the officers made their approach to request general information. Absent reasonable suspicion of criminal activity, the officers could not forcibly detain or constructively stop him from driving his vehicle or exiting his vehicle. The Court finds that defendant was effectively seized before Officer Lee had an opportunity to approach the car and request general information and smell what appeared to be marijuana emanating from the defendant and his vehicle.

Even if this Court were to find that the officers did not constructively stop and seize the defendant when they pulled up alongside of his vehicle and activated the police lights, the testimony and evidence failed to establish that the officers had an objective credible reason to approach defendant's legally parked vehicle. An anonymous tip has been held reliable to provide the basis for an officer to approach a parked vehicle to inquire.

Officer Lee did not have firsthand knowledge of the source of the tip and did not specify during her testimony what date and time the tip was received and whether the source of the tip was from an anonymous 911 call, or a telephone call, or a face-to-face encounter with an undisclosed civilian. In this Court's opinion, this lack of specificity about the source of the tip taints the credibility and reliability of the anonymous tip. *Navarette v. California*, 572 U.S. 393 (2014); *Florida v. J.L.*, 529 U.S. 266 (2000).

In *Navarette v. California*, the United States Supreme Court held that police are justified in relying on an anonymous 911 call in encounters with motorists where the call is (i) made by an eyewitness, (ii) nearly contemporaneous with the event, and (iii) recorded and traced by the 911 system. 572 U.S. 393, 398-401 (2014). In *Navarette v. California*, a person called 911 to report that a truck driver was driving dangerously and had just run the person off the road. The person gave the make, model, color, and license plate number to California highway patrol. A police officer saw the truck being driven by Defendant Navarette on the highway and followed it for five minutes before pulling it over. The officer did not observe any reckless driving at the time he was following the truck. Upon approaching the truck, the officer smelled marijuana. The officer searched the truck and found thirty pounds of marijuana. Defendant challenged the constitutionality of the traffic stop and incident search. In upholding the constitutionality of the stop and search, the Supreme Court found that an anonymous 911 call has an inherent indicium of reliability because the caller uses the 911 system, which generally has "some features that allow for identifying and tracing callers" such that "a false tipster would think twice before using the system."

Based on the foregoing, the Court finds that the officer's conduct was not justified from its inception. Officer Lee's vague testimony about receiving information about an anonymous tip "maybe" one week prior from her supervisor was insufficient to provide the police with the requisite objective credible reason, not necessarily indicative of criminality to justify a level one encounter. Here the police failed to simply exercise their objective credible reason to approach. Instead, in pulling beside defendant's vehicle, blocking him in both by their vehicle and Officer Lee standing right in his doorway as he opened the door, and activating their police lights as soon as they exited their vehicle, the officers effectively stopped and seized defendant, at which time they lacked reasonable suspicion for a level three encounter. Again, here, this court finds the anonymous tip was not 1) reliable due to the fact that a) there was no indication how the tip was made—was it by a call, a 911 call, in person by someone who observed the alleged actions; b) it was not made contemporaneous to the actual approach in that the tip allegedly came in "maybe" one week prior to the actual arrest of the Defendant, nor 2) corroborated by the officer in that beyond the fact that the defendant was sitting in a car with the license plate provided by the anonymous tipster, the officer testified to no further confirmatory observations of the defendant that drew her attention. Thus, the tip information was not reliable and not corroborated. Accordingly, the officers lacked the requisite probable cause to make an arrest and seize evidence. The physical evidence and statements obtained by the People as a result of this vehicle encounter, is the fruit of the poisonous tree and must be suppressed.

This constitutes the Decision and Order of this Court.

---

1   What details were provided in the anonymous tip to the police in this case?
2   What did the officer do, based on this tip?
3   What is the rule about stopping an automobile to speak to the occupants?
4   What did the police officer do wrong in this encounter?

CASE QUESTIONS

CHAPTER SUMMARY

Arrests must be supported by probable cause. The definition of probable cause is a reasonable belief that a crime has occurred or is about to. The Fourth Amendment requires probable cause before anyone can be arrested or before a search can be conducted. Determining the precise point when a person is placed under arrest is a critical component in analyzing the situation for probable cause. There are specific types of instances that can give rise to probable cause, including descriptions over the radio, suspicious or unusual behavior, information provided by confidential informants, stops at roadsides sobriety checks, and flight. A person is considered to be under arrest when he or she is no longer free to leave. Only police officers are allowed to make arrests. There are some provisions for so-called citizen's arrests, but these only occur in limited circumstances.

When a police officer applies for an arrest warrant, he or she appears before a local magistrate. The officer will fill out an application and provide sworn testimony in the form of an affidavit to support the facts contained in the warrant application. The magistrate then decides that probable cause to arrest exists and authorizes the police officer to serve the arrest warrant and take the suspect into custody.

KEY TERMS AND CONCEPTS

Probable cause	Fresh pursuit doctrine	Affidavit
Pretextual stops	Citizen's arrest	"Four Corners" test
Arrest	Warrant	
Venue	Magistrate	

END OF CHAPTER EXERCISES

Review Questions

See Appendix A for answers

1 This chapter mentions that there is a preference for warrants, but that courts give police officers greater latitude to arrest without a warrant. Explain this difference.
2 What purpose does an affidavit serve in a warrant application?
3 Who is authorized to make an arrest once an arrest warrant has been issued?

4   What is the "Four Corners" test?

5   Explain probable cause.

6   Can probable cause be based on gut feelings or hunches? Explain your answer.

7   What degree of proof is required to establish probable cause?

8   List specific types of acts that can create probable cause.

9   What rules must be in effect for sobriety checkpoints?

10   What is a pretextual stop?

11   Does flight rise to probable cause? Explain your answer.

12   What is the legal test to determine if a person is under arrest?

13   What rights are afforded to a person who is under arrest?

14   Which persons are authorized to carry out an arrest?

15   What is a citizen's arrest?

16   Explain venue.

17   What is the fresh pursuit doctrine?

18   Why is it important to determine the precise point at which a person is placed under arrest?

Web Surfing

1   There are some websites that discuss probable cause that offer questionable interpretations of the law, at best. Find some of these sites and then compare them to ones where the law is better stated. What is the most common misconception about probable cause?

2   Can you locate federal or state statistics of the number of arrests in recent years for major felonies?

Question for Analysis

Aram is walking on the sidewalk in a gated community. He has very dark skin. A resident calls the police to report him. Officer Tad arrives and puts Aram in the back of the police car to question him. He doesn't like Aram's defiant answers and takes him to headquarters for additional questioning. Is Aram under arrest?

Hypothetical

Officer Nancy sees a car that she recognizes. It is owned by a person who Officer Nancy knows has been arrested before for drug possession. The current driver of the car looks like the person that Nancy has arrested before for possession of methamphetamine. She pulls the car over and while questioning the driver, observes what she believes to be narcotics on the floor of the car. She arrests the driver. Did she have probable cause to pull over the car in the first place?

PRACTICE QUESTIONS FOR TEST REVIEW

See Appendix A for answers

Essay Question

What is probable cause and why is it required?

True-False

1   T   F   Arrests must be supported by proof beyond a reasonable doubt.

2   T   F   The test for when an arrest occurs is that a reasonable person would believe that the detained person was not free to leave.

3   T   F   Citizens are allowed to detain people who have committed a crime.

Fill in the Blank

1   The constitutional requirement that law enforcement officers have reasonable belief that a person has committed a crime is ____.

2   The detention or arrest of a person for a minor offense when the officer really suspects that the defendant has committed a more serious crime is ____.

3   The ____ is the particular geographic area where a court or an official can exercise power; an example would be a county's borders.

Multiple Choice

1   A court-created doctrine that allows police officers to arrest suspects without warrants and to cross territorial boundaries while they are still pursuing the suspect.

   A   Citizen's arrest doctrine.
   B   Plain view doctrine.
   C   Right time, right place doctrine.
   D   Fresh pursuit doctrine.

2   An order, issued by a judge that authorizes a police officer to arrest a suspect or conduct a search.

   A   Request.
   B   Motion.
   C   Warrant.
   D   Certification.

3 A judicial requirement that a warrant affidavit contain all necessary information in the materials before the warrant was issued.

   A The paperwork test.

   B The "Four Corners" test.

   C The take it or leave it test.

   D The caveat emptor test.

ENDNOTES

1. *People v. Davis*, 36 N.Y.2d 280, 282, 367 N.Y.S.2d 256, 326 N.E.2d 818, cert. denied 423 U.S. 876, 96 S.Ct. 149, 46 L.Ed.2d 109 (1975).
2. *U.S. v. Lopez*, 482 F.3d 1067 (9th Cir. 2007).
3. *Denson v. State*, 159 Ga. App. 713, 285 S.E.2d 69 (1981).
4. *Brinegar v. United States*, 338 U.S. 160, 69 S.Ct. 1302, 93 LE 1879 (1948).
5. *Carroll v. United States*, 267 U.S. 132, 45 S.Ct. 280, 69 LE 543 (1925).
6. *Clark v. State*, 189 Ga. App 124, 375 SE2d 230 (1988).
7. *People v. Gomcin*, 697 N.Y.S.2d 93, 265 A.D.2d 493 (N.Y. App. Div. 1999).
8. *Bost v. State*, 406 Md. 341, 958 A.2d 356 (2008).
9. *Clark v State*, 189 Ga. App 124, 375 SE2d 230 (1988).
10. *Whiteley v. Warden*, 401 U.S. 560, 91 S.Ct.1031, 28 L.Ed.2d 306 (1971).
11. *Chambers v. Maroney*, 399 U.S. 42, 90 S.Ct.1975, 26 L.Ed.2d 419 (1970).
12. *Brinegar v. United States*, 338 U.S. 160, 69 S.Ct.1302, 93 LE 1879 (1948).
13. 462 U.S. 273, 103 S.Ct.2317, 76 L.Ed.2d 527 (1983).
14. *Id.*
15. *Brinegar v. United States*, 338 U.S. 160, 69 S.Ct.1302, 93 LE 1879 (1948).
16. *Quinn v. State*, 132 Ga. App 395, 208 SE2d 263 (1974).
17. *Florida v. J.L.*, 529 U.S. 266 (2000).
18. *Id.*
19. *Alabama v. White*, 496 U.S. 325, 110 S.Ct.2412, 110 L.Ed.2d 301 (1990).
20. *Michigan Dept. of State Police v. Sitz*, 496 U.S. 444, 110 S.Ct.2481, 110 L.Ed.2d 412 (1990).
21. *U.S. v. Randolph*, 628 F.3d 1022 (8th Cir. 2011).
22. *U.S. v. Laville*, 480 F.3d 187 (3d Cir. 2007).
23. *Jewett v. Anders*, 521 F.3d 818 (7th Cir. 2008).
24. *U.S. v. Wali*, 811 F. Supp. 2d 1276 (N.D. Tex. 2011).
25. *U.S. v. Castro-Gaxiola*, 479 F.3d 579 (8th Cir. 2007).
26. *U.S. v. Hastamorir*, 881 F.2d 1551, 1556 (11th Cir.1989); *United States v. Hammock*, 860 F.2d 390, 393 (11th Cir.1988).
27. *State v. Garcia*, 146 Wash. App. 821, 193 P.3d 181 (Div. 3 2008).
28. 232 U.S. 383 (*1914*).
29. *State v. Tucker*, 262 Neb. 940, 636 N.W.2d 853 (2001).
30. *Mowrer v. State*, 447 N.E.2d 1129 (Ind. Ct. App. 4th Dist. 1983).
31. *Draper v. U.S.*, 358 U.S. 307 (1959).
32. *Morrow v. State*, 140 Neb. 592, 300 N.W. 843 (1941).
33. *Harvey v. Commonwealth*, 226 Ky. 36, 10 S.W.2d 471 (1928).
34. *U.S. v. Ventresca*, 380 U.S. 102, 85 S. Ct. 741, 13 L.Ed.2d 684 (1965).
35. *Kerns v. Board of Com'rs of Bernalillo County*, 707 F. Supp. 2d 1190 (D.N.M. 2010).
36. *Whiteley v. Warden, Wyo. State Penitentiary*, 401 U.S. 560, 91 S. Ct. 1031, 28 L.Ed.2d 306 (1971).

37. *State v. Dabney*, 264 Wis. 2d 843, 2003 WI App 108, 663 N.W.2d 366 (Ct. App. 2003).
38. *State v. Penalber*, 386 N.J. Super. 1, 898 A.2d 538 (App. Div. 2006).
39. *Hopper v. City of Prattville*, 781 So. 2d 346 (Ala. Crim. App. 2000).
40. *State v. Garcia*, 146 N.C. App. 745, 553 S.E.2d 914 (2001).
41. *Burke v. Town of Walpole*, 405 F.3d 66 (1st Cir. 2005).
42. *State v. Wilson*, 6 S.W.3d 504 (Tenn. Crim. App. 1998).
43. *State v. Davidson*, 260 Neb. 417, 618 N.W.2d 418 (2000).
44. *Fulgencio v. City of Los Angeles*, 131 Fed. Appx. 96 (9th Cir. 2005).
45. Fed. R. Crim. P. 4(b)(1)(A).

Fourth Amendment: Search and Seizure

- Explain the process that law enforcement officers use to obtain arrest warrants
- Define the role of the magistrate in issuing a warrant
- Explain the details that a warrant must have to make it legally sufficient
- Describe situations in which search warrants are not required
- Discuss the various ways that a warrant may be challenged

I. Search Warrants
   A. Standards for Issuing Search and Seizure Warrants
   B. The Good Faith Exception
   C. Exceptions to the Search Warrant Requirement

II. Searches Without a Warrant
   A. Plain View
   B. Open Fields
   C. Dropped Evidence
   D. Abandoned Property
   E. Contraband
   F. Stop and Frisk
   G. U.S. Border Searches
   H. Canine Officers
   I. Consent
   J. Exigent Circumstances

III. Search Warrant Limitations
   A. General Searches Not Allowed
   B. Stale Warrants
   C. Vagueness
   D. Overbreadth
   E. Challenging a Warrant
   F. The Exclusionary Rule

SEARCH WARRANTS

Search warrant
A court order authorizing law enforcement to enter, search, and remove evidence of a crime.

A **search warrant** is a warrant issued by a judge that authorizes the police to search a private residence or other area and seize particular kinds of property. To be more precise, a search warrant should be described as a search and seizure warrant, because it authorizes police to search a specific area and to seize evidence of a crime. When they have a warrant, police are authorized to enter the private residence of a person, conduct a search, and take away items described in the warrant. When the police arrive at a person's home with a valid search warrant, the homeowner cannot legally interfere with the police. Police officers are not required to wait until the homeowner contacts his or her attorney or calls the magistrate court to make sure that the warrant was issued there.

A. STANDARDS FOR ISSUING SEARCH AND SEIZURE WARRANTS

In the last chapter, we saw that police officers have wide latitude to arrest persons without a warrant. However, the opposite situation occurs when law enforcement conducts searches. Here, the courts will presume that a warrant was required unless and until the police and prosecutors can show that warrantless search was valid. The reason behind this is simple: Police can secure a location and obtain a warrant to search it, but they often do not have the same option when it comes to a human being.

Just as we saw with arrest warrants, before a magistrate can issue a search warrant, he or she must have reviewed all of the sworn testimony and made a determination that there is sufficient probable cause to believe that evidence of a crime will be found in a certain location. For instance, is a warrant to search even necessary? To answer that question, the judge must look at the issue of expectation of privacy. When the location to be searched enjoys a high degree of expectation of privacy, then police must obtain a warrant before conducting a search. However, if the expectation of privacy is very low, police might not be required to obtain a search warrant at all. What then is **expectation of privacy?**

Expectation of privacy
The Constitutional standard that a court must determine before issuing a search warrant. If an area has a high expectation of privacy, then a warrant will be required; if low or nonexistent, then no warrant is required.

The phrase "expectation of privacy" does not appear in the U.S. Constitution. In fact, the Fourth Amendment makes no reference to privacy at all. The interpretation of the Fourth Amendment was left to the courts. Those courts created the expectation of privacy test as a way to evaluate when or if a search warrant is required.

The expectation of privacy test was created in *Katz v. U.S.*[1] The test has both subjective and objective components. What the U.S. Supreme Court did in *Katz* was first to see if the suspect who was searched had a subjective expectation of privacy in the item or place to be searched. The second part of the test was to evaluate the search from an objective, hypothetical third party's perspective. Would this hypothetical third party believe that the area to be searched would have a high expectation of privacy? If the answer to both of these questions is yes, then the police must obtain a search warrant. An expectation of privacy is a person's belief in how secure and private an area should be. For the courts and for most individuals, the place with the highest expectation of privacy is the home. Examples of places with the least expectation of privacy are public areas where a person's actions can be seen by anyone.

If a suspect has a high degree of expectation of privacy, then the police have a higher burden to meet before search warrants will be issued. A person has an expectation of privacy in personal papers, his or her residence, and any other private areas. People do not have a high expectation of privacy in items that can be clearly seen in public. If we were to create a bar graph with the highest level of expectation of privacy on one end and the lowest expectation of privacy on the other end, most of us would agree that our homes should have the highest degree of expectation of privacy. An area with a no expectation of privacy would not require a search warrant. This explains why there are very few instances in which courts will allow warrantless searches of a person's home, but frequently find warrantless searches of items fully exposed to view and in public to be constitutionally permissible. Before police may enter your home, a magistrate must issue a search warrant authorizing them to do so. Police and magistrates face these issues every day in trying to determine what areas have a high degree of expectation of privacy and then establishing sufficient probable cause for a magistrate to issue a warrant to search that area.

When it comes to interpreting the language of a search warrant, courts follow rules that are similar to the way that arrest warrants are evaluated. Numerous court decisions have established that warrants should be read in a commonsense fashion. The U.S. Supreme Court does not impose highly technical rules on search warrants. Common misspellings, for instance, will not invalidate a search warrant. A warrant will not be ruled invalid because of a minor technicality. The U.S. Supreme Court has approved of this more lenient treatment of affidavits and search warrants, reasoning that a highly technical requirement would only work to discourage police officers from applying for search warrants in the first place.

B. THE GOOD FAITH EXCEPTION

Several cases have upheld technically faulty warrants when the police officers were obviously acting in good faith. When a police officer has no reason to suspect that a warrant is technically flawed, the courts will not rule that the warrant is invalid. However, the good faith exception is not a panacea for all insufficient warrants. Before they will apply the good faith exception, courts must also look to other features of the case.[2] A police officer must have an objective, reasonable ground to believe that the warrant was validly issued. Where a warrant is so obviously defective that no trained police officer could reasonably believe that the warrant was correct, the good faith exception does not apply.[3] Obviously, if the officer deliberately caused the error, then he or she cannot take advantage of the good faith exception. We discuss the good faith exception in much greater detail in Chapter 7.

C. EXCEPTIONS TO THE SEARCH WARRANT REQUIREMENT

Although courts have a preference for searches conducted with a warrant, there are instances where appellate courts have allowed searches without a warrant, but only in narrow circumstances. From plain view to contraband, these searches can be conducted without a warrant, as long as they fall into one of the prescribed categories.

SEARCHES WITHOUT A WARRANT

Despite the fact that courts have a stated preference for search warrants, there are times when obtaining one is not feasible. The refrain from the appellate courts remains a distinct, "When in doubt, get a warrant," but courts have also recognized specific times when a search without a warrant is the only way for police to proceed. Examples of situations where a search can be performed without a warrant include:

- Plain view
- Open fields
- Dropped evidence
- Abandoned property
- Contraband
- Stop and frisk
- U.S. border searches
- Canine officers
- Consent
- Exigent circumstances

A. Plain View

Plain view doctrine
A court principle that allows police to search without a warrant when they see evidence of a crime in an unconcealed manner.

Courts developed the **plain view doctrine** in response to a common problem. Suppose that an officer pulls over an automobile and while talking with the suspect, the officer sees an item that is evidence of a crime. Because the officer had a legal reason to be where he or she was at the time that the evidence was observed, the officer is not required to obtain a warrant. A similar problem occurs when police officers execute a search warrant looking for specific items, but come across other items that are clearly illegal. In both cases, the evidence may be seized without a warrant because the items were in "plain view" or available for anyone to see. "It has long been settled that objects falling in the plain view of an officer who has a right to be in the position to have that view are subject to seizure and may be introduced into evidence."[4] The plain view doctrine does not permit police officers to seize any evidence at any time. The officers must have a legitimate reason to be in position to see the object. Consider Scenarios 5-1 and 5-2.

TWO JOBS

Officer Tango is working his off-duty job as a security officer at an apartment building. The apartment complex is built into the side of a steep hill and as Officer Tango walks along a sidewalk, he is actually even with the second floor of the apartment complex. He hears a sound and glances toward an open window. Inside, he sees four people snorting a white, powdery substance off a small mirror and then laughing very loudly. He goes to the door of the apartment and knocks. When a woman answers the door, she is carrying a small mirror in her hand that is smeared with a white, powdery substance. He arrests her for possession of cocaine and then searches the apartment. He finds more cocaine and some marijuana and then charges the others present. Is the search valid under the plain view doctrine?

Answer: Yes. Because the officer had a legitimate reason to be where he was when he saw the criminal activity, the subsequent search is constitutional.

KICKING IN THE DOOR

Officer Cash knows that the resident of a certain apartment has been in trouble with the law before. Officer Cash believes that the resident may be in possession of cocaine. He climbs up the back stairs of the apartment and peeks in through the back window through a drape, which almost, but not completely covers the window. He sees the suspect snorting a white, powdery substance. Officer Cash kicks in the back door and arrests the suspect. He subsequently searches the apartment and finds more suspected cocaine and some marijuana. Is the search valid under the plain view doctrine?

Answer: No. Because the officer had no legitimate reason to be on the suspect's back stairs or to be looking into his apartment, the officer's subsequent search was a violation of the Constitution and the evidence cannot be used at trial.

B. OPEN FIELDS

In addition to plain view, there is also a doctrine called **open fields** according to which officers are not required to obtain a warrant before conducting a search. Unlike plain view, the open fields doctrine revolves around expectation of privacy. An open field, fully exposed to view by anyone, has virtually no expectation of privacy. "An individual may not legitimately demand privacy for activities conducted out of doors in fields, except in the area immediately surrounding the home."[5] See Scenario 5-3.

Open fields doctrine
A court principle that allows police to search without a warrant when the evidence is located in a public setting, such as farmland or beside a road.

SCENARIO 5-3	MARIJUANA GROWING

MARIJUANA GROWING

Steve has a home in the country, and directly behind his home he has a plowed field. He grows herbs in this field, but he also grows marijuana plants. Growing and selling marijuana is not legal in his state. The field is within ten feet of his back door and cannot be seen from the driveway of his home. It is, in fact, surrounded by a high privacy fence. A police officer visiting the neighborhood on an unrelated matter decides to walk on to Steve's property and peek over his privacy fence. Is this an example of an open fields exception to a search warrant requirement?

Answer: No. Because the marijuana was growing close to Steve's home and not a "field" in the traditional sense, the most likely result will be a ruling that the police must obtain a warrant before looking over Steve's fence.

C. DROPPED EVIDENCE

When police officers are chasing a fleeing suspect and he drops or throws away some evidence, police do not have to obtain a search warrant to seize it. The suspect has surrendered any property rights to the evidence. Many courts refer to these cases as "dropsy" cases, because many suspects will drop incriminating evidence when confronted by the police. The inherent problem with these cases is making the connection between the recovered evidence and the suspect. For instance, police chase a suspected drug dealer and see him fling out an arm. The police then retrieve a bag containing three rocks of crack cocaine. How can the police be sure that this bag belongs to this suspect? Generally, a police officer will testify about the circumstances of the arrest, the area in which the item was thrown, and the condition of the item when it was recovered. If it was a rainy night, for example, but the bag was still relatively dry when it was recovered, that would indicate that the bag was not lying on the ground for a long period of time.

D. ABANDONED PROPERTY

There is no requirement for law enforcement to obtain a warrant to search and seize abandoned property. Garbage is a perfect example. In *California v. Greenwood*,[6] the U.S. Supreme Court held that there is no privacy expectation in garbage. If an item—for example, drug paraphernalia—has been thrown into a communal trash receptacle, or even into a private trash receptacle subsequently taken to the curb for collection, then the person throwing it out has also tossed away any constitutional objections to having the item seized. The U.S. Supreme Court has ruled that there is no reasonable expectation of privacy for discarded garbage.[7] Of course, there are limits to the rule for the police obtaining abandoned property. They cannot, for instance, commit trespass to get to a suspect's trash. In that case, they would have to wait until the trash can has been placed on the curb for collection and is off the suspect's property.

E. CONTRABAND

The Fourth Amendment does not protect items that are illegal to possess. Contraband encompasses items such as illegal weapons or narcotics, which can be seized by law enforcement without a warrant whenever they are discovered. Under the Fourth Amendment, there is no reasonable expectation of privacy in items that are illegal to possess in the first place.

F. STOP AND FRISK

In Chapter 3, we discussed the law of stop and frisk. In that chapter, we saw that a police officer can briefly detain a person and pat that person down for weapons. If, during that pat down, an officer discovers evidence of a crime, that evidence can be retained and used against the suspect at trial. Stop and frisk does not require a warrant.

G. U.S. BORDER SEARCHES

U.S. Customs and Border Patrol officers and others who monitor the U.S. borders have much greater freedom to search without a warrant than do police officers. Because these officers are charged with preventing items from coming into the United States, they can search many more items. These searches can be carried out without a search warrant, but they do not give the officers involved complete freedom to search anyone and everything. As a general rule, these officers can perform a cursory search. Any additional or intrusive searches would likely require a search warrant.

H. CANINE OFFICERS

The U.S. Supreme Court has stated that the use of specially trained dogs to detect narcotics, explosives, or other items does not fall within the protections of the Fourth Amendment. There is, according to the court, no expectation of privacy in air, but there are cases pending before the court that will test that maxim. The court recently ruled that these specially trained dogs are not permissible around private residences without a warrant.[8] However, the court ruled that they can be used in open areas.[9]

I. CONSENT

Consent
When a person gives knowing and voluntary permission to a search carried out by law enforcement.

When a person knowingly and voluntarily gives law enforcement officers **consent** to search his or her belongings or residence, then there is no longer a need to obtain a search warrant. The consent cannot be coerced. If a suspect does give consent, he or she cannot revoke it once the police have recovered evidence of a crime. However, a person who has given consent can withdraw it before police have located such evidence.

In cases where police testify that a suspect gave them consent to search, the issue is often whether or not the consent was given knowingly and intelligently. Consent that is obtained by force or threats is not consent at all and any evidence obtained may be suppressed.

J. EXIGENT CIRCUMSTANCES

Exigent circumstance
An emergency situation requiring aid or immediate action.

An **exigent circumstance** is some kind of emergency that threatens the lives of people or the existence of evidence. Police are not required to obtain a search warrant if they can show that an emergency (exigent) circumstance existed. An exigent circumstance is one that poses some danger to property or people such that waiting to obtain a warrant might result in the loss of evidence or injury to a person. One example is a situation in which police officers hear two people having a violent fight inside their home. They do not have to wait for a warrant before entering and stopping one person from killing the other.

 SEARCH WARRANT LIMITATIONS

As Figure 5-1 shows, the Fourth Amendment calls for specific steps before a search can be conducted, including the provision for an oath or affidavit as well as the requirement that the warrant must state with particularity the person or place to be searched. One type of search is specifically prohibited in the Constitution: general searches.

FIGURE 5-1

Fourth Amendment, U.S. Constitution

The right of the people to be secure in their persons, houses, papers, and effects, against unreasonable searches and seizures, shall not be violated, and no Warrants shall issue, but upon probable cause, supported by Oath or affirmation, and particularly describing the place to be searched, and the persons or things to be seized.

A. GENERAL SEARCHES NOT ALLOWED

The Fourth Amendment does not permit a general search. This is the type of search where law enforcement goes through a person's home or other belongings looking for evidence of some crime. The framers of the U.S. Constitution had had some experience with general searches authorized under British law and they wanted to make sure that no such search would be carried out in the United States. This is why they insisted that all search warrants must have probable cause and describe with particularity the place to be searched. Consider Scenario 5-4.

SEARCHING FOR A KILLER

A suspect is wanted for detonating a bomb in a large urban area. Someone has reported seeing a person who meets the description in a neighborhood. Police arrive and cordon off the area, and then begin searching the front and backyards of everyone in the area. Then, police enter every home in the neighborhood without seeking permission or consent. They do not find the suspect, but they do find a methamphetamine lab in Darryl's house. When Darryl challenges the search on the grounds that it is unconstitutional and qualifies as a general search, how is the judge likely to rule?

Answer: The judge will probably rule that the search that resulted in locating the meth lab was unconstitutional and any evidence seized is not admissible. If this is the only evidence against Darryl, then the case against him will be dismissed.

B. STALE WARRANTS

A search warrant must be executed within a reasonable time period after it is issued. If not, it becomes stale. A **stale warrant** is no longer valid. A warrant becomes stale when the circumstances originally involved in issuing it have changed substantially. For instance, a magistrate judge issues a warrant authorizing the search of a home for narcotics. Because drugs tend to be moved or consumed very quickly, a one-month delay between the issuance and execution of a search warrant would be far too much time. There are many things that may have changed in the intervening time and the officers who waited such a long period of time would be required to apply for a new search warrant.

Stale warrant
When too much time has passed between the application and issuance of a warrant and the search that it authorizes.

Staleness is an issue that is very much dependent on the facts and the items to be searched. Two days between issuance and execution of a search warrant for drugs might be too long, but in one case, a court held that a seven-month wait between the issuance and execution of a search warrant for child pornography did not make the warrant stale.[10]

To avoid this problem, a warrant may have to be executed quickly. Narcotics, for example, are produced for the express purpose of being

Anticipatory warrant
A warrant issued for contraband or evidence that has not yet arrived at its final destination.

consumed.[11] Staleness may not be such an issue when the goods are more permanent in nature (e.g., illegal automatic weapons). In some cases, law enforcement may apply for an **anticipatory warrant**, a warrant authorizing a search and seizure of illegal items at some future time.

C. VAGUENESS

A warrant must state with "particularity" the places to be searched and the items to be seized. If a warrant fails to meet this standard, then the subsequent search may be ruled unconstitutional. A warrant authorizing the seizure of "all suspected items" would be vague to the point of absurdity. Such a warrant would give the police the power to seize anything and everything they wished, and would be considered too vague to be enforceable.

D. OVERBREADTH

Overbroad
When a search warrant allows police far too much discretion in what they may search; similar to the prohibition against general searches.

The requirement of particularity also means that a warrant cannot be **overbroad** in its description of items to be seized. This is another way of restraining police by requiring that they search for specific evidence of a crime. Police are not allowed to engage in a "'fishing expedition'" that would search for any evidence of a crime. This resembles general searches far too closely.

E. CHALLENGING A WARRANT

The question of a legal challenge to a search warrant involves the issue of standing. Broadly speaking, standing is the requirement that the person making the challenge must have some personal interest in the search. The personal interest has more to do with expectation of privacy than ownership rights. This explains why a renter may have standing to challenge a search where the landlord might not. A renter actually lives on the premises and has an obvious expectation of privacy, whereas the landlord who does not live on the premises may lack such an expectation. Only those who have an expectation of privacy in an area that was searched can challenge the constitutionality of the search.[12]

F. THE EXCLUSIONARY RULE

The consequences of an unconstitutional search are simple: The evidence obtained cannot be used at trial. This is the premise of the exclusionary rule, which we will address in much greater detail in Chapter 7.

U.S. v. YOUNG

—— F3D. —— (W.D.MO., 2020)

Case No. 18-00175-01-CR-W-DGK.

REPORT AND RECOMMENDATION

This matter is currently before the Court on the Motion of Defendant Paris Young to Suppress Evidence (Doc. #43). For the reasons set forth below, it is recommended that the portion of the motion seeking the suppression of a statement the defendant made at the scene, which statement was made in response to questioning initiated by a law enforcement officer, be granted. The remainder of the motion should be denied.

I. BACKGROUND

On June 18, 2018, a Criminal Complaint was filed against defendant Paris B. Young. On June 26, 2018, the Grand Jury returned a four-count Indictment against defendant Young. On July 17, 2019, the Grand Jury returned a four-count Superseding Indictment against defendant Young. The Superseding Indictment charges that on June 16, 2018, defendant Young possessed with intent to distribute "crack" cocaine (Count One), possessed a firearm in furtherance of a drug trafficking crime (Count Two), was a felon in possession of a firearm (Count Three), and possessed a firearm with an obliterated serial number (Count Four).

II. FINDINGS OF FACT

On the basis of the evidence presented at the evidentiary hearing, the undersigned submits the following proposed findings of fact:

1. On June 16, 2018, Officers Kelsey Wingate and Christopher Lear were on routine patrol. Officer Lear was driving the patrol car and Officer Wingate was the passenger in the car. At approximately 6:55 p.m., the officers observed a maroon BMW turning northbound from 41st onto Garfield, failing to use a turn signal.

2. Failure to use a turn signal when making a turn in the City of Kansas City, Missouri, is a traffic violation.

3. The officers made the decision to pull the vehicle over. The officers initiated their emergency lights and siren. The BMW pulled to the side of the road. There was one person in the vehicle, later identified as Paris Young. As Officer Lear approached the vehicle, he saw the driver leaning over the center console area making movements consistent with altering or placing an object there. Officer Lear testified that these movements indicated to him that there was something the driver did not want him to see. The driver had opened the car door and was wanting to get out of the vehicle. Officer Wingate testified that when people immediately try to get out of the car when they are pulled over, it usually indicates that they are trying to get themselves away from contraband inside the vehicle. Officer Lear testified that it indicates to him that there might be something in the car that the person does not want to be associated with. Officer Lear testified that the driver was not listening to his

commands to shut the door and to get back in the car, so Officer Lear told the driver that if he wanted to get out, they could go talk by the officers' car. Officer Lear directed the driver (defendant Young) to stand in front of the police vehicle so that they were out of traffic and could talk safely. The door to the BMW was left open.

4. While Officer Lear was explaining to defendant Young why he had been pulled over, Young was looking around kind of nervous and antsy, consistent with someone looking for a place to run. Defendant Young then pushed off Officer Lear and tried to run across the street. The officers testified that it is a crime to run away from a traffic stop. Defendant Young was placed under arrest for resisting a lawful traffic stop. The officers considered the BMW abandoned, given Young's attempt to run from the car, leaving the car door open.

5. The officers testified that in their experience, when people flee on foot from traffic stops, they are fleeing because there is contraband in the car, they have warrants, or they are driving while suspended or revoked.

6. When asked why he ran, defendant Young told the officers that he was "dirty." Officer Wingate testified that she took this to mean that Young had narcotics, a gun, or warrants. Officer Lear testified that he took this to mean that Young had either warrants or items of contraband on him, something that would get him in trouble with the law.

7. The officers testified that it is police policy to tow a vehicle if the driver is arrested and the vehicle is parked on a public street. (Tr. at 17, 50.) The Kansas City, Missouri Police Department tow policy provides in part:

E. Custodial Arrest of Driver of Vehicle

1. When a vehicle is stopped on private or public property and the operator (arrestee) is placed under custodial arrest, the members will allow the operator (arrestee) time to arrange for the vehicle's timely removal unless:

a. The arrestee's physical condition, active resistance, or disorderly conduct prevents such an arrangement; or
b. The person operating the vehicle eludes arrest for an alleged offense for which the member would have taken the operator into custody (RSMo 304.155)1 . . . .

Officer Wingate testified that both subsections (a) and (b) applied in that defendant Young actively resisted by trying to run away and that the officers would have placed Young under arrest for possession of the firearm and crack cocaine later found in the vehicle and on his active warrants which were subsequently discovered.

8. The officers testified that when a vehicle is towed, officers are required to do a content inventory of the vehicle. (Tr. at 17, 50.) The tow policy provides in part:

A. Custodial Arrest Content Inventory

If the vehicle is towed from the scene pursuant to a custodial arrest, a complete content inventory of the interior, engine compartment, and trunk will be completed to prevent any article of valuable property from being overlooked.

In conjunction with towing a vehicle, officers also must fill out a tow form, Form 36. A content inventory and a tow form were filled out in this case.

9. The officers testified that they also believed they had probable cause to search the vehicle given that defendant Young was seen fumbling around with the center

console as the officers approached the vehicle, that Young fled from the vehicle, and given Young's statement that he was "dirty."

10. The officers discovered 46 small baggies of crack cocaine in the center console of the BMW. A loaded Taurus, Model Judge .45-caliber revolver was recovered from under the driver's seat. Part of the serial number on the revolver was scratched off.

11. After the inventory search of the BMW was completed, the vehicle was towed to the city tow lot.

12. Subsequent to his arrest, defendant Young made an incriminatory statement during interrogation.

III. DISCUSSION

Defendant Young seeks to suppress all statements and evidence, and testimony related to such statements and evidence, obtained as a result of an unlawful arrest, search, and seizure of the defendant. Specifically, defendant Young argues that there was no lawful basis for the stop because he put on his turn signal when he made the turn. Defendant Young further argues that the sun reflected on the rear window of the car in front of the officers' vehicle, which made it impossible for the officers to see Young's blinker. Given the invalidity of the stop, defendant Young argues that all statements and evidence which came after the stop must be suppressed.

A. THE STOP

As the Eighth Circuit Court of Appeals has observed, "any traffic violation, however minor, gives an officer probable cause to stop a vehicle." *United States v. Arciniega*, 569 F.3d 394, 397 (8th Cir. 2009).

Prior to stopping defendant Young, the officers observed that Young failed to signal when making a right turn. Officer Wingate testified that her vision of the BMW's turn signal was blocked in part by another vehicle until the BMW had completed the turn, but that she could see through the glass of the vehicle between them to see that the BMW did not have a turn signal on.

B. THE ARREST

As Officer Lear approached the vehicle, he saw the driver leaning over the center console area making movements consistent with altering or placing an object there. Officer Lear testified that these movements indicated to him that there was something the driver did not want him to see. Officer Lear testified that the driver had opened the car door and was wanting to get out of the vehicle. Officer Lear testified that the driver was not listening to his commands to shut the door and to get back in the car, so Officer Lear told the driver that if he wanted to get out, they could go talk by the officers' car. Defendant Young did exit the vehicle, and while Officer Lear was explaining to Young why he had been pulled over, Young was looking around kind of nervous and antsy, consistent with someone looking for a place to run. Defendant Young then pushed off Officer Lear and tried to run across the street. Defendant Young was placed under arrest for resisting a lawful traffic stop.

The United States Supreme Court has held that "[i]f an officer has probable cause to believe that an individual has committed even a very minor criminal offense in his presence, he may, without violating the Fourth Amendment, arrest the offender."

Atwater v. City of Lago Vista, 532 U.S. 318, 354 (2001). The officers were justified in arresting defendant Young for resisting a lawful traffic stop.

C. THE WARRANTLESS SEARCH OF THE VEHICLE

The government first justifies the warrantless search of the BMW as a valid inventory search. "It is well-settled that a police officer, after lawfully taking custody of an automobile, may conduct a warrantless inventory search of the property to secure and protect vehicles and their contents within police custody." *United States v. Rehkop*, 96 F.3d 301, 305 (8th Cir. 1996). A warrantless inventory search of a vehicle is valid if it is conducted pursuant to standardized police procedures and not done in bad faith or for the sole purpose of investigation. As set forth above, defendant Young was arrested for resisting a lawful traffic stop. The vehicle Young had been driving was parked on Garfield, a public street. It is police policy to tow a vehicle if the driver is arrested and the vehicle is parked on a public street. The Kansas City, Missouri Police Department tow policy requires that an officer complete an inventory of a vehicle if the vehicle is going to be towed.

The Court finds that the officers' decision to tow the vehicle was made and the resulting inventory search was conducted pursuant to standardized police procedures and not in bad faith or for the sole purpose of investigation. Thus, the Court finds that an inventory search of the vehicle was appropriate.

IV. CONCLUSION

Based on the foregoing, it is RECOMMENDED that the motion should be denied.

CASE QUESTIONS

1 What was the original reason for stopping the defendant and then why did the police arrest him?
2 The police officers believed that they had probable cause to search for two separate reasons. What were they?
3 What impact does a valid vehicle stop give to the subsequent search of the car?
4 What is the position of the U.S. Supreme Court concerning probable cause for minor offenses?
5 What limitations are placed on a police officer in conducting a warrantless search of a vehicle?

CHAPTER SUMMARY

Although it is common to arrest individuals without a warrant, seizing evidence without a warrant is generally frowned upon. In situations where individuals have a high expectation of privacy, the police will almost always be required to obtain a search warrant before they can enter a home or other structure. However, there are exceptions to the search warrant requirement. Searches can be conducted without a warrant when the facts fit within specific categories, such as open fields, plain view, dropped evidence, abandoned property, contraband, stop and frisk, U.S. border searches, canine involvement, consent, and exigent circumstances.

When a search warrant is issued, police officers are protected by the good faith exception when the warrant has a technical problem but otherwise appears to be valid. Warrants may also be challenged when they are overbroad or after too much time has passed since they were issued, making them stale. There are also situations in which the wording of the warrant is so vague as to render it unenforceable.

KEY TERMS AND CONCEPTS

Search warrant   Consent   Overbroad
Expectation of privacy Exigent circumstance
Plain view doctrine   Stale warrant
Open fields doctrine   Anticipatory warrant

END OF CHAPTER EXERCISES

Review Questions

See Appendix A for answers

1   What is the expectation of privacy?
2   Why do courts have a preference for search warrants?
3   Explain the plain view exception to the search warrant requirement.
4   Compare and contrast abandoned property and dropped evidence rules regarding search warrant requirements.
5   What is contraband?
6   What are exigent circumstances?
7   What are general searches and why are they specifically prohibited by the U.S. Constitution?
8   Under what circumstances may a search warrant grow stale?
9   Provide an example of a vague warrant.
10 Why are canine police officers exempt from needing a search warrant?

Web Surfing

Locate statistics from state or federal sources about the most common type of search warrant. What crime gets the most search warrant applications?

Question for Analysis

Although the U.S. Constitution specifically prohibits general searches, can you make a good argument for why this prohibition should be removed?

Hypotheticals

1   Officer Theo obtains a search warrant for a house at 123 Maple Street, however, the focus of his surveillance and investigation has always been 123 Mable Street. He executes the warrant at 123 Mable Street and finds evidence of a crime. Will the good faith exception protect him or will the evidence be ruled inadmissible?

2   Detective Nancy needs DNA from a suspect in a series of rapes. She has spoken with the suspect, who has refused to provide any evidence and invoked his right to remain silent. He has also hired an attorney. One day, while Detective Nancy is observing the suspect, she sees him spit out some chewing gum. She immediately picks it up and submits it to the crime lab. The DNA is a match for the suspect in the rapes. Should this evidence be admissible? Does the prosecution have a specific exception they can argue to request that the judge admit the evidence? Explain.

PRACTICE QUESTIONS FOR TEST REVIEW

See Appendix A for answers

Essay Question

List and explain at least three exceptions to the general rule that all searches must be carried out with a warrant.

True-False

1   T   F   Police can search without a warrant when they see evidence of a crime in an unconcealed manner.

2   T   F   General searches are constitutional.

3   T   F   When too much time has passed since a search warrant was issued, it will be considered invalid.

Fill in the Blank

1   A court principle that allows police to search without a warrant when the evidence is located in a public setting, such as farmland or beside a road is called _____.

2   A ⎯⎯ is a court order authorizing law enforcement to enter, search, and remove evidence of a crime.

3   The constitutional standard that a court must determine before issuing a search warrant is called ⎯⎯. If it is high, then a warrant will be required; if it is low or nonexistent, then no warrant is required.

Multiple Choice

1   An emergency situation requiring aid or immediate action.

   A   Desperate situation.
   B   Full-scale issue.
   C   Exigent circumstance.
   D   Normal circumstance.

2   Warrants issued for contraband or evidence that has not yet arrived at its final destination.

   A   Destination warrants.
   B   Issuance warrants.
   C   Prohibitory warrants.
   D   Anticipatory warrants.

3   Items that are illegal to possess, including child pornography, narcotics, and certain types of automatic weapons.

   A   Hereditaments.
   B   Titles.
   C   Facets.
   D   Contraband.

ENDNOTES

1.   389 U.S. 347 (1967).
2.   *U.S. v. Leon*, 468 U.S. 897 (1984).
3.   *Lo-Ji Sales, Inc. v. New York*, 442 U.S. 319 (1979).
4.   *Harris v. U.S.*, 390 U.S. 234 (1968).
5.   *Oliver v. U.S.*, 466 U.S. 170 (1984),
6.   486 U.S. 35 (1988).
7.   *California v. Greenwood*, 486 U.S. 35 (1988).
8.   *Florida v. Jardines*, 569 U.S. 1 (2013).
9.   *U.S. v. Place*, 462 U.S. 696 (1983).
10.   *U.S. v. Seiver*, 692 F.3d 774, 775 (C.A.7 (Ill.),2012).
11.   *U.S. v. Beltempo*, 675 F. 2d 472 (2d Cir. 1982), cert. denied 457 U.S. 1135 (1982).
12.   *U.S. v. $40,955.00 in U.S. Currency*, 554 F.3d 752, 756 (C.A.9 (Cal.), 2009).

Constitutional Issues in the Use of Evidence

- Describe the impact of the First Amendment on obscenity cases
- Explain the relationship of the exclusionary rule to the Fourth Amendment
- Define the rule against self-incrimination provided in the Fifth Amendment
- Explain when a suspect has a right to an attorney under the Sixth Amendment
- List and describe the privacy issues involved with the use of DNA

I. Evidence Law

II. The First Amendment and Evidence
   A. Establishment and Free Exercise Clauses
   B. Freedom of Speech
      Freedom of Speech and Incitement to Riot
      Freedom of Speech vs. Freedom of Expression
      Prosecutions for Pornography
   C. The Right of the Press

III. Fourth Amendment Evidentiary Issues

IV. Fifth Amendment and Evidentiary Issues
   A. The Grand Jury
      Use of Hearsay Evidence at Grand Jury
   B. Self-Incrimination and Pleading the "Fifth"
   C. Self-Incrimination and Identification

V. Sixth Amendment and Evidentiary Issues
   A. The Right to Confront Witnesses

B. The Right to an Attorney
   Right to an Attorney at a Lineup
   Constitutional Limits on Lineups
   Right to Counsel at a Lineup
   Participants in a Lineup
   Photographic Lineups
   Constitutional Sanctions for Improper Lineups
C. The Right to a Public Trial
   Closing a Trial to the Public

VI. Other Evidentiary Issues with Constitutional Implications
   A. DNA
      Using DNA as Evidence
      Gathering DNA Samples into a Database
   B. Fingerprinting
   C. Polygraph Tests

FIGURE 6-1

Defining Relevant
Evidence Under the
Federal Rules

Rule 401. Definition of "Relevant Evidence"

"Relevant evidence" means evidence having any tendency to make the
existence of any fact that is of consequence to the determination of the
action more probable or less probable than it would be without the evidence.

EVIDENCE LAW

Evidence is what prosecutors use to prove that a defendant committed a crime.
During the course of a trial, both the state and defense may introduce a wide
variety of evidence to attempt to establish the basic elements of their cases.
When prosecutors use evidence, there are several hurdles that the government
must clear before it can be introduced at trial and considered by the jury. The
first of those considerations deals with relevance.

On the federal level, the Federal Rules of Evidence govern what, how and
when evidence can be admitted at trial. The Federal Rules can be found in the
U.S. Code, but many private companies also publish them as a separate volume.
The Federal Rules, abbreviated FRE, govern the evidence used in both civil and
criminal cases. The rules are very comprehensive and have served as a model for
many states (see Figure 6-1).

However, there are other concerns that rise above relevance. There are
many constitutional issues surrounding the use of specific types of evidence.
In this chapter, we will examine many types of evidence that have constitutional
implications. We will address constitutional issues in the order of the Bill of
Rights, beginning with the First Amendment and the wording of that amendment that can affect the course of a criminal case.

THE FIRST AMENDMENT AND EVIDENCE

The First Amendment to the U.S. Constitution provides for freedom of speech,
freedom of religion, and freedom of the press, among others. In this section we
will examine how the First Amendment arises in the context of evidence and
charges brought against an individual and how it can be used as a defense in
a criminal case (see Figure 6-2).

A. ESTABLISHMENT AND FREE EXERCISE CLAUSES

The specific wording in the First Amendment prohibits the government from
enacting laws that bar groups from worshiping in whatever way they choose.

> Congress shall make no law respecting an establishment of religion, or prohibiting the free exercise thereof; or abridging the freedom of speech, or of the press; or the right of the people peaceably to assemble, and to petition the government for a redress of grievances.

FIGURE 6-2

First Amendment, U.S. Constitution

The real issue that arises in criminal cases is not so much about dogmas or teachings, but actions. The U.S. Supreme Court has consistently held that behavior, not beliefs, can be regulated. For example, in *Employment Division v. Smith*,[1] the Court ruled that although peyote was an important part of some Native American worship practices, its use could be proscribed. The Court ruled that the use of the drug, not the underlying belief, could be regulated. When it comes to other practices, such as "snake handling," courts are divided, with some states allowing the practice in tightly contained spaces and others outlawing the practice.[2]

Perhaps the most important takeaway from the consideration of the First Amendment's guarantee of freedom of religion is that there are not many prosecutions brought under the rubric of either the establishment or the free exercise clause. The same cannot be said for freedom of speech.

B. FREEDOM OF SPEECH

Prosecuting people for speech or expression is a great deal more common than prosecuting them for their religious beliefs and practices. There are many things that a person can say or do that could be considered dangerous. Because of this, there is a constant tension between the First Amendment's guarantees and the needs of society to regulate behavior. Consider Scenario 6-1.

FREE SPEECH?

SCENARIO 6-1

Ulysses is attending a local community college and received a grade on his criminal procedure test that he doesn't like. Instead of complaining to the instructor, he decides to hold a rally in the parking lot. As he stands on the roof of his own car, he encourages other students to "fight the system." Has he committed a crime? Is he protected by the First Amendment?

Answer: It depends.

FREEDOM OF SPEECH AND INCITEMENT TO RIOT

The question in Scenario 6-1 essentially asks if Ulysses is engaged in incitement to riot. A person's freedom of speech is always balanced against the needs of society. The First Amendment does not always trump societal concerns. The reverse is also true. Instead, the courts review the actions and criminal charges in each case to determine if the individual exceeded the protections guaranteed in the First Amendment. If the First Amendment does not protect the defendant, then he or she can be charged and prosecuted. If the First Amendment does protect the defendant, then the charges against him or her must be dismissed.

In Scenario 6-1, the question then becomes, "Is Ulysses inciting others to commit a riot?" A riot is defined as a public disturbance involving a group of three or more people who engage in destruction of personal property or who injure people. The problem with prosecuting individuals for riot is not what to do with them once the riot has begun, but when police officers are permitted to make an arrest for inciting a riot. There is an inherent tension between protecting the public from property destruction and danger to human beings and the First Amendment's guarantee of freedom of expression and the right to lawfully assemble. To create a test that assists law enforcement and citizens with a guideline to determine when an action crosses the line from constitutionally protected speech into riot, the court used the case of *Brandenburg v. Ohio,* 89 S.Ct. 1827 (1969), to create the "imminent lawless action test." Under this test, police may arrest individuals for incitement to riot when they can show that:

1 The defendants are actively advocating behavior that is likely to produce imminent lawless action, and
2 The defendants' actions are likely to incite or produce imminent lawless action.

Under this test, for the prosecution to be successful in a charge of incitement to riot, it must show not only that the defendants advocated unlawful behavior, but also that their advocacy was closely tied to circumstances where violence was likely. Without both elements, an incitement to riot charge will fail.

ANSWER TO

SCENARIO 6-1

Now that we have considered the U.S. Supreme Court's definition of incitement to riot, does the speech given by Ulysses rise to the level of incitement? Almost certainly not. His statement to "fight the system" could hardly be said to meet the standard of advocating for imminent lawless action. He might be in violation of campus policies, but arresting him for incitement to riot is far-fetched.

FREEDOM OF SPEECH VS. FREEDOM OF EXPRESSION

Courts have long held that freedom of speech applies to freedom of expression. The First Amendment protections have expanded on the definition of speech to include other forms of expression such as political cartoons, parody,[3] and even flag burning,[4] whereas other forms of expression, such as nude dancing,[5] receive limited constitutional support.

However, the question gets murkier when the state charges someone with possession of pornography. Does it qualify as free expression or is it material that, like contraband, should be illegal whenever and wherever it is located?

PROSECUTIONS FOR PORNOGRAPHY

The First Amendment to the U.S. Constitution guarantees the right of freedom of speech for all citizens. The difficulty in analyzing crimes that have First Amendment implications is to know when a statute or police action has crossed the line between enforcement and a guaranteed constitutional right. One example of a crime carrying enormous First Amendment concerns is the area of obscenity law.

Pornography and Obscenity. Obscenity law has triggered a vast amount of court decisions. Drawing a line between what is obscene and what is not is sometimes difficult to do. One person's obscenity could easily be another person's art. The First Amendment gives citizens freedom of expression, but the question has always been how far that expression can be taken before it crosses the line into criminal behavior. Before considering prosecutions of obscenity law and potential First Amendment issues, we must first define our terms. **Pornography** is a general term, referring to material that is sexual in nature; **obscenity** refers to material that is lewd, patently offensive, and involves sexual acts.

One of the most challenging aspects of analyzing First Amendment protections and society's interest in protecting exploited persons is deciding what qualifies as pornography. If an item is deemed to be pornographic, then it can be seized and the person who possesses it can be charged with an offense. If the material is not deemed to be pornographic, then a person can freely possess it and cannot be charged. However, one person's pornography is another person's art. Demonstrating the difficulty with defining pornography is Justice Stewart's concurrence in *Jacobellis v. Ohio*,[7] where he stated,

> I have reached the conclusion, which I think is confirmed at least by negative implication in the Court's decisions since *Roth* and *Alberts,* that under the First and Fourteenth Amendments criminal laws in this area are constitutionally limited to hard-core pornography. I shall not today attempt further to define the kinds of material I understand to be embraced within that shorthand description; and perhaps I could never succeed in intelligibly doing so. But I know it when I see it, and the motion picture involved in this case is not that.[8]

Because defining pornography can be so difficult, the U.S. Supreme Court wrestled with several definitions before finally settling on one that they found workable. In *U.S. v. Miller,* the court created the *Miller* test, which was supposed to assist prosecutors and defense attorneys in being able to define what is obscenity and when a person can be prosecuted for possessing obscene materials.

Pornography
Material depicting sexual behavior to cause sexual excitement. When it is nonobscene, it is protected by the First Amendment, but child pornography is not.

Obscenity
Material that an average person would consider appeals to a prurient interest, displays patently offensive sexual acts, and lacks serious artistic, political, scientific, or political value.

The Miller Test. The U.S. Supreme Court has wrestled with the legal standard of obscenity for decades. In *Miller v. California,*[9] the court announced some guiding principles to help others know when something is obscene or not. The *Miller* test has three basic components:

1 Whether the average person, applying "contemporary community standards" would find that the work, taken as a whole, appeals to prurient interest.
2 Whether the work displays or describes, in a patently offense way, sexual contact specifically defined by a state statute.
3 Whether the work, again taken as a whole, lacks serious literary, artistic, political, or scientific value.

Possession of Obscene Material. One of the more unusual aspects of obscenity law is that simply possessing obscene materials in one's home (in most situations) is not a crime. Sending it by mail, selling it, or even giving it away may all be violations of state or federal obscenity laws, but simply possessing it is not a violation. One could easily argue that the only way to get obscene materials is to acquire them from some other source, but simple possession is constitutionally protected. This exemption does not apply to child pornography.

Child Pornography. The constitutional protections on obscenity disappear when the subject matter concerns **child pornography**. The U.S. Supreme Court has recognized that states have a compelling interest in the protection of children. States are given greater latitude when dealing with child pornography as opposed to pornography involving consenting adults. States can pass statutes limiting children's access to obscene material and can also completely ban material depicting children as sexual objects. Statutes may also criminalize the possession of child pornography, unlike adult pornography. The *Miller* test does not apply to child pornography. The government does not have to show that the material involving children appeals to the prurient interest. All that the state must show is that the material displays a lewd exhibition of the child's sexual organs and that the defendant knew that the material contained such exhibitions. All states have enacted statutes outlawing child pornography.

C. THE RIGHT OF THE PRESS

> Congress shall make no law abridging the freedom of speech, or of the press.
>
> *—First Amendment*

Because criminal trials are open to the public, they are also open to the press. But press coverage brings with it a whole host of other issues that are not seen when members of the general public are in attendance at a public trial. It is not

---

Child pornography
Any visual depiction of sexually explicit conduct involving a minor (persons less than 18 years old).

uncommon for intensive press coverage to make it difficult for a defendant to receive a fair trial. As a result, there is an inherent conflict between two constitutional values: the right of the defendant to receive a fair trial and the freedom of the press. Neither right is ascendant over the other. In each case, the judge must weigh the constitutional values and reach some type of accommodation and balance the freedom of the press with the defendant's right to a fair trial. A judge cannot, for example, bar any press coverage of the trial, but a judge can prevent news organizations from bringing in cameras to televise or photograph the trial.[10] The defendant's right to a fair trial does not always trump the freedom of the press, so a judge must take both concerns into account in conducting the trial.

FOURTH AMENDMENT EVIDENTIARY ISSUES

We discuss the importance of the Fourth Amendment in Chapters 3, 4, 5, and 7. The Fourth Amendment requires that all searches and seizures be conducted with probable cause. What happens when law enforcement violates the terms of this amendment? The answer is both simple and complex: the exclusionary rule.

The U.S. Supreme Court has created a rule that goes to the very heart of Fourth Amendment violations. If the police violate the Fourth Amendment in obtaining evidence, then they are barred from using it. This seemingly simple remedy has spawned years of litigation and appeals. Evidence discovered from unconstitutionally seized evidence is also ruled unconstitutional under the "fruit of the poisonous tree" doctrine.

Please see Chapter 7 for a complete discussion of the exclusionary rule, its implications, and the important exceptions that apply to seized evidence.

FIFTH AMENDMENT AND EVIDENTIARY ISSUES

A. THE GRAND JURY

The Fifth Amendment (see Figure 6-3) requires that a person who is accused of a felony be indicted by a grand jury. Most states also follow this model. A presentation before the grand jury is a lopsided affair. The grand jury only hears from the government, not the defendant. The defendant has no right to testify before the grand jury or present any favorable evidence. This limitation has led to the most severe criticism of the grand jury system. Because the state is not obligated to present the defendant's version of the facts, it is highly likely

> No person shall be held to answer for a capital, or otherwise infamous crime, unless on a presentment or indictment of a grand jury, except in cases arising in the land or naval forces, or in the militia, when in actual service in time of war or public danger; nor shall any person be subject for the same offense to be twice put in jeopardy of life or limb; nor shall be compelled in any criminal case to be a witness against himself, nor be deprived of life, liberty, or property, without due process of law; nor shall private property be taken for public use, without just compensation.

that, having heard only the state's version of the events, the grand jury will decide that there is sufficient probable cause to continue the case. The defendant's attorney is not permitted to attend or make any statements to the grand jury. In addition, the state is not required to present a balanced account of the case. The U.S. Supreme Court has even held that the prosecution is under no obligation to present evidence that is favorable to the defendant during a grand jury hearing.[11]

The presentation of evidence and testimony before the grand jury depends very much on state law. In some states, for example, the prosecutor will coordinate the hearing by calling witnesses, swearing them in, and asking them questions in the presence of the grand jurors. Once the prosecutor has completed the questioning process, he or she then turns the questioning over to the grand jurors themselves. If they have no questions, the state may call additional witnesses before retiring and requesting that the grand jury rule on the evidence as presented. However, there are states that do not allow prosecutors to go into the grand jury room. In that case, a police or district attorney investigator may present the case. Among the more interesting evidentiary issues that arise in a grand jury proceeding is the use of hearsay.

USE OF HEARSAY EVIDENCE AT GRAND JURY

In some states, the prosecutor attends the grand jury meeting, questions the witnesses, and presents evidence. In other states, the grand jury conducts its own investigation and questioning. In either situation, grand jury members always have the right to ask questions of any witness.

Unlike other court proceedings, the rules of evidence do not apply to grand jury proceedings. This means that the grand jury can consider illegally obtained evidence and listen to hearsay evidence. However, the grand jury does have some limitations. It is not permitted to take unlimited fishing expeditions through people's lives and randomly subpoena documents trying to find evidence of some crime. The grand jury must focus on a specific investigation or risk having the indictment quashed.

B. SELF-INCRIMINATION AND PLEADING THE "FIFTH"

> [No person] shall be compelled in any criminal case to be a witness against himself . . . .

> —*Fifth Amendment, U.S. Constitution*

The Fifth Amendment, which is the source of so many other rights for criminal defendants, also provides that persons cannot be compelled to give evidence against themselves. This protection follows defendants who are questioned before or after arrest, and includes every step of the process, including grand jury proceedings. If a defendant is asked a question at any point in the criminal process, he or she can refuse to answer by stating that the answer might incriminate him or her and that it therefore is protected by the Fifth Amendment. A defendant does not have to admit to any criminal actions or give any testimony that might be incriminating.

C. SELF-INCRIMINATION AND IDENTIFICATION

Closely linked to the invocation of the Fifth Amendment to refuse to answer a potentially incriminating question, a defendant also has the right to avoid other questions that would incriminate him or her in a crime. The Fifth Amendment to the U.S. Constitution prohibits criminal defendants from being coerced into giving testimony against themselves. In Chapter 8, we will see that a defendant cannot be coerced into providing incriminating statements. The defendant must also be advised of his or her *Miranda* rights before being questioned by law enforcement, but does the same rule apply to evidence not based on testimony? Is it a violation of the Fifth Amendment to have the defendant stand up in trial and show the jury the facial scar that the victim described as belonging to his or her attacker? According to the U.S. Supreme Court, the answer is no. Physical traits, especially those that can be seen by ordinary observation, do not fall under the protection of the Fifth Amendment.[12] Making a defendant demonstrate a physical trait, such as a scar or tattoo, is not the same thing as compelling the defendant to admit to a crime.[13] However, there are some states that do not permit this kind of action because of the potential conflict it will cause with the defendant's constitutional rights.

V SIXTH AMENDMENT AND EVIDENTIARY ISSUES

The Sixth Amendment does, among other things, guarantee the right of criminal defendants to a speedy trial, jury trials for specific offenses, the right to be informed of the charges against him or her, and attorney representation, among

FIGURE 6-4

Sixth Amendment, U.S. Constitution

In all criminal prosecutions, the accused shall enjoy the right to a speedy and public trial, by an impartial jury of the State and district wherein the crime shall have been committed, which district shall have been previously ascertained by law, and to be informed of the nature and cause of the accusation; to be confronted with the witnesses against him; to have compulsory process for obtaining witnesses in his favor, and to have the Assistance of Counsel for his defence [sic].

others. One of the most important rights provided by the Sixth Amendment is the right to confront witnesses (see Figure 6-4).

A. THE RIGHT TO CONFRONT WITNESSES

The right of a criminal defendant to confront witnesses and also to cross-examine them is considered to be one of the fundamental rights guaranteed by the U.S. Constitution. Without the ability to confront witnesses and ask them questions, there can be no due process.[14] The provisions of the Sixth Amendment, especially the right to confront witnesses in a criminal trial, have been made applicable to the states through the passage of the Fourteenth Amendment.[15] It is common for courts to say that the right of the defendant to face-to-face confrontation of a witness is one of the most important rights guaranteed under the U.S. Constitution, but this right is not absolute. Like many other rights, it must be balanced against other interests. There are several situations in which a defendant does not have the right of face-to-face confrontation, but instead can watch the victim's testimony through closed-circuit television or watch as a child victim is seated at a small table in front of the jury box, where he or she testifies directly to the jury and not directly to the defendant.

The confrontation clause of the Sixth Amendment actually provides two rights: (1) the right of the defendant to confront witnesses against him or her and (2) the right to cross-examine these witnesses to show bias or prejudice.[16] Included in this concept is the idea that a defendant can use cross-examination to develop evidence of a witness's biases or even a motive that the witness might have to lie about the events.[17] Defendants have the right to cross-examine the state's witnesses to show that the witness is biased or prejudiced or that the witness simply does not have personal knowledge of the facts to which he or she is testifying.[18]

B. THE RIGHT TO AN ATTORNEY

For decades, the Sixth Amendment's guarantee of the right to assistance of counsel was narrowly interpreted to mean that a defendant could hire any attorney he or she could afford. If defendants could not afford one, then they would have to represent themselves. The first change to this area of law came in a recognition that in cases where the defendant faced the death penalty, not allowing him or her an attorney was tantamount to an automatic guilty verdict. That was not the only change in the interpretation of the Sixth Amendment, though. In a series of decisions, the U.S. Supreme Court, especially the Warren Court in the 1960s, addressed the issue of when a person should be allowed to have an attorney and, more important, when the state must provide counsel when the defendant could not afford to hire an attorney. The most famous—and in many ways, the most popular—U.S. Supreme Court case in this field is *Gideon v. Wainwright*.

We examine the *Gideon* case in detail in Chapter 10. Here, we will simply state that the Sixth Amendment now provides that all defendants charged with felonies on the state and federal level must be allowed to have an attorney to represent them. If the defendant cannot afford to hire his or her own attorney, then the government must provide one. The same rule does not apply to those charged with misdemeanors.

RIGHT TO AN ATTORNEY AT A LINEUP

Because identification of the defendant is such an important part of the case, courts have given close scrutiny to the various methods used by law enforcement to identify the defendant. There are very stringent rules about how such identifications are carried out. This is especially true in the area of lineups and show-ups.

A **lineup** is often depicted in television and movies. Several people, all roughly similar in appearance, are lined up in front of a two-way mirror. The victim of the crime is then asked to identify the perpetrator. Because the consequences of this lineup are so serious—the person identified will be charged with a crime—the U.S. Supreme Court has placed numerous limitations on how lineups are conducted. For example, police are not permitted to "suggest" which member of the lineup the victim should identify. In addition, the lineup cannot be unduly suggestive. This means that law enforcement cannot place a suspect with dark hair in a lineup with five or six other individuals with blond hair, making one person stand out from the others. The height and general body appearance of all members of the lineup should be approximately equal. A lineup that suggests the identity of the perpetrator is a violation of a defendant's due process guarantees under the Constitution.[19] The penalty for a suggestive lineup is that the identification of the suspect will be inadmissible at trial.

Lineup
A group of persons, placed side by side in a line, shown to a witness of a crime to see if the witness will identify the person suspected of a committing the crime. It should not be staged so that it is suggestive of one person.

The Importance of an Eyewitness Identification. Witnesses are often asked to identify the perpetrator from some form of lineup. These days, the most common form of lineup is a photographic lineup (discussed below). At the trial, the witness will again be asked to identify the perpetrator and to point him or her out to the jury. This has a profound psychological effect on the jury.

Just How Accurate Is Eyewitness Testimony? One area fraught with difficulty for the prosecution and one that should be closely scrutinized by the defense is the identification of the defendant by the victim or witnesses. Eyewitness testimony is notoriously unreliable, yet there is hardly a more dramatic moment in the trial than when the witness points to the defendant and says, "That's the man." Unfortunately, there are numerous studies showing that eyewitness testimony is generally unreliable.[20]

CONSTITUTIONAL LIMITS ON LINEUPS

One of the most important Supreme Court cases in the area of lineups is *U.S. v. Wade.*[21] Wade was placed in a lineup without his attorney's knowledge and identified as the suspect. Prior to the lineup, however, the witness saw Wade standing in the courtroom. The witness knew that Wade was the person charged with the offense before he identified him in the lineup. The Supreme Court held that the subsequent identification was unduly suggestive and testimony about the identification should not have been allowed.

RIGHT TO COUNSEL AT LINEUP

The defendant's attorney should be present for any postindictment lineups. The attorney has the right to observe how the witness responds and to hear anything that the witness says during the identification process. However, the attorney does not have a right to be present when the lineup occurs prior to a formal charge.

PARTICIPANTS IN A LINEUP

The people chosen to stand with the suspect at the lineup are selected on the basis of similarity to the suspect: same approximate age, same race, build, hair and skin coloring, and so on. The members of the lineup are allowed to pick where they will stand. Each position has a corresponding number so that no names will be used. Police are not permitted to draw the witness's attention to the suspect in any way, such as dressing him in different clothing or selecting people to serve in the lineup who do not resemble the defendant. The entire procedure in the pretrial lineup should be reliable. Without some indicia of reliability, the identification is useless.[22] Members of a lineup may also be asked to say certain words or phrases to aid the witness in voice recognition.

Single-Suspect Lineups. The U.S. Supreme Court has stated that one-person lineups are obviously impermissibly suggestive and should not be used.[23] The simple reasoning behind this is that when a witness is presented with only a single person to identify, he or she routinely identifies that person as the perpetrator. Such a procedure is rife with potential abuse and therefore unconstitutional.

Show-up
A pretrial identification procedure in which only one suspect and a witness are brought together.

One-Person Show-ups. If physical lineups are a potential legal minefield, one-person **show-ups** are even worse. Generally, a one-person show-up occurs when the police arrest a suspect and present him or her to the witness with the question, "Is this the person?" The primary justification for the police using show-ups is the belief that the brief time lapse between the witness's observation of the suspect committing the crime and coming face-to-face with him or her can enhance accuracy of identification. Still, these situations could certainly fall into the category of unduly suggestive, and the identifications are often ruled inadmissible.

PHOTOGRAPHIC LINEUPS

In many situations it is not practical to arrange a live lineup. In those situations, a police officer will go through the mug-shot books and arrange a photographic lineup to show to the eyewitness. Whether a lineup is done using persons or photographs, the same rules apply. The individuals in the photographs should all look approximately like the suspect. When a photographic lineup is presented to a witness, the photos are often taped to a file folder and numbered. Like a live lineup, no names are provided. The witness must pick out the suspect from the photographs. The defendant's attorney does not have the right to be present during a photographic lineup.[24]

In either physical lineups or photographic lineups, there can be nothing especially suggestive about the defendant. An unduly suggestive lineup (one that sets the suspect off in some way from the others) could invalidate the entire identification process.

CONSTITUTIONAL SANCTIONS FOR IMPROPER LINEUPS

When the defendant's right to have his or her attorney present at a physical lineup has been violated or the lineup has been unduly suggestive, the punishment imposed on the state is that the testimony about the identification is ruled inadmissible.[25] This is very similar to the exclusionary rule, discussed earlier and also in much greater detail in Chapter 7.

C. THE RIGHT TO A PUBLIC TRIAL

The Sixth Amendment also provides that a trial must be conducted in public. The Supreme Court has stated that the right to a public trial is one of the most important guaranteed to a criminal defendant. "Without the freedom to attend such trials, which people have exercised for centuries, important aspects of freedom of speech and of the press could be eviscerated."[26] Conducting trials in secret has been one of the many tools of despots and authoritarian regimes throughout history. By allowing anyone from the public to attend a trial, the court system can be said to be truly transparent. Having an open and public criminal trial is a simple and efficient way to ensure that justice is served.

CLOSING A TRIAL TO THE PUBLIC

Despite the wording of the Sixth Amendment, there are times when a judge is authorized to close a portion of a trial. No judge is authorized to close the entire proceedings to the public, but if one of the parties requests that part of a trial be closed to the public, the judge is allowed to make that ruling. Even in the situations where a judge has legislative authority to close a portion of a trial to the public, the judge may only do so for a brief period of time. The judge must show a "compelling interest" to close a portion of the trial from the public. The two most common instances involve testimony by rape victims or testimony by children about sexual acts committed on them. There is no standing rule that requires a case to be closed at a certain point in any trial. In fact, the government must show a compelling reason to close the trial before the judge will authorize it. The preference under U.S. law is for all trials to remain open.

OTHER EVIDENTIARY ISSUES WITH CONSTITUTIONAL IMPLICATIONS

Although we have spent some time examining the issues surrounding the various amendments found in the Bill of Rights, there are also other evidentiary issues that carry constitutional issues. Some of them do not fit easily within a particular amendment, but still carry constitutional implications for suspects and defendants. One type of evidence that has become a staple of murder and rape prosecutions in recent decades is **DNA evidence.** There is no amendment or other constitutional provision that expressly provides for the "right to privacy," but the use of tools like DNA does carry clear issues about how evidence that is used to identify suspects can be abused in other areas of people's lives.

DNA evidence
Comparing body tissue samples (e.g., blood, skin, hair, or semen) to see if the genetic materials match. It is used to identify criminals by comparing their molecular composition with that found at a crime scene; it is also used to identify a child's parents.

A. DNA

In 1953, in work that would later earn them the Nobel Prize, James Watson and Francis Crick discovered the chemical and structural arrangement of DNA. They had spent several years trying to discover how the basic building block of almost all life worked. Although a different researcher finally discovered that the shape was a double helix, Watson and Crick discovered the most important features of DNA. Years after their discovery, scientists realized that DNA could be used to identify suspects in criminal cases. Like fingerprints before them, the use of DNA was initially ridiculed but eventually adopted as an effective way to single out or, in some cases, exclude suspects from a criminal inquiry.

DNA is composed of two strands of molecules arranged in the now famous double helix configuration. The double helix is like a spiral staircase, in which the handrails are composed of sugars and phosphates and the steps are composed of matching pairs of four (and only four) chemical compounds. These bases are adenine, cytosine, guanine, and thymine. Normally abbreviated A,

T, G and C, these bases only combine in the following sequences: A – T and C – G. They are referred to as base pairs. The human genetic code, which contains all of the information required to develop a human being from a single cell, consists of 3 billion base pairs. It is the arrangement or sequence of the base pairs that is so important. Base pair arrangements determine the ultimate shape of the animal: cat, dog, or human being.

USING DNA AS EVIDENCE

The use of DNA as a forensic tool began in the mid-1980s. Researchers realized that because each person's DNA is different (with the exception of identical twins), there should be a way to harness this feature for identification purposes. Like fingerprints, DNA was seen as a method to link a suspect with a crime scene in a way that could either eliminate or implicate him or her as a suspect with a relatively simple test.

Whether the DNA comes from a person's skin, hair, or body fluid, it will contain identical DNA. This means that DNA forms the basis of the ultimate fingerprint: Every cell, no matter where it originates in a person's body, has exactly the same DNA. This principle underlies the use of DNA as a means of identifying a person. When law enforcement has an identified specimen of a person's DNA, it can be compared with an unknown sample recovered from a crime scene and compared. If they match, it can be said quite conclusively that the suspect was at the scene.

DNA cannot show motive or bent of mind or planning. It can show, however, that the suspect was present or that he or she left incriminating evidence behind. In rape cases, sperm can be checked against the suspect's DNA type and can tell whether or not the sperm is his.

Technicians can now obtain useful DNA from a wide variety of sources, including hair, saliva, blood, semen, tissue, and even badly decomposed bodies. Researchers have obtained DNA from corpses buried for decades, or even centuries. DNA can be obtained from the bloodstained clothing of a victim or from any source where a person has left behind some cells from his or her body.

GATHERING DNA SAMPLES INTO A DATABASE

Many states and federal agencies have begun storing the results of DNA tests in computer databases. Similar to the creation of the FBI fingerprint database, the DNA database permits law enforcement to compare an unknown DNA sample with any of the known samples stored in the nationwide database.

> Sidebar
>
> *The FBI maintains records of DNA in its Combined DNA Index System (CODIS).*

B. FINGERPRINTING

Everyone is familiar with fingerprints. As early as 1605, scientists had noted that the patterns of grooves and whorls on a person's fingertips were as individual as faces. It wasn't until the early 1900s, however, that law enforcement began using this fact as a means to identify perpetrators.

Fingerprints can be left behind on a wide variety of surfaces, including human skin. Specially trained technicians search for fingerprints in likely places: doorknobs, tabletops, or anywhere else a person was likely to put his or her hand.

The FBI maintains a nationwide database of fingerprints, which can now be computer matched in a short period of time.

C. POLYGRAPH TESTS

Polygraph machines, or lie detectors, have been around in one form or another for decades. The basic principle behind any lie detector is that when a person tells a lie, it causes him or her physical stress. A polygraph machine allows a person to monitor the test subject's blood pressure, heart rate, respiration, and skin conductivity as a person is asked a series of questions. Some of the questions are control questions, providing a baseline, and some are incriminating questions, designed to see what response the subject's body gives to deceit. The polygraph machine measures various physiological indicators, allowing the machine operator to tell when someone is telling a truth and when the person is lying. However, because of their notorious unreliability, few courts have ever allowed them to be used as evidence. Occasionally, defense attorneys will attempt to use them to show that the defendant has been telling the truth, but in almost all cases, polygraph results remain inadmissible in criminal trials.

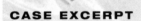

CASE EXCERPT

STATE v. HOMAN
191 WASH.APP. 759, 364 P.3D 839 (WASH. APP. 2015)

MAXA, J.

Russell Homan appeals his conviction for luring under RCW 9A.40.090. He argues that RCW 9A.40.090 is unconstitutionally overbroad both facially and as applied to the facts of his case. We hold that the luring statute as written is facially overbroad. However, pursuant to our obligation to adopt a limiting construction that will render the statute constitutional, we imply a criminal intent element for the crime of luring under RCW 9A.40.090. Because the trial court was not aware that it was required to find criminal intent in order to convict Homan, we reverse Homan's conviction and remand for a new trial.

FACTS

In August 2010, Homan rode past nine-year-old CCN on his bicycle and said "Do you want some candy? I've got some at my house." CCN said nothing in response, but reported the incident to his mother and the police. Homan was charged and convicted of luring under RCW 9A.40.090 in a bench trial.

Homan appealed his conviction, arguing that there was insufficient evidence to support his conviction and that RCW 9A.40.090 was unconstitutionally overbroad. This court held that there was insufficient evidence to support Homan's luring conviction, and therefore did not reach Homan's overbreadth argument. The State appealed to the Supreme Court. The Supreme Court held that there was sufficient evidence to support Homan's luring conviction, and remanded the case to this court to determine whether RCW 9A.40.090 is unconstitutionally overbroad.

ANALYSIS

A. STATUTORY LANGUAGE

RCW 9A.40.090 provides in part, that a person commits the crime of luring if the person:

(1)(a) Orders, lures, or attempts to lure a minor or a person with a developmental disability into any area or structure that is obscured from or inaccessible to the public, or away from any area or structure constituting a bus terminal, airport terminal, or other transportation terminal, or into a motor vehicle;

(b) Does not have the consent of the minor's parent or guardian or of the guardian of the person with a developmental disability; and

(c) Is unknown to the child or developmentally disabled person.

(2) It is a defense to luring, which the defendant must prove by a preponderance of the evidence, that the defendant's actions were reasonable under the circumstances and the defendant did not have any intent to harm the health, safety, or welfare of the minor or the person with the developmental disability.

For purposes of this statute, "minor" refers to a person under the age of 16 and a "person with a developmental disability" means a person with a developmental disability as defined in RCW 71A.10.020(5). RCW 9A.40.090(3)(a)–(b).

The legislature has not defined the terms "lure" and "luring." *State v. McReynolds*, 142 Wash.App. 941, 947, 176 P.3d 616 (2008). However, case law defines "lure" as an invitation accompanied by an enticement.

RCW 9A.40.090 does not require a defendant to engage in any conduct to commit the crime of luring. Luring may be committed with words alone. In addition, RCW 9A.40.090 as written contains no criminal intent requirement.

B. FACIAL OVERBREADTH CHALLENGE

Homan argues that RCW 9A.40.090 is facially overbroad under the First Amendment because it criminalizes a substantial amount of constitutionally protected speech. The State argues that although RCW 9A.40.090 does apply to some constitutionally protected speech, it does not prohibit a substantial amount of such speech. The State also argues that the affirmative defense in RCW 9A.40.090(2) cures any overbreadth problems. We hold that the statute as written is facially overbroad and that the affirmative defense in RCW 9A.40.090(2) does not cure the statute's overbreadth.

1. Burden of Proof

A facial challenge to a law on First Amendment grounds does not require us to address the specific facts of the case—whether the defendant's actual speech was constitutionally protected. The question is whether the law improperly infringes on protected speech in general.

We presume that statutes are constitutional, and the party challenging the statute generally bears the burden of proving its unconstitutionality. However, the Supreme Court in *Immelt* stated that the burden shifts when a statute is challenged in the free speech context, and the State usually bears the burden of justifying a statute that restricts free speech.

Because Homan is challenging RCW 9A.40.090 as an infringement on free speech, the State bears the burden of justifying the statute's restriction on protected speech.

2. Legal Principles

The First Amendment to the United States Constitution, which applies to the states through the Fourteenth Amendment's due process clause, provides in relevant part that "Congress shall make no law . . . abridging the freedom of speech." U.S. CONST. amend. I; amend. XIV, §1.

A law is unconstitutionally overbroad under the First Amendment if two requirements are satisfied. First, the law must actually implicate constitutionally protected speech. A defendant may invoke the First Amendment only if a law places some burden on free speech.

The First Amendment does not extend to "unprotected speech." See *State v. Allen,* 176 Wash.2d 611, 626, 294 P.3d 679 (2013) ("true threats" are unprotected speech).

3. Overbreadth Analysis

We engage in a four-part analysis to determine whether a law is facially overbroad under the First Amendment. First, we must determine whether the challenged law actually prohibits speech. See *Immelt*, 173 Wash.2d at 7, 267 P.3d 305 (holding that horn honking may rise to the level of speech). Here, RCW 9A.40.090 clearly prohibits certain types of speech. The Supreme Court recognized in this case that the crime of luring may be committed with words alone.

Second, we must determine the legitimate sweep of the challenged law—whether the law legitimately prohibits certain speech. The First Amendment does not protect certain types of speech, including "libelous speech, fighting words, incitement to riot, obscenity, and child pornography," and true threats. *State v. Kilburn,* 151 Wash.2d 36, 43, 84 P.3d 1215 (2004). A law that prohibits such unprotected speech does not violate the First Amendment.

Another type of unprotected speech is speech made with the intent to facilitate criminal conduct. The United States Supreme Court has listed "speech integral to criminal conduct" as one of the traditional categories of unprotected speech. *United States v. Stevens*, 559 U.S. 460, 468, 130 S.Ct. 1577, 176 L.Ed.2d 435 (2010).

Courts in other jurisdictions specifically have concluded that the First Amendment does not protect speech in the furtherance of criminal conduct involving a child, particularly in the context of luring children either in person or over the Internet.

Finding that speech made with the intent to facilitate criminal conduct is unprotected is consistent with RCW 9A.40.090's clear purpose of preventing a minor under age 16 or a developmentally disabled person from being alone with a stranger in a secluded place, where that vulnerable person could be abducted or harmed. Undoubtedly, protecting particularly vulnerable members of the public from strangers who intend to harm them is an important and legitimate government interest. In furtherance of this interest, RCW 9A.40.090(1) can legitimately prohibit speech designed to lure minors under age 16 and developmentally disabled persons when that speech is made with the intent to facilitate criminal conduct. The First Amendment does not protect such speech.

Third, we must determine whether the challenged law also prohibits constitutionally protected speech. Although speech made with the intent to facilitate criminal conduct is unprotected, "innocent" speech that falls within the definition of luring is protected. It is clear that RCW 9A.40.090(1) prohibits some protected speech.

Homan and the ACLU provide several examples of constitutionally protected speech that would violate RCW 9A.40.090(1). Homan identifies these scenarios: (1) political speech, where a student invites minors or developmentally disabled people to his or her house to discuss school district policies with an enticement of cupcakes; (2) a statement made in an attempt at humor by a student comedian at a talent show; (3) a genuine offer of help, where a good Samaritan offers to drive an injured child to the hospital for aid; (4) statements misunderstood as orders, where a school bus driver would be in violation for telling a child to "Hop in!" absent parental consent; and (5) an invitation from one child to another to play inside his or her home.

In addition, Homan notes that RCW 9A.40.090(1) prohibits mere jests and idle talk. And the ACLU points out that a person could violate RCW 9A.40.090(1) by using hyperbole, such as telling someone to "take a long hike off a short pier" or to "go to the moon." The First Amendment prohibits criminalization of communications that are "merely jokes, idle talk, or hyperbole." *State v. Schaler*, 169 Wash.2d 274, 283, 236 P.3d 858 (2010).

Fourth, we must determine whether the challenged law prohibits a substantial amount of such speech. This involves weighing the amount of unprotected speech that the law legitimately prohibits against the amount of prohibited protected speech.

The United States Supreme Court has stated there are "serious constitutional difficulties with seeking to impose on the defendant the burden of proving his speech is not unlawful." *Ashcroft v. Free Speech Coal.*, 535 U.S. 234, 255, 122 S.Ct. 1389, 152 L.Ed.2d 403 (2002).

Here, individuals who meet the elements of RCW 9A.40.090(1) can be charged with the crime of luring even if their motivations are entirely innocent. These individuals must either rely on the mercy of an understanding prosecutor, or repress speech that meets the elements of RCW 9A.40.090(1) to avoid being pulled into the criminal justice system. RCW 9A.40.090 is unconstitutional.

---

1 Does the legislation in this case ever define what "luring" is?
2 Is it necessary for a defendant to take some action to commit the crime of luring?
3 What presumptions are raised when a defendant challenges a statute based on the First Amendment?

CASE QUESTIONS

4   The court states that the First Amendment does not protect certain types of speech. What are they?

5   Ultimately, what was the deciding factor the court used to overturn the statute and rule it unconstitutional?

CHAPTER SUMMARY

Evidence plays a pivotal role in criminal cases. It also carries with it many constitutional issues. In cases where a person is charged with incitement to riot, for example, the defendant may interpose the defense that the speech is protected by the First Amendment. Similarly, a person charged with the possession of obscene materials may claim that the *Miller* test, developed by the U.S. Supreme Court as a way of evaluating First Amendment claims in pornography cases, also requires dismissal of all the charges.

The Fourth Amendment requires probable cause before any person or item of evidence is seized. If the police violate the terms of the Fourth Amendment, they may be subject to the exclusionary rule. This rule provides that any evidence seized in violation of the Constitution cannot be used at trial.

The Fifth Amendment provides a whole host of protections for individuals charged with crimes. Persons charged with a felony must be indicted by a grand jury. Defendants cannot be forced into giving statements that incriminate them. Similarly, the Sixth Amendment requires the state to provide an attorney to a person charged with a felony. The attorney must also be present at any lineups conducted to attempt to identify the defendant as the person who committed the crime.

Other evidentiary tools, like DNA, raise a host of privacy concerns. Although DNA and fingerprinting have become ubiquitous, law enforcement was originally slow to adopt these technologies.

KEY TERMS AND CONCEPTS

Pornography   Lineup
Obscenity   Show-up
Child pornography   DNA evidence

END OF CHAPTER EXERCISES

Review Questions

See Appendix A for answers

1   What is the reason that polygraph tests are not admissible as evidence in a criminal trial?

2 What is DNA?

3 Can a grand jury consider hearsay testimony? Explain your answer.

4 What is the *Miller* test and how does it apply to obscenity prosecutions?

5 What is incitement to riot and what important U.S. Supreme Court case put limitations on the prosecution of this offense?

6 What is the exclusionary rule?

7 Which amendment to the U.S. Constitution guarantees the right to an attorney at trial?

8 What is a lineup?

9 What is a show-up?

10 Explain the right to confront witnesses.

11 Is eyewitness testimony reliable? Explain your answer.

12 Is child pornography different than pornography? How?

13 Is a judge permitted to close an entire trial to the public? Explain.

14 What are photographic lineups?

15 Compare and contrast DNA and fingerprints.

Web Surfing

1 Search for information about how DNA evidence is obtained and how it is encoded into the FBI database.

2 Do all states use the grand jury system? Search online to see if you can locate any that do not.

Questions for Analysis

Are there privacy concerns with the use of DNA? Although it has proven to be an effective tool for law enforcement, is there a danger that people whose DNA reveals pre-existing vulnerabilities to certain diseases might end up being discriminated against?

Hypotheticals

1 Can you change the facts in Scenario 6-1 to make it clear that Ulysses has crossed the line into incitement to riot?

2 Ricky has a Facebook page where he proudly displays the names of women he has slept with. Nancy has gone to the police to report that Ricky sexually battered her. Should the police be allowed to look at Ricky's Facebook page to see if Nancy's name is there?

PRACTICE QUESTIONS FOR TEST REVIEW

See Appendix A for Answers

Essay Question

Explain the *Miller* test.

True-False

1 **T F** Child pornography is not, by itself, illegal to possess.

2 **T F** A suspect does not have the right to an attorney at a lineup.

3 **T F** The First Amendment protects not only speech but expression.

Fill in the Blank

1 Material that an average person would consider appeals to a prurient interest, displays patently offensive sexual acts, and lacks serious artistic, political, scientific or political value is called ____.

2 ____ is a pretrial identification procedure in which only one suspect and a
witness are brought together.

3 The ____ Amendment to the U.S. Constitution requires a fair and impartial
jury.

Multiple Choice

1 The U.S. Supreme Court test created to help identify and distinguish
pornography cases from obscenity cases.

   A The Steven Inquiry.
   B The Breadbox Question.
   C The Cat in the Box Test.
   D The *Miller* Test.

2 The U.S. Constitutional amendment that requires probable cause before a
search or seizure can occur.

   A First Amendment.
   B Second Amendment.
   C Fourth Amendment.
   D Fifth Amendment.

3 Any visual depiction of sexually explicit conduct involving a minor (persons less than 18 years old).

    A Child pornography.
    B Pornography.
    C Scandal sheet.
    D Visual representation.

ENDNOTES

1. 494 U.S. 872 (1990).
2. *State ex rel. Swann v. Pack*, 527 S.W.2d 99 (Tenn. 1975).
3. *Hustler Magazine v. Falwell*, 485 U.S. 46, 108 S.Ct. 876 (1988).
4. *Texas v. Johnson*, 491 U.S. 397 (1989).
5. *Barnes v. Glen Theatre, Inc.*, 501 U.S. 560 (1991).
6. *Terminiello v. City of Chicago*, 337 U.S. 1, 69 S.Ct. 894, 93 L.Ed. 1131 (1949).
7. 378 U.S. 184 (1964).
8. *Jacobellis*, 378 U.S. at 197 (Stewart, J., concurring).
9. 413 U.S. 15, 93 S.Ct. 2607, 37 L.Ed.2d 419 (1973).
10. *Bridges v. California*, 314 U.S. 252 (1941).
11. *U.S. v. Williams*, 112 S.Ct. 1735 (1992).
12. *State v. Roy*, 220 La. 1017, 58 So. 2d 323 (1952); *State v. Moore*, 308 S.C. 349, 417 S.E.2d 869 (1992).
13. *Holt v. U.S.*, 218 U.S. 245, 31 S. Ct. 2, 54 L. Ed. 1021 (1910).
14. *Chambers v. Mississippi*, 410 U.S. 284, 93 S.Ct. 1038, 35 L.Ed.2d 297 (1973).
15. *Shorter v. U.S.*, 792 A.2d 228 (D.C. 2001).
16. *U.S. v. Eagle*, 498 F.3d 885, 74 Fed. R. Evid. Serv. 257 (8th Cir. 2007).
17. *Commerford v. State*, 728 So.2d 796 (Fla. Dist. Ct. App. 4th Dist. 1999).
18. *Com. v. Avalos*, 454 Mass. 1, 906 N.E.2d 987 (2009).
19. *Moore v. Illinois*, 434 U.S. 220, 98 S.Ct. 458, 54 L.Ed.2d 424 (1977); *Foster v. California*, 394 U.S. 440, 89 S.Ct. 1127, 22 L.Ed.2d 402 (1969).
20. https://www.scientificamerican.com/article/do-the-eyes-have-it/. Retrieved on April 17, 2020.
21. 388 U.S. 218 (1967).
22. *Manson v. Brathwaite*, 432 U.S. 98, 97 S.Ct. 2243, 53 L.Ed.2d 140 (1977).
23. *Stovall v. Denno*, 388 U.S. 293, 87 S.Ct. 1967, 18 L.Ed.2d 1199 (1967) (disapproval on other grounds *Griffith v. Kentucky*, 479 U.S. 314, 107 S.Ct. 708, 93 L.Ed.2d 649 (1987)).
24. *Milholland v. State*, 319 Ark. 604, 893 S.W.2d 327 (1995).
25. *Gilbert v California*, 388 U.S. 263, 18 L.Ed.2d 1178 (1951).
26. *Richmond Newspapers, Inc. v. Virginia*, 100 S.Ct. 2814 (1980).

The Exclusionary Rule

Chapter Objectives

- Explain the state of the law before the exclusionary rule was created
- Describe the historical development of the exclusionary rule in the federal system
- Define how the exclusionary rule was extended to the state
- Demonstrate an understanding of the various exceptions to the exclusionary rule
- Describe the fruit of the poisonous tree doctrine

Chapter Outline

I. The Exclusionary Rule
   A. Practical Aspects of the Exclusionary Rule
      Motions to Suppress
      Standing
   B. Historical Development of the Exclusionary Rule
   C. The Purpose of the Exclusionary Rule
   D. Does the Exclusionary Rule Work?
   E. Fruit of the Poisonous Tree

II. Exceptions to the Exclusionary Rule
   A. Independent Source Doctrine
   B. Attenuation
   C. Inevitable Discovery
   D. Good Faith

THE EXCLUSIONARY RULE

Exclusionary rule
A court-created rule that forbids the use of any evidence to be used that was acquired in violation of the Fourth Amendment.

The **exclusionary rule** is a rule created by the U.S. Supreme Court that dictates the punishment for failing to follow the correct procedures in obtaining evidence. Illegal or unconstitutional evidence cannot be used at trial. By providing such a sanction, the U.S. Supreme Court hoped to effectively force all law enforcement agencies to abide by constitutional provisions in seizing evidence. The exclusionary rule is the device used in numerous movies and television dramas as the "technicality" that allows an obviously guilty suspect to go free. However, because the court's ruling actually states that the police violated the Constitution in obtaining the evidence, to allow unconstitutionally seized evidence to be used in one case would invite the police to circumvent the Constitution in future cases, too. A ruling that specific evidence was obtained unconstitutionally does not mean that the charges against the defendant are dropped. However, if all evidence against a defendant is ruled illegal, then for all practical purposes, there is nothing that the prosecution can use that links the defendant to the crime.

The exclusionary rule has always been controversial. The idea behind the rule is deceptively simple: When police violate the Constitution in obtaining evidence, they are prohibited from using that same evidence at trial. The primary purpose of the exclusionary rule has always been to deter police misconduct.[1] If a police officer violates a person's constitutional rights in carrying out a search and seizure, then the officer, and by extension, the government, is punished by not being able to use that evidence at trial.

The Fourth Amendment guarantees a person's right "to be secure in their persons, houses, papers, and effects, against unreasonable searches and seizures."[2] Because the Fourth Amendment contains no explicit enforcement provision of its own, the Supreme Court created the exclusionary rule as a means of addressing tactics that police had been using for decades that were violating both the letter and the spirit of the Fourth Amendment.[3] However, the Court has consistently maintained that excluding evidence is an extreme measure and should only be used as a last resort.[4]

There are some basic issues that should be resolved in discussing the exclusionary rule. First of all, the rule only applies to Fourth Amendment issues. The rule focuses on searches and seizures, and although there have been suggestions to apply a similar rule to other constitutional protections, such as freedom of speech or the right to remain silent, the rule has remained squarely in the category of Fourth Amendment search and seizure law.

As we saw in a previous chapter, the Fourth Amendment requires probable cause before police officers can conduct a search and seizure. Performing a search without a warrant is generally frowned upon and the courts have been consistent in stating that the default approach to a search is, when in doubt, get a warrant.

The exclusionary rule comes into play after the search and seizure have been carried out. Law enforcement is now in possession of evidence that

Sidebar

"The Fourth Amendment of the United States Constitution requires that a search warrant be based upon probable cause. . . . Generally, where law enforcement officers illegally search private premises or seize property without probable cause in violation of the Fourth Amendment, the illegally seized evidence will be excluded from evidence in a criminal prosecution."[5]

it intends to use against the defendant at his or her trial. The defendant wishes to challenge the admissibility of this evidence. The argument the defendant makes is that it was seized in violation of the Constitution. If the defendant can establish that the police acted improperly, then the evidence cannot be used.

A. PRACTICAL ASPECTS OF THE EXCLUSIONARY RULE

The most common way of asserting the exclusionary rule is through a pretrial motion, usually a **motion to suppress** the evidence that was seized and is being used by the prosecution to prove its case against the defendant. When the defense files a motion to suppress, it puts the prosecution on notice that it must present sufficient facts to justify the search and seizure of the materials. The motion puts the parties in an unusual situation. Generally, the party who brings a motion must present evidence to substantiate it. However, in a motion to suppress evidence under the exclusionary rule, the defense is obligated only to raise the motion, whereas the state is obligated to disprove it. As a result, in a pretrial motion, a defense attorney will bring a motion to suppress, declare that the search was unconstitutional, and then the burden falls to the prosecution to produce witnesses to show that the search and seizure were conducted lawfully.

MOTIONS TO SUPPRESS

During a motion to suppress hearing, police officers will take the stand in the pretrial hearing and testify about the circumstances that led up to the search and seizure. During their testimony, they must testify to specific facts that indicated to them that evidence of a crime was in the defendant's possession and what they did based on that belief. The defense will attempt to show that the police exceeded their authority either because they did not have sufficient probable cause to begin the inquiry or they exceeded the scope of their authority once the search began. After both sides have presented their evidence and arguments, it is up to the trial judge to make a ruling. If the judge rules that the evidence is admissible, then it can be used against the defendant at the later trial. If the judge rules that the evidence is inadmissible, and this falls under the exclusionary rule, then the prosecution and state witnesses are forbidden to refer to the evidence in any way. Essentially, during the trial, the prosecution must act as though the evidence never existed. If a prosecutor or a prosecution witness does refer to the excluded evidence, the judge is authorized to declare a mistrial.

It is extremely rare for all evidence against a defendant to be ruled unconstitutional. Even in cases where some of the evidence was obtained illegally, the prosecution may still continue with the case. The government cannot use that evidence and will instead rely on other evidence that was obtained constitutionally. See Figure 7-1 for a sample motion to suppress.

FIGURE 7-1

Sample Motion to
Suppress

[Insert Style here]

DEFENDANT DARRYL D. DEFENDANT MOTION TO SUPPRESS EVIDENCE AND STATEMENTS

COMES NOW, Darryl Defendant, the defendant in the above-styled action and files this, his Motion to Suppress any and all tangible evidence, including, but not limited to physical evidence including a "hatchet style axe, a bloody shirt, a pair of sneakers and an Android Series K cell phone" registered to the above-styled defendant.

In addition, the defendant hereby moves to suppress any and all statements made by the defendant to any law enforcement official before, during or after his arrest on May 14, 2020.

Respectfully submitted, attorney for Defendant
Clarence D. Arrow
State Bar No. 00664

STATEMENT OF FACTS
MEMORANDUM OF AUTHORITIES

Even if the statements were deemed by the court to be admissible, counsel for Mr. Hunt will challenge the accuracy of the statements at adjudication. Mr. Hunt does not concede that the substance of the statements and surrounding circumstances were accurately captured in the police report.

OFFICER THEO VIOLATED THE DEFENDANT'S GUARANTEED FOURTH AMENDMENT RIGHTS BY SEIZING ITEMS BELONGING TO AND IN THE POSSESSION OF THE DEFNDANT AT THE TIME OF HIS ARREST; OFFICER THEO HAD NO PROBABLE CAUSE TO SEIZE SUCH ITEMS AND HIS SEIZURE DOES NOT FALL INTO EXCEPTION TO THE EXCLUSIONARY RULE RECOGNIZED BY THIS STATE.
ALL EVIDENCE OBTAINED FROM MR. HUNT'S UNLAWFUL DETENTION IS A FRUIT OF THAT STOP AND MUST BE SUPPRESSED.

Where illegality is established for a stop, by, for instance, violating the Fourth Amendment, all evidence seized from that stop by exploitation of that illegality is "fruit of the poisonous tree," unless the evidence was obtained by, " . . . means sufficiently distinguishable to be purged of the primary taint." Wong Sun, 371 U.S. at 488. Officer Theo did not have a reasonable articulable suspicion that a crime had been committed. As such, his actions in seizing personal items belonging to and in the possession of the defendant was without legal or constitutional justification.

CONCLUSION
FOR ALL OF THE FOREGOING REASONS, the defendant hereby moves this court to enter an order granting this, his motion to suppress, as to any and all physical evidence, defendant's statements, defendant's alleged confession

and any other evidence secured as a result of the constitutionally tainted manner in which it was obtained from the defendant.

Respectfully Submitted,

_____

Clarence D. Arrow,
Attorney for Darryl Defendant

FIGURE 7-1

Sample Motion to
Suppress *(continued)*

STANDING

Before a court considers the merits of a motion to suppress, it must first address a basic question: Does the person have the right to complain about the seizure? This is the question of standing. In any court hearing, only persons who are directly affected by the court's ruling can participate in the litigation. The legal term for this requirement is **standing**. Individuals who are charged with a criminal offense always have standing. However, others, even those closely associated with the defendant, may not. Suppose that police pull over a car and conduct an unconstitutional search. Later, they charge the driver. Others in the car, who were upset by the police tactics and behavior, also want to complain about what happened. However, none of them were charged and none of their property was confiscated. Do the others in the car have standing?

No. To have standing to challenge a search and seizure, the person's liberty, property, or some other thing of value must have been seized or impacted. Simply being in a car where another person was charged does not confer standing. Consider Scenario 7-1.

Standing
The requirement that before persons challenge a court's action they must show an adverse effect on their personal interest; a recognized legal right to bring suit to challenge a legal decision.

STANDING?

Dale currently lives in a long-term hotel. He lists the hotel's address as his domicile and receives all of his bills and other correspondence there. He keeps his personal possessions in the room and has done so since moving in six months ago. Yesterday, while he was at work, the police came to the hotel and spoke with the hotel manager. The police told the manager that they suspected that Dale was dealing drugs. The hotel manager opened Dale's door and let the police inside. While searching, they came across several pill bottles containing oxycodone. Dale has no prescription for the drug and when he arrived home, the police arrested him for possession of a Schedule II/IIN Controlled Substance without a prescription. Does Dale have standing to challenge the search?

Answer: Absolutely. Even though Dale's address is a hotel, a person has an expectation of privacy in his room. Dale also has standing because his personal items were seized and he was charged with a crime.

Some of the elements that a court considers before accepting that a party has standing include:

- Does the individual have a possessory interest in the seized evidence?
- Does the individual have an expectation of privacy in the area that was searched?
- Did the suspect suffer a specific constitutional invasion?
- Is the individual's expectation of privacy reasonable under the circumstances?[8]
- Is the individual the person charged in the case? (Defendants always have standing.)[9]

Sidebar

Another way of viewing standing is to require the court to make an inquiry into "whether the disputed search and seizure has infringed an interest of the defendant in violation of the protection afforded by the Fourth Amendment."[10]

B. HISTORICAL DEVELOPMENT OF THE EXCLUSIONARY RULE

For most of the history of the United States, no exclusionary rule existed. However, problems with evidence had been a common enough occurrence that some method for putting teeth into the provisions of the Fourth Amendment was often sought. The amendment (see Figure 7-2) does not provide any mechanism for enforcing its provision.

You will notice that nowhere in the language of the Fourth Amendment is there a provision about what courts or other authorities are supposed to do when the clear language of the amendment is violated. As is true in many other clauses of the Constitution, the framers left it to others to implement the philosophy expressed.

The exclusionary rule was first proposed and made applicable to all federal prosecutions in *United States v. Weeks.*[11] In that case, the courts finally decided that there had to be some mechanism to prohibit law enforcement from violating the express terms of the Fourth Amendment. Their solution was elegantly simple: Evidence obtained in violation of the Fourth Amendment could not be used. The solution struck at the very core of the problem. By making the evidence inadmissible, it took away any incentive for the police to violate the Fourth Amendment. For almost 50 years, courts ruled that the exclusionary rule only applied to federal prosecutions. However, it was applied to all of the states in *Mapp v. Ohio.*[12]

In *Mapp v. Ohio*, several police officers forced their way into the defendant's residence without a search warrant. They struggled with the defendant and then later searched her home. Although the officers claimed that they had a search

FIGURE 7-2

Fourth Amendment, U.S. Constitution

The right of the people to be secure in their persons, houses, papers, and effects, against unreasonable searches and seizures, shall not be violated, and no Warrants shall issue, but upon probable cause, supported by Oath or affirmation, and particularly describing the place to be searched, and the persons or things to be seized.

warrant, none was ever obtained. Mapp was convicted of possession of lewd and lascivious materials, including books and photographs. The U.S. Supreme Court used the facts of this case as the basis to apply the exclusionary rule to all states. They based their decision not only on the *Weeks* case, but also on a broader interpretation of the Fourth and Fourteenth Amendments of the U.S. Constitution.

C. THE PURPOSE OF THE EXCLUSIONARY RULE

Courts have been very specific about the purpose of the exclusionary rule. It is a method "to deter law enforcement officers from committing Fourth Amendment violations."[13] There might have been other methods to attempt to control police behavior. For example, the courts could have encouraged disciplinary actions against offending officers. They could have authorized some kind of civil action by the defendant against an officer who violated the Fourth Amendment. However, the exclusionary rule had several advantages. Courts have no power over departmental sanctions and punishments. They also do not have the authority to create legislation authorizing broad-ranging civil actions against the police. However, they do have control over the admission of evidence. So, they tailored their rule to meet the practicalities of what courts were facing all over the country and they fashioned a remedy that was completely within their control. In many ways, it was a master stroke of judicial activism.

D. DOES THE EXCLUSIONARY RULE WORK?

There is an interesting question about the exclusionary rule. It was designed to deter police from engaging in unconstitutional searches and seizures, but has it been successful? One could argue that the answer is yes. Police officers are trained to conduct searches in a proper way and to obtain a warrant when the seizure of evidence is in question. However, that does not mean that all searches and seizures are carried out in a legally proper way. There might be instances where a police officer does not abide by the exclusionary rule. Some reasons for that activity include the following:

- There are times when police officers are willing to gamble that specific evidence may be ruled admissible.
- Contraband that has been seized by the police will not be returned to the defendant.
- Police officers are rarely fired or even disciplined for violations of the exclusionary rule.
- Some police officers see the rule as highly technical and do not modify their behavior based on subsequent court rulings.
- Most cases end with the defendant pleading guilty and never go to trial.

E. FRUIT OF THE POISONOUS TREE

Fruit of the poisonous tree doctrine
The rule that evidence gathered as a result of evidence gained in an illegal search or questioning cannot be used against the person searched or questioned even if later evidence was gathered lawfully.

Occasionally, when evidence has been obtained in violation of the Constitution, this evidence will lead to the discovery of additional evidence. What happens when other evidence is located, but this evidence was derived from a constitutionally tainted source? The courts have said that for the exclusionary rule to have any binding effect, it must be applied to this new evidence as well. When new evidence is discovered only through unconstitutionally obtained evidence, this new evidence will be excluded at trial. This is the so-called **fruit of the poisonous tree doctrine**. This doctrine holds that if the original evidence was tainted, any additional evidence obtained from it is also tainted and suffers the same penalty: exclusion at trial. Say, for example, that a key to a safe deposit box was found during an illegal search. The key itself (the poisonous tree) cannot be admitted into evidence during the trial, nor can the contents of the safe deposit box (the fruit). Consider Scenario 7-2.

SCENARIO 7-2

FRUIT OF THE POISONOUS TREE?

An FBI agent has been working undercover for some time, advertising his services as a *sicario* or hitman in various posts on the Dark Web. Recently, a woman calling herself Darla made contact with him and inquired how much he would charge for killing her husband. The agent reported the contact with his supervisor who learned the woman's full name and her location. Without obtaining a warrant, the supervisor authorized a team to intercept the woman on her way to work. While she was being arrested, police noticed that she had a smartphone. They forced Darla to put her thumb on the phone to open it up and discovered that Darla had been using the phone to conduct scams on local businesses. Is the phone and the subsequent information retrieved from the phone considered to be fruit of the poisonous tree?

Answer: Yes. To arrest Darla, police needed probable cause. Based on the facts presented here, there is none. Confirming the woman's name and address is not the same thing as conducting a detailed surveillance and confirming that the woman is serious about hiring someone to kill her husband. As a result, her arrest is not supported by probable cause. That also means that any subsequent evidence is also tainted and would fall into the category of fruit of the poisonous tree.

When a claim has been made that evidence is "fruit" of an unlawful search, the evidence might nevertheless be admissible if it fits within one of several recognized exceptions to the exclusionary rule. We will examine exceptions to the exclusionary rule next.

EXCEPTIONS TO THE EXCLUSIONARY RULE

There are several exceptions to the exclusionary rule—although the exact number remains open to debate. The exceptions include:

- Independent source doctrine
- Attenuation
- Inevitable discovery
- Good faith[14]

A. INDEPENDENT SOURCE DOCTRINE

Under the independent source doctrine, the court is presented with evidence that was located in two ways: one that violated the Constitution and one that did not. Because one path was free of any violations of the Fourth Amendment, the court will permit the evidence to be used. "In the classic independent source situation, information which is received through an illegal source is considered to be cleanly obtained when it arrives through an independent source."[15]

B. ATTENUATION

The **attenuation doctrine** arose in situations where considerable time had passed between the seizure of evidence, which was obtained in violation of the Fourth Amendment, and the proposed use of the evidence. The idea is that time and intervening events removed some of the taints of the evidence. Under the attenuation doctrine, evidence may be admitted at trial, if the "connection between unconstitutional police conduct and the evidence is remote or has been interrupted by some intervening circumstance, so that the interest protected by the constitutional guarantee that has been violated would not be served by suppression of the evidence obtained."[16]

The attenuation doctrine is a way for the government to claim that sufficient time has passed from the constitutional violation that the harm of admitting the evidence is no longer as severe as it once was, and the evidence remains as relevant as it ever was. Consider Scenario 7-3. The court will consider several factors before allowing the exception to the exclusionary rule, including these:

- How much time has passed since the seizure?
- Have there been intervening factors since the original seizure, such as another prosecution or court ruling?
- How severe was the original violation? If it was particularly egregious, then this may weigh in favor of continuing to exclude the evidence.[17]

> ## Sidebar
>
> *Under the independent source doctrine, a court recognizes that the exclusionary rule does not apply when there were two different paths to evidence. One was tainted by a constitutional violation; one was not.*

Attenuation doctrine
The connection between the constitutional violation and the evidence has been interrupted by some intervening event, such as time or distance, so that a constitutional violation is no longer as severe as it was originally.

ATTENUATION?

SCENARIO 7-3

Officer Adams sees a car driven by a Hispanic male and has a gut feeling that the man is up to no good. He stops the car without any probable cause. As he speaks with the man, he sees a handgun in the passenger seat. The officer charges the man with failure to yield right of way and, when the gun is logged into evidence, it is discovered that the gun has been stolen. Police add an additional count against the man for possession of a stolen handgun. Is there sufficient attenuation from the unconstitutional stop to charge the man with possession of a stolen weapon?

Answer: Maybe. Attenuation is a relatively new doctrine and some of the details are being worked out in the court system, but courts have held that a subsequent investigation revealing that the defendant had committed an offense separate and distinct from the original offense might qualify under the attenuation doctrine. However, the general rule about attenuation usually involves time and there is very little time between the original stop and the discovery of the illegal item to make this a close case. The courts might just as easily decide that the exclusionary rule applies to the stolen handgun.

C. INEVITABLE DISCOVERY

Inevitable discovery rule
An exception to the exclusionary rule by which the evidence would have been discovered one way or another, even if one of the methods violated the Fourth Amendment.

Under the **inevitable discovery rule**, the prosecution may present evidence during the defendant's trial even though it was obtained in violation of the Constitution if the prosecution can show that the evidence would have come to light anyway. The most common example is a dead body. In one notable instance, police violated the Fourth Amendment provisions by getting a defendant to show them where the victim's body was, but the court ruled that because the body would have been discovered by others, the inevitable discovery rule allowed the evidence of the body to be used. The court held that "the inevitable discovery doctrine provides that illegally obtained information may nevertheless be admissible if the prosecution can establish by a preponderance of the evidence that the information would have ultimately been discovered by lawful means."[18]

The inevitable discovery exception "allows for the admission of evidence that would have been discovered even without the unconstitutional source, because punishment for an act that does no harm is not required in order to deter harmful acts."[19] When the evidence is challenged, it is up to the government to prove by a preponderance of the evidence that the unlawfully obtained evidence would have ultimately or inevitably been discovered.[20]

D. GOOD FAITH

Good faith exception
A court-created doctrine that holds that evidence will not be suppressed under the exclusionary rule when officers were acting in good faith and had no reason to know that the warrant was invalid.

When officers are acting on a reasonable belief that the search warrant they have been given to execute is valid, the courts will not invalidate the evidence that they recover when it turns out the warrant was invalid. This is the **good faith exception**, first put forth in the U.S. Supreme Court case of *United States v. Leon.*[21] As long as there is no reasonable way that the officer would know that the warrant was invalid, the evidence will not be suppressed. Obviously, this exception to the exclusionary rule does not operate when the officer caused the warrant to be invalid in the first place or where the officer could obviously tell that the warrant was invalid.

Under the good faith exception, a court may suppress evidence obtained in violation of the Fourth Amendment, "only if it can be said that the law enforcement officer had knowledge, or may properly be charged with knowledge, that the search was unconstitutional under the Fourth Amendment."[22] If they did not, then the evidence obtained by the search will be allowed at trial.

The good faith exception protects a police officer who has an "objectively reasonable belief that the issuing magistrate had probable cause to issue the search warrant" and the officer can rely on the magistrate's determination that probable cause exists. Police officers are not required to second-guess the magistrate's decision.[23]

COLLINS v. COMMONWEALTH
RECORD NO. 0765-17-2 2018

CASE EXCERPT

The Circuit Court of the City of Richmond convicted Terence Lamont Collins, Jr., of aggravated malicious wounding, attempted robbery, and two counts of using a firearm in the commission of a felony. On appeal, Collins maintains that the circuit court erred by denying his motion to suppress evidence obtained from the search of his cell phone. Collins also challenges the sufficiency of the evidence supporting his convictions. For the following reasons, we affirm Collins's convictions.

I. A. THE SHOOTING AND INITIAL IDENTIFICATION OF COLLINS

Around 11:00 a.m. on February 5, 2016, David Johnson saw Collins at a convenience store in downtown Richmond. Johnson knew Collins from "the street." Collins offered to give Johnson a ride to a nearby barbershop, and Johnson accepted the offer. Johnson bought heroin from Collins in a parking lot near the barbershop. During the transaction, Collins saw that Johnson possessed a substantial amount of money.

Collins followed Johnson through the parking lot after the heroin transaction. At some point, Collins pointed a pistol at Johnson and told him to "kick the money." Collins then shot Johnson in both of his legs. Johnson refused to give his money to Collins. Collins shot Johnson in the buttocks as he was running toward an alley. Collins also fired a shot at Johnson's torso, but the bullet got caught in Johnson's jacket and did not actually hit him. As he was running, Johnson's leg buckled and he fell to the ground. After Johnson fell, Collins shot him again in the right leg. He then demanded Johnson's money and hit him in the face with the pistol. When Johnson cried for help, Collins ran to his car and drove away from the area.

Police officers and emergency medical personnel promptly arrived at the scene of the shooting in response to a 9-1-1 call. Johnson initially told the police officers that he did not know who shot him. After he was transported to the hospital, however, Johnson told the police that someone named "Tee" shot him with a "pink and black .380" caliber pistol. Johnson also provided a detailed physical description of his assailant, and told the police that the shooter was wearing an "Army fatigue jacket." Based on Johnson's description, the police identified Collins as a suspect. Johnson subsequently identified Collins as the shooter from a photo lineup. The police obtained warrants for Collins's arrest, and he was taken into custody five days after the shooting.

Collins denied any involvement in the shooting. He told the police that he did not know Johnson or own any firearms. Collins had two cell phones with him when he was taken into custody. He was also wearing a camouflage jacket.

B. THE SEARCH OF THE CELL PHONE AND THE MOTION TO SUPPRESS

Detective Mark Godwin, the lead investigator in the present case, applied for two search warrants pertaining to Collins's cell phones. Godwin initially requested a warrant allowing him to search the personal property held by the jail in which Collins was an inmate and seize the cell phones that he possessed when he came into police custody. Godwin submitted this request to a magistrate in Prince George County, the jurisdiction where the jail was located.

In the affidavit supporting the warrant, Godwin described the shooting and explained how Collins was identified as a suspect. The affidavit also noted that Collins had cell phones in his possession when he was taken into custody. The affidavit then stated:

> Based on your affiant's training and experience investigating weapons offenses, as well as violent crimes, your affiant knows that offenders communicate with cellular devices by means of phone conversations, text messages, email, and social media applications. Your affiant has investigated numerous violent criminal cases in which cell records, to include call detail lists, contact lists, text message content were instrumental in understanding how a violent crime occurred and who was involved. Therefore, . . . your affiant requests a search warrant be issued to further this investigation.

Additionally, the affidavit discussed Godwin's law enforcement training and experience. The affidavit stated that Godwin had been a police officer for nine years and that he was currently an aggravated assault detective. The affidavit also explained that Godwin had investigated numerous crimes involving violence.

The magistrate issued the requested warrant. Pursuant to the warrant, Godwin searched Collins's personal property and seized two cell phones. Godwin then applied for an additional warrant allowing him to search the contents of one of the cell phones. As the search of the cell phone was to be conducted within the City of Richmond, Godwin submitted his request for the second warrant to a circuit court judge sitting in that jurisdiction. Godwin submitted an almost identical affidavit to support the second warrant. Notably, the affidavit contained the statement regarding the role of cell phones in violent crimes previously quoted in this opinion. After reviewing the affidavit, a circuit court judge issued the requested warrant.

The police found several images on the cell phone when they executed the search warrant. One of the images showed a hand holding a pink and black Ruger .380 caliber pistol. Another image showed Collins. Both images were created within eleven minutes of each other on December 8, 2015, approximately two months before the shooting.

Collins filed a motion to suppress the evidence obtained from the cell phone. Collins argued that the warrant authorizing the search of the cell phone was not supported by probable cause. Specifically, Collins maintained that the affidavit supporting the warrant failed to establish any factual connection between the charged offenses and the cell phone or any reason to believe that evidence pertaining to the shooting would be found on the cell phone. In addition, Collins contended that the warrant was overbroad because it allowed the police to search all of the data on the cell phone.

Following a hearing on Collins's motion to suppress, the circuit court determined that "the affidavit for the search warrant, and the search warrant itself, lacked sufficient particularity and were facially overbroad." Nevertheless, the circuit court concluded that the evidence obtained from the search of the cell phone was admissible under the good faith exception set forth in *United States v. Leon*, 468 U.S. 897 (1984). The circuit court acknowledged that the law regarding cell phone searches was in a "state of uncertainty and flux." The circuit court also noted that a circuit court judge issued the warrant authorizing the search. Under these circumstances, the circuit court concluded that the police reasonably relied on the search warrant in good faith and denied Collins's motion to suppress.

C. COLLINS'S JURY TRIAL

Johnson testified about the events of the shooting at Collins's trial. He unequivocally identified Collins as his assailant, and testified that Collins shot him with a "pink and black .380" caliber pistol. He also testified that Collins drove a small blue four-door car with "donut tires" on the day of the shooting and that Collins was wearing an "Army fatigue jacket" on that day. Johnson explained that he did not identify Collins as his assailant at the scene of the shooting because a crowd of people had gathered around him and he feared further bodily harm if he identified Collins as the shooter in public.

The images obtained from Collins's cell phone were admitted into evidence, including the image of the pink and black Ruger .380 caliber pistol. Additionally, the camouflage jacket that Collins was wearing when he came into police custody was admitted into evidence.

Collins presented defense evidence following the Commonwealth's case-in-chief. Collins testified on his own behalf. Collins acknowledged that he knew Johnson and that he gave him a ride on the day of the shooting. Collins explained that he initially lied to the police about the shooting because he had sold heroin to Johnson. Collins denied that he owned a pink and black pistol, and explained that the image on his cell phone was the cover of his rap mix tape. Collins admitted that he had previously been convicted of five felonies and three misdemeanors involving moral turpitude.

Collins testified that a man wearing a black jacket and a black "du-rag" approached Johnson in the alley near the barbershop on the day of the shooting. When the man said "something like I got you, got your ass, got you," Collins turned and ran back to his car. He then heard a gunshot. Collins suggested that the shooting was related to Johnson's gang affiliation.

The jury ultimately convicted Collins of aggravated malicious wounding, attempted robbery, and two counts of using a firearm in the commission of a felony. This appeal followed.

II. ANALYSIS

On appeal, Collins contends that the circuit court erred by denying his motion to suppress the evidence obtained from the search of his cell phone. Collins argues that the warrant authorizing the search only stated generalized suspicions and failed to establish the required nexus between the cell phone and the shooting. Collins maintains that the affidavit supporting the warrant was so lacking in indicia of probable cause that an objective police officer could not have reasonably relied on it in good faith. Therefore, Collins contends that the circuit court erred by determining that the evidence obtained from his cell phone was admissible under the good faith exception established by *Leon* and subsequent cases.

Upon review, we conclude that the circuit court did not err by admitting the evidence obtained from Collins's cell phone pursuant to the *Leon* good faith exception. We also conclude that the evidence presented in this case was sufficient to support Collins's convictions.

A. THE CIRCUIT COURT DID NOT ERR BY DENYING COLLINS'S MOTION TO SUPPRESS THE EVIDENCE OBTAINED FROM HIS CELL PHONE

"A defendant's claim that evidence was seized in violation of the Fourth Amendment presents a mixed question of law and fact that we review de novo on appeal." *McCain v. Commonwealth*, 275 Va. 546, 551, 659 S.E.2d 512, 515 (2008). "In considering such questions, we are required to give deference to the factual findings of the trial court and to determine independently whether, under the law, the manner in which the evidence was obtained satisfies constitutional requirements." *McCain v. Commonwealth*, 261 Va. 483, 490, 545 S.E.2d 541, 545 (2001). "The defendant has the burden to show that, considering the evidence in the light most favorable to the Commonwealth, the trial court's denial of his suppression motion was reversible error." *McCain*, 275 Va. at 552, 659 S.E.2d at 515.

"The Fourth Amendment of the United States Constitution requires that a search warrant be based upon probable cause." *Sowers v. Commonwealth*, 49 Va. App. 588, 595, 643 S.E.2d 506, 510 (2007). Generally, "where law enforcement officers illegally search private premises or seize property without probable cause in violation of the Fourth Amendment, the illegally seized evidence will be excluded from evidence in a criminal prosecution." *Colaw v. Commonwealth*, 32 Va. App. 806, 810, 531 S.E.2d 31, 33 (2000).

In *Leon*, "the United States Supreme Court established a good-faith exception to the exclusionary rule, applicable when a search is conducted pursuant to a warrant subsequently determined to be defective for Fourth Amendment purposes." *Ward v. Commonwealth*, 273 Va. 211, 222, 639 S.E.2d 269, 274 (2008). "Under the good faith exception, 'where a police officer has an objectively reasonable belief that the issuing magistrate had probable cause to issue the search warrant, the officer may rely upon the magistrate's probable cause determination and the evidence obtained pursuant to the defective warrant will not be excluded.'" *Sowers*, 49 Va. App. at 602, 643 S.E.2d at 513.

"The exclusionary rule is designed to deter police misconduct rather than to punish the errors of judges and magistrates." Id. (quoting *Leon*, 468 U.S. at 916). "An officer ordinarily cannot be expected to question the magistrate's determination of probable cause." *Adams*, 48 Va. App. at 747, 635 S.E.2d at 24. "Evidence seized pursuant to a warrant should be suppressed 'only in those unusual cases in which exclusion will further the purposes of the exclusionary rule.'" Id. at 746, 635 S.E.2d at 24 (quoting *Leon*, 468 U.S. at 918). "Penalizing the officer for the magistrate's error, rather than his own, cannot logically contribute to the deterrence of Fourth Amendment violations." *Leon*, 468 U.S. at 921.

"The good-faith exception is not without limitations. In *Leon*, the Supreme Court outlined four circumstances in which the good-faith exception to the exclusionary rule would not apply." Ward, 273 Va. at 222, 639 S.E.2d at 274. A police officer cannot have an objectively reasonable belief that probable cause exists for a search and suppression is an appropriate remedy:

> "1) When the magistrate 'was misled by information in an affidavit that the affiant knew was false or would have known was false except for his reckless disregard of the truth'; (2) when 'the issuing magistrate wholly abandoned his judicial role . . .'; (3) when 'an affidavit is so lacking in indicia of probable cause as to render official belief in its existence entirely unreasonable'; or (4) when 'a warrant is so facially deficient . . . that the executing officers cannot reasonably presume it to be valid.' "

Id. at 222-23, 639 S.E.2d at 274.

Collins bases his appellate argument on the third limitation to the *Leon* good faith exception. Collins argues that the affidavit supporting the warrant authorizing the search of his cell phone was so lacking in indicia of probable cause that a reasonable police officer could not have relied on it in good faith. Collins emphasizes that the only statements contained in the affidavit suggesting that evidence pertaining to the shooting would be found on his cell phone were Godwin's generalized statements about the behavior of violent criminals. Therefore, Collins contends that the affidavit failed to establish any factual nexus between the shooting and the data contained on the cell phone.

Assuming without deciding that the circuit court correctly determined that the warrant at issue was not supported by probable cause, we find that the circuit court correctly concluded that the evidence obtained from the search of Collins's cell phone was admissible pursuant to the *Leon* good faith exception. Although the affidavit supporting the warrant may have failed to establish the requisite nexus between the cell phone and the shooting, it was not "so lacking in indicia of probable cause as to render official belief in its existence entirely unreasonable." *Leon*, 468 U.S. at 923.

"As long as there is some indicia of probable cause in the underlying affidavit, we will apply the good faith exception as long as a reasonable police officer, after assessing the facts set forth in the affidavit, could have believed that the warrant was valid." *Anzualda*, 44 Va. App. at 781, 607 S.E.2d at 757. In the present case, the affidavit supporting the warrant at issue contained some indicia of probable cause. The affidavit contained a description of the shooting, and stated that the victim identified Collins as his assailant. The affidavit also indicated that Collins had a cell phone in his possession when he was taken into police custody following the shooting. The affidavit then explained that the data contained in a suspect's cell phone was often "instrumental in understanding how a violent crime occurred and who was involved."

While conclusions based on a police officer's training and experience are not sufficient in themselves to provide a basis for probable cause, a magistrate may consider such conclusions when determining whether to issue a search warrant. Based on Godwin's training and experience, he concluded that Collins's cell phone likely contained evidence pertaining to the shooting. In the affidavit supporting the warrant, Godwin explained that violent offenders often communicated with their cell phones and that their cell phones frequently contained evidence of their crimes. The affidavit also described Godwin's prior law enforcement experience, and indicated that he had investigated numerous violent crimes. These statements established a nexus, "however slight," between the shooting and Collins's cell phone. Moreover, additional circumstances supported police reliance on the warrant at issue. "In determining whether police officers relied in good faith on a judicially issued warrant, we may 'take into account information known to police officers that was not included in the search warrant affidavit.'" *Midkiff v. Commonwealth*, 54 Va. App. 323, 332, 678 S.E.2d 287, 292 (2009). In this case, Godwin obtained two warrants regarding the cell phones. A magistrate in Prince George County issued a warrant authorizing Godwin to search Collins's property and seize any cell phones that he found, and a circuit court judge sitting in the City of Richmond issued a warrant authorizing the search of the contents of the cell phone. Thus, two different officials had previously determined that Godwin's affidavit established a sufficient nexus between the shooting and Collins's cell phone.

We conclude that a reasonable police officer could have relied in good faith on the warrant authorizing the search of Collins's cell phone. The warrant contained some indicia of probable cause establishing that evidence of the shooting would be found on the cell phone, and both a magistrate and a circuit court judge concluded that probable cause supported the search. Under these circumstances, the circuit court did not err by determining that the evidence obtained from Collins's cell phone was admissible under the *Leon* good faith exception.

III. CONCLUSION

For the reasons stated, we affirm Collins's convictions.
Affirmed.

CASE QUESTIONS

1 The defendant was detained related to a shooting. What were the circumstances surrounding obtaining a search warrant for his cell phones?
2 Was there any evidence on the phones that linked the defendant to the shootings?
3 At trial, the defendant filed a motion to suppress the evidence from the cell phones. What was the basis of his argument?
4 How did the trial court rule on the defendant's motion to suppress?
5 The defendant claimed that the exclusionary rule should apply in this case and that any evidence obtained from the phone should be suppressed. How did the court rule on this issue?

CHAPTER SUMMARY

In this chapter, we examined the exclusionary rule. Before the twentieth century, jurists and others had been struggling with a way of encouraging the police to follow the dictates of the Fourth Amendment and to find some way to deter bad behavior of officers who routinely violated the Constitution when they were performing searches and seizures. In *U.S. v. Weeks*, the Supreme Court created a simple yet very effective remedy for situations where law enforcement violated an individual's Fourth Amendment protections. The court ruled that any evidence seized without probable cause would be subject to the exclusionary rule. This simple rule turned out to be very effective. It struck at the very heart of a prosecution case. If evidence could not be used, then the prosecution faced a serious challenge in getting a conviction. The primary reason for the adoption of the exclusionary rule was to deter police misconduct in carrying out searches and seizures. Originally, the exclusionary rule applied only to federal prosecutions, but in its decision in *Mapp v. Ohio*, the U.S. Supreme Court applied the exclusionary rule to all states. The exclusionary rule also applies to any evidence that is discovered after unconstitutionally seized evidence has been discovered. This is referred to as the fruit of the poisonous tree doctrine.

When a defendant wishes to challenge evidence that will be used against him or her at trial, the most common method is to file a motion to suppress. This motion seeks to suppress, on the grounds of violation of the Fourth Amendment, all evidence acquired by law enforcement. To bring a motion to suppress, a person must have standing. This is a term that refers to a situation where a person's property or liberty could be affected by the admission of the evidence.

There are some exceptions to the exclusionary rule. For instance, if the prosecution can show that the evidence was obtained from an independent source, one that was independent of the tainted procedure that acquired the evidence, the independent source rule will allow the evidence to be used at trial. Under the attenuation doctrine, unconstitutionally seized evidence can be used when sufficient time has passed since the evidence was seized. Under the inevitable discovery rule, evidence that was obtained in violation of the Fourth Amendment can be used if the prosecution can show that the evidence would have been discovered by other means. Finally, the good faith exception allows the admission of evidence when police officers had no knowledge that the search warrant they were executing was not legally sufficient.

KEY TERMS AND CONCEPTS

Exclusionary rule	Fruit of the poisonous	Inevitable discovery rule
Motion to suppress	tree doctrine	Good faith exception
Standing	Attenuation doctrine	

END OF CHAPTER EXERCISES

Review Questions

See Appendix A for answers

1   What is the fruit of the poisonous tree doctrine?
2   List four exceptions to the exclusionary rule.
3   Explain the attenuation doctrine.
4   Explain the valid independent source exception to the exclusionary rule.

5   What is standing?

6   What is a motion to suppress?

7   Explain the good faith exception to the exclusionary rule.

8   Explain the significance of *United States v. Weeks* (1914).

9   Has the exclusionary rule been extended beyond Fourth Amendment, such as the First or Fifth Amendment? Explain your answer.

10   What is the independent source rule as it relates to the exclusionary rule?

11   What is the significance of *Mapp v. Ohio*?

12   Why was the exclusionary rule created?

13   For almost 50 years, the exclusionary rule only applied to the states. Explain why.

Web Surfing

Visit Justia (www.supreme.justia.com) and review the case of *United States v. Leon*, 468 U.S. 897 (1984). What provisions does the court create for the use of the good faith exception?

Question for Analysis

Can you make a case for discontinuing the exclusionary rule? What would be your main points?

Hypothetical

Detective Theo has applied for a warrant and received a copy of it from the magistrate. The warrant clearly states that it is limited to authorizing only the search of a specific automobile to be found at the residence. Even a cursory look at the warrant would have revealed this. However, the detective does not read the warrant and when he arrives at the residence proceeds to search the house. He seizes evidence of a crime. Would this evidence be admissible as an exception to the exclusionary rule? Does it fall under the category of good faith?

PRACTICE QUESTIONS FOR TEST REVIEW

See Appendix A for answers

Essay Question

Explain the exclusionary rule.

True-False

1   T   F   The exclusionary rule only applies to Fourth Amendment cases.

2   T   F   Originally, the exclusionary rule only applied to federal prosecutions.

3   T   F   Family members who have not been charged can challenge unconstitutional searches and seizures.

Fill in the Blank

1   A motion filed by the defense that seeks to suppress the admission of testimony or evidence during the trial of the accused is a(n) _____.

2   _____ is a court-created doctrine that holds that evidence will not be suppressed under the exclusionary rule when officers had no reason to know that the warrant was invalid.

3   The requirement that before persons challenge a court's action they must show an adverse effect on their personal interest; a recognized legal right to bring suit to challenge a legal decision is known as _____.

Multiple Choice

1   The case that applied the exclusionary rule to all states.

   A   *Miranda v. Arizona.*
   B   *Roe v. Wade.*
   C   *Gideon v. Wainwright.*
   D   *Mapp v. Ohio.*

2   The rule that evidence gathered as a result of evidence gained in an illegal search or questioning cannot be used against the person searched or questioned even if later evidence was gathered lawfully.

   A   Fruit of the poisonous tree doctrine.
   B   The wishful thinking doctrine.
   C   The year and the day rule.
   D   The rule against perpetuities.

3   Which of the following is an exception to the exclusionary rule?

   A   Attenuation doctrine.
   B   Independent source rule.
   C   Good faith exception.
   D   All of the above.

ENDNOTES

1. *United States v. Janis,* 428 U.S. 433 (1976).
2. U.S. CONST. Amend. IV.
3. *Herring v. United States,* 555 U.S. 135, 139, 129 S.Ct. 695, 699 (2009).
4. *Hudson v. Michigan,* 547 U.S. 586, 591, 126 S.Ct. 2159, 2163 (2006).
5. *Colaw v. Commonwealth,* 32 Va. App. 806, 810, 531 S.E.2d 31, 33 (2000).

6. *Wong Sun v. United States,* 371 U.S. 471, 485, 83 S.Ct. 407, 9 L.Ed.2d 441 (1963).
7. *Katz v. United States,* 389 U.S. 347, 357 (1967).
8. *Rakas v. Illinois,* 439 U.S. 128 (1978).
9. *State v. Stott,* 243 Neb. 967, 503 N.W.2d 822 (1993).
10. *State v. Van Ackeren,* 194 Neb. 650, 235 N.W.2d 210 (1975).
11. 232 U.S. 383 (1914).
12. 367 U.S. 643 (1961).
13. *Davis v. United States,* 564 U.S. 229 (2011).
14. *State v. Adams,* 409 S.C. 641, 763 S.E.2d 341 (2014).
15. *Murray v. United States,* 487 U.S. 533, 538-39 (1988).
16. *Utah v. Strieff,* 579 U.S. ----, 136 S.Ct. 2056, 2061, 195 L.Ed.2d 400 (2016).
17. *Utah v. Strieff,* 579 U.S. ----, 136 S.Ct. 2056, 2061, 195 L.Ed.2d 400 (2016).
18. *Nix v. Williams,* 467 U.S. 431, 444 (1984).
19. *Strieff,* 136 S.Ct. at 2059.
20. *Utah v. Strieff,* 579 U.S. ----, 136 S.Ct. 2056, 2061, 195 L.Ed.2d 400 (2016).
21. 468 U.S. 897 (1984).
22. *Illinois v. Krull,* 480 U.S. 340 (1987).
23. *U.S. v. Leon,* 468 U.S. 897 (1984).

Fifth Amendment: Grand Jury and Indictment

Chapter Objectives

- Explain the role of the grand jury
- Describe the role of the prosecutor in the charging decision
- Contrast the differences and similarities between indictments and accusations
- Define the procedure followed during a grand jury hearing
- Explain the various challenges that a defendant can bring to an indictment

Chapter Outline

I. Charging Decision
   A. Ask for Additional Investigation
   B. Bring Additional Charges Against the Defendant
   C. Dismiss the Case

II. Grand Jury
   A. True Bill vs. No Bill
   B. History of the Grand Jury
   C. The Purpose of the Grand Jury
   D. How Is the Grand Jury Composed?
      Challenging the Composition of the Grand Jury
   E. Function of the Grand Jury

F. Presenting a Case to the Grand Jury
   Only the State's Witnesses Appear Before the Grand Jury
G. Subpoena Powers of the Grand Jury
   Objecting to a Grand Jury Subpoena: Witness Privilege
   Pleading the "Fifth Amendment" Before the Grand Jury
   Motion to Quash
H. Immunity Powers of Grand Juries

III. After the Grand Jury Proceedings

CHARGING DECISION

After arrest, initial appearance, and preliminary hearing, one might be tempted to think that the next phase of a criminal case would be simply to present the case that was bound over in magistrate court to the grand jury. However, when the case is bound over from magistrate court to superior court, the case also comes under the power and authority of the prosecutor, whom this text will refer to as the district attorney (acknowledging that prosecutors can also be known as state's attorneys, people's attorneys, solicitors, and other names). When a case is bound over to superior court, the district attorney is permitted to review the case and to add, change, or dismiss the charges against the defendant. This process is loosely defined as the **charging decision** and involves a review of the facts and the law to decide not only what would be the most successful charge that the state can bring against the defendant, but also what is the most just way to proceed. Prosecutors are not charged with the duty to obtain convictions, but to seek justice. The charging decision involves several steps. Usually, the elected district attorney delegates charging decisions to his or her assistant district attorneys. In large cities, there could be hundreds of assistant district attorneys, all handling thousands of cases. In small communities, on the other hand, there might only be a few assistants. In either situation, it is up to the prosecution to decide how best to proceed in the case. An assistant district attorney might do some or all of the following:

Charging decision
The process that a prosecutor goes through to determine what is the appropriate and just charge to bring against a defendant based on the law and the facts in the case.

- Ask for additional investigation
- Bring additional charges against the defendant
- Dismiss the case

A. ASK FOR ADDITIONAL INVESTIGATION

A prosecutor is empowered to request additional investigation of the case by the police or through investigators employed directly by the district attorney. Many district attorneys' offices have their own body of investigators and support staff whose sole purpose is to conduct additional investigations into cases brought by the police. Why might such additional investigation be necessary? The simple answer is that the police may have overlooked some important issue, or the prosecutor believes that he or she can add more charges in the case, but must have the facts to support them. The charging decision by the prosecutor always focuses on the facts and law in a case. Without the facts, and the evidence to support them, there can be no case.

B. BRING ADDITIONAL CHARGES AGAINST THE DEFENDANT

Although the police have brought specific charges against a defendant, the prosecutor may add other charges as he or she sees fit. A prosecutor can add, delete, modify, or dismiss the original charges brought by law enforcement. This gives the prosecutor a great deal of authority. A prosecutor often will consult with the police officers involved in the case before taking any of these actions, but the prosecutor is not compelled to do so. The prosecutor acts independently of the police. Just as a prosecutor has no power to hire or fire police officers, law enforcement officials have no right to dictate what charges should or should not be brought against defendants. Having said this, however, a prosecutor who routinely disregards the input of the police will find himself or herself isolated and ignored by the police. Although it is rarely depicted in fictional portrayals of criminal cases, there can be a certain amount of animosity between police and prosecutors. They have different approaches to cases. For example, police officers often consider a case "closed" when an arrest is made, whereas for the prosecutor, the case has just begun. There are other differences to consider in the approach of police officers and prosecutors to criminal cases. Although fictional portrayals usually show police and prosecutors working in a harmonious partnership, that is not always the case. Police officers work odd hours and are almost universally poorly paid. They face danger on a daily basis and must often interact with people and situations that most of us would eagerly avoid. They are also obligated to look after their communities and not to abuse that trust, especially in terms of the minority members of that community. Prosecutors, on the other hand, focus on the elements of proof and are not always as aware of the situations that police must face. At worst, police and prosecutors can despise one another, with police officers believing that prosecutors are pampered law graduates with no sense of the real world, whereas prosecutors believe that police officers are brutes with little consideration for constitutional principles or the pressures brought to bear on a trial attorney. However, this extreme viewpoint is not common. In the typical scenario there are prosecutors and police who get along very well together and others who do not. However, it would be a mistake to believe that police officers subjugate themselves to the whims of prosecutors or that prosecutors blindly follow the recommendations of police officers. The relationship can often be complicated. Consider Scenario 8-1.

ALTERING THE CHARGES

SCENARIO 8-1

Detective Letisha has brought charges against John Doe for forgery and fraud. The assistant district attorney assigned to the case reviews the file and decides to dismiss those charges and bring entirely different charges. Can Detective Letisha force the prosecutor to bring the original charges?

Answer: No. The decision about what crimes to charge against the defendant are exclusively the province of the prosecutor and, although the police officer may have strong feelings about a case, it is ultimately the prosecutor's decision about how to proceed.

C. DISMISS THE CASE

Nolle prosequi
An order dismissing a criminal charge.

Prosecutors have the right to dismiss a case prior to presenting it to the grand jury. They actually have the right to dismiss their case at any point, but after a case has been presented to a grand jury, the dismissal must usually be signed by a judge. However, a prosecutor may seek a dismissal of a case, referred to as a **nolle prosequi**, if the prosecutor does not believe that there is sufficient evidence in the case to prove that the defendant is guilty beyond a reasonable doubt. The prosecutor can take this action against the wishes of the victim in the case, the police officer's desires, and even the community's interest in the case. In most cases, of course, the prosecutor will discuss a dismissal of a case with a victim and also engage the police officer, but there is no requirement that he or she do so. A prosecutor should be guided by conscience and the law, and a prosecutor who believes that a defendant is innocent should dismiss a case. A prosecutor has an ethical duty not to prosecute someone that he or she believes is innocent.

Accusation
A document that charges a defendant with a misdemeanor in most state courts.

Information
A document that charges a defendant with a misdemeanor in federal court.

Once a prosecutor has decided what the appropriate criminal charges in a case should be, he or she will draft a charging document. Most states make a strict distinction between misdemeanor and felony cases. As shown in Chapter 2, a felony is any charge where the potential punishment is more than one year in custody. In such a case, the prosecutor would draft an indictment. The indictment lists the facts of the charge and the code section that the defendant has violated. When the charge is a misdemeanor, the charges are brought in an **accusation** (referred to as an **information** on the federal level and in some state jurisdictions).

The indictment must give the defendant notice of the charges against him or her, list the crimes committed, and give the defendant details about the circumstances surrounding the charges. Generally, an indictment is sufficient if it answers the question words: who, when, where, and how. (Indictments do not answer the question of why.) See Figure 8-1 for a sample indictment.

Once the prosecutor has gone through the charging decision and drafted the indictment, the case is ready to be presented to the grand jury.

GRAND JURY

No person shall be held to answer for a capital, or otherwise infamous crime, unless on a presentment or indictment of a Grand Jury. . . .

—*Fifth Amendment, U.S. Constitution*

Grand jury
A group of citizens who consider felony charges against defendants and make a determination that there is sufficient evidence to warrant further prosecution.

If a defendant is charged with a felony, the next step in the criminal process is to convene a **grand jury** to consider the charges against him or her. Grand juries are required under the U.S. Constitution, and most states, but not all, follow this example.

The grand jury is not the same as the jury that hears a criminal charge. Instead, the grand jury is composed of 16 to 23 persons, and they consider

BILL OF INDICTMENT

Grand Jury Witnesses: R. L. Queen, Prosecutor

State of Placid
Placid Superior Court
March Adjourned Term

State of Placid
versus
Mark William Finnegan

Offense (s):

Count 1:	**Kidnapping**
Count 2:	**Aggravated Assault**
Count 3:	**Stalking**
Count 4:	**Simple Battery**
Counts 5-12:	**Stalking**

———————————— Bill

This ———— day of ————, 20 ————.

—————————————————

Howard D. Purcell, Jr.
Grand Jury Foreperson

===================================

Received in open court from the swc Grand Jury bailiff and filed in office.

This ———— day of ————, 20 ————.

—————————————————

Deputy Clerk, Placid Superior Court.

=================================

Sean J. Turlow, District Attorney
Placid Judicial Circuit
Special Presentment.

We the jury find the defendant

———————————————
———————————————
———————————————
———————————————
———————————————

Foreperson
This ———— day of ————, 20 ————.

The defendant herein waives a copy of indictment, list of witnesses, formal arraignment and pleads ———— guilty.
This ———— day of ————, 20 ————.

—————————————————

Defendant

—————————————————

Attorney for the Defendant

—————————————————

Assistant District Attorney

FIGURE 8-1

Sample Indictment

continued

FIGURE 8-1

Sample Indictment
(continued)

STATE OF PLACID, COUNTY OF PLACID
IN THE SUPERIOR COURT OF SAID COUNTY

Count 1 of 12

The GRAND JURORS selected, chosen and sworn for the County of Placid, to wit:

1. Howard D. Purcell, Jr., Foreperson	12. Virginia E. Driskell
2. Marion Fred Walden, Jr., Vice Foreperson	13. Dennis Eckman
	14. Billie Ellis
3. Teresa Ann Morris, Clerk	15. William B. Francis, III
4. Wendy Ball, Asst. Clerk	16. Elizabeth Hawkins
5. Alice V. Banks	17. Cynthia J. Hope
6. Kathleen M. Barrett	18. Venita Masters
7. Dennis F. Boyd	19. Bennie W. Moorehead
8. Lois M. Cragin	20. Mrs. Martha A. Nunnally
9. Charlotte C. Crosland	21. Helen Phillips
10. Faye P. Crowe	22. Doris F. Stone
11. Samuel E. Couch	23. Diane Young

in the name and behalf of the citizens of Placid, charge and accuse **Mark William Finnegan** with the offense of **Kidnapping** in that the said accused, in the State of Placid and County of Placid, on the **20th day of April, 2013**, did then and there unlawfully abduct Hilda River, a human being, without lawful authority and hold said person against her will, contrary to the laws of said State, the peace, good order and dignity thereof.

Count 2 of 12

and the GRAND JURORS, aforesaid, in the name and behalf of the citizens of Placid, further charge and accuse **Mark William Finnegan** with the offense of **Aggravated Assault** in that the said accused, in the State of Placid and County of Placid, on the **20th day of April, 2013**, did then and there unlawfully make an assault upon the person of Hilda River, with a knife, a deadly weapon by holding said knife and threatening her with it, contrary to the laws of said State, the peace, good order and dignity thereof.

Count 3 of 12

and the GRAND JURORS, aforesaid, in the name and behalf of the citizens of Placid, further charge and accuse **Mark William Finnegan** with the offense of **Stalking** in that the said accused, in the State of Placid and County of Placid, **between the dates of the 1st day of August, 2013 and the 30th day of September, 2013, the exact date being unknown to the Grand Jurors**, did then and there unlawfully contact Wilma Johnson at a public place, to wit: the Ingles Market, Inc. parking lot, 2850 Gant-Suwanee Road, Suwanee, Placid, without her consent and for the purpose of harassing and intimidating her, contrary to the laws of said State, the peace, good order and dignity thereof.

Count 4 of 12

and the GRAND JURORS, aforesaid, in the name and behalf of the citizens of Placid, further charge and accuse **Mark William Finnegan** with the offense of **Simple Battery** in that the said accused, in the State of Placid and County of Placid, on the **29th day of October, 2013**, did then and there unlawfully and intentionally make contact of an insulting and provoking nature to Chula Smith by grabbing her skirt, contrary to the laws of said State, the peace, good order and dignity thereof.

Count 5 of 12

and the GRAND JURORS, aforesaid, in the name and behalf of the citizens of Placid, further charge and accuse **Mark William Finnegan** with the offense of **Stalking** in that the said accused, in the State of Placid and County of Placid, on the **29th day of October, 2013**, did then and there unlawfully contact Chula Smith at a public place, to wit: the Annexter Wire and Cable Co., 550 Old Peachtree Road, Suwanee, Placid, without her consent and for the purpose of harassing and intimidating her, contrary to the laws of said State, the peace, good order and dignity thereof.

Count 6 of 12

and the GRAND JURORS, aforesaid, in the name and behalf of the citizens of Placid, further charge and accuse **Mark William Finnegan** with the offense of **Stalking** in that the said accused, in the State of Placid and County of Placid, on the **15th day of February, 2013**, did then and there unlawfully contact Silvia Swenson at a public place, to wit: the Ingles Market, Inc. parking lot, 2850 Gant-Suwanee Road, Suwanee, Placid, without her consent and for the purpose of harassing and intimidating her, contrary to the laws of said State, the peace, good order and dignity thereof.

Count 7 of 12

and the GRAND JURORS, aforesaid, in the name and behalf of the citizens of Placid, further charge and accuse **Mark William Finnegan** with the offense of **Stalking** in that the said accused, in the State of Placid and County of Placid, on the **30th day of March, 2013**, did then and there unlawfully contact Jessica Wilhoit at a public place, to wit: the Ingles Market, Inc. parking lot, 2850 Gant-Suwanee Road, without her consent and for the purpose of harassing and intimidating her, contrary to the laws of said State, the peace, good order and dignity thereof.

Count 8 of 12

and the GRAND JURORS, aforesaid, in the name and behalf of the citizens of Placid, further charge and accuse **Mark William Finnegan** with the offense of **Stalking** in that the said accused, in the State of Placid and County of Placid, **between the dates of the 2nd day of April, 2013 and the 10th day of April, 2013, the exact date being unknown to the Grand Jurors**, did then and there unlawfully contact Nicole Parker at a public place, to wit: the Ingles Market, Inc. parking lot, 2850 Gant-Suwanee Road, Suwanee, Placid, without her consent and for the purpose of harassing and intimidating her, contrary to the laws of said State, the peace, good order and dignity thereof.

FIGURE 8-1

Sample Indictment
(continued)

Count 9 of 12

and the GRAND JURORS, aforesaid, in the name and behalf of the citizens of Placid, further charge and accuse **Mark William Finnegan** with the offense of **Stalking** in that the said accused, in the State of Placid and County of Placid, on the **10th day of April, 2013**, did then and there unlawfully contact Sasha Sasha at a public place, to wit: the Ingles Market, Inc. parking lot, 2850 Gant-Suwanee Road, Suwanee, Placid, without her consent and for the purpose of harassing and intimidating her, contrary to the laws of said State, the peace, good order and dignity thereof.

Count 10 of 12

and the GRAND JURORS, aforesaid, in the name and behalf of the citizens of Placid, further charge and accuse **Mark William Finnegan** with the offense of **Stalking** in that the said accused, in the State of Placid and County of Placid, on the **between the dates of the 12th day of April, 2013, and the 14th day of April, 2013, the exact date being unknown to the Grand Jurors**, did then and there unlawfully contact Kim Kimberly at a public place, to wit: the Ingles Market, Inc. parking lot, 2850 Gant-Suwanee Road, Suwanee, Placid, without her consent and for the purpose of harassing and intimidating her, contrary to the laws of said State, the peace, good order and dignity thereof.

Count 11 of 12

and the GRAND JURORS, aforesaid, in the name and behalf of the citizens of Placid, further charge and accuse **Mark William Finnegan** with the offense of **Stalking** in that the said accused, in the State of Placid and County of Placid, on the **17th day of April, 2013**, **said date being a material element**, did then and there unlawfully contact Juana Juan at a public place, to wit: the Ingles Market, Inc. parking lot, 2850 Gant-Suwanee Road, Suwanee, Placid, without her consent and for the purpose of harassing and intimidating her, contrary to the laws of said State, the peace, good order and dignity thereof.

Count 12 of 12

and the GRAND JURORS, aforesaid, in the name and behalf of the citizens of Placid, further charge and accuse **Mark William Finnegan** with the offense of **Stalking** in that the said accused, in the State of Placid and County of Placid, on the **2nd day of May, 2013, said date being a material element**, did then and there unlawfully contact Kim Kimberly at a public place, to wit: the Ingles Market, Inc. parking lot, 2850 Gant-Suwanee Road, Suwanee, Placid, without her consent and for the purpose of harassing and intimidating her, contrary to the laws of said State, the peace, good order and dignity thereof.

Sean J. Turlow, District Attorney

Prima facie
Facts that are considered true as presented until they are disproven by some contrary evidence.

the basic facts of the prosecution's case. The purpose of the grand jury is to act as a buffer between the state and the defendant. The grand jury considers witness testimony and then makes a ruling as to whether or not the case should continue. If the grand jurors determine that there is a **prima facie** case of guilt, then they will authorize continued prosecution.

The U.S. Constitution requires a grand jury indictment for a person charged with a capital offense (one punishable by death) or "otherwise infamous crime." This phrase has come to mean any felony offense. However, the U.S. Supreme Court has never held that this provision of the Fifth Amendment applies to the states. In fact, there are some states that do not use grand juries at all; however, because most states do, this text will spend some time examining the functions and procedures of the grand jury.

A. TRUE BILL VS. NO BILL

When the grand jurors reach a decision that the prosecution against a particular defendant should continue, they record their vote as a **true bill**. A true bill authorizes the prosecution to bring formal charges against the defendant and to summon him or her to trial. On the other hand, if the grand jurors do not believe that a case should continue, then they vote **no bill**. A vote of no bill effectively stops the prosecution in its tracks. At this point, the prosecution can either wait until a new grand jury is empaneled, which could be as long as a year or more, or seek to charge the defendant with a misdemeanor.

If the grand jury returns a true bill against a defendant, the next step in the prosecution is the arraignment.

B. HISTORY OF THE GRAND JURY

Grand juries have been part of both the U.S. and English systems for centuries. The primary reason for the creation of a grand jury was to interpose a barrier between the government and the individual. Prosecutors must present their version of the criminal case to a grand jury and receive its permission to continue with the prosecution. Grand juries were traditionally seen as a way of allowing the community to protect innocent individuals from being persecuted by overzealous government officials and to prevent the government from using its power to bring criminal charges as a way to intimidate and silence those who disagreed with government policy.[1] Grand juries do not exist in civil cases. There are also no grand juries authorized under the Military Code of Justice or in juvenile cases. Misdemeanor cases are not presented to grand juries and some states even allow specific types of minor felonies to bypass the grand jury system (see Figure 8-2).

Even in states that follow a grand jury system, there are variations in how the grand jurors are selected and how the case is presented. When a state does have a grand jury system, it is authorized and governed by statutes. Often, the grand jury requirement is set out in the state constitution.

Grand juries do not decide whether a person is guilty or not guilty of a crime. Instead, they reach a decision that is partially based on probable cause and partially on the opinions of the individual jurors. It is easy to confuse a grand jury with a regular or petit jury. A regular jury is what is normally portrayed on courtroom television dramas. These jurors decide the guilt or

Sidebar

Cases involving misdemeanors are not presented to grand juries.

True bill
A grand jury's determination that there is sufficient probable cause to continue the prosecution against the accused.

No bill
A grand jury's determination that there is insufficient probable cause to continue the prosecution against the accused.

FIGURE 8-2

Sample Statute
Authorizing the
Prosecution of Some
Felonies Through
Accusations Bypassing
the Grand Jury (Georgia)

TITLE 17. CRIMINAL PROCEDURE
CHAPTER 7. PRETRIAL PROCEEDINGS
ARTICLE 4. ACCUSATIONS

O.C.G.A. §17-7-70 (2013)

§17-7-70. Trial upon accusations in felony cases; trial upon accusations of felony
and misdemeanor cases in which guilty plea entered and indictment waived

(a) In all felony cases, other than cases involving capital felonies, in which
defendants have been bound over to the superior court, are confined in jail or
released on bond pending a commitment hearing, or are in jail having waived a
commitment hearing, the district attorney shall have authority to prefer
accusations, and such defendants shall be tried on such accusations, provided
that defendants going to trial under such accusations shall, in writing, waive
indictment by a grand jury.

(b) Judges of the superior court may open their courts at any time without the
presence of either a grand jury or a trial jury to receive and act upon pleas of
guilty in misdemeanor cases and in felony cases, except those punishable by
death or life imprisonment, when the judge and the defendant consent thereto.
The judge may try the issues in such cases without a jury upon an accusation
filed by the district attorney where the defendant has waived indictment and
consented thereto in writing and counsel is present in court representing the
defendant either by virtue of his employment or by appointment by the court.

---

innocence of the defendant. The grand jury does not make that determination.
Instead, it simply returns a vote stating whether or not the case against the
defendant should proceed. If the grand jury believes that the prosecution has
made a sufficient showing, it will return a vote of "true bill." This authorizes
the state to bring the defendant to trial. If the grand jury returns a "no bill"
the case is dismissed, and the only way that the state can proceed is either
by charging the defendant with a misdemeanor or by waiting until a new
grand jury is seated and present the case to them. Figure 8-3 shows a breakdown
of the differences between grand juries and regular juries.

C. THE PURPOSE OF THE GRAND JURY

The grand jury was devised to act as a buffer between the state and the defendant. Developed in England and later transplanted to the New World, the original concept of the grand jury has existed for more than 700 years. The grand
jury is composed of citizens who sit in secret session and listen to evidence about
specific cases. The essential function of the grand jury is to determine that there
is probable cause to believe that a crime has occurred. Once they do, the grand
jurors allow the prosecutor to continue with his or her case.[2] The grand jury

FIGURE 8-3	Differences Between a Grand Jury and a Regular (Petit) Jury

Grand Jury	Regular Jury
16–23 members	12 members
Do not determine guilty or not guilty verdicts	Return guilty or not guilty verdicts
Do not recommend sentences	May recommend sentences
Meet regularly for a set period of time, e.g., every month for six months	Meet only once to consider a specific case

FIGURE 8-4

Sample Indictment with True Bill Determination

Grand Jury witnesses:
Detective Able
	State of Yuma
	Gannett Superior Court
	March Adjourned Term
	
	State of Yuma
	  versus
	Christine Lynn Kline
	  Offense(s):
	Count 1: Murder
	
	[True] Bill
	_____
	
	This the ___ day of April, this year
	Seamus Kadirka (signature)
	_____
	Seamus Kadirka,
	Grand Jury Foreperson
	============================
	Received in open court from the sworn Grand Jury Bailiff and filed in office.
	
	This the ___ day of April, this year
	Irma Friendly (signature)
	_____
	Irma Friendly, Deputy Clerk
	Gannett Superior Court
	===========================
	Derrick Young, District Attorney
	Gannett Judicial Circuit

We the jury find the defendant: _____ _____ _____ _____ Foreperson This ___ day of _____, _____	The defendant herein waives a copy of indictment, list of witnesses, formal arraignment and pleads ___ guilty. This ___ day of _____, _____ _____ Defendant _____ Attorney for Defendant _____ Assistant District Attorney

---

Count 1 of 1

The GRAND JURORS selected, chosen and sworn for the County of Gannett, to
wit:

1. Seamus Kadirka, Foreperson
2. Randall Makepeace
3. Mary Manz
4. Jessica Etters
5. Janae Freeman
6. Melodie Sisk
7. Yolanda Price
8. Starla Hoke
9. Debra Holbrook
10. Deborah Bolstridge
11. Sharon Ferguson
12. Lisa Mazzonetto
13. Brenda Timmerman
14. Richard Garrison
15. John Farthing
16. Paul Dellinger
17. Paula Barnes
18. Patsy Dellinger
19. Betsy Bevans
20. Christy Wallace
21. Gayle Hartung
22. Marianne Simpson
23. Star Hand

In the name and behalf of the citizens of Yuma, charge and accuse Christine
Lynn Kline, with the offense of Murder in that the said accused, in the state of
Yuma and County of Gannett, on or about the 19th day of November, last year,
did then and there unlawfully and with malice aforethought, kill Douglas Betters
by smothering him to death, contrary to the laws of said State, the peace, good
order and dignity thereof.

Derrick Young, District Attorney
Gannett Judicial Circuit

---

writes its decision on the indictment. See Figure 8-4 for an example of a case that
has been true billed by a grand jury.

D. HOW IS THE GRAND JURY COMPOSED?

A grand jury is selected in various ways in different jurisdictions. The most
common method of selecting individual grand jurors is by using the same
pool of jurors that would be used for a normal jury trial. Grand jurors must
meet the following criteria:

- Must be members of the jurisdiction
- Cannot have been convicted of a felony
- Must be citizens

A grand jury is made up of citizens of the county or federal district. They must be
selected from a cross-section of the community, including factors such as race,
sex, occupation, and so on.[3] Citizens cannot be excluded from a grand jury on
the basis of their race, ethnic origin, or their sex.[4] The usual number of jurors is
between 12 and 23, again depending on the jurisdiction. Neither the federal system nor any state allows a grand jury to proceed with fewer than 12 members,[5]

but many states allow a grand jury to convene if some of its members are temporarily absent. Members are selected by the chief judge of the district.

When it comes to the actual composition of the grand jury, the members must represent a fair and impartial cross-section of the jurisdiction, with the percentages of minorities reflected as closely as possible in the composition of the grand jury itself. There is no requirement that the exact percentages of race and ethnicity found in the jurisdiction must be represented in the composition of the grand jury. As long as no minority group is deliberately excluded, a defendant has no claim of improper grand jury composition if it turns out that a specific minority group was not represented on his or her particular grand jury. Beyond that, states vary considerably on who may serve as a grand juror. Most states specifically prohibit the victim from being a grand juror in his or her own case for obvious reasons. Many, but not all, states prohibit actively serving law-enforcement officers from serving on a grand jury, and obviously the arresting officer is not permitted to act as a grand juror in his or her own case.[6]

CHALLENGING THE COMPOSITION OF THE GRAND JURY

A defendant may challenge the composition of the grand jury as not representing a fair cross-section of the community, but unless the defendant can show a clear pattern of exclusion of individuals on the basis of ethnicity or race, the court is unlikely to rule that the composition was improper. To successfully challenge the composition of the grand jury, a defendant must show that there was some irregularity in the way that the grand jury was compiled, such as government officials deliberately ignoring statutory procedures or deliberately excluding individuals on the basis of race, religion, or ethnicity.

E. FUNCTION OF THE GRAND JURY

The grand jury actually has several functions. The primary purpose of the grand jury is to determine if a crime has occurred. If the government can establish probable cause to believe that the defendant committed the crime presented, the grand jury has the power and duty to authorize further prosecution of the case.[7] As such, it is a key element of the criminal justice process. Witnesses appear before the grand jury and are asked questions to establish the basic merits of the case. In many states, an assistant DA is permitted to enter the grand jury room long enough to question the witness and establish the legal basis of the claim; in other states, the prosecutor is not permitted to be present at all, and law enforcement officers present the case. In all states, however, the grand jury votes in secret, with no one else present.

Beyond its strictly "bill or no bill" role, the grand jury is also empowered to conduct its own investigations into criminal allegations. The grand jury can investigate people or activities to determine if crimes have occurred. To this end, the grand jury can subpoena witnesses and documents and does not have to establish probable cause before doing so. As such, the grand jury has more latitude than police or prosecutors when investigating a case.

Sidebar

The grand jury does not determine if the person charged is guilty or not guilty. It simply makes a determination that there is probable cause to believe that the defendant is guilty.

In its role as a supervisory body, the grand jury also oversees many local government offices and procedures. The grand jury is often called on to make a written report about the condition of the buildings and other facilities found in the county.

Grand juries also have limitations on their power. They cannot, for example, randomly subpoena witnesses to determine if some crime has occurred. The grand jury must be focused on a particular crime and does not function as an extension of the police department. The grand jury must confine its investigating and accusatory powers to investigating criminal cases. Grand juries do not involve themselves in civil cases.

F. PRESENTING A CASE TO THE GRAND JURY

Unlike criminal trials, where prosecutors must prove that a defendant is guilty of a crime beyond a reasonable doubt, prosecutors have a much lower standard of proof for a grand jury. After all, the grand jury does not reach a verdict about a defendant's guilt, only whether the case should proceed.

The actual procedure to present a case to the grand jury varies from state to state and on the federal level. In many states, the district attorney may appear before the grand jury and question witnesses and present evidence. In other states, the prosecutor is barred from entering the grand jury room at any time and must wait outside while an investigator or a police officer presents the case to the grand jurors. In still other instances, the grand jurors may initiate their own investigations and obtain legal advice from the district attorney.

The rules of evidence for a grand jury are different than in a criminal trial. In cases presented before the grand jury, the evidentiary rules do not apply. Grand juries may consider evidence that may or may not be ruled unconstitutionally seized as well as consider hearsay testimony. (Hearsay was covered in Chapter 6).

Given this wide latitude in what the grand jury may consider, it may come as a surprise that the grand jury has some limitations, as previously mentioned. The grand jury cannot, for example, decide to investigate anyone for anything. It cannot randomly issue demands for people to appear before it to see if a crime has occurred. It cannot issue orders for individuals who are not suspected of a crime to appear before it in an effort to discover if they have committed some crime. The grand jury must focus on a specific investigation or risk having the indictment quashed.

Another limitation on the grand jury is that the government must present enough evidence to justify a vote of true bill. The state must make a prima facie showing of the defendant's guilt, meaning that the prosecution must present enough evidence to convince the jury that the basic facts of the case are true. The prima facie standard requires the state to present a basic case to the grand jury, showing that the defendant is the person who most likely committed the crime and providing enough evidence to support this contention. Because the grand jury only hears from the state's witnesses (in most cases), it is not difficult for the state to make out a prima facie showing of the defendant's guilt.

The grand jury system has come under criticism over the years by groups claiming that it simply functions as a rubber stamp for the prosecutor. Critics claim that the prosecutor has too much control over the grand jury and can obtain indictments on anyone he or she chooses. However, others push back by pointing out that there are frequent examples of grand juries refusing to indict cases brought before them. If the grand jury were a rubber stamp for the prosecution, then a vote of no bill would never occur. Whether the grand jury still functions as a bulwark between the individual and the vast power of the state or simply as a rubber stamp for the prosecutor probably depends on one's point of view. The truth is probably somewhere between these two opposing views.

ONLY THE STATE'S WITNESSES APPEAR BEFORE THE GRAND JURY

Critics of the grand jury system also claim that the grand jurors only hear the state's version of the case. Defendants do not appear before the grand jury. The defendant has no right to testify before the grand jury or present any favorable evidence. Because the state is not obligated to present the defendant's version of the facts, it is highly likely that, having heard only the state's version of the events, the grand jury will decide that there is sufficient probable cause to continue the case. The defendant's attorney is not permitted to attend or make any statements to the grand jury. In addition, the state is not required to present a balanced account of the case. The U.S. Supreme Court has even held that the prosecution is under no obligation to present evidence that is favorable to the defendant during a grand jury hearing.[8]

Although state law often invests the grand jury with the sole power to drive the investigation, it is not uncommon for a prosecutor to guide a grand jury in such a way that it would appear that the prosecutor is taking the lead. A grand jury is supposed to be independent of the prosecutor's office, but the reality is somewhat different. To maintain the separation between prosecution and grand jury, courts have held that a prosecutor must at least inform the grand jury that the defendant wishes to testify.[9] Prosecutors are barred from giving closing arguments before a grand jury to convince them to rule in a particular way.[10]

When there is a question about improprieties in the way that the grand jury conducted its investigation, the defendant has the burden of showing that the grand jury failed to act properly. This is one of the few instances in which the burden is on the defendant instead of the state to prove wrongdoing.[11] The defendant will face some difficult hurdles to meet this standard. The grand jury meets in secret and no one, other than the grand jurors, is allowed to be present when they vote on a case.

G. SUBPOENA POWERS OF THE GRAND JURY

A grand jury has the power to issue subpoenas. A **subpoena** is a court order requiring a person to appear and testify or for a person to appear with specific evidence, such as documents, records, or other tangible objects. Once issued and

Subpoena
A court order demanding that a person or item be produced to the court at a specific date and time.

served on a person, the subpoena cannot be ignored. A person who fails to abide by a grand jury subpoena is subject to a finding of contempt of the grand jury and may be held in custody until he or she complies or until the grand jury's term ends, whichever comes first. This gives the grand jury great power, but this power is subject to some limitations. The party who receives the subpoena may always contest it on the grounds that the subpoena calls for material that is protected by a witness privilege or by invoking the provisions of the Fifth Amendment to the U.S. Constitution.

OBJECTING TO A GRAND JURY SUBPOENA: WITNESS PRIVILEGE

The law has always protected specific types of communications from being revealed in open court and before a grand jury. Some relationships are protected under law by a privilege. A **privilege** is a legal right that protects a person from being compelled to testify about certain matters. Attorney-client discussions are privileged, which means that most discussions between a client and his or her attorney are protected from disclosure. If an attorney receives a grand jury subpoena and is asked to reveal confidential information shared with him or her by a client, the attorney can refuse to answer the question on the grounds of the attorney-client privilege. There are other privileged communications, including those between:

Privilege
A right to refuse to answer questions and to prevent disclosure of information communicated within a legally recognized confidential relationship.

- Pastor and member of a church
- Doctor and patient
- Psychiatrist and patient
- Spouse and spouse

PLEADING THE "FIFTH AMENDMENT" BEFORE THE GRAND JURY

In addition to refusing to answer a question on the basis of a legally recognized privilege, a person may also raise the Fifth Amendment as a reason not to answer specific questions, in an action known as **pleading the Fifth**. Among other rights, the Fifth Amendment to the U.S. Constitution provides that no none "shall be compelled in any criminal case to be a witness against himself. . . ."[12] The Fifth Amendment guarantees that persons cannot be compelled to give evidence against themselves. This right protects not only defendants, but also witnesses who are called to testify before the grand jury. If a person believes that by answering a specific question, he or she may be admitting to a crime, then the person may state to the grand jury, "I refuse to answer on the grounds that I might incriminate myself." The grand jury is not authorized to override the witness's constitutional rights.

Pleading the Fifth
When a person refuses to answer on the grounds that the answer might tend to incriminate him or her.

MOTION TO QUASH

A motion to **quash** a subpoena is filed with the court and describes the material that has been subject to subpoena and the reason that the party objects to

Quash
Do away with, annul, overthrow, cease.

producing those documents. In such a case, a judge would quash the subpoena and refuse to allow the grand jury to review the materials.

H. IMMUNITY POWERS OF GRAND JURIES

There are times when federal grand juries wish to hear testimony from individuals who might also be facing charges themselves. To avoid the witness invoking his or her Fifth Amendment rights, the only way to get necessary testimony is to grant immunity to the witness. When a person has been granted **immunity**, it means that the testimony given before the grand jury cannot be used as the basis to prosecute that person. In some states, the grand jury is empowered to grant immunity as a way of encouraging a witness to give evidence against others. In other states, the prosecutor must bring a motion before a court to have immunity granted. No matter how it is granted, once immunity is given, the witness may testify about specific criminal activity without fear that the testimony will be taken down and then used against him or her at a later date.

Immunity
A grant to an individual that exempts him or her from being prosecuted based on the testimony that the person gives.

The problem with granting immunity is that if the grand jury confers that benefit on the wrong person, then they are effectively preventing the prosecution from bringing a case. Suppose, for example, that the grand jury is investigating organized crime, and they grant immunity to the person who turns out to be the head of the organization. In that situation, any testimony that the crime boss gave before the grand jury would be immunized, and the state would be unable to use it against him or her.

 AFTER THE GRAND JURY PROCEEDINGS

The role of the grand jury ends with a return of a true bill. The individual grand jurors are not permitted to sit on the jury that determines the defendant's verdict, and they will not have any input on the judicial decision after the case proceeds to trial. Often, the individual grand jurors have no idea how a particular case was resolved.

STATE v. BENT
263 P.3D 903 (N.M.APP., 2011)

CASE EXCERPT

KENNEDY, JUDGE.

Defendant stands convicted of various counts of criminal sexual contact of a minor and contributing to the delinquency of a minor as a result of which he was sentenced to prison. Of the many issues he raises on appeal, one defect in the grand jury proceedings deprives the district court of its jurisdiction and is, accordingly, dispositive of all other issues.

Defendant was indicted by a grand jury, which was convened on October 3, 2007, and whose statutory term would have ended on January 4, 2008, but for an order extending the statutory term issued verbally by a district judge. Defendant's case was presented to the grand jury on May 20, 2008. Since NMSA 1978, Section 31–6–1 (1983) provides that a "grand jury shall serve for a period of no longer than three months," we hold that this statutory term is a mandatory limitation on the grand jury's jurisdiction. An indictment returned after the grand jury's term expires is void ab initio. Therefore, Defendant's motion to quash the indictment should have been granted, as the grand jury was without legal authority to consider his case and return an indictment. As a result, the indictment issued by the grand jury was void, and the district court did not have jurisdiction to proceed with the trial in this case.

I. FACTUAL AND PROCEDURAL BACKGROUND

Defendant, the apparent leader of a religious community in northeastern New Mexico, was charged with various crimes centering around what he maintained were religious practices intended to be cleansing ceremonies. The State argued that such practices amounted to criminal sexual contact of minors and contributing to the minors' delinquency. The case was presented to the grand jury of Union County on May 20, 2008. Defendant was indicted and arraigned on the indictment.

There is no dispute in this case as to the facts pertaining to this issue. The grand jury that heard Defendant's case had been convened on October 3, 2007. An almost indecipherable pleading bearing a file stamp from that date appears to have summoned grand jurors for service on November 12, 2007. At the hearing on Defendant's motion to quash the indictment, the prosecutor stated to the court that the grand jury's term had been verbally extended "sua sponte" by District Judge Sam Sanchez without the entry of any written order. There is no documentary evidence concerning such an extension, nor does the record contain any explanation as to why the extension was made. We are left to rely on assertions by counsel and the district court that it happened. The parties agree that the grand jury only sat twice, once in November, and again on May 20, 2008. The date in May was beyond three months past the date of any previous grand jury activity.

Defendant's motion to quash the indictment was heard on August 12, 2008, alleging that, under NMSA 1978, Section 31–6–3(A) (2003), the grand jury was not selected and seated in accordance with the law. Specifically, Defendant alleged that the grand jury had been convened on October 3, 2007, and had convened again on May 20, 2008, in violation of Section 31–6–1, which mandates a maximum period of grand jury service of "no longer than three months."

The district court responded to the portion of the motion related to the grand jury term by stating that the statute "doesn't provide for any relief if there's a violation." Defendant responded that the remedy for an illegal indictment is that it be "quashed, and a new grand jury seated properly." The court further inquired as to whether a showing of prejudice to Defendant was required before an indictment may be quashed. Defendant responded that the indictment was deficient on its face and should be quashed because the grand jury exceeded its term, the State denied discovery, and the State did not present exculpatory evidence to the grand jury that had been requested by Defendant. The State responded that the district court had already noted that the statute was only advisory in nature. The State then asserted, without citation to the record, that Judge Sanchez had explained to the grand jury that he extended their tenure sua sponte for an additional three months without issuing a written order on the record. The prosecutor, without having them admitted, showed to the court certified pay records indicating the grand jury served on two days.

The State was aware and informed the district court of case law indicating that an indictment handed down by a grand jury after the expiration of its statutory period would in some states render the indictment "void ab initio." The State mentioned that there are such things as "de facto" grand juries that are allowed to proceed past their terms. At the end of the argument, the district court ruled:

> With respect to the first issue, that the grand jury was empaneled or served beyond the three-months time period as provided by Section 31-6-1, it appears that within that section, there is no remedy provided for a jury that serves longer than its term. And at this point in time, there's been no prejudice shown by . . . Defendant with respect to that issue by itself. And so, the motion to quash with respect to that violation or apparent violation of the statute will be dismissed.

II. DISCUSSION

When an indictment is presented by a grand jury in open court, the presumption is that it is legally presented; that the jurors were properly summoned, legally qualified, and competent, and that the required number, at least concurred in the finding. These facts are essential to the lawful finding and presentment.

In this case, the questions are (1) whether the term of the grand jury had expired; and (2) if the term expired, what was the expiration's effect on the validity of the grand jury's indictment of Defendant. Challenges to the validity of the grand jury are specifically limited by statute to three enumerated grounds: (1) the grand jury was not legally constituted, (2) an individual grand juror was not legally qualified to serve as a juror, and (3) an individual juror was a witness against the person indicted. Section 31-6-3. It is to the legal constitution of the grand jury that Defendant directs his appeal.

THE REQUIREMENT OF THE FILING OF AN INDICTMENT OR INFORMATION IS A CONSTITUTIONAL REQUIREMENT UPON WHICH THE JURISDICTION OF THE DISTRICT COURT DEPENDS

"A court obtains no jurisdiction to proceed and render judgment in an action brought without authority." The New Mexico Constitution, Article II, Section 14 and the Fifth Amendment to the United States Constitution require the State to file an indictment or information before commencing a felony prosecution. In such cases, the district court has no jurisdiction to try a defendant without an indictment. The failure of jurisdiction in this regard may not be waived. Nor, in the absence of a proper indictment conferring jurisdiction on the district court, may a defendant be sentenced. Thus, if the indictment in this case is void for having been issued by a grand jury that was not empowered to sit, the indictment cannot confer jurisdiction on the court to consider the case and would require dismissal.

Section 31-6-1 constitutes the statutory framework applicable to grand juries and states: "The district judge may convene one or more grand juries at any time, without regard to court terms. A grand jury shall serve for a period of no longer than three months." The Supreme Court, in adopting the Uniform Jury Instructions, uses this construction. The district court judge swears in a grand jury with an oath, which contains the following instruction: "Your term as members of the grand jury expires _____ unless you are discharged or excused by the court prior to this time." UJI 14–8002 NMRA. Use Note 2 states: "Members of a grand jury may not serve for a period longer than three months." We read the statute and jury instruction as being in parity, establishing and recognizing in turn that a grand jury cannot by law be convened for a period "longer than three months." There is no exception to this mandate contained in the statute, nor provision for an extension of the statutory period. The language is clear and unambiguous.

The clear language of the statute limits the term of a grand jury to not more than three months. There being no statutory language for extending the period of a grand jury's service, we hold that, in the absence of any legislative expression to the contrary, a grand jury may not be empaneled to serve under Section 31–6–1 for a period longer than three months. To ask it to engage in further work on another matter after the end of its three-month term was beyond the power of the prosecutor or district court.

Statutory provisions concerning the nature of what is fundamental in empaneling, convening, and providing structure to the grand jury are generally mandatory, and provisions concerning its administration once empaneled are directory. In *State v. Ulibarri*, 1999–NMCA–142, 8, 15–25, 128 N.M. 546, 994 P.2d 1164, we held that compliance with the statutes, requiring the preparation of a verbatim record of grand jury proceedings, setting the number of concurring jurors necessary to issue an indictment, and requiring instruction of the grand jurors on the record concerning the elements of offenses they were considering, were mandatory preconditions to an indictment. There, statutes mandated the existence of an adequate record of the proceedings and proper instruction on the law and ensured the overall legal adequacy of the process of the grand jury's work as protecting "the very heart of the grand jury system." Id. ¶15. When a person appeared to prosecute before the grand jury who was not properly authorized by statute to do so, we held that the violation of the mandatory statute compelled dismissal of the indictment.

OBTAINING AN INDICTMENT AFTER THE GRAND JURY'S TERM EXPIRES RESULTS IN AN INDICTMENT THAT IS VOID AB INITIO AND CONFERS NO JURISDICTION TO TRY DEFENDANT

Other jurisdictions that set specific terms for their grand juries have held them to have no power after the expiration of their terms. Under federal law, "an indictment returned by a grand jury sitting beyond its legally authorized time is a nullity. The uniform rule is that in the absence of statute to the contrary the grand jury is discharged by operation of law at the end of the term of court for which it was called."

We therefore construe the statute in this case as unambiguously mandatory in limiting the term of grand juries to not more than three months. We are provided with no legislative history, but note that, in most other jurisdictions, the terms of grand juries are limited by statute, and we impute what we know of their intent in limiting grand jury terms to our situation in New Mexico. The policy considerations employed elsewhere are illustrative of why a limited term of service is considered mandatory elsewhere, and why we have come to regard it as such in this case.

Thus, for a grand jury to act without authorization beyond the term during which it is empowered to sit, is fatal to the indictment. An unauthorized extension of the term of a grand jury beyond its term is a defect which "goes to the very existence of the grand jury itself." There is no statutory provision for extending the term of a grand jury in New Mexico contained in Section 31–6–1 or otherwise and, in that absence, we cannot legislate the existence of one. The jurisdiction of any proceeding in which Defendant is charged with a felony depends on the "presentment or indictment of a grand jury." N.M. Const. art. II, §14. Without a properly constituted grand jury returning a valid indictment charging Defendant with a crime, we hold that the district court was without jurisdiction to proceed against him.

III. CONCLUSION

The indictment in this case is void because the group of citizens that issued the purported indictment was not a legally constituted grand jury, as it had finished its term some months before and had ceased to exist. Any extension of its term by the district court was undertaken without statutory authority. Legally speaking, there was no grand jury convened in this case. Therefore, there was no indictment under the law in this case to confer jurisdiction on the district court to try, convict, or sentence Defendant. We note that Defendant's acquittal in a court lacking proper jurisdiction did not violate the constitutional prohibitions against double jeopardy and would not in and of itself bar retrial. Therefore, we remand this case to the district court and instruct that the charges and conviction be set aside without prejudice, the indictment be quashed, and Defendant be discharged from custody.

IT IS SO ORDERED.

WE CONCUR: JONATHAN B. SUTIN and TIMOTHY L. GARCIA, Judges.

CASE QUESTIONS

1 When was the defendant indicted in this case, and why is that date important?
2 How was the grand jury's term supposedly extended?
3 Was the statute in this case "advisory" in nature or mandatory? Explain.
4 What presumption normally greets an indictment?
5 What effect did the filing of this indictment have, considering that the term of the grand jury had expired?

CHAPTER SUMMARY

Once a case is bound over from a preliminary hearing, the prosecutor reviews the case to see if any additional investigation is required and also to determine if the original charge should remain in place or if the charge should be changed to something else. The prosecutor is also free to add any additional charges supported by the evidence and to dismiss the case if the prosecutor does not believe that there is sufficient evidence. Once the prosecutor drafts the indictment, it is presented to the grand jury for consideration.

A grand jury is a group of citizens who meet periodically to consider felony cases. They are not required in all states, but in the ones where they are, the purpose of the grand jury is to decide if there is prima facie evidence that the defendant should be charged with the crime. If the grand jury determines that the case against the defendant should continue, they return a true bill. If not, they dismiss the case with a vote of no bill.

KEY TERMS AND CONCEPTS

Charging decision	Prima facie	Pleading the Fifth
Nolle prosequi	True bill	Quash
Accusation	No bill	Immunity
Information	Subpoena	
Grand jury	Privilege	

END OF CHAPTER EXERCISES

Review Questions

See Appendix A for answers

1 What are some of the issues that a prosecutor considers in making a charging decision?
2 What is the purpose of the grand jury?
3 Explain the historical background of the grand jury.
4 Describe the composition of the grand jury.
5 How and why would a defendant challenge the composition of the grand jury?
6 Does a grand jury reach a verdict? Explain.
7 Explain how a case is usually presented to a grand jury.
8 What is a prima facie showing?
9 Explain the subpoena powers available to the grand jury.
10 How does a prosecutor decide what crime to charge against a defendant?
11 What is a motion to quash?
12 Explain what it means for a witness to invoke the Fifth Amendment before the grand jury.

Web Surfing

Do a search to determine which states use grand juries for felony charges. How many can you locate that follow the grand jury system?

Question for Analysis

Given the criticism leveled at grand juries (that they are simply rubber stamps for prosecutors), does the grand jury still serve an important function?

Hypothetical

Detective Dan has charged John Doe with aggravated assault. The prosecutor, Paula, decides that there is no real evidence that the John Doe committed the crime. Detective Dan insists that the case continue. The detective is well known in the community and has a great deal of political support. What should Paula do?

PRACTICE QUESTIONS FOR TEST REVIEW

See Appendix A for answers

Essay Question

What is the purpose and function of the grand jury?

True–False

1   T   F   The document that charges a person with a felony is an indictment.

2   T   F   Grand juries are used in all states.

3   T   F   When a grand jury decides that a case should continue, it issues a true bill.

Fill in the Blank

1   A(n) ——is filed with the court to describe the material that has been subject to subpoena and the reason that the party objects to producing those documents. In such a case, a judge would refuse to allow the grand jury to review the materials.

2   A right to refuse to answer questions and to prevent disclosure of information communicated within a legally recognized confidential relationship is called ——.

3   —— is a grant to an individual that exempts him or her from being prosecuted based on the testimony that he or she gives.

Multiple Choice

1 The process that a prosecutor goes through to determine what is the appropriate and just charge to bring against a defendant based on the law and the facts in the case.

  A Voluntary encounter.
  B Charging decision.
  C Probable cause.
  D Reasonable suspicion.

2 An order dismissing a criminal charge.

  A Nolle prosequi.
  B Waiver.
  C Sequester.
  D Jurisdiction.

3 A document that charges a defendant with a misdemeanor in most state courts.

  A Attachment.
  B Answer.
  C Assignment.
  D Accusation.

ENDNOTES

1. *In re Grand Jury Appearance Request by Loigman*, 183 N.J. 133, 870 A.2d 249 (2005).
2. *State v. Hall*, 152 N.H. 374, 877 A.2d 222 (2005).
3. *Campbell v. Louisiana*, 118 S.Ct. 1419 (1998).
4. *Taylor v. Louisiana*, 95 S.Ct. 692 (1975); *Castaneda v. Partida*, 97 S.Ct. 1272 (1977).
5. Fed. R. Crim. P. 6(f).
6. *Stinski v. State*, 281 Ga. 783, 642 S.E.2d 1 (2007).
7. *State v. Kuznetsov*, 345 Or. 479, 199 P.3d 311 (2008).
8. *U.S. v. Williams*, 112 S.Ct. 1735 (1992).
9. *Cameron v. State*, 171 P.3d 1154 (Alaska 2007).
10. *State v. Penkaty*, 708 N.W.2d 185 (Minn. 2006).
11. *State v. Francis*, 191 N.J. 571, 926 A.2d 305 (2007).
12. Amendment V, U.S. Constitution.

Fifth Amendment: Interrogation and Confessions

Chapter Objectives

- Define when a person is considered to be under arrest
- Describe the rules governing when a person can be interrogated
- Explain the significance of *Miranda v. Arizona* for interrogations and confessions
- Define when an interrogation must cease
- Describe the rights of suspects during interrogation

Chapter Outline

I. Actions Following Arrest
   A. Interrogation
      Oral and Written Statements
      Miranda
      When Miranda *Does Not Apply*
   B. Invoking the Right to Remain Silent
   C. Requesting an Attorney
   D. Reinitiating Questioning
   E. Procedure after Arrest

II. Special Rules Regarding Interrogation
   A. Instances Where Defendant Will Not Be Interrogated
   B. *Jackson v. Denno* Hearing

ACTIONS FOLLOWING ARREST

Although you might think that police interrogate everyone after arrest, this is not true. There are many suspects who the police have no need to interrogate. A person who has been arrested for driving under the influence, for instance, will usually not be interrogated. There is very little that the defendant could tell police that would be helpful to the prosecution. Why the defendant chose to drink that night or where he or she got drunk is not going to be an issue in the case.

However, there are numerous other circumstances in which the police will want to question a suspect after he or she has been arrested. In that event, police must follow a specific procedure or risk violating the Constitution.

The first step in a valid interrogation of a suspect is that he or she must be read the *Miranda* rights. Television and movies often portray these rights being read to suspects, and most people can actually quote the *Miranda* rights from memory. The reason that the *Miranda* warnings are required is that police must inform the defendant that he or she has the right to remain silent, and if the suspect gives up that right to remain silent, anything that the defendant says can and will be used against him or her during a trial.

A. INTERROGATION

Interrogation
Questioning of a suspect to determine if he or she has committed a crime.

Police usually interrogate a suspect in a room or some other secure location, often private. This setting allows the police officers to concentrate on what the defendant is saying and to design questions that will hopefully keep the defendant talking. There are some common misconceptions about **interrogations**. For one thing, police officers are not allowed to use violence against a suspect. Police cannot deprive a person of sleep or food or bathroom privileges as a means to "break" the suspect. Although police can use loud tones of voice, they are not allowed to use any physical violence. Another common misconception concerns who is present at the interrogation. If the defendant requests that an attorney be present while he or she is being questioned, then the attorney must be present. Police are not allowed to delay or trick the attorney into going to another location and then to question the defendant "while the attorney is on the way." If a defendant invokes his or her right to remain silent, then questioning must cease. If the defendant states that he or she does not wish to answer any more questions, then questioning must cease.

In addition to these misconceptions, there is at least one other that should be addressed. Prosecutors are generally not present during an interrogation. They do not participate in questioning a suspect, and they rarely observe the questioning while it is going on. The reasons for this are very simple: Unlike police officers, prosecutors are not trained to interrogate anyone. Prosecutors have a different skill set. In addition, should the prosecutor actually decide to be present when an interrogation is being conducted and the defendant says something that will be used in evidence against him or her, then the prosecutor may well become a witness. Because an attorney cannot be both a witness and an attorney in a case, most prosecutors opt not to be present when the interrogation occurs.

ORAL AND WRITTEN STATEMENTS

When the police question a suspect, they do so verbally. They often use recording devices, such as audio or video recorders, but even with this technology, officers usually write down the defendant's statement after he or she has made it. Officers have the defendant review the written statement to make sure that it is actually what the defendant said, then ask for the defendant to sign it.

MIRANDA

Once a defendant has been placed under arrest, a number of important constitutional rights are triggered, including the right to have an attorney, the right to a trial by jury, the right to be presumed innocent, the right not to incriminate oneself and the right to remain silent, among others. These are collectively referred to as *Miranda* **rights** based on the case through which they were developed.

> *Miranda* **rights**
> The rights that must be read to a person who has been arrested and then questioned by the police.

Before the decision in *Miranda v. Arizona*, there was an open question about these rights. Police officers acknowledged that suspects had these rights and courts were in agreement that suspects should be made aware of them, but the question was who would advise the defendant. Police officers argued that they were in the worst position to advise the suspect of his or her rights. They are not lawyers and have no pretense to understanding the nuances of constitutional interpretation. In briefs submitted during the appeal in *Miranda v. Arizona*, police agencies urged that the court require that defense attorneys be responsible for advising suspects. However, the court determined that although many defendants might have access to defense counsel, many would not. Nevertheless, the court could be sure that there would be at least two people present in every interrogation: the police officer and the suspect. Because of this certainty, the U.S. Supreme Court ruled that police officers were responsible for advising suspects of their *Miranda* rights before they began any post-arrest questioning. One version of the *Miranda* rights is provided in Figure 9-1.

Miranda v. Arizona[1] was a highly controversial case when it was first decided, but it did put an end to speculation about when a suspect should be advised of his or her constitutional rights and who should do the advising. As anyone who watches television or movie legal dramas knows, police officers are responsible for advising suspects, and they must be advised before they are interrogated.

You have the right to remain silent. If you give up this right to remain silent, anything you say can and will be used against you at trial. You have the right to an attorney during any questioning. If you cannot afford an attorney, one will be appointed to represent you. Do you understand these rights?

FIGURE 9-1

The *Miranda* Rights Warning

Background on the Miranda *Decision.* Ernesto Miranda was arrested for the kidnapping and rape of a young woman. After his arrest, he was interrogated by police officers for several hours and eventually confessed to the crime. The *Miranda* decision came about when Miranda's attorney appealed his conviction on the basis that his confession should not have been used in his trial because he had never been informed of his rights under the law. The U.S. Supreme Court consolidated Miranda's case with several others in which the same issue was raised and then reached its famous decision. Because Miranda's name was first on the Court's opinion, the ruling became known as the *Miranda* decision, and the requirements imposed by the Court on police became known as *Miranda* warnings.

Under the ruling, the prosecution may not use any statement that was made by the defendant until the state has proven that the defendant knew all of his or her constitutional rights, had the ability to invoke them, then waived them and gave a statement to police. Among these rights, police must specifically tell a suspect that the Fifth Amendment provides the right to remain silent and not incriminate oneself, and if a person waives that right, any statement that he or she makes may be used against that person during the trial to prove that he or she committed the crime. Before the prosecution can introduce the defendant's confession at trial, the prosecutor must call police witnesses to testify that they read the defendant his or her rights, that he or she appeared to understand them, that he or she was not coerced or promised anything to waive those rights, and that he or she gave a statement after waiving those constitutional rights.

The *Miranda* decision gives little latitude to police officers. The rights must be read, even if the suspect is an attorney, a police officer, or a judge. It does not matter how many times the suspect has been arrested before; he or she must be read the rights again before being questioned in the present case. The only variation that the Court allows is that, as long as the substance of the rights is conveyed to the suspect, it does not matter in what order they are read to him or her.[2]

WHEN *MIRANDA* DOES NOT APPLY

Miranda rights must be read to a suspect who is taken into custody or arrested, if he or she is going to be questioned. An arrest is not unconstitutional if the police fail to read a suspect his or her *Miranda* rights. A suspect must be read the rights before being questioned, but there are circumstances, as noted previously, in which the police have no intention of questioning a defendant and therefore do not read the suspect *Miranda* warnings. There is also no requirement that the police must read a person the *Miranda* warnings before he or she is arrested. *Miranda* applies only to post-arrest questioning and interrogation. One might be tempted to think that the police would wish to question everyone who they arrest, but there are numerous circumstances when such questioning never occurs.

There are also other circumstances in which the *Miranda* rights warnings are not required:

- Background or routine police questioning
- Exigent circumstances

■ Voluntary statements
■ Traffic stops

Background or Routine Police Questioning. When police arrive at the scene of a crime, they will likely ask some typical questions: What happened? Who did it? Where is the person who did the crime? What is the relationship of the people to one another, the victim and the defendant? In these situations, the police are not required to preface their questions with the *Miranda* warnings. When they focus their attention on a specific suspect and begin to ask questions that could incriminate him or her, they have moved beyond background or routine questioning, and *Miranda* rights apply. However, until that time, officers may question people at the scene without any need to Mirandize everyone they meet.

Exigent Circumstances. The U.S. Supreme Court has ruled that *Miranda* warnings are not required in exigent circumstances. An **exigent circumstance** is a situation that is inherently dangerous to people or evidence. In an emergency situation, officers are permitted to ask questions that will help them prevent harm to others or prevent evidence from being destroyed. There is no requirement to read the *Miranda* warnings in this situation. Of course, once the situation has been resolved and there is no longer an emergency, the *Miranda* warning requirement resurfaces.

Exigent circumstance
An emergency situation requiring aid or immediate action.

Voluntary Statements. If a suspect voluntarily agrees to speak with police, then *Miranda* does not apply. By volunteering, the suspect is waiving his or her constitutional rights—the very rights spelled out in the *Miranda* warnings. A suspect always has the right to waive the application of those rights to his or her case and freely discuss it with the police. However, law enforcement officers are not permitted to use subterfuge to trick the defendant into giving a "voluntary" statement. For instance, police cannot address one another within earshot of the suspect and say that the suspect is hiding behind his rights or that a "real man would own up to what he had done." Unfortunately, this rule is routinely and almost universally abused by television detectives.

When It Is Lawful to Use Trickery. We have just established that law enforcement cannot use trickery or deceit to make a suspect give up his or her constitutional rights. However, that prohibition does not extend to other areas. Police may lie to a defendant, so long as the lie is not designed to overcome any constitutional protections. Law enforcement might lie to a suspect and tell him or her that a witness saw the suspect or that they have evidence tying him to the scene when they actually do not. Trickery and deception are not commonplace during most interrogations because of the difficulties involved in maintaining the deception. Lies often lead to other lies. If the defendant knows that he wore gloves during the crime and the detectives claim that they recovered his fingerprints from the scene, the defendant will realize that they are lying and may question just how much evidence they actually have that incriminates him. In cases where police use trickery, courts always examine the officers' actions closely, and that is yet another reason to avoid wandering into this legal minefield.

Traffic Stops. When police officers pull over automobile drivers for routine infractions, such as speeding or improper passing, this stop is not considered to be an arrest, and therefore *Miranda* warnings are not required.[3] However, *Miranda* warnings would apply if the police officer were to remove the driver from his or her automobile and place the driver under arrest or transport the driver back to police headquarters for questioning.[4]

B. INVOKING THE RIGHT TO REMAIN SILENT

A criminal suspect has an absolute right to remain silent. When a defendant states that he or she has nothing to say, police are not permitted to force the suspect to make incriminating statements. A statement obtained in a coercive way is not admissible at trial. When the suspect states that he or she does not wish to say anything until he or she speaks with an attorney, questioning must also stop at that point. Police officers are not allowed to try to talk the suspect out of his or her need for an attorney or to continue questioning him or her until that attorney arrives. The Supreme Court has held, however, that a defendant must tell the police that he or she intends to remain silent.[5] The suspect cannot simply refuse to answer and have the police infer that he or she intends to remain silent.

C. REQUESTING AN ATTORNEY

During questioning, the suspect has the right to request an attorney. Police officers are not allowed to try to talk the defendant out of that right to an attorney or to state that only someone who was guilty would want an attorney. However, if the suspect's request for an attorney is vague, police may continue to question him or her until he or she either refuses to answer any more questions or makes an unequivocal request for an attorney. Consider Scenarios 9-1 and 9-2.

SCENARIO 9-1	UNEQUIVOCAL REQUEST FOR AN ATTORNEY (1)

Tad is being questioned by the police in connection with a series of burglaries. During the questioning, Tad says, "I wonder if I should to talk to my lawyer."

The officer responds that he certainly has that right, but they would like to get some more information from him to clear up the charges. Is any continued questioning by the police constitutional?

Answer: Yes. Because the defendant did not give an unequivocal request for an attorney, questioning can continue.

UNEQUIVOCAL REQUEST FOR AN ATTORNEY (2)

It's about an hour later, and Tad is still being questioned.

The police officer asks Tad, "Why did you commit these burglaries? Did you need the money?"

Tad responds, "I want my lawyer."

Can police continue questioning Tad?

Answer: No. Tad's request is now definitely unequivocal, and all questioning must cease until Tad's attorney arrives.

In most situations, when an attorney arrives at the interrogation, he or she usually advises the suspect to stop answering any questions and to end the interview.

D. REINITIATING QUESTIONING

A question often arises during the course of repeated interrogations of a suspect: How long are the *Miranda* rights "good" for? Put another way, is it sufficient to read the suspect his or her *Miranda* rights once and then never read them again? Do the rights eventually expire? When police officers initially question a suspect and read that suspect the *Miranda* warnings, must they be read every time that they question the suspect after that?

Police officers are not required to re-Mirandize a suspect each and every time that they question him or her. However, once the suspect has invoked the right to remain silent, the situation changes. In one case, *Edwards v. Arizona,*[6] a suspect (Edwards) was arrested on burglary and murder charges. During questioning, Edwards said that he wanted to consult with an attorney before making any further statements. The police officers stopped the interview and returned Edwards to his cell. At this point, the officers had acted in accordance with *Miranda*. However, the following day, two other police officers appeared at the jail and asked to see Edwards. He refused to speak with the officers but was told by a guard that he must. He was read his *Miranda* rights again, and during this interrogation made incriminating statements that were later used against him at trial. The U.S. Supreme Court held that the use of his statement violated his right to have an attorney present during his questioning. Edwards, according to the Court, had made an unequivocal request for an attorney. His questioning the next day did not waive that right.

A suspect must knowingly and intelligently relinquish his or her rights. The U.S. Supreme Court has placed the burden for showing compliance with its decisions squarely on the shoulders of the state. Therefore, the state must show that the defendant voluntarily waived his or her rights before the statement can be read to the jury. When police reinitiate questioning of a suspect, they may rely on the fact that they Mirandized the suspect the first time; however, if any appreciable period of time has passed between the first questioning and the second, police must read the suspect his or her *Miranda* rights again. Courts have been vague on just how long this appreciable period is. The safest course for a police officer to follow when there is any doubt about whether the first reading of *Miranda* rights was sufficient is to Mirandize the suspect again.

E. PROCEDURE AFTER ARREST

Once a person is placed under arrest, he or she is then transported to the local detention facility where the typical book-in procedures take place. The person will be fingerprinted, have all belongings taken away and stored for safekeeping, issued a jail uniform with sandals, and then assigned to a cell. However, there are numerous instances in which this procedure is not followed. For instance, suppose that a suspect has been arrested on a misdemeanor count. Many jail facilities post bond amounts for specific types of offenses. For example, a first-offense theft by shoplifting might carry a bond of $500. If the defendant can pay the bond, then he or she will be released on the bond after being fingerprinted. If the defendant cannot make bond, then he or she will be held at the local detention facility until the initial appearance.

SPECIAL RULES REGARDING INTERROGATION

We tend to think that everyone who is arrested is immediately interrogated by the police. However, this is not the case. There are numerous instances in which a defendant will not be interrogated.

A. INSTANCES WHERE DEFENDANT WILL NOT BE INTERROGATED

Before an interrogation can be carried out, police must determine that the defendant is not under the influence of drugs or alcohol, which would affect the accuracy, quality, and veracity of his or her statements. Consider Scenario 9-3.

SCENARIO 9-3   UNDER THE INFLUENCE

Sally has been arrested for driving under the influence of alcohol. She is very intoxicated, as a breath test has confirmed. Can or should the police interrogate Sally?

Answer: No. First of all, police will not need to question Sally. Why should they? She has been arrested for operating a motor vehicle under the influence. What additional questions do they need to ask? Even if they did, Sally is demonstrably acting under the influence of alcohol. If the police wished to question her, then they would have to wait until she sobered up.

However, when police do wish to interrogate someone who has been arrested, there are strict rules that they must follow. The most obvious—and most famous—is administering the *Miranda* warnings. There are other protocols that the police and prosecution must establish before a defendant's statement can be admitted during a trial. A successful interrogation is based on first ensuring that the defendant understands his or her rights and then he or she knowingly waives them before making a statement. Among the factors that the state must show before a defendant's confession can be admitted during the trial are that the defendant:

- Was advised of his or her *Miranda* rights
- Was able to ask questions and verbalize questions and responses
- Demonstrated his or her ability to understand the nature of the rights
- Voluntarily waived his or her right to remain silent and to speak with an attorney
- Was not promised a reward or benefit
- Was not threatened into making a statement[7]

In addition to these elements, courts will also focus on "the totality of all the surrounding circumstances, including the accused's characteristics, the conditions of interrogation, and the conduct of law enforcement officials" before ruling that a confession was given voluntarily and knowingly.[8] Another factor was whether the defendant was hungry or tired. If the defendant requests food, he or she should be fed. If the defendant states that he or she is too tired to continue, the police should discontinue questioning until he or she has slept.[9] The government always bears the burden of showing that all of these safeguards were put in place and that the defendant's statement was voluntary.[10]

B. *JACKSON v. DENNO* HEARING

As we will see in Chapter 12, one way for the defense to challenge the admissibility of a defendant's statement is by bringing a motion to suppress. Sometimes in what is referred to as a **Jackson v. Denno hearing**, the defense is permitted to challenge the use of the defendant's confession during the trial based on the fact that it was not voluntarily given or that it was the product of coercion, promises, or other improper procedures.[11]

Jackson v. Denno **hearing**
A pretrial hearing where the government must show that the defendant gave a knowing, voluntary statement after being advised of his or her rights and that he or she was not compelled to do so by promises, threats, intimidation, or other means.

CASE EXCERPT

STATE v. PERRY

——— WA. ——— (2020) NO. 35476-8-III

UNPUBLISHED OPINION

SIDDOWAY, J.

Donna Perry appeals her convictions for three counts of first-degree premeditated murder, with the aggravating circumstance in each case that the murder was part of a common scheme or plan involving more than one victim. We affirm the convictions but remand with directions to strike a criminal filing fee from Perry's judgment and sentence.

FACTS AND PROCEDURAL BACKGROUND

Between February and May 1990, Yolanda Sapp, Nickie Lowe, and Kathleen Brisbois were murdered. All worked as prostitutes, and all were found dead along the Spokane River with gunshot wounds, the first two within the Spokane City limits and the third in what was then an unincorporated part of the county. The three women knew each other. The Spokane Police Department and the Spokane County Sheriff's Office came to believe these were serial murders, because of the women's similar lives, the perpetrator's use of a small caliber firearm, and the bodies' location near the river. The departments conducted a joint investigation. Many suspects were considered, including Robert Yates and, for a brief time, the Green River killer, but evidence did not support charges against any suspect. In the mid-1990s the investigations into the murders went cold.

Following improvements in DNA analysis, law enforcement renewed review of evidence of the murders and in 2008 submitted several items of evidence for DNA testing. A forensic scientist was able to develop a male DNA profile from blood found under one of Ms. Brisbois's fingernails and entered it into the Combined DNA Index System (CODIS) in 2009. There was no immediate hit.

Several years later, however, CODIS returned a potential hit for the blood sample: Douglas Perry, also known as Donna Perry. The gender disparity in the names was later explained by the fact that in 2000, Douglas Perry underwent gender reassignment surgery in Thailand and became Donna Perry. Perry had not previously been identified as a suspect in the murders.

Investigation into Perry's background revealed prior associations with prostitutes in Spokane and prior contacts with law enforcement. He could be placed in the Spokane area in 1990 based on a police report documenting contact with Perry for soliciting a prostitute and a report from NCIC3 that the Spokane Police Department ran his name in February 1990.

The investigation revealed that in 1994, law enforcement obtained a search warrant to search Perry's house on East Dalton Avenue in Spokane for weapons, which he could not legally possess. A search conducted with the Bureau of Alcohol, Tobacco, Firearms and Explosives (ATF) produced 33 firearms and a substantial amount of ammunition, all of which was confiscated. During the search, ATF Agent Lance Hart spoke with Perry, whom he described as extremely knowledgeable about firearms and very protective of the ones in his possession. Asked by Hart how he obtained money to purchase firearms, Perry responded that he was a woman trapped inside a man's body, and made money by dressing up as a woman and engaging in prostitution. Among firearms confiscated from Perry's house were three that used .22 caliber bullets, the type that had been recovered from the bodies of Ms. Lowe and Ms. Brisbois. One was a 10/22 Ruger rifle. Police later learned that Perry had purchased two .22 caliber pistols in the 1970s that were not confiscated by ATF in 1994, one being an Iver Johnson pistol. A firearm expert later determined that the bullets and fragments recovered from the bodies of Ms. Lowe and Ms. Brisbois could have been fired by a 10/22 Ruger rifle or an Iver Johnson pistol.

It was also determined that in 1998, a prostitute reported her concern to a police officer about a "date" she had just concluded at Perry's home on East Empire Avenue in Spokane that she would later describe as "the creepiest thing I've ever been through in my life." She described "mannequins and crossbows and weapons and things everywhere in his house, everywhere." While voicing her concern to the officer, Perry drove by and the prostitute pointed him out. The police officer stopped Perry's car and in patting him down, located two knives and a stun gun. In a search of the car to which Perry consented, the officer found papers explaining how to obtain gender reassignment surgery. The officer took no action against Perry other than the stop and search.

In November 2012, county Sheriff's Detective James Dresback and Spokane Police Detective Mark Burbridge arranged to visit Perry, who was being held as a federal inmate at the Spokane County Jail. They were armed with a search warrant for Perry's DNA. At the outset of the interview, the detectives told Perry they were working on old cases, wanted to see if Perry could help them, and needed to first advise her of her rights. Perry stated "I should probably have an attorney here if you're going to question me about something."

Detective Dresback proceeded to read Perry her *Miranda* rights and then asked if she wanted to answer questions. Perry again told the detectives "I think I should have a lawyer here if you're going to ask questions." Detective Dresback, who had been reading the rights from a card, pointed out to Perry that he had noted her response on the card, and Perry signed the card.

Detective Dresback then stated, "Okay, we have another order of business we have to take care of today," and told Perry he had a search warrant to obtain a sample of her DNA. When Perry asked, "In conjunction with what?" the detective answered that it was "in conjunction with some old cases that we're investigating." When Perry asked what the detectives meant by "old cases" the following exchange occurred:

Dresback: Well, I want to make sure that you want to talk to me about this, okay?

Perry: Well, I should have a lawyer here if you're going to take DNA and all of this.

Burbridge: Your lawyer doesn't get to be here while we serve the search warrant.

Perry asked why the detectives wanted her DNA and Detective Burbridge responded that they had a search warrant for first degree murder, and that they believed Perry had information about the murder. When Perry asked additional questions Detective Burbridge told Perry:

Burbridge: And again, you wanted a lawyer so I can't talk to you. If you want to talk to us then. . . .

Perry: Yeah, I need a lawyer for something like this.

Burbridge: . . . then you need to tell me that.

Perry then repeated, "Yeah, I think I better have a lawyer. This is crazy."

Perry was provided with the search warrant but said she couldn't read it without glasses, so Detective Dresback read it to her. He then instructed her how to swab her cheek to provide samples. Handing the swabs back to the detective, Perry asked, "Am

I being accused of murder or something?" and Detective Dresback responded that she was the prime suspect in multiple murders. After Perry stated that she did not understand what was going on, the following exchange occurred:

Burbridge: Again, Donna. We can't talk to you. You've asked for a lawyer. Unless you tell us you want to sit down and talk.

Dresback: And you do understand that the rights of you having an attorney and your right to remain silent, these are your rights. All they do is restrict me, they don't restrict you in any way. You have the right to talk and you have the right to not talk, okay? So, I'm absolutely going to honor your right to an attorney at this time. Which is why we're not really, freely, discussing the whole thing with ya. Um, but it is your right.

Detective Dresback then said that he was going to tape up the box with the DNA samples and would be back with a copy of a return for Perry.

The detectives left the room, returning five minutes later. After being given her copy of the search warrant, Perry told the detectives "Tell me what's going on. I don't understand a thing. I need a lawyer or somebody to explain what actually is going on." The detectives gave her a brief description of the crimes and the CODIS hit that led them to her. Perry asked additional questions and expressed that she was paranoid and "in a total panic mode" and had "a million questions." Detective Dresback responded:

Dresback: Well, I have about a thousand. So, you've got more than me. And a . . . and like I said before, it's your right if you at any time you decide that you want to discuss this, you have the right to do that. But until that happens, I'm not too terribly comfortable asking you anything about it, to clarify things. So, that's where we're at. Do you have any other questions for me?

Perry: What are the names of these people?

Burbridge: I'm not comfortable going down that road.

Dresback: Not yet.

Perry expressed again how upset she was about being a suspect. The detectives said they were going to give her time to finish the soda they had provided and would be back to take her back to the jail.

Detective Dresback returned six minutes later and gave Perry his business card, telling her to let him know if she decided she wanted to talk. Perry reiterated how upset she was, including to ask for the detective's pistol and one round so that she could "finish it," but then said, "Let's talk. Let's sit down and work this out of my head." Detective Burbridge entered the room and Detective Dresback said that before they could talk, he needed to reread her rights. He reread Perry her rights and asked her if she understood them, to which she answered, "Yes." Asked if she wanted to answer his questions, Perry said, "I'll try to answer your questions." Told that the detective needed her signature on his advice of rights card, Perry signed it.

During the questioning that followed, Perry told the detectives "I did pick up some prostitutes, yes. But I always let them out and they were alive and well when I let them out."

Notwithstanding Perry's denials, Detective Burbridge suggested that something made Perry stop killing, and the following exchange occurred:

Burbridge: Here's . . . here's the real thing the question to me is, people that kill people, multiple people over periods of time, they generally keep going once it starts.

Perry: Yeah.

Burbridge: So the question to me is [sic] a law enforcement officer who's studied this in depth?

Perry: Um hm.

Burbridge: What made Donna stop? So then I asked myself. . . .

Perry: Douglas didn't stop. Donna stopped it. The gender change operation.

Burbridge: Do you think that's what stopped it?

Perry: I have . . . yeah . . . I'm convinced of it.

Dresback: I hadn't thought of that. That's a good question.

Burbridge: Well, here's . . . here's another one I'm wondering too, is where is she?

Dresback: There's no more testosterone to fuel the anger.

Shortly thereafter, as the detectives continued to question Perry as if she had committed the murders, she stated:

Perry: I'm not going to admit I killed anybody. I didn't. Donna has killed nobody.

Burbridge: Doug did?

Perry: I don't know if Doug did or not. It's 20 years ago and I have no idea whether he did or didn't.

While Perry denied many times in the remainder of the interview that Doug had murdered any of the victims, she later repeated that she "got rid of violence with the sex change operation."

The DNA sample obtained from Perry was analyzed by the Washington State Patrol Crime Laboratory and was compared with other evidence obtained from the murder victims and their surroundings. It proved to be a definitive match to the blood found under Ms. Brisbois's fingernail; a match, but weaker, to a floral blanket found near Ms. Sapp's body; and a weak match to a vaginal swab of Ms. Brisbois.

The State charged Perry with three counts of premeditated first degree murder, with the aggravating circumstance that the murder was part of a common scheme or plan involving more than one victim. When officers traveled to Texas to bring Perry to Spokane for trial, Perry reportedly told officers during the flight, "I'm never going to get out of this," "instead of jail, I hope they send me to Eastern State Hospital," "I'm not violent now," and that the plane ride would be "the last time she would be outside of concrete walls." RP at 1562-63, 1569.

In addition to the foregoing matters, evidence at trial included the following evidence specific to the three victims:

As to Yolanda Sapp, evidence that her body, naked except for some jewelry, was found on the morning of February 22, 1990, on the north Spokane River bank. A forensic expert testified to a common profile between Perry's DNA and DNA found on the floral blanket found near Ms. Sapp's body and that "one in 3300 men at most, probably less than that, would also share that profile." RP at 1666. Ms. Sapp had scrapes on her forehead and on one of her armpits, and three gunshot wounds to her back from small caliber bullets. The medical examiner concluded that the bullets entered Ms. Sapp's back and exited through her front side. They were not recovered.

As to Nickie Lowe, evidence that her body was found on the morning of March 25, 1990, under the Greene Street Bridge. Her body was positioned with her legs up on the guardrail and her back on the ground. Her pants had been pulled down to her knees and her top had been pulled up, exposing her genital area and her trunk up to a breast. She had marks and bruising on her backside suggesting that she had been dragged or pulled to the guardrail. She had a single gunshot wound to her chest; the bullet, which was recovered, was a .22 caliber bullet. The medical examiner concluded from tears and bloodstains on Ms. Lowe's clothing that she was normally clothed when she was shot, while the markings and bruising on her body occurred after her pants had been pulled down and her top pulled up.

A wallet containing Ms. Lowe's driver's license was reported found in a dumpster on Sprague Avenue. Police searched the dumpster and retained several items for testing. A fingerprint lifted from a tube of lubricating jelly found in the dumpster was a match for Perry's fingerprint.

As to Kathleen Brisbois, evidence that her body was found in the late afternoon on May 15, four or five feet down an embankment by the river. A forensic expert testified to the definitive match of Perry's DNA to DNA from the blood found under Ms. Brisbois's fingernail and the weaker match of his DNA to DNA from her vaginal swab. Ms. Brisbois's autopsy revealed that she had been struck at least eight times in the head with a blunt object and sustained three gunshot wounds to her head, chest, and right shoulder area, all inflicted from close range.

At the conclusion of the several week trial, the jury found Perry guilty as charged, answering yes to special verdict forms asking if the murders had been part of a common scheme or plan. The trial court sentenced Perry to three life sentences, to be served consecutively, without the possibility of parole or early release. It imposed $710 in legal financial obligations (LFOs) consisting of the $500 crime victim assessment fee, the $100 DNA collection fee, and the $110 criminal filing fee in effect when the crimes were committed. Additional factual and procedural background is provided in connection with specific assignments of error.

ANALYSIS

Perry assigns error to (1) the trial court's ruling that Perry's statements made during the interview by Detectives Dresback and Burbridge were admissible at trial,

I. THE TRIAL COURT PROPERLY ADMITTED PERRY'S STATEMENTS FROM THE NOVEMBER 2012 INTERVIEW

Perry contends that the trial court improperly admitted her statements made during the interview by Detectives Dresback and Burbridge because she had unequivocally invoked her right to counsel. A suspect's decision to cut off questioning does not raise a presumption that she is unable to proceed without a lawyer's advice, but an unequivocal request for a lawyer does. *Arizona v. Roberson*, 486 U.S. 675, 683, 108 S. Ct. 2093, 100 L. Ed. 2d 704 (1988). The presumption raised by a suspect's request for a lawyer is that she considers herself unable to deal with the pressures of custodial interrogation without legal assistance. Id. After a request for a lawyer, "reinterrogation may only occur if 'the accused himself initiates further communication, exchanges, or conversations with the police.'" Id. at 680-81 (quoting *Edwards v. Arizona*, 451 U.S. 477, 485, 101 S. Ct. 1880, 68 L. Ed. 2d 378 (1981)).

The State argues that Perry's requests for a lawyer were equivocal, and alternatively that she initiated further conversation about the investigation. The trial court, which made a record of the fact that it watched the entire videotaped interview of Perry, appears to have found her statements admissible because she initiated the further conversation about the investigation. Among the court's findings of fact were the following:

7   Initially during the November 15, 2012 interview, Ms. Perry stated that she thought she should consult with an attorney.

8   The detectives did not question Ms. Perry, given her request. The detectives did retrieve her DNA pursuant to a search warrant previously authorized.

9   Ms. Perry continued to ask questions of the detectives. The detectives advised that they couldn't speak with her regarding her concerns because she had wanted a lawyer. The detectives provided Ms. Perry with their business card if she wanted to contact them in the future.

10 Upon telling Ms. Perry that she would be transported back to the jail, Ms. Perry stated "No. You don't need to do that. I want to talk to you, let's talk."

11 The detectives then readvised Ms. Perry of her rights, which she again stated she understood, and agreed to waive.

12 The detectives did not force or coerce the conversation on November 15, 2012. They remained professional for the entirety of the interview. The detectives did not raise their voices or make any sort of threats during the interview.

Clerk's Papers (CP) at 205. The trial court concluded "Ms. Perry was properly advised of her rights and . . . freely and voluntarily waived those rights and chose to speak with law enforcement" during the interview. CP at 206.

Perry does not assign error to any of the trial court's findings of fact. She nonetheless argues on appeal that the detectives' conduct was manipulative and their interrogation never ceased, because "interrogation" includes words or actions that are reasonably likely to elicit an incriminating response. But one of the findings to which no error is assigned, and that is a verity on appeal, is that "the detectives did not question Ms. Perry, given her request to consult with an attorney." CP at 205. And the detectives' statements to Perry before she said she wished to talk did not elicit incriminating statements. While the information they provided piqued Perry's curiosity to the point that she wanted to talk, that does not violate the Fifth Amendment right of a suspect whose decision to answer questions is voluntary. Perry does not assign error to the trial court's finding that the detectives did not force or coerce the conversation.

In *Roberson*, the Supreme Court states, "As we have made clear, any further communication, exchanges, or conversations with the police that the suspect himself initiates, are perfectly valid." 486 U.S. at 687. The trial court's findings support its conclusion that Perry's statements were admissible.

The convictions are affirmed and the case is remanded with directions to strike the criminal filing fee from the judgment and sentence.

CASE QUESTIONS

1   Although the murders in this case occurred in 1990, police did not arrest the suspect until 2012. Why was there such a substantial delay?

2   After the detective read the suspect her *Miranda* rights, did she request an attorney?

3   Did the appellate court view the defendant's statement as an unequivocal request for an attorney?

4   What is the rule about defendants who cut off questioning versus those who make an unequivocal request for an attorney?

CHAPTER SUMMARY

This chapter focused on the events that occur after arrest, specifically questioning and interrogation of the suspect. A post-arrest interrogation carries with it many constitutional questions. Before the police can question the suspect, they must first determine if he or she has the ability to answer questions. Obviously intoxicated individuals will not be questioned until they have sobered up. Before the questioning can begin, police must read the suspects their *Miranda* rights and ensure that they understand these rights. *Miranda* rights must be read to all suspects the police intend to question, even if they are police officers or attorneys.

There are times when officers can ask questions and *Miranda* rights do not apply. *Miranda* rights are not required for routine or background questions of a suspect. They are also not required in emergency (exigent) circumstances. Police are not required to give *Miranda* warnings before a suspect gives a voluntary statement; they are also not required to give *Miranda* warnings at traffic stops. When a person requests an attorney or invokes his or her right to remain silent, then all police questioning must stop. To show that the police complied with constitutional procedures, the state will present evidence in a *Jackson v. Denno* hearing that the defendant was advised of his or her rights, that he or she was not promised or threatened, and that he or she gave a knowingly and voluntary waiver of his or her *Miranda* rights before giving a confession.

KEY TERMS AND CONCEPTS

Interrogation   Exigent circumstance
Miranda rights   *Jackson v. Denno* hearing

END OF CHAPTER EXERCISES

Review Questions

See Appendix A for answers

1 What is the first thing that a police officer must do before asking the defendant questions about the crime?
2 Can police deprive the defendant of sleep or food in an effort to break his or her will?
3 If the suspect makes an unequivocal request for an attorney, what must happen?
4 The text states that prosecutors are usually not present during an interrogation. Why?

5   Summarize the *Miranda* rights that must be read to a suspect before being questioned about a crime.

6   Why was the *Miranda* decision so controversial when it was announced?

7   How did the *Miranda* case develop?

8   List and explain some situations where the *Miranda* rights do not apply.

9   What are exigent circumstances?

10 Can the police lie to a suspect during an interrogation? If so, what lies are they not allowed to say?

11 Does a suspect have to speak to invoke his or her right to remain silent? Explain.

12 What is a *Jackson v. Denno* hearing?

Web Surfing

1   Do an Internet search with the search phrase, "requesting an attorney." How much information can you locate that seems questionable? Are there sites that provide correct information? If so, what are they?

2   Visit the Legal Information Institute (www.law.cornell.edu/) and do a search for *Jackson v. Denno* hearings. What does the site have to say about who has the burden of bringing the motion and who has the burden of proving that the state's questioning was done correctly?

Question for Analysis

Occasionally, there are movements to do away with the *Miranda* rights. Several years ago, legislation was proposed in the U.S. Congress to overturn the *Miranda* decision. Is that a good idea? Explain your answer.

Hypotheticals

1   Carl has been arrested for armed robbery. Before his questioning at police headquarters begins, Detective Carol reads Carl the *Miranda* warnings. Carl says that he understands and that he wants to talk. However, a few minutes into the questioning, Carl says, "I'm wondering if maybe I need an attorney." Is Detective Carol obligated to stop the questioning?

2   Same facts as the preceding hypothetical, however after several minutes of questioning, Carl says, "I want my lawyer. I'm not answering anything else." Is there a different resolution to this situation than the previous hypothetical? Why?

PRACTICE QUESTIONS FOR TEST REVIEW

See Appendix A for answers

Essay Question

What are the *Miranda* rights and why are they important?

True-False

1   **T   F**   Prosecutors are usually present during an interrogation.

2   **T   F**   *Miranda* warnings are required at traffic stops.

3   **T   F**   *Miranda* warnings are required during exigent circumstances.

Fill in the Blank

1   An ——— is an emergency situation that poses a threat to persons or to evidence.

2   Questioning of a suspect to determine if he or she has committed a crime is called ———.

3   The rights that must be read to a person who has been arrested and then questioned by the police are known as ———.

Multiple Choice

1   Who is responsible for reading a suspect his or her *Miranda* rights?

   A   The magistrate.
   B   The defense attorney.
   C   The police officer.
   D   None of the above.

2   A pretrial hearing where the government must show that the defendant gave a knowing, voluntary statement after being advised of his or her rights and that he or she was not compelled to do so by promises, threats, intimidation, or other means.

   A   *Jackson v. Denno* hearing.
   B   *Miranda* hearing.
   C   Ex post facto hearing.
   D   Motion in opposition.

3   Meryl is being questioned by the police. She states, "I refuse to answer any more questions until my attorney is present." What happens next?

    A   The police can talk Meryl out of her request.

    B   The police officer says, "Okay, but you have to talk with us until she gets here."

    C   The police officer says, "Okay, but what kind of a person would hide behind a lawyer?"

    D   The police stop asking questions and leave.

ENDNOTES

1. 384 U.S. 436, 86 S.Ct. 1602, 16 L.Ed.2d 694 (1966).
2. *Florida v. Powell*, 559. U.S. 722 (2010).
3. *Pennsylvania v. Bruder*, 488 U.S. 292 (1990).
4. *Berkemer v. McCarty*, 103 S.Ct. 3138 (1984).
5. *Berghuis v. Thompkins*, 560 U.S. 370 (2010).
6. 451 U.S. 477 (1981).
7. *Jackson v. Denno*, 378 U.S. 368, 376 (1964).
8. *United States v. Anderson*, 929 F.2d 96, 99 (2d Cir. 1991).
9. *United States v. Haak*, 884 F.3d 400, 415-16 (2d Cir. 2018).
10. *Lego v. Twomey*, 404 U.S. 477 (1972).
11. *Jackson v. Denno*, 378 U.S. 368, 376 (1964).

Sixth Amendment: Right to Trial and Associated Rights

Chapter Objectives

- Describe when a defendant is entitled to an attorney
- Explain the presumption of innocence
- Explain the significance of the *Gideon v. Wainwright* case
- Describe the rights that a defendant has in a criminal trial
- Describe the defendant's right to present evidence

Chapter Outline

I. The Defendant's Rights Prior to Trial
   A. The Right to an Attorney
      Hiring an Attorney
      Gideon v. Wainwright
      Court-Appointed Attorney vs. Public Defender Systems
      When the Defendant Cannot Afford an Attorney
      The Right of a Defendant to Represent Himself
   B. The Right to Be Presumed Innocent
      Presumptions vs. Inferences

II. The Defendant's Rights During a Trial
   A. The Right to a Fair Trial
   B. The Right to a Jury Trial
      Number of Jurors Used in the Trial

Times When Nonunanimous Verdicts Are Permitted
Exceptions to the Right to a Jury
   C. The Right to a Public Trial
      When Can a Judge Close a Trial to the Public?
   D. The Right to Confront Witnesses
   E. The Right to Be Present
      Trials in Absentia
      Continuing a Trial After the Defendant Flees
      When the Defendant Waives His or Her Right to Be Present
      When the Judge May Remove the Defendant from the Courtroom

F. The Right to Wear Civilian Clothing During
    the Trial
    Prison Attire Not Permitted
G. The Right to Present Evidence
H. The Right to Present a Defense

III. Proving the Defendant Guilty
      A. Proof Beyond a Reasonable Doubt
      B. Explaining the State's Burden of Proof
IV. Criminal Trials and the Press

 THE DEFENDANT'S RIGHTS PRIOR TO TRIAL

The rights that protect a defendant prior to trial include the following:

- The right to an attorney
- The right to be presumed innocent

A. THE RIGHT TO AN ATTORNEY

In all criminal prosecutions, the accused shall enjoy the right . . . to have the
Assistance of Counsel for his defense.

—*Sixth Amendment, U.S. Constitution*

For decades, the Sixth Amendment's guarantee of the right to assistance of
counsel was narrowly interpreted to mean that a defendant could hire any attorney he or she could afford, but the state was under no obligation to provide one
free of charge. If defendants could not afford an attorney, then they would have
to represent themselves. The first change to this area of law came in a recognition
that in cases where the defendant faced the death penalty, not allowing him or
her an attorney was tantamount to an automatic guilty verdict. Then in a series
of decisions, the U.S. Supreme Court, especially the Warren Court in the 1960s,
addressed the issue of when a person should be allowed to have an attorney and,
more important, when the state must provide counsel if the defendant could not
afford to hire one. The most famous case in this field is *Gideon v. Wainwright*,
which will be examined in greater detail later in this chapter.

Before beginning a discussion of the rights of a defendant during and after
the trial, an important question must be answered: At what point do suspects
have the right to have an attorney represent them? Much of the case law about
this question focuses on a discussion of whether or not a particular stage is "critical." If the stage of the prosecution is critical, then the defendant should have an
attorney representing his or her interests. But what is a critical stage? In most
prosecutions, a critical stage is a hearing where the prosecutor, judge, and possible witnesses appear. One such hearing is the preliminary hearing. However,
this is not the first point in a criminal proceeding where a defendant has the
right to request an attorney.

This text has already discussed *Miranda* rights and how they are critical to
interrogating a suspect. One of the rights provided for in *Miranda* is that a

defendant must be told that he or she has the right to an attorney and can refuse to answer any questions until that attorney appears. So, a defendant has the right to an attorney at any critical stage in a criminal case and during interrogation—whenever his or her legal rights are in jeopardy or during any adversarial hearing. This essentially means that a defendant has the right to an attorney beginning at interrogation and proceeding forward. In some jurisdictions, the right is triggered even earlier. In those jurisdictions, a defendant has the right to an attorney the moment that the investigation focuses on him or her.[1]

HIRING AN ATTORNEY

Before discussing the implications of the *Gideon* decision, it is important to note that a defendant who can afford to hire a private attorney is always free to do so. One might wonder how a person who is incarcerated can contact an attorney. The defendant might ask a friend or a family member to contact a specific attorney, but some attorneys who are already visiting a client at the local jail might meet with a defendant who is currently unrepresented. Attorneys who handle criminal cases usually charge a **retainer**—an upfront fee to represent a defendant. The amount of the fee varies with the complexity and seriousness of the case. Some attorneys have also been known to accept private property as payment instead of cash, but there are problems with this practice. The attorney must avoid receiving any merchandise that is stolen. Because of this, most attorneys prefer to deal on a currency basis.

Retainer
A fee charged at the beginning of a case to pay an attorney for all actions carried out.

GIDEON V. WAINWRIGHT

Clarence Earl Gideon was charged with felony burglary in the state of Florida. He was forced to represent himself at trial because he could not afford to hire his own attorney. At that time, Florida only appointed counsel in death penalty cases, not in felony cases. Gideon represented himself throughout the trial. When it concluded, he was found guilty. The judge sentenced Gideon to five years in prison.

Gideon appealed his case all the way to the U.S. Supreme Court. The basis of the appeal, which he brought himself, was that a felony sentence, by itself, is serious enough to warrant the application of the Sixth Amendment. The Supreme Court agreed with him and created a ruling that radically changed the way that attorneys were appointed throughout the United States.

In ruling in favor of Gideon, the court said that the "assistance of counsel is one of the safeguards of the Sixth Amendment deemed necessary to insure fundamental human rights of life and liberty. . . . The Sixth Amendment stands as a constant admonition that if the constitutional safeguards it provides be lost, justice will not . . . be done."[2] The Court ruled that Gideon should be retried and that this time the state of Florida should provide him with an attorney, paid for by the state. Interestingly enough, when he was retried, this time with an attorney appointed by the state, he was found not guilty and set free.

Gideon was the first in a series of U.S. Supreme Court decisions that expanded the guarantees of the Sixth Amendment's right to counsel and helped expand the public defender system in places that already had it and to create other systems of providing attorneys, free of charge, to those who could not afford them and were facing felony charges anywhere in the United States. As the law now stands, any person facing a potential maximum sentence of greater than six months in prison must have representation. If the person cannot afford to hire an attorney, then the state must provide one for him or her. Consider Scenario 10-1

SCENARIO 10-1

MUST THE STATE PROVIDE AN ATTORNEY?

Theo is charged with a misdemeanor count of theft by taking an item that is less than $500 in value. However, after he makes bond, the case is reinvestigated and the police and prosecutors determine that the item that Theo is alleged to have taken is actually worth more than $1,000. They present the case to the grand jury and Theo is indicted for a felony. Does he qualify to have an attorney represent him if he cannot afford one?

Answer: Yes. Even though Theo was originally arrested for a misdemeanor—which would not qualify him for attorney representation in most states—the fact that the charge was changed to a felony would mean that he is now entitled to an attorney.

COURT-APPOINTED ATTORNEY VS. PUBLIC DEFENDER SYSTEMS

Court-appointed attorney
A private, local attorney who is selected by a judge to handle a criminal case; this attorney is paid by the state, usually on an hourly basis.

Public defender
A government attorney who works for an office in the court system whose sole responsibility is to provide legal representation to those individuals who are charged with crimes.

There are essentially two systems for providing legal representation for those who cannot afford it. Although some jurisdictions take a different approach, the most common arrangement is a **court-appointed attorney** or **public defender** offices.

States use different systems in different counties. The reason that there are variations is that in smaller counties, with a correspondingly lower tax base, there may not be sufficient funds to hire and staff a public defender's office. In those situations, courts often turn to local attorneys who already have their own offices and staffs and appoint them to criminal defendants on a case-by-case basis. The private attorneys in the court-appointed system are usually paid on an hourly basis by the court system. The money that the government pays to these local, private attorneys is usually far less than they make in other types of cases. Why, then, would a local attorney agree to serve on a court-appointed list? The answer is deceptively simple: An attorney on the court-appointed list will get a great deal of experience in trials. Most people are not aware of the fact that private attorneys actually spend very little time in courtrooms. They do most of their work in their offices, but to become good at anything, a person needs practice; for a trial attorney, experience inside the courtroom is valuable. Another reason may be economics. An attorney, especially one who is recently out of law school, has a lot of bills to pay (including student loans), and a ready source of income is always welcome. Finally, there is political pressure. A local judge may ask attorneys to take cases on the appointed list, and when a judge makes such a request, it is difficult to turn down.

The other side of the equation from court-appointed lawyers is the public defender. A public defender is a government employee, just like an assistant district attorney. In fact, both are often paid the same wage. The sole duty of the public defender is to represent persons who have been charged with a crime and who cannot afford to hire their own attorneys. Where public defenders exist, there is no need for an extensive court-appointed attorney system. However, this is not to say that court-appointed cases are never arranged in counties that have public defender offices. There are times when the public defender is overwhelmed with cases, or when the public defender has a conflict of interest, and in those situations the judge may seek a local private attorney to act in a particular case. However, in counties that have public defender offices, very few cases are ever handled by court-appointed attorneys.

WHEN THE DEFENDANT CANNOT AFFORD AN ATTORNEY

Before a judge will appoint an attorney to represent a defendant, he or she must inquire about the defendant's finances. The state has specific financial guidelines that a person must meet before an attorney will be appointed to represent him or her. Generally, if the defendant is in custody and cannot afford to make bail or bond, an attorney will be appointed to represent him or her. Defendants who are not in custody must often complete a questionnaire, providing details about how much money they make. Different states have different guidelines that a defendant must meet. If the defendant does not meet the financial criteria—because he or she makes too much money—then the defendant may not qualify for a court-appointed attorney or a public defender. A great many people have well-paying jobs but huge debt loads that prevent them from raising the up-front retainer for a skilled criminal defense attorney. They find themselves unable to pay for an attorney, even though they make too much money to qualify for a public defender or court-appointed attorney. Defendants who are charged with felonies will get attorney representation, although they may be required to pay back some of the money if their income is too large to initially qualify. Defendants who are charged with a misdemeanor may not have any options: If they cannot afford to hire an attorney, cannot negotiate some payment plan with a local attorney, and do not meet the financial criteria for the public defender's office, they may end up having to represent themselves.

THE RIGHT OF A DEFENDANT TO REPRESENT HIMSELF

Even after the safeguards of *Gideon* and other cases became bedrock law in the U.S. legal system, there was nothing that required a defendant to accept an attorney provided for free by the government. Defendants always have the right to represent themselves. When a person conducts a trial and acts as his or her own attorney, this is referred to as **pro se** representation. However, such an approach is rarely successful. In fact, a pro se defendant often does himself or herself more harm than good. A person might, reasonably enough, conclude that no one could better represent his or her interests than himself or herself, but in law, that conclusion is faulty. Pro se defendants are not familiar with the rules of evidence or the proper way to subpoena witnesses and evidence.

Pro se
Latin; "by oneself;" a person who chooses to represent himself or herself in a legal proceeding.

They do not know the correct way to give an opening statement or how to conduct a case. The pro se defendant also has a very skilled and experienced opponent in the person of the prosecutor. This mismatch usually results the way one might expect: The pro se defendant is found guilty. Consider Scenario 10-2.

SCENARIO 10-2

PRO SE REPRESENTATION

David is charged with first-degree murder and the state is seeking the death penalty. The judge in the case has appointed an attorney to represent David but David does not want to be represented. He wants to represent himself. The judge reminds David that he is facing a possible death sentence. Can the judge force David to have an attorney represent him in this case?

Answer: No. A person has the absolute right to represent himself. In this case, the judge may appoint an attorney to sit with David in case he has some questions, but David can represent himself if he so chooses.

B. THE RIGHT TO BE PRESUMED INNOCENT

Presumption
A conclusion about a fact that must be made unless and until refuted by other evidence.

Acquit
Finding the defendant in a criminal case not guilty.

In addition to the right to an attorney, another important right protects the defendant from the moment that he or she is arrested: the **presumption** of innocence. In any prosecution, there is a presumption that a defendant is innocent until proven guilty. This is a very powerful presumption. What this means is that, barring any evidence showing the defendant's guilt, the jury must **acquit** the defendant. This presumption follows the defendant throughout the trial. Judges inform the members of the jury about this presumption, telling them they must find the defendant not guilty unless the state proves its case beyond a reasonable doubt. The presumption of innocence can only be overcome by evidence produced against the defendant. If there is insufficient evidence, then the defendant must be set free. The presumption of innocence is one of the cornerstones of the U.S. legal system. Consider Scenario 10-3.

SCENARIO 10-3

QUESTIONING A JUROR IN A CASE

Andy has been called for jury duty. During jury selection, the judge advises the entire panel that the defendant is presumed to be innocent unless and until the state has proven the charges against him. As jury selection proceeds, the judge asks Andy, "What is your opinion about the defendant's guilt or innocence?"

Andy responds, "I don't have one, Your Honor. I haven't heard any evidence in the case yet."

The judge responds: "You are dismissed from this jury panel. A juror must always believe that a defendant is not guilty."

Is this action proper?

Answer: Yes. Although this a more literal interpretation of the presumption of innocence than most judges follow, it is a correct statement of the law and a juror is supposed to take this presumption very seriously.

SCENARIO 10-3

(continued)

PRESUMPTIONS VS. INFERENCES

We have said that a criminal defendant is always presumed innocent. A presumption is a conclusion that a judge or jury must make in certain situations. For instance, when a defendant is charged with a crime, the jury has no choice in the matter: They must presume that the defendant is not guilty. If, during jury selection, a potential juror states that he or she cannot make this presumption, then that person will be dismissed from the panel.

An **inference** is an assumption that may be made from the facts. If your friend comes to visit you and he has severe sunburn, you can infer that he has spent too much time outside. Even though a criminal defendant is protected by numerous presumptions, these presumptions can be overcome by the state's case. The jurors are told that they can make inferences based on the facts presented, but they are also told that they are never to presume that the defendant is guilty until the state proves it.

Inference
A fact that a person can believe is probably true.

 ## THE DEFENDANT'S RIGHTS DURING A TRIAL

There are several critical rights that protect a defendant during a criminal trial. We will examine each of these in detail. They include the right to:

- A fair trial
- A jury trial
- A public trial
- Confront witnesses
- Be present
- Wear civilian clothing during the trial
- Present evidence
- Present a defense

A. THE RIGHT TO A FAIR TRIAL

In all criminal prosecutions, the accused shall enjoy the right to a speedy and public trial, by an impartial jury of the State and district wherein the crime shall have been committed, which district shall have been previously ascertained by law, and to be informed of the nature and cause of the accusation; to be confronted with the witnesses against him; to have compulsory process for obtaining witnesses in his favor, and to have the Assistance of Counsel for his defense.

—*Sixth Amendment, U.S. Constitution*

One of the most basic rights granted in the U.S. criminal justice system is that a defendant must receive a fair trial. The judge is the person who must ensure this right, and a conviction can be overturned on appeal if the judge or the prosecutor acts in an unfair manner or does something to unfairly prejudice the jury against the defendant before or during the trial.

B. THE RIGHT TO A JURY TRIAL

Jury trial
A trial with a judge and jury, not just a judge.

The Sixth Amendment guarantees that individuals who are charged with certain crimes must be given a **jury trial**. This does not mean, however, that everyone charged with any type of criminal offense must receive a jury trial. Instead, the U.S. Supreme Court has interpreted this amendment to mean that jury trials are warranted in some types of cases, but not in others. For instance, there are no jury trials in juvenile cases, primarily because the hearings are not considered to be adversarial or criminal. The entire juvenile court system is built around a different concept than the focus of the rest of criminal law: the rehabilitation of the juvenile.

Trials are also not guaranteed under the Sixth Amendment for petty offenses. The U.S. Supreme Court has interpreted that amendment to be reserved for "serious offenses."[3] What the Court means by this phrase is that a defendant is entitled to a jury trial when he or she faces a potential sentence that is more than six months in custody. If the potential punishment for an offense is less than six months, a state does not have to provide a jury trial for the defendant.[4] This ruling applies even in situations where the defendant is charged with several crimes, none of which can be punished by more than six months in custody but, taken as consecutive sentences, could result in the defendant serving more than six months in prison.

To determine whether a defendant's charge is considered a serious offense and therefore one for which he or she must receive a jury trial, the court will consider the maximum sentence allowed by law. Almost all statutes that criminalize behavior list not only the elements of each offense, but the range of punishments for those offenses. In that situation, the judge would simply refer to the applicable statute to decide if a jury trial is warranted. However, there are situations in which the state legislature has made a certain action criminal but has failed to provide a maximum sentence for the offense. In that case, the judge must determine what the possible maximum sentence is by researching similar offenses or by referring to common law. Consider Scenario 10-4.

SCENARIO 10-4   ## STEALING WIRE

Helen is charged with theft of copper wire. There is no maximum sentence stated for the offense, and the trial judge rules that the charge is a misdemeanor punishable by a maximum of three months in custody; therefore Helen has no right to a jury trial. Helen is given a bench trial, where the judge acts as the fact finder instead of a jury.

After her conviction, Helen is sentenced to twelve months in the prison system. She appeals her conviction on the grounds that she should have been given a jury trial. How is the appellate court likely to rule?

SCENARIO 10-4

(continued)

Answer: The appellate court will almost certainly rule that Helen's conviction should be overturned and that she should be retried, this time with a jury. The fact that there was no maximum sentence stated in the statutes does not allow a judge to arbitrarily decide to exclude the possibility of a jury trial, especially where the judge by his or her own actions demonstrates that the maximum sentence is clearly beyond the six-month threshold.[5]

NUMBER OF JURORS USED IN THE TRIAL

Everyone knows that a jury is composed of 12 persons. Many would be surprised to learn, however, that this number is not mentioned in the U.S. Constitution nor is it guaranteed in the Bill of Rights. There is, in fact, no constitutional requirement for 12 people to sit on a jury. The U.S. Supreme Court has stated that, "the 12-person requirement . . . is not an indispensable component of the right to trial by jury."[6] Many states allow six-person juries to hear misdemeanor cases. Despite the fact that 12-person juries are not a constitutional requirement, most states have opted for that number and require 12 people to sit as the jury in felony cases. Having 12 jurors has been a tradition for so long, at least in felony cases, that changing the number is unlikely.

Why was the number 12 originally chosen? The simple answer is that the U.S. court system is based on the English system, and that system used 12 as the number of jurors. Why the English adopted this number is more difficult to answer.

As early as 1164, an English king required juries to be composed of 12 men.[7] Twelve has always been a number of special significance. There are 12 months in the year. Roman law, which forms an important foundation of our own legal system, was first promulgated in the Twelve Tables.[8] Because 12 was the original number, the tradition has held and will likely continue to do so for the foreseeable future.

TIMES WHEN NONUNANIMOUS VERDICTS ARE PERMITTED

It was once true that two states allowed non-unanimous verdicts in felony cases. In those states, if 11 out of the 12 jurors reached a specific verdict, then that would have been the verdict for the entire jury. However, all of that changed in 2020, with the U.S. Supreme Court's ruling in *Ramos v. Louisiana*, 590 US _____ (2020). In that case, the court ruled that non-unanimous verdicts were a violation of the Constitution. Of course, the vast majority of states already required unanimous verdicts. In states where jurors cannot reach agreement and declare themselves unable to ever reach a unanimous verdict are referred to as a **hung jury**, and the case is declared to be a **mistrial**.

Hung jury
A jury that is unable to reach a unanimous verdict.

Mistrial
A trial that the judge ends and declares will have no legal effect.

Six-Person Juries. Prior to the court's ruling in *Ramos v. Louisiana*, the Supreme Court's had already ruled that nonunanimous verdicts for six-person juries was unconstitutional. In *Burch v. Louisiana*,[9] the Court held that nonunanimous verdicts by six-person criminal juries pose a threat to constitutional principles and will not be allowed.

EXCEPTIONS TO THE RIGHT TO A JURY

Although there is no right to a jury trial for minor offenses or any offense where the possible sentence is less than six months, there are other types of prosecutions where defendants do not have the right to jury trials. In juvenile cases, for example, juries are not used. Instead, a juvenile court judge hears all evidence and reaches a decision in the case.[10] Traffic-citation cases are another example. In most cases where the possible punishment is only a fine, there is no requirement or authorization for a jury trial.

Criminal Infractions Where the Sentence Is Six Months or Less. Despite the fact that they are not required to do so, many states provide jury trials for people charged with minor offenses. In some states, the defendant is tried first without a jury, and only if convicted does he or she have the right to a jury trial.

To determine the maximum sentence for a particular offense, the criminal sentencing statute should be reviewed. The state legislature sets the maximum sentence for an offense. The legislature generally includes the nature of the punishment in the statute making a certain action illegal. Where the maximum sentence is set at six months or greater, a jury trial would be required. Consider Scenario 10-5.

SCENARIO 10-5   ## JURY TRIAL REQUIRED?

Cary is charged with several offenses. They are all misdemeanors, and the maximum sentence for each is only four months in custody. However, there are 10 such counts and the maximum sentence adds up to 40 months of a possible sentence. Is Cary entitled to a jury trial because of the maximum possible sentence?

Answer: No. A jury trial is based on the maximum sentence for each charge, not the total charges. If any of the charges had a maximum possible sentence of more than six months, then Cary would be entitled to a jury trial.

C. THE RIGHT TO A PUBLIC TRIAL

The Sixth Amendment also provides that a trial must be conducted in public. The Supreme Court has stated that the right to a public trial is one of the most important guaranteed to a criminal defendant. "Without the freedom to attend such trials, which people have exercised for centuries, important aspects of freedom of speech and of the press could be eviscerated."[11] Secret trials are the staple of totalitarian governments around the world. Opening a criminal trial to the public is a simple and efficient way to ensure that justice is served. When judges and prosecutors know that their actions can be monitored by any member of the public or the press, they tend to behave more responsibly. Even though a trial is open to the public, the trial judge may bar specific people from attending if they prove to be disruptive or dangerous to the proceedings.[12]

WHEN CAN A JUDGE CLOSE A TRIAL TO THE PUBLIC?

There are only a few instances in which a trial judge is allowed to close a jury trial to the public, and even in these instances the judge may only do so for a brief period of time. The judge must show a "compelling interest" to close a portion of the trial to the public. The two most common instances involve testimony by rape victims or testimony by children about sexual acts committed on them. There is no standing rule that requires a case to be closed at a certain point in any trial. In fact, the government must show a compelling reason to close the trial before the judge will authorize it. The preference under U.S. law is for all trials to remain open. For instance, in a case where a state passed a statute that required a trial to be closed whenever a child sexual assault victim testified, the U.S. Supreme Court ruled it an infraction of the defendant's right to a public trial, and before any such closing is made, the judge must weigh the state's compelling interest (in this case, protecting the identity of the child) against the defendant's constitutional right to have an open and public trial. In the case of the mandatory statute, the rule that required closure in all such cases was ruled to be unconstitutional. There is no one factor that will always justify the closing of a trial. The trial judge must weigh the defendant's rights against other factors and there is no one right that always outweighs another. The judge must make some accommodation short of closing the trial if at all possible. Consider Scenario 10-6.

CLOSING THE TRIAL TO THE PUBLIC

SCENARIO 10-6

There is a trial pending before Judge S in which 10 different defendants are charged with child molestation of dozens of children. Each of these children will testify, essentially meaning that there will be days and days of testimony by underage children who will be testifying about intensely personal, sexual, and humiliating acts perpetrated on them. Can the judge rule that the trial will be closed during the entire phase where witnesses will be testifying?

Answer: No. A judge can choose to close the trial each time a child testifies, but a judge cannot close most of a trial to the public because of the nature of the charges. The judge must weigh the rights of the defendants against the rights of the children and come up with some alternative to closing the entire witness testimony phase of the case.

Jury Selection. It is not simply the trial that must remain open to the public, but also the jury selection process.[14] If jury selection involves some sensitive

> ## Sidebar
>
> *Closing a trial to the public is only allowed in limited circumstances. A trial can only be closed for a "compelling interest."[13] To close a trial, the state must show that some overriding interest is at stake.*

issues, the jurors can be questioned in the judge's chambers. Although jury selection must remain a public affair, there are some practical issues to be considered. When a large jury pool is summoned for a case, there might not be any additional seating left for anyone to sit and view the selection process. In some instances, the size of the courtroom itself is the limiting factor, not the parties' intention of closing an otherwise open trial.

Preliminary Hearings. The rule about open trials also applies to preliminary hearings and many other hearings, including motions, where important issues are decided. The only situation in which the Supreme Court has allowed a preliminary hearing to be closed to the public is when the hearing may actually impinge on the defendant's right to a fair trial, such as when the case involves intense pretrial publicity.[15]

Sensitive or Underage Witnesses. There are provisions that allow the judge to close a public trial, briefly, while a child or sexual assault victim testifies. However, even then, the prosecution must show a compelling reason to do so. Despite the fact that the testimony in such cases is of a sensitive nature, it is not common for a prosecutor to request that the trial be closed during the entire testimony of a rape or child abuse victim. Instead, they conduct the trial in public, despite the fact that sensitive or embarrassing details may emerge. Prosecutors do not do this to make the victim even more uncomfortable, but to emphasize just how serious the case is and how everyone should know what the defendant is accused of doing. Leaving a trial open to the public, even when it involves extremely sensitive information and a sensitive victim, helps to educate not only the jurors, but also the public at large that the state will not shirk its duties to protect victims. Hopefully it sends a message to those considering such a crime that they will not avoid prosecution. However, the decision to request closing a portion of a trial is a question left to each individual prosecutor; some may routinely request closure, whereas others never do.

D. THE RIGHT TO CONFRONT WITNESSES

The right of a criminal defendant to confront witnesses and also to cross-examine them is considered to be one of the fundamental rights guaranteed by the U.S. Constitution. Without the ability to confront witnesses and ask them questions, there can be no due process.[16] Consider Scenario 10-7.

SCENARIO 10-7	DISCOVERING THE DEAL

During the defendant's trial for armed robbery, Juan, the defense attorney, learns that one of the other codefendants has struck a deal with the prosecution where he will testify against Juan's client. When the codefendant takes the stand, Juan begins to question the codefendant about whether or not he has made a deal with the state. The prosecution objects and the judge sustains the objection, preventing Juan from asking any questions along these lines. Is this an unfair restriction on the defendant's right to cross-examine?

Answer: Yes. Juan must be allowed to confront the state's witnesses, especially with information that so intimately affects their possible testimony.[17]

SCENARIO 10-7

(continued)

The provisions of the Sixth Amendment, especially the right to confront witnesses in a criminal trial, have been made applicable to the states through the passage of the Fourteenth Amendment.[18] It is common for courts to say that the right of the defendant to face-to-face confrontation of a witness is one of the most important rights guaranteed under the U.S. Constitution, but this right is not absolute. Like many other rights, it must be balanced against other interests. There are several situations in which a defendant does not have the right of face-to-face confrontation. Many states allow rape and child abuse victims to testify through closed-circuit television from another room. In other situations, a child victim might not be seated at the actual witness stand, but may testify at a smaller (child-sized) table in front of the jury box, where he or she faces the jury and does not speak directly to the defendant.

The confrontation clause of the Sixth Amendment provides two rights: (1) the right of the defendant to confront witnesses against him or her, and (2) the right to **cross-examine** these witnesses to show bias or prejudice.[19] Included in this concept is the idea that a defendant can use cross-examination to develop evidence of a witness's biases or even a motive that the witness might have to lie about the events.[20] Cross-examination is used to show that a state's witness does not know what he or she claims to know, that the witness lacks personal knowledge, that the witness is biased or prejudiced against the defendant, or that the witness has been coached.[21]

Cross-examine
To question a witness for the opposition about his or her possible bias, prejudice, or lack of knowledge about the issues in the case.

Although the defendant has the right to a cross-examination, this does not mean that the defendant (or defendant's attorney) has the right to ask any question about any topic. Instead, the defendant is guaranteed the opportunity for a full and effective cross-examination. What he or she does with that opportunity is left to the defendant and the defense attorney. Defendants are not given free rein to ask any question that they wish. Their questions must be limited to the issues pending in the case and must still survive the test of relevancy that we discussed in Chapter 6. The judge has the final say about when the defendant has exhausted all relevant questions and can even stop the defense from asking any more questions about a particular topic, once the issue has been thoroughly examined.[22]

Finally, the right to confront witnesses changes with the status of the defendant. During a jury trial, the defendant has the right to confront witnesses as part of the guarantees of the Due Process Clause of the Constitution. However, when the defendant is convicted, and the status of the person charged changes from defendant to probationer or convict his or her constitutional right of confrontation is considerably less. During a probation-revocation hearing, for example, the state has a relaxed standard and can use witness statements, hearsay, and other documentary evidence that might not be admissible during trial but is admissible during a probation-revocation hearing. The defendant's right of confrontation is considerably curtailed after being found guilty.

E. THE RIGHT TO BE PRESENT

In addition to a fair and public trial, the right to a jury trial, and the right to confrontation, the defendant also has the right to be present during the trial. Although this might seem obvious, there are many countries that prosecute individuals but do not allow them to be present for the proceedings. Fortunately, the U.S. legal system requires the defendant to be present, unless certain specific circumstances are present.

TRIALS IN ABSENTIA

In absentia
Latin; the defendant is not present.

Although there are instances where a trial may be conducted against an individual when he or she is not present, or **in absentia**, it is much more common and often required for the defendant to be present during all phases of a jury trial. What happens in situations where the defendant absconds before the trial begins? In that situation, the court will continue the defendant's case until such time as the defendant is arrested and brought back before the court. There will be no trial until the defendant is located.

CONTINUING A TRIAL AFTER THE DEFENDANT FLEES

Once the trial is underway, a defendant who is out on bond is free to come and go, just like the witnesses and attorneys. What happens when a defendant abuses this privilege and flees the jurisdiction after the trial begins? Is the judge required to declare a mistrial? The answer depends on the nature of the case. When the case is a misdemeanor, the judge may opt to continue the case against the defendant, even though he or she is no longer present. This would be a classic case of a trial in absentia. However, if the defendant absconds during a felony case, the court may call a recess to see if the defendant can be arrested and brought back to the courtroom. If the defendant cannot be located, the most common result is for the judge to declare a mistrial and wait for the defendant to be rearrested and a new trial scheduled. In such a situation, the judge would issue a bench warrant for the defendant's arrest, and that would authorize any law enforcement officer to seize the defendant and bring him or her back to the courtroom so that the trial could continue. A bench warrant will often contain a "no bond" provision, which prevents the defendant from obtaining a bail bond before the next trial date. It would not make much sense to allow a defendant who has absconded on his or her first bond to be able to make bail again.

WHEN THE DEFENDANT WAIVES HIS OR HER RIGHT TO BE PRESENT

In minor cases, such as misdemeanor charges, the defendant can waive his or her presence during the trial, but only with the judge's permission. Most states have statutes or court rules that allow this for certain minor offenses. However, this rule does not apply to felonies and certainly never to capital murder cases (where the death penalty can be imposed). Although a defendant cannot waive his or her presence at a felony jury trial, some states do allow the defendant to waive his or her presence during earlier stages in the prosecution, such as preliminary hearings or arraignments.

If the defendant is not available when the trial is scheduled to begin—for example, because he or she is hospitalized—the court must wait until the defendant is able to be present before the jury trial can commence. Although many foreign countries allow defendants to be tried in absentia, it is rare in the U.S. court system.

WHEN THE JUDGE MAY REMOVE THE DEFENDANT FROM THE COURTROOM

In situations where the defendant disrupts the order and propriety of the courtroom setting, a judge may remove the defendant from the courtroom. In situations where the defendant continually interrupts the proceedings or acts out in a violent way, the judge is authorized to bind and gag the defendant or to remove the defendant and keep him or her someplace nearby.[24] The defendant can be informed about the various stages of the trial by his or her attorney or can listen (or watch) the trial through a closed-circuit system. This is a better alternative to gagging or binding the defendant to prevent him or her from acting out in court. In fact, if the defendant is put in chains or handcuffs, he or she must be restrained in such a way that the jury cannot see that the defendant is shackled. Given the choice between handcuffing the defendant to his or her chair or simply removing him or her to a nearby cell where he or she can listen to the proceedings over an intercom, most judges would opt for the latter choice.

F. THE RIGHT TO WEAR CIVILIAN CLOTHING DURING THE TRIAL

One of the more important rights for a defendant is to be tried in regular or civilian clothes during the trial. A defendant who appeared before a jury in a prison tunic might give the jury the impression that his or her guilt has already been determined.

PRISON ATTIRE NOT PERMITTED

It is common practice for jails to confiscate all of a defendant's personal items, including his or her clothing, and hold it in safekeeping. In such situations, defendants are issued uniforms, often brightly colored so that they may be identified at a distance. However, a defendant has the right to appear before the jury without a prison uniform. In fact, numerous appellate court decisions have held that putting a defendant on trial in prison attire would jeopardize his or her right to a fair trial.[25] Instead, the state must provide the defendant with suitable clothing if he or she does not have any. A defendant may not appear at a jury trial in a prison uniform. In many cases, the defense attorney often provides his or her client with suitable clothing for the duration of the trial.

G. THE RIGHT TO PRESENT EVIDENCE

Our discussions so far have focused on the rights that protect the defendant, but in this section, we will examine the right of a defendant to be proactive in his or her defense. The ability to present evidence during the trial is probably as important as the right to cross-examine the state's witnesses. If a defendant decides to present evidence, then he or she is bound by the same rules that bind the prosecutor. The defendant must follow the same rules of evidence. A defendant has the right to take the stand and tell his or her side of the story even if the defendant refused to speak to the police after being arrested.

The defendant also has the right to subpoena other witnesses to testify, and this subpoena carries the same weight as the subpoena issued by the government to compel witness testimony on its behalf. A defendant can subpoena both people and records and once issued, it must be obeyed. However, just as with the state, a defendant who requests information to which he or she is not entitled may be subject to having the subpoena quashed. When a defendant issues a subpoena, the prosecutor is allowed to challenge it and ask for a court ruling on whether or not the material should be produced. For instance, if the defendant's subpoena is too broad or calls for violating an evidentiary privilege, the defendant can no more receive this information than can the state.

Although the right to present evidence means that the defendant is permitted to take the stand and to testify on his or her own behalf, most defendants choose not to do so for several reasons. The most obvious is that if the defendant takes the stand, he or she will be subject to cross-examination by the prosecutor. These attorneys are skilled in cross-examining witnesses, and few defendants bear up well to a blistering cross-examination.

Placing character into evidence
When a criminal defendant testifies and his or her previous criminal record is allowed into evidence through the cross-examination of the defendant.

Another reason is that in some jurisdictions, and in the federal system, a defendant who takes the stand is **placing character into evidence**. This deceptively simple phrase conceals a complex procedure. Normally, a prosecutor is not allowed to tell the jury about the defendant's criminal record. The prosecutor cannot, for example, tell the jury that the defendant has been convicted of other crimes because it would prejudice the jury. (They might well decide that a person who has been convicted of a crime similar to the one for which he or she is currently being tried is probably guilty and might be tempted to ignore the evidence. As seen many times in this text, criminal cases must stand on their own.) However, in jurisdictions that follow the character into evidence rule, when defendants take the stand in their own trials, the prosecutor is allowed to question the defendants about their previous convictions. The jury will then hear that the defendant has a criminal past. (Some jurisdictions modify this rule, and the prosecutor must wait until the defendant says something about his or her previous criminal record before being allowed to introduce this evidence.)

If a defendant chooses not to take the stand during the trial, then the prosecutor is barred from bringing up the defendant's criminal history. The prosecutor certainly cannot tell the jury in either opening statements or closing arguments that the defendant has a long criminal history—this would result in a mistrial and perhaps even sanctions against the prosecutor by the State Bar. It is up to the judge, defense attorney, and prosecutor to ensure that no witness attempts to bring up the defendant's criminal history.

A defendant is under no obligation to present evidence and is certainly not obligated to take the stand and deny the charge before the jury. Defendants are not even under an obligation to present a defense and may actually remain silent during the entire trial, although that is unusual. When a defendant exercises the right to remain silent, the jurors are instructed that they are to draw no negative inference from this and that they must, in fact, presume that the defendant is innocent until proven guilty. The right to remain silent is so central to the constitutional rights guaranteed to those accused of a crime that a prosecutor is not even permitted to comment to the jury that the defendant invoked it. A prosecutor cannot even imply that if the prosecution's version is not correct, then the defendant should have refuted it. Consider Scenario 10-8.

PROSECUTOR'S MISTAKE?

During Phil's trial, he chose not to take the stand and testify. Phil's attorney presented some other witnesses and some evidence, but the jury never heard from Phil. During the prosecutor's closing argument, she says to the jury, "If the state is wrong, then why hasn't the defendant said so? Why hasn't he taken the stand and told you what he says is the real truth? You want to know why? Because we are right. He is guilty and he knows it."

Phil's attorney immediately objects and moves for a mistrial. Is he likely to get it?

Answer: Yes. The defendant's right to remain silent is one of the bedrock principles of U.S. law. The fact that the prosecutor violated that principle will almost certainly mean that the judge will declare a mistrial.

H. THE RIGHT TO PRESENT A DEFENSE

Although we have seen that the defendant's constitutional guarantees are so profound that he or she may choose to remain silent throughout the entire trial, most defendants present some kind of a defense, even if it is simply to suggest alternative explanations for the crime by cross-examining the state's witnesses.

PROVING THE DEFENDANT GUILTY

While discussing the rights of the defendant, it is important to point out that there are burdens on the state. One of the biggest is that the state must always prove that the defendant committed the offense beyond a reasonable doubt.

A. PROOF BEYOND A REASONABLE DOUBT

Reasonable doubt
The standard of proof that the prosecution must meet to prove that a defendant committed a crime.

Under the U.S. legal system, the defendant is never under any burden to prove his or her innocence. Instead, that burden remains on the state throughout the trial. As we have already seen, the defendant is protected by many different rights, including the presumption of innocence. That presumption requires that the state prove every material allegation against the defendant beyond a **reasonable doubt**. Failure to meet this burden means that the case against the defendant will fail. Reasonable doubt can be a difficult term to quantify. Beyond a reasonable doubt is a much higher standard than that used in civil cases. Proving a case beyond a reasonable doubt does not mean that the state has to prove the case beyond all doubt, or beyond a shadow of a doubt. Reasonable doubt means a doubt based on a commonsense reason, not some capricious or ill-advised opinion. If, at the end of the trial, a juror is still unsettled in his or her mind, or has qualms about the proof, this is a reasonable doubt. The judge's instruction to the jury leaves little doubt about what should happen if a juror has a reasonable doubt. In any situation where a reasonable doubt exists, the juror must vote to acquit the defendant.

Jurors are repeatedly instructed, during the course of the trial, that the state's burden is proof beyond a reasonable doubt. They are even told that if they believe that the defendant committed the crime, but the state did not prove it beyond a reasonable doubt, it is their duty to acquit the defendant.

The standard the prosecutor must meet in all criminal trials is proof beyond a reasonable doubt.

B. EXPLAINING THE STATE'S BURDEN OF PROOF

If a defendant presents a defense, such as an alibi or insanity, it continues to be the state's obligation to disprove the defense beyond a reasonable doubt. The burden in a criminal case never rests on the defendant to prove that he is not guilty. In cases where the defense is insanity, for instance, the state must present rebuttal evidence establishing that the defendant was legally sane at the time of the crime.

CRIMINAL TRIALS AND THE PRESS

Congress shall make no law abridging the freedom of speech, or of the press.

—*First Amendment, U.S. Constitution*

Because criminal trials are open to the public, they are also open to the press. But press coverage brings with it a whole host of other issues that are not seen when members of the general public are in attendance at a public trial. It is not uncommon for intensive press coverage to make it difficult for a defendant to receive a fair trial. As a result, there is an inherent conflict between two constitutional values: the right of the defendant to receive a fair trial and the freedom of the press. Neither of these rights outbalances the other. They must be weighed, one against the other. In each case, the judge must weigh the constitutional values and reach some type of accommodation and balance the freedom of the press with the defendant's right to a fair trial. A judge cannot, for example, bar any press coverage of the trial, but a judge can prevent news organizations from bringing in cameras to televise or photograph the trial. The defendant's right to a fair trial does not always outweigh the freedom of the press, so a judge must take both concerns into account in conducting the trial.

SHORTER v. U.S.

792 A.2D 228, 229-236 (D.C., 2001)

CASE EXCERPT

REID, ASSOCIATE JUDGE:

Appellant Richard A. Shorter challenges his convictions for child sexual abuse of and threat to injure T.J. He claims, primarily, that the trial court violated his constitutional Sixth Amendment right of confrontation by refusing his request to cross-examine T.J., or to conduct a voir dire of T.J. and her mother, about T.J.'s alleged prior allegation of sexual abuse which she later recanted. He also contends that the trial court erred by: 1) denying him the right to examine psychological reports regarding the complaining witness and her siblings; 2) failing to grant a mistrial during the complaining witness' testimony; 3) allowing the government to introduce photographs of rooms in his home that were in disarray; and 4) denying his D.C.Code §23-110 motion (ineffective assistance of counsel) without a hearing and without appointing counsel for him. We remand this case for further proceedings with respect to appellant's primary contention, but reject his remaining arguments.

FACTUAL SUMMARY

The government's trial evidence showed the following facts. Between September 2, 1996 and May 14, 1997, T.J., who at the time was seven years of age, complained that Shorter, her mother's fiancé, whom she called "Uncle Rick," and who is the appellant in this case, had sexual contact with her on three different occasions. On one of those occasions, he threatened to injure her.

ANALYSIS

We turn to Shorter's contention that the trial court erred by denying him the opportunity to cross-examine T.J., or to conduct a voir dire of T.J. and her mother, concerning a recanted allegation of a prior sexual assault against her by Shorter. Shortly before trial, the government filed a motion in limine to exclude irrelevant evidence, including "evidence of prior reports of sexual abuse made by T.J. . . . ." The government stated, in pertinent part: "The defendant may seek to cross-examine T.J. on a prior report of sexual abuse made to her mother. . . ." The issue of cross-examination concerning T.J.'s alleged prior report of sexual abuse was joined late on a Friday evening during the cross-examination of T.J. Defense counsel advised the trial judge that:

> Last year, T.J. accused Shorter of doing something similar in the nature of sexual molestation or abuse, and after she made that report to her mother—I believe the same day—she recanted and said that's not true.
>
> What I would like to do is cross-examine her about that, ask her if there was a time apart from the three times that she's talked about that she accused her uncle and then said it wasn't true.

When the trial court pointed out that a recantation did not establish falsity of the prior sexual assault allegation and that Shorter would have to show convincingly its falsity, his counsel asked for a voir dire of T.J. and her mother. In response to the trial court's request for the government's view regarding voir dire of T.J. and her mother, the prosecutor gave a proffer of what T.J. would say about the prior allegation:

The trial judge made a tentative ruling, allowing Shorter to "cross-examine T.J. about the particulars of the charged sexual assaults and whether T.J. previously made any statements that were different than the particulars that she testified to today." On the other hand, the judge explained her reasons for proposing to deny the defense request to conduct a voir dire of T.J. and her mother: 1) the mother did not witness the recanted incident; and 2) "given the Government's proffer, and the fact that this is a child, I think it would be both not necessary and arguably detrimental to the child were the Court to conduct a voir dire on the matter that is not going to be the subject of the trial." The trial judge was convinced that "the voir dire would not establish the falsity of the prior accusations," and that a mini-trial during the trial would be "confusing" to the jury, whether conducted in or outside the jury's presence.

On the Monday morning following the exchange between counsel and the trial judge regarding the prior allegation of sexual molestation that T.J. recanted, Shorter filed a written memorandum, citing his constitutional Sixth Amendment right to confrontation, and claiming that the prior allegation was admissible: "(a) as substantive evidence of his defense theory that T.J. had fabricated these allegations of other sexual assaults; (b) to show T.J.'s state of mind, credibility and bias against Mr. Shorter; and (c) to rebut the inference that T.J.'s mother, a defense witness, disbelieved T.J.'s allegations without reason and to rehabilitate T.J.'s mother as a defense witness." The trial judge decided that "this issue of alleged prior false accusations will not be admitted"; in part because: 1) T.J.'s mother's disbelief of her daughter's allegation "had not been introduced as substantive evidence"; 2) "even if T.J.'s recantation is shown convincingly, it is not convincing evidence that the underlying accusations were false"; and 3) T.J. could be cross-examined about "prior inconsistent statements about what happened in the kitchen the day before the report in school. . . ."

When defense counsel continued to press the recantation issue, the trial judge asked for a proffer as to her cross-examination of T.J. Defense counsel attempted to link the alleged October recantation incident to the kitchen incident about which T.J. had testified, and to show that T.J.'s report of the kitchen sexual molestation was false, in part because of an alleged inconsistency as to whether there had been a touching or a penetration. As defense counsel put it:

It is our belief that it is an October report that she made to her mother and then recanted. And I think it would be appropriate for me to cross-examine her by asking something along the lines of what you say happened in the kitchen and you told your mother about that and then later told her that wasn't true. And I'm asking the Court whether that falls into the Court's ruling of appropriate examination.

The trial court responded: "It does not." When defense counsel asked why, the judge explained:

You are trying to slip in a prior false allegation that has not been demon-strably shown to be false. . . .
　If you simply want to cross-examine her about the timing you may. But to try to bring before the jury a claim of a prior false allegation cannot be done in this case given my ruling as to the lack of substantial evidence of . . . fal-sity and the balancing issue of it being a mini-trial on another issue.

In reaction to the trial judge's statement, defense counsel reiterated her request for a voir dire of T.J. or her mother, based on a good faith basis to question one or the other about the recantation. The government opposed the voir dire of both, pointing out, first, that: T.J.'s mother was not present when the alleged sexual molestation took place; and second, proffering what T.J. would say. When defense counsel continued to link the kitchen incident with the alleged October recantation, the trial judge made her final ruling: "You may cross-examine about the particulars and whether she pre-viously made any statements that were different than the particulars that she testified to today. You may not based on what's been said so far ask anything about a prior recantation. . . ." The judge also denied the request for the voir dire of the mother because she was not present during the kitchen incident. She also refused to permit the voir dire of T.J. on the grounds that it was unnecessary, and "arguably would be detrimental to the child . . . and would not establish the falsity of the accusations." Following the bench conference, defense counsel conducted rather extensive cross-examination of T.J.

On appeal, Shorter contends that the trial court violated both his Sixth Amendment right of confrontation and his Fifth Amendment right to present a defense by excluding evidence of the prior sexual abuse allegation. It is beyond dis-pute that a defendant has a constitutional right to be confronted with the witnesses against him. Indeed, "prejudicial error may result from limiting a defendant's right to cross-examine a crucial government witness, especially a witness without whose testimony the government could not prove guilt." Moreover, "although the extent of cross-examination is within the discretion of the trial court, the trial court's wide lat-itude in the control of cross-examination . . . cannot justify a curtailment which keeps from the jury relevant and important facts bearing on the trustworthiness of crucial testimony." We recognized these fundamental principles both in *Roundtree v. United States*, 581 A.2d 315 (D.C.1990) and *Lawrence*, supra, cases which the government and Shorter, respectively, advance as controlling the outcome of this case. *Roundtree* affirmed the trial court's preclusion of the cross-examination of the complaining witness about prior allegations of sexual assaults, and Lawrence concluded that the trial court violated the appellant's Sixth Amendment confronta-tion right by disallowing such cross-examination.

In claiming trial court error, Shorter relies primarily upon Lawrence, supra, and distinguishes *Roundtree*, supra, on the ground that in *Roundtree*, there was corroborating evidence to show that the prior allegation was true; the prior allegation involved others rather than the defendant; and the trial court conducted a voir dire examination. Further, Shorter insists that T.J.'s recantation itself establishes the falsity of her prior allegation, and that, "the failure of the trial court to allow examination of this issue at least through a voir dire of T.J. and her mother . . . deprived him of a fair trial." In response, the government argues that there was no violation of Shorter's constitutional rights, and the trial court did not abuse its discretion in excluding evidence of the prior assault allegation. Relying on *Roundtree*, supra, the government maintains that Shorter failed to show convincingly that the allegation of a prior sexual assault was false; that the government's proffer as to what T.J. would say about the prior assault allegation showed that it was not false; and that the "barebones" defense proffer was inadequate to show falsity of the prior allegation.

Roundtree, supra, is a case involving a conviction for sodomy under a District statute that has since been repealed. There, the defendant, a correctional officer at the D.C. Jail, sought to cross-examine the seventeen-year-old complaining witness, who was an inmate at the jail when the officer sexually molested her, about her prior allegations of sexual abuse by other men, including her brother, in the State of Minnesota. After examining Minnesota documents, "the trial court indicated that there was 'no basis for inquiry into prior accusations' because there had been no 'firm determination' as to whether any of the complaining witness's allegations 'were false or true.' Id. at 319. However, the trial judge decided, apparently without the request of either party, to conduct a voir dire of the complaining witness before reaching a final conclusion. During the voir dire, the complaining witness explained her recantation and reasserted her allegations of prior sexual molestation by others. After the voir dire, and based on the Minnesota documents and the trial judge's assessment of the complaining witness's testimony . . . ," id. at 320, the judge stated: "'there is no substantial basis for concluding that these assaults are fabrication.'" Id. Thus, cross-examination about the prior allegations was precluded, because "appellant had failed to 'show convincingly' that the complaining witness's allegations were false." Id.

On appeal, this court explained that, with respect to credibility, the complaining witness's allegations of prior sexual molestation "would be probative . . . only if they were fabricated." Id. at 321. We stated:

> Where an accused seeks to impeach the credibility of a witness by offering evidence that the witness has made a false claim under similar circumstances, the confrontation clause mandates that the trial court give defendant leave to cross-examine about the prior claim only where it is "shown convincingly" that the prior claim is false.

The *Roundtree* court recognized that in *Lawrence*, supra, we had "found reversible error in a trial court's refusal to permit the defendant to cross-examine a witness to a sexual assault on a minor about 'prior false accusations of sexual activity made by the witness against other family members.'" That decision, however, had been premised on an apparent assumption—shared by the parties—that the prior allegations were indeed false. No such assumption prevailed in *Roundtree*, where the trial court had conducted a voir dire and "observed the complainant's testimony first hand" before concluding that the defense had failed to show the falsity of the accusations convincingly.

In applying the foregoing principles and cases to Shorter's situation, we are first mindful of the fact that T.J. was a "crucial government witness." Moreover, when the trial judge considered the defense request for a voir dire examination of T.J. and her mother about the prior alleged sexual assault which T.J. recanted, T.J.'s mother was a potentially critical defense witness. The jury's determination of Shorter's guilt or innocence would rest primarily on its perception of the credibility of T.J.'s testimony, as well as the later testimony of T.J.'s mother and Shorter. Equally important, whether T.J. had made a prior false accusation of sexual abuse against Shorter, in October of 1996, which T.J. later recanted, as alleged in Shorter's motion, was also probative of T.J.'s bias against Shorter.

Second, Shorter's proposed cross-examination pertaining to T.J.'s alleged October 1996 recantation of a prior false report of his sexual abuse would be, if the falsity were established, neither "'repetitive nor marginally relevant.'" If Shorter could show convincingly that T.J. fabricated a prior charge of sexual abuse against him, a jury arguably could question her credibility regarding the three charged incidents of child sexual abuse by Shorter, and could deem T.J. to be a biased witness. Third, unlike in *Sherer,* supra, Shorter's proffer of facts supporting the claimed false allegation in the past was not "scanty," "conclusory," or supported only by "inadmissible hearsay." The government did not dispute that the child had made and then withdrawn the prior claim of sexual abuse; its counter-proffer was an explanation for why she had made the about-face. Finally, the trial court's concern about a mini-trial and jury confusion could have been alleviated through a limited voir dire examination outside the presence of the jury, and depending upon the results of the voir dire, limited cross-examination of T.J. about the October 1996 alleged incident and her recantation. The trial court's understandable worry about T.J. could not defeat Shorter's Sixth Amendment right to confrontation, in the absence of some objective indication that T.J.'s safety would be compromised, or that she would be harassed because of her trial testimony about the October 1996 incident and her recantation. See *Roundtree,* supra.

At the same time, contrary to Shorter's position and based on *Roundtree,* supra, we agree with the trial judge that a complaining witness's recantation of an alleged prior sexual assault, by itself, is insufficient to show convincingly that the accusation is false. Indeed, in this case, the government's proffer concerning T.J.'s testimony about the alleged prior sexual assault indicated that T.J. recanted, not because her accusation was untrue, but because she was afraid of her mother and Shorter, and because her mother threatened to punish her when she made the prior allegation.

Nevertheless, on the record before us, which contains no precise dates for two of the three charged instances of child sexual abuse, we cannot say as a matter of law that, as a result of a voir dire of T.J. and her mother, Shorter would be unable to show convincingly that T.J.'s allegation of a prior, October 1996, sexual assault by him was false, and thus, that T.J. was neither a credible witness nor without bias against him. In contrast with *Roundtree,* supra, where "exploration into prior false accusations made by a witness . . ." was permitted through the voir dire process, id. at 322, in Shorter's case, no direct exploration of the witnesses into the prior, October 1996 allegation of sexual assault, and the subsequent recantation, was allowed. Our decisions discussed above lead us to conclude that the government's proffer of T.J.'s testimony, by itself, could not establish the truth or the falsity of the uncharged October 1996 allegation of sexual misconduct; nor could the trial court assume its truth or falsity based solely on the government's proffer. Thus, we hold that Shorter had a good faith basis for at least a limited voir dire examination of T.J. and her mother about the alleged and recanted prior sexual abuse in October 1996.

Since "prejudicial error may result from limiting Shorter's Sixth Amendment right to cross-examine a crucial government witness, especially a witness without whose testimony the government could not prove guilt . . . ," *Wright,* supra, 508

A.2d at 923, we are constrained to "remand this case for the trial court to exercise proper discretion . . . ," by conducting a limited voir dire of T.J. and her mother concerning the alleged prior assault of October 1996. If, following the voir dire, "the court concludes that cross-examination about the prior sexual abuse allegation should have been permitted at trial, the court shall order a new trial, for we cannot say that the omission of relevant cross-examination of T.J. relating to her credibility and bias . . . would be harmless." Should the court determine that the falsity of the prior allegation has not been shown satisfactorily under the *Roundtree* standard, Shorter's "conviction . . . shall stand affirmed—subject to the right to appeal the trial court's ruling."

Accordingly, we remand this case to the trial court for further proceedings consistent with this opinion.

Second, Shorter argues that the trial court erred in failing to declare a mistrial when T.J. made comments pertaining to her sister's role in telling their mother about Shorter's sexual abuse incident in the kitchen. The denial of a motion for a mistrial is committed to the sound discretion of the trial judge. The challenged comments were inadvertent and the trial court promptly, and also during final jury instructions, told the jury to disregard them. Under the circumstances, there was no abuse of discretion.

Third, Shorter contends that the trial court abused its discretion by denying his motion to exclude prejudicial photographs of his home that had "little probative value." The record shows that the trial court spent time reviewing each of the government's proposed photographic exhibits before deciding whether a photograph, which reflected a dirty room, would be admitted into evidence. The court determined that some of the pictures would be useful in "illustrating the testimony" of T.J. "It is well settled that a decision to admit or exclude photographs as demonstrative evidence is within the trial court's sound discretion." We see no abuse of discretion.

Fourth, Shorter asserts that the trial court committed error by denying his D.C.Code §23-110 pro se motion to vacate his conviction and sentence, without holding a hearing or appointing counsel. The judge who decided Shorter's §23-110 motion was the trial judge in his case, and thus, was " 'in a far better situation, than an appellate court to determine whether there is any appreciable possibility that a hearing could establish either constitutionally defective representation or prejudice to the defendant. . . .' " Moreover, a hearing is not "automatically required . . . ," especially "where the existing record provides an adequate basis for disposing of the §23-110 motion. . . ." Nor is the appointment of counsel required where the appellant fails to state adequate grounds for relief under §23-110. Our review of the record in this case, as well as the trial court's order denying Shorter's §23-110 motion (which responds to each of the points raised by Shorter), convinces us that Shorter has not met his burden to show deficient trial counsel performance and prejudice under *Strickland v. Washington*, 466 U.S. 668, 687-88, 104 S.Ct. 2052, 80 L.Ed.2d 674 (1984).

CASE QUESTIONS

1 What was the defendant's claim concerning the confrontation clause in his appeal?
2 How did the trial court rule about T.J.'s supposed prior recantation?
3 How did the appellate court decide this issue?
4 What was the basis of the defendant's claim regarding a request for mistrial based on statements by T.J.'s sister?
5 What type of pro se motion did the defendant make in this case?

CHAPTER SUMMARY

Among the important rights that protect a defendant before and during a criminal trial are the right to an attorney and the right to the presumption of innocence. After the decision in *Gideon v. Wainwright*, the U.S. Supreme Court requires that any person facing a felony charge must be provided with an attorney if he or she cannot afford to hire one. States have created two basic systems to deal with the standard created in *Gideon*. Some areas have created a public defender system, where attorneys who work for the government have the job of representing people charged with crimes. In other areas, there is a court-appointed list, where private attorneys take on criminal cases and are paid hourly. A defendant can still choose to represent himself or herself, called pro se. During the trial, the defendant has the right to a fair and public trial and to confront the witnesses against him or her. A defendant cannot be tried before a jury while he or she is wearing prison clothing. Civilian clothing must be provided. In most cases, the defendant must be present for his or her trial. If a defendant absconds after the trial begins, there are times when he or she can be tried in absentia. The burden on the government is to prove that the defendant is guilty beyond a reasonable doubt, and this burden never shifts to the defendant. During the trial, members of the press have as much right to be present as any other member of the public, and the rights of the press do not outweigh the rights of the defendant to receive a fair trial.

KEY TERMS AND CONCEPTS

Retainer	Acquit	In absentia
Court-appointed attorney	Inference	Placing character into evidence
Public defender	Jury trial	Reasonable doubt
Pro se	Hung jury	
Presumption	Mistrial	
	Cross-examine	

END OF CHAPTER EXERCISES

Review Questions

See Appendix A for answers

1 How are most private criminal attorneys paid?
2 Explain the importance of the *Gideon* decision.
3 What is the difference between court-appointed and public defender systems?

4   What financial restraints are placed on defendants who wish to obtain court-appointed attorneys but are charged with misdemeanors?

5   What is pro se representation?

6   Explain the presumption of innocence.

7   What is the difference between a presumption and an inference?

8   Are 12 people always required to sit on a jury? Why or why not?

9   When are six-person juries permitted?

10   What types of cases do not allow jury trials?

11   Are juries permitted in juvenile cases? Why or why not?

12   When can a trial judge close a trial to the public?

13   Is it permissible to try a defendant while he or she is wearing prison clothing? Why or why not?

14   Under what circumstances can a trial that began when the defendant was present continue without him or her?

15   What has been called the "greatest legal engine ever invented for the discovery of truth?"

16   What is the confrontation clause?

17   Can a prosecutor comment on a defendant's failure to testify in his or her own defense?

18   Does the right of the press to see a trial always outweigh the defendant's right to a fair trial? Explain your answer.

19   Explain what proof beyond a reasonable doubt means.

20   What does the phrase "placing character into evidence" mean?

Web Surfing

1   Visit the Legal Information Institute (www.law.cornell.edu) and do a search for "right to counsel."

2   Do an online search to see which states and cities have public defender offices and which rely on appointed lists for criminal defense attorneys.

Questions for Analysis

1   Should the state's burden in criminal cases be lowered? Is "beyond a reasonable doubt" too high a standard to meet? Explain your answer.

2   Some have said that criminal defendants in the United States have too many rights. What is your view? Provide examples to support your argument.

Hypotheticals

1   Danny is charged with burglary and faces a possible maximum sentence of 20 years. He does not qualify for representation by the public defender because he makes too much money per year, however he claims that he does not have any savings and no equity in his home to borrow against. Essentially, he has no way to pay for an attorney and no local attorney is willing to take his case. What is the judge likely to do in this situation?

2 Tonya is in the state legislature and decides to introduce a bill making all 12- person juries into 15-person juries. Is there a constitutional argument against this proposal? Is there a practical argument against this proposal? Is it a good idea?

3 During the trial of an alleged child sexual assault, the prosecutor asks that the trial be closed to the public from the point of his first statement to the jury until the defense rests its case. Is the judge likely to grant that request? Why or why not?

PRACTICE QUESTIONS FOR TEST REVIEW

See Appendix A for answers

Essay Question

Why is the *Gideon* case so important to the U.S. criminal justice system?

True-False

1 T F There are instances where an adult defendant can be tried in secret in the U.S. system.

2 T F Some states seat six-person juries for certain types of criminal cases.

3 T F No state permits nonunanimous verdicts in criminal cases.

Fill in the Blank

1 A(n) ⎯⎯ is the fee charged at the beginning of a case to pay an attorney for all actions carried out.

2 A government attorney who works for an office in the court system whose sole responsibility is to provide legal representation to those individuals who are charged with crimes is a(n) ⎯⎯.

3 A conclusion about a fact that must be made unless and until refuted by other evidence is ⎯⎯.

Multiple Choice

1 The standard of proof that the prosecution must meet to prove that a defendant committed a crime.

   A Proof beyond all doubt.
   B Proof beyond a shadow of a doubt.
   C Proof beyond a reasonable doubt.
   D Proof to a preponderance of the evidence.

2   When a criminal defendant testifies and his or her previous criminal record is allowed into evidence through the cross-examination of the defendant.

    A   Record of witness impeachment.
    B   Placing character into evidence.
    C   Showing the state's case is weak.
    D   All of the above.

3   Which of the following are circumstances where a judge is authorized to remove a defendant from the courtroom during his or her trial?

    A   Defendant is unruly.
    B   Defendant refuses to follow the judge's orders.
    C   Defendant acts aggressively.
    D   All of the above.

ENDNOTES

1. *State v. Armfield*, 214 Mont. 229, 693 P.2d 1226 (1984).
2. *Gideon v. Wainwright*, 372 U.S. 335, 343, 83 S.Ct. 792, 796 (U.S. Fla., 1963).
3. *Lewis v. U.S.*, 518 U.S. 322, 116 S.Ct. 2163, 35 L.Ed.2d 590 (1996).
4. *Baldwin v. New York*, 399 U.S. 66 (1970).
5. *Codispoti v. Pennsylvania*, 418 U.S. 506, 94 S.Ct. 2707 (1974).
6. *Williams v. Florida*, 399 U.S. 78, 90 S.Ct. 1893, 26 L.Ed.2d 446 (1970).
7. *Foundations of Modern Jurisprudence*, William Seal Carpenter, 1958, page 114.
8. *The Grandeur That Was Rome*, J.C. Stobart, 4th Edition, 1961.
9. 441 U.S. 130, 139, 99 S.Ct. 1623, 60 L.Ed.2d 96 (1979).
10. *McKeiver v. Pennsylvania*, 403 U.S. 528, 91 S.Ct. (1976).
11. *Richmond Newspapers, Inc. v. Virginia*, 100 S.Ct. 2814 (1980).
12. *Estes v. Texas*, 381 U.S. 532 (1965).
13. *Globe Newspaper Co. v. Superior Court*, 457 U.S. 596, 102 S.Ct. 2613 (1982).
14. *Press Enterprise Co. v. Superior Court (Press Enterprise I)*, 464 U.S. 501 (1984).
15. *Press Enterprise Co. v. Superior Court (Press Enterprise II)*, 478 U.S. 1 (1986).
16. *Chambers v. Mississippi*, 410 U.S. 284, 93 S.Ct. 1038, 35 L.Ed.2d 297 (1973).
17. *Burbank v. Cain*, 535 F.3d 350 (5th Cir. 2008).
18. *Shorter v. U.S.*, 792 A.2d 228 (D.C. 2001).
19. *U.S. v. Eagle*, 498 F.3d 885, 74 Fed. R. Evid. Serv. 257 (8th Cir. 2007).
20. *Commerford v. State*, 728 So. 2d 796 (Fla. Dist. Ct. App. 4th Dist. 1999).
21. *Com. v. Avalos*, 454 Mass. 1, 906 N.E.2d 987 (2009).
22. *U.S. v. Orisnord*, 483 F.3d 1169 (11th Cir. 2007).
23. 5 J. Wigmore, Evidence §1367, p. 32 (J. Chadbourn rev.1974).
24. *Illinois v. Allen*, 397 U.S. 337, 90 S.Ct. 1057, 25 L.Ed.2d 353 (1970).
25. *Estelle v. Williams*, 425 U.S. 501 (1976).

Eighth Amendment: Initial Appearance, Bail, and Preliminary Hearings

- Explain the purpose of the initial appearance
- Describe the role of the preliminary hearing in a prosecution
- Define how a court decides on a bail and bond amount
- Describe at what point in pretrial proceedings a suspect is guaranteed to have an attorney
- Explain the rules of evidence as they apply at preliminary hearings vs. criminal trials

I. Initial Appearance
   A. Purpose of the Initial Appearance
   B. Right to an Attorney at Initial Appearance

II. Bail and Bond
   A. Bonding Companies
      Bounty Hunters
   B. Recognizance Bond
   C. Factors to Consider in Setting Bond
      Defendant's Ties to the Community
      Seriousness of the Offense
      Defendant's Likelihood of Flight to Avoid Prosecution
      Danger of the Defendant to Victim or Community

Defendant's Burden in a Bail Hearing
   D. Bond Forfeiture
   E. The Push to Eliminate Bond

III. Preliminary Hearing
   A. The Purpose of the Preliminary Hearing
   B. The Procedure Followed at the Preliminary Hearing
   C. Evidentiary Issues and Rules During Preliminary Hearings
   D. Decision at the Preliminary Hearing
   E. The Defendant's Role at the Preliminary Hearing
   F. Negotiations Between Prosecutors and Defense Attorneys at Preliminary Hearings

INITIAL APPEARANCE

Initial appearance
A hearing that takes place within days of the suspect's arrest, where the suspect is advised of his or her constitutional rights and given the opportunity to request a court-appointed attorney, and where the court can confirm the defendant's identity.

In some jurisdictions, the **initial appearance** is also called the preliminary examination. No matter what the term, the purpose of the hearing is the same. Shortly after the defendant is arrested, the defendant is brought before a judge—often a magistrate judge—and again reminded of his or her rights and also asked if it will be necessary to appoint an attorney to represent the defendant.

During the initial appearance, the magistrate will often advise the defendant of the charges currently pending against him or her. These are often preliminary charges, and the defendant may have additional charges added once the prosecution team has had an opportunity to review the defendant's case.

The final purpose of the initial appearance is to ensure that the defendant has been correctly identified. The judge will confirm that the person the state believes that it has in custody is in fact the person being held. To that end, the judge may order fingerprint comparisons or some other procedure to properly identify the defendant.

A. PURPOSE OF THE INITIAL APPEARANCE

At the initial appearance, a magistrate or some other court official will notify the accused of his or her rights, as well as any additional information, such as:

- The seriousness of the charge against him or her
- The consequences of the hearing and future hearings
- The right to the assistance of counsel

The initial appearance hearing is specifically designed to ensure that the defendant is aware of his or her constitutional rights as early in the legal process as possible. The person who informs the defendant of his or her rights is often a magistrate judge. The magistrate may appoint an attorney to represent the defendant if the defendant cannot afford to hire his or her own.

At the initial appearance, the judge will advise the defendant of the charge against him or her. The judge will also inform the defendant that this is a preliminary charge and that additional charges may be brought against the defendant. The defendant will be told if he or she is charged with a felony or a misdemeanor and the maximum possible sentence (although not all jurisdictions follow this last procedure).

The judge will also confirm the defendant's identity, making sure that the person the police have charged and placed under arrest is the same person referred to in the arrest warrant. To that end, the judge may sometimes require fingerprint analysis to confirm that the person in custody is in fact the person the police believe him or her to be. If the defendant contests his or her identity, then the court may order DNA evidence to be obtained.

B. RIGHT TO AN ATTORNEY AT INITIAL APPEARANCE

Although some initial appearance hearings are conducted by other officials, for the sake of clarity this text will continue to refer to the presiding official at the initial appearance hearing as a magistrate judge. This judge will read the defendant his or her constitutional rights. The rights sound similar to the *Miranda* rights read to the defendant shortly after being placed under arrest, and that similarity is by design. The *Miranda* decision, as well as subsequent Supreme Court decisions, requires that the defendant be made aware of his or her rights to be presumed innocent, that the defendant has the right to remain silent, that the defendant has the right to a jury trial, and that the defendant has the right to an attorney. If the defendant cannot afford an attorney, the magistrate at the initial appearance hearing may appoint one at that time or advise the clerk's office or other administrator that the defendant's case should be routed to the public defender's office or to the appointed attorney list, depending on the procedure followed in that jurisdiction.

A defendant may hire an attorney at any point following the arrest. The defendant may have contacted an attorney before the arrest warrant was served, assuming that the defendant was aware of the warrant. In any event, as soon as an attorney is hired for the defendant, the attorney's first bit of advice to the client is usually to say nothing to the police. Defense attorneys know that it is far more likely that the defendant, in trying to explain his or her actions, will only give law enforcement and the prosecution more evidence that they can later use against him or her. However, once the defendant has invoked his or her right to remain silent, the police cannot question the suspect any further. If an attorney is either retained to represent the defendant or is appointed to represent the defendant, that attorney will normally handle the defendant's case from that point onward. The attorney will discuss the case with the prosecutor, attend the preliminary hearing and any other hearings, as well as conduct the jury trial, should it come to that. A defense attorney may enter the picture at any of several different steps in the post-arrest process.

One of the first duties of a defense attorney is to attempt to have the defendant released from jail on bond. We will discuss the role of bond in the next section.

 BAIL AND BOND

There is wide variation among the states and the federal government regarding **bail** or **bond**. Although criminal defendants cannot be subject to "excessive bail" (as shown in the Eighth Amendment in Figure 11-1, the Amendment does not explain what is meant by excessive. We will begin our discussion with a definition of what exactly bail or bond is, then discuss how it is used in criminal cases, and finally examine the parameters of the Eighth Amendment as they apply to bail and bond. For the purposes of simplicity,

Bail
The posting of a monetary amount to guarantee the return of the defendant for subsequent court hearings.

Bond
A promise of specific monetary amount promised to the state and offered as a guarantee for the defendant's return to court at a later date.

FIGURE 11-1

**Eighth Amendment, U.S.
Constitution**

> Excessive bail shall not be required, nor excessive fines imposed, nor cruel
> and unusual punishments inflicted.

this text will refer only to bail and then later explain the difference between bail
and bond.

Bail may be set at the initial appearance hearing, but usually this issue
comes up more often at the preliminary hearing stage, discussed later in this
chapter. In many jurisdictions, a judge has wide latitude in deciding on bail.
The accused is entitled to a hearing where evidence will be presented to determine the amount of bail required. In serious cases, there is no set monetary
amount for each case. The nature of the charge will determine the monetary
amount of bail. The arresting officer has no authority to set the amount of
bail. A judge will often consider the officer's recommendation but is not
bound to follow the officer's wishes. Similarly, a prosecutor may make a bail
recommendation, but the court may disregard the prosecutor's desires as
well. The reason bail is required is to ensure the defendant's appearance at
trial or other proceeding.

Posting bail serves two purposes: It releases the defendant and allows him
or her to return to gainful employment and to ensure that the defendant has a
vested interest in returning for his or her court hearing. If the defendant does
not return for court, then his or her bail is forfeited and a warrant will issue for
the defendant's arrest. There are several factors that weigh into a bail decision.
The concept of bail arises under the presumption in U.S. law that a person is
innocent until proven guilty and should, therefore, not be held in jail until
trial unless there is some overriding reason for doing so.

The words bail and bond have been used and misused so often that they
have become confused with one another. Bail is a person's assurance that he
or she will return to court at a specific date and time. As such, there are some
bails that do not involve money or property at all. Bail can mean several different things. A person released on bail might be released with no conditions
or might be released on supervised bail, where he or she must check in with a
court clerk or other official periodically. Defendants may also receive conditional bail or conditional release, where their release from jail contains specific
provisions that, if broken, will land the person back in jail. One of the most
common requirements of conditional bail is that the accused stay away from
the victim in the case. Bond, on the other hand, is a monetary guarantee by
the defendant or someone else that offers the promise that the defendant
will return for court. If he or she fails to return, the bond will be forfeited.
In addition to setting monetary amounts as a condition of release, some
judges may turn to property bonds in lieu of cash. A **property bond** is the
posting of an individual's title to his or her home or other land as a guarantee
of the defendant's return. If the defendant flees the jurisdiction and does
not return for court hearings, then the court has the unenviable task of
seizing someone's home as forfeiture of the bond. In such a case, the owners

Property bond
Posting of real estate to
guarantee the defendant's
return for a subsequent court
appearance.

are removed from their home and the house and land become the property of the local government.

Because bonds can involve real estate as well as money or other items of value, the consequences for the person who owns the property, especially if the property belongs to someone other than the defendant, can be disastrous. Consider Scenario 11-1.

PROPERTY BOND

Ralph has been arrested, and the court is requiring that someone post a property bond for his release. This means that someone who owns real estate outright can pledge the property as a guarantee for Ralph's return to court. Ralph's grandmother, Tia, posts her own home for Ralph's bond. Unfortunately, Ralph immediately flees the jurisdiction and does not return for his court date. What are the consequences for Grandma Tia?

Answer: She will lose her home. The state will bring a forfeiture action against her, and because she posted her personal residence as bond for Ralph, she will lose it because he failed to appear.

Bail can be set by magistrate judges or trial judges. The appellate courts have said, time and again, that the trial judge is in the best position to review all of the available facts and to know the case "on the ground" better than an appellate court. As such, appellate courts are generally reluctant to overturn a trial judge's decision regarding the amount of bail or even if bail should be set at all.

The ultimate purpose of bail is to prevent or at least discourage people accused of crimes from fleeing the jurisdiction. Having to forfeit a large sum of money is enough to keep most people from running, but there are other forms of bail that can achieve the same ends.

Another purpose of bail is to allow the defendant to help his or her attorney prepare his or her defense. That is considerably easier to do when the defendant is out in the community rather than being held at the local jail. The defendant, while out on bail, can continue to work, which will help him or her pay for legal services, and the defendant can help the attorney to locate witnesses beneficial to the defense. Bail or bond is not intended to punish the defendant before the case has been concluded. It is not, as has sometimes been portrayed in various media, a means for the court to financially cripple the accused before the trial ever occurs. Although there are many situations where the court might deny bail, those reasons must be based on factors independent of the person's supposed guilt.

A. BONDING COMPANIES

A **bonding company** is in the business of posting monetary bail bonds for people who cannot afford to pay their own bail. Usually, these companies will charge a 10 percent, nonrefundable fee to the defendant for this service. In the case where

Bonding company
A private business that posts bonds for individuals who have been charged with crimes and will be forced to pay the balance of the defendant's bond if the defendant flees the jurisdiction or otherwise does not appear for a court date.

a judge sets a bond at $20,000, the bonding company will charge the defendant $2,000 in exchange for posting a promissory bond that it will pay in the event that the defendant fails to appear for court. In addition to posting a monetary amount for bail, a judge may impose other conditions, such as:

- Defendant must maintain gainful employment
- Defendant will have no contact with the victim in the case

In states that allow the use of bonding companies, the individuals who work for the bonding company may periodically check up on the defendant before his or her court date to make sure that the defendant has not fled the jurisdiction. States tend to like this arrangement because it keeps a second pair of eyes on the defendant to make sure that he or she will appear for a subsequent court date. On the other hand, there are many critics that point out that bonding companies may take a far more intrusive interest in their clients and may engage in questionable, if not violent, tactics to ensure that the defendant appears for his or her court date.

Some states have eliminated bonding companies entirely. Citing concerns about abusive practices by bonding company employees, some states allow defendants to post bond through the state government, which in many ways acts in the same capacity as a bonding company. In states that continue to allow the use of bonding companies an interesting profession has arisen: the so-called bounty hunter.

BOUNTY HUNTERS

Bounty hunter
An employee of a bonding company who works to locate defendants who have absconded and to return these defendants to face their court dates.

Bonding companies often employ individuals to hunt down and return defendants who have fled the jurisdiction. State law usually gives a grace period to the bonding company to produce the individual who has not appeared for court. This grace period might be 72 hours to 10 days, depending on the circumstances. If the bonding company is able to locate the defendant and return him to the jail, then the bonding company will not be required to forfeit the defendant's bond. This creates a system in which the bonding company has a strong interest in keeping tabs on its client, and also gives law enforcement another tool to help locate defendants who have absconded. This is where the **bounty hunter** enters the picture. The bonding company may pay a flat fee to an individual to find the defendant and bring him or her back to the jurisdiction. In other cases, the bounty hunter may be paid on a percentage basis, such as 10 percent of the bonding company's fee. In either event, the bounty hunter is employed by the bonding company to locate the defendant, return him or her to the jurisdiction, and surrender him or her off bond to the local authorities.

The use of bounty hunters has been called into question, prompted by several instances in which bounty hunters have used excessive force to subdue defendants and return them. In one notable case, a bounty hunter crossed into Mexico, kidnapped a defendant, and returned him to the United States. The Mexican government charged the bounty hunter with kidnapping, causing no end of confusion for all parties concerned.

B. RECOGNIZANCE BOND

Recognizance bond is a type of bond procedure that once was quite common, but is not seen as frequently in modern times. When someone posts a recognizance bond, he or she is simply giving a promise to return and not posting any money to ensure that return. Basically, the person is giving his or her word. In the past, when communities were smaller, such a process worked with reasonable efficiency. The person who posted an own recognizance (OR) bond would simply promise to return to court and then would be released. Because the person was known in the community, tracking him or her down did not involve much effort if the person failed to appear. Recognizance bonds are used with much lower frequency in bigger cities and even in smaller communities where the populace is more mobile than it once was.

Recognizance bond
The person accused simply gives his or her word that he or she will return for a specific court date.

C. FACTORS TO CONSIDER IN SETTING BOND

Before a judge sets bail, he or she must consider several different factors. Obviously, no judge wishes to release a defendant who then commits another crime, such as murdering the witness in the case. On the other hand, the Eighth Amendment prohibits excessive bail. To juggle these competing interests, a judge will consider all of the following factors before setting bail:

- Defendant's ties to the community
- Seriousness of the offense
- Defendant's likelihood of flight to avoid prosecution
- Danger of the defendant to victim or community

DEFENDANT'S TIES TO THE COMMUNITY

One important factor in setting bail is the defendant's ties to the community. If the defendant is a stranger or someone simply passing through the area on his or her way to some other locale, then there is a greater likelihood that the defendant will abscond from the jurisdiction when he or she is released. However, a defendant with strong ties to the community, such as family members who live in the area, children who attend school in the jurisdiction, or long-term employment in the area is less likely to flee. All of these factors will weigh in the defendant's favor. If the defendant cannot show any of these ties to the area, then the bail amount will undoubtedly be larger than that for someone charged with the same offense who can boast of these connections to the community. Consider Scenario 11-2.

HISPANIC ORIGIN

SCENARIO 11-2

Juan has been arrested for shoplifting. At his bond hearing, the judge says that because Juan is Hispanic, it's likely that he will flee the jurisdiction and return to his home country if he is set free on bond. The judge makes no inquiry into what country Juan is from or even his citizenship status. Is this a valid consideration for a bond?

Answer: No. The judge may consider a defendant's ties to the communities, but may not simply assume that because someone is of a particular race that he or she is a flight risk. In this case, the judge did not even determine if Juan was a U.S. citizen.

SERIOUSNESS OF THE OFFENSE

Presumption of innocence
A basic tenet of U.S. law that a defendant enters the criminal process clothed in the assumption that he or she is innocent unless and until the prosecution proves that he or she is guilty beyond a reasonable doubt.

Although a defendant enters all courts with the **presumption of innocence**, a judge may take into account the nature of the charge before setting a bail amount. There are certain offenses, such as rape and murder, where the court may deny bail. In such a situation, the danger to the community, or to specific individuals, may be such that it outweighs the defendant's need for freedom pending trial. There are also certain offenses, including rape and murder, where many states will not allow a magistrate to set bail. In these cases, the bail must be set by a superior or trial court judge.[1] The trial judge has exclusive jurisdiction in these types of cases to set the bail amount. The defendant must remain in custody until he or she is brought before the trial judge for a bond hearing. See Scenario 11-3.

SCENARIO 11-3

SERIOUSNESS OF THE OFFENSE

Cyril is charged with several counts of first-degree murder. There are allegations that Cyril is involved with a gang and that these murder charges were gang-related. When Cyril's defense attorney brings a motion for bond, the trial judge summarily rejects it, stating that given the seriousness of the offense, she will not set any bond. Is this a valid ruling?

Answer: Yes. Although a judge must consider several factors, seriousness of the offense alone may be enough to deny bond. However, the judge should also review other factors in the case.

DEFENDANT'S LIKELIHOOD OF FLIGHT TO AVOID PROSECUTION

Closely linked with the consideration of the defendant's ties to the community is the issue of whether or not the defendant is likely to flee the jurisdiction once he or she is released. A defendant who has fled while on bond in previous cases is unlikely to be granted bail at all. It is not always easy for the judge to decide who is or is not a likely candidate to flee the jurisdiction. The defendant's attorney will certainly argue that he or she will not, whereas the prosecutor may just as forcefully argue that he or she might. The judge must make up his or her own mind about this issue.

DANGER OF THE DEFENDANT TO VICTIM OR COMMUNITY

A defendant who has threatened police or victims in a case is unlikely to be granted bail. A judge must consider the danger to the community, to specific individuals, and even to the defendant, if bail is set and the defendant is released pending trial. There have been cases in which a defendant who was released on bond killed the witness against him or her or otherwise caused bodily injury and property damage. Judges do not have crystal balls; they must rely on their own experiences and the law as they weigh this element in with the other factors that must be considered before setting a bond amount.

DEFENDANT'S BURDEN IN A BAIL HEARING

A defendant requests bail so, unlike in other hearings, he or she will often take the stand to offer testimony on the limited subject of bail. A prosecutor may cross-examine the defendant but will be limited to questions surrounding the four basic issues of bail, not issues related to the underlying case. Even with this limited interaction, many defense attorneys prefer testimony from individuals other than the defendant. Defense attorneys are well aware that many bail hearings are transcribed and that the defendant might make some statement that could be used against him or her at a later date—although some jurisdictions do not allow statements made in bail or bond hearings to be used at trial.

D. BOND FORFEITURE

Once a defendant has been released on bail, a judge has full discretion to revoke bail and have the defendant returned to jail pending trial. A judge can base this **bond forfeiture** decision on allegations that the defendant has attempted to intimidate or injure witnesses in a case or has committed another offense.[2]

Bond forfeiture
A judicial determination that the defendant has violated the conditions of his or her release and that the defendant should be placed into custody pending further hearings.

E. THE PUSH TO ELIMINATE BOND

Just as there have been attempts to eliminate bonding companies, other states have entertained legislation to eliminate bond entirely, at least for low-level offenses. Proponents of this legislation say that when someone cannot pay a low bond amount, the alternative, placing this person in custody until a trial date, is a waste of both time and money. The state must provide room and board for this person, as well as guards and security. In many cases, when the defendants in these types of cases are brought to court, they are often released on "time served." This phrase refers to the amount of time that the defendant has spent in jail awaiting a trial date. In many situations, the time spent awaiting trial is longer than the sentence would have been had these defendants pled guilty on the day they were arrested.

PRELIMINARY HEARING

Preliminary hearing
A court hearing that determines if there is probable cause to believe that the defendant committed the crime with which he or she is charged.

Within a few days of the initial appearance (the actual time period varies by state), the defendant will be brought before another magistrate or other court officer. However, this hearing is not an initial hearing. Instead, the court will hold a hearing to determine if there is sufficient probable cause to believe that the defendant committed the crime. The **preliminary hearing** (also known as a probable cause hearing) is held within days of the defendant's arrest. It is a hearing where the defendant will appear, represented by an attorney, and the case will be presented by a prosecutor. Preliminary hearings are usually reserved only for felony cases. Misdemeanor cases, in most states, do not have preliminary hearings.

The preliminary hearing, unlike the initial appearance hearing, is adversarial in nature. The prosecutor will be present, as well as the defendant, defendant's attorney, and state's witnesses. The defendant also has the opportunity to testify at the preliminary hearing, although this rarely happens.

A. THE PURPOSE OF THE PRELIMINARY HEARING

The preliminary hearing has one purpose: to establish that there is sufficient probable cause for the defendant's arrest and continued detention. At the preliminary hearing, the government, through the prosecutor, is required to present witness testimony to establish probable cause. Normally, a preliminary hearing is held before a magistrate judge. The judge has the responsibility of deciding whether or not the prosecution has met the burden of showing probable cause. The actual procedure for carrying out a preliminary hearing varies somewhat from jurisdiction to jurisdiction, but the basic elements are the same everywhere: The state must present evidence to prove probable cause for the defendant's arrest.

B. THE PROCEDURE FOLLOWED AT THE PRELIMINARY HEARING

Because the purpose of a preliminary hearing is to establish probable cause that the defendant committed the crime with which he or she is charged, the state must present some evidence to meet its burden. This burden never shifts to the defendant to prove his or her innocence. The state meets its burden by calling witnesses, often police officers, but frequently civilian witnesses as well. These witnesses will testify about the facts surrounding the crime and the defendant's arrest. The prosecutor calls his or her witnesses first, and then the defense attorney has the right to cross-examine the witnesses about their testimony. This cross-examination is supposed to be limited to the issue of probable cause, but many defense attorneys see this as a perfect opportunity to learn more about the case. They will often ask questions outside the scope of the hearing to learn these facts. There is no requirement to prove probable cause beyond a reasonable doubt. Instead, the state must establish probable cause by a preponderance of evidence.

During a preliminary hearing, the state's burden is simply to show that it is more likely than not that the defendant committed the crime. The state does not have to prove that the defendant committed the crime beyond a reasonable doubt, because that standard is reserved for trials. It is also not required because the defendant will not be sentenced at the conclusion of the hearing, and the defendant continues to enjoy the full spectrum of constitutional protections. However, because the burden of proof at a preliminary hearing is much lower than that required at trial, there are some practical issues that heavily favor the prosecution. One such issue concerns the rules of evidence that are used in preliminary hearings.

C. EVIDENTIARY ISSUES AND RULES DURING PRELIMINARY HEARINGS

The rules of evidence at a preliminary hearing are more relaxed than those used at a trial. For instance, hearsay testimony, which is generally inadmissible during a trial, can be used in a preliminary hearing. The reason that the rules of evidence are not as rigorous goes to the very heart of the preliminary hearing. The defendant will not be found guilty or sentenced at the conclusion. The jury in the defendant's case will never be told about the result of the preliminary hearing. As such, the standard of proof is much lower. Prosecutors routinely win preliminary hearings, and it is rare for a judge to rule that there is insufficient probable cause, given such a low standard of proof.

Preliminary hearings are not difficult to present, and this explains why many new prosecutors are assigned to this duty. The hearing superficially resembles a trial, and inexperienced prosecutors can gain valuable insights into the adversarial process without the prospect of losing a major trial.

D. DECISION AT THE PRELIMINARY HEARING

There are only two decisions at a preliminary hearing: a finding that the state has established probable cause or that it has not. In the vast majority of cases, the magistrate will find that probable cause exists. This result can be explained by various factors, including good police work, the prosecutor's preparation, and the very low standard of proof. Beyond that, if a magistrate rules that there is no probable cause and the prosecutor disagrees with this ruling, then the prosecutor may still present the case to the grand jury.

When a magistrate decides that the state has met the burden of probable cause in a preliminary hearing, the judge issues a ruling **binding over** the case to a higher court. In many states, that means the defendant's case will be transferred to superior court, although not all states use that term to refer to a trial court empowered to hear felony cases. On the other hand, if the magistrate rules that there is insufficient probable cause, then the defendant will be ordered

Binding over
A determination that probable cause exists in a preliminary hearing, triggering a transfer of the case to a higher court, usually superior court.

to be released. Assuming that there are no other charges pending against the defendant, the holding facility will release him or her. Consider Scenario 11-4.

| SCENARIO 11-4 | PROOF BEYOND A REASONABLE DOUBT |

PROOF BEYOND A REASONABLE DOUBT

Sandy is charged with aggravated assault and represents herself at her preliminary hearing. The police officer testifies that the victim told him that Sandy hit him with a shovel and then fled the scene. Sandy objects that the victim is not present to testify, but the judge overrules the objection. The officer identifies Sandy as the person he later found running through the neighborhood, holding a shovel. The victim also identified Sandy. The judge allows Sandy to offer testimony and, when she finishes, the judge rules that there is probable cause to bind the case over. Sandy objects that based on this evidence no jury would convict her. She requests that the judge dismiss the case on these grounds. Is she correct?

Answer: No. The standard of proof at a preliminary hearing is not the same as that required in a jury trial. Therefore, a judge can rule based solely on probable cause to believe that Sandy committed the crime and bind the case over.

E. THE DEFENDANT'S ROLE AT THE PRELIMINARY HEARING

A defendant sits with his or her counsel during the preliminary hearing, and the two are allowed to confer with one another as the hearing proceeds. Many defense attorneys will meet with their clients shortly before the hearing to explain what will happen, to discuss the merits of the case, and also to explain that the hearing will not result in the defendant going to prison or being found guilty.

Defendants are permitted to testify at a preliminary hearing, but they are normally counseled to remain silent because establishing probable cause is an easy thing to do and the chances are extremely high that the court will rule against the defendant. Given those facts, having the defendant testify—and then be subject to cross-examination by the prosecutor—could only help the state's case.

F. NEGOTIATIONS BETWEEN PROSECUTORS AND DEFENSE ATTORNEYS AT PRELIMINARY HEARINGS

Even though a case is on the docket for a preliminary hearing, there still may not be a hearing. There is a certain amount of give and take between prosecutors and defense attorneys, and the negotiations between them can become intense. What are they negotiating? On the surface, there may appear to be very little that a prosecutor could offer a defendant or anything that the defendant would want, but appearances can be deceiving. Prosecutors often have dozens of cases pending on a particular day's calendar. It is also the prosecutor's role to make bail recommendations in cases, although the magistrate is not bound to follow those recommendations. The prosecutor and the defense may enter into some hard-nosed bargaining about two issues: waiver and bail recommendations.

If a defendant waives the preliminary hearing, then he or she admits that there is sufficient probable cause to bind the case over. This admission cannot be used against the defendant at trial, so there is little danger to the defendant to simply avoid the hearing. However, a defense attorney may negotiate with the prosecutor over the issue of the bail recommendation. The bargaining might go something like this:

> Prosecutor: My bail recommendation on your client is $10,000.
> Defense attorney: If I get my client to waive the hearing, will you consider lowering that recommendation to $5,000?
> Prosecutor: If you can get your client to waive the hearing, I'll go to $7,500.
> Defense attorney: I'll talk to my client.

In such a scenario, the prosecutor lowers his or her bail recommendation to the court in exchange for a waiver of the preliminary hearing. The prosecutor will have one less case to worry about and may be able to release one or two witnesses. The defense attorney can tell his or her client that the prosecutor is lowering the bail recommendation. Of course, both parties realize that a judge is not compelled to follow the prosecutor's recommendation, but in the vast majority of cases, the judge will follow the mutually agreed upon resolution, reasoning that the defense attorney and prosecutor are both in the best position to know the issues in the case. Their compromise saves valuable court time and resources.

For purposes of clarity, this text will continue to refer to the trial court as superior court, keeping in mind that there is some variation among the states, and not all states use the term "superior court" to refer to the trial court. Following the preliminary hearing, when the case is bound over to superior court—and the overwhelming majority will be bound over—the next phase is the charging decision by the prosecutor.

ATKINS v. STATE
DECEMBER 18, 2017—UNPUBLISHED OPINION

CASE EXCERPT

MEMORANDUM OPINION BY CHIEF JUSTICE MORRISS [SIC]

MEMORANDUM OPINION

In mid-2016, Texarkana, Texas, Police Officer Johnny Lee Bailey, Jr., responded to a report of a disturbance at the residence of Marilyn Eason. When Bailey arrived at Eason's residence, he saw Eason, Eason's son (Kourtney Atkins), and a small child in a car seat on the front porch, where Atkins and Eason were exchanging heated words with each other. After a brief struggle, which included all adults present and during which Atkins tossed an item inside the house, Atkins was secured in the patrol car.

What happened after Atkins was placed in the patrol car is subject to conflicting testimony, but Bailey's version is that Eason consented to Bailey looking inside the residence for whatever Atkins tossed there. Bailey's testimony that Eason gave him consent to search inside the house was the subject of Atkins' objections at trial and his arguments here on appeal that such testimony was improper hearsay and violated Atkins' confrontation rights. Because pretrial proceedings such as this suppression hearing do not support confrontation claims or the exclusion of hearsay, we affirm Atkins' conviction and sentence.

In his testimony, Bailey recounted Eason's report that Atkins did not have permission to be at the house and she wanted him to leave; however, Eason had testified at the suppression hearing that Atkins and his infant son, her grandson, lived with her. Atkins was not following the officer's instructions, so Bailey pushed the door to prevent Atkins from entering the house. Bailey saw "somewhat of a white and orange object, similar to what a pill bottle would be" in Atkins' right hand, the hand pinned by the door. When Bailey and another officer were struggling with Atkins to try to get him under their control, Atkins, using his right hand, threw something hard into the house. Bailey's subsequent search inside the house yielded a pill bottle that proved to contain methamphetamine.

On appeal, Atkins contends that the trial court erred in denying his motion to suppress because Bailey's testimony at the suppression hearing was hearsay and violated Atkins' rights under the Confrontation Clause. We affirm the trial court's judgment because neither the Texas Rules of Evidence nor the Confrontation Clause apply in a suppression hearing.

Except as they would apply to privileges, the Texas Rules of Evidence do not apply during suppression hearings because such hearings involve preliminary questions. In *Granados*, appellant complained that, at the suppression hearing, the trial court erred in admitting into evidence a police officer's testimony of what another officer told him about what the victim's family said about the victim's whereabouts. *Granados*, 85 S.W.3d at 226-27. Granados claimed that testimony constituted inadmissible hearsay. Id. at 227. The court concluded that the officer's testimony, in which "he testified as to the facts that he . . . believed constituted probable cause," was not hearsay and, thus, was admissible. Id. at 230. Moreover, the court noted that the testimony would have been admissible, even if it had been hearsay, because courts are permitted to rely on hearsay and other inadmissible evidence in suppression hearings even though it would not otherwise be admissible at trial. Id. at 227 n.29 (citing *United States v. Raddatz*, 447 U.S. 667, 679 (1980) ("At a suppression hearing, the court may rely on hearsay and other evidence, even though that evidence would not be admissible at trial.")). The leading cases on the Confrontation Clause, such as *Melendez-Diaz* and *Crawford*, involve the admissibility of evidence against an accused at trial, not in a preliminary hearing. The Supreme Court has never extended the reach of the Confrontation Clause beyond the confines of a trial. Thus, the right of confrontation does not apply to a pretrial suppression hearing. *Ford v. State*, 268 S.W.3d 620, 621 (Tex. App.—Texarkana 2008), rev'd on other grounds by 305 S.W.3d 530, 534 (Tex. Crim. App. 2009).

Thus, Atkins' complaint—that the trial court erred in denying his motion to suppress because the officer's testimony constituted hearsay under the Texas Rules of

Evidence and violated his constitutional rights under the Confrontation Clause—fails. We overrule this point of error.

We affirm the trial court's judgment.

Josh R. Morriss [sic], III

Chief Justice

CASE QUESTIONS

1 The defendant contends that the police officer gave hearsay testimony during the preliminary hearing. What testimony is the defendant referring to?

2 According to the appellate court, does it matter if this was hearsay testimony or not?

3 Can courts rely on hearsay and other inadmissible evidence at a preliminary hearing?

4 Does the confrontation clause extend beyond jury trials?

CHAPTER SUMMARY

In this chapter, we examined the first procedural step that occurs after a defendant has been placed under arrest. An initial appearance is a court hearing where the defendant appears before a judge—often a magistrate—and is advised of his or her constitutional rights. During the initial appearance hearing or at any subsequent time, the judge may also set bail for the defendant. Bail is the posting of money or sometimes real property as a guarantee that the defendant will return for future court hearings. Judges must consider several factors before setting bail, including the seriousness of the offense charged, the defendant's ties to the community, and the defendant's likelihood of fleeing the jurisdiction should he or she be released on bail.

Following the initial appearance hearing, the next procedural step is the preliminary hearing. At a preliminary hearing, the prosecutor will present testimony from a witness to establish that there is probable cause to believe that the defendant committed the crime with which he or she is charged. The defense attorney has the right to cross-examine the witness, and the judge makes a determination of whether the state has met its burden. Because the rules of evidence are much more liberal and because the standard of proof is usually preponderance of the evidence—not beyond a reasonable doubt—the state usually wins this hearing, and the defendant's case is bound over to the superior court.

KEY TERMS AND CONCEPTS

Initial appearance   Bond   Bonding company
Bail   Property bond   Bounty hunter

Recognizance bond   Bond forfeiture
Presumption of   Preliminary hearing
   innocence   Binding over

END OF CHAPTER EXERCISES

Review Questions

See Appendix A for answers

1   What is the purpose of the initial appearance?
2   Explain how an attorney may be appointed at an initial appearance.
3   What are some factors that a court considers when setting bail or bond?
4   What is the difference between bail and bond?
5   How do bonding companies function?
6   Explain the role of bounty hunters.
7   What is a property bond?
8   Explain how a defendant would receive a recognizance bond.
9   What is bond forfeiture?
10   Explain the purpose of a preliminary hearing.
11   What procedure is followed at a preliminary hearing?
12   How are the evidentiary rules different at preliminary hearings when compared to trials?
13   What is the significance of binding over after a preliminary hearing?
14   What negotiations typically occur between prosecutors and defense attorneys before and during preliminary hearings?

Web Surfing

1   Visit www.justice.gov/usao and search for "preliminary hearings."

2   Do an online search for "eliminating bail" or "eliminating bail bond."

3   Visit www.law.cornell.edu/ and search for "initial appearance."

Questions for Analysis

1   Some states have done away with bonding companies. Should all states make bond an issue for the government and not for private enterprise? Explain your answer.

2   Can you make a case for not having bail or bond in any cases? Explain.

Hypotheticals

1   Judge Henao is presiding at a preliminary hearing. A witness testifies that she overheard a person in her neighborhood say that the defendant wanted to kill the victim and then later, when she saw the victim's body, she knew that the defendant must have done it. Is this evidence admissible in a preliminary hearing?

2   At the same hearing, another witness testifies that she is in contact with the "spirit world," and last night, the victim's ghost contacted her and told her the defendant was the person who murdered her. Is this testimony admissible at a preliminary hearing?

PRACTICE QUESTIONS FOR TEST REVIEW

See Appendix A for answers

Essay Question

Compare and contrast initial appearance hearings and preliminary hearings.

True-False

1   T   F   A judge can take a defendant's race into account in determining the amount of bail.

2   T   F   All defendants are presumed innocent, even at preliminary hearings.

3   T   F   The court hearing that decides if there is sufficient probable cause to detain the defendant is called the initial appearance hearing.

Fill in the Blank

1   A(n) _____ is a hearing that takes place within days of the suspect's arrest, where the suspect is advised of his or her constitutional rights and given the opportunity to request a court-appointed attorney, and where the court can confirm the defendant's identity.

2   The posting of a monetary amount to guarantee the return of the defendant for subsequent court hearings is known as _____.

3   An employee of a bonding company who works to locate defendants who have absconded and to return these defendants to face their court dates is called a(n) _____.

Multiple Choice

1 A judicial determination that the defendant has violated the conditions of his or her release and that the defendant should be placed into custody pending further hearings.

   A Guilt.
   B Bond forfeiture.
   C Preliminary hearing.
   D Probable cause.

2 Posting of real estate to guarantee the defendant's return for a subsequent court appearance.

   A Property bond.
   B Bond.
   C Surety.
   D Beneficiary.

3 The person accused simply gives his or her word that he or she will return for a specific court date.

   A Promise to return.
   B Self-bail.
   C Recognizance bond.
   D None of the above.

ENDNOTES

1. *State v. Dodson*, 556 S.W.2d 938 (Mo. Ct. App. 1977).
2. *Stiegele v. State*, 685 P.2d 1255 (Alaska Ct. App. 1984).

Arraignment and Discovery

- Explain the purpose of the arraignment
- List and explain the types of motions that a defendant might file at or before arraignment
- Explain how discovery proceeds in criminal cases
- Discuss the significance of the *Brady* decision in discovery
- Describe the types of motions that prosecutors might file in a criminal case

I. Arraignment
  A. Importance of the Arraignment
  B. Purpose of the Arraignment
  C. Filing Motions at Arraignment
  D. Waiving Arraignment
  E. Bench Warrants

II. Discovery
  A. Purpose of Discovery
    Changes to Discovery Rules
  B. Material Provided in Discovery
    Witness List
    Statement of Defendant
    Statement of Codefendant
    Defendant's Criminal Record
    Documents and Tangible Objects
    Scientific Reports

Statements of Witnesses
  C. Open File Policy
  D. Variations Among States in Discovery Rules
  E. Information That Is Normally Not Discoverable by the Defendant
    Work Product
    Criminal Records of State Witnesses
  F. *Brady* Material
    In Camera *Inspections*

III. Defense Motions Based on Discovery
  A. Motions to Suppress
  B. Motion to Sever
  C. Motion *in Limine*
  D. Motion to Reveal the Deal (*Giglio*)
  E. Motion to Reveal Identity of Confidential Informants

IV. Other Defense Motions
  A. Motion to Change Venue
  B. Motion for Continuance
  C. Plea of Former Jeopardy
  D. Bill of Particulars
  E. Speedy Trial Demand
    Dismissing a Case for Failure to Receive a Speedy Trial

    How Speedy Must a "Speedy Trial" Be?
    When the Defendant May Not Want a Speedy Trial After All
    When Is the Right to a Speedy Trial Triggered?
V. Prosecution Motions
  A. Similar Transactions
  B. Aggravation of Sentence
  C. Motion to Join

ARRAIGNMENT

Arraignment
A court hearing where the defendant is informed of the charge against him or her and given the opportunity to enter a plea of guilty or not guilty.

As we saw in Chapter 8, the grand jury has the responsibility of deciding whether or not a case should proceed. When they return a true bill of indictment, it means that the case will continue. The next step after the indictment is the **arraignment**. In some jurisdictions, initial appearances and arraignments are held at the same time. See Chapter 11 for a discussion of initial appearances. There is a difference in the procedural steps in many states based on whether a case is a misdemeanor or a felony. For the sake of clarity, we will continue our discussion of the criminal procedural steps as though all charges involved felony charges. The arraignment is normally scheduled several weeks or even months after the grand jury meets. In some jurisdictions, a defendant can be arraigned on the day of the trial, but most follow a pattern that sets the arraignment several weeks before the next scheduled trial date. At the arraignment, the defendant is told exactly what the charges are against him or her and is given an opportunity to enter an official plea. If the defendant has hired his or her own attorney, the attorney will respond for the defendant. Many defendants appear at the arraignment without an attorney and request that the judge appoint one for them. The court is authorized to appoint an attorney when the defendant's financial status indicates that the defendant is not able to afford one. The defendant may plead guilty or not guilty. If the defendant pleads guilty, he or she may be sentenced immediately. However, if the defendant enters a not guilty plea, the case will be scheduled for trial.

A. IMPORTANCE OF THE ARRAIGNMENT

The arraignment is important for several reasons. At the arraignment, the defendant and his or her attorney are given a copy of the formal charges pending against the defendant; in felony cases, the formal charge is embodied in the indictment. Traditionally, the indictment and the state's list of witnesses were the only items that the state was required to serve on the defendant at the arraignment. However, as we will see later in this chapter, the traditional rules have been changed, and the state is not only often required to present additional discovery materials to the defendant, but also must do so at the arraignment.

B. PURPOSE OF THE ARRAIGNMENT

The procedure followed at an arraignment is very simple. A list of cases (called a **calendar** or **docket**) is published. This docket contains the names of all the defendants who will be called on a particular day's arraignment calendar. The cases are normally announced according to their case file number or sometimes in alphabetical order based on the defendant's last name. "Calling" the calendar refers to the process of simply calling out the names of the defendants. This case file number or docket number has been assigned by the clerk's office after the grand jury returned a true bill of indictment. Defendants are instructed that they must respond when their names are called. Failure to appear for the scheduled arraignment can have severe consequences for the defendant, which we will discuss later in this chapter.

> **Calendar or docket**
> A listing of the cases currently pending before the court, usually by the defendants' names, case file number, and charges brought against them.

At the arraignment, once the defendant's case has been called, the defendant is brought before a judge and officially informed of the charges pending against him or her. This hearing might seem redundant, but for important reasons it is not. The defendant has already been arrested, so why does he or she need to be informed of the charges? The simple answer is that the prosecutor may have amended those charges during the prosecutor's charging decision. The arraignment is the point during the case when the defendant receives the final word about the pending charges. The defendant is given a copy of the indictment (for felonies) or an accusation (for state-level misdemeanors). The judge will also use the arraignment as an additional opportunity to inform the defendant of his or her rights and to inquire whether or not the defendant has an attorney. If the defendant cannot afford an attorney, the judge may appoint one or have the public defender review the defendant's status to see if he or she qualifies for their services. In some jurisdictions, the judge also informs the defendant of the maximum sentence possible for each of the charges pending against him or her.

The defendant is required to enter a plea at the arraignment. If the defendant pleads not guilty, he or she will be scheduled to return at a later time for a trial. If the defendant chooses to plead guilty, the judge may impose sentence that day or defer sentencing for a later date.

C. FILING MOTIONS AT ARRAIGNMENT

In the past, the arraignment procedure had greater significance than it has today. For instance, it was common for defendants to request *formal arraignment*. A formal arraignment consists of either the judge or the prosecutor reading the entire indictment, out loud, before the defendant and the others present in the courtroom. The defendant would then have the opportunity to challenge the sufficiency of the indictment. However, modern practice has tended away from formal arraignment to a more informal procedure where the defense counsel expressly waives formal arraignment, requests a copy of the indictment and discovery, and reserves the right to file additional **motions**, including those challenging the sufficiency of the indictment at a later time. The defendant may

> **Motion**
> An oral or written request to a court to take some action.

also decide to file additional motions after going through the indictment and whatever discovery the state may have served on him or her at the arraignment.

D. WAIVING ARRAIGNMENT

Waiving arraignment
A defendant surrenders the right to have the indictment read in open court; however, the defendant does not surrender any other rights.

A defendant is always free to waive both formal and informal arraignment through his or her counsel or by filing a written notice waiving arraignment and filing motions about specific issues in the case.[1] As noted, formal arraignment refers to the prosecutor or the judge actually reading the indictment aloud in court. This practice dates back centuries and was probably instituted in a time when most people could not read. These days, it is very common for a defense attorney to announce that the defendant is **waiving arraignment** (or the full reading of the indictment) and agrees to proceed with an informal arraignment. See Scenario 12-1.

| SCENARIO 12-1 | WAIVING ARRAIGNMENT |

George has his arraignment scheduled for today. He hired an attorney several weeks ago and when George's name is called from the listed cases on the docket, George's attorney stands and says, "Your Honor, Tamara Tigani representing George McKesson. We hereby waive formal arraignment, request a copy of the indictment, discovery, and request 10 days to file any motions related to the case." What is the practical effect of this announcement?

Answer: George's attorney has just told the judge that the formality of reading the indictment in open court is not necessary. The attorney has also requested a copy of the indictment charging George with a crime as well as any discovery that the state is obligated to turn over to the defense. The last part of the announcement gives the attorney the right to file additional motions, such as a motion to suppress the statement that George gave when he was being interrogated.

E. BENCH WARRANTS

Bench warrant
A warrant issued for the arrest of a person who was scheduled to appear in court but failed to do so.

When a defendant has been officially notified of his or her arraignment date and fails to appear, the judge is empowered to issue a **bench warrant** for his or her arrest. When a defendant makes bond after his or her arrest, one of the notifications he or she receives is the date of arraignment. The jail personnel usually give this notification to the defendant. However, the prosecutor's office may also send the defendant a certified letter, informing him or her of the arraignment date, along with a letter informing the defendant of the consequences should he or she fail to appear.

In the past, a defendant was always required to be physically present for an arraignment, but some jurisdictions have softened this requirement, either by allowing an attorney to appear on behalf of the defendant or by conducting arraignments through closed-circuit television.[2] Defendants may not actually be in the courtroom during a video arraignment. Instead, they may be several miles away at the local jail, and they "appear" in court by stepping before a camera and answering the judge's questions.

If a defendant fails to appear for an arraignment at all, the judge is authorized to issue a bench warrant for the defendant's arrest. A bench warrant permits any law enforcement officer to arrest the defendant and place him or her in custody pending a new court date. The defendant's bond is revoked, and if a bonding company posted bail for the defendant, the bond amount is forfeited to the state. Many states allow a grace period after the issuance of a bench warrant for a bonding company to locate and surrender the defendant to the authorities without forfeiting the entire bond amount. Although the amount of time varies, 72 hours is common. During that time, if the bonding company can locate the defendant, they can save themselves the entire bond amount, which gives them a strong interest in locating the defendant.

 ## DISCOVERY

Discovery refers to the process through which both sides in a case exchange information. In civil cases, the rules of discovery are quite liberal and the parties exchange a great deal of information. Both the civil plaintiff and defendant know the identities of each side's witnesses, what documents will be relied on, and what evidence will be presented. In addition to this wealth of information, civil litigants can also depose witnesses. In a civil deposition, the attorneys are allowed to question witnesses prior to trial, under oath, and to have this testimony recorded or transcribed. Later, at the trial, the attorneys may rely on transcripts of these depositions when questioning the witness.

This extensive exchange of information is not mirrored in criminal cases. Historically, very little discovery was allowed in criminal cases. Trials were conducted in the past by surprise and ambush. Whereas a civil litigant will know virtually every aspect of the case before the trial ever starts, a modern-day prosecutor might not know who the defense is going to call as a witness, or even what the defense to the crime may be until the defense attorney gives his or her opening statement. Modern changes to criminal discovery rules have attempted to change this age-old pattern.

Under the traditional criminal law system, where pretrial discovery procedures common to civil cases were not permitted in criminal trials, both the prosecutor and the defense attorney often began a trial with no clear idea of what the other side's witnesses would say. No doubt it made for an exciting trial, but it was not the most efficient use of court time. In many states, this traditional approach to discovery still exists.

The trial by "surprise" aspect of criminal cases has been modified in recent years with some changes in discovery rules that force the prosecutor to give the defendant far more information than the prosecutor was ever required to provide in the past. These changes in discovery rules also now place some

Discovery
The exchange of information, witness statements, and other evidence between the state and the defense attorney in a criminal case.

burden on the defense to produce information for the prosecutor, however. In the past, except in rare circumstances, this was unheard of. Historically, the defendant was not required to provide any discovery to prosecutors, and only in cases of insanity or alibi were they even required to tell the prosecution what the defense would be.

Under traditional rules of discovery, the state had to produce certain items for the defendant, but there was no requirement for the defendant to produce anything. The result of this limited discovery was that a prosecutor often began a trial with nothing other than an educated guess about how the defense would proceed or what evidence the defense would seek to admit. The information that the state provided to the defense attorney was little better. The defense attorney would know the names of the state's witnesses but would not know what these witnesses would say.

A. PURPOSE OF DISCOVERY

The purpose of discovery in criminal cases is very similar to that in civil cases: to provide information to the opposing side that will ensure better and more efficient use of court time. The more the parties know about the facts of the case before they come to trial, the less time they will need during the trial to discover important information. However, there has always been an enormous difference between discovery in civil cases and discovery in criminal cases. Part of this has to do with the nature of a criminal case itself, but the rules of discovery are different in criminal cases for other reasons. Even though there was very little statutory guidance about what a prosecutor should produce for the defense, there were at least two guiding principles that compelled prosecutors to act, even in the absence of statutes mandating certain actions. These two principles are a prosecutor's ethics and U.S. Supreme Court cases.

A prosecutor is not merely an advocate for a client. Prosecutors have moral and ethical duties to seek justice, not simply to convict as many people as possible. Some courts have stated that a prosecutor has a moral, if not a legal, obligation to produce evidence for the defendant prior to trial to allow the defendant to present an adequate defense. This often placed the prosecutor in the position of having to decide how much evidence to give to the defense to make sure that the prosecutor has met his or her obligation. It is the prosecutor's duty to ensure that full discovery, at least to the extent required by statute, is met. Courts have held, time and again, that the prosecutor's duty is to seek justice, not to guarantee convictions. Faced with this dilemma, most prosecutors decided, and continue to decide, to give more rather than less information in the discovery process. Some prosecutors even realize that by providing more information than is actually required by statute, they may convince the defense that it would be better to plead guilty than face trial, given the sheer volume of evidence against the defendant.

The prosecutor has both legal and ethical obligations to ensure a fair trial and cannot pick and choose among the evidence that he or she will provide to the defendant to make sure that the prosecutor secures a guilty verdict.[3] Balanced against that ethical and legal responsibility is the concept that there is no general right to discovery in criminal cases at all.[4] There is considerable variation among states about how much information the defendant should be provided with prior to trial. As we will see later in this chapter, some Supreme Court cases have preempted state law and require the state to produce certain types of information whether they are required by state law or not. The famous *Brady* case is a perfect example, and we will address that case in depth later in this chapter.

CHANGES TO DISCOVERY RULES

Many states have recognized the discrepancy between civil and criminal discovery and have made changes in their criminal discovery statutes. For instance, many states have amended their rules about what information a prosecutor must serve on a defendant. These statutes were amended to protect defendants from the consequences of unfair surprise at trial and to assist them in locating evidence that they could offer in their defense.

> Sidebar
>
> *The prosecutor should always err on the side of giving the defense too much information, rather than too little.[5]*

These new discovery statutes are designed to encourage voluntary disclosures of information like the information exchange that takes place in civil cases every day. These statutes also give the court the power to compel either side to disclose relevant facts to the other side. The judge may order such disclosure prior to trial. Many of these new changes require the state to turn over far greater portions of its prosecution and police files to the defendant than was ever required before. This means that the state is now compelled to give the defendant copies of witness statements, police reports, and many other items traditionally withheld by the state.

Among the changes to the discovery rules is the requirement that the defense provide some information to the state. Traditionally, discovery in criminal cases was almost always one-way. In some limited circumstances, discussed below, a criminal defendant might be required to provide some minimal information to the state, but in most situations, the criminal defendant was not compelled to provide any discovery whatsoever. That rule changed under the new discovery statutes.

B. MATERIAL PROVIDED IN DISCOVERY

Although many states have modified their criminal discovery rules in recent years, this is certainly not true in all states. In states that have not changed their discovery rules, a defendant must request discovery before he or she will receive most items from the prosecution. In such states, if the defendant fails to file discovery motions, then the prosecution is under no obligation to give him or her anything, except for *Brady* material, which we will discuss later in this chapter.

A criminal defendant does not have to produce the same amount of material, nor to such an extent as the state, but requiring the defendant to produce any information at all is a novelty in criminal law. Here is a sample of the kind of information a defendant must produce prior to trial:

- Specifics about alibi or other legal defenses, especially insanity defense
- List of defense witnesses, known addresses, and telephone numbers

In redrafting their criminal discovery statutes, many states have followed the model set out in the federal rules of criminal procedure.

When the defendant makes a discovery request under the new rules, the state normally produces the following kinds of information:

- Witness list
- Statement of defendant (both written and oral)
- Statement of a codefendant
- Defendant's criminal record
- Documents and tangible objects (books, papers, documents, photographs, motion pictures, mechanical or electronic recordings, buildings and places or any other crime scene, etc.)
- Scientific reports
- Statements of witnesses

WITNESS LIST

State and federal prosecutors are required to give the defendant a list of the witnesses that the government intends to call during the trial. This list consists of not only the names of each witness, but also their addresses and phone numbers (if known). Witnesses are often troubled by the fact that the defendant will know their complete name, residence, and telephone number. This would seem to ensure that the defendant will take retribution against the witnesses, especially now that he or she knows exactly where to find the people who will testify in the case. Although witnesses have been harassed and even murdered prior to trial, in most cases the defendant does not contact the witnesses or try to intimidate them. Defense attorneys will certainly attempt to contact these witnesses to find out their version of the facts, but it is rare for a defendant to attempt to do so. Witnesses are under no compulsion to actually speak with the defense attorney prior to trial.

STATEMENT OF DEFENDANT

If the police have questioned the defendant, then the written statement they made of that interrogation must be provided to the defense. One might wonder, because the defendant was present when he or she made his statement, why he or she would need a copy of it. The answer is that it is really for the defendant's attorney. One of the defense attorney's obligations is to review police actions to make sure that the defendant was not coerced, promised, or threatened into giving a confession. If a video or audio recording of the interrogation was made, then the defense gets a copy of that, too.

STATEMENT OF CODEFENDANT

The rule about providing the defendant's statements to the defense team also applies to statements by codefendants. It is important to note that the prosecution may not be able to admit the statement of codefendant A in the trial of codefendant B. The statement by codefendant B[6] might unfairly prejudice defendant A's case, so a court might rule that the state cannot use it.

DEFENDANT'S CRIMINAL RECORD

In the past, the defendant's own criminal record was not provided to the defense attorney. However, that rule has changed in many jurisdictions. It is now common for a state's discovery package to contain the defendant's statement, any statements by codefendants, and a complete breakdown of the defendant's criminal record. This information might help the defense to do a better job in advising his or her client, especially if the client has not been forthcoming with information. Providing the criminal history also factors into the state's decision to file a similar transactions motion, which we will discuss later.

DOCUMENTS AND TANGIBLE OBJECTS

In addition to receiving a copy of the defendant's statement and his or her criminal history, the defense also has the right to see and inspect the state's evidence prior to trial. This includes weapons, documents, photographs, and even scenes of the crime, depending on the nature of the case. The defense can inspect any piece of evidence before the trial occurs. If the state attempts to bar the defense from visiting a scene or viewing evidence, the defendant can file a motion requesting the court give the defense team permission to do so. The defense also has the right to request independent testing of certain items, including blood samples, DNA and other scientific evidence.

SCIENTIFIC REPORTS

All states require the prosecution to give the defendant copies of any and all scientific reports prepared by prosecution witnesses. These scientific reports must be produced at least 10 days prior to trial in most jurisdictions. This 10-day rule allows the defense time to hire its own experts to review the tests and also to request permission to conduct tests on physical evidence. In an era where shows like *CSI* dominate nightly TV schedules, it is surprising to note that in many cases there are no scientific reports to turn over at all. In many cases, there are no scientific tests even conducted. Crime scene technicians may be unable to lift fingerprints from various objects, and there is no other evidence to test. In that situation, there is no scientific report to pass along to the defendant. However, it must also be said that in high-profile cases, usually murder cases, law enforcement often pulls out every tool in their arsenal, and they conduct DNA tests, carpet-fiber analysis, blood-spatter pattern analysis, and fingerprint testing, to name just a few. Furthermore, if the defendant has received a mental evaluation, a copy of the report of this evaluation will also be given to the defendant. All of these tests must be copied and made available to the defendant.

STATEMENTS OF WITNESSES

Traditionally, the defense was not permitted to obtain statements of witnesses from the police or prosecutors' files. That rule has been eliminated with modern changes to discovery rules. Now, all states that have revised their discovery laws require the prosecution to provide witness statements to the defense. This is true even if the statement was given to a prosecutor instead of a police officer. In the past, the rules made no such provisions, and defense attorneys were left to their own devices to find out what the state's witnesses said to the police. Even though modern discovery rules require the prosecution to provide these statements, many defense attorneys still make the request in their motions for discovery. See Figure 12-1.

C. OPEN FILE POLICY

Open file policy
A policy in some prosecution offices that the defense is entitled to review the entirety of the state's case against the defendant, with the exclusion of work product and memoranda from the prosecutor about trial tactics and strategy.

Although discovery rules have changed over the years, many prosecution offices have maintained a separate system from what is required under discovery statutes. Some prosecutors' offices have made standard procedure out of their **open file** policy. Under this approach, the prosecution provides the defense complete access to its files, including witness statements, police reports, detectives' reports, and any other information that might be relevant to the case. The advantage of such a system is that it completely sidesteps any claim that the prosecution is attempting to hide information. Open file policies are not mandated by law but are set up by individual district attorneys. Some prosecutors favor these policies, but some do not. The fact that one district attorney's office operates under an open file policy cannot be used to force a district attorney in another county or state to open up his or her files.[7]

D. VARIATION AMONG STATES IN DISCOVERY RULES

The discussion in this chapter has made an assumption that all states follow basically the same discovery rules. That is not actually true. There is considerable variation among the states in what they typically provide to the defense and even what information is required to be handed over to the prosecution by the defense. Our discussion has focused on the minimum material that a state must provide, but there are states that require the prosecution (and the defense) to produce considerably more information. In states that have not changed their discovery rules, a defendant must request discovery before he or she will receive most items from the prosecution. In such states, if the defendant fails to file discovery motions, then the prosecution is under no obligation to give him or her anything, except for material that the U.S. Supreme Court requires in all criminal cases.

FIGURE 12-1

Defendant's Motion for Discovery

NOW COMES the defendant in the above criminal action and files this MOTION FOR DISCOVERY AND INSPECTION OF PHYSICAL EVIDENCE. Pursuant to the State of Grace's Rules of Criminal Discovery, 4-102, defendant prays for discovery and inspection of the following items:

I.

1. The Defendant moves the Court to order and require the District Attorney to produce and permit by the Defendant or Defendant's counsel the inspection of and the copying and/or photographing of the following:

- Any and all documents, papers, books, accounts, letters, photographs, objects, digital recordings in any format or other tangible things not protected by a recognized legal privilege, which constitute, contain or could be construed as evidence relevant and material to any matter involved in the above-styled criminal action and which are in the possession, custody or control of the State or any of its agencies, including police departments and civilian witnesses acting on behalf of the State;
- Any written or oral statements of the Defendant;
- The Defendant's criminal record consisting of any criminal conviction in this or any other state, territory or other recognized jurisdiction of the United States.
- Criminal records of each and every of the State's witnesses;
- Personnel records and internal memoranda relating to disciplinary actions taken by the lead police officers and/or detectives in this case.
- Any evidence that could be construed under *Brady v. Maryland* as exculpatory or mitigating for the defendant's benefit.
- All statements made by any witness intended to be called by the state, whether reduced to writing or recorded in an audio or video format.

WHEREFORE, the Defendant respectfully prays and submits that this Court grant the Defendant's Motion for Discovery and Inspection.

Respectfully submitted,
Clarence D. Arrow, Esq.

E. INFORMATION THAT IS NORMALLY NOT DISCOVERABLE BY THE DEFENDANT

The defendant is not allowed to use the discovery process as a fishing expedition; that is, as a means to go through all of the prosecution's files, hoping to find something useful. The defendant can request specific items, or any exculpatory information (see *Brady* material below), but is not permitted to submit a general request for "all information." In fact, the following materials are not generally provided by the state in discovery:

- Work product
- Criminal records of state witnesses

WORK PRODUCT

Work product
An attorney's personal notes about strategy, weaknesses, strengths, and general ideas about how to proceed in a case.

The prosecuting attorney's mental notes and strategy ideas about the case are not discoverable. The prosecuting attorney's ideas and mental impressions about a case are referred to as **work product** and this material is not discoverable, either in criminal or civil cases. This is based on the premise that mental notes, ideas, and impressions form the very core of the service provided by an attorney and requiring the disclosure of such information would severely limit the attorney's effectiveness. The general exception to this rule, however, comes when these notes focus on witness testimony that may be exculpatory to the defendant, which would bring it within the scope of *Brady*.

CRIMINAL RECORDS OF STATE WITNESSES

In most states, the criminal records of the witnesses, other than the defendant, are not made discoverable. This means that prosecutors do not make a habit of running criminal records on all of their witnesses and then making them available to the defendant. However, this rule can have several major exceptions, not the least of which comes when this information falls under *Brady*. Consider Scenario 12-2.

SCENARIO 12-2   ## CRIMINAL RECORDS

In a trial for burglary, it turns out that the state's main witness, and the person who saw the defendant at the scene coming out of the house with stolen goods, is also a convicted burglar. Should this witness's criminal history be turned over to the defendant?

Answer: Yes. Most interpretations of *Brady* would require that this information be provided to the defense.

The situation outlined in Scenario 12-2 is not all that unusual. It is quite common for one or more of the state's witnesses to have a criminal record. In fact, this person may have been a codefendant or could be someone who is facing unrelated criminal charges and has agreed to testify for the state in exchange for a more lenient sentence recommendation. As we will see in the section on motions filed by the defense, such an arrangement must be made known to the defense.

In the real world of prosecutions, the prosecutor might not only voluntarily hand over this information to the defense, but also will make the jury aware of the witness's criminal history at the beginning of the trial. Why would the state volunteer this information to the jury? The primary reason is because the jury is going to hear about it anyway. Because the defense attorney is aware of the witness's criminal history, he or she will bring the state's witness's criminal record up at every opportunity. It is better that the jury hear about this from the prosecution first.

The topic of the state's witness's criminal records has been controversial for years. Many states have never required the state to produce any criminal records of its intended witnesses for the defense, whereas others have required it for decades. Even in the states that require the state to hand over any criminal records of its witnesses, there is no uniformity about how much information is provided to the defense. For instance, in some states the defense must be given a copy of the witness's criminal history, showing any convictions but not necessarily any arrests. In other states, all arrests and convictions must be produced.

F. *BRADY* MATERIAL

Regardless of whether a particular state has changed its discovery rules in criminal cases, the U.S. Supreme Court has mandated that certain kinds of information must be turned over to the defendant prior to trial in all criminal prosecutions. In the *Brady v. Maryland*[8] decision, the Court ruled that when the state has evidence or information tending to show the defendant is not guilty of the crime (**exculpatory information**), the state must produce such evidence for the defendant, whether or not the defendant has requested it. The Supreme Court reasoned that because the role of the prosecutor was not simply to convict a defendant but to seek justice, it was only proper that the state turn over such evidence to the defense to ensure the defendant has a fair trial.

The *Brady* decision has been expanded over the years to include not only exculpatory information, but also any evidence or information that might mitigate the defendant's guilt. *Brady*'s effect has been far-reaching. Most prosecutors now serve on the defendant a *Brady* notice, including all ***Brady* material** detailing any evidence that has come to light during the state's investigation that might even arguably tend to mitigate the charges against the defendant. Consider Scenario 12-3.

Exculpatory information
Evidence that tends to provide an excuse or a justification for the defendant's actions or that shows that the defendant did not commit the crime charged.

***Brady* material**
Information available to the prosecutor that is favorable to the defendant, either because it mitigates his or her guilt or sentence. This material must be provided to the defense prior to trial.

DISCOVERY

SCENARIO 12-3

As Keisha is preparing to defend Sam for armed robbery of a jewelry store, she finds an indication that the entire armed robbery was recorded on a computer hard drive. The only items that she has received through discovery from the state are still photographs showing her client waving a gun around and pointing it at people inside the jewelry store. The note in her file indicates that the video showed the defendant actually striking several victims inside the jewelry store. Keisha files a motion alleging that the state has violated *Brady*.

In the hearing on her motion, Keisha learns from a witness that the hard drive on the computer crashed shortly after the photos were downloaded and no one has been able to retrieve the entire video. Is this a violation of *Brady*?

Answer: No. *Brady* was designed to force the state to produce any evidence that might tend to exculpate or mitigate the defendant's guilt. The DVD, in contrast, would have actually further incriminated the defendant. There is no *Brady* violation.[9]

The U.S. Supreme Court in *Brady* held, "the suppression by the prosecution of evidence favorable to an accused upon request violates due process where the evidence is material either to guilt or to punishment, irrespective of the good faith or bad faith of the prosecution."[10] This evidence must be revealed to the defendant even if the defendant does not request it.[11]

IN CAMERA INSPECTIONS

In camera
(Latin) In chambers; a review of a file by a judge carried out in his or her private office.

When a judge receives a request by a defense attorney under *Brady*, the judge must conduct an ***in camera*** inspection of the state's file. An *in camera* inspection is carried out by the judge in his or her chambers. The state provides the judge with its entire file, and the judge goes through all of the witness statements, police reports, and other material looking for anything that might be construed under the *Brady* decision to be exculpatory. If the judge does find some material, he or she provides it to the defense. In this manner, the defense can be assured that an impartial party has reviewed the state's file, and the defense attorney does not have to take the prosecutor's word that all exculpatory information has been provided. The judge must make appropriate findings of fact, detailing that he or she has reviewed the state's file and found nothing that might be exculpatory to the defense that has not been already provided to the defendant.

DEFENSE MOTIONS BASED ON DISCOVERY

Defendants may raise a wide variety of motions before trial. These motions may involve evidentiary issues, but can also involve many other issues. Some defense attorneys will file dozens of motions before trial and insist that each motion be argued. Some of these motions might include motions to suppress and motions *in limine*.

A. MOTIONS TO SUPPRESS

A motion to suppress is a motion requesting the judge to rule that certain evidence is inadmissible at trial. The most common reason for this request is that the evidence was seized in violation of the defendant's constitutional rights. In situations where evidence has been seized illegally, the judge is authorized to rule the evidence inadmissible and therefore unusable at trial. This is the famous exclusionary rule, first enunciated in the early 1900s and expanded by later U.S. Supreme Court decisions. Under the exclusionary rule, if law enforcement officials violate constitutional principles in obtaining evidence, their punishment is that they cannot use it at trial.

Defendants often file motions to suppress evidence in cases even when there is no clear constitutional violation. Many defense attorneys believe that there is nothing to lose by filing such a motion. If the judge denies the motion, the defendant is in no worse a position than he or she was already. If the judge grants the motion, a crucial piece of evidence will be excluded from the trial. However, if the judge rules against the government on a motion to suppress, the government is permitted to appeal that decision.

A motion to suppress can be focused on any of a number of issues raised in the case, from the defendant's confession to the photographic lineup used to identify the defendant as the person responsible for the crime. Defense attorneys routinely file motions to suppress the following:

- Physical evidence
- Defendant's statement
- Photographic lineup
- Warrantless searches
- Searches with warrants
- Wiretaps

B. MOTION TO SEVER

In some cases, the defendant may request a motion to **sever** offenses or parties. A motion for severance asks the court to try different counts of an indictment as separate trials or different codefendants in separate trials. A defendant requests severance when he or she believes that being tried together with several other defendants will unduly prejudice the case and prevent the defendant from receiving a fair trial. In a similar fashion, a motion to sever offenses requests a separate trial for offenses that may be unrelated in time or action to each other. The jury might not separate out the proof of one offense from the other, but might instead be more likely to assume that the defendant is guilty simply by the sheer number of offenses against him or her.

Sever
Separate or cut off into constituent parts.

C. MOTION *IN LIMINE*

In addition to motions to suppress, a defendant will also file numerous motions *in limine*. A **motion *in limine*** is a motion requesting a ruling on the use of a particular piece of evidence or a limitation on the kind of testimony that a witness may give on the stand. For instance, if a defense attorney has reason to believe that a particular state's witness will refer to the defendant's criminal history during his or her testimony, the defense attorney may file a motion *in limine* requesting the judge to order the witness to make no such references. Because a defendant's prior criminal record is normally not admissible at trial, such a motion will usually be granted. The defense may also file a motion *in limine* to restrict the use of other kinds of evidence or testimony. Each such motion will be argued by the attorneys and may involve the testimony of a witness at a motion hearing prior to trial. These motion hearings are often days or even weeks before the

Motion *in limine*
(Latin) At the beginning. A motion by one party that requests specific judicial rulings at the outset of the trial.

actual trial. Some motions may also be argued shortly before the trial begins. Still other motions may also be raised during the course of the trial.

D. MOTION TO REVEAL THE DEAL (*GIGLIO*)

Motion to reveal the deal
Also known as a *Giglio* motion, a request from the defense for any information about any offers, inducements, or sentence recommendations made to any of the state's witnesses against the defendant.

When a defense attorney suspects that a prosecution witness has been offered a deal for his or her testimony at trial, the attorney can file a motion requesting the details of the arrangement. When a defense attorney requests information about any arrangements between the prosecution and a witness, it is commonly referred to as a **motion to reveal the deal.** This is a motion asking that the state be ordered to reveal any deal entered into with any witness in which the state has offered immunity or some other benefit in exchange for testimony. It is fairly common for a state's witness to be granted some form of immunity or the promise of a light recommendation on sentencing in exchange for the witness's testimony against anther codefendant. Defense attorneys rightly assume that such promise could have an effect on the witness's performance on the stand. Although a prosecutor would probably feel that any such promise would have to be revealed to the defense attorney because of the *Brady* decision (see above), a defense attorney might decide to cover his or her bases by filing a motion anyway.

E. MOTION TO REVEAL IDENTITY OF CONFIDENTIAL INFORMANTS

Confidential informant
A person who works with the police, providing them information about illegal activities.

Defense attorneys may file a motion to reveal the identity of a **confidential informant** (CI) who was involved in the case. Generally, police and prosecutors protect CIs because to release their names to the defendant might put them in danger of being killed. Discovery rules allow a prosecutor to conceal the identity of a CI, but this right is not absolute. The court is allowed to weigh the right of the government to protect its CIs from retribution against the right of the defendant to receive a fair trial. If a judge decides that the only way to make sure that the defendant receives a fair and proper trial is to release the name of the CI to the defense, then the judge is authorized to do so.[12] This is another example where the judge would review the state's file *in camera* before making a decision on whether or not to reveal the CI's name.

 OTHER DEFENSE MOTIONS

In addition to bringing motions to suppress and motions to reveal any deal between a witness and the state, defense attorneys are free to file as many motions as they see fit. In high-profile cases, the defense may file literally dozens of motions. One of the most common in such a case would be a motion for change of venue.

A. MOTION TO CHANGE VENUE

A defendant who wants to move the location of the trial will request a change of venue. Generally, a defendant must show that his or her chances of receiving a fair trial in the original area have been diminished or completely negated, usually by intense pretrial publicity. Defendants will often present evidence of newspaper or other media reports that have focused on the case in a negative way. Because the potential jurors for the trial will be drawn from the same area, a **motion for change of venue** alleges that the jury pool for this case has been influenced before they ever hear any testimony. If the judge grants a change of venue motion, it usually means that the trial will be moved to some other jurisdiction. The jury will be selected from the new area, but the prosecutor, judge, and defense attorney remain the same.

Motion for change of venue
A motion to transfer the location of the trial to another area, often brought when there is extensive pretrial publicity.

B. MOTION FOR CONTINUANCE

A **motion for continuance** is a motion that can be made by either side in a criminal case, the prosecution or the defense. When the party moves for a continuance, it is requesting that the case be taken off the current calendar and rescheduled for a later date. There are many reasons why a party might request a continuance. The party might not be prepared for the trial, a key witness might not be available, or some other factor could weigh heavily against trying the case now and waiting to try it at a later date. A judge must approve the motion for a continuance, but if the opposing side does not object to the continuance, more often than not the judge will grant it.

Motion for continuance
A request by one party to postpone a trial or other hearing for a future date.

C. PLEA OF FORMER JEOPARDY

A **plea of former jeopardy** is a motion filed by a defendant that states that he or she was prosecuted in a former case and that prosecution also was involved in the current charges. Essentially, the defendant is saying that the state is barred from prosecuting the defendant because the defendant has already been sentenced on a related charge and because the Fifth Amendment bars a person from being tried twice for the same offense. Pleas of former jeopardy are often seen in cases where a defendant is charged with a traffic offense and with some other offense, such as transporting narcotics. The defendant enters a plea to the underlying traffic offense and then brings a plea of former jeopardy attempting to claim that the first prosecution bars the charge on the narcotics. Occasionally, these pleas are successful, but in many cases they are not.[13]

Plea of former jeopardy
A defendant's motion stating that he or she has already been prosecuted for the underlying offense, and any further prosecution is barred by the Fifth Amendment.

D. BILL OF PARTICULARS

Bill of particulars
A defendant's motion requesting dates, names, locations, and addresses for the charges set out in the indictment.

Another tool available to a criminal defendant is a motion for a **bill of particulars**. A bill of particulars requests additional information about the counts of the indictment. For instance, a defendant might request in his or her bill of particulars "information concerning any oral statements of the defendant relied upon by the government to support the charge in the indictment." In the alternative, a defendant's bill of particulars might request additional information about the evidence relied on to support specific allegations in the indictment. In essence, the defendant is requesting that the government provide background information on specific charges to enable the defendant to better prepare his or her defense. However, a defendant might also file a bill of particulars simply to gather any additional information, whether pertinent to the defense or not.

E. SPEEDY TRIAL DEMAND

> . . . the accused shall enjoy the right to a speedy and public trial . . .
>
> —*Sixth Amendment, U.S. Constitution*

Speedy trial
A constitutional guarantee that a person must receive a trial within a reasonable period of time after being arraigned.

The right of an accused to a **speedy trial** has a long history. Originally mentioned in the Magna Carta in the year 1215, the defendant's right to a speedy trial was considered to be an important, if often ignored, right. The right to a speedy trial was embodied in the Virginia Declaration of Rights of 1776, then incorporated into the later U.S. Constitution and then all state constitutions. In *Klopfer v. North Carolina*,[14] the Supreme Court declared that the right to a speedy trial was as important as any other right guaranteed in the Sixth Amendment, calling it "one of the most basic rights preserved by our Constitution."

All states have laws that are commonly referred to as speedy-trial-demand statutes. Speedy-trial statutes seek to enforce the Sixth Amendment guarantee of a speedy trial. These statutes allow a defendant to serve on the state a demand that the defendant be tried in this or the next **term of court**. If the trial is not held, then the defendant's case must be dismissed.

Term of court
The period of time slates for court hearings; it can be as short as a week or as long as a year.

DISMISSING A CASE FOR FAILURE TO RECEIVE A SPEEDY TRIAL

If the defendant serves a speedy-trial demand and is not tried in the specified time, then the charges against the defendant must be dismissed and the defendant released from confinement. Serving a "speedy" on a prosecutor often has a galvanizing effect on the state. Because a prosecutor knows that if the defendant is not tried, he or she must be released, the practical effect of serving a speedy-trial demand is usually that the defendant's case is moved up to the number one trial in the next trial week. Even when the defendant is already in prison serving a sentence on an unrelated offense, he or she is still entitled to receive a speedy trial on another charge.[15]

Although this right is considered one of the fundamental rights guaranteed in the Constitution, defining what exactly constitutes a "speedy" trial has been difficult to quantify. The U.S. Supreme Court has grappled with this issue in many different cases.

HOW SPEEDY MUST A "SPEEDY TRIAL" BE?

The Supreme Court has held that a delay of eight years between indictment and trial is too long;[16] five years may also be too long.[17] The problem is that each case must be considered on its own facts. The Supreme Court has been reluctant to state a maximum period that will always mean a violation of the Sixth Amendment. Despite the Court's reluctance to name a specific period of time in which a defendant must always be tried, the Court has been specific about the sanction imposed for failing to try a defendant. Where the defendant's right to a speedy trial has been violated, only one sanction is allowed: dismissal of the state's case. This drastic remedy was authorized in *Strunk v. United States*.[18]

WHEN THE DEFENDANT MAY NOT WANT A SPEEDY TRIAL AFTER ALL

Although each state has a statute authorizing the filing of a speedy-trial demand to enforce the Sixth Amendment guarantee, a speedy trial might actually work against the defendant. Often, a delay in bringing the case to trial will help the defendant. Memories fade over time. Evidence may be lost. In fact, taking a case to trial sooner rather than later may only be helpful to the defendant when the prosecution is not prepared. Otherwise, a quick trial might actually work against the defendant. The defense team should evaluate these potential difficulties before filing a statutory speedy-trial demand.

WHEN IS THE RIGHT TO A SPEEDY TRIAL TRIGGERED?

A question often arises in the context of speedy-trial demands: When is the right triggered? Put another way, at what point during the proceedings does the prosecution pass the point of no return, where the state fails to prosecute the defendant and the provisions of the speedy-trial demand will necessitate dismissing the case? Courts have wrestled with that question for many years and have finally settled it at a specific point during the case. The right to receive a speedy trial is triggered when an indictment has been lodged against the defendant.[19] The right to a speedy trial also attaches when a defendant has been accused—that is, when he or she is charged with a misdemeanor. Of course, this assumes that the defendant has not filed a motion for continuance. If the defendant files such a motion, he or she waives the right to a speedy trial. After all, the defendant is requesting a trial to be held immediately and then, by his or her own request, wishes to put the trial off.

PROSECUTION MOTIONS

The state may also bring motions against the defendant. The prosecutor, however, has much greater limitations on the types of motions that he or she can file. The relatively few motions that a prosecutor can bring are the following:

- Similar transactions
- Aggravation of sentence
- Motion to join

A. SIMILAR TRANSACTIONS

Similar transactions motion
A motion brought by the state showing that the defendant has committed similar offenses, and this shows his or her bent of mind, motive, or course of conduct.

In many states the prosecution is allowed to bring a **similar transactions motion** so that the jury can hear evidence of the defendant's prior crimes. Although the defendant's prior criminal record is normally inadmissible at trial, similar transaction laws do allow a limited use of such prior convictions. In situations where the current charge against the defendant is very similar to a previous conviction, the state is permitted to present evidence of the prior conviction to show a common method, plan, or scheme by the defendant to carry out certain kinds of crimes. "If the defendant is proven to be the perpetrator of another . . . crime and the facts of that crime are sufficiently similar or connected to the facts of the crime charged, the separate crime will be admissible to prove identity, motive, plan, scheme, bent of mind, or course of conduct."[20]

However, before the state is allowed to present any such evidence to the jury, the court must rule on the evidence. A similar transactions hearing must be held in which the witnesses from the prior conviction testify, and the state builds a case showing how the prior conviction has many of the same features as the current charge. If the judge rules that there is sufficient similarity between the two offenses to establish the defendant's common motive, plan, or conduct, the evidence of the prior conviction can be used in the current case. The judge must give a limiting instruction to the jury, telling them that this evidence is only being admitted for the limited purpose of showing the defendant's common approach to similar crimes. Under this limitation, a prosecutor can only admit evidence of crimes substantially similar to the current charge. A similar transactions motion does not allow the prosecutor to put the defendant's entire criminal record into evidence.

A prosecutor will often file a notice that he or she intends to use similar transactions in any case where they might possibly apply. The practical effect of similar transactions testimony is to taint the defendant in the eyes of the jury. When a defense attorney learns that the prosecutor intends to use similar transactions, this puts even greater pressure on the defendant to plead guilty to the charge. The defense reasons that if the jury should learn that the defendant has been convicted of a similar crime before, they will be far more likely to convict him or her of the present crime.

B. AGGRAVATION OF SENTENCE

In addition to filing a motion for similar transactions, a prosecutor may also file a motion in aggravation of sentence. The prosecutor may file this motion prior to the trial or wait and file it after the defendant has been found guilty. A **motion in aggravation of sentence** is a document that shows that the defendant has a lengthy criminal record or has a history of violence or harming others. In addition to filing the written motion, the prosecutor will also provide certified copies of the defendant's prior convictions. The judge may or may not take the convictions into account when sentencing the defendant. Generally, when a defendant has a lengthy criminal record, he or she will receive a longer sentence on conviction than someone who has no prior record. One way of ensuring that the court is aware of the defendant's criminal record is for the prosecution to file a motion in aggravation of sentence.

Motion in aggravation of sentence
A motion filed by the state that seeks to enhance the defendant's sentence based on his or her prior convictions.

C. MOTION TO JOIN

A motion to join is exactly the opposite of the defendant's motion to sever (see Figure 12-2). In a motion for joinder, the state requests that a series of crimes or multiple defendants be tried together. State and federal rules allow a prosecutor to move the court to combine several cases into a single prosecution under special circumstances. If there is one crime or a series of crimes committed by the same individuals, it might make more sense—both in terms of time and economy—to try all of the individuals at the same time, rather than try them one by one. In situations where the government has separately indicted individuals for the same crime, a prosecutor can file a motion to join the defendants together and have them tried in one trial. Of course, the defense will often fight this motion, reasoning that if a jury sees a group of people charged, it will be harder for a single defendant to stand out as an innocent party.

The court may order that separate cases be tried together as though brought in a single indictment or information if all offenses and all defendants could have been joined in a single indictment or information.[21]

FIGURE 12-2

Rule 13. Joint Trial of Separate Cases

OHIO v. MAGWOOD

2019 OHIO 5238

PATRICIA ANN BLACKMON, J.:

1} Jonathan Magwood ("Magwood") appeals from the trial court's denial of his petition for postconviction relief and assigns the following errors for our review:

I. The trial court erred by denying Magwood relief on his post-conviction petition when the evidence presented with the petition showed that Mr. Magwood received ineffective assistance of counsel.

II. The trial court erred by denying Magwood relief on his post-conviction petition when the evidence presented with the petition showed that the state withheld *Brady* material.

Having reviewed the record and pertinent law, we affirm the trial court's judgment. The apposite facts follow.

On May 3, 2017, the trial court found Magwood guilty of three counts of rape in violation of R.C. 2907.02(A)(2), a first-degree felony, kidnapping with a sexual motivation specification in violation of R.C. 2905.01(A)(4), a first-degree felony, and petty theft. These convictions stemmed from an incident that occurred on August 20, 2016, at a Taco Bell on the west side of Cleveland. According to the victim, T.J., she went into the women's restroom at the Taco Bell, Magwood forced his way into the bathroom after her, and then he raped her. DNA evidence confirmed that Magwood and T.J. engaged in sexual conduct, and video surveillance evidence showed that Magwood followed T.J. into the Taco Bell and forced his way into the women's bathroom. Magwood's defense throughout the trial was that this conduct was consensual.

On June 7, 2017, the court sentenced Magwood to 22 years in prison. Magwood filed a direct appeal, and this court reversed the petty theft conviction and affirmed Magwood's remaining convictions as well as his prison sentence. *State v. Magwood*, 8th Dist. Cuyahoga No. 105885, 2018-Ohio-1634.

On July 24, 2018, Magwood filed a petition for postconviction relief, arguing that the state failed to disclose *Brady* material, and his trial counsel was ineffective for failing to investigate T.J.'s credibility and failing to present mitigating evidence at sentencing. On December 21, 2018, the court held a hearing on Magwood's petition, and on December 27, 2018, the court denied the petition. It is from this order that Magwood appeals.

POSTCONVICTION RELIEF

Pursuant to R.C. 2953.21(A)(1)(a),

any person who has been convicted of a criminal offense . . . who claims that there was such a denial or infringement of the person's rights as to render the judgment constitutionally void or voidable . . . may file a petition in the court that imposed sentence, stating the grounds for relief relied upon, and asking the court to vacate or set aside the judgment or sentence or to grant other appropriate relief.

A postconviction petition does not provide a petitioner a second opportunity to litigate his or her conviction. *State v. Steffen*, 70 Ohio St.3d 399, 410, 639 N.E.2d 67 (1994). Rather, it is a means to reach constitutional issues that would otherwise be impossible to reach because the evidence supporting those issues is not contained in the record. Id. at ¶12.

BRADY CLAIM

Brady v. Maryland, 373 U.S. 83, 87, 83 S.Ct. 1194, 10 L.Ed.2d 215 (1963), governs situations when the state withholds evidence that tends to exculpate a criminal defendant. "When the prosecution withholds material, exculpatory evidence in a criminal proceeding, it violates the due process right of the defendant under the Fourteenth Amendment to a fair trial." *State v. Johnston*, 39 Ohio St.3d 48, 60, 529 N.E.2d 898 (1988). *Brady* violations may be found regardless of whether the defense requested the evidence and "irrespective of the good faith or bad faith of the prosecution." *Brady* at 83, 87. In determining whether suppressed evidence is material, courts consider whether "there is a reasonable probability that, had the evidence been disclosed to the defense, the result of the proceeding would have been different." *United States v. Bagley*, 473 U.S. 667, 682, 105 S.Ct. 3375, 87 L.Ed.2d 481 (1985). "A 'reasonable probability' is a probability sufficient to undermine confidence in the outcome." Id.

The "defendant bears the burden to show that the evidence not produced was materially exculpatory, or that the failure to produce the evidence was based on bad faith, in order to demonstrate a due-process violation." *State v. Hartman*, 2d Dist. Montgomery No. 26609, 2016-Ohio-2883, ¶84, 64 N.E.3d 519.

For *Brady* purposes, the United States Supreme Court "disavowed any difference between exculpatory and impeachment evidence." *Kyles v. Whitley*, 514 U.S. 419, 433, 115 S.Ct. 1555, 131 L.Ed.2d 490 (1995). "When the 'reliability of a given witness may well be determinative of guilt or innocence,' nondisclosure of evidence affecting credibility falls within this general rule." *Giglio v. United States*, 405 U.S. 150, 154, 92 S.Ct. 736, 31 L.Ed.2d 104 (1972).

The linchpin of a *Brady* violation follows: "evidence is material, and constitutional error results from its suppression by the government, 'if there is a reasonable probability that, had the evidence been disclosed to the defense, the result of the proceeding would have been different.'" Id., quoting *Bagley* at 682.

In the case at hand, Magwood argues that the state failed to disclose relevant information relating to Cleveland Police Detective Morris Vowell ("Detective Vowell"), who took T.J.'s statement as part of the investigation in this case. At the December 21, 2018 hearing, Magwood introduced into evidence Detective Vowell's 2011 internal affairs report that the state disclosed as *Brady* material in another matter. The gist of the report was that Detective Vowell had been indicted for using a police computer for personal reasons. Ultimately, the charges against Detective Vowell were dismissed. Magwood argued that the "information in question goes to the heart of the professional integrity and credibility of the investigating detective in this case," and the state's failure to disclose the information deprived Magwood of the opportunity to impeach Detective Vowell.

The state, on the other hand, argues that the 2011 charges against Detective Vowell were public record as evidenced by news articles outlining the detective's legal troubles. According to the state, this information—albeit not the internal affairs report—was not in the exclusive control of the police or the prosecution. Although the state conceded that it turned the report over to the defense in another case subsequent to the case at hand, the state did not concede that Detective Vowell's 2011 internal affairs report was *Brady* material. Rather, the state argued that the evidence was given to other defense counsel as a precaution; it was not suppressed in the case at issue, because it was known to the public; it was not material in that it would not have changed the outcome of the proceedings; and it was not admissible because it did not result in a conviction.

In *Cindric v. Edgewater Yacht Club*, 8th Dist. Cuyahoga No. 68365, 1996 Ohio App. LEXIS 1793 (May 2, 1996), this court held that "evidence of a theft, whether alleged or admitted, is not probative—and certainly not 'clearly' probative—on the issue of a party's truthfulness (that is a theft does not necessarily involve the telling of a falsehood)." Furthermore, in denying Magwood's postconviction relief petition, the trial court stated in its journal entry that "even if the information contained within the Internal Affairs log regarding Detective Vowell had been disclosed by the State prior to Magwood's trial, there is no reasonable probability that this Court's verdict would have been different." Additionally, prior to issuing the journal entry, the court stated the following at the hearing on Magwood's petition: "I can represent a hundred percent that Detective Vowell's testimony played no role in reaching the conclusion that I did. His credibility or lack of credibility was irrelevant."

In Magwood's direct appeal, this court summed up Detective Vowell's role in this case and testimony at trial as follows:

Detective Vowell took T.J.'s statement approximately one week after the incident. He testified that she was crying, upset, and very emotional during the statement. At one point, the detective turned off the recorder and called a rape advocate to sit with T.J. because she was "crying and upset and shaken up." When T.J. regained her composure, the detective continued with the interview.

As part of his investigation, Detective Vowell obtained the video surveillance footage from Taco Bell and the assault evidence kit collected by the SANE nurse. Through the DNA obtained from the sexual assault kit, Detective Vowell identified Magwood as a suspect, and T.J. later identified Magwood from a photo array as the person who attacked her.

Upon review, we find that Magwood's *Brady* claim lacks merit, because allegations that Detective Vowell used a work computer for personal reasons is not material to Magwood's guilt in the case at hand. See *State v. Brown*, 115 Ohio St.3d 55, 2007-Ohio-4837, 873 N.E.2d 858, ¶49 ("As a rule, undisclosed evidence is not material simply because it may have helped the defendant to prepare for trial").

Accordingly, Magwood's second assigned error is overruled.

Judgment affirmed.

CASE QUESTIONS

1   What is the underlying theory of *Brady v. Maryland*?
2   Does it matter to the analysis whether or not the defense counsel requested the potentially exculpatory evidence from the state?
3   Does the Supreme Court, in *Brady*, make any distinction between exculpatory evidence and impeachment evidence?

4 What is the linchpin of the *Brady* case?

5 The defendant alleges that the lead detective in the case was brought up on charges of using a computer in violation of department policy. Did the failure to deliver that information to the defendant rise to the level of a *Brady* violation? Explain.

CHAPTER SUMMARY

The arraignment is the court hearing where a defendant is brought before the court and officially informed of the charges against him or her. At the arraignment, the defendant has the opportunity of entering a plea: either guilty or not guilty. If the defendant pleads not guilty, he or she is given a trial date and told to return for trial. If the defendant pleads guilty, then he or she will usually be sentenced that day. Discovery is often provided at arraignment, or at least 10 days prior to trial, depending on the custom found in the jurisdiction. Traditionally, very little information was exchanged between the state and the defendant in discovery; however, that has changed in recent years. These days, it is common for the state to produce numerous documents, including the defendant's and witness's statements, physical evidence, and scientific reports, among others. Whether a jurisdiction has updated its discovery statutes or not, all states must abide by the decision in *Brady v. Maryland*, which requires states to turn over any exculpatory or mitigating information to the defense. Defense attorneys routinely file motions in cases, requesting that specific evidence be suppressed or making other requests of the court. Although it is not as frequent, the state may also file its own motions, such as alerting the defense to the fact that it intends to seek a longer prison term against the defendant or a similar transactions motion, which will show that the defendant has committed similar crimes in the past.

KEY TERMS AND CONCEPTS

Arraignment
Calendar or docket
Motion
Waiving arraignment
Bench warrant
Discovery
Open file policy
Work product
Exculpatory information

Brady material
In camera
Sever
Motion *in limine*
Motion to reveal the deal
Confidential informant
Motion for change of venue
Motion for continuance

Plea of former jeopardy
Bill of particulars
Speedy trial
Term of court
Similar transactions motion
Motion in aggravation of sentence

END OF CHAPTER EXERCISES

Review Questions

See Appendix A for answers

1 What is arraignment?
2 What is a court docket?
3 What motions might a defense attorney file at or before arraignment?
4 What is the difference between formal arraignment and arraignment?
5 Explain bench warrants.
6 Provide a brief overview of criminal discovery.
7 Explain the basic information provided by the state in discovery.
8 What is an open file policy?
9 When would a judge conduct an *in camera* inspection?
10 What is exculpatory evidence?
11 How have discovery rules changed over the years?
12 What is *Brady* material?
13 What is work product?
14 When would the state provide criminal records of its witnesses?
15 What is a motion to suppress?
16 Explain motions to sever.
17 Why would a defendant bring a motion *in limine*?
18 Explain the function of a motion to reveal the deal.
19 When would a defendant bring a motion to change venue?

Web Surfing

1 Visit Criminal Defense Lawyer (www.criminaldefenselawyer.com) and search for "Criminal arraignment: What to expect."

2 Visit www.findlaw.com and search for "What is the process for an arraignment hearing?"

3 Visit www.justia.com and search for "Discovery in criminal cases."

Questions for Analysis

1 Should criminal discovery be made the same as civil discovery? Can you think of reasons why they should remain different?

2 Can you construct an argument for the premise that everything in the state's file should be available to a criminal defendant, no matter what?

Hypotheticals

1 While a case is pending against a defendant charged with murder, the state receives information that a very similar murder has occurred since the defendant was arrested and incarcerated awaiting trial. Should the prosecution reveal details of the new cases to the defendant's attorney?

2 *Brady* has been extended from simply providing exculpatory material to evidence that could mitigate the defendant's sentence. If the prosecution has evidence that the defendant was the victim of abuse as a child, does *Brady* require that the prosecutor turn this information over to the defense?

PRACTICE QUESTIONS FOR TEST REVIEW

See Appendix A for answers

Essay Question

What is the importance of the *Brady v. Maryland* case?

True-False

1 **T   F**   There is no requirement for the state to provide a copy of the defendant's confession to him or her prior to trial.

2 **T   F**   Some states follow open file policies when it comes to discovery.

3 **T   F**   Work product is generally not available through discovery.

Fill in the Blank

1 The exchange of information, witness statements, and other evidence between the state and the defense attorney in a criminal case is known as _____.

2 _____ is an attorney's personal notes about strategy, weaknesses, strengths, and general ideas about how to proceed in a case.

3 Evidence that tends to provide an excuse or a justification for the defendant's actions or that shows that the defendant did not commit the crime charged is called _____.

Multiple Choice

1 A court hearing where the defendant is informed of the charge against him or her and given the opportunity to enter a plea of guilty or not guilty.

   A Initial appearance.
   B Preliminary hearing.
   C Arraignment.
   D Sentencing.

2 A listing of the cases currently pending before the court, usually by the defendants' names, case file number, and charges brought against them.

    A Schedule.

    B List.

    C Docket.

    D None of the above.

3 An oral or written request to a court to take some action.

    A Demand.

    B Filing.

    C Ruling.

    D Motion.

ENDNOTES

1. *Shivers v. State*, 188 Ga. App. 21, 372 S.E.2d 2 (1988).
2. *State v. Phillips*, 74 Ohio St. 3d 72, 1995-Ohio-171, 656 N.E.2d 643 (1995).
3. *U.S. v. Consolidated Laundries Corp.*, 291 F.2d 563 (2d Cir. 1961); *State v. Spano*, 69 N.J. 231, 353 A.2d 97 (1976); *State v. Reiman*, 284 N.W.2d 860 (S.D. 1979).
4. *Weatherford v. Bursey*, 429 U.S. 545, 97 S.Ct. 837, 51 L.Ed.2d 30 (1977).
5. *State v. Reiman*, 284 N.W.2d 860 (S.D. 1979).
6. *Bruton v. United States*, 391 U.S. 123 (1968).
7. *State v. Moore*, 335 N.C. 567, 440 S.E.2d 797, cert. denied, 513 U.S. 898, 115 S.Ct. 253, 130 L.Ed.2d 174 (1994).
8. *Brady v. Maryland*, 373 U.S. 83, 83 S.Ct. 1194, 10 L.Ed.2d 215 (1963).
9. *U.S. v. Drake*, 543 F.3d 1080 (9th Cir. 2008).
10. *Brady*, 373 U.S. at 87.
11. *State v. Hunt*, 615 N.W.2d 294, 296-302 (Minn. 2000).
12. *Drouin v. State*, 222 Md. 271, 160 A.2d 85 (1960).
13. *United States v. Sabella*, 272 F.2d 206, 207 (C.A.2 1959).
14. 386 U.S. 213, 87 S.Ct. 988, 18 L.Ed.2d 1 (1967).
15. *Smith v. Hooey*, 393 U.S. 374, 89 S.Ct. 575, 21 L.Ed.2d 607 (1969).
16. *Doggett v. United States*, 5 U.S. 647, 112 S.Ct. 2686, 120 L.Ed.2d 520 (1992).
17. *Barker v. Wingo*, 407 U.S. 514, 92 S.Ct. 2182, 33 L.Ed.2d 101 (1972).
18. 412 U.S. 434 (1973).
19. *United States v. Marion*, 404 U.S. 307 (1971).
20. *Hatcher v. State*, 224 Ga.App. 747, 752(3), 482 S.E.2d 443 (1997).
21. Rule 13. F.R.C.P.

The Trial

- Explain the layout of the courtroom
- Identify the various professionals who play a role before, during, and after the trial
- Describe the jury selection process
- Detail the similarities and differences between direct and cross-examination
- Explain the purpose of a motion for directed verdict
- Define the function of jury instructions

I. The Courtroom
   A. The Jury Box
      Jury's Deliberation Room
   B. Witness Stand
   C. Judge's Bench
   D. Location of Defense and Prosecution Tables
   E. Clerk of Court
   F. Court Reporter

II. Jury Selection
   A. Peremptory Challenges
   B. Challenges for Cause
   C. *Batson* Challenges
   D. Striking the Jury
      Silent Strikes
   E. Alternate Jurors
   F. Final Steps for the Jury Before the Trial

III. Opening Statements

IV. Direct Examination
   A. Questioning Witnesses During Direct Examination
   B. Introducing Evidence During Direct Examination

V. Cross-Examination
   A. How Is Cross-Examination Different from Direct Examination?
   B. Impeachment

VI. Redirect Examination

VII. Directed Verdict

VIII. Defense Case-in-Chief

IX. Rebuttal

X. Mistrial

XI.   Charge Conference   XV.   Verdict
                                              A. Various Types of Verdicts in Criminal Cases
XII. Closing Arguments   *Guilty*
                                                  Guilty but Mentally Ill
XIII. Jury Instructions   *Not Guilty*
                                                  Not Guilty by Reason of Insanity
XIV. Deliberations   B. Polling the Jury
                                              C. Excusing the Jury

THE COURTROOM

When it comes to a discussion of the layout of the trial courtroom, it is important to keep in mind that there are many different types of courthouses. Attorneys find themselves in vastly different courthouses, all with their own styles of architecture and peculiarities. However, when it comes to the trial courtroom, there are some basic features that will always be present, even if they are in different locations in every courtroom. You will notice that we make a distinction between a trial courtroom and other types of courtrooms. A room that has been designed for jury trials is different from other judicial rooms. There are features that all trial courtrooms have in common. All jury trial courtrooms have judge's benches, witness stands, tables for attorneys, and so on. For a jury trial, certain elements must be present. The most obvious of these is the jury box.

A. THE JURY BOX

Jury box
An area that is separated from the rest of a courtroom and is reserved exclusively for jurors during a trial.

Recess
A short break in the proceedings in a trial.

The **jury box** is the area where the jurors who have been selected in the voir dire process are seated during the trial. (Some jurisdictions may use a different term to refer to this area, but we will continue to use this term throughout the chapter.) The jurors are restricted to this area during the trial and they are not allowed to leave it, unless directed to do so. Jurors cannot, for example, leave the jury box to get a better look at evidence or to sit in a more comfortable chair. When the judge calls a **recess** or the trial has finished for the day, the bailiff will guide the jurors back to a jury room. If they are on a recess, this is the area where they can relax and talk. They are forbidden to discuss the case until the end of the trial, so they must discuss other matters. Although all felony cases require 12 jurors, there are usually extra seats in the jury box. These extra seats are for alternate jurors. As we will see later in this chapter, it is common in any jury trial that may last for a few weeks to have alternate jurors. Alternate jurors are not allowed to deliberate at the end of the trial, but they do sit and hear all evidence and arguments.

JURY'S DELIBERATION ROOM

The jury room, sometimes called the jury deliberation room, is usually a small room adjacent to the courtroom where the jury will go on recesses and where they will retire to decide the verdict when the trial is over. Jury rooms are not known for their comfort or luxury. This is done purposefully. No one wants the jurors to enjoy the jury room too much; they might be tempted to stay in there longer. Instead, if the room is cramped, perhaps with no window and uncomfortable seating, there is a good chance that the jurors will reach a quick verdict and conclude the case. Televisions, cell phones, media players, and other electronic devices are all barred from the jury room. The jurors are not permitted access to outside media for fear that they might base their verdict on coverage in the news and not what they heard in the courtroom. The room is private, and no one but the jurors and the bailiff are permitted to enter.

B. WITNESS STAND

Returning to our tour of the courtroom and using the jury box as the beginning point, the next most obvious feature is the witness stand. It is always located fairly close to the jury box so that the jurors can see and hear the witnesses with no difficulty. The witness stand is often a seat inside a closed area with one side open to admit the witness. Most modern courtrooms have microphones set up at face level for the witnesses, even though the witness stand is close to the jury box. The microphone enables everyone in the courtroom to hear the witness testify and also to record the testimony. The witness may be requested to step out of the witness stand to point out some feature on a diagram or to address some other piece of evidence, but the vast majority of the witness's remarks will be made while seated in the witness stand.

C. JUDGE'S BENCH

The judge sits on an elevated platform called the **bench**. It is always the highest position in the courtroom and helps to emphasize the judge's power and authority. The judge's bench is always positioned so that the judge can get a clear view of the entire courtroom, including the jury box, witness stand, and attorney tables. In modern courtrooms, the judge might have a laptop available at the bench with real-time transcription of the testimony as it is being taken down by the court reporter. The judge may also use the laptop to access legal databases should a question of law come up during the trial. When the judge calls the attorneys to the bench during the trial, it is called a **bench conference**. In situations where a defendant waives a jury trial, then the judge will act as both the judge and jury and will reach a verdict on his or her own. This type of trial is referred to as a **bench trial**.

Bench
The place in the courtroom reserved for the judge.

Bench conference
A private conference held at the judge's bench between the attorneys and the judge.

Bench trial
A trial where the judge decides both questions of law and the final verdict in the case; no jury is present.

D. LOCATION OF DEFENSE AND PROSECUTION TABLES

There are usually at least two tables set aside for the attorneys. One table is used by the prosecution, and the other is reserved for the defense. These tables are positioned so that they face the judge's bench and also so that both sides can get a clear view of the witness stand and the jury. In many jurisdictions, there is an old tradition that the prosecutor always uses the table closest to the jury box and the defendant gets the table furthest from the jury box. However, like many traditions, practical issues might dictate a different setup in a courtroom.

Just like the judge's bench, modern courtrooms have wireless hotspots that allow attorneys to access the Internet through their laptops or other devices. This not only gives the attorneys the ability to do real-time legal research, but also gives them access to a real-time transcription of the witness testimony, as well as access to any other technology available in the courtroom, including a projector in case they wish to display photos, diagrams, or slide presentations during closing arguments.

E. CLERK OF COURT

Clerk
A court official who maintains records of dispositions in both civil and criminal cases.

Usually located in front of or on the far side of the bench are spaces for the court reporter and the **clerk** of court. The clerk is usually only present during calendar calls where he or she notes dispositions in cases that day. The clerk will return to the court if the defendant is found guilty. At that point, the clerk will make notes in the public record about the verdict and the sentence that the defendant received. The notations about the outcome of the case will become a part of the public record where anyone may see the results.

F. COURT REPORTER

Court reporter
A trained professional who is responsible for taking down every spoken word in the courtroom during a hearing and reproducing those words as a transcript.

A **court reporter** is the person is responsible for taking down every spoken word in the courtroom. Court reporters are trained to use various types of technology, including computerized stenographic machines. In the past, court reporters wrote out everything that was said in shorthand, but that has given way to advanced technology. Nowadays, court reporters use a machine that allows them to type as fast 200 words per minute. However, when a court reporter types in a courtroom, he or she is actually recording the spoken words phonetically. Someone who is not trained to be a court reporter would find it impossible to read the printout. A computer chip inside the machine automatically converts the phonemes into English and this written transcript is made available to the attorneys and the judge within seconds of the person having testified on the witness stand. A court reporter takes down everything that anyone in the courtroom says. It is a challenging and repetitive occupation that can be financially rewarding, but it is clearly not a profession for everyone. It takes a certain amount of dedication and concentration to work as a court reporter.

⫟⫟⫟ JURY SELECTION

A trial begins in a very formal fashion. The judge will call the case and ask the parties if they are ready for trial. If they answer that they are, then the judge will ask the parties to **join issue**. To join issue is similar to boxers touching gloves before a bout and probably predates that custom. When the parties join issue, they are signifying that they are ready to start the trial. The defendant will sign the indictment under the plea: not guilty. Once issue has been joined, the next step is to select a jury.

Join issue
The parties officially submit the case to a jury for a determination and verdict.

The process of selecting a jury is also known as **voir dire**. This is a French phrase meaning look-speak. The term is quite expressive of the process of selecting a jury. The attorneys in the case look over the prospective jurors, ask them questions, and then eliminate the ones that they believe will not be favorable to their case. It is not an exact science. Prospective jurors are questioned by both the prosecutor and defense attorney. Their responses are noted and used to determine which members of the panel will be removed from the panel and which ones will stay. For the sake of clarity, we refer to this group of citizens from whom a jury is selected as the panel. The term **venire** is often used, but panel will serve just as well. The attorneys listen to the responses and take this opportunity to look the panel members over and decide which ones they wish to strike from the panel and which ones they would like to keep.

Voir dire
(French) To see, to say; the questioning of a jury panel member to determine if the person is competent to serve on a jury.

Venire
The group of local citizens who are summoned for jury duty and from whom a jury will be selected.

Although in the past there were many restrictions to jury service, including the deliberate exclusion of women and minorities from panels, modern practice allows almost anyone to serve on a jury. The only people who are barred from jury duty are those who have been convicted of a felony, minors, noncitizens, or anyone who cannot or will not follow the judge's orders and the law.

Panel members are selected from a wide variety of sources. Although it was true in the past that jury administrators would cull voter registration rolls for names of people to be summoned for jury duty, modern practice has expanded this to motor vehicle department records, tax rolls, and other public records.

The actual process of selecting a jury varies from state to state and even county to county, but there are some general provisions that occur in all jury selection. For instance, there is always a general question session.

General questions are asked of the entire panel and often consist of questions designed to make sure that everyone who is present is legally qualified to serve on the jury. The judge or the prosecutor might ask the panel if there are any convicted felons seated in the panel or anyone under the age of 18. Beyond that, general questions might include more nuanced inquiries about whether panel members can follow the judge's directions and the law. Panel members will also be asked a series of broad-based questions to make sure that all members are not biased or prejudiced against one side or the other. In some states, attorneys question the potential jurors; in others, and in federal court, the judge asks all of the questions. In most courts, the judge will explain what the jury selection process is and how it will proceed. Following that explanation, the prosecutor usually goes first with his or her general questions. Then the defense attorney will do the same.

Prosecutors and defense attorneys have different general questions for the panel. The prosecutor will focus on issues such as seeking jurors who will follow the law, whereas the defense attorney might ask the panel members if they have had bad experiences with police officers or whether they would tend to put more faith in police officers than in other witnesses. The purpose of these questions is twofold: The attorneys really want to know if there are panel members who clearly side with the prosecution or the defense, but there is a secondary agenda. Because the attorneys know that the 12 people who will sit on the jury are seated somewhere in the room, they take the opportunity to make a good impression on them and to get them thinking about specific issues.

In recent years, many of the most common general questions asked by attorneys have been reduced to juror questionnaires and given to the panel members when they are summoned for jury duty. Each panel member's answers are provided to the prosecutor and defense attorney, which frequently helps speed up the jury-selection process. A common question might be this: Have you ever been the victim of a crime? Both attorneys will want to know the answer to that question. The prosecutor would like to know because a person who has been a victim of a crime might be more willing to return a guilty verdict than someone who has not. The defense attorney might wish to strike that person during selection for the same reason.

Once general questioning is over, the attorneys are then allowed to move on to individual questions. Here, they follow up on any indications or answers that panel members gave in general questioning. The attorneys might wish to know more specifics about the panel member's response to a general question and also to try to evaluate the person more closely to see if he or she would make a good juror for the prosecution or defense. Just as we saw with general questioning, the prosecutor goes first in asking individual questions. Attorneys often see this as an opportunity for establishing a personal rapport with the panel members. This rapport may carry over to the trial if this panel member ends up as a juror on the case. Attorneys also wish to see how interested the panel members are, whether they make eye contact, and the numerous other body language clues that people give off. Jury selection often boils down to an intuitive feeling about a panel member instead of a mathematical appraisal. Barring any openly hostile panel member—who will undoubtedly be eliminated—in the end the attorney removes people often based on nothing more than a negative feeling about a particular panel member.

When we use the phrase jury selection, we are not being accurate. Attorneys do not select the jurors that they want. Instead, they remove panel members that they do not want until they have 12 remaining. The process of removing panel members is called **striking a jury**. When a panel member is struck, this person will not serve on the jury. In many jurisdictions, the panel might consist of 48 persons. The defense has the right to remove 24 and the prosecutor 12, leaving 12 people who will serve on the jury. In many jurisdictions, the parties have an equal number of strikes. In those jurisdictions, for example, the jury administrator might bring in 36 people on a panel. Both sides have the right to remove or strike 12, for a total of 24 strikes. The remaining 12 would then serve on the jury. Panel members may be struck in two different ways: (1) challenge for cause, and (2) peremptory strike.

Striking a jury
The process of questioning and removing panel members until 12 jurors are left; these 12 will serve on the jury.

A. PEREMPTORY CHALLENGES

A **peremptory challenge** is the right of a party to strike a panel member for almost any reason. One of the attorneys might not like the way that the person answers a question, or the attorney just has a gut feeling about the panel member. See Scenario 13-1. Peremptory strikes do not have to be justified, except in certain instances (set out below). Both sides are given a specific number of peremptory strikes, as we previously outlined. In some jurisdictions, the defendant is given twice as many peremptory strikes as the state, whereas in other jurisdictions, they receive the same number. When either side has used up their allotted number of peremptory strikes, they are not permitted to strike any additional members of the panel.

Peremptory challenge
A strike of a juror for any reason, except based on race or sex.

JURY SELECTION

SCENARIO 13-1

During the jury selection process, Paula Prosecutor asks the general question, "Is there anyone here who believes that the drug cocaine should be legalized?" One person, Dale, raises his hand. Paula decides to strike him from the panel because of that answer. Can she do so?

Answer: Yes, peremptory strikes can be used for almost any reason.

B. CHALLENGES FOR CAUSE

A member of the panel may be removed or challenged for cause. A **challenge for cause** is the process of removing a panel member because the person has demonstrated some prejudice to one of the parties or has indicated that he or she will not follow the judge's instructions. When either the state or the defense uncovers any of these attitudes, that party normally moves to have the panel member dismissed for cause. A challenge for cause does not count against a side's number of peremptory strikes. See Scenario 13-2.

Challenge for cause
A formal objection to the qualifications or attitude of a prospective juror.

CHALLENGE FOR CAUSE

During jury selection, Paula Prosecutor asks the following question: "Is there anyone here who cannot sit on a jury for religious or other reasons?"

Diana raises her hand. In follow-up questioning, Diana responds that it is against her religious principles to judge other human beings and no matter what the judge tells her to do, she will not participate in the jury and will not vote to return either a guilty or a not guilty verdict. Can she be removed for cause?

Answer: Yes. Her answer clearly indicates that she will not follow the rules or obey the judge's instructions. She can be removed for cause and this removal will not count against Paula's peremptory strikes.

C. *BATSON* CHALLENGES

In recent decades, the power to use a peremptory challenge for any reason has been substantially curtailed. In the past, a prosecutor might use a peremptory challenge to remove members of a specific race in the mistaken belief that jury members who are the same race as the defendant will not return a guilty verdict against him or her. Eventually those types of practices were dealt with by the U.S. Supreme Court. In the case of *Batson v. Kentucky*, 476 U.S. 79 (1986), the Court ruled that peremptory strikes could not be used by a prosecutor to remove all African American panel members simply because of their race. The Court reasoned that because the court system is a function of the government, it could not be used to further discriminatory practices. The *Batson* decision has been extended to other types of discriminatory peremptory strikes. For instance, *Batson*-type decisions have forbidden striking panel members on the basis of any racial affiliation, as well as gender-based discrimination. In the past few years, so-called reverse *Batson* **challenges** have been made as well. In a reverse *Batson* challenge, the state challenges the defense for striking panel members for a discriminatory reason.

Batson **challenge**
A challenge to the strikes used by a party during jury selection that claims the party used discriminatory practices in removing members of the panel.

D. STRIKING THE JURY

When all of the questioning of the panel has been concluded, striking the jury is the next phase. Courts handle this process in different ways, but there are two generally accepted procedures to strike a jury. In the first scenario, the clerk of court reads off the panel member's name, and he or she stands. The prosecutor will either strike this juror (using one of his or her peremptory strikes) or accept the juror. This is done out loud. The prosecutor may say, "The state strikes this juror," or, a little more politely, "The state excuses this juror." This eliminates the panel member from serving on the jury. If the state accepts the juror, then the defendant has the right to strike the panel member. If the defendant accepts, this person becomes a member of the trial jury. Each panel member's name will be called until 12 jurors have been selected. If either the prosecutor or the defendant uses all of his or her allotted peremptory strikes, he or she has lost the right to strike any more panel members.

SILENT STRIKES

In some jurisdictions, striking the jury is done on paper with silent strikes. Under this system, the attorneys do not announce their acceptance or rejection of the panel member out loud. Instead, they simply mark the panel list with their strikes. The list is handed back and forth between each attorney until 12 jurors have been selected. Many judges prefer the silent strike because it moves the jury selection along at a faster pace and causes less inconvenience for the panel members. One might argue that it also creates less discomfort for jurors because they do not have to stand and then either be accepted or rejected.

E. ALTERNATE JURORS

There are times when, in addition to selecting 12 members of the jury, the court may select one or more **alternate jurors**. Although alternates are not used in most trials, there are times when a trial is projected to last several days or even weeks. In that situation, it is wise to select one or two alternate jurors who would take the place of one of the 12 jurors, should he or she become sick or otherwise be unable to carry on in the trial. Alternate jurors sit in the jury box during the trial but do not retire with the jury at the end to deliberate. Only the main 12 jurors are allowed to deliberate. Alternate jurors are normally released when the case is over and the jury retires to the jury room to reach a verdict. The process of selecting alternate jurors is exactly like the process for selecting the 12 main jurors. Once the 12th juror has been selected, the judge will announce that selection will continue for one or two alternates. The prosecutor and the defendant have the right to use peremptory strikes to eliminate panel members, just as they did when selecting the main jury. Once accepted, these alternate jurors join the main group in the jury box. Jury selection has then concluded.

Alternate juror
A person selected to sit on the jury, but who will have no right to participate in the deliberations and will not be able to vote to return a verdict.

F. FINAL STEPS FOR THE JURY BEFORE THE TRIAL

When a jury has been selected and seated in the jury box, the rest of the panel is excused. The people who were not selected to serve on the jury return to the jury administration area, where they may be released from any further jury duty or be called to sit on another panel in a different case. The jurors who have been selected to sit on the trial will now be given badges identifying them as jurors in an ongoing trial. They will be given pads and pencils to take notes. The judge will also give them some preliminary instructions, such as informing them about their duties in the trial. One of the most important instructions that a judge gives the jurors is that they must wait until the end of the case before they reach a decision about the defendant's guilt or innocence. The judge tells the jurors that they will hear testimony from witnesses and will also see physical and other evidence that is admitted during the trial. They are not to make up their minds about the guilt or innocence of the defendant until all evidence and testimony has been tendered. Whether jurors actually follow that admonition has been subject to a great deal of debate in recent years, with studies showing that many jurors begin to make up their minds as early as opening statements and most have reached a conclusion about the case before the closing argument phase.

The judge will also tell the newly sworn-in jurors that they are forbidden to discuss the details of the case with anyone, even each other, while the case is pending. They may not talk about the case with friends or family and may not discuss the case with the media or anyone else. In fact, most judges tell the jurors that if anyone approaches them and questions them about the case or tries to persuade them, they should report that fact to the judge immediately and the judge will launch an investigation into the possibility of jury tampering.

Jurors are also told to avoid watching media accounts of the trial (if any) and reading anything about the case in newspapers or online. (In the vast majority of cases, there will be no media attention at all.) In addition to these instructions, the judge will also tell the jury that neither the attorneys nor the witnesses in the case are allowed to speak with them outside the courtroom. Most attorneys take this instruction so seriously that they will not even greet a juror if they should see one in the hallway during a break in the trial.

OPENING STATEMENTS

Once jury selection has been completed and the jurors who will decide in the trial are seated in the jury box, the trial can begin. The first phase of a criminal trial is the opening statements.

Opening statement
A preliminary address to the jury by the prosecutor and defense attorney, outlining the general facts of the case.

Opening statements are made by both the prosecutor and the defense attorney. They are short speeches to the jury where the attorneys outline the facts and evidence of the case—as they see them. Attorneys cannot testify or offer opinions during an opening statement. Instead, they often explain what will happen during the course of the trial. After all, most jurors have no idea what to expect, and telling them what to expect can alleviate some tension. Some attorneys go so far as to explain who will testify and what they expect that witness to say. They cannot show the jury any evidence (because it has not yet been admitted), but they can certainly state what evidence they believe will be admitted during the trial.

An opening statement is not a persuasive argument and a judge will admonish an attorney who attempts to argue that the defendant is or is not guilty during the opening statement. Such persuasion is reserved for the closing argument. The opening statement is only intended as a mechanism for the attorneys to explain the trial process. Instead, the attorneys will outline each of their cases and ask the jury to return a verdict. For the prosecutor, the verdict requested will always be a finding of guilty on all counts against the defendant. After the prosecutor has given his or her opening statement, the defense attorney will give one as well. Defense attorneys often ask the jurors to keep an open mind throughout the case and to remember that there are two sides to every story. Because the state will go first, the defense attorney will remind the jurors that they should not reach a conclusion in the case until they have heard from the defense in the case.

Opening statements are supposed to be short statements that outline the general facts of the case, but this is also the first time that an attorney has to speak to the jurors, so within the confines of the structure of the opening statement, the attorneys will do what little they can to persuade the jurors to their viewpoint. Attorneys are not allowed to give impassioned speeches or to plead with the jury; they must limit their remarks to the evidence, but within that framework a clever attorney can attempt to both deliver a factual overview and also slip in a few remarks intended to persuade the jury. Consider Scenario 13-3.

OPENING STATEMENT

SCENARIO 13-3

During defense attorney Tamara's opening statement, she makes the following remarks:

"Ladies and gentlemen, the evidence in this case will show that the defendant did not participate in the robbery. The evidence will show that he is a good and decent man who was at home when the robbery occurred, surrounded by his five children and his loving wife. The evidence will also show that because he is gainfully employed as a city worker for 20 years, he had no need of any money and that none of the money from the robbery was ever traced to him. We will also show that as a volunteer member of Habitat for Humanity who has built over 20 homes for indigent people, he has sustained an injury to his right shoulder that would make it impossible for him to aim a shotgun, as the state has alleged."

Is this an improper opening statement?

Answer: Probably not. Although Tamara has inserted several points in her opening statement that should not be there, such as telling the jury about what a good and decent man her client is, she has cleverly couched these terms as an expression of what the evidence will show. As a result, the judge will be hard pressed to say that she is going outside the purpose of an opening statement, although she is certainly coming very close to crossing the line.

 **DIRECT EXAMINATION**

Once opening statements have been concluded, the judge will turn to the prosecutor and ask him or her to begin the case. The prosecutor always goes first in the U.S. system because the state has the burden of proving that the defendant is guilty beyond a reasonable doubt. This stage of the trial is often referred to as the state's **case-in-chief**. This is where the prosecution presents its entire case, including all witnesses and evidence, to show that the defendant committed the crime. Although there are times when the state may present additional evidence at the end of the trial, in most cases, the state gets a single shot to make its case. Testimony from witnesses will come in the form of **direct examination**.

Case-in-chief
The body of evidence and testimony offered by a party during its presentation of a jury trial.

Direct examination
The questions asked of a witness by the attorney who has called him or her to the stand.

A. QUESTIONING WITNESSES DURING DIRECT EXAMINATION

When prosecutors begin their cases, they do so by calling witnesses. Like all attorneys in criminal and civil cases, prosecutors are not allowed to make their own statements to the jury about evidence or offer opinions about the truth of a witness or the quality of the evidence. Those are decisions that must be made by the jury. In most cases, the only way for an attorney to present evidence and prove the allegations in a case is by calling live witnesses to the stand. To do so, the prosecutor will call a witness to the stand and the witness will be sworn. Then the witness takes the stand and is asked questions by the prosecutor in what is referred to as direct examination. The questions that the prosecutor asks on direct examination attempt to prove the elements of the offense, establish the basic facts of the case, and also provide a platform for the prosecutor to introduce evidence that also establishes the defendant's guilt beyond a reasonable doubt.

The witnesses who testify on direct examination are generally considered to be friendly to that side. State's witnesses often include police officers, coroners, victims, and others who have knowledge of the case. The rules about direction examination are strict: An attorney is not allowed to ask leading questions, questions that suggest an answer. For instance, an attorney cannot ask a witness, "The man sitting over there, he was the one who hit you, wasn't he?" That question is not permissible because it leads the witness to the answer. Instead, the attorney who conducts direct examination must stick to general questions, usually ones that begin with the standard question words: who, what, when, and where. (Attorneys usually do not ask why because a witness cannot testify what the defendant was thinking.)

B. INTRODUCING EVIDENCE DURING DIRECT EXAMINATION

As the prosecutor questions each witness on direct, he or she may also introduce evidence during the examination. In earlier chapters, we saw that there are specific foundation questions that an attorney must ask a witness that establish the relevance and admissibility of particular evidence. These questions must be asked before the evidence is tendered to the court for admission into evidence. Just as we saw with opening statements, an attorney cannot simply produce evidence and begin waving it about in front of the courtroom. A witness must be questioned to establish the relevance of the evidence and then the judge must rule that the evidence is admissible, often over the objection of the opposing attorney.

When the attorney who is questioning the witness has asked all the questions necessary, he or she usually announces, "No further questions." This is the signal to the judge and the other attorney that cross-examination is to begin.

V CROSS-EXAMINATION

As we have seen, the prosecution always goes first in a criminal trial and presents its witnesses and evidence, but that does not mean that the defense attorney has no role to play. In fact, the defense attorney is involved in every part of the state's case. The defense attorney may object to a particular question of a witness, such as objecting to a leading question. The attorney will almost certainly object to the admission of specific types of evidence and the judge must make a determination if the evidence should be admitted over the defense attorney's objection. The defense attorney has one other major role to play during the state's case, though: He or she will **cross-examine** each of the state's witnesses.

Cross-examine
Asking questions of a witness to determine, bias, lack of knowledge, prejudice, or some other failing.

Although there is no requirement that all witnesses must be cross-examined, most of the state's witnesses will face cross-examination by the defense counsel. Once direct examination has been completed, the judge will give the defense attorney the opportunity to cross-examine the witness. A judge may not bar or otherwise prevent a defense attorney from conducting a cross-examination, but the judge may prevent the attorney from asking certain types of questions. For instance, if the judge does not believe that a particular question on cross is relevant, the judge may instruct the defense attorney to move on to another question. The prosecutor may object to a question and the judge will rule on the question before allowing the witness to answer it. However, within these guidelines, an attorney has wide latitude on cross-examination. If the attorney can show relevance, then he or she can ask virtually any question.

A. HOW IS CROSS-EXAMINATION DIFFERENT FROM DIRECT EXAMINATION?

Attorneys are also not constrained on cross-examination the way that they are on direct examination. As we have already seen, an attorney who asks questions during direct examination cannot ask leading questions. An attorney who is carrying out a cross-examination, however, not only can ask leading questions, but is actually encouraged to do so. An excellent attorney can almost always bring up some serious issues on cross-examination or at least some questions for the jury to consider.

Attorneys often use cross-examination as a way of developing a particular theme of the trial. The defense attorney may emphasize the fact that there is some question about the eyewitness identification of the defendant, for example, or establish some evidence of alibi. Defense attorneys rarely use the tactics portrayed on TV or in movies, such as screaming at witnesses or physically intimidating them. These tactics rarely work and often turn the jury against the defense attorney and, by extension, the defendant. Instead, most attorneys focus on the details of the question, not the loudness of the delivery. However, there are times when an attorney may take a more aggressive approach to a witness, such as impeaching the witness.

> **Sidebar**
>
> *Cross-examination is both an art and a skill. Attorneys spend many years developing good cross-examination skills.*

B. IMPEACHMENT

Impeachment
Showing that a witness is not worthy of belief.

Impeachment of a witness shows that he or she is not worthy of belief. The most common way to impeach a witness is to show that he or she has a criminal record or has no personal knowledge of the case. Calling the witness's credibility into question is a tried and true tactic of both prosecutors and defense attorneys to discredit a witness. A witness may be impeached for any of the following reasons:

- Bias
- Inconsistent statements
- Previous conviction
- Not competent to testify

REDIRECT EXAMINATION

Redirect examination
The process of questioning a witness who was originally called on direct examination to clear up any issues raised during cross-examination.

At the conclusion of each cross-examination, the attorney who originally presented the witness on direct examination has the right to ask question on **redirect examination**. Such questioning is usually limited to points raised on cross-examination and is not designed to allow the attorney to repeat the entire direct examination. The attorney will ask questions to help clear up any apparent contradictions the witness may have made during the cross-examination and then conclude redirect.

DIRECTED VERDICT

Directed verdict
A ruling by a judge that there is not sufficient evidence of the defendant's guilt to present to the jury.

At the conclusion of the state's case, once the prosecutor has presented all the witnesses and evidence that he or she believes has proven the defendant's guilt beyond a reasonable doubt, the state announces the following to the court: "Your Honor, the State rests."

This announcement signals the next phase of the trial: the defense. However, before the defendant puts up any evidence or witnesses, if any, the defendant will first make a motion for a **directed verdict**. A motion for directed verdict requests the court to enter a verdict of not guilty on some or all of the charges against the defendant. The basis of the motion is that the state has failed to meet its burden of proof on the charges and that there is not sufficient evidence for the jurors to even consider the case in their deliberations at the end of the trial. The defense attorney is essentially asking the court to dismiss the case because of lack of proof. Normally, the court will only grant such a motion when the prosecution has failed to present any evidence to support the various charges against the defendant. If it is a question of the sufficiency or how much weight to give the evidence that has been presented, then the court will usually defer to the jury to make those determinations. The judge will, in that event, deny the motion for directed verdict and allow the jury to decide the issues in the case.

In most cases, the motion for directed verdict fails, but that does not stop defense attorneys from bringing it. In fact, in almost any criminal trial, a defense attorney would be considered remiss—and perhaps ineffective in his or her representation—if the motion were not brought. After all, the defense has nothing to lose by bringing the motion and a lot to gain. If the judge denies the motion, then the defense is in no worse a position than it was before the motion was made. If the judge grants the motion, then some or all of the charges against the defendant will be dismissed. Assuming that the normal result prevails—that the defendant's motion for directed verdict is denied—then we move to the next phase of the trial: the defense.

 ## DEFENSE CASE-IN-CHIEF

The defense is under no obligation to present any evidence or testimony. In fact, there are very good reasons for the defense to stand mute. The defendant might not make a very good witness. Other defense witnesses may also might make a good impression on the jury. Despite the judge's instructions to the jurors that they may not make any negative inference against the defendant for failing to testify, it is human nature that they would like to hear the defendant proclaim his or her innocence. However, in most situations, the defense attorney counsels the defendant not to take the stand. If the defendant takes the stand, he or she will then be subject to cross-examination.

In addition to whether or not the defendant will do well during direct and cross-examination, the defense must also consider an issue that we have already discussed: placing the defendant's character into evidence. As we saw in an earlier chapter, in the federal system and in many state systems, the defendant is open to questions about his or her criminal convictions if he or she takes the stand. Answering these questions could have a devastating effect on the defense. The defense attorney must weigh all of these factors before deciding to put the defendant on the stand. If the defendant has an unpleasant personality, or could easily be led astray on cross-examination, the best course is not to put the defendant on the stand.

If the defense decides to put up witnesses and admit testimony, the defense attorney must follow the same rules as the prosecutor. Witnesses must be sworn in. The defense attorney must conduct direct examination with the same limitations placed on the state during its direct examination. After each witness for the defense testifies, the prosecutor has the right to cross-examine that witness. In addition to direct and cross-examination, a defense attorney who wishes to admit evidence must ask the correct foundation questions and deal with any objections raised by the prosecutor.

In many ways, the defense case is a mirror image of the state's version. Witnesses will be called and testify on direct, and the defense attorney will admit evidence during that testimony. When the defense attorney has presented what he or she believes is sufficient evidence to create a reasonable doubt with the jury, the defense will rest its case in exactly the same way that the prosecution did. There is one important difference, however. The state is not allowed to move for a directed verdict at the end of the defense case. Instead, the case must be submitted to a jury for their decision. There are some rare instances where the state can present additional evidence at the conclusion of the defense case. This is referred to as rebuttal.

REBUTTAL

Rebuttal
Denying or taking away the effect of the other party's presentation; a rebuttal attacks claims made by one party with evidence presented by the other.

At the conclusion of the defense case, the prosecutor has a decision to make. The rules of court allow the prosecutor to make a **rebuttal** to the defense. Rebuttal is used to attack a point raised during the defense. If the defense presents no evidence and raises no new issues, there is little need for the prosecutor to go back over its testimony and present the same witnesses who testified during the prosecution's case-in-chief. In fact, a judge would not allow this. However, there are times when the prosecution must present a rebuttal, such as when the defense is insanity or alibi. We will discuss those defenses in Chapter 14, but when such defenses are raised, the jury will be instructed that as long as the defense has raised some evidence to support its defense, the prosecution must rebut the testimony or the jury will be compelled to find the defendant not guilty. Rebuttal, then, is testimony that directly refutes the defendant's claims made in his or her case-in-chief. Even in situations where the defense has raised several issues, the judge may still restrict the state to rebutting specific points only and prevent the state from presenting evidence on other issues.

MISTRIAL

There are many events that may cause a mistrial. Declaring a case to be a mistrial means that the judge has determined that the case cannot go on, either because the jury cannot reach a decision or because something has occurred in the case that is prejudicial to the defendant.[1] An order of mistrial simply means that all of the parties act as though the trial never occurred. The state is free to try the case all over again. This means that all of the witnesses must testify again, all evidence must be admitted, and everything, in fact, must be repeated as though it had never happened.

CHARGE CONFERENCE

When the evidentiary part of the trial is over, the next phase consists of the closing arguments. However, before those arguments can be made, the attorneys and the judge will meet to discuss the jury charges.

> I hereby charge you that the state must prove each and every material allegation against the defendant by proof beyond a reasonable doubt. The burden in this case never shifts to the defendant to prove his or her innocence. The defendant has presented a defense in this case. It is not the duty of the defendant to prove the defense beyond a reasonable doubt; it is the state's burden to disprove the defense beyond a reasonable doubt.[2]

FIGURE 13-1

Standard Jury Charge on Reasonable Doubt

During the **charge conference**, the attorneys will request that specific charges be read and may oppose charges proposed by the other side. A charge is a statement about the law. The most common one used in criminal cases is this: "Ladies and gentlemen, I charge you that the defendant in this case is presumed innocent unless and until the state has proven his guilt beyond a reasonable doubt." There are many other statements of the law, though, that the judge will read to the jury to help guide them in their deliberations. Because this is the last thing that the jurors will hear before they go into the jury room to deliberate, the attorneys are concerned about what they hear. Both attorneys are permitted to offer their own versions of particular charges, and there are often objections by one side to the other's jury instructions. In a major case, there could dozens of different statements about the law that the judge will either read to the jury or provide to them in written form. In addition to the parties' suggested jury charges, there are also standard jury instructions that a judge must give in every jury trial. Eventually, the judge will rule on proposed charges and also inform the attorneys about the standard charges that he or she will read to the jurors (see Figure 13-1). At the conclusion of the charge conference, the judge will allow the attorneys a brief recess to review the instructions. The attorneys need to know what instructions the judge plans to give because they will refer to some of these statements of the law during their closing argument.

Charge conference
A meeting held after the close of evidence in a trial and before the closing arguments where the attorneys and the judge discuss what jury instructions will be given to the jurors.

CLOSING ARGUMENTS

When all testimony has been heard and all evidence admitted, including any rebuttal, and the charge conference is concluded, the trial moves to the closing argument phase. In a **closing argument**, each attorney will urge the jury to return a verdict in his or her favor. The prosecutor will argue that each of the elements of the crime has been proven and that the defendant is guilty beyond a reasonable doubt. The defense attorney will argue, just as forcefully, that the state has failed to meet its burden, either because they have prosecuted the wrong person or because the defendant is legally insane or that he or she had an alibi or is not guilty by virtue of some other reason. The defense attorney will inevitably ask the jury members to carefully consider the case and to consider

Closing argument
An attorney's summation of his or her case during which the attorney seeks to convince the jury to a return a verdict favorable to his or her side.

that the state has failed to prove the case to the high standard of proof beyond a reasonable doubt.

Unlike the fictional portrayals of closing arguments that we often see in movies and TV shows, real-life closing arguments are not conducted in the span of a few minutes. In previous decades, a closing argument might last for hours. Some famous cases had closing arguments that lasted for days. Nowadays, attorneys are usually limited to one or two hours for a closing argument. (Death penalty cases frequently allow greater time for closing arguments.) One hour is a considerably long time for any one person to speak about any topic, and attorneys are aware of this. Many of them have become as technologically savvy as any other professional. Instead of simply speaking to the jurors—and risk boring them or, even worse, losing their attention—attorneys now routinely rely on slide presentations, graphics, videos, computer simulations, and almost any other type of visual media available.

Despite the advances in technology and presentation, studies continue to show that jurors have almost always made up their minds about the verdict in the case before the closing arguments ever start. A closing argument, no matter how brilliantly delivered or flawlessly performed, is more often than not ignored by the jurors who have decided to return a different verdict. This is not to say that a brilliant closing argument cannot win a case. In some situations, it probably does. However, the idea that the jurors have not thought through the facts of the case prior to the closing argument and reached some type of conclusion, even tenuous, flies in the face of both research and common sense.

Unlike in the opening statement and direct and cross-examination, attorneys are given considerable latitude in how they present their closing arguments. They cannot introduce evidence or facts that were not brought out in trial; they cannot offer their personal opinion that the facts in the case are true. Beyond that, though, an attorney has an enormous range of activities that he or she can do during a closing argument. An attorney can make a logical, consistent argument, but is also permitted to offer a completely illogical and inconsistent position. Attorneys can appeal to emotions, to logic, and to altruism; they can appeal to the worst or best in us all.

One practical issue that often comes up is which party gets to give the closing argument first. The general answer is that the prosecution goes first and the defendant goes second, mirroring the opening statement. This arrangement can be affected by several factors, though. In some jurisdictions, for instance, if a defendant presents no evidence or testimony, then the defendant has the right to go first. After the state presents its closing argument, the defense attorney is permitted to give a final summation, commenting on the points raised by the state. However, this rule is not followed in all jurisdictions and the exact order of who goes first can vary depending on local court rules.

Regardless of who goes first or second in the closing argument, both sides will ask the jury to do the one thing that they are required to do: return a verdict. The prosecution will obviously ask the jury to return a guilty verdict, and the defense will just as forcefully ask the jury to return a not guilty verdict.

 **JURY INSTRUCTIONS**

As we have already seen, during the charge conference, the judge and attorneys will meet and discuss the **jury instructions** (what we referred to as charges earlier) that the judge will provide to the jurors. A jury instruction is a statement about the law in the case. Jury instructions give the jurors the statutory guidelines and elements of the offense with which the defendant is charged and also direct them in practical matters, such as how to select a foreperson and how to complete the verdict. Among the charges that the judge will provide to the jurors is an explanation that the state has the burden of proof in the case and must prove the case beyond a reasonable doubt. The tradition has been, for hundreds of years, for the judge to read all of these instructions to the jury, probably stemming from a time when most people were illiterate. However, in the days of modern technology (and limited attention spans) sitting through an hour or two of someone reading the law is an excruciating experience. That is why many judges have begun to defy convention and provide copies of the entire charge to the jury. However, there are still courtrooms all across the country where the judge reads the entire set of charges to the jury, despite the fact that the process could take several hours.

> **Jury instructions**
> A judge's directions to the jury about the law that pertains to the issues in the trial and the jury's function once they retire to the jury room.

There is a rather famous jury charge that judges sometimes give when jurors indicate that they are deadlocked and unable to reach a unanimous verdict. Rather than declare a mistrial, the judge can give an "Allen" or "dynamite" charge.[3] This jury instruction uses blunt language to tell the jurors that they have entered into an obligation to act as jurors and that they should follow their sworn duty. The jury instruction does not tell the jurors what verdict to reach, only that they should reach one and soon.

 **DELIBERATIONS**

All of the evidence and testimony have been presented. The closing arguments are over. The judge has either read or provided the jurors with written copies of the instructions. The final act of the trial is about to commence: jury deliberations.

When the jury begins its deliberations, the jurors are escorted from the courtroom to the jury room. The evidence that has been admitted during the trial is brought to them and the bailiff then leaves the jurors alone to consider the case. The jury deliberation process consists of the jurors reviewing the evidence, discussing the case, and deciding on a verdict. One of the first things that the jury does is to elect one of the members to act as the foreperson. This person will generally keep things organized and will act as the jury's spokesperson when dealing with the judge. The jury deliberation period can last for a few minutes or can go on for days. There are numerous instances in which the jury deliberation actually takes longer than it took to try the case.

What happens in the jury room? The attorneys for the case would desperately like to know, but the only people allowed to be present while they deliberate are the jurors themselves. No doubt they discuss the case and sometimes have heated arguments with one another. In most jurisdictions, the jurors are compelled to reach a unanimous verdict. In fact, one of the judge's first instructions to the jurors is that they should select a jury foreperson and then decide on a verdict. If the jurors can reach a unanimous verdict, they will write it down and then tell the bailiff they have reached a decision. They do not tell the bailiff what their decision is. Instead, they must come back into the courtroom for the announcement.

VERDICT

Juries are charged with the duty of reaching a verdict in the case. A verdict is what the jury has determined to be the facts in the case. In criminal cases, there are several different verdicts that a jury may return, including:

- Guilty
- Guilty but mentally ill
- Not guilty
- Not guilty by reason of insanity

Reading of the verdict in open court is one of the most dramatic moments in a trial. The format is often, "In case of *State v. John Doe*, we the jury find the defendant. . . ." If the defendant is found not guilty, the jury will be dismissed and assuming that the defendant has no other charges pending, he or she will be immediately released. If the verdict is guilty, then the trial moves into the final phase, sentencing.

In almost all jurisdictions, there has been a requirement that the jury's verdict must be unanimous. However, for several decades, the states of Louisiana and Oregon allowed nonunanimous verdicts in felony cases. The juror vote could drop as low as 10-2, either to acquit or convict, and the verdict would be acceptable. The U.S. Supreme Court originally authorized the use of nonunanimous verdicts in *Apodaca v. Oregon*.[4] That ruling stood for 48 years until *Ramos v. Louisiana*, 139 S. Ct. 1318 (2019) overturned it. Although the rule of *stare decisis* should be followed in all cases, the Court in *Ramos* stated that sometimes bad precedent makes for bad decisions. In *Ramos*, the court ruled that allowing nonunanimous verdicts in felony cases is a violation of the Sixth Amendment.

A. VARIOUS TYPES OF VERDICTS IN CRIMINAL CASES

Traditionally, there were only three possible verdicts in a criminal case: guilty, not guilty, and not guilty by reason of insanity. However, some states have expanded by one the possible verdicts in a criminal case.

GUILTY

If the verdict is guilty, then the judge will enter a judgment that the defendant was found guilty and will either sentence the defendant immediately or defer sentencing to some later date.

GUILTY BUT MENTALLY ILL

As we saw in a previous chapter on defenses, when a defendant raises the claim of insanity, many jurisdictions allow a jury to return a verdict of guilty, but mentally ill. The only difference between these two verdicts is that with a guilty, but mentally ill decision the defendant must be sentenced to some facility that provides counseling or psychiatric services. The defendant is still convicted and will serve a sentence. States that have this verdict option may require that defendants found guilty, but mentally ill receive psychiatric treatment during their imprisonment.

NOT GUILTY

A not guilty verdict is the jury's determination that the state has failed to prove the defendant's guilt beyond a reasonable doubt. Once a jury returns a not guilty verdict, the state is barred by the provisions of the Fifth Amendment from retrying the defendant. The Double Jeopardy Clause of that amendment forbids retrying a person who has been found not guilty. Assuming that the defendant has no other charges pending, perhaps in another case, the defendant will be released directly from the courtroom.

NOT GUILTY BY REASON OF INSANITY

When a defendant raises the defense of insanity, a jury is authorized to return a verdict of not guilty by reason of insanity. In such a situation, the defendant is not convicted of a crime because the jury has determined that he or she lacks the ability to distinguish right from wrong and therefore cannot form the necessary *mens rea* to commit a crime. There are those who think that a person found not guilty by reason of insanity are immediately released. That is usually not the case. Instead, such a person may be committed to a mental institute for evaluation.

B. POLLING THE JURY

When the jury reaches a verdict of guilty, the defense attorney has the right to ask that the jurors be polled. **Polling** means that each juror will be asked if this verdict is his or her personal decision in the case. This means that the judge will ask each and every juror the following series of questions: "Mr. Juror, was this your verdict in the jury room? Is this your verdict now?" Assuming that everyone answers "Yes" to that question, then the judge will excuse the jury from any further attendance in the case.

Polling
Requesting the jurors to provide a verbal assurance that the verdict each person reached in the jury room is the still the verdict that they maintain when they return after deliberations.

C. EXCUSING THE JURY

Once the verdict has been returned, the jury is told that they are now free to discuss the case with anyone. The prohibitions about talking about the case are lifted. The attorneys who tried the case will, in many instances, talk to the jury so that they can learn what the jury thought was important in the case. This is a great way for young attorneys to learn how to improve their performance in the courtroom, assuming that they get forthright answers from the jury.

CASE EXCERPT

PEOPLE v. MURPHY
79 A.D.3D 1451, 1454, 913 N.Y.S.2D 815, 818) (N.Y.A.D. 3 DEPT., 2010)

CARDONA, P.J.

Appeal from a judgment of the County Court of Albany County (Breslin, J.), rendered May 18, 2009, upon a verdict convicting defendant of the crime of manslaughter in the second degree.

On the night of April 29, 2006 and into the early morning hours of April 30, 2006, defendant was engaged in two incidents with Joseph Jerome on Hudson Avenue in the City of Albany. Jerome's companions, Hector Perez and Rob Desantola, were also present. During the first encounter, defendant exchanged words with the group on the sidewalk outside his home. Perez then punched defendant twice, knocking him down and injuring his lip. The second encounter occurred shortly thereafter when Jerome, Perez, and Desantola returned to the area outside defendant's home. During that encounter, defendant fatally stabbed Jerome. The details surrounding both incidents are sharply disputed.

Defendant was convicted of murder in the second degree. Subsequently, this Court reversed that conviction on the ground that the admission into evidence of certain tape-recorded statements by defendant, in conjunction with other circumstances at the trial, violated defendant's right against self-incrimination and right to counsel, and we remitted the matter for a new trial. Following a retrial, defendant was convicted of manslaughter in the second degree and sentenced to 5 to 15 years in prison. He now appeals, and we affirm.

Initially, we are not persuaded by defendant's contention that County Court should have denied the People's reverse-*Batson* objection to his peremptory challenge of an African-American juror. While defense counsel offered a race-neutral explanation for the challenge—specifically, that the juror indicated that one of the reasons she kept a dog was for security—our review of the record supports the court's factual finding that the reason was pretextual In particular, we note that defense counsel had stricken every other African-American juror up to that point, and the court had previously put counsel "on notice" and warned him that his proffered explanation as to one of those jurors was only "marginally acceptable." Under these circumstances, and mindful that the court's evaluation of counsel's motivation in making the specific challenge at issue herein turned largely on its assessment of counsel's credibility, which is entitled to great deference, we find no error in the court's decision to strike the peremptory challenge.

Defendant next argues that County Court erred in excluding both the testimony of a mental health counselor who would have testified that defendant exhibits two symptoms of posttraumatic stress disorder (hereinafter PTSD), and the testimony of a psychiatrist who diagnosed defendant with "subclinical PTSD" based upon his opinion that defendant exhibits three symptoms of PTSD. Defendant argues that such expert testimony was necessary to assist the jury in understanding his state of mind at the time of the stabbing, which was crucial to his justification defense.

" 'It is for the trial court in the first instance to determine when jurors are able to draw conclusions from the evidence based on their day-to-day experience, their common observation and their knowledge, and when they would be benefitted by the specialized knowledge of an expert witness' " (*People v. Lee*, 96 N.Y.2d 157, 162, 726 N.Y.S.2d 361, 750 N.E.2d 63 (2001)). Here, after extensive oral argument and written submissions by both parties, County Court excluded the testimony based upon its conclusions that subclinical PTSD is not a recognized syndrome, disease, or mental defect, and that the specific symptoms at issue—hypervigilance, emotional numbing, and a sense of helplessness in the face of stress—were within the jury's range of knowledge and intelligence, particularly since defendant himself would be able to testify about his military experience and other events purportedly underlying his symptoms. Under the particular circumstances presented, we find that the court did not abuse its discretion in this regard.

Defendant next contends that the testimony of a police detective briefly noting that defendant "refused to talk about the fight," as well as the People's fleeting reference to that testimony during summation, violated defendant's right against self-incrimination. Notably, however, counsel raised no objection to the summation. Furthermore, when objecting to the testimony, counsel did not contend that the offending testimony impermissibly implicated defendant's invocation of his right to remain silent. Rather, counsel stated that his objection was based upon his belief that the line of questioning being pursued by the prosecutor would "ultimately" result in testimony that defendant invoked his right against self-incrimination and his right to counsel. When the prosecutor assured him that he would take the questioning in another direction, counsel stated, "That is fine," and no curative instruction was requested. Accordingly, the arguments made herein are not preserved for appellate review. In any event, in light of the evidence presented, we find that any such errors were "harmless beyond a reasonable doubt" inasmuch as there is "no reasonable possibility that the errors might have contributed to defendant's conviction" (*People v. Crimmins*, 36 N.Y.2d 230, 237, 367 N.Y.S.2d 213, 326 N.E.2d 787 (1975)).

We are also not persuaded by defendant's claim that the prosecutor violated his rights by noting during summation that defendant failed to provide an exculpatory version of events. Not only did defendant fail to object, rendering the issue unpreserved, but the prosecutor's comments in that regard referenced defendant's tape-recorded conversation with his father and sister, not his interaction with police. Finally, with respect to defendant's challenge to the redacted version of the tape-recorded conversation that was admitted at the retrial, we note that defendant asks this Court to reverse its previous holding that his statements were spontaneous (see *People v. Murphy*, 51 A.D.3d at 1057-1058, 856 N.Y.S.2d 713), which we decline to do.

ORDERED that the judgment is affirmed.

PETERS, SPAIN, KAVANAGH and EGAN JR., JJ., concur.

CASE QUESTIONS

1 With what crime is the defendant charged?
2 Is this the first time that the defendant was tried on this charge?
3 What is the reverse-*Batson* claim brought by the defendant?
4 What pattern had defense counsel followed during jury selection?
5 Did the prosecutor violate the defendant's rights during the prosecutor's closing argument (or summation?)

CHAPTER SUMMARY

There are many phases of a criminal trial. Jury selection is the first phase. Attorneys are allowed to strike or remove members of the panel until 12 jurors remain. An attorney can use a peremptory strike to remove a panel member for almost any cause. However, in the U.S. Supreme Court decision in *Batson v. Kentucky*, the Court barred attorneys on either side from removing jury members for discriminatory reasons. Once the jury is selected, the attorneys address the jurors in a short speech called an opening statement. Following the opening statement, the state must proceed first, calling witnesses and introducing evidence to prove that the defendant is guilty beyond a reasonable doubt. After each of the state's witnesses is questioned on direct examination, the defense attorney has the right to conduct cross-examination. When the state's case is concluded, the defense will almost always move for a directed verdict. A motion for directed verdict asserts that the state has failed to present enough evidence to sustain the charges. If the judge rules in favor of the defendant's motion, the charges against the defendant are dismissed. If the judge denies the motion, the case continues. At this point, the defense must decide to put up witnesses or evidence of its own. The prosecutor is entitled to cross-examine any defense witnesses who take the stand. When the defense concludes, the attorneys and the judge meet briefly to discuss the jury instructions that the judge will give to the jury members. The attorneys are then allowed to give a closing argument to the jury. At the conclusion of the closing arguments, the judge will provide instructions to the jury and the jurors will retire to the jury room to deliberate and reach a verdict in the case. Jurors must vote unanimously—in most states— and their verdict can be guilty, not guilty, not guilty by reason of insanity, or guilty, but mentally ill. Once a verdict has been returned and if the defendant has been found guilty, the judge will sentence the defendant.

KEY TERMS AND CONCEPTS

Jury box	Bench conference	Court reporter
Recess	Bench trial	Join issue
Bench	Clerk	Voir dire

Venire	Case-in-chief	Charge conference
Striking a jury	Direct examination	Closing argument
Peremptory challenge	Cross-examine	Jury instructions
Challenge for cause	Impeachment	Polling
Batson challenge	Redirect examination	
Alternate juror	Directed verdict	
Opening statement	Rebuttal	

END OF CHAPTER EXERCISES

Review Questions

See Appendix A for answers

1   What is the jury box?
2   What is the function of the jury deliberation room?
3   Explain where the witness stand is in relation to the judge's bench.
4   Explain the function of the judge's bench.
5   Where are the defense and prosecution tables located in the courtroom?
6   What functions does the clerk of court carry out?
7   What is the purpose of the court reporter?
8   Explain how a jury is selected.
9   What does it mean to join issue?
10   What is voir dire?
11   What is the venire?
12   What is a peremptory challenge?
13   Explain a challenge for cause.
14   What is a *Batson* challenge?
15   Explain the process for striking a jury.
16   What is the opening statement?
17   Explain how a direct examination is carried out.
18   What is a cross-examination?
19   What is a redirect examination?
20   What is a directed verdict?
21   What is the purpose of rebuttal?
22   Explain the function of the jury charge.
23   How is a charge conference carried out?
24   How is a typical closing argument carried out?
25   Explain the possible verdicts that a jury may reach.
26   What is "polling" a jury?

Web Surfing

1   Go to criminal.findlaw.com and do a search for "Criminal trial overview."

2   Visit www.uscourts.gov and search for articles about types of juries.

Questions for Analysis

1 Should all peremptory challenges to juries be eliminated? If a person qualifies for jury service, is it really necessary to ask him or her a lot of personal questions to see if he or she might be a good juror for one side or the other?

2 Have court rulings gone too far in regard to *Batson* challenges? Should the philosophy of antidiscriminatory practices in striking jurors be expanded to other categories? Explain your answer.

Hypotheticals

1 During an opening statement, attorney Matt Lock takes a bloody knife out of his coat pocket and displays it to the jury, telling them that this is the real murder weapon and that the prosecutor has the wrong knife. Is this an improper opening statement? Why or why not?

2 During a closing argument, attorney Matt Lock argues to the jury that the murder victim in this case "deserved to die and whoever killed him did the world a great service." Based on what you have learned in this chapter, is this a proper closing argument? Why or why not?

3 It is the middle of a trial for armed robbery and the judge learns that one of the jurors has been talking with the defense attorney and even helping the defense attorney investigate the case. What should the judge do?

PRACTICE QUESTIONS FOR TEST REVIEW

See Appendix A for answers

Essay Question

Explain the basic steps in a trial.

True-False

1 **T F** Impeachment is a showing that the witness is not worthy of belief.

2 **T F** At the conclusion of the defendant's case (if there is one), the state may present rebuttal evidence.

3 **T F** A mistrial is finding that the defendant is not guilty.

Fill in the Blank

1 A trial where the judge decides both questions of law and the final verdict in the case and no jury is present is called a(n) _____.

2   A(n) _____ is a trained professional who is responsible for taking down every spoken word in the courtroom during a hearing and reproducing those words as a transcript.

3   _____ is a French term meaning to see, to say; this refers to the questioning of a jury panel member to determine if the person is competent to serve on a jury.

Multiple Choice

1   An area that is separated from the rest of a courtroom and is reserved exclusively for jurors during a trial.

   A   Jury box.
   B   Jurors' station.
   C   Jurors' mainstay.
   D   Jury stand.

2   A short break in the proceedings in a trial.

   A   Judicial intervention.
   B   Recess.
   C   Absentia.
   D   Reservation.

3   The place in the courtroom reserved for the judge.

   A   Judicial table.
   B   Judge's bench.
   C   Judge's suite.
   D   Judge's position.

ENDNOTES

1. *United States v. Kramer*, 955 F.2d 479, 488-89 (7th Cir. 1992).
2. *Allen v. State*, 263 S.W.3d 168 (Tex. App. 2007).
3. *United States v. LaVallee*, 439 F.3d 670, 689 (10th Cir. 2006).
4. 406 U.S. 404 (1972).

Defenses to Criminal Prosecutions

Chapter Outline

I. Simple Defenses
  A. Constitutional Defenses
    Double Jeopardy
    Privilege Against Self-Incrimination
    Due Process
    Equal Protection
    First Amendment
  B. Technical Defenses
    Vagueness and Overbreadth
    Ex Post Facto
    Statute of Limitations
    Errors in Charging Documents

II. Affirmative Defenses
  A. Asserting Affirmative Defenses

  B. Specific Affirmative Defenses
    Age
    Alibi
    Battered Woman's Syndrome
    Coercion
    Consent
    Defending Property
    Duress
    Entrapment
    Insanity
    Intoxication
    Mutual Combat
    Necessity
    Self-Defense
    Other Defenses

SIMPLE DEFENSES

In this chapter, we will discuss the wide variety of defenses available to a person who has been accused of a crime. Some of these defenses are provided directly by the U.S. Constitution and statutes, whereas others are the product of the creativity of defense attorneys.

A. CONSTITUTIONAL DEFENSES

The Fifth and Fourteenth Amendments to the U.S. Constitution provide numerous protections to a person accused of a crime, including:

- Double jeopardy
- Privilege against self-incrimination
- Due process
- Equal protection

However, there was an interesting (and far-reaching) problem that arose after the U.S. Constitution was ratified: Did the provisions of the Bill of Rights actually apply to the individual states? Many states, which had held enormous power under the Articles of Confederation, argued that the provisions of the U.S. Constitution functioned more like guidelines than mandates. That question remained open until the Civil War finally provided an answer. The southern states had always maintained that they could, under a supposed agreement of mutual independence, secede from the various United States when they no longer supported the positions taken by the federal government. Although there were many causes of the Civil War and many outcomes, there is no doubt that it settled some questions of constitutional law. The ratification of the Fourteenth Amendment clearly decided some specific issues that had been left unresolved since the founding of the country. For our purposes, one of the most important is that the protections guaranteed in the Fifth Amendment to the U.S. Constitution applied to all of the states, regardless of what their individual constitutions guaranteed. See Figure 14-1 for the text of both the Fifth and the Fourteenth Amendments to the U.S. Constitution.

Under the provisions of the Fifth and Fourteenth Amendments, we can see that the original list of constitutional defenses available to a criminal defendant expanded to include not only the protections of double jeopardy, self-incrimination, and due process, but also equal protection. We will discuss each of these defenses in turn.

DOUBLE JEOPARDY

A person who has been prosecuted for a crime and found not guilty cannot be tried for that offense again. That provision is at the very core of the Fifth Amendment and made applicable to the states through the Fourteenth Amendment. The law on this point has been refined over many decades. One

FIGURE 14-1

Fifth and Fourteenth
Amendments, U.S.
Constitution

The Fifth Amendment
No person shall be held to answer for a capital, or otherwise infamous crime, unless on a presentment or indictment of a Grand Jury, except in cases arising in the land or naval forces, or in the Militia, when in actual service in time of War or public danger; nor shall any person be subject for the same offence to be twice put in jeopardy of life or limb; nor shall be compelled in any criminal case to be a witness against himself, nor be deprived of life, liberty, or property, without due process of law; nor shall private property be taken for public use, without just compensation.

The Fourteenth Amendment, Section 1
All persons born or naturalized in the United States, and subject to the jurisdiction thereof, are citizens of the United States and of the State wherein they reside. No State shall make or enforce any law which shall abridge the privileges or immunities of citizens of the United States; nor shall any State deprive any person of life, liberty, or property, without due process of law; nor deny to any person within its jurisdiction the equal protection of the laws.

of the key points in analyzing **double jeopardy** is answering this question: When does it apply? Clearly, a defendant cannot be retried if the jury finds him or her not guilty. Not all cases end in this manner, though. There are times when the court may declare a mistrial because of some irregularity that occurred during the trial. Because a mistrial resets the parties and the issues back to a point as though the trial never occurred, does this bar the defendant from being retried? The answer is no, but the law concerning double jeopardy has some subtleties to it that have come out over time. Suppose that during the trial, the prosecutor realizes that things are going badly and deliberately causes a mistrial? Does this mean that the defendant can be tried again? Conceivably, a prosecutor could cause a mistrial in the subsequent trials as well, retrying the defendant until the prosecutor believed that he or she had finally gotten it right. Obviously, there must be some guidelines about double jeopardy that apply in situations like this.

When courts talk about when a defendant can assert the defense of double jeopardy, they phrase the question in terms of when does the right apply. Put another way, if the double jeopardy applies to a specific case, then the defendant cannot be retried. Courts then have been wrestling with the issue of when the double jeopardy provision applies in cases where the defendant has not been found guilty, but some other irregularity has occurred in the trial.

The general rule is that double jeopardy attaches when the jury is sworn and enters the jury box. A clever defendant, knowing this, might try to cause a mistrial. Many states have addressed this issue by declaring that if the prosecution deliberately causes a mistrial, the case cannot be retried, but if the defendant deliberately causes a mistrial, the case can be retried. On the other hand, double jeopardy as a defense does not apply when a defendant has been found guilty and his or her case goes up on appeal. If the defendant should win the appeal,

Double jeopardy
A provision of the Fifth Amendment that forbids the retrial of a person who has already been tried for an offense and found not guilty.

the state has the right to retry him. Is this a violation of double jeopardy? No. In this situation, the original trial has been vacated and the new trial will take the place of the original. If the defendant is retried and found guilty, then he or she may still appeal that conviction, so the defendant has not lost any rights.

PRIVILEGE AGAINST SELF-INCRIMINATION

Self-incrimination
A provision of the Fifth Amendment that prohibits a person from being forced to give evidence against himself or herself.

Technically speaking, the privilege against **self-incrimination** is not a defense so much as it is a right of the defendant to refuse to answer questions or to be forced into giving evidence against himself or herself. Defense attorneys do not use the right against self-incrimination as a defense so much as they use it as a means to suppress the defendant's statement when evidence shows that it was obtained in an unconstitutional manner. However, we discuss it here because it is mentioned in the Fifth Amendment.

DUE PROCESS

Due process
A clause in the Fifth Amendment that guarantees that each and every defendant will receive the same procedural safeguards throughout a criminal case, regardless of the charge.

Due process, as stated in the Due Process Clause, requires that the same procedures be used in all criminal cases. The rules do not change when someone is "obviously" guilty as opposed to someone who "may" be guilty. A claim of violation of due process is usually raised on appeal and not during the trial. On appeal, the defendant may claim that specific, required procedures were either not followed or were somehow curtailed or prejudiced in his or her case.

EQUAL PROTECTION

The Fifth and Fourteenth Amendments require that all citizens be treated fairly. As far as criminal law is concerned, this means that people falling into different socioeconomic, religious, or racial categories cannot be treated differently under the law. Any law that contains classifications based on these factors is immediately suspect and may be found unconstitutional.

FIRST AMENDMENT

For certain types of crimes, a defendant may also use the First Amendment as a protection. As we have already seen earlier in this text in prosecutions involving obscenity, a defendant may urge the defense that what the government considers to be obscene, he or she considers to be an expression that is protected under the First Amendment. In such cases, it is the judge who must make a determination whether the amendment bars the prosecution or if it should proceed.

B. TECHNICAL DEFENSES

When a defendant raises what could be called a technical defense, he or she is saying that there is something wrong with the law that makes the action a crime or there is something wrong with the charging document that alleges that the defendant committed a crime. In the first category are defenses such as:

- Vagueness and overbreadth
- Ex post facto

Under the second category of challenges to the charging documents themselves are defenses such as:

- Statute of limitations
- *Allegata* vs. *probata*

VAGUENESS AND OVERBREADTH

When a defendant raises the defense of vagueness and overbreadth, the defendant is actually challenging the statute that criminalizes the behavior. A defendant may challenge the statute under which he or she has been charged by claiming that the statute is worded in such a vague manner that people of common intelligence would have to guess at its meaning. The underlying principle in criminal law is that people must be able to figure out what is and is not illegal. When a statute fails to make this notice clear, a court may declare it unconstitutional. Consider Scenario 14-1.

CELL PHONE

Because of numerous complaints and a great deal of press coverage, the State of Placid's legislature has decided to take on the issue of cell phone use. The legislature voted on and the governor passed a statute that reads:

> In this state, it shall be illegal for any person to use any electronic device while carrying out any activity that could be deemed unsafe.

Is this statute one that could be challenged for vagueness?

Answer: Yes. If the standard for vagueness is whether a person of average intelligence would have to guess at its meaning, then this statute clearly fails the test. Although it was obviously intended to deal with such things as texting while driving, the wording is so vague that it could also apply to listening to an iPod, using a hearing aid, having a heart pacemaker, and any of a number of other electronic devices, all while doing an activity that is considered "dangerous." There are many activities that people carry out every day that could meet this definition, including mowing a yard, driving a car, and conducting surgery, to name just a few. The statute is too vague to be enforceable.

In a similar vein, a court may strike down a statute if it is overbroad. A statute that is overbroad is one that makes constitutionally protected and unprotected activities equally illegal. A statute that criminalizes the homeless, for example, when they carry out inoffensive conduct, is considered overbroad.[1]

EX POST FACTO

No Bill of Attainder or ex post facto Law shall be passed.

—Article I, Section 9, U.S. Constitution.

A bill of attainder is a legislative action attempting to short-circuit a criminal trial and declare an individual guilty of a crime (usually treason). Bills of attainder are not permitted in the United States. Challenges to a law based on a claim that it is a bill of attainder are extremely rare. Instead, it is far more common to base a claim on **ex post facto** laws.

Ex post facto
An action that is criminalized only after it has been committed.

An ex post facto law is one that criminalizes behavior or increases punishment for an action after it has already occurred. In many cases, a person may carry out an activity that is not technically illegal at the time, but one that many people consider to be criminal in nature. When they are surprised to learn that there is no law against the activity, they lobby for one. For instance, when the crime of computer hacking first began, most states had no statute on the books that made this illegal. The prohibition against ex post facto laws prevents the legislature from making that action illegal—after the fact—just to punish that individual. The legislature can, and often does, address the situation by enacting laws, but these laws only apply to people who commit the crime after the statute has been enacted. Ex post facto defenses also apply to sentences. A person's sentence must reflect the law at the time he or she committed the action. The legislature cannot, in a fit of outrage, seek to enhance the punishment for a particularly gruesome crime. The legislature can only enhance the sentence for others who commit it. The constitutional limit of ex post facto means that these new statutes cannot be applied to a defendant who committed the crime before the new law was created.

STATUTE OF LIMITATIONS

Statute of limitations
The time period in which a criminal case must be commenced or is barred forever.

Almost all crimes have a statutorily determined time period in which the government must bring charges against an individual or the case cannot be prosecuted. Some people question why the state would impose a limitation on itself to bring a prosecution or have it barred forever. There are some very practical reasons for a **statute of limitations**. First, there is the simple issue that over time, witness memory fades, evidence disappears, and the likelihood of returning a verdict against the correct person for an old crime gets more and more difficult. There is also the issue that for some crimes, there should be a point where all concerned realize that no case can ever be brought against anyone and all parties concerned can move on with their lives. Generally, less serious crimes have shorter statutes of limitations. For crimes such as shoplifting, for example, the statute of limitations is often two years. For battery, it could be one year. When we deal with more serious crimes, though, we find that the statute of limitations increases dramatically. For armed robbery cases, the statute of limitations is between five and ten years, depending on the jurisdiction. In rape cases many states have a 10- or 15-year statute of limitations. When it comes to the worst of crimes, murder, there is no statute of limitations at all. A person can be charged with murder decades after it was committed.

Like constitutional defenses and other technical defenses, a defendant would bring a claim that a particular prosecution was barred by the statute of limitations to the trial court, not the jury. In situations dealing with the law, the judge has the final say. In issues of fact, it is the jury.

ERRORS IN CHARGING DOCUMENTS

In addition to bringing a claim that the prosecution is barred by the passage of time, a defendant might also challenge the sufficiency of the charging document. Because we have used the term indictment to refer to the charging document used in felony cases, we will continue with that use, keeping in mind that a defendant is perfectly free to challenge the sufficiency of a misdemeanor charge in exactly the same way, also by alleging that the charging document (which can be an accusation or an information) can also be challenged because it is facially deficient.

Allegata *vs.* Probata. The terms ***allegata*** and ***probata*** are the Latin terms for allegations and proof, respectively. Essentially, this defense is based on what the state has alleged is the crime and what the state has proven at trial. There are times when the proof does not match up to the allegations. A motion for directed verdict is often based on the simple premise that the crime charged against the defendant does not match the evidence produced against him or her at trial. In such a situation, the defendant might claim that although the state has produced evidence that the defendant committed a crime, it was not the crime originally alleged in the indictment. In most cases, such claims are not successful. It is rare for the state to bring charges against a defendant and then seek to prove some other crime instead. This is not to say that the state cannot bring additional evidence against a defendant to support a lesser included offense. As we saw in a previous chapter, a lesser included offense is one that has almost all of the same elements as a greater offense. Kidnapping is an example. The elements of kidnapping are:

Allegata
Latin; the allegations contained in a charging document.

Probata
Latin; the proof elicited in a trial.

- The unlawful
- Restraint
- And transportation
- Of a person
- Against his or her will

The lesser included offense of false imprisonment consists of the following elements:

- The unlawful
- Restraint
- Of a person
- Against his or her will

In such a case, a defendant's claim that the allegations do not match the proof would fail because false imprisonment contains the same elements (but one) of kidnapping.

Technical Deficiencies in Charging Documents. Similar to a claim of *allegata* vs. *probata,* a defendant can also offer the defense that the indictment itself is insufficient. For instance, a defendant might claim that the indictment does not provide sufficient information to show that the defendant committed a crime. Many states require that the indictment must provide sufficient information, on its face, to put the defendant on notice of the crime he or she is alleged to have committed, including dates, persons, locations, and other information that the defendant will need to prepare a defense. As we saw in Chapter 12, a defendant can file a bill of particulars requesting additional information about the charges in the case. If the state fails to comply, then the judge is authorized to dismiss the indictment.

AFFIRMATIVE DEFENSES

As we have already seen, the state always has the burden of proving that the defendant is guilty beyond a reasonable doubt. A defendant enters a criminal trial with certain defenses already in place. He or she is not required to raise them at the trial. These are the legal or constitutional defenses that all defendants have and are often referred to as **simple defenses**. Among these simple defenses is the right to be considered not guilty until his or her guilt is proven beyond a reasonable doubt. With technical and constitutional defenses, the state must sustain its case by showing that the constitutional provisions were provided and that there were no irregularities. There is little or no burden on the defendant when it comes to offering these defenses. However, the same cannot be said of **affirmative defenses**.

Simple defenses
Defenses that are automatically triggered when a defendant is charged with a crime. A defendant is not required to submit any evidence or testimony to raise a simple defense.

Affirmative defenses
Defenses that are something more than a mere denial and that require that the defense present evidence or testimony to prove, either by a preponderance of evidence or by clear and convincing evidence, that the defense is true.

A. ASSERTING AFFIRMATIVE DEFENSES

As the name suggests, the defendant must put forth some evidence or testimony to affirmatively state these defenses. Affirmative defenses require the defense to make a presentation at trial and produce enough evidence to warrant a serious consideration by the judge and jury. If a defendant wishes to raise the affirmative defense of alibi, for example, then the defendant must present testimony that he or she was somewhere else when the crime occurred. It is not enough for a defense attorney to simply state that the defendant was not present when the crime occurred. The defense attorney must present testimony, either from the defendant or someone else, to substantiate this defense to a preponderance of the evidence. Affirmative defenses do not require that the defendant take the stand, but someone must. An affirmative defense attempts to explain, refute, or excuse the defendant's criminal conduct. If the jurors believe the affirmative defense to a preponderance of the evidence, then they would be authorized to find the defendant not guilty of the charges.

Is a defendant required to prove his or her affirmative defense beyond a reasonable doubt? The answer is clearly no. That burden is reserved for the state. There must be some minimal level that a defendant must meet, however, to qualify for the defense. If the standard is not proof beyond a reasonable doubt, then what is it? The answer in most jurisdictions is preponderance of evidence. Preponderance of evidence is a burden of proof that requires a party to simply show that his or her version of facts is more likely to be true than not true. We examined preponderance as a standard of proof in an earlier chapter in our discussion of civil cases. This is one of the few times that a civil standard of proof enters into a criminal case. Preponderance of evidence is a much lower standard than proof beyond a reasonable doubt, but it does serve as a high enough threshold to prevent the defense from simply stating a defense and providing no evidence to back it up. It should be noted that not all states follow the preponderance of evidence standard for defenses. In those jurisdictions, the standard is **clear and convincing evidence**. In those jurisdictions, defendants have a higher standard than preponderance of evidence and must establish that there is a high likelihood that the defense is true.

Clear and convincing evidence
The version presented by the party is highly probable to be true and is a higher standard than preponderance of the evidence.

One of the more interesting aspects of an affirmative defense is that the defendant is often placed in the unenviable position of having to admit to committing the crime before claiming specific types of defenses. In the case of self-defense, age, or insanity, for example, the defendant must admit that he or she carried out the crime, but that the action was excused in some way. With other affirmative defenses, however, the defendant is not placed in that position. With alibi, a defendant raises the defense that he or she was somewhere else when the crime occurred and therefore could not have committed it.

Once an affirmative defense is presented, it is the duty of the prosecution to disprove the defense beyond a reasonable doubt. The burden in a criminal trial never shifts to the defendant to prove his or her innocence. Instead, the burden of proving the case beyond a reasonable doubt applies both to the state's case and to the defendant's affirmative defense.

In almost all jurisdictions, defendants are required to notify the state when they intend to bring specific types of affirmative defenses such as alibi or insanity. The defendant is required to serve written notice on the government that he or she intends to bring these defenses. This notice allows the state to prepare additional witnesses to rebut the defense. The idea behind the notification requirement is not limited to giving the state additional time to prepare to attack the defense. When the defendant places the state on notice of a specific type of defense, such as alibi, it also allows the state additional time to investigate the defense to determine if it is accurate. The theory is that if the state should confirm that the defendant's affirmative defense is correct, the state will be saved the expense of taking an innocent person to trial. In the real world, however, the defense presented is not as clear or as obvious as one would hope. If the state received irrefutable evidence that the defendant's alibi was correct, then the state would be obligated to dismiss the case. However, such concrete evidence is not normally forthcoming from the defendant. Instead, the defense produces an indication that someone might be able to place the defendant at some other location at the approximate time when the crime occurred. This evidence is hardly conclusive.

Just as the state is required to present evidence on specific elements of criminal charges, defendants are also obligated to present evidence or testimony to meet the specific elements of their defenses. However, the defendant's burden is never as great as the state's and it is usually left to the jury to determine how much weight and credence to give to the defendant's evidence. Of course, if the defendant fails to present any evidence to support the defense, then the judge can refuse to instruct the jury on the defense and they will not be able to consider it during their posttrial deliberations.

B. SPECIFIC AFFIRMATIVE DEFENSES

There are any number of ways to present the various affirmative defenses. For the sake of clarity, they are listed here in alphabetical order. Among the affirmative defenses are:

- Age
- Alibi
- Battered woman's syndrome
- Coercion
- Consent
- Defending property
- Duress
- Entrapment
- Insanity
- Intoxication
- Mutual combat
- Necessity
- Self-defense

AGE

One affirmative defense that a defendant can raise is age. When the defendant is below a specific age, the law presumes that he or she is incapable of forming *mens rea* and therefore cannot be guilty of a crime. In most jurisdictions, that age is seven or below. Society has made a decision that young children should not be treated in the same manner as adults and that children, at least children below a certain age, cannot be guilty of crimes. That is not to say that the state cannot intercede. The juvenile justice system is specifically designed to operate in this situation, but the child will not be prosecuted in an adult court. For children between the ages of 7 and 14, the presumption is rebuttable, meaning that the prosecution can present evidence that a particular child could form *mens rea*. Over the age of 14, a child is presumed to be able to form *mens rea*. In some situations, a child between the age of 14 and 18 can be certified as an adult, usually only for purposes of prosecuting a major felony such as rape or murder, and actually be tried in adult court.

ALIBI

Alibi is the defense that asserts that the defendant was not present when the crime occurred. Unlike many other affirmative defenses, alibi does not admit to the underlying crime and then seek to mitigate or excuse it. When a defendant raises the defense of alibi, the defendant is claiming that he or she was somewhere else when the crime occurred and therefore cannot be guilty. Alibi is a **complete defense**, meaning that if the defendant presents sufficient proof, the jury is not only authorized to reach a not guilty verdict, but must do so. A complete defense is one that shows that the defendant is not guilty of the crime and leaves the jury with no other option than finding the defendant not guilty.

BATTERED WOMAN'S SYNDROME

Battered woman's syndrome is not recognized as a legitimate defense in all states, but in those where it is, it can be offered as an affirmative defense by a defendant who has committed an act of violence against a husband or intimate partner. Battered woman's syndrome developed as a refinement of self-defense. In that defense, which we will discuss in this chapter, a person may take violent action to protect himself or herself. However, battered woman's syndrome takes this analysis one step further. The controversial aspect to battered woman's syndrome is that unlike self-defense, where the person being attacked immediately acts violently to protect himself or herself, battered woman's syndrome allows a battered spouse or significant other to retaliate against repeated abuse at a time when the person is not actually being attacked. The most common example of battered woman's syndrome is when a woman who has been repeatedly battered waits until her attacker falls asleep or is otherwise incapacitated and then attacks him, sometimes even killing him. Such an action would not be justified under traditional self-defense, where the response must be contemporaneous with the threat. Advocates of battered woman's syndrome point to the fact that it is only when the abuser is vulnerable that the victim can respond in some way to end the abuse. Just as we will see with so many affirmative defenses, a person who raises battered woman's syndrome must first admit to the act and then seek to mitigate or excuse it because of the surrounding circumstances.

In states that recognize battered woman's syndrome, a woman who can show that she was the subject of repeated beatings can be found not guilty for retaliating against her abuser, even though he was not a threat when she acted violently.

COERCION

Coercion is the use of intimidation, physical threats, or psychological pressure, all designed to force a person to commit a crime that he or she ordinarily would

Alibi
A defense that the defendant was not present when the crime occurred.

Complete defense
A defense that would completely exonerate the defendant of the crime charged, assuming the defendant presents sufficient evidence to meet his or her burden of proof (usually preponderance of the evidence).

Battered woman's syndrome
An affirmative defense that asks the jury to excuse a woman's attack on her supposed longtime abuser or asks the judge to mitigate her sentence in reflection of the fact that she was responding to a long period of abuse at the hands of the "victim."

Coercion
The direct threat of physical violence to make a person commit a crime that he or she would not ordinarily commit.

not commit. In coercion, if the defendant can show that he or she was physically threatened with violence unless he or she committed a crime, then a defense of coercion can be sustained. If proven, the jury is authorized to find that the defendant is not guilty because he or she was forced to commit the crime by someone else.

CONSENT

Consent is a defense that states that the victim agreed to the actions carried out by the defendant. In a case of assault and battery, for example, a defendant might claim that the victim acquiesced to the attack and even encouraged it. If the victim gives voluntary and knowing consent, it is a complete defense to some crimes. However, consent is not a defense to many crimes. A child molester, for example, cannot claim consent as a defense because children are legally barred from giving consent to sexual activity. Consent is also not available in murder convictions. A person cannot consent to being murdered. The most common use of the consent defense is in cases of rape and sexual battery, where the defendant claims that the victim agreed to the sexual contact.

Because consent requires a knowing and voluntary agreement, there are individuals who cannot consent to a crime for the simple reason that they are incapable of doing so. Mentally handicapped individuals and those who have been found to be legally incompetent cannot give valid consent.

Consent is also not a defense in a crime like statutory rape, where one partner is legally incapable of giving consent. Third parties cannot consent for others. A husband cannot give consent to another man to have sex with his wife. People do not have the authority to allow another person to be the victim of a crime. Consent law also requires that consent must be given freely and voluntarily. Without such a showing, consent is not a valid defense

DEFENDING PROPERTY

A question often arises in the context of theft cases: How far can a theft victim go to protect property? A person can take reasonable steps to prevent property from being stolen, but these actions cannot extend to deadly force. Violence, especially deadly force, is not permitted to protect property, only people.

DURESS

Duress
Unlawful psychological and mental pressure brought to bear on a person to force him or her to commit a crime that the person would ordinarily not commit.

A claim of **duress** is one in which the defendant claims that some other person used intimidation, psychological control, or other means short of outright threats to force a defendant to commit a crime. Unlike coercion, where there is a direct correlation between the crime and the threat of physical violence to the defendant, duress operates more as subtle mental manipulation—even what some might term verbal and mental torture. Because of this, duress is often more difficult to prove than coercion. In coercion, a person physically threatens the well-being of another unless they commit a crime, but in duress, the defendant must show that another person used psychological pressure, torment, and manipulation to force him or her to carry out a crime. Because people respond differently to psychological pressure, the jurors are often left with a question as to whether or not the abuse alleged by the defendant was sufficient to cause a reasonable person to respond by committing a crime.

ENTRAPMENT

Entrapment is an interesting defense in that the defendant claims that he or she was tricked or manipulated into committing a crime by the police. Unlike coercion or duress, entrapment can only be carried out by law enforcement officers. When a person is entrapped, he or she has been given both the idea for the crime and the means to carry it out by law enforcement or prosecutors. Essentially, the defendant is saying that the police made him or her do it. The idea behind making entrapment a valid defense is that we, as a society, do not want the police in the business of thinking up crimes and then encouraging others to carry them out. Because the government should not be in the business of creating crime, jurors are authorized to punish the government for doing so by finding the defendant not guilty.

Entrapment can be a confusing defense, however. Defendants often claim that they have been entrapped when police work as undercover police officers, sometimes even providing defendants with drugs so that they can continue the illusion that the undercover officer is actually a fellow criminal. The question often becomes this: When do the government's actions cross the line between acceptable police work and entrapment?

There are two ways of testing whether entrapment exists in a particular case. This involves answering two separate questions: (1) Did the idea for the crime originate with the police? (2) Did the police provide the defendant the means to carry the crime out? If the answer to both questions is yes, then there is a solid case for entrapment. If the answer to either question is no, then there is no case of entrapment.

As we have seen with all affirmative defenses, the prosecution must disprove entrapment beyond a reasonable doubt, assuming that the defendant has met the relatively low burden of presenting it. When a defense of entrapment is presented, the government must present rebuttal testimony refuting that the idea of the crime originated with the police or that the police provided the means to the defendant to consummate the crime. The most common way to rebut a defense of entrapment is to show that the defendant was already disposed to commit the crime, and the police simply provided the defendant with the opportunity to put his or her wish into action. Some states have a further requirement to disprove entrapment beyond a reasonable doubt: The state must prove that it did not overcome the defendant's free will and force him or her to carry out the crime.[2]

INSANITY

The **insanity** defense has been portrayed in movies, books, and TV for decades. As a result, there are many misconceptions concerning its use. Insanity is an

Entrapment
A defense that claims government agents induced a defendant to commit a crime when he or she was not predisposed to do so.

Insanity
A defense that claims that at the time that the defendant committed the crime, he or she did not know the difference between right and wrong.

affirmative defense and a defendant must admit to committing the underlying crime before claiming that he or she was legally insane at the time. The reason that the insanity defense can be confusing is that the legal standard to determine when a person is insane is not the same standard used by psychiatrists or medical professionals to make the same determination. At its core, the test for legal insanity is relatively simple: Did the defendant know the difference between right and wrong when he or she committed the crime? If the answer to that question is yes, then the defendant is legally sane, even though he or she may suffer from very debilitating mental problems. A person can suffer from any number of different psychological problems, including schizophrenia and multiple-personality disorder, and still not meet the legal test for insanity.

A defendant offers the insanity defense by presenting expert testimony during the defense case to show that the defendant did not know or understand the difference between right and wrong when he or she committed the crime. This requires either a psychiatrist or a psychologist to testify that at the time the defendant committed the crime he or she met the legal standard for insanity.

There are many misconceptions about the defense of insanity. One common misconception is that people who have a mental illness will automatically be considered not guilty by reason of insanity. This is not true. No matter what form of mental illness the defendant may or may not have, the legal standard remains the same: Did the defendant understand the difference between right and wrong? Another common misconception about the defense of insanity is that if the defense is raised successfully, and a verdict of not guilty by reason of insanity is entered, the defendant is then released. This is also not true. If a defendant has been found not guilty by reason of insanity, the defendant is usually placed in a mental hospital for the criminally insane.

Like alibi, insanity is a complete defense and if the jury finds that the defendant is not guilty by reason of insanity, he or she is relieved of all criminal liability. The defendant is not guilty of the crime for the simple reason that when he or she committed it, the defendant lacked the ability to form *mens rea*. There are essentially two basic elements to all crimes: *mens rea* (intent) and *actus reus* (act). A person who cannot form *mens rea* cannot commit a crime.

Historical Development: M'Naghten Rule. The ancient Romans recognized that insanity was a valid defense. However, over time under the English and U.S. legal systems, the pendulum has swung very far in both directions, with occasional periods where the standard for the determination of insanity was quite liberal and others where it has been extremely difficult to prove. No discussion of the insanity defense would be complete without its most famous example: the M'Naghten case.

In 1843, M'Naghten attempted to kill Sir Robert Peel, the prime minister of England. Instead, he killed Peel's private secretary, a man named Edward Drummond. He was found not guilty by reason of insanity, and this controversial verdict started a national debate in both England and the United States over what the definition of legal insanity should be. The findings of a British court of inquiry into the case established the first conclusive test for legal insanity: "To establish a defense on the ground of insanity, it must be clearly proved that, at

A defendant is considered to be legally insane when:

- He or she cannot distinguish between right or wrong
- A person suffers from an irresistible impulse that precludes him or her from choosing between right and wrong
- His or her lawful act is the product of a mental disease or defect (Durham Test)

FIGURE 14-2

Durham Test for Insanity

the time of the committing of the act, the party accused was laboring [sic] under such a defect of reason, from disease of the mind, as not to know the nature and quality of the act he was doing; or, if he did know it, that he did not know he was doing what was wrong."[3] Since the M'Naghten case there have been many modifications to the insanity defense. Various states have sought their own standards and the Model Penal Code has also weighed in on the issue.

Modern Definitions of Insanity After M'Naghten. In most states, the modern definition of insanity is either the standard M'Naghten test or some variant on the definition shown in Figure 14-2.

A growing dissatisfaction with the plea of not guilty by reason of insanity brought about legislative initiatives in many jurisdictions that modified this defense. Some of these initiatives included creating new verdicts in criminal cases, such as guilty but mentally ill. When the jury returns this verdict, the defendant will be incarcerated in a regular prison facility but must have some access to psychiatric or psychological services and treatment.

Determining the Moment of Insanity. To bring a defense of insanity, the defense attorney plays an active role in having the defendant evaluated by mental professionals. There is a disconnect between a defendant actively participating in his or her own defense at the time that his or her attorney believes that he or she is legally insane. At various points throughout the trial, the defense attorney's role is critical. He or she will interact with the client, psychologist, psychiatrists, and others to make a determination of the client's mental status. Unlike for other defenses, a client who is insane may often dispute raising this as a defense. Many people who suffer from mental illness do not necessarily believe that there is anything wrong with them.

There are two different points at which the defendant's sanity can become a factor in the trial. A defendant can be found legally insane at the time that he or she committed the crime or the defendant can be found to be legally insane at the time of the trial. When a defendant claims that he or she is insane at the time of the trial—and not when the crime occurred—the defendant may raise the "special plea" of insanity at the time of the trial. Although these two defenses sound very similar, in practice they are quite different. When a defendant pleads insanity at the time of the trial, he or she is alleging that he or she is not competent to understand the legal process and cannot assist in his or her defense. However, when a defendant raises the defense of insanity at the time that the crime was committed, the defendant is maintaining that he or she cannot be guilty of a crime. Defendants who claim that they are insane at the time of trial do not get the benefit of the insanity defense. The jury is not authorized to find them not guilty by reason of insanity, because they are not alleging that they were insane at the time that the crime was committed. A defendant who is not competent to stand trial may be remanded into a state facility until such time that he or she is able to stand trial. In many cases, a defendant may claim both forms: insanity at the time of the crime and insanity at the time of the trial. If it is proven that the defendant is incompetent to be tried, then the court will wait and make further determinations in the future. If, at some time, the defendant is declared to be fit for trial, then the trial will proceed. The defendant can then raise any affirmative defense he or she wishes, including legal insanity.

Raising the Insanity Defense. The defendant who wishes to use the defense of insanity must serve notice on the state prior to trial that he or she plans to do so—the notice period is usually a minimum of 10 days prior to trial. This notice allows the state to bring in its own experts to evaluate the defendant and offer their own opinion about the state of the defendant's sanity at the time that the crime occurred. At the trial, the defense will present its own expert witnesses to testify that the defendant was not legally sane at the time that he or she committed the crime, and the state will then, in rebuttal, present evidence that the defendant was legally sane when the defendant committed the crime. In the end, it becomes a battle of the experts, and the jurors are left to decide which expert to believe. If they believe the defense expert, then they must find the defendant either not guilty by reason of insanity or, in the states that have this verdict alternative, guilty, but mentally ill.

Having said all of this, the insanity defense is rarely used and is even less likely to be successful. Part of this rests with the burden placed on the defense to present believable evidence that the defendant did not know the difference between right and wrong when the crime occurred. Any action that a defendant took to conceal the crime, dispose of evidence, or flee indicates that the defendant understood all too well that what he or she did was wrong.

Burden of Proof for the Defendant When Raising the Insanity Defense. As is true with many other affirmative defenses, the defendant who raises the defense of insanity must present enough evidence to establish by a preponderance of evidence that he or she is legally insane. In some jurisdictions the standard the defendant must meet is clear and convincing evidence of legal insanity. Once the defendant has presented this evidence, the prosecution must rebut the defendant's evidence. The government must show that the defendant was legally sane at the time of the crime.

Diminished capacity
Inability of the defendant to understand the actions that he or she took and why his or her actions constituted a crime.

Diminished Capacity. The defense of **diminished capacity** is a form of insanity defense. Although it is not recognized in all jurisdictions, the defense of diminished capacity allows a defendant to offer testimony and evidence about his or her mental condition. This evidence is intended to mitigate or excuse the defendant's guilt in the crime. Often, diminished capacity defenses focus on the *mens rea* element of a crime. A defendant presents evidence of lower than normal IQ or slow mental development as a way to show the jury that he or she lacked the ability to form *mens rea*. In specific intent cases, such as murder, diminished capacity may be used as a defense to show that the defendant lacked the ability to form specific intent and therefore could not be guilty of first-degree murder.[4] The problem with diminished capacity defenses is defining exactly what diminished capacity is. For instance, courts have held that a defendant does not fall under the category of diminished capacity if or she he suffers from mood swings, feelings of insecurity, overwhelming fear of disease, or inability to care about others.[5]

INTOXICATION

Voluntary **intoxication** is not a defense to most crimes. Permitting a defendant to avoid responsibility for a crime by getting drunk would not serve society's interests. However, there are times when voluntary intoxication does affect criminal liability. For example, voluntary intoxication might help reduce a crime from the most severe to a lesser included offense. In the crime of murder in the first degree, for example, the state must prove that the defendant specifically intended to cause the death of another human being with malice and premeditation. A defendant who is intoxicated, even if this intoxication is the result of his or her own actions, may be unable to form specific intent or premeditation to murder. This does not mean that the defendant cannot be charged with murder; it simply means that it might reduce a charge of first-degree murder to second-degree murder. Except for this narrow exception, voluntary intoxication is not a defense to a crime and will not lessen the defendant's culpability or the ultimate sentence.

> **Intoxication**
> When a person is acting under the influence of alcohol or other drugs to the extent that judgment and motor reflexes are impaired.

However, there are situations where a form of intoxication can be a defense. Involuntary intoxication can be an affirmative defense. The defense of involuntary intoxication results when a person is overcome by fumes or chemicals to such an extent that he or she is no longer capable of rational thought. When the defendant is overcome with these substances, and has not voluntary submitted to the condition, he or she may not be criminally liable. Situations that bring about involuntary intoxication are rare and might include a worker in a factory where dangerous chemicals have been accidentally released or a defendant who has been unknowingly exposed to fumes or toxins.

MUTUAL COMBAT

The affirmative defense of **mutual combat** arises when the defendant and the victim agree to fight one another. Similar to consent, when a victim agrees to enter into a fight, he or she essentially surrenders his or her right to bring charges for battery against the other fighter. However, mutual combat has some strict limitations. If the defendant exceeds the understanding of what weapons will be used in the fight, or uses excessive force, then mutual combat as a defense may not be available. Consider Scenario 14-2.

> **Mutual combat**
> A defense that claims that the defendant and the victim voluntarily entered into a physical confrontation.

MUTUAL COMBAT?

Kim and Khloe are at a party and get into a disagreement. They begin shoving each other and Kim says, "Let's take it outside." Khloe agrees and they get into a fight next to their limousine in the parking lot. During the tussle, Kim pulls a knife and cuts her sister. The police are called and Kim is charged with aggravated battery. Will she have the defense of mutual combat?

Answer: No. Mutual combat assumes that both parties have the same weapons and defenses. There was nothing to indicate that either Kim or Khloe had a knife when they left the party to go the parking lot. When Kim pulled the knife, she went beyond the implied ground rules of the fight. As a matter of law, Kim is not allowed to raise the defense of mutual combat.[6]

NECESSITY

Necessity
The defense that a defendant committed a crime to avoid an act of nature or of God.

The affirmative defense of necessity is similar to duress. When a defendant claims **necessity**, he or she admits committing the crime, but in this case, he or she did so to avoid some catastrophe or some force of nature. A common example of necessity is when someone breaks into a cabin to avoid a blizzard. Normally, that person would be guilty of trespass or criminal damages to property; however, the offense is excused by his or her need to stay alive. In this case, breaking into the cabin was the lesser of two evils: committing a crime or dying. In applying the defense of necessity, most jurisdictions require that the danger to the defendant outweigh the damage he or she does in committing the crime. A defendant could not use the defense of necessity in attempting to excuse a murder, for example, because all jurisdictions have held that no danger outweighs the value of another person's life.

SELF-DEFENSE

Self-defense
The defense that the defendant injured or killed another, but only as a direct threat to the defendant's well-being.

Self-defense is, perhaps second only to insanity, the most misunderstood of all defenses. Under the law, a person always has the right to defend himself or herself against a physical threat. However, there are severe limitations on this affirmative defense. In most situations, the response of the person raising the claim of self-defense must be comparable to the threat. This means that when someone is threatening the defendant with bare fists, the defendant is not permitted to retaliate with a weapon. The claim of self-defense seeks to excuse the defendant's actions by showing that they were necessary to keep the defendant alive. To use self-defense, the defendant must admit that he or she used force, but only for protection. When self-defense is raised, most jurisdictions require the jury to make a determination as to whether or not the defendant acted reasonably when he or she used force. If the jury finds that the defendant did not act reasonably, the jury could refuse to take self-defense into account.[7]

What if the victim had a reputation for being a violent and aggressive person? Could the defendant present such evidence to prove that the defendant acted reasonably? The answer is maybe. In most jurisdictions, if the defendant was aware of the victim's violent history, then it may be admissible. However, if the defendant did not know the victim's history, it probably would not be admissible. The reason for this discrepancy is simple. Self-defense has a great deal to do with what was in the defendant's mind at the time of the attack. If the defendant didn't know that the victim was a violent person, then he or she couldn't have based his or her actions on this fact.

Defendant as Aggressor. A defendant cannot use the defense of self-defense when he or she is the person who started the fight. Aggressors are not permitted to raise the claim of self-defense when they attack a person and that person fights back. There are also other times when a defendant cannot use self-defense. Individuals who are trained in the martial arts or are professional fighters or have advanced military training may be considered to use deadly force even when they respond with their bare hands. These individuals must be much more cautious before they engage in physical confrontations because their greater skill and training makes their hands and feet "deadly weapons" as far as self-defense is concerned.

Defense of Others. Does self-defense apply to protecting other people? Under the common law, a person could only defend another person with whom he or she had a close, legally recognized relationship. Parents could defend children; husbands could defend wives. At common law, though, a stranger could not use force to defend another stranger. That rule is no longer followed in most jurisdictions. Like self-defense, however, the other person must be faced with the immediate threat of bodily injury before the stranger acted to defend him or her. The threat must be one that a reasonable person would perceive as a threat.

"Stand Your Ground" Laws. Some recent cases have highlighted an interesting—and some would argue, dangerous—change in the law of self-defense. Traditionally, states followed the retreat doctrine. Under this doctrine, a person who is presented with violence, even deadly force, must retreat if he or she can reasonably do so. The reasons for the retreat doctrine are easy enough to understand: If a person can avoid being injured by a simple action, then he or she should do so. However, the doctrine has never required a person to retreat in all circumstances, only when it was reasonable to do so. If a person would put himself or herself in greater jeopardy by retreating, then the doctrine did not apply. However, some states have, in recent years, decided to repeal the retreat doctrine and replace it with "stand your ground" laws. Under these new laws, a person who is presented with violence, including deadly force, is not obligated to retreat, even when it is reasonable to do so. In these states, if a judge makes a determination that the person was under a threat, and the person responds with deadly force to a perceived deadly force attack, the person is protected under the laws of self-defense. It is important to note that not all states have stand your ground laws. Consider Figure 14-3.

FIGURE 14-3

States That Have Some Form of Stand Your Ground Laws

States that have passed stand your ground laws include:

Alabama	Louisiana	Pennsylvania
Alaska	Michigan	South Carolina
Arizona	Mississippi	South Dakota
Florida	Missouri	Tennessee
Georgia	Montana	Texas
Idaho	Nevada	Utah
Indiana	New Hampshire	West Virginia[8]
Kansas	North Carolina	
Kentucky	Oklahoma	

Rebutting a Claim of Self-Defense. Like all affirmative defenses, the state has the burden of disproving one or more of the elements of the self-defense beyond a reasonable doubt. To do this, the state must present evidence in rebuttal showing that the defendant's actions were not justified, either because the defendant used excessive force or because the defendant was the aggressor or because of some other reason.

OTHER DEFENSES

The variety of defenses presented in criminal cases is almost as varied as the crimes and the people who are charged with committing them. Over the years, defendants and defense attorneys have presented legions of unusual, even bizarre defenses to crimes including defendants driven to violent actions by telephone shows or video games to imbibing certain drinks or foods that cause defendants to supposedly act in criminal ways. Among the more unusual and generally ineffective defenses are claims that antidepressant drugs caused the defendant to black out and commit murders.[9] Although these defenses are interesting to note and watch unfold, most of them are unsuccessful.

CASE EXCERPT

McELRATH v. STATE
——— GA. ——— (2020)

MELTON, CHIEF JUSTICE.

On December 11, 2017, a jury found Damian McElrath guilty but mentally ill of the felony murder and aggravated assault of his adoptive mother, Diane, whom McElrath killed by stabbing over 50 times in a single episode. Based on the same episode, McElrath was also found not guilty of the malice murder of Diane by reason of insanity. McElrath now appeals, contending among other things that the jury's verdicts were repugnant and that his conviction for felony murder must be reversed or vacated. Under the specific facts of this case, we conclude that McElrath's verdicts are repugnant. Accordingly, we vacate both verdicts and remand McElrath's case for a new trial.

1. THE EVIDENCE AT TRIAL

(a) The evidence presented at trial showed that McElrath, who was 18 at the time of the stabbing, had suffered from either schizophrenia or a related schizoaffective disorder. As a result of this disorder, McElrath had a long history of disciplinary problems, including difficulties with Diane. Over time, McElrath began to believe that Diane was poisoning his food and beverages. Although the timeline is not exact, this delusion began approximately three years before Diane's death. The week before the stabbing occurred, McElrath had to be hospitalized in a mental health facility because of his behavior and thoughts, which included delusions that he was an FBI agent who regularly traveled to Russia and who had killed a number of people as such an agent. On the day before the stabbing, or slightly earlier, McElrath believed that Diane confronted him and admitted that she had been poisoning him.

On July 16, 2012, McElrath stabbed Diane more than 50 times in an attack that began in an upstairs bedroom of the home Diane and McElrath shared and ended at the front door. There, Diane collapsed and died. After the stabbing, McElrath changed his clothes, cleaned Diane's blood off of his body, and washed a wound on his hand that he sustained during the stabbing. He wrote a note titled "My Antisocial Life," claiming that Diane told him that she had been poisoning him. In the note, McElrath stated that he was not sorry about what he had done and that "she poisoned me so I killed her." He added that "I think I am right for doing it." McElrath then called 911 and reported that he killed his mother because she poisoned him. McElrath asked the dispatcher if he was wrong to do that.

Shortly thereafter, police arrived at the scene. McElrath was transported to the police station for interrogation, where he admitted that "I killed my Mom because she poisoned me." When the detective attempted to clarify any difficulties McElrath may have had with Diane, McElrath stated that he was only mad that she poisoned him. When the detective asked him if he thought stabbing Diane was right or wrong, McElrath stated, "It was right to me."

A number of experts testified at McElrath's trial. There was a general consensus that McElrath was, in fact, mentally ill and suffering from at least some delusions, including the delusion that he was being poisoned by Diane. Dr. Kevin Richards, the defense expert, testified that, at the time McElrath stabbed Diane, McElrath was acting under the delusion that he was in imminent danger of death. In other words, McElrath was acting under the false belief, though real to him, that he would die if he did not immediately protect himself against Diane.

(b) As an initial matter, this evidence authorized the jury to find that McElrath was not guilty of malice murder by reason of insanity at the time that he stabbed his mother.

In Georgia, a defendant is presumed to be sane and "a defendant asserting an insanity defense has the burden to prove by a preponderance of the evidence that he was insane at the time the crime was committed." *Buford v. State*, 300 Ga. 121, 793 S.E.2d 91 (2016). A defendant may prove insanity by showing that, at the time of the incident, he lacked the mental capacity to distinguish right from wrong or that he was suffering from a delusional compulsion.

The delusional compulsion defense is available only when the defendant is "suffering under delusions of an absurd and unfounded nature and was compelled by that delusion to act in a manner that would have been lawful and right if the facts had been as the defendant imagined them to be." *Lawrence v. State*, 265 Ga. 310, 313, 454 S.E.2d 446 (1995).

Here, Dr. Richards testified specifically that McElrath was suffering from a multifaceted delusion, one in which he believed both that Diane was poisoning him and that he was in imminent danger of death at the time that he attacked Diane. This "absurd or unfounded" delusion authorized the jury to determine that, under the facts as McElrath believed them to be, his actions were justified.

(c) But there was also sufficient evidence to allow the jury to find beyond a reasonable doubt that McElrath was guilty but mentally ill of felony murder based on aggravated assault for stabbing Diane. As to guilt, McElrath admitted that he stabbed Diane, and his confession was amply corroborated by the forensic and other evidence. As to mental illness, it is largely undisputed that McElrath was mentally ill at the time of the crime and, in fact, had been so for years. And, while there was evidence that McElrath suffered from delusions at times, the jury was authorized to determine that McElrath was not delusional at the time of the stabbing or that, even if he was, any delusion that he was experiencing did not justify the stabbing. For example, the jury could have accepted that McElrath suffered from the delusion that Diane had been poisoning him, but rejected that he had any delusion that his life was in imminent danger. Under such a scenario, the stabbing would not be justified, and the jury could have concluded that McElrath stabbed Diane because he was admittedly angry with her. The evidence thus supported the jury's alternative determination that McElrath was guilty but mentally ill of the felony murder of Diane based on aggravated assault under the standard set forth in *Jackson v. Virginia*, 443 U.S. 307, 99 S.Ct. 2781, 61 L.E.2d 560 (1979).

2. CLASSIFICATION OF MCELRATH'S CONTRADICTORY VERDICTS

The jury's verdicts in this case are marked by an inherent contradiction. As such, it becomes necessary to determine how to characterize those verdicts. There are three main classes of contradictory verdicts: "inconsistent verdicts," 'mutually exclusive verdicts," and "repugnant verdicts." We will analyze each in turn.

(a) Inconsistent verdicts: As a general rule, inconsistent verdicts occur when a jury in a criminal case renders seemingly incompatible verdicts of guilty on one charge and not guilty on another. In Georgia, as explained below, we have abolished the rule that inconsistent verdicts require reversal. *Milam v. State*, 255 Ga. 560, 562 (2) (341 SE2d 216) (1986). Perhaps the classic example of inconsistent verdicts occurred in *United States v. Powell*, 469 U.S. 57 (105 S.Ct. 471, 83 L.E.2d 461) (1984). In *Powell*, the defendant was acquitted of conspiring to possess cocaine with the intent to distribute but convicted of the "compound offenses of using the telephone in 'committing and in causing and facilitating' certain felonies—'conspiracy to possess with intent to distribute and possession with intent to distribute cocaine.'" Id. at 60. Though the Supreme Court recognized the internal inconsistency in these verdicts, it nonetheless allowed them to stand, explaining that where truly inconsistent verdicts have been reached, "the most that can be said . . . is that the verdict shows that either in the acquittal or the conviction the jury did not speak their real conclusions, but that does not show that they were not convinced of the defendant's guilt." *Dunn v. United States*, 284 U.S. 390, 393 (52 S.Ct. 189, 76 L.E. 356) (1932).

For reasons that will be made clear in Division 2 (c), infra, McElrath's verdicts cannot be classified simply as "inconsistent verdicts."

(b) Mutually exclusive verdicts: The term "mutually exclusive" generally applies to two guilty verdicts that cannot legally exist simultaneously. In such cases, where it is "both legally and logically impossible to convict on both counts, a new trial should be ordered." *Dumas,* supra, 266 Ga. at 799 (2).

As McElrath's verdicts are not two contradictory guilty verdicts, his verdicts cannot be classified as "mutually exclusive."

(c) Repugnant verdicts: Though they do not involve two guilty convictions, repugnant verdicts suffer from a similar infirmity as mutually exclusive verdicts; they occur when, in order to find the defendant not guilty on one count and guilty on another, the jury must make affirmative findings shown on the record that cannot logically or legally exist at the same time. Where a jury renders repugnant verdicts, both verdicts must be vacated and a new trial ordered for the same reasons applicable to mutually exclusive verdicts.

This case falls into the category of repugnant verdicts, as the guilty and not guilty verdicts reflect affirmative findings by the jury that are not legally and logically possible of existing simultaneously. This is because the not guilty by reason of insanity verdict on malice murder and the guilty but mentally ill verdict on felony murder based on aggravated assault required affirmative findings of different mental states that could not exist at the same time during the commission of those crimes as they were indicted, proved, and charged to the jury. Put simply, it is not legally possible for an individual to simultaneously be insane and not insane during a single criminal episode against a single victim, even if the episode gives rise to more than one crime.

In this case, the jury must have determined that McElrath was legally insane at the time that he stabbed Diane in order to support the finding that he was not guilty of malice murder by reason of insanity. Nonetheless, the jury went on to find McElrath guilty but mentally ill of felony murder based on the same stabbing—a logical and legal impossibility. For this reason, the verdicts in this case are repugnant, both verdicts must be vacated, and McElrath's case must be remanded for a new trial.

Judgment vacated and case remanded with direction. All the Justices concur.

---

1 What reason did the defendant give for stabbing his adoptive mother?
2 When is the defense of delusional compulsion available to a defendant?
3 The court states that there is an issue of inconsistent verdicts in this case. What are the three main classes of contradictory verdicts?
4 If inconsistent verdicts do not require mandatory reversals, what about repugnant verdicts?
5 Why did the court rule that the verdicts in this case qualified as repugnant verdicts?

CHAPTER SUMMARY

Defendants have a wide variety of defenses available to them. A defendant is not required to present any evidence to support a simple defense. These types of defenses are available to all defendants and include the presumption of innocence and various constitutional defenses. However, if the defendant decides to present an affirmative defense, he or she must present evidence to support the claim. Affirmative defenses include alibi, consent, coercion, duress, and insanity, to name just a few. When a defendant raises the defense of alibi or insanity, he or she must give notice to the state of the intent to do so. Insanity is one of the more controversial defenses and requires that the defendant establish, by a preponderance of the evidence, that he or she did not know the difference between right and wrong when the crime was committed. A defendant must present expert testimony to this effect and the state must rebut this evidence with its own expert testimony showing that the defendant did understand the difference between right and wrong. Ultimately, the question of the defendant's sanity, like all affirmative defenses, rests with the jury.

KEY TERMS AND CONCEPTS

Double jeopardy
Self-incrimination
Due process
Ex post facto
Statute of limitations
Allegata
Probata
Simple defenses
Affirmative defenses

Clear and convincing
  evidence
Alibi
Complete defense
Battered woman's
  syndrome
Coercion
Duress
Entrapment

Insanity
Diminished capacity
Intoxication
Mutual combat
Necessity
Self-defense

END OF CHAPTER EXERCISES

Review Questions

See Appendix A for answers

1 Explain the difference between *allegata* and *probata*.
2 Describe simple defenses as compared to affirmative defenses.
3 What standard of proof must a defendant meet in presenting an affirmative defense?
4 What is clear and convincing evidence and how does it differ from preponderance of the evidence?

5   Explain the defense of alibi.

6   What is battered woman's syndrome?

7   What is the difference between coercion and duress?

8   When can a person's age be considered a defense?

9   Define complete defense.

10   Can a victim consent to murder? Why or why not?

11   Is it possible to use deadly force to protect property? Explain.

12   What are stand your ground laws?

13   List and explain the two elements of entrapment.

14   What is the legal test for insanity?

15   How does a defendant raise the defense of insanity?

16   What is the Durham test as that test applies to the defense of insanity?

Web Surfing

1   Visit the Legal Information Institute (www.law.cornell.edu) and search for "legal definition insanity." Review what the site has to say about the various approaches to the insanity defense in the various states.

2   Go to Findlaw.com (criminal.findlaw.com) and search for material on "stand your ground" laws.

Questions for Analysis

1   Should the insanity defense be modified or even eliminated? Why or why not?

2   This chapter has listed numerous defenses. Should the defenses available to a criminal defendant be limited or expanded? Justify your answer.

Hypotheticals

1   Danny has an overwhelming fear of reptiles. As he is driving home one night, he sees a large alligator in the road. Danny is particularly afraid of alligators. He sees a car coming in the opposite direction and is faced with a choice: He can run over the alligator or enter the oncoming lane and hit the approaching car. He chooses to hit the car, killing the driver. At trial for vehicular manslaughter, Danny claims necessity. You are a juror on the case. How do you vote?

2   Troy enters a department store and a strange man begins following him around. The man continually stares at Troy, making Troy feel very uncomfortable. As Troy approaches the register to pay for his belongings, the man steps forward and Troy punches him. At trial, Troy claims self-defense. Has Troy met his burden for this defense?

PRACTICE QUESTIONS FOR TEST REVIEW

See Appendix A for answers

Essay Question

Explain the insanity defense.

True-False

1   **T   F**   It is not unconstitutional to criminalize behavior after it has already occurred.

2   **T   F**   Most crimes do not have a statute of limitations.

3   **T   F**   If the defendant can prove that he or she was not present when the crime occurred, it is a complete defense.

Fill in the Blank

1   Defenses that are automatically triggered when a defendant is charged with a crime are known as ———.

2   ——— is a provision of the Fifth Amendment that forbids the retrial of a person who has already been tried for an offense and found not guilty.

3   The ——— Clause in the Fifth Amendment guarantees that each and every defendant will receive the same procedural safeguards throughout a criminal case, regardless of the charge.

Multiple Choice

1   A provision of the Fifth Amendment that prohibits a person from being forced to give evidence against himself or herself.

    A   Stand Your Ground.
    B   Attorney-client privilege.
    C   Self-incrimination.
    D   Pro se representation.

2   Defenses that are something more than a mere denial and that require that the defense present evidence or testimony to prove, either by a preponderance of evidence or by clear and convincing evidence, that the defense is true.

    A   Affirmative defenses.
    B   Statutory claims.
    C   Warranty defense.
    D   Standard disclosure.

3 A defense that would completely exonerate the defendant of the crime charged, assuming the defendant presents sufficient evidence to meet his or her burden of proof (usually preponderance of the evidence).

    A Absolute term.
    B Definitive determination.
    C M'Naghten rule.
    D Complete defense.

ENDNOTES

1. *Pottinger v. Miami*, 810 F Supp. 1551 (S.D. Fla. 1992).
2. *Quick v. State*, 660 N.E.2d 598 (1996).
3. M'Naghten's Case, 10 Clark & Finnelly 200, 210, 8 Eng. Rep. 718, 722 (HL 1843).
4. *State v. Warden*, 133 Wash. 2d 559 (1997).
5. *State v. Wilburn*, 249 Kan. 678, 822 P.2d 609 (1991).
6. *Martin v. State*, 258 Ga. 300, 368 S.E.2d 515 (1988).
7. *State v. Adams*, 52 Conn. App. 643, 727 A.2d 780 (1999).8. See criminal.findlaw.com; downloaded on March 24, 2020.
9. *State v. Clemons*, 82 Ohio St. 3d 438, 696 N.E.2d 1009 (1998).

Eighth Amendment: Sentencing

- Explain the basic procedure involved when a defendant enters a plea
- Describe the various types of pleas available to defendants
- Define the purpose of plea bargaining
- Explain the role of victim impact statements in sentencing
- Define *Alford* and conditional pleas

I. Guilty Pleas
  A. Procedure
    Voluntariness of the Plea
  B. *Alford* Plea
  C. *Nolo Contendere*
  D. Conditional Plea
  E. First Offender Treatment

II. Plea Bargaining
  A. Federal Sentencing Negotiations
    Federal Sentencing Guidelines
  B. State Plea Negotiations
    State Sentencing Guidelines
  C. The Controversy Surrounding Plea Bargaining

III. Sentencing
  A. Judicial Discretion
    Judicial Procedure in Imposing Sentences

B. Presentence Investigation
C. Sentencing Hearing
    Victim Impact Statements
    Aggravation of Sentence
    Mitigation of Sentence
D. Possible Punishments
    Death
    Life in Prison Without the Possibility of Parole
    Life in Prison
    Sentence for Years
    Probation or Parole
    Fines
    Community Service
    Restitution

IV. Constitutional Issues in Sentencing
  A. Cruel and Unusual Punishment
  B. "Three Strikes and You're Out"

This chapter focuses on sentencing issues, including how and under what circumstances a defendant enters a plea of guilty and what happens on appeal following a conviction. We begin by addressing the issue of procedures involved in entering a guilty plea.

GUILTY PLEAS

Before addressing the process involved in entering a guilty plea, it's important to understand the significance of pleading guilty. At its simplest, a plea of guilty is the defendant's admission that he or she committed the crime.[1] Once the plea is made and accepted by the court and the defendant begins serving his or her sentence, the defendant is barred from retracting it. A person accused of a crime always has the right to plead guilty to it, even when the crime is capital murder and the defendant is facing a possible death sentence. (Some states do not allow a defendant to enter a plea of guilty in capital murder cases.[2])

Even though a defendant has the right to plead guilty, it does not mean that the judge is compelled to accept the plea. Why would such a rule exist?

A judge may reject a defendant's guilty plea if the defendant claims that he or she did not commit the activity. A defendant cannot have it both ways: He or she either admits guilt and accepts the sentence of the court or pleads not guilty and goes to trial. With the sole exception of *Alford* pleas (discussed below), a defendant cannot maintain his or her innocence while pleading guilty to the infraction.

A. PROCEDURE

Sidebar

Before a defendant is permitted to enter a plea of guilty, the judge must determine that the defendant has done so freely, voluntarily, and without any duress, threat, or intimidation.

Before a judge can accept a defendant's plea, the judge must make a determination that the plea is given voluntarily and not as the result of coercion, threats, or other inducements.[3] A guilty plea must be given knowingly and voluntarily. To establish the voluntary nature of the plea, the judge (or the prosecutor) will question the defendant on the record to determine that the plea has not been forced. (In some misdemeanor cases, the defendant may simply initial statements on a plea form that state, "This plea is not the result of force, threat, or coercion.") In felony cases, the traditional method of accepting a guilty plea is to do so in open court, with the entire proceeding taken down by a court reporter and subsequently made part of the record. To establish that a guilty plea is voluntarily and knowingly given, many courts have established a standard set of questions that defendants must answer, out loud, in open court. If a defendant refuses to respond to any of the questions or retracts any statement, the court will reject the defendant's guilty plea and set the

FIGURE 15-1

Interrogatories of
Defendant During Plea

1. Please state your name for the record.
2. What is your age?
3. Are you now under the influence of alcohol, medicine, drugs, or any other substance?
4. Can you read and write?
5. Have you read and examined the indictment charging you in this case?
6. Do you understand that you are charged with the following offenses?
7. Do you understand that there are certain rights that you would have at trial and that by pleading guilty you give up those rights? Do you understand that you are giving up the right to:

   - A trial by a jury
   - Be presumed innocent
   - Confront the witnesses against you
   - Subpoena any witnesses to appear on your behalf
   - Testify yourself and offer other evidence
   - Have an attorney represent you during your trial?

8. Do you understand that if you plead not guilty or if you remain silent and enter no plea at all you will have the right to a trial by jury?
9. Do you understand that for the offense of _____ you can be sentenced to a maximum sentence from _____ to _____ years and a fine of $_____?
10. The State has recommended a sentence to the judge of _____. Other than this recommendation, has anyone made any promises to cause you to plead guilty?
11. Do you understand that the judge is not required to follow this recommendation but can give you any sentence allowed by law?
12. Has anyone used any force or threats against you to cause you to plead guilty?
13. Are you satisfied with the services of your attorney in this case?
14. Do you understand all of the questions that you have answered so far?
15. Understanding all of your rights, do you want to enter a plea of guilty to the offense(s) listed in the indictment?
16. Is your decision to plead guilty made freely and voluntarily?
17. Did you in fact commit the offense of _____ as it is stated in the indictment?

case for a trial. Defendants are not railroaded into pleading guilty by overzealous judges or prosecutors, despite what may be portrayed on television and in movies. See Figure 15-1 for a list of questions that the defendant must answer.

VOLUNTARY PLEA?

Dora has been charged with larceny and when her case is called for trial, she tells the court that she wants to plead guilty. When the court goes through the standard questions with her, she tells the judge, "I really don't want to plead guilty, but my boyfriend says that if I don't, he'll run off with my children."

Is this a valid guilty plea that the judge can accept?

Answer: No. The answer indicates that the defendant is not giving her plea freely, voluntarily, and without intimidation.

VOLUNTARINESS OF THE PLEA

The judge must always consider any statements made by the defendant during the questioning process to determine that the plea was made voluntarily, knowingly, and without coercion. If a defendant gives an equivocal answer to one of the plea interrogatories set out in Figure 15-1, then the judge will be required to suspend the sentencing. During the suspension, the defendant will have the opportunity to speak to his or her counsel and restart the sentencing phase. If the defendant continues to make statements that seem to indicate he or she is not guilty of the crime, then the judge must halt the sentencing process, enter a plea of not guilty, and place the defendant's case back on the active trial roster.

B. *ALFORD* PLEA

Alford **plea**
A plea, authorized by the U.S. Supreme Court, that allows a defendant to enter a guilty plea, but basing the plea on the amount and quantity of evidence against him or her instead of the defendant's belief in his or her actual guilt.

An *Alford* **plea** allows a defendant an alternative to pleading either guilty or not guilty. Under an *Alford* plea, a defendant can continue to maintain his or her innocence but tender a guilty plea and be sentenced as though he or she had said he or she was guilty. A defendant might decide to use an *Alford* plea when the government's case against him or her seems strong and the possible defenses weak. The Supreme Court first recognized the possibility of a defendant choosing to plead guilty while protesting his or her innocence in the case of *North Carolina v. Alford*, 91 S.Ct. 160 (1970), and it has since been referred to as an *Alford* plea.

Alford pleas are common, although there are no statistics that reveal exactly how often they are used. Judges and legal scholars alike support the use of the *Alford* plea as an efficient, constitutional way of resolving cases. Furthermore, when defendants enter an *Alford* plea, it can be a benefit when they seek future employment. They can explain to their potential employer that they were innocent, but the evidence was stacked against them.

C. NOLO CONTENDERE

Nolo contendere
Latin; "I do not contest;" a plea offered in a criminal case where the defendant does not contest his or her guilt and asks for the court's mercy.

A plea of **nolo contendere** literally means, "I do not contest." For purposes of sentencing, a plea of nolo contendere has the same requirements and the same implications as a guilty plea. If that is the case, why would a person bother to present such a plea? In some instances, a plea of nolo contendere can prevent points from being assessed against the defendant's driver's license. Pleas of nolo contendere are routinely accepted in first-offense driving under the influence (DUI) cases for that reason. Because a plea of nolo contendere does not admit guilt, a defendant may also wish to use this plea instead of a plea of guilty because of a pending civil case. Because a nolo plea does not admit guilt, this plea cannot be used against the defendant in a civil case the same way that a guilty plea can. A certified copy of a defendant's guilty plea to a traffic violation may be the only thing that a plaintiff in a civil case needs to prove that the defendant is liable for medical and property damages. A nolo plea cannot be used in that manner.

It should be noted that many states do not allow a defendant to use the plea of nolo contendere or, if they do, its use is limited to specific types of offenses, usually minor ones like traffic violations or a first-offense DUI. The judge always has the option to accept or reject a nolo contendere plea. If the judge rejects the plea, then the defendant must either change the plea to guilty or proceed to trial on a plea of not guilty.

D. CONDITIONAL PLEA

In some states, a defendant is allowed to enter what is referred to as a **conditional plea**. This is an alternative to an *Alford* plea, and in many ways they are similar. A defendant enters a plea of guilty, including a condition that although he or she continues to maintain his or her innocence, the facts and the law are such that the chances of the defendant actually winning at trial are virtually nonexistent. In the face of such overwhelming evidence, the defendant enters a conditional plea of guilty. The practical consequences between a conditional plea, an *Alford* plea, and a guilty plea are identical. For purposes of crime records, employment applications, security clearance, and any other jobs that require someone without a criminal record, the person who has entered a conditional plea is considered to have pleaded guilty—exactly as the person who offered an *Alford* plea of guilty.

Conditional plea
A plea entered by the defendant who maintains his or her innocence but states that the evidence against him or her is overwhelming.

E. FIRST OFFENDER TREATMENT

Another possible outcome for a defendant who decides to plead guilty is a request to be enrolled in the state's first offender program. All states have some form of this program, although it is not available for all types of crimes. Generally, first offender programs are reserved for youthful offenders for relatively minor crimes. Rather than have these people carry a criminal conviction for the rest of their lives, a judge might decide to enroll them into the first offender program. Under the terms of the program, a defendant must sign an agreement to complete various activities. If he or she is successful, at the completion of the first offender program, the judge will rescind the defendant's guilty plea. At this point, a defendant can truthfully say that he or she has not been convicted of a crime. The judge will order that the defendant's conviction be expunged from the record. However, to earn this generous benefit, a defendant will have to complete some or all of the following activities:

- Attend education classes
- Complete substantial amounts of community service
- Pay all fines and restitution to victims
- Attend psychological, drug, or narcotics counseling on a regular basis
- Commit no further crimes during his or her time in the first offender program

PLEA BARGAINING

The vast majority of criminal cases end in some kind of negotiated plea of guilty. The process of plea bargaining has been going on for hundreds of years in this country, although it has not always gone by that name. A plea bargain is essentially an agreement between the defendant and the state. The prosecutor promises that he or she will recommend a lower **sentence** than what the defendant might ordinarily receive in exchange for the defendant's promise to plead guilty. Plea bargaining works differently in different jurisdictions. In some states and on the federal level, prosecutors cannot recommend a specific sentence, because sentencing guidelines demand specific sentences for specific crimes, but prosecutors can negotiate the number and type of charges that they will bring against a defendant. In other states, a plea bargain is as simple as first stated: The state (in the person of the prosecutor) makes a promise to the defendant to recommend a sentence in exchange for a guilty plea.

In most jurisdictions, the judge has specific restrictions on the ultimate sentence that he or she can impose on the defendant. For instance, all crimes carry maximum sentences. In some states, a conviction for armed robbery could carry a maximum sentence of 20 years. Following a conviction for this crime, the judge could not sentence a defendant to any sentence that exceeds this period, even if the judge wanted to set an example for the community and impose a harsher sentence than allowed by law. There are also additional constitutional prohibitions that a judge faces when imposing a sentence that will be addressed later in this chapter.

Although the prosecutor can make a recommendation to the judge about the defendant's sentence—at least in those states that do not follow mandatory sentencing guidelines—the judge is the final authority on the sentence that the defendant receives. If the state's recommendation seems inadequate to a judge, then the judge will announce to the defendant that he or she does not intend to follow the recommendation. The judge is not compelled to tell the defendant what sentence he or she is inclined to give. However, the defendant has one option: When the judge announces an intention not to follow the recommendation, the defendant is free to withdraw his or her guilty plea and proceed to trial instead. The defendant's attorney may meet with the prosecution again to determine a new plea bargain in hopes that the judge will accept a different arrangement.

Sentence
The punishment, such as a prison sentence or fine, that is imposed on a convicted defendant by a judge.

Sidebar

The vast majority of criminal cases are disposed of through some type of plea bargaining.

A. FEDERAL SENTENCING NEGOTIATIONS

Many states and the federal government have imposed sentencing guidelines for individuals convicted of crimes. These sentencing guidelines have been imposed, in many situations, as a way of reaching more uniform results in sentencing. Essentially, these statutes take away some of the judge's discretion in imposing a sentence and require specific sentences for specific crimes.

The rationale for sentencing guidelines is that they provide more consistent sentences. When a judge has wide discretion in the sentence to be meted out, the judge may give a sentence that is considerably less or considerably more than the sentences other individuals have received for the same offense. This gives the criminal justice system the appearance of being arbitrary and capricious. Under sentencing guidelines or "structured sentencing" as it is sometimes called, judges have far less discretion in the sentence imposed on the defendant. When the judge is confronted with a defendant convicted of a crime, the judge must refer to a schedule that determines the sentence, based on the kind of infraction and the defendant's prior criminal record. In many cases, the guidelines were imposed by legislatures eager to show a "get tough on crime" stance.[4]

FEDERAL SENTENCING GUIDELINES

The U.S. Congress, after finding that there were large discrepancies in the length of sentences that defendants received for the same crime in different parts of the country, enacted the Federal Sentencing Guidelines. The U.S. Sentencing Commission was created by Congress in 1984. The commission's job was to develop guidelines for sentencing all federal offenders. These guidelines became the law of the federal courts in 1987 and withstood a constitutional challenge in 1989.[5] One can hardly claim that the Federal Sentencing Guidelines were a success. They have been attacked from all sides, by defense attorneys and prosecutors, and even by federal judges.

A big change came in the use of Federal Sentencing Guidelines in the Supreme Court case of *U.S. v. Booker*, 543 U.S. 220 (2005). That case held that the mandatory provisions of the Federal Sentencing Guidelines were unconstitutional because they took power away from juries to determine key facts in a case and gave that responsibility solely to the federal judge. However, the Supreme Court did not rule that the Federal Sentencing Guidelines are unconstitutional in all ways. They may be used as guidelines for judges when they impose sentences. The basic claim raised in the *Booker* case was that the judge made additional factual findings during Booker's sentencing phase concerning facts that the jury had not considered in the case-in-chief. This put the judge in the impermissible position of being both fact finder and judge in a jury trial. In the aftermath of the *Booker* case, the Federal Sentencing Guidelines are no longer considered mandatory but do provide guidance for federal prosecutors and judges.

B. STATE PLEA NEGOTIATIONS

On the state level, prosecutors face the same pressures as federal prosecutors. As discussed later in this section, there is a genuine need to reduce caseloads on both the state and federal level. States have addressed this problem in different ways. Some states allow a judge great latitude in the sentence that he or she may impose, risking a claim of disproportionate sentencing. Other states have attempted to follow the federal model and enacted their own state sentencing guidelines.

STATE SENTENCING GUIDELINES

Many states have followed the federal model by enacting sentencing guidelines for individuals convicted of crimes. These sentencing guidelines have been imposed, in many situations, as a way of reaching more uniform results in length of prison term and fine imposed. Essentially, these statutes take away some of the judge's discretion in imposing a sentence and require specific sentences for specific crimes.

The rationale for sentencing guidelines is that they provide more consistent sentences. When a judge has wide discretion in the sentence that he or she can impose, the judge may give a sentence that is considerably less or considerably more than the sentences other individuals have received for the same offense. Under sentencing guidelines, or structured sentencing as it is sometimes called, judges have far less discretion in the sentence imposed on the defendant. When the judge is confronted with a defendant convicted of a crime, the judge must refer to a schedule that determines the sentence, based on the kind of infraction and the defendant's prior criminal record.

C. THE CONTROVERSY SURROUNDING PLEA BARGAINING

Sidebar

Sentencing guidelines remove much of a judge's discretion in sentencing convicted defendants.

Many claim that allowing defendants to plead guilty to lesser sentences does nothing to advance the cause of justice and merely sets up a system in which an offender is doomed to become a repeat offender. Prison should be made more difficult, the conditions worsened, critics argue, so that no one would want to risk becoming a recidivist. However, others argue that without plea bargaining, the criminal justice system in the United States would grind to a halt. There are simply too many cases for every defendant to receive a jury trial. If prosecutors did not offer some incentive to defendants to get them to plead guilty, then they would all opt for a jury trial. There is already considerable delay between a defendant's arrest and his or her trial, and this gap would only become longer as more and more defendants requested jury trials. There is also the question of economics. All of those jurors must be paid, even if it is only $25 per day. Moreover, in high-profile cases, jurors may be sequestered, meaning that they are sent to hotels at night during the trial instead of being allowed to go home and possibly see news coverage of the trial that could affect their verdict.

Despite the naysayers, plea bargains are a daily fact of every prosecutor's life, and through skillful negotiation, a prosecutor might reduce his or her monthly trial docket by as much as 90 percent by using them.

Of course, there are some cases where plea bargains are simply not appropriate. In states that have enacted "three strikes and you're out" provisions (discussed below), a defendant faces a mandatory life sentence on a third felony conviction. There is no offer that a prosecutor can make to induce the defendant to plead guilty. The sentence is mandatory and the prosecutor cannot alter it. In other cases, such as capital murder cases where a defendant is facing a possible death sentence, there is also very little room—and often very little inclination—for a prosecutor to offer a deal to a defendant.

 # SENTENCING

The judge sentences defendants who are found guilty at trial. Because there are no further proceedings in cases where defendants are found not guilty, this chapter concentrates on the sentencing and appeals phase of criminal prosecutions. In most jurisdictions, the judge has specific restrictions on the ultimate sentence that he or she can impose on the defendant. The statute that criminalizes the behavior usually includes a provision for a minimum and maximum sentence and a judge is bound to impose a sentence within those limits.

A. JUDICIAL DISCRETION

Sentencing guidelines were imposed as a way of curbing a judge's discretion. In jurisdictions where sentencing guidelines do not exist, the judge has broad discretion. The judge can take a wide range of factors into account in fashioning a sentence, including the maximum sentence permissible under the statute, the defendant's prior history, and any aggravating or mitigating factors.

JUDICIAL PROCEDURE IN IMPOSING SENTENCES

In most situations, it is the judge's sole responsibility to impose the sentence on the defendant. However, there are jurisdictions that allow the jury to have some input on the sentence. This is especially true in death penalty cases where the jury must actually recommend a death sentence to the judge.[6]

When it comes time to sentence, the judge must address the defendant and also allow the defendant the opportunity to make any statements that he or she wishes, as long as these statements do not cross the line into verbal abuse or disrupt the court proceedings.[7]

Statutory Minimum and Maximum Sentences. In most situations, when a defendant is convicted of a crime, the statute will provide the maximum, and in some cases the minimum, sentence permissible under law. A judge may not exceed the maximum sentence. In the absence of mandatory sentencing guidelines, a judge has the power to impose any sentence between the minimum and the maximum.

Concurrent sentence
One or more sentences that are served at the same time.

Concurrent Sentencing. A **concurrent sentence** is one that will be served at the same time as any other prison term. When sentences run concurrently, a defendant serves time for two or more offenses at the same time. Obviously, a defendant would prefer to be sentenced to a concurrent sentence instead of a consecutive sentence.

Consecutive Sentencing. A consecutive prison term is one that is added to a current prison term. If a defendant has been sentenced to a five-year prison term on one offense, then his or her new sentence will begin when the first prison term has ended. Judges often sentence defendants to **consecutive sentences** to increase the overall time that a defendant will serve in custody.

Consecutive sentences
Sentences that are served one after the other.

B. PRESENTENCE INVESTIGATION

Presentence investigation
An investigation by court-appointed social workers, probation officers, and others, into a criminal's background to determine the criminal's prospects for rehabilitation.

Once the judge has accepted the plea of guilty, sentence may be imposed. In most situations, the sentence will be entered immediately. In other situations, a sentencing hearing may be scheduled. This is especially true if the judge orders a **presentence investigation** (PSI). A PSI is a report prepared by the defendant's probation officer. This report will detail the defendant's circumstances, including the details of the crime, the defendant's upbringing, his or her criminal history, and any other factors in mitigation or aggravation of sentence. Defense attorneys are given an opportunity to supplement the probation officer's materials with anything they believe relevant. However, the judge still has the final decision on sentencing.

C. SENTENCING HEARING

At the conclusion of a trial, or as part of the defendant's guilty plea, the judge may hold a sentencing hearing to determine what sentence the defendant should receive. A sentencing hearing allows the prosecution to present evidence to justify a harsher sentence. The defense also has the opportunity of presenting any evidence that might mitigate the sentence. This hearing is like a mini-trial. Witnesses may testify and both sides may introduce evidence to support their positions.

VICTIM IMPACT STATEMENTS

Victim impact statement
The right of a victim of a crime to address the court during the defendant's sentencing and to testify about the effect that the defendant's crime has had on the victim.

A victim is permitted and often encouraged to file a statement that can be read at the hearing and is made a part of the defendant's file. A **victim impact statement** allows the victim to tell the judge what effect the defendant's crime has had on the victim's life. Victim impact statements are often an important part of the healing process that occurs in the aftermath of a crime, especially a violent crime. The victim is permitted to read the statement in open court or the statement may be read by a prosecutor for a victim who does not wish to appear in court on the sentencing day.

AGGRAVATION OF SENTENCE

During a sentencing hearing, the prosecutor may seek to introduce a wide range of evidence to justify a harsher, or **aggravation of sentence** for the defendant. For example, the prosecution might show that:

- The defendant has prior criminal convictions.
- The defendant's actions have had an adverse impact on the victim or victim's family.
- The defendant poses a significant threat to the community or is likely to commit more crimes in the future.

Aggravation of sentence
Evidence offered by the state to enhance or lengthen the defendant's sentence.

Many states have enacted statutes that allow victims of specific kinds of crime to recover money from state or federal funds. These funds are designed to help defray some of the costs associated with obtaining replacement goods (or to meet insurance deductibles when insurance coverage exists). In these states, a victim must file a claim under the applicable legislation and show how the defendant's actions affected the victim's life and also prove any monetary losses that were not covered by insurance.

In general, when the state seeks to enhance a defendant's sentence, it must bring out the underlying aggravating factors during the trial so that they can also be proven beyond a reasonable doubt. In that way, the judge can consider them in the sentencing phase.[8]

MITIGATION OF SENTENCE

The defense may also present evidence in **mitigation of sentence** for the defendant. For instance, the defense may show that the defendant has a poor education or a bad childhood to help explain why the defendant resorted to crime. In addition to family life and education, the defense might introduce evidence of the defendant's mental stability or intelligence. In addition, the defendant may take the stand and testify about the circumstances of his or her life as a way to explain why he or she committed the crime.

Mitigation of sentence
Evidence offered by the defense to lessen or shorten the defendant's sentence.

D. POSSIBLE PUNISHMENTS

There are a wide range of punishments that a defendant can receive at the conclusion of a trial, including:

- Death
- Life in prison without the possibility of parole
- Life in prison
- Sentence for years

- Probation or parole
- Fines
- Community service
- Restitution

DEATH

Originally, the prohibition of cruel and unusual punishment was enacted to prohibit torture, but not the death penalty. The Founding Fathers had seen enough of practices such as "pressing" or putting someone in a stock in the village square. The Eighth Amendment forbids these types of corporal and psychological torture, but does not forbid a sentence of death; it simply means that the sentence must be carried out with as little pain as possible. Most "innovations" in the mechanisms of executing a human being have been based on making the death as painless as possible. The invention of the electric chair was originally put forward as a "painless" way to carry out a death sentence.

Procedures in Death Penalty Cases. Issues surrounding the imposition of the death penalty could fill an entire volume. Sentencing a person to execution at the hands of the state has always been considered to be the most extreme sanction in law. As such, death penalty or capital murder cases have different safeguards and procedures than are seen in other prosecutions. As we have seen, a death sentence itself is not necessarily "cruel and unusual" punishment, but the manner in which it is carried out could be. Many jurisdictions limit the possible methods of execution to proven methods. For instance, some states no longer permit the use of hanging or the use of the electric chair.[9]

Sentencing in Death Penalty Cases. Sentencing in death penalty cases raises a whole host of crucial issues. Death penalty trials are always bifurcated, meaning that there are two trials. When a defendant is charged with capital murder and the government announces its intention to seek the death penalty, special rules are triggered to protect the defendant. The **bifurcated trial** consists of the guilt phase, where the jury decides whether or not the defendant is guilty of the crime, and the sentencing phase, where the judge or jury is called on to decide if the defendant's actions warrant a death sentence. In most jurisdictions the only crime that warrants a death sentence is murder. Although in the past it was possible to be sentenced to death for crimes such as rape, most jurisdictions limit a death sentence to cases involving homicide. In some states only a jury can decide to impose a death sentence. In other jurisdictions, the judge decides to impose death. In either situation, the fact-finder must not only decide that the defendant is guilty of the crime, but also decide that the defendant's actions warrant a death sentence. The only way to reach this conclusion is to find that certain aggravating factors were present. Simply killing another person is not enough to warrant a death sentence. For a defendant to be sentenced to death, the murder must have been committed during the commission of another crime (such as rape) or in a particularly gruesome way.

Bifurcated trial
Separate hearings for different issues in the same case; for example, for guilt and sanity or guilt and punishment in a criminal case.

Aggravating Factors. To put a convicted murderer to death, the defendant must have committed the murder under special circumstances, often referred to as aggravating factors. These factors authorize the use of the death penalty, and include murders that were:

- Done in a particularly heinous, cruel, or depraved manner, including torture
- Committed during the course of a felony, such as rape or kidnapping
- Carried out for money
- Killed two or more people
- Committed when the defendant was escaping from legal confinement
- Committed against a child
- Acts of terrorism
- Committed by a defendant who had a prior conviction for first-degree murder
- Committed against a victim who was an elected official or a police officer

In states that formally punished other types of offenses—such as the rape of a child—with the death penalty, the U.S. Supreme Court has ruled that the death penalty can only be used in cases where the victim died.[10]

LIFE IN PRISON WITHOUT THE POSSIBILITY OF PAROLE

The U.S. Supreme Court has also held that sentences of life without **parole** do not violate the Eighth Amendment for certain offenses. These include murder, kidnapping, bank robbery, narcotic offenses, and aggravated rape. Except for murder, life sentences without parole are only authorized when the other listed crimes (kidnapping, rape, etc.) involve violence or repeated convictions. A life sentence without the possibility of parole means that the defendant will never be released. Such a sentence is often the alternative for a person who is facing a potential death sentence. In states that allow a person facing a capital murder charge to plead guilty, this is usually the sentence that they receive. The defendants give up the possibility of ever being released from prison in exchange for not facing the death sentence at trial. In most situations, life without parole means exactly what it says and the defendant will never leave the correctional system alive.

Parole
A release from prison, before a sentence is finished, that depends on the person's "keeping clean" and doing what he or she is supposed to do while out.

LIFE IN PRISON

For serious crimes—including murder, kidnapping with violence, and cases where the defendant has a long criminal history—a defendant may be sentenced to life in prison. Although there is a well-known (and incorrect) saying that a life sentence simply means a maximum of seven years in custody, the facts are more complicated. For instance, it makes a great deal of difference in what state the defendant is sentenced to life. In some states, for instance, a life sentence may actually mean that the defendant serves the rest of his or her life in prison, whereas in other states it means that the although the defendant has received a life sentence, his or her first parole hearing will not be scheduled until the seventh year of incarceration, at which time the defendant could be released or could be held for a longer period of time.

SENTENCE FOR YEARS

When the judge sentences a defendant to a term in prison, he or she may order that the sentence be served consecutively to other prison terms or concurrently with other terms. A sentence for years can be as low as a few days in the local jail or decades spent behind bars. Usually, a sentence short of life in prison without the possibility of parole always gives the prisoner the right to gain credit for good behavior that will shorten his or her sentence. Similarly, negative or disruptive behavior may see additional time added to the balance of the sentence.

When a defendant is sentenced to prison, it is important to keep in mind that there are many different types of prisons. The Federal Bureau of Prisons lists five distinct categories:

- Administrative
- Minimum security
- Low security
- Medium security
- High security

Administrative facilities house individuals who have been charged, but not yet processed by the criminal justice system. Minimum security prisons are usually dormitory-style facilities, with relatively little security or guards. Low-security prison facilities have double-fenced perimeters surrounding the unit, dormitory housing, and work programs. High-security prisons are what most people think of as prisons, with barred doors on the cells (or thick doors), numerous security guards, thick walls, and often double layers of fencing around the entire outside of the facility, usually topped with razor wire.

Alternative Prisons. In some situations, a judge may consider an alternative form of punishment. For instance, in appropriate cases, a judge may order that a defendant be held under house arrest. There are several private companies that specialize in monitoring services, some of which use advanced technology such as electronic ankle bracelets and computer terminals to confirm that a defendant remains within the confines of the home.

Other alternative forms of punishment include boot camps and shock incarceration. Someone who has been sentenced to a boot camp is normally sent there for a maximum period of 90 days. The conditions are stricter than those found in typical prisons. In these facilities, modeled on military boot camps, prisoners must abide by a strict code of conduct. The advantage for a prisoner is that with successful completion of the boot camp program, he or she will be released much sooner than he or she would have been normally.

Of course, if the defendant cannot abide by the limitations of the boot camp, his or her sentence will convert to a more conventional prison sentence.

PROBATION AND PAROLE

After release from prison, a defendant will often continue to serve the balance of his or her sentence on **probation** or parole. Probation officers ensure that the defendant follows the conditions of his or her sentence. For instance, if the defendant has been ordered to pay fines or restitution, the probation officer is the person who monitors these payments. In addition, the probation officer also makes sure that the probationer obtains employment, refrains from drug use, and follows other rules. If the probationer commits another crime while serving probation, the probation officer can seek to have the original probation revoked and the defendant returned to prison. Although this text has used the terms "probation" and "parole" interchangeably, they actually describe two different phases of supervision.

Probation
Allowing a person convicted of a criminal offense to avoid serving a jail sentence imposed on the person, so long as he or she abides by certain conditions (including being supervised by a probation officer).

Probation is usually given in place of a prison sentence. When a convict is placed on probation, it means that he or she will be monitored to see that he or she does not commit any new crimes, doesn't engage in the use of drugs, or other harmful practices, and is gainfully employed. Probation is often seen as a benefit to the defendant, who can remain in society and avoid serving time in custody. Parole, on the other hand, is the term used when a person is released from prison before serving his or her full sentence. The balance of the sentence will be served on parole. While he or she is on parole, the convict will be subject to many of the same conditions that the probationer has faced: supervision, employment requirements, and so on.

Probation and parole are both confinement sentences. For example, suppose that a person receives a five-year sentence. If he or she is released from prison early because of good behavior, he or she will serve the balance of that sentence on parole. Probation is usually given to people who are not sentenced to confinement. It is important to note that the use of these terms varies from state to state. In some states, parole has been completely eliminated and all noncustody sentences are simply referred to as "probation."

When a probationer violates one or more conditions of his or her probation, the probation officer is authorized to file a petition with the original sentencing judge, asking that the probation be revoked. In many states, prosecutors can also file such petitions. Probation revocation hearings are similar to trials. The state presents evidence to justify revoking the defendant's probation and the defense is permitted to present evidence to show that the defendant should be allowed to continue on probation. The judge makes the final determination about whether or not the defendant has violated the terms of probation and the judge may then resentence the defendant to his or her original sentence or modify the sentence in other ways. The one thing that a judge cannot do is resentence the defendant to more time in custody than he or she originally received. The judge can order the defendant returned to prison to serve out the balance of his or her sentence, but cannot sentence him or her to a new term in custody as though the first sentence was never imposed.

FINES

The Eighth Amendment to the U.S. Constitution not only forbids cruel and unusual punishment; it also prohibits excessive fines. Many states have enacted minimum fines that a convicted defendant must pay as part of his or her sentence. For instance, some states require a minimum fine of $1,000 on a third conviction for DUI in a five-year period. Other offenses, such as trafficking in narcotics, carry much stiffer fines. Fines for some narcotics offenses are as high as $250,000 and in some states may be even higher. However, the fine must be proportional to the nature of the offense. A minor offense should not be assessed a huge fine.

Once a defendant is sentenced and begins serving his or her sentence on probation, he or she must make regular payments on the imposed fine to the probation office. When a probationer fails to make payments on an outstanding fine, his or her probation can be revoked and he or she can be placed back into incarceration. A person serving time in custody does not have to make any payments on fines, court costs, or restitution.

COMMUNITY SERVICE

For misdemeanors and some types of minor felonies, a court may sentence a defendant to community service. A sentence served on community service usually puts the defendant to work picking up trash on roads around the county, working in local government offices, or carrying out light labor, such as trash collection or processing materials at a state-run recycling plant. Community service is frequently required in DUI cases and for some first-time offenders.

RESTITUTION

In addition to fines, a defendant may also be ordered to compensate the victim for damages or items taken. Restitution acts like damages in civil cases, where the defendant pays money to compensate the victim for injuries. The restitution amount must normally be proven during the sentencing hearing, unless the defendant agrees to pay the restitution as part of a plea agreement. As the defendant makes payments to his or her probation officer on his fines and fees, the probation department will also collect restitution for the victim. In many cases, the victim will receive the final restitution amount as one lump payment.

 CONSTITUTIONAL ISSUES IN SENTENCING

Excessive bail shall not be required, nor excessive fines imposed, nor cruel and unusual punishments inflicted.

—Eighth Amendment, U.S. Constitution

A judge is permitted to sentence a defendant who has either pled guilty or been found guilty, and the judge often has broad discretion in the sentence that can be imposed, but there are some constitutional limits that a judge may not exceed. When it comes to sentencing in criminal cases, the most important consideration is the Eighth Amendment, which prohibits cruel and unusual punishment.

A. CRUEL AND UNUSUAL PUNISHMENT

One of the most important restrictions placed on the kind of sentence that can be imposed on a defendant is set out in the Eighth Amendment to the U.S. Constitution. In very few words, that amendment prohibits any punishment deemed "cruel and unusual." This amendment was made applicable to the states through the Fourteenth Amendment. Many state constitutions have similar provisions. Because the amendment does not define exactly what constitutes cruel and unusual punishment, the U.S. Supreme Court has been called on to interpret it. The Court's decisions have established that a sentence cannot involve torture, and that the sentence given must be in **proportionality** to the crime.[11] This means that all states are prohibited from engaging in practices that are considered to be cruel and unusual punishment, including torture, whipping, and corporal punishment.

Proportionality
The U.S. Supreme Court has mandated that a sentence must be proportional to the crime to satisfy the Eighth Amendment. For instance, without some other aggravating circumstance, a life sentence for a petty infraction would be out of proportion and would be a violation of the Eighth Amendment.[12]

B. "THREE STRIKES AND YOU'RE OUT"

So-called three strikes statutes generally require a lengthy prison sentence (sometimes even life in prison) for a third felony conviction. These statutes have been deemed constitutional by the Supreme Court because they place conditions on imposing such a severe sentence (namely, two prior felony convictions before the statute is triggered).[13] In practice, this could mean that a defendant's third felony conviction could be for a relatively minor felony, yet still satisfy the minimum requirements of the statute and trigger a mandatory life sentence.

THREE STRIKES?   SCENARIO 15-2

Leonard has two previous convictions for theft and burglary in a state that has a three strikes law. This time he is charged with possession of five pounds of marijuana, another felony. Is he facing life in prison if he is convicted?

Answer: Yes. Most states do not make a distinction between the types of felonies needed to qualify for the three strikes laws and Leonard will almost certainly face a life sentence.

CASE EXCERPT

McCLOON v. STATE

669 S.E.2D 466, 294 GA. APP. 490 (GA. APP. 2008)

JONATHAN MCCLOON, PRO SE.

Timothy Grady Vaughn, Dist. Atty., and Russell Paradise Spivey, Asst. Dist. Atty., for Appellee.

BLACKBURN, PRESIDING JUDGE.

Following his guilty plea to three felony counts (armed robbery, burglary, and aggravated assault), Jonathan McCloon appeals the trial court's denial of his motion for an out-of-time appeal. He argues that his counsel's failure to appeal the armed robbery conviction constituted ineffective assistance and that the record failed to show that he entered into the plea freely and voluntarily. Because the record supports neither argument, we hold that the trial court did not abuse its discretion in denying his motion for an out-of-time appeal.

McCloon and two co-defendants were indicted for armed robbery, aggravated assault, and burglary. At their guilty plea hearing before Telfair County Superior Court, the court informed them of the details of the charges, of the potential sentences associated therewith, and of their constitutional rights, including the privilege against compulsory self-incrimination, the right to trial by jury, and the right to confront one's accusers. After ensuring that each understood these rights, that each was under no coercion nor receiving any benefit or threat to plead guilty, and that each was uninfluenced by intoxicants or narcotics, the court received their guilty pleas as to all charges.

At their sentencing hearing, the prosecutor gave the court the following factual basis for the pleas. Armed with guns, McCloon and his co-defendants broke into a residence and began stealing items, including a shotgun. The owner of the residence returned home, whereupon the threesome hid in a back bedroom (which had a back outside door through which they could have exited but did not). As they heard the owner approach the back bedroom, McCloon opened fire through the closed bedroom door, striking the owner with four bullets. The owner managed to escape out the front door, leading one of the co-defendants to use the owner's shotgun to fire at the owner as he drove away in his truck (twice hitting the truck). The owner soon found police and reported the incident, leading police to descend upon the area of the residence and within hours to find the threesome, each of whom confessed to the above facts.

At the sentencing hearing, the State also submitted photos and diagrams substantiating many of the facts, and the defendants confirmed their guilty pleas. After sentencing the three men, the court informed them of their right to move to withdraw their guilty pleas and of their right to appeal their convictions. The sentence was filed with the clerk on August 29, 2003.

After the term of court had expired (see OCGA §15-6-3(29)(E)), McCloon in March 2004 moved to withdraw his plea, which the court denied as untimely. Several years later in 2008, McCloon moved to file an out-of-time appeal, which the court denied as lacking merit. McCloon now appeals the denial of his motion for an out-of-time appeal.

A defendant who has pled guilty to a crime may obtain an out-of-time appeal only "if the issues he seeks to raise can be resolved by facts appearing on the record and if his failure to seek a timely appeal was the result of ineffective assistance of counsel." *Colbert v. State.* "Where the record shows that the attacks on the guilty plea that a defendant seeks to raise in an out-of-time appeal are without merit, trial counsel cannot have been ineffective in failing to pursue such an appeal, and a trial court thus does not err in denying an out-of-time appeal." Id. at 81-82, 663 S.E.2d 158.

Here, McCloon attacks the guilty plea on two fronts: the armed robbery conviction is unsupported by the factual record set forth by the State, and the transcript fails to show he entered the plea freely and voluntarily. As the record reflects that these attacks are without merit, we find no abuse of discretion in the trial court's denial of his motion for an out-of-time appeal.

1. Citing *State v. Evans*, McCloon first claims that the court failed to make an inquiry on the record to establish a factual basis for the armed robbery plea. Specifically, he claims that the facts recited by the State during the sentencing hearing did not show the elements of armed robbery in that the theft of the shotgun and other items took place prior to the home owner arriving at the premises and therefore were not taken (i) by use of an offensive weapon (ii) from his person or immediate presence. We disagree.

(a) The element of using an offensive weapon. OCGA §16-8-41(a) provides that "a person commits the offense of armed robbery when, with intent to commit theft, he or she takes property of another from the person or the immediate presence of another by use of an offensive weapon. . . ." Interpreting this statute, *Moore v. State* held regarding the weapon that "the offensive weapon be used as a concomitant to a taking which involves the use of actual force . . . against another person. . . . The force . . . essential to robbery must either precede or be contemporaneous with, not subsequent to, the taking." Here, the threesome were in the process of stealing the home owner's shotgun and other items when the owner stumbled upon them and was shot with a gun and shot at with the shotgun. Thus, the force essential to the armed robbery here was contemporaneous with the taking.

(b) The element of taking the items from the person or immediate presence of the victim. Regarding the element that the stolen items be taken from the person or immediate presence of the victim, "one's 'immediate presence' in this context stretches fairly far, and robbery convictions are usually upheld even out of the physical presence of the victim if what was taken was under his control or his responsibility and if he was not too far distant." *Maddox v. State.* Here, the victim was present in his residence at the time his shotgun was being stolen in a nearby room, which shotgun the thieves used to shoot at him as he escaped in his truck. This factual record establishes the two allegedly missing elements of the crime of armed robbery.

2. McCloon next argues that no record establishes he made the guilty plea freely and voluntarily. Specifically, McCloon points to the transcript of the sentencing hearing, in which the court made no reference to McCloon's constitutional rights at trial but instead focused only on his rights to move to withdraw his guilty plea and to appeal.

However, McCloon completely ignores the transcript of the plea hearing, during which the court reviewed with McCloon his right to a jury trial, to a presumption of innocence, to the State's burden of proof, to his right to counsel, to his right to confront the State's witnesses and to cross-examine them, to his right to subpoena witnesses, to his right to testify, and to his privilege against compulsory self-incrimination. At that plea hearing, McCloon told the court he understood he was giving up all those rights by pleading guilty. The court explained the charges in detail against McCloon and the possible sentences. After confirming with McCloon that he had not been threatened or frightened or promised any benefit to plead guilty (other than the State's agreement to recommend a certain sentence) and that he was acting freely and voluntarily, the court received McCloon's guilty plea. This procedure complied with the court's obligations when taking a guilty plea. See *Beckworth v. State* ("the entry of a guilty plea involves the waiver of three federal constitutional rights: the privilege against compulsory self-incrimination, the right to trial by jury, and the right to confront one's accusers. It is the duty of a trial court to establish that the defendant understands the constitutional rights being waived, and the record must reveal the defendant's waiver of those constitutional rights"); *Maddox v. State* ("the trial court must determine that the plea is voluntary, the defendant understands the nature of the charges, and there is a factual basis for the plea. In addition, the trial court must inform the defendant of the rights being waived, the terms of any negotiated plea, and the minimum and maximum possible sentences").

Based on this record, even if McCloon were able to present some evidence showing that his attorney had failed to file an appeal on his behalf, such a failure would not amount to ineffective assistance of counsel because it is apparent from the transcript of the plea hearing that the issues he now seeks to raise in an out-of-time appeal are completely without merit. An attorney's failure to file an appeal frivolously attacking the indisputable facts proved by the transcript could not be deemed ineffectiveness.

Accordingly, we hold that the trial court did not abuse its discretion in denying McCloon's motion for an out-of-time appeal.

Judgment affirmed.

MILLER and ELLINGTON, JJ., concur.

CASE QUESTIONS

1 McCloon and two co-defendants were indicted for armed robbery, aggravated assault, and burglary. How did they plead when the case came to trial?

2 After entering his plea, what action did McCloon take? What was the basis of his action?

3 Did the appellate court find that there was a factual basis for the charges against the defendant?

4 What rights was the defendant made aware of during his sentencing?

5 Did the trial court follow the correct procedures in accepting McCloon's guilty plea? Specifically, what procedure is required?

CHAPTER SUMMARY

This chapter examines the various issues related to sentencing in criminal cases. As part of the procedure and accepting a guilty plea, a judge must determine that the defendant is acting voluntarily. There are a series of questions that the court will ask of a defendant to ensure this voluntariness. There are times when a defendant wishes to plead not guilty but realizes that the evidence against him or her is overwhelming. In such a situation, a defendant may wish to enter an *Alford* plea. Based on the U.S. Supreme Court case of *North Carolina v. Alford*, an *Alford* plea allows a defendant to maintain his or her innocence while also pleading guilty to the crime. In addition to pleading guilty, the defendant can also plead nolo contendere, which means I do not contest the charges.

The vast majority of criminal prosecutions end in a plea of guilty, usually as a result of plea bargaining. On the federal level, federal sentencing guidelines restrict a judge's discretion about the minimum and maximum sentence that can be imposed on a defendant. Many states also follow similar sentencing guidelines. There are times when a judge may order a presentence investigation before imposing a sentence. This investigation will focus on the nature of the crime, the defendant's remorse, mitigating factors, and aggravating factors involved in the case. An essential part of any sentencing is the victim impact statement. This is the victim's opportunity to detail the effect that the crime had on the victim and the victim's family.

There are many different punishments available under the U.S. system. The most extreme, the death penalty, is only available when a defendant has murdered someone and done so in a particularly cruel or heinous fashion. Before a death penalty can be imposed, a bifurcated trial must be held. The first part of the trial focuses on the guilt or innocence of the defendant. The second part of the trial, only held after the defendant is found guilty of homicide, focuses on whether the jury will recommend a sentence of death. In addition to the death sentence, defendants may also face life in prison without the possibility of parole for certain violent offenses. However, it is far more likely for defendants to receive a sentence of years for the crimes to which they have either pled guilty or been found guilty of committing. In addition to serving sentences in custody, many defendants also serve time on probation or parole after they are released. During their probationary period, defendants are required to pay fines, pay restitution to victims, and complete any community service that may have been ordered.

The Eighth Amendment to the U.S. Constitution prohibits cruel and unusual punishment. The death penalty is not considered to be a violation of the Eighth Amendment. There are also many states that impose a mandatory life sentence for permitting three or more felonies in a defendant's lifetime. These punishments have also been found to be constitutional under the Eighth Amendment.

KEY TERMS AND CONCEPTS

Alford plea	Consecutive sentences	Bifurcated trial
Nolo contendere	Presentence investigation	Parole
Conditional plea	Victim impact statement	Probation
Sentence	Aggravation of sentence	Proportionality
Concurrent sentence	Mitigation of sentence	

End of Chapter Exercises

Review Questions

See Appendix A for answers

1   What is the procedure involved in entering a guilty plea?
2   Why is plea bargaining considered to be controversial?
3   What type of discretion do judges have in imposing sentences?
4   What are statutory minimum and maximum sentences?
5   Compare concurrent and consecutive sentences.
6   What is a presentence investigation?
7   Explain the procedure at a sentencing hearing.
8   What is a victim impact statement?
9   What evidence might a prosecutor introduce in aggravation of a defendant's sentence?
10 What is first offender treatment?
11 What is a conditional plea?
12 Why is it necessary for a judge to determine that a plea was entered voluntarily?
13 What is a plea of nolo contendere?
14 What are the procedures followed in death penalty cases?
15 What is the difference between fines and restitution?
16 What is meant by the phrase "cruel and unusual punishment?"
17 Explain the legislation entitled "Three Strikes and You're Out."
18 What provisions does the Eighth Amendment have regarding punishment?

Web Surfing

1   Visit www.law.cornell.edu and search for federal sentencing guidelines.

2   Visit www.hg.org and do a search for "*Alford* plea."

3   Go to www.nolo.com; do a search there for "Pleading Guilty: What Happens in Court."

Questions for Analysis

1   Would it be possible for someone to "accidentally" plead guilty to a crime?

2   Does it make sense to take away a judge's discretion in entering a sentence and by using sentencing guidelines instead?

Hypotheticals

1   Halfway through entering his guilty plea, Barry decides that he wants to withdraw his plea. Can he?

2 At the conclusion of opening statements, Alfonzo's attorney realizes that the evidence against his client is overwhelming. He decides to enter a guilty plea on his client's behalf. As you understand the material outlined in this chapter, would that be possible?

PRACTICE QUESTIONS FOR TEST REVIEW

See Appendix A for answers

Essay Question

What is an *Alford* plea?

True-False

1 **T** **F** A defendant is not allowed to plead "no contest" to a criminal charge.

2 **T** **F** There are times when a defendant continues to proclaim his or her innocence but decides to plead guilty because of the overwhelming evidence against him or her.

3 **T** **F** The U.S. Supreme Court has mandated that a sentence must be proportional to the crime to satisfy the Eighth Amendment.

Fill in the Blank

1 A _____ plea is entered by a defendant who maintains his or her innocence but states that the evidence against him or her is overwhelming.

2 The punishment, such as a prison sentence or fine that is imposed on a convicted defendant by a judge is known as _____.

3 The _____ is the right of a victim of a crime to address the court during the defendant's sentencing and to testify about the effect that the defendant's crime has had on the victim.

Multiple Choice

1 A plea, authorized by the U.S. Supreme Court, that allows a defendant to enter a guilty plea, but basing the plea on the amount and quantity of evidence against him or her instead of the defendant's belief in his or her actual guilt.

    A *Alford* plea.
    B Guilty but mentally ill.
    C Declaration of liability.
    D Mea culpa.

2 A Latin phrase that means, "I do not contest."

   A Quid pro quo.
   B Caveat emptor.
   C Sine qua non.
   D Nolo contendere.

3 Evidence offered by the state to enhance or lengthen the defendant's sentence.

   A Mitigation of sentence.
   B Evidence of remorse.
   C Similar transactions.
   D Aggravation of sentence.

Endnotes

1. *State v. Merino*, 81 Haw. 198, 915 P.2d 672 (1996).
2. *People v. Coates*, 337 Mich. 56, 59 N.W.2d 83 (1953).
3. *Woods v. Rhay*, 68 Wash. 2d 601, 414 P.2d 601 (1966).
4. *Fear of Judging: Sentencing Guidelines in the Federal Courts*, Kate Stith and Jose A. Cabranes. Chicago: The University of Chicago Press, 1998.
5. *Mistretta v. U.S.* 488 U.S. 361 (1989).
6. *U.S. v. Bishop*, 412 U.S. 346, 93 S.Ct. 2008, 36 L.Ed.2d 941 (1973).
7. *Ross v. State*, 676 N.E.2d 339 (Ind. 1996).
8. *Southern Union Co. v. U.S.*, 132 S.Ct. 2344 (2012).
9. *Woodson v. North Carolina*, 428 U.S. 280, 96 S.Ct. 2978, 49 L.Ed.2d 944 (1976).
10. *Kennedy v. Louisiana*, 128 S.Ct. 2641, 171 L.Ed.2d 525 (2008).
11. *Miller v. Alabama*, 132 S.Ct. 2455 (2012).
12. *Solem v. Helm*, 463 U.S. 277, 103 S.Ct. 3001, 77 L.Ed.2d 637 (1983).
13. *Ewing v. California*, 538 U.S. 11, 123 S.Ct. 1179, 155 L.Ed.2d 108 (2003).

Appeals

- Explain the function of a motion for new trial
- Describe the basis of appellate jurisdiction
- Explain the purpose of the record
- Define certiorari
- List and describe the contents of an appellate brief

I. The Appellate System
   A. Motion for New Trial
   B. Notice of Appeal
      The Record
      Docket Number
   C. Appellate Procedure
      The Brief
      Contents of the Appellant's Brief
      The Appellee's Brief
      Moving Through the Appellate System
      Certiorari
   D. The Powers of the Appellate Courts
   E. *Habeas Corpus*

II. Organization of the Appellate System
   A. The U.S. Supreme Court
   B. The U.S. Supreme Court Is the Final Authority for Both Federal and State Courts

THE APPELLATE SYSTEM

Appeal
Asking a higher court to review the actions of a lower court to correct mistakes or injustice.

A defendant who has been found guilty always has the right to **appeal** the conviction. The precise rules and procedures for bringing a criminal appeal vary from state to state. For the sake of clarity, we will assume that a defendant has been found guilty in a state court of a major felony (sexual assault, for example), because there is more uniformity from state to state in such cases than in other types of charges.

At the conclusion of the trial, and assuming that the defendant has been found guilty, he or she is permitted to appeal the conviction. Part of the appellate process is establishing that the appellate court has jurisdiction to hear the case. In criminal cases, that is usually a simple statement in a brief that the defendant was tried, found guilty, and sentenced in state court. Before an appellate court will make any ruling on an appeal, it always reviews applicable laws and cases to ensure that it has the authority to do so. This authority is jurisdiction.

All states allow defendants to appeal their felony convictions. The same cannot be said for the prosecutor. Barring an adverse ruling on a pretrial motion, the government is not permitted to appeal a finding of not guilty by a jury.

After the verdict has been returned and the defendant has been sentenced, he or she usually has only a small window of opportunity to bring an appeal. In most jurisdictions, for example, a defendant must begin the appeals process within 10 to 30 days following the entry of sentence. Failure to bring an appeal essentially waives it forever. How the defendant begins his or her appeal is the subject of the next section.

A. MOTION FOR NEW TRIAL

Motion for new trial
A motion, filed by the defendant after sentencing, that requests a new trial based on errors or irregularities in the trial; if denied, it begins the appellate process.

A **motion for new trial** states specific irregularities that occurred in the trial that justify a new trial for the defendant. In most jurisdictions the same judge who heard the trial also hears the motion for a new trial. If the judge grants the request, then a new trial is ordered and everything starts over as though the first trial never occurred. If the judge denies the request, then the defendant's appellate rights are triggered. In most situations, the motion for new trial is denied. At this point, the defendant would then docket his or her appeal in the appellate court, called the Court of Appeals in many states. We will continue to use that name to refer to this first level of the appellate courts, keeping in mind that not all states call this court by that name.

B. NOTICE OF APPEAL

Notice of appeal
The official docketing and commencement of the appeals process.

After the motion for new trial has been denied, a defendant files a **notice of appeal**. This places the state on notice that the defendant intends to appeal his or her conviction to the Court of Appeals. The filing of a notice of appeal with the Court of Appeals triggers the deadlines that both the state and the defense must follow to have a legal appeal. The time limits vary from state to state, but most states have a specific time period from the time of filing of a notice of appeal until the time that the appeal is docketed with the Court of Appeals. Once the defendant files his or her brief, the state will have a set number of days to respond to that filing.

As the parties prepare for the appeal, there are some important components that must be included when the case is transferred from the trial court to the court of appeals. The notice of appeal will include the record and the docket number.

THE RECORD

The notice of appeal not only informs the appellate court that an appeal will be forthcoming, it also requests that the trial court forward the **record** to the appellate court. The record consists of all the evidence and pleadings that have been admitted at trial. This record, along with the transcript of the witness testimony, will be forwarded to the appellate court and stored there while the appeal is pending.

Record
The evidence, pleadings, motions, transcript of the trial, and any other documents relevant to the case.

DOCKET NUMBER

When a case is filed with the appellate court, it receives a **docket number** similar to the case file number that was given to the case when the complaint was originally filed in the trial court. This appellate docket number should appear on all documents filed in the appellate court, especially the briefs.

Docket number
The number assigned to a case on appeal; all subsequent briefs and other documents must bear this number.

C. APPELLATE PROCEDURE

Once a case has been docketed in the State Court of Appeals, the appellate process has officially begun. From this point forward, many of the terms and procedures associated with a criminal case change dramatically. First, there is the issue of establishing the appellate court's jurisdiction. As we have already seen, jurisdiction refers to a court's power and authority. An appellate court does not have the jurisdiction to make rulings in any prosecution until the jury has returned a verdict, the judge has entered a judgment, the defendant has been sentenced, a motion for new trial has been denied, and a notice of appeal has been filed. More important, before an appellate court will accept a case for review, the party bringing the appeal must establish that a final ruling has been made in the trial court and that there are no additional issues to be resolved in that court. The party must also establish that the ruling has an adverse impact on his or her life, liberty, or property. A criminal conviction qualifies in all of these areas.

Along with establishing jurisdiction for the State Court of Appeals, there are some additional changes that occur on appeal. One such change is that the parties are renamed. In the trial court, the state prosecuted the defendant. The

Appellant
The party bringing the current appeal from an adverse ruling in a lower court.

Appellee
The party who won in the lower court.

Brief
A written statement prepared by one side in a lawsuit to explain its case to the judge.

Reversible error
A mistake made by a judge in the procedures used at trial, or in making a legal ruling during the trial.

Statement of facts
Section of an appellate brief that contains an accurate and detailed breakdown of the specific facts that gave rise to the original lawsuit.

parties were referred to as simply the government or the state versus the defendant. Appellate courts do not use that terminology. Instead, the party bringing an appeal is referred to as the **appellant**. The winning party in the lower court is referred to as the **appellee**.

THE BRIEF

Cases are appealed by the filing of a written **brief** in a case. Although the parties can request an oral argument before the court, in the vast majority of appeals there is no such argument, only a brief prepared by both sides of the case that argues their positions and asks the court to rule in their favor. A brief is often dozens of pages long and contains an exhaustive discussion of the facts of the case and how legal precedent applies to those facts. The appellant's brief (the original defendant) would list the evidence, testimony, and rulings in the trial court and state why some or all of these were wrong, prejudicial, or counter to prevailing case law. The appellant will make a claim for **reversible error**, showing that some action taken by the trial court so prejudiced his or her case that the only valid remedy is reversal and a new trial. In a similar vein, the appellee's brief (the prosecutor) will also provide details about the trial and just as conclusively attempt to show that all actions taken by the trial court were correct and do not warrant a reversal. The brief is a formal, written argument that not only discusses the facts of the case and the applicable law, but also seeks to advocate for the client. It attempts to persuade. The person to be persuaded is usually a judge or a justice of the appellate court.

The purpose of the appellant's brief is to explain the party's position and argue a position. This argument is based on an analysis of the facts of the case and the law that applies to those facts. Appellate court briefs have a specified format, often set out in the state's rules of appellate procedure.

CONTENTS OF THE APPELLANT'S BRIEF

An appellate brief has specific subsections, including:

- Title page
- Statement of facts
- Enumerations of error
- Argument
- Conclusion

Title Page. A brief must have a title or cover page, listing the names of the parties, the appellate docket number, and the name of the court.

Statement of Facts. After the cover sheet, the legal team prepares a **statement of facts** that describes the incident that gave rise to the lawsuit and the events of the trial that feature prominently in the appeal. The statement of facts provides an overview of all relevant details that occurred between the parties that eventually gave rise to the lawsuit. In addition to the circumstances of the original incident, occasionally the statement of facts also includes details about the court case and subsequent actions on appeal. The statement of facts is supposed to be an objective recitation of what occurred between the parties. However, in preparing the brief, the parties may attempt to emphasize certain facts over others as part of their overall persuasive argument.

Enumerations of Error. Once the party has set out the basic facts of the case, the next section of the appellate brief contains the **enumerations of error**. This is usually a single, bold-faced paragraph that explains why the court's ruling was wrong. Most appeals have several enumerations of error.

> **Enumerations of error**
> The specification of an error committed in the trial court that an appellate seeks to overturn on appeal.

In the enumerations of error, the party on appeal states what it believes to be the error, if any, committed at the trial court. Enumerations of error are often phrased in such a way that they not only attempt to point out an error but also try to persuade at the same time.

There are several ways that the appellant in an appeal can phrase an enumeration of error. Suppose that the defendant was convicted of possession of narcotics. The brief advocating for the appellant might read like this:

- **The Trial Committed Reversible Error in Admitting the Defendant's Confession.**

However, this enumeration of error misses a chance at persuasion. Another way of listing an enumeration of error, covering the same ground, also provides some context and a bit of persuasion:

- **The Trial Court Committed Reversible Error by Ignoring the Coercion and Threatening Behavior by Law Enforcement in Forcing the Defendant to Confess to a Crime He Did Not Commit.**

As you can see, both of the enumerations set out above contend that the trial court committed an error, but the second enumeration also provides the defendant's argument encapsulated in a few words. In an appellate brief, attorneys try to find as many opportunities to persuade as they possibly can, so why not use the enumeration of errors as another point of argument?

Argument. The real meat of an appellate brief is the argument. Everything up to this point has been mere preparation. The argument is where the parties set out the facts and the law that support their contentions. This is the point where extensive legal research pays off. In Chapter 1, we saw that *stare decisis* binds courts. *Stare decisis* dictates that an appellate court must reach a similar decision as a previously decided case that had similar facts and similar issues.

The argument section of a brief can go on for many pages, setting out the facts and the previous case law and showing it supports the parties' contentions. The appellant would certainly argue that the current law either is not correct or that the facts of this case do not jibe with previously decided cases. The appellee, on the other hand, will argue the exact opposite. Ultimately, the appellate court will decide the case based on what it reads in the argument section of the brief and after reviewing the applicable statutes and case law.

Conclusion. The conclusion is usually a brief statement at the end of the brief that reiterates the party's position and requests specific relief. In a criminal case, the original defendant, now the appellant, would no doubt request a new trial based on the errors that occurred in the trial court.

THE APPELLEE'S BRIEF

The appellee's brief will be very similar in appearance to the appellant's brief. It will contain the same elements. The only differences are in the way that the statement of facts and argument are presented. The appellee's statement of facts will tend to emphasize the state's position in the case and will encourage the appellate court to leave the judgment as it stands.

MOVING THROUGH THE APPELLATE SYSTEM

It is quite common for appeals in criminal cases to last for years. Although the process outlined above sounds relatively straightforward, in daily practice each of the steps takes months, sometimes years, to complete. Once a defendant is sentenced, he or she will file a motion for a new trial. It may be weeks before that motion is heard. If the motion is denied, then the defendant can file a notice of appeal. Pulling together all of the necessary information can take months. Once filed, the docketing process can also take months. So, even before the first appeal in the case is heard, these time periods often have already added up to a year or more. After the State Court of Appeals receives the briefs, it may take up to a year to make a decision. The Court has hundreds of other cases pending and it decides the cases in the order in which they were received. Patience is a virtue in appellate work.

There is another feature of an appeal that should be considered. Suppose that the defendant who was found guilty and sentenced filed a proper notice of appeal and then brought an appeal in the appellate court. For the sake of clarity, we will call this court the State Court of Appeals, recognizing that this nomenclature is not used in all states. In this situation, at the first level of appeal, the person who was the defendant at the trial becomes the appellant on appeal. The state would be the appellee. However, suppose that the appellant wins the first round of appeals. If the state decides to appeal to a higher court, the parties' names switch. Because the state lost in the State Court of Appeals, the state now becomes the appellant and the original defendant is the appellee. Because of this, a person reading an appellate decision cannot automatically assume that the appellant is always the original criminal defendant. Depending on the level of the appellate court system, the party titles can change.

When the State Court of Appeals reaches its decision, whatever it might be, either party may appeal the decision to a higher court. This adds more time to the course of an appeal. Unlike the original verdict, if the defendant wins a reversal on appeal, the state is permitted to appeal that decision to the next highest court. In most states, that court is referred to as the State Supreme Court. The defendant is also free to appeal to this court, assuming that he or she loses at the State Court of Appeals. However, the rules change again at this point. The State Supreme Court (again, this text will use this name because it is the most common name for this court, but it can be called by another name in some states) has the right to decide which cases it will hear. Unlike the State Court of Appeals, which must hear all appeals brought to it, the State Supreme Court, like the U.S. Supreme Court, has the power to choose which cases it will accept for appeal. This power is referred to as *certiorari*.

CERTIORARI

State Supreme Courts have the right to decide which cases they will hear. All litigants must pass an administrative hurdle before the court will consider the case. This hurdle is **certiorari**. *Certiorari* is almost universally referred to as cert, not only because the word itself is difficult to pronounce, but also because appellate courts commonly abbreviate the term that way in reporting decisions, as in "petition for cert. denied."

Certiorari (cert)
Latin, "To make sure;" a court's authority to decide which cases it will hear on appeal and which it will not.

State Supreme Courts mirror the U.S. Supreme Court in that they all have the power to grant or deny cert, and in the vast majority of cases that petition for cert, the Court refuses to grant it. Ninety-five percent or more of the cases that apply for cert in both the state and U.S. Supreme Courts are denied.

Standards Used to Determine Granting Cert. A **petition for cert** is filed by the party wishing the court to hear the appeal and sets out why this case is important. To be granted cert, a party must show that the case involves a matter that falls into one or more of the following categories:

Petition for cert
A petition filed by a party on appeal requesting a court to consider its appeal and grant cert.

- There is a conflict among the courts about how a statute has been interpreted.
- The case involves an interpretation of the U.S. Constitution.
- One state has ruled a particular action legal, whereas another has ruled it illegal.
- The case involves issues of national importance.

Nowhere on the list of issues to be considered in granting cert is a discussion of why the case is important to the individual parties. That is not one of the considerations that courts use in deciding whether to grant cert. The U.S. Supreme Court, like state supreme courts, does not grant cert simply because the case has vital importance to the defendant or the state in an individual prosecution. In fact, the case must present issues that are important to the community at large, not just the litigants, for the court to grant cert.

The U.S. Supreme Court follows the "rule of four" in deciding whether or not to grant cert. If four out of the nine justices believe that cert should be granted, then the case will be heard. If that minimum is not reached, then the case is denied cert and the decision in the most recent appeal stands as the final decision.

Granting Cert. When the State Supreme Court grants cert, it means that the court has agreed to hear the case. The appeal will now proceed in an almost identical fashion as it followed in the State Court of Appeals. The parties will submit written briefs and again ask the court to rule in their favor. However, there are some important differences between the State Court of Appeals and the State Supreme Court. For one thing, **oral argument** is more common. The justices of the State Supreme Court, like those who serve on the U.S. Supreme Court, may wish to question the litigants in person, and the only way to do that is through oral argument before the court. Although oral argument is not that frequent, it does pose a special challenge to the litigants. During the oral argument, the attorneys for both sides will present their reasoning for why they should win the case. They present their case before the panel of justices, which can be as many as nine if the parties appear before the U.S. Supreme Court. The justices are free to interrupt the proceedings at any point and ask questions of the attorneys.

Oral argument
A presentation of an appeal done orally before a panel of judges or justices.

It is important to note that the decision to grant cert has no bearing on the court's ultimate decision. A court might grant cert to a party and then rule against him or her. A grant of cert simply authorizes the continuation of the appeal. The Court is free to rule any way that it sees fit once it considers the merits of the case.

Denial of Cert. When the State Supreme Court denies cert, it means that the Court has refused to hear the appeal. At this point, the appellate process is essentially over. The appellant can file a motion for rehearing requesting the Court to reconsider its ruling, but that is highly unlikely. If the party has been denied cert before the State Supreme Court, then he or she has one more option: the U.S. Supreme Court. Appeals from State Supreme Courts go to the U.S. Supreme Court. However, if the State Supreme Court has denied cert, it is unlikely that the U.S. Supreme Court will grant it.

D. THE POWERS OF THE APPELLATE COURTS

Appellate courts can only review the record of the case on appeal. No witnesses testify before the Court of Appeals or Supreme Court. An appeal is not a new trial. Appeals consist of a review of the record and then an in-depth examination of applicable case law. An appellate court reviews the actions of a lower court to determine if the court has committed reversible error. If the court finds no error, then no action is taken. Appellate courts are important because they evaluate the precedents in law and explain, enlarge, or reverse those precedents. Occasionally, an appellate court, especially one as important as the U.S. Supreme Court, may come out with an interpretation of law that creates entirely new procedures. Consider the earlier discussion of the *Miranda* rights as only one of many such examples. Although some people are tempted to think that appellate courts have enormous power, their authority is actually limited. There are only a few actions that an appellate court may take. Essentially, an appellate court can only take some combination of the following actions:

- **Affirm**
- **Reverse**
- **Remand**

When an appellate court affirms a decision, it enters a judgment in favor of the finding in the lower court. Whatever the decision may have been in that lower court, a higher court's finding that it affirms that decision will leave the previous decision in place.

However, the opposite occurs when a court reverses a decision. An appellate court issues a reversal when it finds that some improper action occurred in the trial court or when the higher court simply disagrees with the reasoning of a lower court. When a case has been reversed, the defendant's conviction is also overturned. This is not quite the great news for a defendant that one might think. When a case has been reversed it means that the state is free to retry the defendant. This is not a violation of the Fifth Amendment's prohibition against double jeopardy because the appellate court has vacated the defendant's conviction. The court's decision means that the original trial had no legal meaning. Under these circumstances, the government is free to bring the case all over again. There are even rare instances where a case has been tried several times. In the original case, the defendant was found guilty and appealed. The appellate court reversed and the state retried the defendant. Again, the defendant appealed and again the appellate court reversed. At this point, most prosecutors would move on to another case, but the state is technically free to bring the case again. In one case, a defendant was tried six times.[1]

There are occasions when an appellate court requires additional information on a case. In such a situation, it orders a remand. The court is not in a position to make a ruling without this additional information and because appellate courts do not hear witness testimony or consider new evidence, the case is sent back to the trial court. The appellate court directs the trial court to hold a hearing, take specific testimony or consider some evidence, transcribe the hearing, and then send the material back to the appellate court. This is the substance of a remand.

E. *HABEAS CORPUS*

Although an appeal essentially ends when a higher court refuses to grant cert, there is one other avenue of appeal open to a person convicted of a crime: ***habeas corpus***. A habeas petition is an appeal that goes through the federal court system, regardless of where the original prosecution occurred. A defendant files a writ of *habeas corpus* under the authority of the U.S. Constitution. The Constitution requires that a criminal defendant must be held for reasonable grounds and the writ of habeas requires the government to prove that the defendant is being held for valid reasons. Although not originally designed to give a criminal defendant a second round of appeals, many criminal convictions are now routinely appealed using *habeas corpus*. In fact, a current issue is whether or not terrorists taken on the field of battle or seized overseas enjoy this right in the

Affirm
When a higher court declares that a lower court's action was valid and right.

Reverse
Set aside; when an appellate court decides that the actions of a lower court were incorrect.

Remand
Send back. For example, when a higher court requires additional information about a case, it returns it to the trial court.

Sidebar

When the defendant loses at trial, he or she is permitted to appeal the conviction to a higher court.

Habeas corpus
Latin, "You have the body;" A judicial order to a prison system ordering that the incarcerated person be brought to court for a hearing; a constitutional mechanism that allows convicts to challenge their sentences.

U.S. court system. An action for *habeas corpus* is based on centuries of legal tradition, extending back through the English system, and this is an integral part of the U.S. court system.

In a *habeas corpus* action a criminal defendant requests the federal court system to remove the defendant from a state prison system based on some alleged unconstitutional action that occurred in the trial. Because a habeas corpus action is brought in federal court, it will follow the federal appellate court system on subsequent rulings. For instance, once filed in U.S. District Court, it would then move up to the U.S. Circuit Court of Appeals for that part of the country. It is even possible that a case that began in the state trial court and was eventually denied cert by the U.S. Supreme Court might find itself at the Court again, this time following a habeas appeal.

Considering the time periods involved in bringing a standard state-based appeal and then factoring in the additional time necessary to bring a habeas petition, it is easy to see how various criminal appeals in a single case can last for more than a decade. That is especially true in death penalty cases.

 ## ORGANIZATION OF THE APPELLATE SYSTEM

The court system in the states has often been described as having a pyramid structure, with the highest court at the top and the lowest courts, the trial courts, at the bottom. The federal appellate system is organized in almost the same way. However, instead of covering a single state, the federal system covers the entire nation. Because of the size of the United States, the country has been divided up into different circuits, with one circuit encompassing several states. Appeals from federal trial courts (called Federal District Courts) are brought to the Federal Circuit Court of Appeals that has jurisdiction over those states. These courts are situated in a major city in one of the states inside that federal circuit.

The federal court system is also arranged as a pyramid, with federal trial courts at the bottom, Federal Circuit Courts of Appeal in the middle, and the U.S. Supreme Court at the top.

A. THE U.S. SUPREME COURT

Like a State Supreme Court, the U.S. Supreme Court has the final say about interpretations of the U.S. Constitution, case law, or statutes. In the United States, there is no court higher than the U.S. Supreme Court. Composed of eight associate justices and one chief justice, the U.S. Supreme Court routinely makes rulings in cases that have national, and sometimes international, impact.

B. THE U.S. SUPREME COURT IS THE FINAL AUTHORITY FOR BOTH FEDERAL AND STATE COURTS

Along with its role as the final arbiter of federal questions, the U.S. Supreme Court has an additional responsibility: It is the court of last resort for all state law questions as well. When a party loses in a State Supreme Court, the only remaining option is to file a petition for cert with the U.S. Supreme Court. State court litigants are not required to start at the bottom of the federal court system and work up. Instead, they go directly from the State Supreme Court to the U.S. Supreme Court. However, in cases in which a State Supreme Court has denied cert because a case lacks sufficient importance, it is highly unlikely that the U.S. Supreme Court would grant cert.

COMMONWEALTH v. O'BRIEN
——— PA. ——— (2019)

CASE EXCERPT

MEMORANDUM BY KUNSELMAN, J.:

Tammy Carley O'Brien appeals pro se from the judgment of sentence imposed following her conviction of operating a motor vehicle without a proper driver's license. See 75 Pa.C.S.A. §1501(a). We affirm.

The relevant factual and procedural history is as follows. On June 15, 2018, Pennsylvania State Police Trooper Patrick Quinn was conducting routine duties as part of a roving detail for the enforcement of driving under the influence laws when he ran a random plate inquiry on a silver Honda Accord. The information in the system indicated that the vehicle had recently been stopped, and a citation had been issued to the operator for driving without a license. Trooper Quinn testified that the description of the individual who had previously been issued a citation for driving without a license matched the profile of the person Trooper Quinn observed operating the vehicle. Thus, the trooper, suspecting that the vehicle was being operated by the same individual, initiated a traffic stop. During the traffic stop, Trooper Quinn requested O'Brien to produce a driver's license. In response, O'Brien initially stated that she forgot it, but then admitted that she did not have a valid driver's license. The trooper then issued her a traffic citation for operating a motor vehicle without a proper driver's license pursuant to section 1501(a).

O'Brien contested the citation, and on August 16, 2018, a magistrate district judge found her guilty of driving without a license. O'Brien filed a timely summary appeal to the Court of Common Pleas of Pike County. On December 12, 2018, the trial court conducted a de novo trial, after which it convicted O'Brien of the summary offense. O'Brien then filed a timely notice of appeal to this Court. The trial court ordered her to file a concise statement of matters complained of on appeal pursuant to Pa.R.A.P. 1925(b). In response, O'Brien filed a "Summary of the Argument." The trial court thereafter filed an opinion pursuant to Pa.R.A.P. 1925(a).

O'Brien raises one issue for our review: "The traffic stop which resulted in a claimed summary offense was not constitutionally justified." Appellant's Brief at 2.

Preliminarily, we note that appellate briefs must materially conform to the requirements of the Pennsylvania Rules of Appellate Procedure. See Pa.R.A.P. 2101. This Court may quash or dismiss an appeal if the appellant fails to conform to the requirements set forth in our appellate rules. Id.; see also *Commonwealth v. Lyons*, 833 A.2d 245 (Pa. Super. 2003). Although this Court is willing to liberally construe materials filed by a pro se litigant, pro se status confers no special benefit upon the appellant. Lyons, 833 A.2d at 252. To the contrary, any person choosing to represent himself in a legal proceeding must, to a reasonable extent, assume that his lack of expertise and legal training will be his undoing. *Commonwealth v. Rivera*, 685 A.2d 1011, 1013 (Pa. Super. 1996).

The Pennsylvania Rules of Appellate Procedure provide guidelines regarding the required content of an appellate brief. See Pa.R.A.P. 2111. Additionally, Rules 2114 through 2119 specify in greater detail the material to be included in briefs on appeal. Instantly, O'Brien's brief falls short of these standards. It does not include a statement of jurisdiction. While O'Brien's brief purports to include a statement of the case, it fails to comply in any respect with our procedural rules. O'Brien's brief appears to be based almost entirely on facts not in evidence; indeed, she makes only one reference to the certified record.

Moreover, whereas O'Brien's brief raises a variety of constitutional claims under the First, Fourth, Fifth, Sixth, Eighth, Ninth, and Fourteenth Amendments, the certified record reveals that she raised only one constitutional challenge before the trial court, namely a Fourth Amendment challenge to the legality of the traffic stop. See Pa.R.A.P. 302 ("Issues not raised in the lower court are waived and cannot be raised for the first time on appeal"). Further, in her concise statement, the sole constitutional challenge that O'Brien raised was whether Trooper Quinn was justified in stopping her vehicle under the Fourth Amendment. See Pa.R.A.P. 1925(b)(3)(vii) (providing that "issues not included in the Statement . . . are waived"). Thus, her additional constitutional claims are waived.

Finally, regarding her sole preserved issue, O'Brien neither identifies controlling Pennsylvania legal precedent, nor explains why the Fourth Amendment entitles her to relief. See Pa.R.A.P. 2119(a) (stating that the parties' briefs must include a discussion of each question raised on appeal and a "citation of authorities as are deemed pertinent"). In this Commonwealth, appellate arguments which are not supported by discussion and analysis of pertinent authority are waived. As O'Brien's argument fails to identify, let alone discuss, the case law relevant to her legal claim, or how the Fourth Amendment entitles her to relief, we deem her claim waived.

Judgment of sentence affirmed.

CASE QUESTIONS

1 What was the reason for stopping the defendant in the first place?
2 What did the court say about the defendant's brief, prepared by herself, pro se?
3 In what ways did the defendant's brief fail to meet the standards?
4 Despite the fact that her brief was poorly written, did the defendant present any issues for the court to rule upon?
5 The court notes that the only defense that the defendant raised adequately was a Fourth Amendment objection to the stop. How did the court rule on this issue?

CHAPTER SUMMARY

The subject of this chapter is criminal appeals. When a defendant has been found guilty, he is allowed to appeal that conviction. The first step in bringing a criminal appeal is to file a motion for a new trial. This motion alleges that some errors occurred during the trial and that the only reasonable remedy is to grant the defendant a new trial on the same charges. The vast majority of these motions are denied and the denial forms the basis for the appeal. When a defendant files a notice of appeal in the appellate courts, he or she must show that the appellate court has jurisdiction to hear the case. Usually, the defendant will allege that something occurred during the trial that caused an infraction of his or her constitutionally guaranteed rights. To bring an appeal, the party must show that the trial court committed reversible error. This means that the trial court error was so severe that the only remedy is to reverse the defendant's conviction or to grant him or her a new trial.

When the parties appeal a case, many terms and phrases change. The parties, formerly referred to as the government versus the defendant, are now changed. The defendant becomes the appellant, and the government becomes the appellee. To bring an appeal, the appellant must file a written brief. A brief contains allegations of error that occurred in the trial. Appellate briefs have a standardized format consisting of a title page, statement of facts, enumerations of error, argument, and a conclusion. Both the appellant and the appellee are permitted to file briefs.

If either party loses in the appellate court, the party can appeal to a higher court. However, many higher courts have a barrier that must be overcome before the court will consider an appeal. This barrier is referred to as cert. For an appellate court to grant cert, the party must show that the case involves an interpretation of the Constitution, some conflict among the courts, or some other important legal issue. If the higher court grants cert it does not mean that the party wins. Instead, a grant of cert means that the higher court will hear the appeal. Denial of cert leaves in place the last appellate decision, whatever it might have been.

KEY TERMS AND CONCEPTS

Appeal	Brief	Affirm
Motion for new trial	Reversible error	Reverse
Notice of appeal	Statement of facts	Remand
Record	Enumerations of error	*Habeas Corpus*
Docket number	*Certiorari* (cert)	
Appellant	Petition for cert	
Appellee	Oral argument	

END OF CHAPTER EXERCISES

Review Questions

See Appendix A for answers

1 Explain the organization of the appellate court system.
2 What is the difference between affirming a decision and reversing one?
3 Explain the purpose of a motion for new trial.
4 What guidelines does a court follow in deciding to grant cert?
5 What is reversible error?
6 What is a remand?
7 Explain the purpose of *habeas corpus.*
8 Why does it normally take so long to appeal a criminal case?
9 What is oral argument?
10 Does a grant of cert mean that a party has won the appeal? Why or why not?

Web Surfing

1 Do a search to locate your state in the broader circuits of the U.S. Courts of Appeal system.

2 For example, the U.S. Court of Appeals for the Eleventh Circuit can be found at http://www.ca11.uscourts.gov/.

3 A map of the Federal Circuit Courts of Appeal, can be found in several places, including the U.S. Courts website: https://www.uscourts.gov/about-federal-courts/court-role-and-structure.

4 Locate your state's appeals courts by doing a web search.

Questions for Analysis

1 Given the fact that many criminal appeals take years to complete, is there a better way to organize the system? If you were suddenly granted the power to change the system, how would you do it, keeping in mind that people under sentence have specific constitutional protections?

2 There are some who argue that algorithms that have been developed for sentencing could also be applied to appeals. Given the formulaic way that briefs are prepared, is there a case to be made for turning the more routine appeals over to a computer system?

Hypotheticals

1 Brandy has been convicted of possession of methamphetamine and other narcotics. She writes a brief in the form of a poem. The poem contains all of the elements of a traditional brief, but in unusual places and nontraditional

presentations. Should her brief be immediately dismissed because it isn't presented in the required way or should the court review it anyway?

2   Toni was convicted of driving under the influence of alcohol. He is currently serving a sentence on probation, which includes the provisions that he obtain gainful employment, avoid narcotics and alcohol, and regularly visit his probation officer. Toni files an appeal and in the statement of facts freely admits that he was under the influence of alcohol as he prepared it. Should the brief be dismissed because Toni has admittedly violated the terms of his probation while writing his brief?

PRACTICE QUESTIONS FOR TEST REVIEW

See Appendix A for answers

Essay Question

What are the minimum requirements of a brief? List and explain each.

True-False

1   **T   F**   When an appellate court agrees with the lower court's determination, it issues a reversal.

2   **T   F**   Appellate courts are authorized to send a case back to the trial court for hearings on specific issues.

3   **T   F**   Appellate courts can dismiss a brief that does not meet the minimum requirements set out in the appellate rules.

Fill in the Blank

1   The power of a court to render a decision on issues and to impose that decision on the parties in the case is called ____.

2   The evidence, pleadings, motions, transcript of the trial, and any other documents relevant to the case are known as the ____.

3   The ____ is the party bringing the current appeal from an adverse ruling in a lower court.

Multiple Choice

1   The official docketing and commencement of the appeals process.

   A   Commencement.
   B   Notice of appeal.
   C   Review.
   D   Supervision.

2   The party who won in the lower court.

   A   Defendant.
   B   Appellee.
   C   Appellant.
   D   Plaintiff.

3   A mistake made by a judge in the procedures used at trial, or in making a
    legal ruling during the trial.

   A   Reversal.
   B   Reversible error.
   C   Mistake.
   D   Cert.

ENDNOTE

1. https://www.nbcnews.com/news/crime-courts/prosecutor-recuses-himself-case-curtis-flowers-tried-six-times-same-n1111611, downloaded on March 11, 2020.

Answers to Review Questions and Practice Questions for Test Review

CHAPTER 1. CRIMINAL LAW AND THE U.S. CONSTITUTION

Review Questions

1 **What is the Supremacy Clause?**

The Supremacy Clause is a provision of the U.S. Constitution that provides that federal law always takes precedence over state law.

2 **Explain statutory law.**

Statutory law refers to laws that have been voted on by the legislature and enacted by the executive branch.

3 **What are ordinances?**

Ordinances are rules and regulations that are promulgated by towns and municipalities to govern issues such as health, noise, and pollution.

4 **Explain case law and its significance.**

Case law is significant because appellate courts apply statutory law to the facts of individual cases and help to explain how the law applies.

5 **Are federal and state agencies able to create their own rules and regulations? Explain.**

Yes, federal and state agencies are able to create their own rules and regulations as a part of their police power inherent in the U.S. Constitution.

6   **What is the common law?**

Common law is the ancient principle of law that existed prior to written or statutory law. Common law consisted of rules and guidelines to assist judges in helping to decide their cases.

7   **Provide an example of a common law rule.**

One example of common law is the ancient expression that "possession is 9/10ths of the law." Under this theory, when a stolen item cannot be clearly identified, the person who possesses the item is allowed to keep it.

8   **What is the function of the judge?**

The judge has several functions: He or she maintains order in the courtroom, interprets the law, and rules on objections raised by counsel. Judges are also frequently called on to sentence defendants who have been found guilty.

9   **What is the role of a defense attorney?**

The defense attorney is responsible for zealously representing the interests of his or her client: the criminal defendant.

10   **How do federal prosecutions differ from state prosecutions?**

One important difference between federal and state prosecutions is that there are many more state prosecutions than federal prosecutions. This is explained by the simple fact that there are 50 states with 50 different sets of criminal statutes. Another important difference between federal prosecutions and state prosecutions is that the federal system is one of limited jurisdiction, whereas state law is general jurisdiction.

11   **Explain "jurisdiction."**

The term jurisdiction refers to the power of the court to make rulings on issues and individuals who appear before the court.

12   **Provide a brief description of the organization of the federal court system.**

The federal court system is arranged in a series of layers with the U.S. Supreme Court at the very top. In the middle are the various federal circuit courts of appeal and below that level are the trial courts of the federal system, known as federal district courts.

13   **What is the name of the highest court in United States?**

The name of the highest court in the United States is the U.S. Supreme Court.

PRACTICE QUESTIONS FOR TEST REVIEW

Essay Question

Explain the concept of *stare decisis*.

Stare decisis is a principle that underlies the entire U.S. judicial system. The idea is simple: Similar cases with similar facts will have similar outcomes as previously decided cases. Also known as the rule of precedent, the system guarantees that the court system remains somewhat predictable and that the various participants can have some idea of why a court reached a particular decision

True-False

1 True
2 True
3 False

Fill in the Blank

1 a statute
2 case law
3 *stare decisis*

Multiple Choice

1 A
2 D
3 D

CHAPTER 2. INTRODUCTION TO THE CRIMINAL JUSTICE SYSTEM

Review Questions

1 **What is the difference between a verdict of guilty and a verdict of liability?**

A guilty verdict means that a jury has found the defendant responsible for committing a crime. After that verdict, the defendant can be sentenced to jail time, a fine, or both. A finding of liability is the jury's determination in a civil case that one of the parties must pay monetary damages to the other.

2   **What is a verdict?**

A jury's verdict is its finding of what the facts in the case are and who is responsible for causing the harm in the case.

3   **What four verdicts are available in criminal trials?**

Jurors in a criminal case can vote that the defendant is not guilty, guilty, guilty but mentally ill, or not guilty by reason of insanity.

4   **What is the burden of proof?**

When a person brings a civil case, the burden on the plaintiff is to prove the allegations raised in the pleadings. Similarly, a prosecutor must prove the allegations in the charging documents against the defendant beyond a reasonable doubt.

5   **Explain preponderance of the evidence.**

This is the standard of proof used in civil cases and it means that the plaintiff must prove that his or her case is more likely to be true than not.

6   **Explain proof beyond a reasonable doubt.**

Although difficult to quantify, a reasonable doubt refers to the type of doubt that a person would have that might prevent him or her from making a major life decision.

7   **What is the style of a case?**

The style is the caption of a case and lists the names and identities of the parties.

8   **How does the style of a criminal case compare to that of a civil case?**

The style in a criminal case lists the government versus a defendant. In a civil case, the parties are the plaintiff versus the defendant.

9   **What is an indictment?**

An indictment is an official document that charges a defendant with a felony.

10   **Explain the difference between felonies and misdemeanors.**

A felony is a crime punishable by more than one year in custody and often a substantial fine. A misdemeanor is a less serious crime, punishable by less than a year in custody.

11   **What is the definition of arrest?**

The definition of arrest is when a reasonable third party would believe that the suspect was no longer free to leave.

12   Explain probable cause.

Probable cause is a reasonable belief that a crime has occurred or is about to occur.

13   Explain *Miranda* warnings.

These are the oral or written warnings that the police must provide to suspects before they are questioned after they have been put into custody.

14   What is the difference between an initial appearance hearing and a preliminary hearing?

An initial appearance hearing is the first time that a defendant is brought before a judge and the primary reason for the hearing is to identify the defendant and to see if the defendant needs an attorney to represent him or her. A preliminary hearing is a hearing where a magistrate judge presides. A prosecutor is present and presents testimony from witnesses to provide sufficient probable cause for the magistrate to believe that the defendant committed the crime and that the case should continue.

15   What is the purpose of the grand jury?

The purpose of the grand jury is to act as a buffer between the state and the individual defendant. The grand jury is empowered to hear the basics of the case and to vote on whether or not the case against the defendant should continue.

16   What is an arraignment?

An arraignment is a court proceeding where the defendant is advised of the charges against him or her, provided with discovery, and given a chance to enter a plea of not guilty or guilty.

17   Explain the difference between prison and probation.

If a defendant is sentenced to prison, he or she will serve time incarcerated in a facility provided by the state. A probationary sentence allows the defendant to live in the community, but he or she must regularly report to the probation officer assigned to his or her case verifying that he or she is employed and not engaging in criminal activity.

PRACTICE QUESTIONS FOR TEST REVIEW

Essay Question

What are three important differences between civil and criminal law?

Criminal and civil law are different on many levels. A civil case is brought by an individual who files a complaint alleging that the defendant committed a civil injury against him or her that justifies the payment of damages. A criminal case begins with an arrest and is prosecuted by an attorney who works for the government. That attorney assembles a case and attempts to prove, beyond a reasonable doubt, that the defendant committed the crime.

True-False

1 True
2 False
3 False

Fill in the Blank

1 indictment
2 verdict
3 damages

Multiple Choice

1 D
2 A
3 A

CHAPTER 3. FOURTH AMENDMENT: STOP AND FRISK AND OTHER DETENTIONS

Review Questions

1 **Is a person who has been asked a question by a police officer during a voluntary encounter obliged to remain in position and answer the question? Why?**

   No, during a voluntary encounter, a person is free to leave and can refuse to answer any questions. A voluntary encounter is not a detention.

2 **What is a *Terry* stop?**

   During a *Terry* stop, police are allowed to ask more invasive questions and to prevent a person from leaving, but this detention does not amount to an arrest.

3 **How would you define reasonable suspicion?**

   Reasonable suspicion consists of specific, articulable facts that a police officer can point to that gave rise to the conclusion that a crime was committed or was about to be committed.

4   **Prior to the decision in *Terry v. Ohio*, what were the two types of interactions permitted between police and individuals?**

Before *Terry,* police could engage in voluntary encounters and full-blown arrests.

5   **In a *Terry* stop, police may detain an individual for a brief period of time. How brief is brief?**

Case law has never addressed specific time periods. The courts consider the time periods on a case-by-case basis.

6   **The *Terry* case authorized a pat down and frisk. Why?**

The idea behind pat down and frisk is that when a police officer briefly detains a suspect, there is a greater chance that violence might ensue. The only way to minimize the potential for violence is to allow police officers to pat down the suspect and remove any weapons that they find.

7   **What is a stop and frisk?**

Police are allowed, while questioning a suspect, to pat him or her down for weapons to protect the officers' safety.

8   **During a stop and frisk, what rules are the police obliged to follow?**

During the frisk, an officer is allowed to pat down the person's outer clothing. If the officer feels something that might be a weapon, he or she is authorized to take it out of the person's clothing.

9   **What is the scope of a stop and frisk?**

The officer is only allowed to check for weapons. It is not to be used as a way of avoiding Fourth Amendment requirements of probable cause to search.

10   **How have stop and frisk policies been abused in some areas of the country?**

Some urban areas have used stop and frisk extensively as a way of lowering crime rates, resulting in claims that the police have disproportionately targeted dark-skinned races over those with lighter skin.

PRACTICE QUESTIONS FOR TEST REVIEW

Essay Question

Explain *Terry* stops.

In *Terry v. Ohio,* 392 U.S. 1, 27 (1968), the Supreme Court held that there was a middle ground between voluntary interactions and full-blown arrests. This category became known as the brief detention and nicknamed the *Terry* stop for the case where it was first implemented. Under *Terry,* police may detain a person when they have reasonable suspicion that a crime has occurred. Appellate courts have specifically held that, "If, from the totality of the circumstances, a law enforcement officer reasonably suspects that criminal activity may be afoot, the officer may temporarily detain a person."

True-False

1 False
2 False
3 True

Fill in the Blank

1 a *Terry* stop
2 stop and frisk
3 contraband

Multiple Choice

1 D
2 A
3 A

CHAPTER 4. FOURTH AMENDMENT: PROBABLE CAUSE AND ARREST

Review Questions

1 **This chapter mentions that there is a preference for warrants, but that courts give police officers greater latitude to arrest without a warrant. Explain this difference.**

Police officers must routinely work with human beings who are unpredictable and can be dangerous. Search warrants are generally issued for homes and other structures that are immobile and therefore there is no time constraint or safety issue involved to wait to obtain the warrant.

2 **What purpose does an affidavit serve in a warrant application?**

An affidavit is required of a police officer for him or her to swear that the facts contained in the warrant application are true and to therefore give a magistrate the basis for issuing the warrant in the first place.

3   **Who is authorized to make an arrest once an arrest warrant has been issued?**

Police officers are the only individuals who are authorized to make arrests once an arrest warrant has been issued.

4   **What is the "Four Corners" test?**

In the "Four Corners" test, a magistrate's decision must be based on the material presented within the four corners of the application and affidavit. The affidavit and accompanying sworn testimony must be sufficient on its face to authorize the magistrate to issue the warrant.

5   **Explain probable cause.**

Probable cause is the reasonable belief that a crime has occurred or is about to occur.

6   **Can probable cause be based on gut feelings or hunches? Explain your answer.**

An officer may well have a feeling that a particular person has committed an offense, but until he or she can present some proof to substantiate it, that feeling cannot form the basis for probable cause, and any arrest based on a hunch will be ruled unconstitutional.

7   **What degree of proof is required to establish probable cause?**

Police officers are not required to establish that a suspect is guilty of a crime beyond a reasonable doubt. They must independently verify facts related to them before they will have sufficient probable cause to make an arrest.

8   **List specific types of acts that can create probable cause.**

Probable cause can be based on the officer's personal observations, descriptions provided to them over the radio, or a tip provided by a reliable confidential informant.

9   **What rules must be in effect for sobriety checkpoints?**

Police must determine how they will stop cars before they set up the roadblock and then follow that procedure during the roadblock. If they have determined that they will stop every car, then they must follow that procedure.

10   **What is a pretextual stop?**

Police officers are authorized to stop motor vehicles, even if the reason that they are doing so is something other than a traffic violation.

11   **Does flight rise to probable cause? Explain your answer.**

Courts have ruled that flight gives the officers probable cause to arrest. When a person flees from the police, they have the right to detain that person.

12 What is the legal test to determine if a person is under arrest?

The legal test is whether a reasonable person, viewing the actions of the police, would believe that the suspect was not free to leave.

13 What rights are afforded to a person who is under arrest?

A person who is under arrest has the right to an attorney, the right to petition for bond, the right to be told about the charges against him or her, and the right to remain silent, among many others.

14 Which persons are authorized to carry out an arrest?

Certified police officers are authorized to carry out arrests.

15 What is a citizen's arrest?

Citizens, or anyone else, can detain a person who has committed a crime and then hand that person over to the police, but citizens do not make arrests.

16 Explain venue.

Venue refers to the particular geographic area where a court or an official can exercise power; an example of venue would be the county's borders.

17 What is the fresh pursuit doctrine?

The fresh pursuit doctrine is a court-created rule that allows police officers to arrest suspects without warrants and to cross territorial boundaries while they are still pursuing the suspect.

18 Why is it important to determine the precise point at which a person is placed under arrest?

Determining the precise point when a person is considered to be under arrest has important constitutional law consequences. At that moment, the person has additional constitutional protections that must be recognized by the police.

PRACTICE QUESTIONS FOR TEST REVIEW

Essay Question

What is probable cause and why is it required?

Probable cause is the reasonable belief that a crime has occurred or is about to occur. The Fourth Amendment requires probable cause before police can arrest or seize evidence of a crime. Probable cause must also support search warrants.

True-False

1 False
2 True
3 True

Fill in the Blank

1 probable cause
2 a pretextual stop
3 venue

Multiple Choice

1 D
2 C
3 B

CHAPTER 5. FOURTH AMENDMENT: SEARCH AND SEIZURE

Review Questions

1 What is the expectation of privacy?

The Constitutional standard that a court must determine before issuing a search warrant. If an area has a high expectation of privacy, then a warrant will be required; if low or nonexistent, then no warrant is required.

2 Why do courts have a preference for search warrants?

Courts have a preference for search warrants because items to be searched can be observed and do not move; people, on the other hand, are mobile.

3 Explain the plain view exception to the search warrant requirement.

If an officer has a legitimate reason for being where he or she is, if he or she observes evidence of a crime, then he or she can seize it because it is in plain view.

4 Compare and contrast abandoned property and dropped evidence rules regarding search warrant requirements.

The U.S. Supreme Court held that there is no privacy expectation in garbage. When police officers are chasing a fleeing suspect and he or she drops or throws away some evidence, police do not have to obtain a search warrant to seize it. The suspect has surrendered any property rights to the evidence.

5 What is contraband?

Contraband is anything that is illegal to possess at any time, such as child pornography, narcotics, and some types of automatic weapons.

6 What are exigent circumstances?

An exigent circumstance is some kind of emergency that threatens the lives of people or the existence of evidence. Police are not required to obtain a search warrant if they can show that an emergency (exigent) circumstance existed.

7 What are general searches and why are they specifically prohibited by the U.S. Constitution?

The framers of the U.S. Constitution had had some experience with general searches authorized under British law and they wanted to make sure that no such search would be carried out in the United States.

8 Under what circumstances may a search warrant grow stale?

A warrant becomes stale when the circumstances originally involved in issuing it have changed substantially.

9 Provide an example of a vague warrant.

A warrant authorizing the seizure of "all suspected items" would be vague to the point of absurdity.

10 Why are canine police officers exempt from needing a search warrant?

The U.S. Supreme Court has stated that the use of specially trained dogs to detect narcotics, explosives, or other items does not fall within the protections of the Fourth Amendment. There is, according to the court, no expectation of privacy in air.

PRACTICE QUESTIONS FOR TEST REVIEW

Essay Question

List and explain at least three exceptions to the general rule that all searches must be carried out with a warrant.

Searches can be conducted without a warrant when the facts fit within specific categories, such as open fields, plain view, and dropped evidence. Courts have ruled that people do not have an expectation of privacy in their fields and therefore police do not require a search warrant to search them. In the case of plain view, if a police officer has a legitimate reason to be in the location where he or she is and then sees evidence of a crime, he or she is not required to obtain a search warrant before seizing the evidence. Finally, a fleeing suspect who drops evidence relinquishes any proprietary interests in property and therefore it has no expectation of privacy.

True-False

1 True
2 False
3 True

Fill in the Blank

1 open fields doctrine
2 search warrant
3 expectation of privacy

Multiple Choice

1 C
2 D
3 D

CHAPTER 6. CONSTITUTIONAL ISSUES IN THE USE OF EVIDENCE

1 **What is the reason that polygraph tests are not admissible as evidence in a criminal trial?**

Because it has been shown that polygraph tests are not reliable and that some individuals have discovered ways of beating them, the tests are not considered to be scientifically valid and therefore not admissible.

2 **What is DNA?**

DNA is composed of two strands of molecules arranged in the now famous double helix configuration. The human genetic code, which contains all of the information required to develop a human being from a single cell, consists of 3 billion base pairs, all of it contained in DNA.

3 **Can a grand jury consider hearsay testimony? Explain your answer.**

Because a grand jury hearing is not an adversarial hearing, grand jurors can rely on evidence that would not normally be admissible in a regular trial.

4   What is the *Miller* test and how does it apply to obscenity prosecutions?

The *Miller* test was developed in the case of *U.S. v. Miller,* where the U.S. Supreme Court came up with a test to evaluate potential obscenity cases. The test consists of three questions: (1) whether the average person, applying "contemporary community standards," would find that the work, taken as a whole, appeals to prurient interest; (2) whether the work displays or describes, in a patently offense way, sexual contact specifically defined by a state statute; and (3) whether the work, again taken as a whole, lacks serious literary, artistic, political, or scientific value.

5   What is incitement to riot and what important U.S. Supreme Court case put limitations on the prosecution of this offense?

Incitement to riot consists of encouraging others to engage in violent or destructive behavior. In the case of *Brandenburg v. Ohio,* 89 S.Ct. 1827 (1969) the court created the "imminent lawless action test." Under this test, police may arrest individuals for incitement to riot when they can show that: (1) the defendants are actively advocating behavior that is likely to produce imminent lawless action, and (2) the defendants' actions are likely to incite or produce imminent lawless action.

6   What is the exclusionary rule?

The exclusionary rule holds that if the police violate the Fourth Amendment in obtaining evidence, then they are barred from using it.

7   Which amendment to the U.S. Constitution guarantees the right to an attorney at trial?

The Sixth Amendment makes this guarantee.

8   What is a lineup?

A lineup is a group of persons, placed side by side in a line, shown to a witness of a crime to see if the witness will identify the person suspected of committing the crime.

9   What is a show-up?

A show-up is a pretrial identification procedure in which only one suspect and a witness are brought together.

10   Explain the right to confront witnesses.

The right of a criminal defendant to confront witnesses and also to cross-examine them is considered to be one of the fundamental rights guaranteed by the U.S. Constitution. Without the ability to confront witnesses and ask them questions, there can be no due process.

11   **Is eyewitness testimony reliable? Explain your answer.**

There are studies that indicate that eyewitness testimony is not as reliable as people are prone to think.

12   **Is child pornography different than pornography? How?**

Pornography refers to graphic depictions of sex. Child pornography refers to any depiction of children engaging in sexual activity. Pornography may or may not be illegal, depending on what is depicted. Child pornography is always illegal.

13   **Is a judge permitted to close an entire trial to the public? Explain.**

A judge can close a portion of a trial to the public, such as when a sensitive witness testifies, but a judge is prohibited from closing an entire trial to the public.

14   **What are photographic lineups?**

Because physical lineups are difficult to stage, police officers often create photographic lineups. When a photographic lineup is presented to a witness, the photos are often taped to a file folder and numbered. Like a live lineup, no names are provided. The witness must pick out the suspect from the photographs.

15   **Compare and contrast DNA and fingerprints.**

DNA and fingerprints are both unique to individuals, with the one exception that identical twins share the same DNA but do not have the same fingerprints. Both are valuable tools to indicate that a person was in a particular location.

Essay Question

Explain the *Miller* test.

The *Miller* test was created in *U.S. v. Miller*. It was supposed to assist prosecutors and defense attorneys in being able to define what is obscenity and when a person can be prosecuted for possessing obscene materials. The elements of the *Miller* test are (1) whether the average person, applying "contemporary community standards" would find that the work, taken as a whole, appeals to prurient interest; (2) whether the work displays or describes, in a patently offense way, sexual contact specifically defined by a state statute; and (3) whether the work, again taken as a whole, lacks serious literary, artistic, political, or scientific value.

True-False

1   F

2   F

3   T

Fill in the Blank

1 obscenity
2 show-up
3 Sixth

Multiple Choice

1 D
2 C
3 A

CHAPTER 7. THE EXCLUSIONARY RULE

Review Questions

1 **What is the fruit of the poisonous tree doctrine?**

   The fruit of the poisonous tree doctrine is an extension of the exclusionary rule. It holds that any evidence that has been derived from unconstitutionally seized evidence is also inadmissible.

2 **List four exceptions to the exclusionary rule.**

   Four exceptions to the exclusionary rule include the attenuation doctrine, the good faith doctrine, the inevitable discovery rule, and the valid independent source rule.

3 **Explain the attenuation doctrine.**

   The attenuation doctrine arose in situations where considerable time had passed between the seizure of evidence, which was obtained in violation of the Fourth Amendment, and the proposed use of the evidence.

4 **Explain the valid independent source exception to the exclusionary rule.**

   Under the independent source doctrine, the court is presented with evidence that was located in two ways: one that violated the Constitution and one that did not. Because one path was free of any violations of the Fourth Amendment, the court will permit the evidence to be used.

5 **What is standing?**

   Standing refers to an individual's right to challenge a particular action by the police. An example of standing would be when a suspect's items have been seized pursuant to a search warrant and he or she seeks to challenge the seizure and the use of those items as evidence against him or her.

6   **What is a motion to suppress?**

A motion to suppress is a motion filed by the defendant that challenges the admissibility of the state's evidence.

7   **Explain the good faith exception to the exclusionary rule.**

The good faith exception refers to situations in which a search warrant has been issued with incorrect information, but the police officer has no reason to suspect that an error exists. In such a situation, the evidence would not be subject to the exclusionary rule and could be used at trial.

8   **Explain the significance of *United States v. Weeks* (1914).**

This case invented the exclusionary rule and made it applicable to all federal prosecutions but not to state-level prosecutions.

9   **Has the exclusionary rule that been extended beyond the Fourth Amendment, such as the First or Fifth Amendment? Explain your answer.**

No. There have been attempts to create a similar rule applying to freedom of speech or to other constitutional guarantees, but thus far the exclusionary rule only applies to the Fourth Amendment.

10   **What is the independent source rule as it relates to the exclusionary rule?**

If the prosecution can show that the evidence obtained was from a source independent of the tainted way that the evidence was obtained, then it can still be used at trial and the exclusionary rule does not apply.

11   **What is the significance of *Mapp v. Ohio*?**

Mapp v. Ohio took the exclusionary rule, originally created in *U.S. v. Weeks,* and extended it to state prosecutions.

12   **Why was the exclusionary rule created?**

Courts recognized that problems with evidence had been a common enough occurrence that some method for putting teeth into the provisions of the Fourth Amendment were often sought. The amendment does not provide any mechanism for enforcing its provision.

13   **For almost 50 years, the exclusionary rule only applied to the states. Explain why.**

The original decision in *U.S. v. Weeks* was only made applicable to federal prosecutions and not state prosecutions. It was applied to the states in *Mapp v. Ohio.*

PRACTICE QUESTIONS FOR TEST REVIEW

Essay Question

Explain the exclusionary rule.

In *U.S. v. Weeks*, the Supreme Court created a simple yet very effective remedy for situations where law enforcement violated an individual's Fourth Amendment protections. The court ruled that any evidence seized without probable cause would be subject to the exclusionary rule. This simple rule turned out to be very effective. It struck at the very heart of a prosecution case. If evidence could not be used, then the prosecution faced a serious challenge in getting a conviction.

True-False

1 True
2 True
3 False

Fill in the Blank

1 motion to suppress
2 Good faith
3 standing

Multiple Choice

1 D
2 A
3 D

CHAPTER 8. FIFTH AMENDMENT: GRAND JURY AND INDICTMENT

Review Questions

1 **What are some of the issues that a prosecutor considers in making a charging decision?**

When a case is bound over to superior court, the district attorney is permitted to review the case and to add, change, or dismiss the charges against the defendant. This process is loosely defined as the charging decision and involves a review of the facts and the law to decide not only what would be the most successful charge that the state can bring against the defendant, but also what is the most just way to proceed. Prosecutors are not charged with the duty to obtain convictions, but to seek justice.

2   **What is the purpose of the grand jury?**

The purpose of the grand jury is to act as a buffer between the state and the defendant, to consider the facts of the case, and to decide whether or not the case against the defendant should continue.

3   **Explain the historical background of the grand jury.**

The concept of the grand jury dates back centuries to the development of the Magna Carta in England. The original purpose of the grand jury was the same as it is today: to act as a buffer between the government and an individual who was charged with a crime.

4   **Describe the composition of the grand jury.**

The grand jury is composed of a cross-section of individual citizens from the county and should reflect, more or less, the racial and ethnic percentages found in the county itself.

5   **How and why would a defendant challenge the composition of the grand jury?**

A defendant might challenge the composition of the grand jury on any of a number of grounds. For instance, the defendant might challenge the composition of the grand jury because it does not reflect an adequate cross-section of the population of the county. Other reasons to challenge the composition of the grand jury include that specific members of the grand jury are not qualified to serve.

6   **Does a grand jury reach a verdict? Explain.**

Grand juries do not reach verdicts. The purpose of the grand jury is to determine that there is sufficient probable cause to believe that the defendant has committed the crime. When they make that determination, they return a vote of "true bill."

7   **Explain how a case is usually presented to a grand jury.**

The presentation of the case to the grand jury varies from state to state. In some states, the prosecutor is present in the grand jury room and makes a presentation to the grand jury through witness testimony. In other states, investigators or others coordinate the appearance of witnesses who testify before the grand jury. However the presentation is made, grand jurors always have the right to ask additional questions of the witnesses who appear before them.

8   What is a *prima facie* showing?

A prima facie showing is a determination that there is, on its face, sufficient evidence to believe that the defendant committed the crime.

9   Explain the subpoena powers available to the grand jury.

Grand juries have extensive subpoena powers and can subpoena both individuals and documents to establish the basic elements of a criminal offense.

10   How does a prosecutor decide what crime to charge against a defendant?

A prosecutor must go through a charging decision. That decision is based on the facts of the case, the charge initially brought by the police officer and any additional investigation that the prosecutor believes is warranted. Finally, the prosecutor must ensure that the charge brought against the defendant matches both the criminal offense and the facts of the case.

11   What is a motion to quash?

A motion to quash is a motion filed by the defense that seeks to quash a subpoena that has been issued by the grand jury or some other authority.

12   Explain what it means for a witness to invoke the Fifth Amendment before the grand jury.

When a witness invokes the Fifth Amendment in testifying before the grand jury, he or she is refusing to answer questions on the basis that the person might tend to incriminate himself or herself.

PRACTICE QUESTIONS FOR TEST REVIEW

Essay Question

What is the purpose and function of the grand jury?

The purpose of the grand jury is to act as a buffer between the state and the defendant. The U.S. Constitution requires a grand jury indictment for a person charged with a capital offense (one punishable by death) or "otherwise infamous crime." The essential function of the grand jury is to determine that there is probable cause to believe that a crime has occurred. Once they do, the grand jurors allow the prosecutor to continue with his or her case.

True-False

1   True
2   False
3   True

Fill in the Blank

1 motion to quash
2 privilege
3 Immunity

Multiple Choice

1 B
2 A
3 D

CHAPTER 9. FIFTH AMENDMENT: INTERROGATION AND CONFESSIONS

Review Questions

1 **What is the first thing that a police officer must do before asking the defendant questions about the crime?**

Police officers must read suspects their *Miranda* rights before questioning them after arrest.

2 **Can police deprive the defendant of sleep or food in an effort to break his or her will?**

No, police are not authorized to use coercive techniques, including sleep deprivation, to break down a suspect's will.

3 **If the suspect makes an unequivocal request for an attorney, what must happen?**

When an unequivocal request for an attorney is made, questioning must cease and cannot resume until the attorney is present.

4 **The text states that prosecutors are usually not present during an interrogation. Why?**

There are several reasons why the prosecutor is not present at an interrogation. For one, prosecutors may not be aware that a person is under arrest. For another, if the defendant does make an incriminating statement, then the prosecutor has become a witness in the case. An attorney cannot be both a witness and an advocate in a trial.

5 **Summarize the *Miranda* rights that must be read to a suspect before being questioned about a crime.**

The suspect must be told that he or she has the right to remain silent, that if he or she waives the right to remain silent anything that he or she says can and will be used against him or her. The suspect has the right to an attorney. If the suspect cannot afford an attorney, the court may appoint one to represent him or her.

6   Why was the *Miranda* decision so controversial when it was announced?

Police officers did not like the *Miranda* decision because it put them in the position of advising a suspect of their rights when they see the interrogation as an adversarial meeting. Police also objected because they could not answer any legal questions that the suspect might have about the various effects of giving testimony.

7   How did the *Miranda* case develop?

Ernesto Miranda was arrested for the kidnapping and rape of a young woman. After his arrest, he was interrogated by police officers for several hours and eventually confessed to the crime. The *Miranda* decision came about when Miranda's attorney appealed his conviction on the basis that his confession should not have been used in his trial because he had never been informed of his rights under the law.

8   List and explain some situations where the *Miranda* rights do not apply.

Miranda does not apply to traffic stops. It also does not apply to background or routine police questioning, exigent circumstances, and voluntary statements.

9   What are exigent circumstances?

An exigent circumstance is a situation that is inherently dangerous to people or evidence. In an emergency situation, officers are permitted to ask questions that will help them prevent harm to others or prevent evidence from being destroyed. There is no requirement to read the *Miranda* warnings in this situation.

10   Can the police lie to a suspect during an interrogation? If so, what lies are they not allowed to say?

Police may lie to a defendant, so long as the lie is not designed to overcome any constitutional protections. Law enforcement might lie to a suspect and tell him or her that a witness saw the suspect or that they have evidence tying him or her to the scene when they actually do not.

11   Does a suspect have to speak to invoke his or her right to remain silent? Explain.

The Supreme Court has held, however, that a defendant must tell the police that he or she intends to remain silent. The suspect cannot simply refuse to answer and have the police infer that he or she intends to remain silent.

12   What is a *Jackson v. Denno* hearing?

A *Jackson v. Denno* hearing occurs when the defense challenges the use of the defendant's confession during the trial based on the fact that it was not voluntarily given or that it was the product of coercion, promises, or other improper procedures.

PRACTICE QUESTIONS FOR TEST REVIEW

Essay Question

What are the *Miranda* rights and why are they important?

The *Miranda* rights are a series of statements that the police must read to a suspect before he or she is questioned. They advise the defendant of his or her various rights and police may only speak with the suspect after he or she has heard and understood the rights and then waived them. The *Miranda* decision was created out of a need to make sure that suspects understood their rights before being interrogated.

True-False

1   False
2   False
3   False

Fill in the Blank

1   exigent circumstance
2   interrogation
3   *Miranda* rights

Multiple Choice

1   C
2   A
3   D

CHAPTER 10. SIXTH AMENDMENT: RIGHT TO TRIAL AND ASSOCIATED RIGHTS

Review Questions

1 **How are most private criminal attorneys paid?**

Most private criminal attorneys are paid by a retainer fee system. The attorney is paid up front and then the attorney assesses his or her fees against that amount until the case is resolved.

2 **Explain the importance of the *Gideon* decision.**

The importance of the *Gideon* decision cannot be overstated. Simply put, it changed the entire fabric of the criminal justice system in regard to access to criminal defense attorneys. After the *Gideon* decision, defendants who could not afford their own attorneys were allowed to have representation, even if this representation was provided by the state.

3 **What is the difference between court-appointed and public defender systems?**

A court-appointed attorney is a private attorney who has been assigned to a particular case. A public defender is a governmental official whose primary job is to represent all criminal defendants charged with offenses.

4 **What financial restraints are placed on defendants who wish to obtain court-appointed attorneys but are charged with misdemeanors?**

Although the *Gideon* decision says that if a person cannot afford an attorney one will be hired to represent him or her, the *Gideon* decision does not apply in misdemeanor cases. In a situation where someone charged with a misdemeanor does not have representation and cannot afford it, he or she must either represent himself or herself or find money to pay for the attorney.

5 **What is pro se representation?**

Pro se representation refers to the situation in which a defendant chooses to represent himself or herself.

6 **Explain the presumption of innocence.**

Presumption of innocence is one of the core values of the U.S. criminal justice system. A defendant is presumed to be innocent until he or she is proven guilty.

7 **What is the difference between a presumption and an inference?**

A presumption is a conclusion that the jury must make, whereas an inference is a conclusion that the jury may make.

8 **Are 12 people always required to sit on a jury? Why or why not?**

Not all states require 12-person juries. In some states, for instance, individuals charged with misdemeanors receive six-person juries.

9 **When are six-person juries permitted?**

Six-person juries are permitted in cases involving misdemeanors, at least in some states.

10 **What types of cases do not allow jury trials?**

Juvenile cases are one example of cases that do not allow juries.

11 **Are juries permitted in juvenile cases? Why or why not?**

There are no juries in juvenile cases for the simple reason that the purpose of juvenile cases is not to determine guilt or innocence, but to determine if the child needs further corrective action or can be released.

12 **When can a trial judge close a trial to the public?**

A trial judge can briefly close a trial to the public during sensitive testimony, such as when a child is testifying about sexual abuse or when a rape victim is on the stand.

13 **Is it permissible to try a defendant while he or she is wearing prison clothing? Why or why not?**

It is not permissible to try a defendant when he or she is wearing prison clothing. Courts have determined that trying a defendant in prison clothing is unduly suggestive to the jury and may result in them finding the defendant guilty on the assumption that the defendant is already serving time in prison.

14 **Under what circumstances can a trial that began when the defendant was present continue without him or her?**

When a trial begins and the defendant is present, but later he or she absconds from the jurisdiction, the trial can proceed without him or her. This is also true when the defendant is unduly disruptive. The defendant can be removed from the courtroom and held in an adjoining cell.

15 **What has been called the "greatest legal engine ever invented for the discovery of truth?"**

Cross-examination has been called the greatest legal engine ever invented for the discovery of truth.

16 **What is the confrontation clause?**

The confrontation clause is contained in the Sixth Amendment of the U.S. Constitution and provides that criminal defendants have the right to confront the witnesses against them, live and in court.

17   **Can a prosecutor comment on a defendant's failure to testify in his or her own defense?**

A prosecutor is barred from commenting on the defendant's failure to testify during the trial.

18   **Does the right of the press to see a trial always outweigh the defendant's right to a fair trial? Explain your answer.**

The right of the press to view the trial does not always outweigh the right of the defendant to a fair trial. In fact, the judge must weigh each right against the other before making a determination on how best to proceed in a particular trial.

19   **Explain what proof beyond a reasonable doubt means.**

Proof beyond a reasonable doubt means proof to the level of certainty that a person would make a major life decision on. It does not mean absolute proof or proof to a mathematical certainty.

20   **What does the phrase "placing character into evidence" mean?**

The phrase "placing character into evidence" refers to a situation where a defendant testifies during his or her trial that he or she has no prior criminal record. At that point, the prosecutor is allowed to introduce the fact of the defendant's prior criminal convictions, if he or she has any.

PRACTICE QUESTIONS FOR TEST REVIEW

Essay Question

Why is the *Gideon* case so important to the U.S. criminal justice system?

In ruling in favor of *Gideon*, the court said that the "assistance of counsel is one of the safeguards of the Sixth Amendment deemed necessary to insure fundamental human rights of life and liberty. The Sixth Amendment stands as a constant admonition that if the constitutional safeguards it provides be lost, justice will not . . . be done." The Court ruled that Gideon should be retried and that this time the state of Florida should provide him with an attorney, paid for by the state.

True-False

1   False

2   True

3   False

Fill in the Blank

1 retainer
2 public defender attorney
3 a presumption

Multiple Choice

1 C
2 B
3 D

CHAPTER 11. EIGHTH AMENDMENT: INITIAL APPEARANCE, BAIL, AND PRELIMINARY HEARINGS

Review Questions

1 **What is the purpose of the initial appearance?**

The purpose of the initial appearance hearing is to advise the defendant of his or her rights shortly after the suspect has been arrested.

2 **Explain how an attorney may be appointed at an initial appearance.**

Attorneys often are appointed at an initial appearance hearing by magistrate judges.

3 **What are some factors that a court considers when setting bail or bond?**

The court will consider the defendant's ties to the community, the seriousness of the offense, and the defendant's prior criminal record, among other factors in considering whether to set bail and how much.

4 **What is the difference between bail and bond?**

Bail is usually considered to be a cash amount that is posted to ensure that the defendant will return to court. Bond, on the other hand, is often classified as the posting of real property to make the same guarantee.

5 **How do bonding companies function?**

Bonding companies normally charge 10 percent of the bail amount as a nonrefundable fee, and they also will locate defendants who have failed to appear for their court hearing to avoid forfeiting the entire bail amounts.

6 **Explain the role of bounty hunters.**

Bounty hunters are hired by bonding companies to locate defendants who have failed to appear for their court hearings.

7   What is a property bond?

A property bond is the posting of real property as a guarantee that a particular defendant will return to court for a hearing.

8   Explain how a defendant would receive a recognizance bond.

A defendant would receive a recognizance bond in a relatively minor case. Under the provisions of a recognizance bond, the defendant simply gives his or her word that he or she will return to court at the appointed day and time.

9   What is bond forfeiture?

Bond forfeiture occurs when a defendant fails to appear for a scheduled court date and the state seizes the cash or the property that has been posted to guarantee his or her return.

10   Explain the purpose of a preliminary hearing.

A preliminary hearing is designed to establish that there is sufficient probable cause to believe that the defendant has committed the crime with which he or she has been charged.

11   What procedure is followed at a preliminary hearing?

The procedure followed at a preliminary hearing is simple: The prosecutor calls a witness, normally the police officer, to testify about the facts surrounding the defendant's arrest. The defense attorney is given the opportunity to cross-examine the police officer to show that there was not sufficient probable cause.

12   How are the evidentiary rules different at preliminary hearings when compared to trials?

The evidentiary rules of preliminary hearings are more relaxed than those that are seen at trial. For instance, hearsay evidence is permitted.

13   What is the significance of binding over after a preliminary hearing?

The significance of binding a case over after a preliminary hearing means that the case is transferred to Superior Court, which will now hear all further matters concerning the case.

14   What negotiations typically occur between prosecutors and defense attorneys before and during preliminary hearings?

It is quite common for prosecutors and defense attorneys to have extensive negotiations before, during, and even after preliminary hearings. The primary negotiation will involve whether or not to have a hearing at all. If the prosecutor can convince the defendant to waive the hearing, the prosecutor will often offer a lower bond recommendation as an incentive to the defendant to waive the hearing.

PRACTICE QUESTIONS FOR TEST REVIEW

Essay Question

Compare and contrast initial appearance hearings and preliminary hearings.

In some jurisdictions, the initial appearance is also called the preliminary examination. No matter what the term, the purpose of the hearing is the same. Shortly after the defendant is arrested, the defendant is brought before a judge—often a magistrate judge—and again reminded of his or her rights and also asked if it will be necessary to appoint an attorney to represent the defendant. Preliminary hearings, on the other hand, occur within several days of the defendant's arrest, where the court will hold a hearing to determine if there is sufficient probable cause to believe that the defendant committed the crime. The preliminary hearing (also known as a probable cause hearing) is held within days of the defendant's arrest. It is a hearing where the defendant will appear, represented by an attorney, and the case will be presented by a prosecutor.

True-False

1 False
2 True
3 False

Fill in the Blank

1 initial appearance
2 bail
3 bounty hunter

Multiple Choice

1 B
2 A
3 C

CHAPTER 12. ARRAIGNMENT AND DISCOVERY

Review Questions

1 **What is arraignment?**

    An arraignment is a core proceeding in which the defendant is informed of the charges against him or her and given an opportunity to enter a plea of guilty or not guilty.

2   What is a court docket?

A court docket is a list of the cases that are currently pending before the court.

3   What motions might a defense attorney file at or before arraignment?

A defendant might file any of a number of motions at or before arraignment, including motions to suppress, motion for change of venue, and motions dealing with the evidence.

4   What is the difference between formal arraignment and arraignment?

A formal arraignment is rarely seen these days, but consists of the prosecutor reading the entire indictment aloud to the assembled courtroom. It is far more common for a defense attorney to request waiver of formal arraignment and accept the indictment without the in-court reading.

5   Explain bench warrants.

A bench warrant is issued by a judge when a defendant fails to appear for court on his or her scheduled court date. It authorizes police officers to arrest the defendant when they come across him or her.

6   Provide a brief overview of criminal discovery.

Criminal discovery is the process of exchanging information between the defense and the prosecution. In criminal cases prosecutors are required to provide a wealth of information to the defendants, but traditionally defendants had very little obligation to provide information to the prosecution. Among the items that the prosecution must provide to the defendant include the indictment, list of witnesses, scientific reports, *Brady* material, and any other material required by statute.

7   Explain the basic information provided by the state in discovery.

The most basic information provided by the state in criminal discovery is the indictment, list of witnesses, and *Brady* material, as well as any scientific reports, if any have been performed in the case.

8   What is an open file policy?

An open file policy is a policy followed by some prosecution offices where they permit the defense attorney to make copies of all of the material currently contained in the prosecution file.

9   When would a judge conduct an *in camera* inspection?

A judge would conduct an *in camera* inspection when a defense attorney files a motion alleging that the state has failed to abide by the required discovery laws. In such an instance, the judge would review the prosecution file personally and supplement discovery with any material that the judge deems necessary for the defense.

10   What is exculpatory evidence?

Exculpatory evidence refers to any evidence that tends to show that the defendant is not guilty of the crime charged. The definition is also been expanded to include any evidence that might mitigate the defendant sentence.

11   How have discovery rules changed over the years?

In the past 20 years, the discovery rules in criminal cases have undergone dramatic changes. State laws now require that the prosecution provide a great deal more information to the defense and have also imposed some obligations on the defense to provide information to the prosecution.

12   What is *Brady* material?

Brady material refers to any evidence that might tend to show that the defendant is not guilty of the crime or any evidence that might mitigate the defendant sentence.

13   What is work product?

Work product refers to the notes, thoughts, and strategies prepared by the attorneys in the case. Work product is not discoverable by either the prosecution or the defense.

14   When would the state provide criminal records of its witnesses?

The state would provide copies of criminal records of its witnesses if a statute required it, but many prosecutors also provide records of some of the state's witnesses even though it is not required, simply because it is a better practice and conforms with the ruling in *Brady*.

15   What is a motion to suppress?

A motion to suppress is a motion filed by the defendant that challenges the admissibility of the state's evidence.

16   Explain motions to sever.

A motion to sever is filed by the defense that seeks an order to try codefendants in separate trials or that seeks separate trials for different offenses against the same defendant.

17   Why would a defendant bring a motion *in limine*?

A motion *in limine* challenges the admissibility of specific types of evidence.

18   Explain the function of a motion to reveal the deal.

When a defense attorney files a motion to reveal the deal, he or she is requesting information about any arrangements between the state's witnesses that offer leniency or the promise of a lighter sentence in exchange for testimony against the defendant.

19   **When would a defendant bring a motion to change venue?**

A defendant would bring a motion to change venue if there were a great deal of pretrial publicity about the case and the defendant's attorney believes that it would be impossible to select a jury that did not already have an opinion about the guilt or innocence of the defendant.

PRACTICE QUESTIONS FOR TEST REVIEW

Essay Question

What is the importance of the *Brady v. Maryland* case?

Regardless of what a particular jurisdiction's statutes provide about criminal discovery, all states must abide by the decision in *Brady v. Maryland,* which requires states to turn over any exculpatory or mitigating information to the defense. This case imposed a fresh burden on the prosecution to provide material to the defendant, even if it wasn't requested, for the prosecution to live up to its sworn duty to provide justice.

True-False

1   False
2   True
3   True

Fill in the Blank

1   discovery
2   work product
3   exculpatory

Multiple Choice

1   C
2   C
3   D

CHAPTER 13. THE TRIAL

Review Questions

1 **What is the jury box?**

   The jury box is the place in the courtroom where all 12 jurors are seated during the course of the trial.

2 **What is the function of the jury deliberation room?**

   The jury deliberation room is where the jury retires to consider its verdict at the conclusion of the trial.

3 **Explain where the witness stand is in relation to the judge's bench.**

   The witness stand is always located next to the judge's bench so that the judge may view the witness and so that the jury may also see the witness.

4 **Explain the function of the judge's bench.**

   The judge's bench is where the judge sits. It is the highest point in the courtroom, allowing the judge to see everything that goes on inside the courtroom during the trial.

5 **Where are the defense and prosecution tables located in the courtroom?**

   The defense and prosecution tables are located across from the witness stand and the judge's bench and are in full view of the jury box.

6 **What functions does the clerk of court carry out?**

   The clerk of court usually attends the first day of a calendar call and makes notations about the resolution of various criminal cases. The clerk may also return at the conclusion of a trial, if the defendant is found guilty, to record what sentence the defendant receives.

7 **What is the purpose of the court reporter?**

   The court reporter's function is to take down everything that is said during the course of the trial and to transcribe it at a later date.

8 **Explain how a jury is selected.**

   To pick a jury, a panel of citizens is brought into the courtroom and members of the panel are eliminated until 12 jurors remain.

9 **What does it mean to join issue?**

   Join issue refers to the point at the trial where the defendant enters an official plea of not guilty. This signals the actual beginning of the jury trial.

10   What is *voir dire*?

This is a French term that means "to look, to speak," and refers to the jury selection process.

11   What is the venire?

This is a term that refers to the panel of citizens that is brought into the courtroom to begin the jury selection process.

12   What is a peremptory challenge?

A peremptory challenge is the dismissal of a member of the panel for essentially any reason at all.

13   Explain a challenge for cause.

A challenge for cause results when a member of the panel indicates that he or she is unwilling or unable to follow the judge's rulings or the law in the case.

14   What is a *Batson* challenge?

A *Batson* challenge results when either the prosecution or the defense alleges that the other party has used discriminatory practices to remove members of the panel during the jury selection process.

15   Explain the process for striking a jury.

Striking a jury is simply the process of removing members of the panel until 12 members remain. These 12 members will become the jury that hears the case.

16   What is the opening statement?

The opening statement is where both the prosecution and defense attorneys outline their case to the jury and describe what the case is about and what evidence the jurors will hear during the course of the trial.

17   Explain how a direct examination is carried out.

Direct examination is carried out by calling a witness to the stand, swearing him or her in, and then asking that witness open-ended questions to help establish the basic facts of the case.

18   What is a cross-examination?

Cross-examination occurs after direct examination when the opposing attorney questions the witness on the stand to establish bias, prejudice, or lack of knowledge on the part of the witness.

19   What is a redirect examination?

Redirect examination occurs after cross-examination and is the point where the original attorney may ask a few follow-up questions of the witness to again establish certain facts in the case.

20 **What is a directed verdict?**

A directed verdict is a request by the defendant to enter a verdict of not guilty based on the fact that the state has failed to prove each and every allegation of the charge against the defendant.

21 **What is the purpose of rebuttal?**

Rebuttal is used by the prosecution to present evidence that directly contradicts evidence that has been brought out by the defense during its case.

22 **Explain the function of the jury charge.**

A jury charge is the point at the trial where the judge informs the jury of the law that is applicable to the case and also explains to the members of the jury what their functions are during the course of jury deliberations.

23 **How is a charge conference carried out?**

A charge conference is carried out between the defense attorney, prosecutor, and judge. They meet and decide what jury charges the judge will read to the jury.

24 **How is a typical closing argument carried out?**

A closing argument is a presentation made to the jury that appeals both to logic and to passions and advocates the jury to take some action. In the case of a prosecution closing argument, it will be to find the defendant guilty. In the case of the defense attorney, it will be to find the defendant not guilty.

25 **Explain the possible verdicts that a jury may reach.**

In a typical criminal case, a jury may reach a verdict of guilty, not guilty, not guilty by reason of insanity, or guilty but mentally ill.

26 **What is "polling" a jury?**

Polling a jury is the process of requesting that each individual member of the jury affirm his or her verdict out loud and in the courtroom.

PRACTICE QUESTIONS FOR TEST REVIEW

Essay Question

Explain the basic steps in a trial.

Criminal trials follow a distinct pattern. Once the jury has been selected, the attorneys for the state and the defense give an opening statement. Then, the prosecution presents its case through evidence and witnesses, all with the goal of proving that the defendant is guilty beyond a reasonable doubt. At the conclusion of the state's case, the defendant may or may not decide to present any evidence. When the defense rests, the attorneys and judge confer to decide on the instructions that the jurors will receive at the conclusion of the case. Then, both attorneys are permitted to give closing arguments to the jury. The members of the jury then receive written or oral instructions from the judge about what their role in the jury room is. The jurors retire, confer with one another, and attempt to reach a unanimous verdict that the defendant is either guilty beyond a reasonable doubt or that he or she is not guilty.

True-False

1 True

2 True

3 False

Fill in the Blank

1 bench trial

2 court reporter

3 *Voir dire*

Multiple Choice

1 A

2 B

3 B

CHAPTER 14. DEFENSES TO CRIMINAL PROSECUTIONS

Review Questions

1 **Explain the difference between *allegata* and *probata*.**

   One refers to the allegations that are made in the indictment. The other refers to the proof that is brought forward at trial to prove that the defendant committed the offense.

2 **Describe simple defenses as compared to affirmative defenses.**

   A simple defense is one that is automatically triggered whenever a defendant is accused of crime. An affirmative defense, on the other hand, requires the defendant to present some type of evidence to support the defense.

3   What standard of proof must a defendant meet in presenting an affirmative defense?

The normal standard of proof required of a defendant who presents an affirmative defense is to present either some evidence or a preponderance of evidence to support the defense.

4   What is clear and convincing evidence and how does it differ from preponderance of the evidence?

Clear and convincing evidence is a higher standard than preponderance of the evidence and requires more facts and evidence to support it.

5   Explain the defense of alibi.

Alibi is a defense that says that at the time that the crimes were being committed, the defendant was in another place.

6   What is battered woman's syndrome?

Battered woman's syndrome is a defense that is an offshoot of self-defense. It is a defense that allows a woman to respond with deadly force to an abuser when he is incapacitated.

7   What is the difference between coercion and duress?

In coercion, a person physically threatens the well-being of another, but in duress a defendant uses intimidation and psychological control to force another to commit a crime.

8   When can a person's age be considered a defense?

A person's age can be a factor in a defense when he or she is below the age of seven. Under that age, a child is considered to be incapable of forming *mens rea* and therefore cannot commit a crime.

9   Define complete defense.

A complete defense is one that, if proven, would completely negate the defendant's guilt.

10   Can a victim consent to murder? Why or why not?

The law does not allow a person to consent to murder. The simple reason is that it would be virtually impossible to prove that the victim consented. Besides that, there is a societal value in not allowing people to consent to their own murders.

11   Is it possible to use deadly force to protect property? Explain.

Most states do not allow the use of deadly force to protect property, only human beings.

12   What are stand your ground laws?

Stand your ground laws are an exception to the general rule that when a person is confronted with force and he or she can reasonably retreat from the situation, then he or she must do so. Under the stand your ground laws, no retreat is required.

13   List and explain the two elements of entrapment.

The two elements of entrapment are that the police came up with the original idea for the crime and also provided the defendant with the means of carrying it out.

14   What is the legal test for insanity?

The legal test for insanity is that the defendant, at the time the crime was committed, was unable to distinguish between right and wrong.

15   How does a defendant raise the defense of insanity?

A defendant raises the defense of insanity by filing a motion claiming that he or she was insane at the time of the crime. This motion must be filed before trial to allow the prosecution sufficient time to engage its own experts to evaluate the defendant to see if the defendant qualifies for the legal test of insanity.

16   What is the Durham test as that test applies to the defense of insanity?

The Durham test consists of one of three components: (1) the defendant could not distinguish between right and wrong; (2) a person suffers from an irresistible impulse that precludes him or her from choosing between right and wrong; or (3) his or her unlawful act is the product of a mental disease or defect.

PRACTICE QUESTIONS FOR TEST REVIEW

Essay Question

Explain the insanity defense.

The insanity defense is a defense that states that at the time that the defendant committed the offense, he or she could tell the difference between right and wrong and therefore did not have the requisite *mens rea* to be convicted of a crime. To bring this defense, the defendant's attorney must present testimony and evidence showing the defendant's mental state at the time that the crime was committed. It is then up to the state to disprove the defendant's insanity defense beyond a reasonable doubt.

True-False

1 False
2 False
3 True

Fill in the Blank

1 simple defenses
2 Double jeopardy
3 Due Process

Multiple Choice

1 C
2 A
3 D

CHAPTER 15. EIGHTH AMENDMENT: SENTENCING

Review Questions

1 What is the procedure involved in entering a guilty plea?

Before a judge can accept a defendant's plea, the judge must make a determination that the plea is given voluntarily and not as the result of coercion, threats, or other inducements. A guilty plea must be given knowingly and voluntarily. To establish the voluntary nature of the plea, the judge (or the prosecutor) will question the defendant on the record to determine that the plea has not been forced. In felony cases, the traditional method of accepting a guilty plea is to do so in open court.

2 Why is plea bargaining considered to be controversial?

Plea bargaining is often seen as controversial because it appears to be unfair, with prosecutors forcing hapless defendants to admit to crimes that they have not committed.

3 What type of discretion do judges have in imposing sentences?

Depending on the jurisdiction, judges have a great deal of discretion in sentencing. If a state (or the federal) government has passed sentencing guidelines, then judicial discretion is drastically removed. In those jurisdictions, judges may only impose minimum or maximum sentences that have been prescribed by the legislative branch.

4   What are statutory minimum and maximum sentences?

In most jurisdictions, the judge has specific restrictions on the ultimate sentence that he or she can impose on the defendant. The statute that criminalizes the behavior usually includes a provision for a minimum and maximum sentence and a judge is bound to impose a sentence within those limits.

5   Compare concurrent and consecutive sentences.

A concurrent sentence is one that will be served at the same time as any other prison term. When sentences run concurrently, a defendant serves time for two or more offenses at the same time. However, consecutive prison sentences function differently. If a defendant has been sentenced to a five-year prison term on one offense, then his or her new sentence will begin when the first prison term has ended.

6   What is a presentence investigation?

This is an investigation conducted by the probation or parole office that reviews the various factors present in the defendant's life that argue to mitigate or increase his or her sentence.

7   Explain the procedure at a sentencing hearing.

At the conclusion of a trial, or as part of the defendant's guilty plea, the judge may hold a sentencing hearing to determine what sentence the defendant should receive. A sentencing hearing allows the prosecution to present evidence to justify a harsher sentence. The defense also has the opportunity of presenting any evidence that might mitigate the sentence.

8   What is a victim impact statement?

A victim impact statement allows the victim to tell the judge what effect the defendant's crime has had on the victim's life. Victim impact statements are often an important part of the healing process that occurs in the aftermath of a crime, especially a violent crime. The victim is permitted to read the statement in open court or the statement may be read by a prosecutor for a victim who does not wish to appear in court on the sentencing day.

9   What evidence might a prosecutor introduce in aggravation of a defendant's sentence?

To show a need for aggravation of sentence, the prosecution might show that the defendant has prior criminal convictions, the defendant's actions have had an adverse impact on the victim or victim's family, or that the defendant poses a significant threat to the community or is likely to commit more crimes in the future

10   What is first offender treatment?

First offender programs are reserved for youthful offenders for relatively minor crimes. Rather than have these people carry a criminal conviction for the rest of their lives, a judge might decide to enroll them into a first offender program. Under the terms of the program, a defendant must sign an agreement to complete various activities. If he or she is successful, at the completion of the first offender program, the judge will rescind the defendant's guilty plea.

11   What is a conditional plea?

This is an alternative to an *Alford* plea, and in many ways they are similar. A defendant enters a plea of guilty, including a condition that although he or she continues to maintain his or her innocence, the facts and the law are such that the chances of him or her actually winning at trial are virtually nonexistent. In the face of such overwhelming evidence, the defendant enters a conditional plea of guilty. The practical consequences of a conditional plea, an *Alford* plea, and a guilty plea are identical.

12   Why is it necessary for a judge to determine that a plea was entered voluntarily?

A judge must show that the defendant was not coerced or tricked into voluntarily stating his or her guilt to the crime charged.

13   What is a plea of nolo contendere?

A plea of nolo contendere literally means, "I do not contest." For purposes of sentencing, a plea of nolo contendere has the same requirements and the same implications as a guilty plea.

14   What are the procedures followed in death penalty cases?

Death penalty cases or capital murder cases have different safeguards and procedures than are seen in other prosecutions. Death penalty trials are always bifurcated, meaning that there are two trials. The bifurcated trial consists of the guilt phase, where the jury decides whether or not the defendant is guilty of the crime, and the sentencing phase, where the judge or jury is called on to decide if the defendant's actions warrant a death sentence.

15   What is the difference between fines and restitution?

A fine is imposed by the legislature for a class of offenses. Restitution is payment to the victim of a crime for her out-of-pocket expenses related to the defendant's criminal behavior.

16   What is meant by the phrase "cruel and unusual punishment?"

This phrase is set out in the Eighth Amendment to the U.S. Constitution. Because the Eighth Amendment does not define exactly what constitutes cruel and unusual punishment, the U.S. Supreme Court has been called on to interpret it. The Court's decisions have established that a sentence cannot involve torture, and that the sentence must be "proportional" to the crime. This means that all states are prohibited from engaging in practices that are considered to be cruel and unusual punishment, including torture, whipping, and corporal punishment.

17 Explain the legislation entitled "Three Strikes and You're Out."

So-called three strikes statutes generally require a lengthy prison sentence (sometimes even life in prison) for a third felony conviction.

18 What provisions does the Eighth Amendment have regarding punishment?

The Eighth Amendment prohibits any type of cruel or unusual punishment, which has been interpreted to mean whipping and other forms of corporal punishment.

PRACTICE QUESTIONS FOR TEST REVIEW

Essay Question

What is an *Alford* plea?

Based on the U.S. Supreme Court case of *North Carolina v. Alford,* an *Alford* plea allows a defendant to maintain his or her innocence while also pleading guilty to the crime. A defendant might decide to use an *Alford* plea when the government's case against him or her seems strong and his or her possible defenses are weak.

True-False

1 False
2 True
3 True

Fill in the Blank

1 conditional
2 sentence
3 victim impact statement

Multiple Choice

1 A
2 D
3 D

CHAPTER 16. APPEALS

Review Questions

1   Explain the organization of the appellate court system.

The appellate court system is essentially arranged like a pyramid. At the bottom of the pyramid are the trial courts. Trial courts report to intermediate appellate courts, which are frequently referred to as courts of appeal. These courts review the actions of the trial courts and make decisions on what occurred in those trial courts. Depending on the outcome in the appellate court, one or more of the parties may appeal to the highest court at the top of the pyramid, usually referred to as the State Supreme Court.

2   What is the difference between affirming a decision and reversing one?

When an appellate court affirms a decision, it means that it agrees with the lower court ruling. When an appellate court reverses a decision, it means it disagrees with a lower court ruling.

3   Explain the purpose of a motion for new trial.

A motion for new trial is filed after a defendant is sentenced and is essentially the beginning of the appeals process. When a trial judge denies the motion for new trial, this gives the defendant the right to appeal to a higher court.

4   What guidelines does a court follow in deciding to grant cert?

In deciding whether or not to grant cert, supreme courts follow strict guidelines including whether or not the case is of national importance or whether there is a split among the jurisdictions about how best to proceed on the law governing the facts of the case.

5   What is reversible error?

Reversible error refers to some error by the trial judge that could have affected the verdict in the case.

6   What is a remand?

A remand is an order by an appellate court sending a case back to the trial court for additional hearings and gathering of evidence.

7   Explain the purpose of *habeas corpus*.

Habeas corpus is a federal proceeding in which the defendant challenges his or her incarceration as an unconstitutional infringement on the defendant's rights.

8   Why does it normally take so long to appeal a criminal case?

Appeals in criminal cases can last for several years. The reason for this is simple: There are many levels on which a defendant can appeal. Because a defendant who loses in the Court of Appeals on the state level is allowed to attempt to appeal to the State Supreme Court, that can add additional time. After that, a defendant who loses on appeal at the state level is allowed to bring his or her case to the U.S. Supreme Court, if that court agrees to the case. All of this takes a great deal of time to process.

9 **What is oral argument?**

An oral argument occurs when the attorneys representing the parties on appeal stand before the appellate court to make their appellate positions in a prepared speech. The attorneys may also be questioned by the appellate justices on the various positions they espouse in their appeal.

10 **Does a grant of cert mean that a party has won the appeal? Why or why not?**

A grant of cert simply means that an appellate court will consider the appeal, but it does not mean that either side has won. With a grant of cert, the court will consider the briefs submitted by both sides and reach a decision at a later point.

PRACTICE QUESTIONS FOR TEST REVIEW

Essay Question

What are the minimum requirements of a brief? List and explain each.

An appellate brief has the minimum requirements of a title page, a statement of facts, various enumerations of error, an argument, and a conclusion

True-False

1 False
2 True
3 True

Fill in the Blank

1 jurisdiction
2 record
3 appellant

Multiple Choice

1 B
2 B
3 B

The Constitution of the United States

We the People of the United States, in Order to form a more perfect Union, establish Justice, insure domestic Tranquility, provide for the common defense, promote the general Welfare, and secure the Blessings of Liberty to ourselves and our Posterity, do ordain and establish this Constitution for the United States of America.

Article I

Section 1

All legislative Powers herein granted shall be vested in a Congress of the United States, which shall consist of a Senate and House of Representatives.

Section 2

The House of Representatives shall be composed of Members chosen every second Year by the People of the several States, and the Electors in each State shall have the Qualifications requisite for Electors of the most numerous Branch of the State Legislature.

No Person shall be a Representative who shall not have attained to the Age of twenty five Years, and been seven Years a Citizen of the United States, and who shall not, when elected, be an Inhabitant of that State in which he shall be chosen.

Representatives and direct Taxes shall be apportioned among the several States which may be included within this Union, according to their respective Numbers, which shall be determined by adding to the whole Number of free Persons, including those bound to Service for a Term of Years, and excluding Indians not taxed, three fifths of all other Persons. The actual Enumeration shall be made within three Years after the first Meeting of the Congress of the United States, and within every subsequent Term of ten Years, in such Manner as they shall by Law direct. The Number of Representatives shall not exceed one for every thirty Thousand, but each State shall have at Least one Representative; and until such enumeration shall be made, the State of New Hampshire shall be entitled to chuse three, Massachusetts eight, Rhode-Island and Providence

Plantations one, Connecticut five, New-York six, New Jersey four, Pennsylvania eight, Delaware one, Maryland six, Virginia ten, North Carolina five, South Carolina five, and Georgia three.

When vacancies happen in the Representation from any State, the Executive Authority thereof shall issue Writs of Election to fill such Vacancies.

The House of Representatives shall chuse their Speaker and other Officers; and shall have the sole Power of Impeachment.

Section 3

The Senate of the United States shall be composed of two Senators from each State, chosen by the Legislature thereof, for six Years; and each Senator shall have one Vote.

Immediately after they shall be assembled in Consequence of the first Election, they shall be divided as equally as may be into three Classes. The Seats of the Senators of the first Class shall be vacated at the Expiration of the second Year, of the second Class at the Expiration of the fourth Year, and of the third Class at the Expiration of the sixth Year, so that one third may be chosen every second Year; and if Vacancies happen by Resignation, or otherwise, during the Recess of the Legislature of any State, the Executive thereof may make temporary Appointments until the next Meeting of the Legislature, which shall then fill such Vacancies.

No Person shall be a Senator who shall not have attained to the Age of thirty Years, and been nine Years a Citizen of the United States, and who shall not, when elected, be an Inhabitant of that State for which he shall be chosen.

The Vice President of the United States shall be President of the Senate, but shall have no Vote, unless they be equally divided.

The Senate shall chuse their other Officers, and also a President pro tempore, in the Absence of the Vice President, or when he shall exercise the Office of President of the United States.

The Senate shall have the sole Power to try all Impeachments. When sitting for that Purpose, they shall be on Oath or Affirmation. When the President of the United States is tried, the Chief Justice shall preside: And no Person shall be convicted without the Concurrence of two thirds of the Members present.

Judgment in Cases of Impeachment shall not extend further than to removal from Office, and disqualification to hold and enjoy any Office of honor, Trust or Profit under the United States: but the Party convicted shall nevertheless be liable and subject to Indictment, Trial, Judgment and Punishment, according to Law.

Section 4

The Times, Places and Manner of holding Elections for Senators and Representatives, shall be prescribed in each State by the Legislature thereof; but the Congress may at any time by Law make or alter such Regulations, except as to the Places of chusing Senators.

The Congress shall assemble at least once in every Year, and such Meeting shall be on the first Monday in December, unless they shall by Law appoint a different Day.

Section 5

Each House shall be the Judge of the Elections, Returns and Qualifications of its own Members, and a Majority of each shall constitute a Quorum to do Business; but a smaller Number may adjourn from day to day, and may be authorized to compel the Attendance of absent Members, in such Manner, and under such Penalties as each House may provide.

Each House may determine the Rules of its Proceedings, punish its Members for disorderly Behaviour, and, with the Concurrence of two thirds, expel a Member.

Each House shall keep a Journal of its Proceedings, and from time to time publish the same, excepting such Parts as may in their Judgment require Secrecy; and the Yeas and Nays of the Members of either House on any question shall, at the Desire of one fifth of those Present, be entered on the Journal.

Neither House, during the Session of Congress, shall, without the Consent of the other, adjourn for more than three days, nor to any other Place than that in which the two Houses shall be sitting.

Section 6

The Senators and Representatives shall receive a Compensation for their Services, to be ascertained by Law, and paid out of the Treasury of the United States. They shall in all Cases, except Treason, Felony and Breach of the Peace, be privileged from Arrest during their Attendance at the Session of their respective Houses, and in going to and returning from the same; and for any Speech or Debate in either House, they shall not be questioned in any other Place.

No Senator or Representative shall, during the Time for which he was elected, be appointed to any civil Office under the Authority of the United States, which shall have been created, or the Emoluments whereof shall have been increased during such time; and no Person holding any Office under the United States, shall be a Member of either House during his Continuance in Office.

Section 7

All Bills for raising Revenue shall originate in the House of Representatives; but the Senate may propose or concur with Amendments as on other Bills.

Every Bill which shall have passed the House of Representatives and the Senate, shall, before it become a Law, be presented to the President of the United States: If he approve he shall sign it, but if not he shall return it, with his Objections to that House in which it shall have originated, who shall enter the Objections at large on their Journal, and proceed to reconsider it. If after such Reconsideration two thirds of that House shall agree to pass the Bill, it shall be sent, together with the Objections, to the other House, by which it shall likewise be reconsidered, and if approved by two thirds of that House, it shall become a Law. But in all such Cases the Votes of both Houses shall be determined by Yeas and Nays, and the Names of the Persons voting for and against the Bill shall be entered on the Journal of each House respectively. If any Bill shall not be returned by the President within ten Days (Sundays excepted) after it shall have been presented to him, the Same shall be a Law, in like Manner as if he had signed it, unless the Congress by their Adjournment prevent its Return, in which Case it shall not be a Law.

Every Order, Resolution, or Vote to which the Concurrence of the Senate and House of Representatives may be necessary (except on a question of Adjournment) shall be presented to the President of the United States; and before the Same shall take Effect, shall be approved by him, or being disapproved by him, shall be repassed by two thirds of the Senate and House of Representatives, according to the Rules and Limitations prescribed in the Case of a Bill.

Section 8

The Congress shall have Power To lay and collect Taxes, Duties, Imposts and Excises, to pay the Debts and provide for the common Defence and general Welfare of the United States; but all Duties, Imposts and Excises shall be uniform throughout the United States; To borrow Money on the credit of the United States; To regulate Commerce with foreign Nations, and among the several States, and with the Indian Tribes; To establish an uniform Rule of Naturalization, and uniform Laws on the subject of Bankruptcies throughout the United States; To coin Money, regulate the Value thereof, and of foreign Coin, and fix the Standard of Weights and Measures; To provide for the Punishment of counterfeiting the Securities and current Coin of the United States; To establish Post Offices and post Roads; To promote the Progress of Science and useful Arts, by securing for limited Times to Authors and Inventors the exclusive Right to their respective Writings and Discoveries; To constitute Tribunals inferior to the supreme Court; To define and punish Piracies and Felonies committed on the high Seas, and Offences against the Law of Nations; To declare War, grant Letters of Marque and Reprisal, and make Rules concerning Captures on Land and Water; To raise and support

Armies, but no Appropriation of Money to that Use shall be for a longer Term than two Years; To provide and maintain a Navy; To make Rules for the Government and Regulation of the land and naval Forces; To provide for calling forth the Militia to execute the Laws of the Union, suppress Insurrections and repel Invasions; To provide for organizing, arming, and disciplining, the Militia, and for governing such Part of them as may be employed in the Service of the United States, reserving to the States respectively, the Appointment of the Officers, and the Authority of training the Militia according to the discipline prescribed by Congress; To exercise exclusive Legislation in all Cases whatsoever, over such District (not exceeding ten Miles square) as may, by Cession of particular States, and the Acceptance of Congress, become the Seat of the Government of the United States, and to exercise like Authority over all Places purchased by the Consent of the Legislature of the State in which the Same shall be, for the Erection of Forts, Magazines, Arsenals, dock-Yards, and other needful Buildings; — And To make all Laws which shall be necessary and proper for carrying into Execution the foregoing Powers, and all other Powers vested by this Constitution in the Government of the United States, or in any Department or Officer thereof.

Section 9

The Migration or Importation of such Persons as any of the States now existing shall think proper to admit, shall not be prohibited by the Congress prior to the Year one thousand eight hundred and eight, but a Tax or duty may be imposed on such Importation, not exceeding ten dollars for each Person.

The Privilege of the Writ of Habeas Corpus shall not be suspended, unless when in Cases of Rebellion or Invasion the public Safety may require it.

No Bill of Attainder or ex post facto Law shall be passed.

No Capitation, or other direct, Tax shall be laid, unless in Proportion to the Census or enumeration herein before directed to be taken.

No Tax or Duty shall be laid on Articles exported from any State.

No Preference shall be given by any Regulation of Commerce or Revenue to the Ports of one State over those of another; nor shall Vessels bound to, or from, one State, be obliged to enter, clear, or pay Duties in another.

No Money shall be drawn from the Treasury, but in Consequence of Appropriations made by Law; and a regular Statement and Account of the Receipts and Expenditures of all public Money shall be published from time to time.

No Title of Nobility shall be granted by the United States: And no Person holding any Office of Profit or Trust under them, shall, without the Consent of the

Congress, accept of any present, Emolument, Office, or Title, of any kind whatever, from any King, Prince, or foreign State.

Section 10

No State shall enter into any Treaty, Alliance, or Confederation; grant Letters of Marque and Reprisal; coin Money; emit Bills of Credit; make any Thing but gold and silver Coin a Tender in Payment of Debts; pass any Bill of Attainder, ex post facto Law, or Law impairing the Obligation of Contracts, or grant any Title of Nobility.

No State shall, without the Consent of the Congress, lay any Imposts or Duties on Imports or Exports, except what may be absolutely necessary for executing it's inspection Laws: and the net Produce of all Duties and Imposts, laid by any State on Imports or Exports, shall be for the Use of the Treasury of the United States; and all such Laws shall be subject to the Revision and Controul of the Congress.

No State shall, without the Consent of Congress, lay any Duty of Tonnage, keep Troops, or Ships of War in time of Peace, enter into any Agreement or Compact with another State, or with a foreign Power, or engage in War, unless actually invaded, or in such imminent Danger as will not admit of delay.

Article II

Section 1

The executive Power shall be vested in a President of the United States of America. He shall hold his Office during the Term of four Years, and, together with the Vice President, chosen for the same Term, be elected, as follows:

Each State shall appoint, in such Manner as the Legislature thereof may direct, a Number of Electors, equal to the whole Number of Senators and Representatives to which the State may be entitled in the Congress: but no Senator or Representative, or Person holding an Office of Trust or Profit under the United States, shall be appointed an Elector.

The Electors shall meet in their respective States, and vote by Ballot for two Persons, of whom one at least shall not be an Inhabitant of the same State with themselves. And they shall make a List of all the Persons voted for, and of the Number of Votes for each; which List they shall sign and certify, and transmit sealed to the Seat of the Government of the United States, directed to the President of the Senate. The President of the Senate shall, in the Presence of the Senate and House of Representatives, open all the Certificates, and the Votes shall then be counted. The Person having the greatest Number of Votes shall be the President, if such Number be a Majority of the whole Number of Electors appointed; and if there be more than one who have such Majority, and have an equal Number of Votes, then the House of Representatives shall immediately chuse by Ballot one of them for President; and if no Person have a Majority, then from the five highest on the List the said House shall in like Manner chuse the President. But in chusing the President, the Votes shall be taken by States, the Representation from each State having one Vote; A quorum for this purpose shall consist of a Member or Members from two thirds of the States, and a Majority of all the States shall be necessary to a Choice. In every Case, after the Choice of the President, the Person having the greatest Number of Votes of the Electors shall be the Vice President. But if there should remain two or more who have equal Votes, the Senate shall chuse from them by Ballot the Vice President.

The Congress may determine the Time of chusing the Electors, and the Day on which they shall give their Votes; which Day shall be the same throughout the United States.

No Person except a natural born Citizen, or a Citizen of the United States, at the time of the Adoption of this Constitution, shall be eligible to the Office of President; neither shall any Person be eligible to that Office who shall not have attained to the Age of thirty five Years, and been fourteen Years a Resident within the United States.

In Case of the Removal of the President from Office, or of his Death, Resignation, or Inability to discharge the Powers and Duties of the said Office, the Same shall devolve on the Vice President, and the Congress may by Law provide for the Case of Removal, Death, Resignation or Inability, both of the President and Vice President, declaring what Officer shall then act as President, and such Officer shall act accordingly, until the Disability be removed, or a President shall be elected.

The President shall, at stated Times, receive for his Services, a Compensation, which shall neither be increased nor diminished during the Period for which he shall have been elected, and he shall not receive within that Period any other Emolument from the United States, or any of them.

Before he enter on the Execution of his Office, he shall take the following Oath or Affirmation: "I do solemnly swear (or affirm) that I will faithfully execute the Office of President of the United States, and will to the best of my Ability, preserve, protect and defend the Constitution of the United States."

Section 2

The President shall be Commander in Chief of the Army and Navy of the United States, and of the Militia of the several States, when called into the actual Service of the United States; he may require the Opinion, in writing, of the principal Officer in each of the executive Departments, upon any Subject relating to the Duties of their respective Offices, and he shall have Power to grant Reprieves and Pardons for Offences against the United States, except in Cases of Impeachment.

He shall have Power, by and with the Advice and Consent of the Senate, to make Treaties, provided two thirds of the Senators present concur; and he shall nominate, and by and with the Advice and Consent of the Senate, shall appoint Ambassadors, other public Ministers and Consuls, Judges of the supreme Court, and all other Officers of the United States, whose Appointments are not herein otherwise provided for, and which shall be established by Law: but the Congress may by Law vest the Appointment of such inferior Officers, as they think proper, in the President alone, in the Courts of Law, or in the Heads of Departments.

The President shall have Power to fill up all Vacancies that may happen during the Recess of the Senate, by granting Commissions which shall expire at the End of their next Session.

Section 3

He shall from time to time give to the Congress Information of the State of the Union, and recommend to their Consideration such Measures as he shall judge necessary and expedient; he may, on extraordinary Occasions, convene both Houses, or either of them, and in Case of Disagreement between them, with Respect to the Time of Adjournment, he may adjourn them to such Time as he shall think proper; he shall receive Ambassadors and other public Ministers; he shall take Care that the Laws be faithfully executed, and shall Commission all the Officers of the United States.

Section 4

The President, Vice President and all civil Officers of the United States, shall be removed from Office on Impeachment for, and Conviction of, Treason, Bribery, or other high Crimes and Misdemeanors.

Article III

Section 1

The judicial Power of the United States shall be vested in one supreme Court, and in such inferior Courts as the Congress may from time to time ordain and establish. The Judges, both of the supreme and inferior Courts, shall hold their Offices during good Behaviour, and shall, at stated Times, receive for their Services a Compensation, which shall not be diminished during their Continuance in Office.

Section 2

The Judicial Power shall extend to all Cases, in Law and Equity, arising under this Constitution, the Laws of the United States, and Treaties made, or which shall be made, under their Authority; — to all Cases affecting Ambassadors, other public Ministers and Consuls; — to all Cases of admiralty and maritime Jurisdiction; — to Controversies to which the United States shall be a Party; — to Controversies between two or more States; — between a State and Citizens of another State; — between Citizens of different States; — between Citizens of the same State claiming Lands under Grants of different States, and between a State, or the Citizens thereof, and foreign States, Citizens or Subjects.

In all Cases affecting Ambassadors, other public Ministers and Consuls, and those in which a State shall be Party, the supreme Court shall have original Jurisdiction. In all the other Cases before mentioned, the supreme Court shall have appellate Jurisdiction, both as to Law and Fact, with such Exceptions, and under such Regulations as the Congress shall make.

The Trial of all Crimes, except in Cases of Impeachment, shall be by Jury; and such Trial shall be held in the State where the said Crimes shall have been committed; but when not committed within any State, the Trial shall be at such Place or Places as the Congress may by Law have directed.

Section 3

Treason against the United States, shall consist only in levying War against them, or in adhering to their Enemies, giving them Aid and Comfort. No Person shall be convicted of Treason unless on the Testimony of two Witnesses to the same overt Act, or on Confession in open Court.

The Congress shall have Power to declare the Punishment of Treason, but no Attainder of Treason shall work Corruption of Blood, or Forfeiture except during the Life of the Person attainted.

Article IV

Section 1

Full Faith and Credit shall be given in each State to the public Acts, Records, and judicial Proceedings of every other State. And the Congress may by general Laws prescribe the Manner in which such Acts, Records and Proceedings shall be proved, and the Effect thereof.

Section 2

The Citizens of each State shall be entitled to all Privileges and Immunities of Citizens in the several States.

A Person charged in any State with Treason, Felony, or other Crime, who shall flee from Justice, and be found in another State, shall on Demand of the executive Authority of the State from which he fled, be delivered up, to be removed to the State having Jurisdiction of the Crime.

No Person held to Service or Labour in one State, under the Laws thereof, escaping into another, shall, in Consequence of any Law or Regulation therein, be discharged from such Service or Labour, but shall be delivered up on Claim of the Party to whom such Service or Labour may be due.

Section 3

New States may be admitted by the Congress into this Union; but no new State shall be formed or erected within the Jurisdiction of any other State; nor any State be formed by the Junction of two or more States, or Parts of States, without the Consent of the Legislatures of the States concerned as well as of the Congress.

The Congress shall have Power to dispose of and make all needful Rules and Regulations respecting the Territory or other Property belonging to the United States; and nothing in this Constitution shall be so construed as to Prejudice any Claims of the United States, or of any particular State.

Section 4

The United States shall guarantee to every State in this Union a Republican Form of Government, and shall protect each of them against Invasion; and on Application of the Legislature, or of the Executive (when the Legislature cannot be convened), against domestic Violence.

Article V

The Congress, whenever two thirds of both Houses shall deem it necessary, shall propose Amendments to this Constitution, or, on the Application of the Legislatures of two thirds of the several States, shall call a Convention for proposing Amendments, which, in either Case, shall be valid to all Intents and Purposes, as Part of this Constitution, when ratified by the Legislatures of three fourths of the several States, or by Conventions in three fourths thereof, as the one or the other Mode of Ratification may be proposed by the Congress; Provided that no Amendment which may be made prior to the Year One thousand eight hundred and eight shall in any Manner affect the first and fourth Clauses in the Ninth Section of the first Article; and that no State, without its Consent, shall be deprived of its equal Suffrage in the Senate.

Article VI

All Debts contracted and Engagements entered into, before the Adoption of this Constitution, shall be as valid against the United States under this Constitution, as under the Confederation.

This Constitution, and the Laws of the United States which shall be made in Pursuance thereof; and all Treaties made, or which shall be made, under the

Authority of the United States, shall be the supreme Law of the Land; and the Judges in every State shall be bound thereby, any Thing in the Constitution or Laws of any State to the Contrary notwithstanding.

The Senators and Representatives before mentioned, and the Members of the several State Legislatures, and all executive and judicial Officers, both of the United States and of the several States, shall be bound by Oath or Affirmation, to support this Constitution; but no religious Test shall ever be required as a Qualification to any Office or public Trust under the United States.

Article VII

The Ratification of the Conventions of nine States, shall be sufficient for the Establishment of this Constitution between the States so ratifying the Same. Done in Convention by the Unanimous Consent of the States present the Seventeenth Day of September in the Year of our Lord one thousand seven hundred and Eighty seven and of the Independence of the United States of America the Twelfth.

Amendment I [1791]

Congress shall make no law respecting an establishment of religion, or prohibiting the free exercise thereof; or abridging the freedom of speech, or of the press; or the right of the people peaceably to assemble, and to petition the Government for a redress of grievances.

Amendment II [1791]

A well regulated Militia, being necessary to the security of a free State, the right of the people to keep and bear Arms, shall not be infringed.

Amendment III [1791]

No Soldier shall, in time of peace be quartered in any house, without the consent of the Owner, nor in time of war, but in a manner to be prescribed by law.

Amendment IV [1791]

The right of the people to be secure in their persons, houses, papers, and effects, against unreasonable searches and seizures, shall not be violated, and no Warrants shall issue, but upon probable cause, supported by Oath or affirmation, and particularly describing the place to be searched, and the persons or things to be seized.

Amendment V [1791]

No person shall be held to answer for a capital, or otherwise infamous crime, unless on a presentment or indictment of a Grand Jury, except in cases arising in the land or naval forces, or in the Militia, when in actual service in time of War or public danger; nor shall any person be subject for the same offence to be twice put in jeopardy of life or limb; nor shall be compelled in any criminal case to be a witness against himself, nor be deprived of life, liberty, or property, without due process of law; nor shall private property be taken for public use, without just compensation.

Amendment VI [1791]

In all criminal prosecutions, the accused shall enjoy the right to a speedy and public trial, by an impartial jury of the State and district wherein the crime shall have been committed, which district shall have been previously ascertained by law, and to be informed of the nature and cause of the accusation; to be confronted with the witnesses against him; to have compulsory process for obtaining witnesses in his favor, and to have the Assistance of Counsel for his defence.

Amendment VII [1791]

In suits at common law, where the value in controversy shall exceed twenty dollars, the right of trial by jury shall be preserved, and no fact tried by a jury, shall be otherwise reexamined in any Court of the United States, than according to the rules of the common law.

Amendment VIII [1791]

Excessive bail shall not be required, nor excessive fines imposed, nor cruel and unusual punishments inflicted.

Amendment IX [1791]

The enumeration in the Constitution, of certain rights, shall not be construed to deny or disparage others retained by the people.

Amendment X [1791]

The powers not delegated to the United States by the Constitution, nor prohibited by it to the States, are reserved to the States respectively, or to the people.

Amendment XI [1798]

The Judicial power of the United States shall not be construed to extend to any suit in law or equity, commenced or prosecuted against one of the United States by Citizens of another State, or by Citizens or Subjects of any Foreign State.

Amendment XII [1804]

The Electors shall meet in their respective states and vote by ballot for President and Vice-President, one of whom, at least, shall not be an inhabitant of the same state with themselves; they shall name in their ballots the person voted for as President, and in distinct ballots the person voted for as Vice-President, and they shall make distinct lists of all persons voted for as President, and of all persons voted for as Vice-President, and of the number of votes for each, which lists they shall sign and certify, and transmit sealed to the seat of the government of the United States, directed to the President of the Senate; — the President of the Senate shall, in the presence of the Senate and House of Representatives, open all the certificates and the votes shall then be counted; — The person having the greatest number of votes for President, shall be the President, if such number be a majority of the whole number of Electors appointed; and if no person have such majority, then from the persons having the highest numbers not exceeding three on the list of those voted for as President, the House of Representatives shall chuse immediately, by ballot, the President. But in chusing the President, the votes shall be taken by states, the representation from each state having one vote; a quorum for this purpose shall consist of a member or members from two-thirds of the states, and a majority of all the states shall be necessary to a choice. [And if the House of Representatives shall not chuse a President whenever the right of choice shall devolve upon them, before the fourth day of March next following, then the Vice-President shall act as President, as in case of the death or other constitutional disability of the President. — The person having the greatest number of votes as Vice-President, shall be the Vice-President, if such number be a majority of the whole number of Electors appointed, and if no person have a majority, then from the two highest numbers on the list, the Senate shall choose the Vice-President; a quorum for the purpose shall consist of two-thirds of the whole number of Senators, and a majority of the whole number shall be necessary to a choice. But no person constitutionally ineligible to the office of President shall be eligible to that of Vice-President of the United States.

Amendment XIII [1865]

Section 1. Neither slavery nor involuntary servitude, except as a punishment for crime whereof the party shall have been duly convicted, shall exist within the United States, or any place subject to their jurisdiction.

Section 2. Congress shall have power to enforce this article by appropriate legislation.

Amendment XIV [1868]

Section 1. All persons born or naturalized in the United States, and subject to the jurisdiction thereof, are citizens of the United States and of the State wherein they reside. No State shall make or enforce any law which shall abridge the privileges or immunities of citizens of the United States; nor shall any State deprive any person of life, liberty, or property, without due process of law; nor deny to any person within its jurisdiction the equal protection of the laws.

Section 2. Representatives shall be apportioned among the several States according to their respective numbers, counting the whole number of persons in each State, excluding Indians not taxed. But when the right to vote at any election for the choice of electors for President and Vice-President of the United States, Representatives in Congress, the Executive and Judicial officers of a State, or the members of the Legislature thereof, is denied to any of the male inhabitants of such State, being twenty-one years of age, and citizens of the United States, or in any way abridged, except for participation in rebellion, or other crime, the basis of representation therein shall be reduced in the proportion which the number of such male citizens shall bear to the whole number of male citizens twenty-one years of age in such State.

Section 3. No person shall be a Senator or Representative in Congress, or elector of President and Vice-President, or hold any office, civil or military, under the United States, or under any State, who, having previously taken an oath, as a member of Congress, or as an officer of the United States, or as a member of any State legislature, or as an executive or judicial officer of any State, to support the Constitution of the United States, shall have engaged in insurrection or rebellion against the same, or given aid or comfort to the enemies thereof. But Congress may by a vote of two-thirds of each House, remove such disability.

Section 4. The validity of the public debt of the United States, authorized by law, including debts incurred for payment of pensions and bounties for services in suppressing insurrection or rebellion, shall not be questioned. But neither the United States nor any State shall assume or pay any debt or obligation incurred in aid of insurrection or rebellion against the United States, or any claim for the loss or emancipation of any slave; but all such debts, obligations and claims shall be held illegal and void.

Section 5. The Congress shall have the power to enforce, by appropriate legislation, the provisions of this article.

Amendment XV [1870]

Section 1. The right of citizens of the United States to vote shall not be denied or abridged by the United States or by any State on account of race, color, or previous condition of servitude.

Section 2. The Congress shall have the power to enforce this article by appropriate legislation.

Amendment XVI [1913]

The Congress shall have power to lay and collect taxes on incomes, from whatever source derived, without apportionment among the several States, and without regard to any census or enumeration.

Amendment XVII [1913]

The Senate of the United States shall be composed of two Senators from each State, elected by the people thereof, for six years; and each Senator shall have one vote. The electors in each State shall have the qualifications requisite for electors of the most numerous branch of the State legislatures.

When vacancies happen in the representation of any State in the Senate, the executive authority of such State shall issue writs of election to fill such vacancies: *Provided,* That the legislature of any State may empower the executive thereof to make temporary appointments until the people fill the vacancies by election as the legislature may direct.

This amendment shall not be so construed as to affect the election or term of any Senator chosen before it becomes valid as part of the Constitution.

Amendment XVIII [1919]

Section 1. After one year from the ratification of this article the manufacture, sale, or transportation of intoxicating liquors within, the importation thereof into, or the exportation thereof from the United States and all territory subject to the jurisdiction thereof for beverage purposes is hereby prohibited.

Section 2. The Congress and the several States shall have concurrent power to enforce this article by appropriate legislation.

Section 3. This article shall be inoperative unless it shall have been ratified as an amendment to the Constitution by the legislatures of the several States, as provided in the Constitution, within seven years from the date of the submission hereof to the States by the Congress.

Amendment XIX [1920]

The right of citizens of the United States to vote shall not be denied or abridged by the United States or by any State on account of sex.

Congress shall have power to enforce this article by appropriate legislation.

Amendment XX [1933]

Section 1. The terms of the President and the Vice President shall end at noon on the 20th day of January, and the terms of Senators and Representatives at noon on the 3d day of January, of the years in which such terms would have ended if this article had not been ratified; and the terms of their successors shall then begin.

Section 2. The Congress shall assemble at least once in every year, and such meeting shall begin at noon on the 3d day of January, unless they shall by law appoint a different day.

Section 3. If, at the time fixed for the beginning of the term of the President, the President elect shall have died, the Vice President elect shall become President. If a President shall not have been chosen before the time fixed for the beginning of his term, or if the President elect shall have failed to qualify, then the Vice President elect shall act as President until a President shall have qualified; and the Congress may by law provide for the case wherein neither a President elect nor a Vice President shall have qualified, declaring who shall then act as President, or the manner in which one who is to act shall be selected, and such person shall act accordingly until a President or Vice President shall have qualified.

Section 4. The Congress may by law provide for the case of the death of any of the persons from whom the House of Representatives may chuse a President whenever the right of choice shall have devolved upon them, and for the case of the death of any of the persons from whom the Senate may chuse a Vice President whenever the right of choice shall have devolved upon them.

Section 5. Sections 1 and 2 shall take effect on the 15th day of October following the ratification of this article.

Section 6. This article shall be inoperative unless it shall have been ratified as an amendment to the Constitution by the legislatures of three-fourths of the several States within seven years from the date of its submission.

Amendment XXI [1933]

Section 1. The eighteenth article of amendment to the Constitution of the United States is hereby repealed.

Section 2. The transportation or importation into any State, Territory, or Possession of the United States for delivery or use therein of intoxicating liquors, in violation of the laws thereof, is hereby prohibited.

Section 3. This article shall be inoperative unless it shall have been ratified as an amendment to the Constitution by conventions in the several States, as provided in the Constitution, within seven years from the date of the submission hereof to the States by the Congress.

Amendment XXII [1951]

Section 1. No person shall be elected to the office of the President more than twice, and no person who has held the office of President, or acted as President, for more than two years of a term to which some other person was elected President shall be elected to the office of President more than once. But this Article shall not apply to any person holding the office of President when this Article was proposed by Congress, and shall not prevent any person who may be holding the office of President, or acting as President, during the term within which this Article becomes operative from holding the office of President or acting as President during the remainder of such term.

Section 2. This article shall be inoperative unless it shall have been ratified as an amendment to the Constitution by the legislatures of three-fourths of the several States within seven years from the date of its submission to the States by the Congress.

Amendment XXIII [1961]

Section 1. The District constituting the seat of Government of the United States shall appoint in such manner as Congress may direct: A number of electors of President and Vice President equal to the whole number of Senators and Representatives in Congress to which the District would be entitled if it were a State, but in no event more than the least populous State; they shall be in addition to those appointed by the States, but they shall be considered, for the purposes of the election of President and Vice President, to be electors appointed by a State; and they shall meet in the District and perform such duties as provided by the twelfth article of amendment.

Section 2. The Congress shall have power to enforce this article by appropriate legislation.

Amendment XXIV [1964]

Section 1. The right of citizens of the United States to vote in any primary or other election for President or Vice President, for electors for President or Vice President, or for Senator or Representative in Congress, shall not be denied or abridged by the United States or any State by reason of failure to pay poll tax or other tax.

Section 2. The Congress shall have power to enforce this article by appropriate legislation.

Amendment XXV [1967]

Section 1. In case of the removal of the President from office or of his death or resignation, the Vice President shall become President.

Section 2. Whenever there is a vacancy in the office of the Vice President, the President shall nominate a Vice President who shall take office upon confirmation by a majority vote of both Houses of Congress.

Section 3. Whenever the President transmits to the President pro tempore of the Senate and the Speaker of the House of Representatives his written declaration that he is unable to discharge the powers and duties of his office, and until he transmits to them a written declaration to the contrary, such powers and duties shall be discharged by the Vice President as Acting President.

Section 4. Whenever the Vice President and a majority of either the principal officers of the executive departments or of such other body as Congress may by law provide, transmit to the President pro tempore of the Senate and the Speaker of the House of Representatives their written declaration that the President is unable to discharge the powers and duties of his office, the Vice President shall immediately assume the powers and duties of the office as Acting President.

Thereafter, when the President transmits to the President pro tempore of the Senate and the Speaker of the House of Representatives his written declaration that no inability exists, he shall resume the powers and duties of his office unless the Vice President and a majority of either the principal officers of the executive department or of such other body as Congress may by law provide, transmit within four days to the President pro tempore of the Senate and the Speaker of the House of Representatives their written declaration that the President is unable to discharge the powers and duties of his office. Thereupon Congress shall decide the issue, assembling within forty-eight hours for that purpose if not in session. If the Congress, within twenty-one days after receipt of the latter written declaration, or, if Congress is not in session, within twenty-one days after Congress is required to assemble, determines by two-thirds vote of both Houses that the President is unable to discharge the powers and duties of his office, the Vice President shall continue to discharge the same as Acting President; otherwise, the President shall resume the powers and duties of his office.

Amendment XXVI [1971]

Section 1. The right of citizens of the United States, who are eighteen years of age or older, to vote shall not be denied or abridged by the United States or by any State on account of age.

Section 2. The Congress shall have power to enforce this article by appropriate legislation.

Amendment XXVII [1992]

No law, varying the compensation for the services of the Senators and Representatives, shall take effect, until an election of representatives shall have intervened.

Glossary

Accusation   A document that charges a defendant with a misdemeanor in most state courts.

Acquit   Finding the defendant in a criminal case not guilty.

Affidavit   A written statement where a person swears an oath that the facts contained are true.

Affirm   When a higher court declares that a lower court's action was valid and right.

Affirmative defenses   Defenses that are something more than a mere denial and that require that the defense present evidence and/or testimony to prove, either by a preponderance of evidence or by clear and convincing evidence, that the defense is true.

Aggravation of sentence   Evidence offered by the state to enhance or lengthen the defendant's sentence.

***Alford* plea**   A plea, authorized by the U.S. Supreme Court, that allows a defendant to enter a guilty plea, but basing the plea on the amount and quantity of evidence against him instead of the defendant's belief in his actual guilt.

Alibi   A defense that the defendant was not present when the crime occurred.

Allegata   (Latin) the allegations contained in a charging document.

Alternate juror   A person selected to sit on the jury, but who will have no right to participate in the deliberations and will not be able to vote to return a verdict.

Answer   The defendant's written response to the complaint, usually containing denials of the defendant's responsibility for the plaintiff's injuries.

Anticipatory warrants   Warrants issued for contraband or evidence that has not yet arrived at its final destination.

Appeal   Asking a higher court to review the actions of a lower court in order to correct mistakes or injustice.

Appellant   The party bringing the current appeal from an adverse ruling in a lower court.

Appellee   The party who won in the lower court.

Arraignment   A court hearing where the defendant is informed of the charge against him or her and given the opportunity to enter a plea of guilty or not guilty.

Arrest   Detention and restraint of a suspect by a law enforcement official; a person who is detained and is not free to leave.

Attenuation doctrine   The connection between the constitutional violation and the evidence has been interrupted by some intervening event, such as time or distance, so that a constitutional violation is no longer as severe as it was originally.

Bail   The posting of a monetary amount to guarantee the return of the defendant for subsequent court hearings.

Batson challenge   A challenge to the strikes used by a party during jury selection that claims the party used discriminatory practices in removing members of the panel.

Battered Woman's Syndrome   An affirmative defense that asks the jury to excuse a woman's attack on her supposed long-time abuser or asks the judge to mitigate her sentence in reflection of the fact that she was responding to a long period of abuse at the hands of the "victim."

Bench   The place in the courtroom reserved for the judge.

Bench conference   A private conference held at the judge's bench between the attorneys and the judge.

Bench trial   A trial where the judge decides both questions of law and the final verdict in the case; no jury is present.

Bench warrant   A warrant issued for the arrest of a person who was scheduled to appear in court but failed to do so.

Bifurcated trial   Separate hearings for different issues in the same case; for example, for guilt and sanity or guilt and punishment in a criminal case.

Bill of particulars   A defendant's motion requesting dates, names, locations and addresses for the charges set out in the indictment.

Binding over   A determination that probable cause exists in a preliminary hearing, triggering a transfer of the case to a higher court, usually superior court.

Bond   A promise of specific monetary amount promised to the state and offered as a guarantee for the defendant's return to court at a later date.

Bond forfeiture   A judicial determination that the defendant has violated the conditions of his or her release and that the defendant should be placed into custody pending further hearings.

Bonding company   A private business that posts bonds for individuals who have been charged with crimes and will be forced to pay the balance of the defendant's bond if the defendant flees the jurisdiction or otherwise does not appear for a court date.

Bounty hunter   An employee of a bonding company who works to locate defendants who have absconded and to return these defendants to face their court dates.

***Brady* material**   Information available to the prosecutor that is favorable to the defendant, either because it mitigates his guilt or his sentence. This material must be provided to the defense prior to trial.

Brief   A written statement prepared by one side in a lawsuit to explain its case to the judge.

Burden of proof   The amount of proof that a party must bring to sustain an action against another party. The burden of proof is different in civil and criminal cases.

Calendar/docket   A listing of the cases currently pending before the court, usually by the defendants' names, case file number and charges brought against them.

Case in chief   The body of evidence and testimony offered by a party during its presentation of a jury trial.

Case law   The written decisions by appellate courts explaining the outcome of a case on appeal.

***Certiorari* (Cert)**   (Latin), "To make sure;" Cert is a court's authority to decide which cases it will hear on appeal and which it will not.

Challenge for cause   A formal objection to the qualifications or attitude of a prospective juror.

Charge conference   A meeting held after the close of evidence in a trial and before the closing arguments where the attorneys and the judge discuss what jury instructions will be given to the jurors.

Charging decision   The process that a prosecutor goes through to determine what is the appropriate and just charge to bring against a defendant based on the law and the facts in the case.

Citizen's arrest   A legal doctrine that holds harmless a citizen who detains a person observed to have committed a crime.

Clear and convincing evidence   The version presented by the party is highly probable to be true and is a higher standard than preponderance of the evidence.

Clerk   A court official who maintains records of dispositions in both civil and criminal cases.

Closing argument   An attorney's summation of his or her case during which the attorney seeks to convince the jury to a return a verdict favorable to his or her side.

Code   A collection of laws.

Coercion   The direct threat of physical violence to make a person commit a crime that he or she would not ordinarily commit.

Common law   All case law or the case law that is made by judges in the absence of relevant statutes or the legal system that originated in England and is composed of case law and statutes.

Complaint   The document filed by the plaintiff and served on the defendant that sets out the plaintiff's factual allegations that show the defendant is responsible for the plaintiff's injuries.

Complete defense   A defense that would completely exonerate the defendant of the crime charged, assuming the defendant presents sufficient evidence to meet his or her burden of proof (usually preponderance of the evidence).

Concurrent sentencing   One or more sentences that are served at the same time.

Conditional plea   A plea entered by the defendant who maintains his or her innocence but states that the evidence against him or her is overwhelming.

Confidential informant   A person who works with the police, providing them information about illegal activities

Consecutive sentencing   One or more sentences that are served on after the other.

Consent   When the victim gives knowing and voluntary to the actions of the defendant. Not allowed in all types of crimes, such as murder.

Contraband   An object that is illegal to possess, including child pornography, certain types of weapons, and illegal narcotics, among others.

Court reporter   A trained professional who is responsible for taking down every spoken word in the courtroom during a hearing and reproducing those words as a transcript.

Court-appointed attorney A private, local attorney who is selected by a judge to handle a criminal case; this attorney is paid by the state, usually an hourly basis.

Cross-examination Asking questions of a witness to determine, bias, lack of knowledge, prejudice or some other failing.

Cross-examine To question a witness for the opposition about his or possible bias, prejudice, or lack of knowledge about the issues in the case.

Damages Money that a court orders paid to a person who has suffered damages by the person who caused the injury.

Diminished capacity Inability of the defendant to understand the actions that he or she took and why his or her actions constituted a crime.

Direct examination The questions asked of a witness by the attorney who has called him or her to the stand.

Directed verdict A ruling by a judge that there is not sufficient evidence of the defendant's guilt to present to the jury.

Discovery The exchange of information, witness statements and other evidence between the state and the defense attorney in a criminal case.

Docket number The number assigned to a case on appeal; all subsequent briefs and other documents must bear this number.

Double jeopardy A constitutional provision that prohibits a person from being tried twice for the same crime.

Due process A clause in the Fifth Amendment that guarantees that each and every defendant will receive the same procedural safeguards throughout a criminal case, regardless of the charge.

Duress Unlawful psychological and mental pressure brought to bear on a person to force him or her to commit a crime that the person would ordinarily not commit.

Entrapment A defense that claims government agents induced a defendant to commit a crime when he or she was not pre-disposed to do so.

Enumerations of error The specification of an error committed in the trial court that an appellate seeks to overturn on appeal.

Ex post facto An action that is criminalized only after it has been committed.

Exclusionary rule A court-created rule that forbids the use of any evidence to be used that was acquired in violation of the Fourth Amendment.

Exculpatory Evidence that tends to provide an excuse or a justification for the defendant's actions or that shows that the defendant did not commit the crime charged.

Exigent circumstance An emergency situation requiring aid or immediate action.

Expectation of privacy The Constitutional standard that a court must determine before issuing a search warrant. If an area has a high expectation of privacy, then a warrant will be required; if low or non-existent, then no warrant is required.

Felony A crime that can be punished with a sentence of one year or more.

Four Corners Test A judicial requirement that a warrant affidavit contain all necessary information in the materials before the warrant was issued.

Fresh pursuit doctrine A court-created doctrine that allows police officers to arrest suspects without warrants and to cross territorial boundaries while they are still pursuing the suspect.

Fruit of the poisonous tree doctrine The rule that evidence gathered as a result of evidence gained in an illegal search or questioning cannot be used against the person searched or questioned even if later evidence was gathered lawfully.

Good faith doctrine A court-created doctrine that holds that evidence will not be suppressed under the Exclusionary Rule when officers were acting in good-faith and had no reason to know that the warrant was invalid.

Grand jury A group of citizens who consider felony charges against defendants and make a determination that there is sufficient evidence to warrant further prosecution.

Guilty The verdict in a criminal case where the jurors have determined that the defendant has committed a crime.

Guilty but mentally ill A finding that the defendant is guilty of the crime charged but has some mental problems or mental disease that mitigate his guilt to a small degree.

Habeas corpus "You have the body;" A judicial order to a prison system ordering that the incarcerated person be brought to court for a hearing; a constitutional mechanism that allows convicts to challenge their sentences.

Hung jury A jury that is unable to reach a unanimous verdict.

Immunity A grant to an individual that exempts him or her from being prosecuted based on the testimony that the person gives.

Impeachment   To show that a witness is not worthy of belief.

In absentia   (Latin) The defendant is not present.

In camera   (Latin) "In chambers"; a review of a file by a judge carried out in his or her private office.

Indictment   A document that charges a defendant with a felony.

Inevitable discovery rule   An exception to the exclusionary rule where the evidence would have been discovered one way or another, even if one of the methods violated the Fourth Amendment.

Inference   A fact that a person can believe is probably true.

Information   A document that charges a defendant with a misdemeanor in federal court.

Initial appearance   A hearing that takes place within days of the suspect's arrest, where the suspect is advised of his or her constitutional rights and given the opportunity to request a court-appointed attorney, and where the court can confirm the defendant's identity.

Insanity   A defense that claims that at the time that the defendant committed the crime, he or she did not know the difference between right and wrong.

Interrogation   Questioning of a suspect to determine if he or she has committed a crime.

Intoxication   When a person is acting under the influence of alcohol or other drugs to the extent that judgment and motor reflexes are impaired.

Jackson v. Denno **hearing**   A pre-trial hearing where the government must show that the defendant gave a knowing, voluntary statement after being advised of his rights and that he was not compelled to do so by promises, threats, intimidation or other means.

Join issue   The parties officially submit the case to a jury for a determination and verdict.

Jurisdiction   The power of a court to render a decision on issues and to impose that decision on the parties in the case.

Jury box   An area that is separated from the rest of a courtroom and is reserved exclusively for jurors during a trial.

Jury instructions   A judge's directions to the jury about the law that pertains to the issues in the trial and the jury's function once they retire to the jury room.

Jury trial   A trial with a judge and jury, not just a judge.

Liable   A finding in a civil case that a party has a duty or obligation to the other party to pay damages or to carry out some other action.

Magistrate   A judge who has limited power and authority.

Miranda **rights**   The rights that must be read to a person who has been arrested and then questioned by the police.

Misdemeanor   A criminal offense that is punished by a maximum possible sentence of one year or less in custody.

Mistrial   A trial that the judge ends and declares will have no legal effect.

Mitigation of sentence   Evidence offered by the defense to lessen or shorten the defendant's sentence.

Motion   An oral or written request to a court to take some action.

Motion for change of venue   A motion to transfer the location of the trial to another area, often brought when there is extensive pretrial publicity.

Motion for continuance   A request by one party to postpone a trial or other hearing for a future date.

Motion for new trial   A motion, filed by the defendant after sentencing, that requests a new trial based on errors or irregularities in the trial; if denied, it begins the appellate process.

Motion in aggravation of sentence   A motion filed by the state that seeks to enhance the defendant's sentence based on his or her prior convictions.

Motion *in limine*   (Latin) "At the beginning." A motion in limine is a motion by one party that requests specific judicial rulings at the outset of the trial.

Motion to "reveal the deal"   Also known as a *Giglio* motion, a request from the defense for any information about any offers, inducements or sentence recommendations made to any of the state's witnesses against the defendant.

Motion to quash   A motion filed with the court that describes the material that has been subject to subpoena and the reason that the party objects to producing those documents. In such a case, a judge would quash the subpoena and refuse to allow the grand jury to review the materials.

Motion to suppress   A motion that requests a court not allow the jury to hear specific information, such as the defendant's confession or other statements based on improprieties in obtaining the information.

Mutual combat   A defense that claims that the defendant and the victim voluntarily entered into a physical confrontation.

Necessity   The defense that a defendant committed a crime in order to avoid an act of nature or of God.

No bill   A grand jury's determination that there is insufficient probable cause to continue the prosecution against the accused.

Nolle prosequi   An order dismissing a criminal charge.

Nolo contendere   (Latin) "I do not contest;" A plea offered in a criminal case where the defendant does not contest his or her guilt and asks for the court's mercy.

Not guilty   The jury's determination that the state has failed to prove that the defendant committed the crime beyond a reasonable doubt.

Not guilty by reason of insanity   A finding that the defendant did not understand the difference between right and wrong when he or she committed the offense and therefore lacks the mental capability to commit a crime.

Notice of appeal   The official docketing and commencement of the appeals process.

Open fields doctrine   A court principle that allows police to search without a warrant when the evidence is located in a public setting, such as farmland or beside a road.

Open file policy   A policy in some prosecution offices that the defense is entitled to review the entirety of the state's case against the defendant, with the exclusion of work product and memoranda from the prosecutor about trial tactics and strategy.

Opening statement   A preliminary address to the jury by the prosecutor and defense attorney, outlining the general facts of the case.

Oral argument   A presentation of an appeal done orally before a panel of judges or justices.

Ordinance   A law passed by a local government, such as a town council or city government.

Overbroad   When a search warrant allows police far too much discretion in what they may search; similar to the prohibition against general searches.

Parole   A release from prison, before a sentence is finished, that depends on the person's "keeping clean" and doing what he or she is supposed to do while out.

Peremptory challenge   A strike of a juror for any reason, except based on race or sex.

Petition for cert   A petition filed by a party on appeal requesting a court to consider its appeal and grant cert.

Placing character into evidence   When a criminal defendant testifies and his previous criminal record is allowed into evidence through the cross-examination of the defendant.

Plain view doctrine   A court principle that allows police to search without a warrant when they see evidence of a crime in an unconcealed manner.

Plea of former jeopardy   A defendant's motion stating that he or she has already been prosecuted for the underlying offense, and any further prosecution is barred by the Fifth Amendment.

Pleading the Fifth   When a person refuses to answer on the grounds that the answer might tend to incriminate him.

Pleadings   1) In a civil case, the pleadings set out the wrong suffered by the parties against one another; 2) in a criminal case, the pleadings are often referred to as indictments (in felony cases) and accusations/informations (in misdemeanor cases), where the state sets out an infraction by the defendant that violates the law.

Preliminary hearing   A court hearing that determines if there is probable cause to believe that the defendant committed the crime with which he or she is charged.

Preponderance of the evidence   The standard of proof most closely associated with civil case where a party proves that his or her version of the facts is more than likely to be true.

Pre-sentence investigation   An investigation by court-appoint social workers, probation officers, and others, into a criminal's background to determine the criminal's prospects for rehabilitation.

Presumption   A conclusion about a fact that must be made unless and until refuted by other evidence.

Presumption of innocence   A basic tenet of American law that a defendant enters the criminal process clothed in the assumption that he or she is innocent unless and until the prosecution proves that he or she is guilty beyond a reasonable doubt.

Pretextual stops   The detention or arrest of a person for a minor offense when the officer really suspects that the defendant has committed a more serious crime.

Prima facie   Facts that are considered true as presented until they are disproven by some contrary evidence.

Privilege A right to refuse to answer questions and to prevent disclosure of information communicated within a legally recognized confidential relationship.

Pro se (Latin) "By oneself;" a person who chooses to represent himself or herself in a legal proceeding.

Probable cause The constitutional requirement that law enforcement officers have reasonable belief that a person has committed a crime.

Probata (Latin) the proof elicited in a trial.

Probation Allowing a person convicted of a criminal offense to avoid serving a jail sentence imposed on the person, so long as he or she abides by certain conditions (including being supervised by a probation officer).

Proof beyond a reasonable doubt The burden of proof in a criminal case; when one has a reasonable doubt, it is not mere conjecture but a doubt that would cause a prudent, rational person to hesitate before finding a defendant guilty of a crime.

Property bond Posting of real estate to guarantee the defendant's return for a subsequent court appearance.

Proportionality The U.S. Supreme Court has mandated that a sentence must be proportional to the crime to satisfy the Eighth Amendment. For instance, without some other aggravating circumstance, a life sentence for a petty infraction would be out of proportion and would be a violation of the Eighth Amendment.

Public defender attorney A government attorney who works for an office in the court system whose sole responsibility is to provide legal representation to those individuals who are charged with crimes.

Quash Do away with, annul, overthrow, cease.

Reasonable doubt The standard of proof that the prosecution must meet in order to prove that a defendant committed a crime.

Rebuttal To deny or take away the effect of the other party's presentation; a rebuttal attacks claims made by one party with evidence presented by the other.

Recess A short break in the proceedings in a trial.

Recognizance bond The person accused simply gives his or her word that he or she will return for a specific court date.

Record The evidence, pleadings, motions, transcript of the trial, and any other documents relevant to the case.

Redirect examination The process of questioning a witness who was originally called on direct examination to clear up any issues raised during cross-examination.

Remand Send back. For example, when a higher court requires additional information about a case, it returns it to the trial court.

Restitution Money that a court orders a criminal defendant to pay to the victim of a crime for damage or destruction of the victim's property.

Retainer A fee charged at the beginning of a case to pay an attorney for all actions carried out.

Reverse Set aside; when an appellate court decides that the actions of a lower court were incorrect.

Reversible error A mistake made by a judge in the procedures used at trial, or in making legal ruling during the trial.

Search warrant A court order authorizing law enforcement to enter, search, and remove evidence of a crime.

Self-defense The defense that the defendant injured or killed another, but only as a direct threat to the defendant's well-being.

Self-incrimination A provision of the Fifth Amendment that prohibits a person from being forced to give evidence against himself.

Sentence The punishment, such as a prison sentence or fine that is imposed on a convicted defendant by a judge.

Sever Separate or cut off into constituent parts.

Similar transactions motion A motion brought by the state showing that the defendant has committed similar offenses, and this shows his bent of mind, motive or course of conduct.

Simple defenses Defenses that are automatically triggered when a defendant is charged with a crime. A defendant is not required to submit any evidence or testimony to raise a simple defense.

Speedy trial A constitutional guarantee that a person must receive a trial within a reasonable period of time after being arraigned.

Stale When too much time has passed between the application and issuance of a warrant, and the search that it authorizes.

Standing The requirement that before persons challenges a court's action they must show an adverse effect on their personal interest; a recognized legal right to bring suit to challenge a legal decision.

Stare decisis The principle that courts will reach results similar to those reached by courts in prior cases involving similar facts and legal issues.

Statement of facts Part of an appellate brief, this section contains an accurate and detailed breakdown of the specific facts that gave rise original lawsuit.

Statute A law that is voted on by the legislature branch of and enacted by the executive branch.

Statute of limitations The time period in which a criminal case must be commenced or is barred forever.

Stop and frisk The right of a law enforcement officer to pat down a person's outer clothing for weapons, whether the person is under arrest or not.

Striking a jury The process of questioning and removing panel members until twelve jurors are left; these twelve will serve on the jury.

Style The caption, title or heading listing the parties to the case.

Subpoena A court order demanding that a person or item be produced to the court at a specific date and time.

Supremacy Clause The provision in Article VI of the U.S. Constitution that the U.S. Constitution, laws and treaties take precedence over conflicting state constitutions or laws.

Term of court The period of time slates for court hearings; it can be as short as a week or as long as a year.

Terry stops A brief detention of a suspect to follow up on specific investigative issues.

True bill A grand jury's determination that there is sufficient probable cause to continue the prosecution against the accused.

U.S. Supreme Court The name for the highest court of the United States federal and state court systems.

Venire The group of local citizens who are summoned for jury duty and from whom a jury will be selected.

Venue The particular geographic area where a court or an official can exercise power; an example of venue would be the county's borders.

Verdict A jury's factual determination; a jury's finding.

Victim impact statement The right of a victim of a crime to address the court during the defendant's sentencing and to testify about the effect that the defendant's crime has had on the victim.

Voir dire (French) To see, to say; the questioning of a jury panel member to determine if the person is competent to serve on a jury.

Voluntary encounter A brief encounter between police and the individual or the individual is not only free to leave but is under no compulsion to answer any of the police officer's questions.

Waiving arraignment A defendant surrenders the right to have the indictment read in open court; however, the defendant does not surrender any other rights.

Warrant An order, issued by a judge that authorizes a police officer to arrest a suspect or conduct a search.

Work product An attorney's personal notes about strategy, weaknesses, strengths, and general ideas about how to proceed in a case.

Index

A

Abandoned property, searches without a warrant, 86–87
Accusation, defined, 146
Acquit, defined, 192
Affidavit, defined, 69
Affirm, defined, 349
Affirmative defenses, 296–308
Affirmative defenses, age, 298–299
Affirmative defenses, alibi, 299
Affirmative defenses, asserting, 296–298
Affirmative defenses, battered woman's syndrome, 299
Affirmative defenses, clear and convincing evidence, 297
Affirmative defenses, coercion, 299–300
Affirmative defenses, complete defense, 299
Affirmative defenses, consent, 300
Affirmative defenses, defending property, 300
Affirmative defenses, defined, 296
Affirmative defenses, diminished capacity, 304–305
Affirmative defenses, duress, 300–301
Affirmative defenses, entrapment, 301
Affirmative defenses, insanity, 301–305
Affirmative defenses, intoxication, 305
Affirmative defenses, mutual combat, 305–306
Affirmative defenses, necessity, 306
Affirmative defenses, self-defense, 306–308
Age, defense, 298–299
Agency rules and regulations, 5–6
Aggravating factors, death penalty, 329
Aggravation of sentence, 253
Aggravation of sentence, defined, 327
Alford plea, defined, 320
Alibi, defined, 299
Allegata v. *probata*, 295–296
Allegata, defense, 295–296
Alternate juror, 269
Alternative prisons, 330–331
Anonymous phone calls, probable cause, 60

Answer, civil case, 24
Anticipatory warrant, search warrant limitations, 90
Appeal, 344
Appeal, appellant, 344
Appeal, brief, 344
Appeal, defined, 342
Appeal, docket number, 343
Appeal, motion for new trial, 342
Appeal, notice of appeal, 342
Appeal, reversible error, 344
Appeal, the record, 343
Appeals, *certiorari*, 347
Appeals, denial of cert, 348
Appeals, granting cert, 348
Appeals, petition for cert, 347
Appellant, defined, 344
Appellant's brief, 344–346
Appellate brief, argument, 345–346
Appellate brief, conclusion, 346
Appellate brief, enumerations of error, 345
Appellate brief, statement of facts, 344–345
Appellate brief, title page, 344
Appellate courts, affirm, 349
Appellate courts, habeas corpus, 349–350
Appellate courts, powers of, 348–350
Appellate courts, remand, 349
Appellate courts, reverse, 349
Appellate procedure, 343–346
Appellate system, 342–350
Appellate system, organization of, 350–351
Appellee, defined, 344
Argument, appellate brief, 345–346
Arguments, closing, 277–278
Arraignment, 234–237
Arraignment, bench warrants, 236–237
Arraignment, calendar, 235
Arraignment, defined, 31, 234
Arraignment, docket, 235
Arraignment, filing motions at, 235–236

Arraignment, importance of, 234
Arraignment, purpose of, 235
Arraignment, waiving, 236
Arrest, 62–67
Arrest, actions following, 168–174
Arrest, citizen's, 65
Arrest, court tests, 66–67
Arrest, defined, 62
Arrest, determining the suspect is, 66
Arrest, fresh pursuit doctrine, 65
Arrest, interrogation, 168–169
Arrest, making, 66
Arrest, *Miranda* rights, 169–172
Arrest, outside of the officer's jurisdiction, 65
Arrest, police officers, 64–65
Arrest, probable cause, 26–27, 63
Arrest, procedure after, 174
Arrest, venue, 64
Arrest, who can?, 64–66
Arrest warrants, 67–72
Arrest warrants, affidavit, 69
Arrest warrants, applying for, 69–72
Arrest warrants, drafting, 70
Arrest warrants, government conduct, 68–69
Arrest warrants, identifying the person to be arrested, 71–72
Arrest warrants, legally sufficient, 70–71
Arrest warrants, magistrate, 69
Arrest warrants, the four corners test, 71
Arrest warrants, what happens after issuance, 72
Attenuation, exclusionary rule, 131–132
Attorney, court-appointed, 190–191
Attorney, *Gideon v. Wainwright*, 189–190
Attorney, hiring a, 189
Attorney, retainer, 189
Attorney, right to, 108–109, 188–192
Attorney, right to an attorney at a lineup, 109

B

Bail and bond, 217–223
Bail hearing, 223
Bail, defined, 217
Bargaining, plea, 322–325
Batson challenges, 268
Battered woman's syndrome,
    defined, 299
Bench conference, defined, 263
Bench trial, defined, 263
Bench warrant, defined, 236
Bench warrants, 236–237
Bench, defined, 263
Bench, judge, 263
Bifurcated trial, defined, 328
Bill of particulars, defined, 250
Binding over, defined, 225
Bond forfeiture, defined, 223
Bond, bonding companies,
    219–220
Bond, bounty hunters, 220
Bond, danger of the defendant to the
    victim more community, 223
Bond, defendant's burden in a bail
    hearing, 223
Bond, defendant's likelihood of
    flight, 222
Bond, defendant's ties to the
    community, 221–222
Bond, defined, 217
Bond, factors to consider in setting,
    221–223
Bond, forfeiture, 223
Bond, property, 218
Bond, push to eliminate, 223
Bond, recognizance, 221
Bond, seriousness of the offense, 222
Bonding companies, 219–220
Bonding companies, bounty
    hunters, 220
Bonding company, defined, 219
Brady material, 245–246
Brief, appellant, 344–346
Brief, defined, 344
Burden of proof, 22–23
Burden of proof, explaining the state's
    burden, 204

C

Calendar or docket, defined, 235
Canine officers, searches without a
    warrant, 87
Case law, 4–5
Case-in-chief, defined, 271
Cert, denial of, 348

Cert, petition for, 347
Certiorari, appeals, 347
Certiorari, defined, 347
Challenge for cause, defined, 267
Challenge, *Batson*, 268
Challenge, peremptory, 267
Character evidence, 202–203
Charge conference, 276–277
Charge conference, defined, 277
Charging decision, accusation, 146
Charging decision, additional charges
    against the defendant, 144–145
Charging decision, additional
    investigation, 144
Charging decision, defined, 144
Charging decision, dismiss the case, 146
Charging decision, information, 146
Charging decision, nolle prosequi, 146
Child pornography, defined, 104
Circumstantial evidence, 29
Citizen's arrest, 65
Civil case, answer, 24
Civil case, complaint, 24
Civil case, pleadings, 23–24
Civil case, style, 24
Civil cases, verdicts in, 21–22
Civilian clothing, defendant, 201–202
Clear and convincing evidence,
    defined, 297
Clerk of court, courtroom, 264
Clerk, defined, 264
Closing arguments, 277–278
Closing trial to the public, 197–198
Closing trial to the public, sensitive or
    underage witnesses, 198
Code, defined, 3
Codefendant, statement of, 241
Coercion, defined, 299
Common-law, 6–9
Common-law, importance of, 7–8
Common-law, uses, 8–9
Community service, 332
Complaint, civil case, 24
Complete defense, defined, 299
Conclusion, appellate brief, 346
Concurrent sentence, defined, 326
Conditional plea, defined, 321
Conference, charge, 276–277
Confidential informants, defined, 248
Consecutive sentences, defined, 326
Consent, defense, 300
Consent, defined, 88
Consent, searches without a
    warrant, 88
Constitution, U.S., 2

Constitutional limits on lineups, 110
Constitutions, state, 2–3
Continuance, motion for, 249
Continuum of contacts and their
    constitutional requirements,
    42–43
Contraband, defined, 46
Contraband, searches without a
    warrant, 87
Court-appointed attorney v. public
    defender, 190–191
Court-appointed attorney, defined, 190
Court reporter, defined, 264
Court rules, 5
Courtroom, 262–265
Courtroom, clerk, 264
Courtroom, court reporter, 264–265
Courtroom, defense table, 264
Courtroom, jury box, 262
Courtroom, jury deliberation room, 263
Courtroom, prosecution table, 264
Courtroom, witness stand, 263
Criminal cases, verdicts in, 20–21
Criminal trial, overview, 32–33
Cross-examination, 273–274
Cross-examination, compared to direct
    examination, 273
Cross-examination, impeachment, 274
Cross-examine, defined, 199
Cruel and unusual punishment, 333

D

Damages, 21
Death penalty, 327–329
Death penalty, aggravating factors, 329
Death penalty, bifurcated trial, 328
Death penalty, procedures in, 328
Death penalty, sentencing, 328
Defendant cannot afford an
    attorney, 191
Defendant flees, jury trial, 200
Defendant waives right to be
    present, 201
Defendant, criminal record, 241
Defendant, removed from the
    court, 201
Defendant, statement of, 240
Defendant's likelihood of flight,
    bond, 222
Defendant's ties to the community,
    bond, 221–222
Defending property, defense, 300
Defense case in chief, 275–276
Defense motions, discovery, 246–248
Defense of others, self-defense, 307

Defense table, courtroom, 264
Defense, right to present a, 203
Defense, self, 306–308
Defenses, affirmative, 296–308
Defenses, age, 298–299
Defenses, alibi, 299
Defenses, *allegata* v. *probata*, 295–296
Defenses, asserting affirmative defenses, 296–298
Defenses, battered woman's syndrome, 299
Defenses, clear and convincing evidence, 297
Defenses, coercion, 299–300
Defenses, complete, 299
Defenses, consent, 300
Defenses, constitutional, 290–294
Defenses, defending property, 300
Defenses, defense of others, 307
Defenses, diminished capacity, 304–305
Defenses, double jeopardy, 290–292
Defenses, due process, 292
Defenses, duress, 300–301
Defenses, entrapment, 301
Defenses, equal protection, 292
Defenses, errors in charging documents, 295–296
Defenses, ex post facto, 294
Defenses, First Amendment, 292
Defenses, insanity, 301–305
Defenses, intoxication, 305
Defenses, mutual combat, 305–306
Defenses, necessity, 306
Defenses, self-incrimination, 292
Defenses, self-defense, 306–308
Defenses, simple, 290–296
Defenses, stand your ground laws, 307–308
Defenses, statute of limitations, 294–295
Defenses, technical, 292–296
Defenses, technical deficiencies in charging documents, 296
Defenses, vagueness and overbreadth, 293
Deliberations, 279–280
Denial of cert, 348
Diminished capacity, defined, 304
Direct evidence, 29
Direct examination, 271–272
Direct examination, defined, 271
Direct examination, introducing evidence, 272

Direct examination, questioning witnesses, 272
Directed verdict, 274–275
Discovery, 237–246
Discovery, *Brady* material, 245–246
Discovery, changes to rules, 239
Discovery, criminal records of state witnesses, 244–245
Discovery, defendant's criminal record, 241
Discovery, defense motions, 246–248
Discovery, defined, 237
Discovery, documents and tangible objects, 241
Discovery, exculpatory information, 245
Discovery, *in camera* inspections, 246
Discovery, information normally not discoverable, 243–245
Discovery, material provided, 239–242
Discovery, open file policy, 242
Discovery, purpose of, 238–239
Discovery, scientific reports, 241–242
Discovery, statement of codefendant, 241
Discovery, statement of defendant, 240
Discovery, statements of witnesses, 242
Discovery, variation amongst states, 242–243
Discovery, witness list, 240
Discovery, witness statements, 242
Discovery, work product, 244
DNA, as evidence, 112–113
DNA, database, 113
Docket number, defined, 343
Documents and tangible objects, discovery, 241
Double jeopardy, 13
Double jeopardy, defined, 291
Dropped evidence, searches without a warrant, 86
Due process, defense, 292
Duress, defense, 300–301
Duress, defined, 300

E
Entrapment, defined, 301
Enumerations of error, appellate brief, 345
Equal protection, defense, 292
Errors in charging documents, defense, 295–296
Evidence, circumstantial, 29
Evidence, defined, 29

Evidence, direct, 29
Evidence, First Amendment, 100–105
Evidence, introducing, 272
Evidence, placing character into, 202–203
Evidence, right to present, 202–204
Evidentiary issues, Fifth Amendment, 105–107
Evidentiary issues, Fourth Amendment, 105
Ex post facto, defense, 294
Ex post facto, defined, 294
Examination, direct, 271–272
Examination, redirect, 274
Exclusionary rule, attenuation, 131–132
Exclusionary rule, defined, 124
Exclusionary rule, does the rule work?, 129
Exclusionary rule, exceptions to, 130–133
Exclusionary rule, fruit of the poisonous tree doctrine, 130
Exclusionary rule, good-faith, 132–133
Exclusionary rule, historical development of, 128–129
Exclusionary rule, independent source rule, 131
Exclusionary rule, inevitable discovery, 132
Exclusionary rule, motion to suppress, 125–126
Exclusionary rule, practical aspects, 125
Exclusionary rule, purpose of, 129
Exclusionary rule, search warrant limitations, 90
Exclusionary rule, standing, 127
Exculpatory information, defined, 245
Exigent circumstances, defined, 88
Exigent circumstances, searches without a warrant, 88
Expectation of privacy, defined, 82
Eyewitness identification, 109
Eyewitness ratification, accuracy, 109–110

F
Federal court, levels of, 9–11
Federal courts of appeal, 10–11
Federal district courts, 9–10
Federal prosecutions v. state prosecutions, 13–15
Federal Sentencing Guidelines, 323
Federal v. state court systems, 9–13
Felonies v. misdemeanors, 24–25

Felony, 24
Fines, 332
Fingerprinting, 113–114
First Amendment, defense, 292
First Amendment, establishment and
    free exercise clauses, 100–101
First Amendment, evidence issues,
    100–105
First Amendment, freedom of speech,
    101–102
First Amendment, freedom of speech v.
    freedom of expression, 102–103
First Amendment, prosecutions for
    pornography, 103–104
First Offender Treatment, 321–322
Flight, Probable cause, 61
Four corners test, arrest warrants, 71
Freedom of speech v. freedom of
    expression, 102–103
Freedom of speech, First Amendment,
    101–102
Fresh pursuit doctrine, 65
Fruit of the poisonous tree doctrine,
    defined, 130

G

General searches, search warrant
    limitations, 89
Gideon v. Wainwright, 189–190
Good-faith exception, defined, 132
Grand jury, 31, 105–106, 145–159
Grand jury, after the proceedings, 159
Grand jury, bill of indictment,
    147–150
Grand jury, challenging the
    composition of, 155
Grand jury, defined, 145
Grand jury, function of, 155–156
Grand jury, history of, 151–152
Grand jury, how composed?, 154–155
Grand jury, immunity powers of, 159
Grand jury, motion to quash, 158–159
Grand jury, objecting to a grand jury
    subpoena, 158
Grand jury, only the state's witnesses
    appear, 157
Grand jury, pleading the "Fifth
    Amendment", 107, 158
Grand jury, presenting a case to,
    156–158
Grand jury, prima facie, 149
Grand jury, privilege, 158
Grand jury, subpoena powers, 157–158
Grand jury, the purpose of, 152–154
Grand jury, true bill v. no bill, 151

Grand jury, use of hearsay
    evidence, 106
Guilty, 20
Guilty but mentally ill, 21
Guilty but mentally ill, verdict, 281
Guilty pleas, 318–322
Guilty pleas, *Alford* plea, 320
Guilty pleas, conditional plea, 321
Guilty pleas, First Offender Treatment,
    321–322
Guilty pleas, nolo contendere, 320–321
Guilty pleas, procedure, 318–320
Guilty pleas, voluntariness, 320
Guilty, verdict, 281
Gut feelings or hunches, probable
    cause, 62

H

Habeas corpus, defined, 349
Historical development of insanity
    defense, 302–303
Hung jury, defined, 195

I

Identification, eyewitness, 109
Immunity, defined, 159
Impeachment, cross-examination, 274
Impeachment, defined, 274
In absentia, defined, 200
In camera inspections, 246
Independent source rule, exclusionary
    rule, 131
Indictment, 24
Inevitable discovery rule, defined, 132
Inference, defined, 193
Inferences, presumptions v., 193
Informants, confidential, 248
Informants, probable cause, 59
Information, defined, 146
Initial appearance, 216–217
Initial appearance, defined, 30
Initial appearance, purpose of, 216
Initial appearance, right to an
    attorney, 217
Insanity, burden of proof, 304
Insanity, defense, 301–305
Insanity, defined, 301
Insanity, determining the moment of,
    303–304
Insanity, diminished capacity, 304–305
Insanity, historical development,
    302–303
Insanity, M'Naghten rule, 302–303
Insanity, not guilty by reason of, 21
Insanity, raising the defense, 304

Instructions, jury, 279
Interrogation, defined, 27
Interrogation, instances where
    defendant will not be
    interrogated, 174–175
Interrogation, *Miranda* rights, 169–172
Interrogation, *Miranda* warnings, 28
Interrogation, oral and written
    statements, 169
Interrogation, special rules regarding,
    174–175
Intoxication, defense, 305
Intoxication, defined, 305

J

Jackson v. Denno, hearing, 175
Jeopardy, plea of former, 249
Join issue, jury selection, 265
Judge's bench, 263
Judicial decisions, 4–5
Jurisdiction, 13
Jurisdiction, state, 14
Jury box, defined, 262
Jury deliberation room, 263
Jury deliberations, 279–280
Jury instructions, defined, 279
Jury selection, 265–270
Jury selection, alternate juror, 269
Jury selection, Batson challenge, 268
Jury selection, challenge for cause,
    267–268
Jury selection, final steps, 269–270
Jury selection, join issue, 265
Jury selection, peremptory
    challenge, 267
Jury selection, silent strikes, 269
Jury selection, striking the jury, 267,
    268–269
Jury selection, venire, 265
Jury selection, *voir dire*, 265
Jury trial, closing to the public, 197–198
Jury trial, defendant flees, 200
Jury trial, defendant waives his right to
    be present, 201
Jury trial, defined, 194
Jury trial, exceptions, 196
Jury trial, hung jury, 195
Jury trial, judge removes defendant
    from the court, 201
Jury trial, mistrial, 195
Jury trial, non–unanimous verdicts,
    195–196
Jury trial, number of jurors, 195
Jury trial, right of defendant to wear
    civilian clothing, 201–202

Jury trial, right of the press, 204–205
Jury trial, right to a, 194–196
Jury trial, right to be present, 200
Jury trial, right to public trial,
    196–198
Jury trial, sensitive or underage
    witnesses, 198
Jury trial, trials *in absentia*, 200
Jury, excusing, 282
Jury, grand, 31
Jury, striking the, 268–269

L
Law, common, 6–9
Liable, 20
Life in prison without possibility of
    parole, 329
Life in prison, sentence, 329–330
Lineup, constitutional limits on, 110
Lineup, constitutional sanctions, 111
Lineup, defined, 109
Lineup, participants in, 110
Lineup, photographic, 111
Lineup, right to counsel, 110

M
Magistrate, defined, 69
Miller test, 104
Miranda rights, 169–172
Miranda rights, background, 170
Miranda rights, background or routine
    police questioning, 171
Miranda rights, defined, 169
Miranda rights, exigent
    circumstances, 171
Miranda rights, trickery, 171–172
Miranda rights, voluntary
    statements, 171
Miranda rights, when *Miranda* does
    not apply, 170–171
Miranda warnings, 28
Miranda, invoking the right to remain
    silent, 172
Miranda, reinitiating questioning,
    173–174
Miranda, requesting an attorney,
    172–173
Miranda, traffic stops, 172
Misdemeanor, 24
Mistrial, 276
Mistrial, defined, 195
Mitigation of sentence, defined, 327
M'Naghten Rule, 302–303
Motion aggravation of sentence,
    defined, 253

Motion for change of venue,
    defined, 249
Motion for continuance, defined, 249
Motion for new trial, 342
Motion for new trial, defined, 342
Motion *in limine*, 247–248
Motion *in limine*, defined, 247
Motion to change venue, 249
Motion to join, 253
Motion to reveal identity of confidential
    informants, 248
Motion to reveal the deal, defined, 248
Motion to sever, 247
Motion to suppress, defined, 125
Motion to suppress, exclusionary rule,
    125–126
Motion, defined, 235
Motions to suppress, 246–247
Motions, prosecution, 252–253
Mutual combat, defense, 305–306
Mutual combat, defined, 305

N
Necessity, defense, 306
Necessity, defined, 306
No bill, 31
No bill, defined, 151
Nolle prosequi, defined, 146
Nolo contendere plea, 320–321
Nolo contendere, defined, 320
Not guilty, 21
Not guilty by reason of insanity, 21
Not guilty by reason of insanity,
    verdict, 281
Not guilty, verdict, 281
Notice of appeal, 342–343
Notice of appeal, defined, 342

O
Obscene material, possession of, 104
Obscenity, defined, 103
Open fields doctrine, defined, 85
Open file policy, defined, 242
Opening statements, 270–271
Oral argument, appeals, 348
Oral argument, defined, 348
Ordinances, 4
Overbreadth, defined, 90
Overbreadth, search warrant
    limitations, 90

P
Parole, defined, 329
Parole, probation and, 331
Particulars, bill of, 250

Peremptory challenge, defined, 267
Placing character into evidence,
    defined, 202
Plainview doctrine, defined, 84
Plea bargaining, 322–325
Plea bargaining, controversy
    surrounding, 324–325
Plea bargaining, federal sentencing, 323
Plea bargaining, sentence, 322
Plea bargaining, state plea
    negotiations, 324
Plea of former jeopardy, defined, 249
Plea, Alford, 320
Pleading the Fifth, defined, 158
Pleadings, 23–24
Pleas, guilty, 318–322
Police officer jurisdiction, 65
Polling, defined, 281
Polygraph tests, 114
Pornography, child, 104
Pornography, defined, 103
Pornography, prosecutions, 103–104
Possession of obscene material, 104
Powers of the appellate courts, 348–350
Preliminary hearing, 224–227
Preliminary hearing, binding over,
    225–226
Preliminary hearing, decision at,
    225–226
Preliminary hearing, defendant's
    role, 226
Preliminary hearing, defined, 30, 224
Preliminary hearing, evidentiary
    issues, 225
Preliminary hearing, negotiations
    between prosecutors and
    defense attorneys, 226–227
Preliminary hearing, procedure
    followed, 224–225
Preliminary hearing, purpose of, 224
Preliminary hearings, closing to the
    public, 198
Preponderance of the evidence, 22
Presence at the crime scene, probable
    cause, 61–62
Presentence investigation, 326
Presumption of innocence,
    defined, 222
Presumption, defined, 192
Presumptions v. inferences, 193
Pretextual stops, 60–61
Prima facie, defined, 31
Prison clothing, 201–202
Prisons, alternative, 330–331
Privilege, defined, 158

Pro se, defined, 191
Probable cause, 26–27
Probable cause, anonymous phone calls, 60
Probable cause, defined, 57
Probable cause, degree of proof needed, 58
Probable cause, flight, 61
Probable cause, Fourth Amendment requirement, 56–62
Probable cause, gut feelings or hunches, 62
Probable cause, informants, 59
Probable cause, presence at the crime scene, 61–62
Probable cause, pretextual stops, 60–61
Probable cause, radio description, 59
Probable cause, sobriety or roadside checkpoints, 60
Probable cause, specific acts that establish, 58–62
Probable cause, suspicious or unusual behavior, 59
Probable cause, what is?, 57–58
Probation, defined, 34
Probation, parole and, 331
Procedure at guilty plea, 318–320
Proof beyond a reasonable doubt, 23
Proof, burden of, 22–23
Property bond, defined, 218
Proportionality, defined, 333
Prosecution motions, 252–253
Prosecution motions, aggravation of sentence, 253
Prosecution motions, motion to join, 253
Prosecution motions, similar transactions, 252–253
Prosecution table, courtroom, 264
Public defender, defined, 190
Public trial, right to, 196–198
Punishments, 327–332

Q
Quash, defined, 158

R
Radio description, probable cause, 59
Reasonable doubt, defined, 204
Reasonable doubt, proof beyond a, 23
Reasonable suspicion, 45
Rebuttal, defined, 276
Rebutting a claim of self-defense, 308
Recess, defined, 262
Recess, trial, 262

Recognizance bond, defined, 221
Record, defined, 343
Redirect examination, defined, 274
Reinitiating questioning, 173–174
Remand, defined, 349
Requesting an attorney, 172–173
Restitution, 22
Retainer, defined, 189
Reverse, defined, 349
Reversible error, defined, 344
Right of the press, 104–105
Right to a fair trial, 193–194
Right to a jury trial, 194–196
Right to a jury trial, hung jury, 195
Right to a jury trial, non-unanimous verdicts, 195–196
Right to a jury trial, six-person jury, 196
Right to a public trial, 108–109, 111–112, 188–192
Right to an attorney, court-appointed, 190–191
Right to an attorney, defendant's right to represent himself, 191–192
Right to an attorney, hiring attorney, 189
Right to an attorney, pro se representation, 191–192
Right to an attorney, public defender, 190–191
Right to an attorney, when the defendant cannot afford, 191
Right to be present, trial, 200
Right to be presumed innocent, 192–193
Right to be presumed innocent, acquit, 192
Right to be presumed innocent, presumption, 192–193
Right to be presumed innocent, presumptions v. inferences, 193
Right to confront witnesses, 108, 198–200
Right to confront witnesses, cross-examine, 199–200
Right to jury trial, exceptions, 196
Right to jury trial, mistrial, 195
Right to present a defense, 203
Right to present evidence, 202–204
Right to public trial, 196–198
Right to public trial, sensitive or underage witnesses, 198
Right to remain silent, 172
Rights during a trial, 193–203
Rights during the trial, right to a fair trial, 193–194

Rights of the press, criminal trials, 204–205
Rules, court, 5

S
Scientific reports, discovery, 241–242
Search warrant limitations, 88–90
Search warrant limitations, anticipatory warrant, 90
Search warrant limitations, challenging a warrant, 90
Search warrant limitations, general searches not allowed, 89
Search warrant limitations, overbreadth, 90
Search warrant limitations, stale warrants, 89–90
Search warrant limitations, the exclusionary rule, 90
Search warrant limitations, vagueness, 90
Search warrants, 82–84
Search warrants, defined, 82
Search warrants, exceptions to, 84
Search warrants, expectation of privacy, 82
Search warrants, standards for issuing, 82–83
Search warrants, the good-faith exception, 83
Searches without a warrant, 84–88
Searches without a warrant, abandoned property, 86–87
Searches without a warrant, canine officers, 87
Searches without a warrant, consent, 88
Searches without a warrant, contraband, 87
Searches without a warrant, dropped evidence, 86
Searches without a warrant, exigent circumstances, 88
Searches without a warrant, open fields, 85–86
Searches without a warrant, plain view, 84–85
Searches without a warrant, stop and frisk, 87
Searches without a warrant, U.S. border searches, 87
Self-defense, defined, 306
Self-defense, rebutting a claim of, 308
Self-defense, stand your ground laws, 307–308
Self-incrimination, 107

Self-incrimination, defense, 292
Self-incrimination, defined, 292
Sentence, defined, 33
Sentencing, 325–332
Sentencing, aggravating factors, 329
Sentencing, aggravation of sentence, 327
Sentencing, alternative prisons, 330–331
Sentencing, bifurcated trial, 328
Sentencing, community service, 332
Sentencing, concurrent sentence, 326
Sentencing, consecutive sentence, 326
Sentencing, constitutional issues in, 332–333
Sentencing, cruel and unusual punishment, 333
Sentencing, death penalty, 327–329
Sentencing, fines, 332
Sentencing, hearing, 326–327
Sentencing, judicial discretion, 325–326
Sentencing, life in prison, 329–330
Sentencing, life in prison without the possibility of parole, 329
Sentencing, mitigation of sentence, 327
Sentencing, possible punishments, 327–332
Sentencing, presentence investigation, 326
Sentencing, prison v. parole, 33–34
Sentencing, probation and parole, 331
Sentencing, proportionality, 333
Sentencing, sentence for years, 329–330
Sentencing, statutory minimum and maximum sentences, 325–326
Sentencing, three strikes and you're out, 333
Sentencing, Victim Impact Statement, 326–327
Seriousness of the offense, bond, 222
Sever, defined, 247
Sever, motion to, 247
Show up, 110–111
Silent strikes, jury selection, 269
Similar transactions motion, defined, 252
Simple defenses, 290–296
Simple defenses, defined, 296
Six-person jury, 196
Sixth amendment, right to an attorney, 188–192
Sobriety or roadside checkpoints, Probable cause, 60
Speedy trial demand, 250–252

Speedy trial demand, dismissing a case, 250–251
Speedy trial demand, how speedy?, 251
Speedy trial demand, term of court, 250
Speedy trial demand, when is the right triggered, 251–252
Speedy trial, defined, 250
Stale warrants, search warrant limitations, 89–90
Stand your ground laws, defense, 307–308
Standing, defined, 127
Standing, exclusionary rule, 127
Stare decisis, 5
State constitutions, 2–3
State court system, 12–13
State sentencing guidelines, 324
State witnesses, criminal records, 244–245
Statement of facts, appellate brief, 344–345
Statement of facts, defined, 344
Statements, opening, 270–271
Statute of limitations, defense, 294–295
Statute of limitations, defined, 294
Statute, defined, 3
Statutory law, 3–4
Stop and frisk, 45–48
Stop and frisk, abuse of, 48
Stop and frisk, contraband, 46
Stop and frisk, defined, 44
Stop and frisk, scope, 47–48
Stop and frisk, searches without a warrant, 87
Stop and frisk, what are the police permitted to do?, 46–47
Striking a jury, defined, 267
Striking the jury, 268–269
Style, civil case, 24
Subpoena, defined, 157
Suppress, motions to, 246–247
Supremacy clause, 3
Supreme Court, U.S., 11
Suspicious or unusual behavior, probable cause, 59

T
Technical defenses, 292–296,
Technical deficiencies in charging documents, defense, 296
Term of court, defined, 250
Terry stop, defined, 44
Terry, detention under, 44–45
Terry, reasonable suspicion, 45

Three strikes and you're out, sentencing, 333
Title page, appellate brief, 344
Traffic stops and Miranda, 172
Trial, closing to the public, 112
Trial, criminal, 32–33
Trial, defendant waives right to be present, 201
Trial, judge removes defendant from the court, 201
Trial, public, 111–112
Trial, right of defendant to wear civilian clothing, 201–202
Trial, right to be present, 200
Trials *in absentia*, 200
Trickery and *Miranda* rights, 171–172
True bill, 31
True bill, defined, 151

U
U.S. border searches, searches without a warrant, 87
U.S. Supreme Court, 11, 350–351
U.S. Supreme Court, final authority, 351
U.S. Constitution, 2

V
Vagueness and overbreadth, defense, 293
Vagueness, search warrant limitations, 90
Venire, defined, 265
Venire, jury selection, 265
Venue, 64
Venue, motion to change, 249
Verdict, 280–282
Verdict, defined, 20
Verdict, directed, 274–275
Verdict, guilty, 281
Verdict, guilty but mentally ill, 281
Verdict, not guilty, 281
Verdict, not guilty by reason of insanity, 281
Verdict, polling the jury, 282
Verdict, various types of verdicts in criminal cases, 280–281
Verdicts in civil cases, 21–22
Verdicts in criminal cases, 20–21
Victim Impact Statement, defined, 326
Voir dire, defined, 265
Voluntariness of guilty plea, 320
Voluntary encounter, defined, 42

W
Waiving arraignment, defined, 236
Warrant, challenging a, 90

Warranties, defined, 67
Warrants, arrest, 67–72
Witness list, discovery, 240
Witness stand, 263,

Witnesses, cross–examine,
    199–200
Witnesses, right to confront, 108,
    198–200

Witnesses, state, criminal records,
    224–245
Witnesses, statements of, discovery, 242
Work product, defined, 244